# THE NAVAJO VERB SYSTEM

# THE NAVAJO VERB SYSTEM

## AN OVERVIEW

ROBERT W. YOUNG

The University of New Mexico Press
Albuquerque

First edition

Library of Congress Cataloguing-in-Publication Data
Young, Robert W., 1912– .
The Navajo verb system: an overview / Robert W. Young
—1st ed., p. cm.
ISBN 0-8263-2172-0 (cloth: alk. paper)
1. Navajo language—Verb.
I. Title.
PM2007.Y77 2000
497'.2—dc21
99-33790
CIP

DEDICATED
to the memory of
Howard W. Gorman
Frank Bradley
Paul Jones
Albert Sandoval

four men who, a few generations ago, at a crossroad in Navajo history, were thrust into a role of critical importance—one for which, at the time, they were uniquely equipped. Drawing on broad bicultural experience, coupled with great bilingual skill and leadership ability, they acted as primary intermediaries to help guide the main body of the tribal populace, inexperienced in the Outside World, as it was herded abruptly into a New Order. They were interpreters par excellence, and I counted them among my most distinguished friends and mentors.

# PREFACE
# AND
# ACKNOWLEDGMENTS

The verb occupies a central position in Navajo, and in the Athabaskan languages generally. Most of the noun lexicon, along with adverbs and adjectivals are verbal in origin or verb related in one way or another. It is little wonder then that the Navajo verb has received so much attention by scholars and students for over a hundred years. Washington Matthews in the closing decades of the 19th century was followed by the Franciscan Fathers, Pliny Earl Goddard, Edward Sapir and his understudy Harry Hoijer, and subsequently by Young and Morgan, Gladys Reichard, Kenneth Hale, Irvy Goosen, James Kari and, most recently, Leonard Faltz. These and a host of others have produced descriptive analytical studies in depth, general or focused on particular facets, in scope.

The Navajo verb constitutes a system, in the true sense of the word, in which multiple morphemes - adverbial, inflectional and root - are linked together to produce meaningful words. This concatenation of components gives rise to a complex of morphophonemic rules of juncture that pose an initial hurdle of major proportions for the Indo-European speaking learner of the language. The verb system differs so radically from the one(s) to which such a student is accustomed that it seems to be composed primarily of "irregular" forms. Fortunately, upon careful analysis, the Navajo verb and its complex rules of stem-prefix juncture emerge as basically simple and "regular."

Hoijer's detailed study of the Apachean Verb, published in a series of articles in IJAL during the period 1945-49, constituted a useful analysis of the Southern Athabaskan verb, including Navajo. Young & Morgan, in their first (1942) Navajo Grammar and Dictionary, and in their more recent Grammar-Dictionary and Analytical Lexicon (1980, 1987, 1991) provided extensive information bearing on verb morpho-phonology. These and Kari's Navajo Verb Phonology (1976) stand in something of a complementary relationship in this regard.

The present treatise draws together most of the descriptive information contained in previous works - especially that contained, in paradigm form, in Young & Morgan's The Navajo Language and in their Analytical Lexicon of Navajo. The present Overview is designed as both an introductory description of the language and as a convenient reference, focused primarily on verb morphology. As such it should prove useful to students of Navajo generally, including native speakers interested in gaining insight into the language they speak, and to users of the several teaching texts currently in use, designed to teach the Navajo verb.

The **Overview** owes its existence, to a very large extent, to the skill and generosity of Dr. Sally Midgette, who patiently did the complex typography and assisted in the organization of charts and other data; and in its final stages of preparation to Anthony and Marilyn Begay, who typed corrections and descriptive matter that was added to the original text.

To these helpers I am most grateful, and to them I must add my longtime colleague Dr. William Morgan, as well as Drs. Mary Ann Willie and Alyce Neundorf --- all of whom were valued consultants.

It is my hope that the **Overview**, along with other studies currently in progress, will generate interest in Navajo as an intriguing modern language, and contribute to its continuing viability and preservation.

Robert W. Young
1999

# TABLE OF CONTENTS

# ABBREVIATIONS

| | | | |
|---|---|---|---|
| Sgl: | singular | O: | object |
| Dpl: | duoplural | S: | subject |
| Dist Pl: | distributive plural | SRO: | solid roundish object |
| 3+: | three or more | AnO: | animate object |
| ~: | same as | LPB: | load, pack, burden |
| SP: | Simple Passive | OC: | object in open container |
| AP: | Agentive Passive | PlO a/b: | plural objects |
| C: | any consonant | SSO: | slender stiff object |
| Ci-: | consonant + vowel /i/ | SFO: | slender flexible object |
| Ca-: | consonant + vowel /a/ | NCM: | non-compact matter |
| Ce-: | consonant + vowel /e/ | FFO: | flat flexible object |
| Ø/Ł-Class: | Theme + Ø- or Ł-classifier | MM: | mushy matter |
| | | Pos.: | position |
| D/L-Class: | Theme + D- or L-classifier | Postpos.: | postposition |

lit: literally

# THE NAVAJO VERB SYSTEM

# CHAPTER ONE:

# INTRODUCTION

## I. ELEMENTS OF THE VERB

Upon analysis the Navajo verb emerges as a composite construction in which abstract meaning, conveyed by a word-final stem, is modified and brought into focus by a variety of prefixes, to function as a meaningful word. The anatomy of the verb is such that its components can be separated and identified in terms of relative position and grammatical function. The stem itself can be dissected and traced to an underlying root.

The Verbal Root is a hypothetical element that embodies verbal meaning in abstract form, and that serves as the foundation upon which to derive the *verbal stems.* There are about 550 verbal roots, from which about 2100 stems are produced, and these in turn form the basis for a virtually limitless verb lexicon.

The Verbal Stem is derived from the underlying root by various processes, including suffixation and changes in vowel quality (oral/nasal, short/long, low/high tone). The stem conveys, not only the root meaning but, in many lexical derivatives, figurative meanings as well.

For purposes of illustration, assume *'A to be the shape of a verbal root meaning "move a solid or compact roundish object." From this root seven stem shapes are derived, corresponding to the Modes and Aspects in which the root is expressed. (Mode: the distinctive manner in which a verbal action or event is conceived, as: incomplete [Imperfective], complete [Perfective], ongoing [Progressive]; Aspect: the distinctive kind of verbal action involved, as: punctual - occurring at a point in time [Momentaneous], continuing [Continuative, Durative], distributed [Distributive]) The seven stems derived from the root *'A have the shapes:

'á (as in naash'á, I'm carrying it around)
'aah (as in bíłák'eesh'aah, I'm in the act of handing it to him)
'ááh (as in náhásh'ááh, I'm turning it around)
'a' (as in bá hooł'a', I made room for him)
'ą́ (as in baa ní'ą́, I gave it to him)
'ááł (as in yish'ááł, I'm carrying it along)
'aał (as in ndeesh'aał, I'll carry it around)

The Stem Sets: The stems usually occur in the form of configurations of particular shapes, corresponding to the Aspect and to the Modes in which a particular Verb Base is expressed. These configurations are called "Stem Sets." All Verb Bases that share the root *'A, the Momentaneous Aspect, and the same set of Modes employ the same Stem Set, as the set:

'aah (Imperfective), 'ááh (Usitative), 'ą́ (Perfective), 'ááł (Future and Optative), that appears in more than 150 lexical derivatives based on the root *'A.

The Aspects crosscut the Modes (i.e. a given Mode can appear in more than one Aspect). Consequently, the Stem shape required by a given Mode for lexical derivation from a common Root may vary. Thus, for the Root * ' A the following Stem shapes occur, marking aspectual distinctions with Imperfective Mode:

| MODE | ASPECT | STEM | EXAMPLE |
|---|---|---|---|
| Imperfective | Momentaneous | 'aah | (as in haash'aah: I'm extracting it) |
| Imperfective | Continuative | 'á | (as in naash'á: I'm carrying it about |
| Imperfective | Distributive | 'a' | (as in bitaash'a': I'm passing it out to them - one each) |
| Imperfective | Reversative | 'ááh | (as in náhásh'ááh: I'm turning it around) |

## II. ROOT / STEM TYPES: THE CLASSIFICATORY STEMS

The Verbal Roots and derived Stems concerned with motion include a category that distinguishes (1) the physical characteristics ( shape, texture, animacy) or (2) the number (singular / plural) of objects to which they refer; and (3) the manner in which the movement is accomplished - whether by "handling," propulsion, or free flight).

1. Handle Stems describe the movement of an object or objects by continuing manual contact (as in carrying, bringing, putting, taking, extracting, inserting, lifting, raising, lowering, setting, hanging, turning over or around - but including, for some, indirect contact, as in hauling or otherwise conveying).

In addition, the "handle" Stems are used in si- Perfective Neuter verbs that describe an object of a particular class at rest - the Positional Neuters (sit, lie, be), and when transitivized "keep or have (the object at rest in a place)."

2. Propel Stems describe the abrupt movement of an object or objects that is/are set in motion by an agent who tosses, throws, or intentionally drops it/them.

3. Fly Stems describe the independent movement of an object or objects of a particular class, as when it flies through the air, falls, or otherwise moves without an agent or causative force.

**Mediopassive** derivatives occur with some "handle" and "propel" Stems, especially in verb constructions that describe movement of the subject's own head. Verbs of this type include a vestigial ni-generic prefix (ni2-6b) that marks "roundness, round shape." The subject of the verb moves "his own roundness"= his own head. A comparable ni-generic prefix has wide use in some of the Northern Athapaskan languages, but it is no longer used productively, in Navajo.

The name and general definition attaching to each classificatory object class reflects a salient feature shared by many of the objects to which it refers, but all objects shared by a given class do not necessarily share the features implied by the class designation. Thus, the SRO (Solid, Compact Roundish Object) class describes a ball, loaf of bread, head and marble - all of which share texture and shape; but the same SRO object class also includes a (calendar) date, a song, a glove, a bicycle and a coin.

In the Classificatory Stem list that follows, the underlying Root is represented by the Stem of the Perfective Mode. It is the main entry, and it is followed by the Perfective Verb Theme Pf.T. (=the Perfective Stem + Classifier Prefix). It is this Theme form that is used in the examples. (V. pp 3 - 17 )

## 1
## SOLID OR COMPACT ROUNDISH OBJECT CLASS - SRO

The SRO Stem class includes a broad range of objects, singular in number, primarily inanimate, usually solid or compact in texture and basically round or roundish in shape. The class includes: a ball, bottle, apple, stone, hat, box, loaf of bread, clock, cup, egg, bulb, seed, grain of sand, head, knife, coin, book, inflated toy balloon, slice of baloney, bed, bicycle, biscuit, buckle, ceremonial mask, song, statement, news.

### HANDLE - SRO

(Root 'Ą́ > Pf. T: Ø'ą́)

shizhé'é tsé shich'į' nayíí'ą́: my father lowered the rock down to me (by continuing manual contact)

shiye' tsits'aa' néidii'ą́ą́ dóó shaa yiní'ą́: my son picked up the box and brought it to me

Neuter Positional: si'ą́: it sits, lies, is (in position) naaltsoos bikáá' adání bikáa'gi si'ą́: the book is on the table

Mediopassive: Pf. T: t'ą́ < d'ą́
tsésǫ'dę́ę́' ch'íninisht'ą́: I stuck my head (slowly) out the window.

## Propel - SRO

(Root: NE' > Pf. T: łne')

shizhé'é tsé léi' shich'į' nayííłne': my father dropped/tossed a rock down to me

'ashkii yázhí bich'ah hashtł'ish yii'jį' nayííłne': the little boy tossed/dropped his hat into the mud

'ashkii léi' tsé yee shííníiłne': some boy threw a stone at me

Mediopassive: Pf. T: łne'
tsésǫ'dę́ę́' ch'íninishne': I stuck my head quickly out the window
dlǫ́ǫ́' 'a'ą́ądę́ę́' hanoolne': the prairie dog stuck its head up out of the hole (quickly)

## Fly; Move Independently - SRO

(Root: TS'ID > Pf. T: lts'id)

hooghan bikáádę́ę́' tsé shik'ijį' naalts'id: a rock fell down on me from the roof of the hogan

tsé yish'áłę́ę shílák'ee haalts'id: the rock that I was carrying fell out of my hand - I dropped it unintentionally.

---

## 2
## NON - COMPACT MATTER - NCM

The NCM class includes anything that is ball-like in shape and/or amorphous in texture (as a loose wad of hair, bunch of hay, a wig - and by extension a cloud of fog, smoke, dust, steam, rain or even a stench). A single Root* JOOL applies to all three motion classes, but the Themes are distinctive.

## Handle - NCM

(Root: JOOL > Pf.T: łjool)

'aghaa' bikáá'adání biyaadę́ę́' háálјool: I took the wool out from under the table

sitsi' sitsiigháshchíín shá shik'iidííłjool: my daughter put my wig on for me

### Propel - NCM

(Root: JOOL > Pf.T: łjool)

kin bikáádę́ę́' 'aghaa' ła' 'adááłjool: I tossed/dropped/lowered some wool down from the roof

### Fly, Move Independently -NCM

(Root: JOOL > Pf.T: Øjool)

níyolgo shich'é'édą́ą́'gi ch'il deeníní naajooł: a tumbleweed is tumbling around in my dooryard

tsiigháshchíín yishjołę́ę shílák'ee háájool: the wig that I was carrying fell out of my hand - I dropped it unintentionally

Neuter Positional: shijool: it lies, is (in position)

sitsiigháshchíín tsásk'eh bikáa'gi dah shijool: my wig is lying on the bed

When the subject of the verb is an amorphous mass (dust, smoke, fog, cloud, snowstorm, stench) it is represented in the verb by the indefinite pronoun 'a-(~ 'i-, ~ 'e-) as: łid hooghan góne' nihił yah 'i'íijool: smoke drifted into the hogan on us

---

## 3
## MUSHY MATTER - MM

The MM class includes anything that is wet and mushy in texture (lard, wet plaster, honey, dough, blood, peanut butter, a scrambled egg, feces), and by extension a wet rag, decrepit hat or loose bag of flour.

### Handle - MM

(Root: TŁÉÉ' > Pf.T: Øtłéé')

sitsi' taos'nii' ła' shílák'eyíítłéé': my daughter handed me some dough - i.e. she put it into my hand

Neuter Positional: sitłéé': it lies, it is (in position)

'atiin bąąhgi béégashii bichaan ła' sitłéé': there is a cow platter by the roadside

## Propel - MM

(Root: TŁÉÉ' > Pf.T: Øtłéé')

tsin bighą́ą́'dę́ę́' sitsilí jeeh bik'iji' 'adáátłéé': I dropped pitch down on my little brother from the treetop

With a d-Theme (d) tłéé' verb constructions are derived that describe the hopping of a frog or toad, as:

ch'ał taah hootłéé': the frog hopped into the water

## Fly, Move Independently - MM

(Root: YĘ́Ę́ZH > Pf.T: łhęęzh)

taos'nii' shílák'ee háálhęęzh: the dough fell out of my hand -- i.e. I dropped the dough unintentionally

tsin bijeeh shik'iji' hadáálhęęzh: pitch fell down on me

---

## 4
## SINGLE FLAT FLEXIBLE OBJECT - FFO

The FFO class includes anything that is flat in shape and flexible in texture (as a sheet of paper, bedsheet, towel, blanket tarpaulin), and by extension a sack or small bag and contents (as a sack of groceries).

## Handle - FFO

(Root: TSOOZ > Pf.T: łtsooz)

gha'diit'aahii naaltsoos shílák'eyíítsooz: the lawyer handed me a document

hane' binaaltsoos ńdiiłtsooz dóó kin góne' yah 'ííłtsooz: I picked up the newspaper and took it into the house

Neuter Positional: siłtsooz: it lies, is in position

shi'éé' tsásk'eh bikáá'gi dah siłtsooz: my shirt it lying on the bed

## Propel - FFO

(Root: 'AH > Pf.T: Ø'ah)

'ashkii yázhí shi'éé' taah yiyíí'ah: the little boy tossed my shirt into the water

shimá naaltsoos bich'į' 'íí'ah: I sent my mother a letter (i.e. I tossed it away out of sight toward her)

Hastiintsoh naaltsoos bá 'íí'ah: I voted for Big Man (i.e. I tossed a paper for him)

## Fly, Move Independently - FFO

(Root: NA' > Pf.T: Øna')

Describes the flight of a FFO (as a sheet of paper) through the air; a sheet of water over a surface; and the oozing of blood from a wound.

deeyolgo naaltsoos bikáá'adání bikáádę́ę́' 'adáána': when the wind came up the paper flew off the tabletop

shíla' shégishgo dił háána': blood oozed out when I cut my finger

naaltsoos naastsoosę́e shílák'ee háána': the paper that I was carrying around fell out of my hand - i.e. I dropped it unintentionally

dziłdi nahałtingo tó nihich'ą́ąh 'íína': we were cut off by a sheet of water with the rain in the mountains

---

## 5
## SLENDER FLEXIBLE OBJECT - SFO

The SFO class applies to a wide range of objects. Basically it describes anything, inanimate or animate, that is slender in shape and flexible in texture (as a string of beads, a piece of rope, a belt, chain, intestine, snake, supple branch), but by extension it is applied to anything that comes in pairs (as socks, gloves, shoes, scissors, pliers, and even crossed legs), and to a conglomerate of plural objects (as constellations, the words of a language, a set of tools or ceremonial paraphernalia, a band of people or herd of animals, the unspecified contents of one's pocket or items taken in a burglary). The SFO Root and derived Stems appear in two forms. (See the Analytical Lexicon, p. 356.)

## Handle - SFO

(Root: LÁ / YÁ > Pf.T: Ølá / lyá)

naalyéhé yá sidáhí yoo' (kélchííh) shá 'adayíílá: the trader took down the string of beads (pair of moccasins) for me

sitsilí Bilagáanaa bizaad bizáálá: I taught English to my younger brother (i.e. I put English words into his mouth)

Diné bizaad sizaalyá: I was taught Navajo (i.e. Navajo words were put into my mouth

Neuter Positional: silá : it is, lies, they are (in position)

siziiz tsásk'eh bikáa'gi dah silá: my belt is lying on the bed

## Propel - SFO

Propel a SFO is derived as a causative - transitive of the corresponding "Fly" verbs.

(Root: DÉÉL > łdéél)

tł'iish ńdiiláá dóó taah yíłdéél: I picked up the snake and tossed / dropped it into the water

'ashkii yázhí chidí yii'dę́ę́' bikee' ch'íiníłdéél: the little boy threw his shoes out of the car

Mediopassive: with the Theme ldéél the Root appears in mediopassive constructions that describe the eating of plural objects (as berries, grapes, sardines. Jeffry Leer suggests that the subject of the verb "tosses the objects into himself").

'ashkii dzidzé t'óó 'ahayóí yooldéél: the boy ate a lot of berries

## Fly, Move Independently - SFO

(Root: DÉÉL > Pf.T: Ødéél)

tł'iish léi' tsin bigąądę́ę́' shik'iįį' 'adáádéél: a snake fell down onto me from the tree limb

siziiz tsídzáádéél: my belt fell into the fire

---

## 6
## SLENDER STIFF OBJECT - SSO

The SSO class includes essentially anything that is elongated in shape (a stick-like object) and rigid (as a bone, match, pencil, stick, pole, stick of gum, cigaret, bow, arrow, broom, ear of corn, rifle, ladder, needle, plank), and by extension a playing card, sheet of tin, saw, frying pan, wedding basket, dentures, bracelet.

### Handle - SSO

(Root: TĄ́ > Pf.T: Øtą́)

Hastiin bibee'eldǫǫh néidiitą́ą́ dóó ch'élwod: the man picked up his rifle and ran out

hastiin tsineheeshjíí' shich'į' nayíítą́, chidítsohdę́ę́': the man lowered the plank down to me from the truck

Neuter Positional: sitą́: it lies, it is ( in position)

bee'ak'e'elchíhí bikáá'adání bikáa'gi dah sitą́: the pencil is lying on the table

### Propel - SSO

(Root: T'E' > Pf.T: łt'e') (The propulsion of a SSO and a single animate object (AnO) is expressed by the same Root (T'E'), and with a d-Theme plus a prefix that marks movement as segmentalized T'E' derives verb constructions with the meaning "hop - as a bird or child.")

'ąą dinítą́ą́ dóó nát'oh yas biih yíłt'e': I opened the door and tossed a cigaret into the snow

'i'íí'ą́ągo nástáán léi' tsídzááłt'e': at sundown I tossed a log onto the fire

### Fly, Move Independently - SSO

(Root: KĘ́ĘZ > Pf.T: Økę́ę́z)

bee'ak'e'elchíhí bikáá'adání bikáádę́ę́' 'adáákę́ę́z: the pencil fell off the table

tsin 'ayóó 'áníłdáás léi' shichidí bik'iikę́ę́z: a heavy pole fell on to my car

---

7

## SINGLE ANIMATE OBJECT - AnO

The AnO class includes any animate object, alive or dead (as a person, animal, insect, microbe), as well as an object made in the form of a living thing (as a doll).

### Handle - AnO

(Root: TĮ > Pf.T: łtį)

'awéé' ńdiiłtįį dóó tł'óó'góó ch'íníłtį: I picked up the baby and carried it outside

chidítsoh biyi'dę́ę́' béégashii yáázh ła' 'adááłtį: I lowered a calf down from the truck

Neuter Positional: Although the ł- component of the łtį Theme is probably thematic (not a transitivizing agent), the Neuter Positionals take a Øtį Theme, as: sitį: it lies, it is in (a reclining) position; sétį: I am lying; and with the addition of ni-terminal (ni[1]-6b) the meaning becomes "lie down," as in nétį: I lay down.

shimá sání tsásk'eh yikáa'gi dah sitį: my grandmother is lying on the bed

shimá sání tsásk'eh yikáa'gi dah neeztį: my grandmother lay down on the bed

### Propel - AnO

(Root: T'E' > Pf.T: łt'e') SSO and AnO share the same Root.)

shizhé'é chidítsoh yii'dę́ę́' dibé yázhí shich'į' 'adayííłt'e': my father tossed/dropped a lamb down to me from the truck

łóó' ła' tééh hóyáanii bizááłt'e': I tossed/dropped a fish into the dolphin's mouth

### Fly, Move Independently - AnO

A number of Roots and derived Stems describe the independent movement of an AnO - it may take the form of falling, crawling, walking, running, flying. However, unintentional flight through the air is described by the Roots TŁIZH and GO' (Pf.T: Øtłizh, Øgo')

TŁIZH suggests "thud," while GO' suggests a rushing passage through the air.

'ashkii hooghan yikáádę́ę́' 'adáátłizh/'adáágo': the boy fell from the hogan roof

'ashkii jooł yikéé' ńdiilwod ńt'éé' chą́ą́h deezgo': the boy started to chase the ball but he stumbled and fell flat on his face

## 8
## LOAD, PACK, BURDEN - LPB

The LPB class includes anything that is bulky, massive, heavy, requiring treatment in the form of a load, burden or pack (as a bed, mattress, armchair, sofa, saddle, heavy log, heavy overcoat, quiver of arrows, truckload of coal or firewood -- but also some classes of small quantities or objects, as a spoonful of something, a medicine pouch, or a bundle of ceremonial paraphernalia).

The Neuter Positional includes not only things of the type listed above, but also a body of water (as a lake, pond, puddle).

Handle and Propel do not have distinctive Stems - both types of motion are represented by YĮ́.

### Handle - LPB

(Root: YĮ́ > Pf.T: Øyį́)

shiye' chidítsoh yii'dę́ę́' 'ak'áán shich'į' 'adayííyį́: my son lowered (or dropped) a bag of flour down to me from the truck

ts'iilzéí t'óó 'ahayóí chidítsoh bee yóó' 'ííyį́: I hauled away a lot of trash with a truck

Neuter Positional: siyį́: it sits, lies, is (in position)

kin góne' bilasáana 'azis bee siyį́: there's a sack of apples in the house

ha''a'aahjígo be'ek'id hatsoh siyį́: on the west there is a big lake

### Propel - LPB

(Root: YĮ́ > Pf.T: Øyį́)

naadą́ą́' 'azis biyi'go tsésǫ'dę́ę́' 'adááyį́: I tossed, dropped (or lowered) the bag of corn out the window

### Fly, Move Independently - LPB

(Root: YĘĘZH > Pf.T: łhęęzh - voiceless ł - devocalizes Stem-initial -y-)

naadą́ą́' 'azis biyi'go naa'ííłhęęzh: the bag of corn toppled over

ni'nahaas' náa'go 'aghaa' 'azis bii' héełgo dah hidiiyínę́ę́ n'diiłhęęzh: when the the earthquake happened the bag of wool that I had hung up broke loose and fell

## 9
## ANYTHING IN AN OPEN CONTAINER - OC

(Root: KĄ́ > Pf.T: Øką́)

The OC class describes the handling of anything in an open container (as a glass of water, bowl of soup, dish of food, bucket of sand, box of apples, corpse in a coffin, baby in a babyboard, water in cupped hands, dirt in a shovel).

### Handle - OC

shimá 'ásaa' yiyi'dóó 'atoo' ła' shá hayííką́: my mother dipped some soup out of the pot for me

tó bee naakáhí bee tó bikáá' adání bikáa'gi dah séką́: I set the bucket of water up on the tabletop

Neuter Positional: siką́: it sits, is (in position)

'atoo' bikáá'adání bikáa'gi dah siką́: the soup is on the table

The Root Ką́ is used (in Themes that include ł-classifier and yi-thematic; yi--łką́: Pf.T) in verb constructions that describe passage of the night and the coming of dawn: yisk ą́: night has passed - a new day has dawned).

### Propel - OC

When the contents of an open container are "propelled" -- tossed, dropped, thrown - they usually spread over the surface on which they land. The Root KAAD, which describes flatness or expansion in other contexts, here describes the scattering of the contents of an open container. Propel is the causative-transitive of "Fly - Move independently" with reference to the OC class, so both employ the same Root and derived Stems.

(Root: KAAD > Pf.T: łkaad)

łeets'a' tááségiz dóó tó ch'íníłkaad: I washed the dishes and threw out the water

'atoo' bikáá'adání bikáagi dah sikánęę hadááłkaad: I knocked over the (container of) soup that was on the table

### Fly, Move Independently - OC

(Root: KAAD > Pf.T: Økaad)

'atoo' naashkáá ńt'éé' shílak'ee háákaad: I was carrying soup around and it fell out of my hand - I dropped it

---

## 10
## PLURAL OBJECTS - Pl0a

There are two Roots that describe the handling of plural objects: NIL and JAA', identified as Pl0a, describes both Handle and Propel, with reference to a plurality of separable objects - i.e. objects of such size that the number can be readily visualized (as several books, eggs, cats, poles, shirts, babies, boxes, beds, mattresses, saddles, corpses).

### Handle - Pl0a

(Root: NIL > Pf.T: Ønil)

tsits'aa' naadlo'í shi'éé bii' háánil dóó dah hidiinil: I took my clothes out of the suitcase and hung them up

kin diiltłago bá'ólta'í 'áłchíní yisdáyiiznil: the teacher rescued the children when the building caught fire (i.e. the teacher moved them to safety)

Neuter Positional: sinil: they lie they are (in position)

łeets'aa' bikáá'adání bikáa'gi dah sinil: the dishes are on the table

### Propel - Pl0a

Root: NIL > Pf.T: Ønil)

Kǫ' k'asdą́ą́' 'ásdįįd lágo łeejin tsídzáánil: when I saw that the fire was nearly out I tossed (put) coal on it

'ałní'ní'ą́ago shilį́į́' łį́į́' bighandę́ę́' ch'íínínil: at noon I put my horses out of the horse corral

shizhé'é gah neistseedę́ę tsits'aa' yiih yiyíínil: my father tossed (put) the rabbits he had killed into the box

### Fly, Move Independently - Pl0a

(Root: DEE' > compound Pf.T: ni--Ødee')

The Root describes the movement through space of plural objects in Themes of the type shown above. The objects can be animate or inanimate, but they are usually separable, not a mass. A mass of plural objects is described by the Root DÁÁZ: (See PlOb.)

bee'eldǫǫh bik'a' ńdiijaa'go shílák'ee haníídee': when I picked up the cartridges they fell out of my hand - i.e. I dropped them.

tózis taah hénilgo táłtł'ááh dahineezdee': when I threw the bottles into the water they sank -- i.e. they fell to the bottom

haidą́ą́' shicheii biwoo' hahineezdee': last winter my grandfather's teeth fell out - he lost his teeth

ni' nahaas'náa'go kin t'óó 'ahayóí naa'aníídee': a lot of buildings fell over when there was an earthquake

tsásk'eh bikáá'góó sétį́įgo siza'azisdę́ę́' béeso hahineezdee': as I lay on the bed coins fell out of my pocket

---

## 11
## PLURAL OBJECTS - PlOb

The PlOb class converges with the PlOa class in some applications that involve the handling of plural objects. PlOa NIL generally implies "severalty" with regard to the number of objects, and the objects are usually relatively large and readily countable, but 10b JAA' has special application to a profusion of objects, ranging in size from small (as seeds, beans, grains of anything, coins, marbles) to larger objects (such as cans, a basket full of kittens, a bunch of arrows, a number of shirts, shoes or boxes).

Convergence also stems from usage, in that Continuative "carry PlO around" and Progressive "carry PlO along" require JAA' derivatives because corresponding forms based on NIL describe "strew, sprinkle, scatter" rather than the normal "handle" action represented by verbs of these types.

### Handle - PlOb

(Root: JAA' > Pf.T: Øjaa')

naadą́ą́' ła' naa'ahóóhai bá niníjaa': I put down some shelled corn for the chickens (as a big handful)

łeejin ła' tsídzáájaa': I put some (small chunks of) coal into the fire sik'is neeshch'íí' t'óó 'ahayóí shílák'eyííjaa': my friend handed me a lot of pinyon nuts - i.e. he put them into my hand

Neuter Positional: shijaa: they lie, there are (in position)

naaltsoos t'óó 'ahayóí bikáá'adání bikáa'gi dah shijaa': There are a lot of books lying on the table

## Propel - PlOb

PlOb class objects and OC (open container) class objects share the same Root to describe propulsion because for both classes the object(s) behave in a similar manner upon contacting a surface: they spread and scatter.

(Root: KAAD > Pf.T: łkaad)

sik'is neeshch'íí' t'óó 'ahayóí 'ázayoolkaad: my friend tossed a bunch of pinyon nuts into his mouth

'ashkii łeezh shik'ijį' nayíítkaad: the boy tossed/dropped dirt down onto me

tsé yadiitł'inęę naa'aníítkaad: I toppled the tower of rocks

## Fly, Move Independently - PlOb

A conglomeration of plural objects can move independently in several manners: (1) it can shower down (like falling snow), (2) it can fall and spread upon contact with a surface, and (3) it can take the form of a mass made up of plural constituents (as a pile of snow on a roof, the dirt in an arroyo bank).

(Root: DEE' > Pf.T: ni -- dee')

tł'éédą́ą́' níyolgo 'at'ąą' naníídee': last night leaves fell (showered down) in the wind

k'eelyéí naashjaahą́ą shílák'ee haníídee': I dropped the seeds that I was carrying around (i.e. they fell out of my hand)

(Root: KAAD > Pf.T: Økaad)

tsé yadiitł'inęę naa'aníkaad: the tower of rocks toppled over (and its plural components scattered on the ground)

tsitł'élí tsits'aa' bee naashjaah ńt'éé' shílák'ee háákaad: I dropped the box of matches that I was carrying (and they scattered on the floor or ground)

(Root: DÁÁZ > Pf.T: łdááz)

ńdíshchíí' biyaadóó sézį́į́ ńt'éé' yas shik'ijį' nááłdááz: I was standing under a pinetree when a pile of snow fell down on me

'azis léi' 'ąą 'ííshłaago biyi'dę́ę́' k'eelyéí t'óó 'ahayóí hááłdááz: when I opened a sack a lot of seeds fell out

(Note: In Neuter derivatives DAAZ describes weight, as in nisdaaz: I'm heavy.)

---

## 12
## MOVE BY STREAMING - (Liquid, granular sustance)

(Root: ZIID > Pf.T: Øziid)

The root ZIID and its derivatives share many of the characteristics of the "handle" verbs, and the object(s) to which it refers move(s) by streaming - as in pouring liquid, raking sand or ashes.

### Handle - streaming matter

tókǫ'í dóó chidí bitoo' 'ahííziid: I mixed kerosene and gasoline together (by pouring)

shimá tsíĺd ch'íidiníziid dóó tsee'é yikáa'gi yiz'ą́: my mother raked out hot coals and set the skillet on them

bá'ólta'í baa níyáago gohwééh shá yayiiziid: when I went to see the teacher he served coffee to me (i.e. he poured it for me)

Neuter Positional: siziid - describes a small puddle of water or a quantity of sand, gravel or seeds that lie (in position)

shich'é'édą́ą'gi tó ła' siziid: there's a little puddle of water in my dooryard

'atiingóó tsézéí siziid: the road is graveled (i.e. pebbles lie on it)

## RECAPITULATION

| | OBJECT CLASS | HANDLE | PROPEL | FLY | BE AT REST | KEEP AT REST |
|---|---|---|---|---|---|---|
| 1. | SRO | Ø'ą́ | łne' | lts'id | Ø'ą́ | ł'ą́ |
| 2. | NCM | łjool | łjool | Øjool | Øjool | łjool |
| 3. | MM | Øtłéé' | łtłéé' | łhęęzh | Øtłéé' | łtłéé' |
| 4. | FFO | łtsooz | Ø'ah | Øna' | łtsooz | łtsooz |
| 5. | SFO | Ølá | łdéél | Ødéél | Ølá | łá |
| 6. | SSO | Øtą́ | łt'e' | Økę́ę́z | Øtą́ | łtą́ |
| 7. | AnO | łtį́ | łt'e' | Øgo' | Øtį́ | Øtį́ |
| | | | | Øgo' | Øtéézh | łtéézh |
| | | | | Øtłizh | Øjéé' | łjéé' |
| 8. | LPB | Øyį́ | Øyį́ | łhęęzh | Øyį́ | łhį́ |
| 9. | OC | Øką́ | łkaad | Økaad | Øką́ | łką́ |
| | | | | łdaaz | | |
| 10. | PlOa | Ønil | Ønil | ni-dee' | Ønil | łnil |
| 11. | PlOb | Øjaa' | łkaad | ni-dee' | Øjaa' | łjaa' |
| | | | | łdaaz | | |
| | | | | Økaad | | |
| 12. | Stream | Øziid | --- | --- | Øziid | --- |

## THE VERB PREFIX CHART

The chart that follows lists the verb prefixes. These elements, predominantly monosyllabic in form, may be transparent in meaning, or they may be meaningless in the modern language; and between these two extremes there is a large number of prefixes whose meaning or function invites speculation. As the chart shows, many elements in this latter category are homophones, sharing a common shape (as the numerous di-/ni- prefixes of Position 6), but they are divergent in meaning or restricted to particular verbal theme types.

Prefixes located nearest the Stem (those in Position 4-8, inclusive) are tightly bound, while those that lie to the left (of 4) are more loosely bound components of the verb complex --- in fact, some prefixes, especially postpositional stems of the type that can occur both independent and bound, are very loosely integrated into the prefix complex.

Some verb prefixes, identified as thematic, are part of the Verb Theme itself. For most of these meaning is lost, in modern Navajo, or highly speculative. However, irrespective of semantic status, a basic understanding of the relationship between the verbal prefixes and the stem is a necessary key to the genius of the language.

## THE VERB PREFIXES

### The Disjunct Prefixes

#### Position 0

Pronominal: represent (1) the object of a postposition, (2) the possessor of a verb-prefixed noun

| Person | SINGULAR | | Person | DUOPLURAL | |
|---|---|---|---|---|---|
| 1. | shi-/shí-/sh-: | me/my. | 1. | nihi-/nihí-/nih-: | us/our |
| 2. | ni-/ní-/n-: | you/your | 2. | nihi-/nihí-/nih-: | you your. |
| 3. | bi-/bí-/b-: | him,her,it/ his,her,its. | 3. | bi-/bí-/b-: | them/their. |
| 3o. | yi-/yí-/y-: | him,her,it/ his,her,its. | 3o. | yi-/yí-/y-: | them/their |
| 3a. | ha-/há-/h- | him,her one,a person/his,her, one's,a person's. | 3a. | ha-/há-/h-: | them/their, people's |
| 3i. | 'a-/'á-/'-: | someone or something unspecified/ someone's,something's. | | | |
| 3s. | ha- ho- hw-: | space, area (rarely in Position 0). | | | |

REFLEXIVE: 'ádi-/'ádí-/'á-~'ád-: self/own.
RECIPROCAL: 'ahi-~'ałhi-/'ahí-~'ałhí-/'ah-~'ałh-: each other/each other's.

P-/P- serve to represent any prefix of Position 0 except 3a, 3i, 3s, Reflexive and Reciprocal

#### Position Ia

The null postposition. Serves various functions, including: (1)represents an indirect object of the verb in the absence of a postposition, (2) represents the subject of an intransitive Inchoative verb construction, and (3) represents the direct object of a transitive Inchoative. The null postposition sometimes contracts with a following ná-ld prefix (the Reversionary) to produce the forms listed below inter-parentheses.

| Person | SINGULAR | Person | DUOPLURAL |
|---|---|---|---|
| 1. | shi- (shéé-): me. | 1. | nihi- (nihéé-): us. |
| 2. | ni- (néé-): you. | 2. | nihi- (nihéé-): you. |
| 3. | bi- (béé-): him,her,it. | 3. | bi- (béé-): them. |
| 3o. | yi- (yéé-): him,her,it. | 3o. | yi- (yéé-): them. |
| 3a. | ho-~hw- (hwéé-): him,her, one, a person. | 3a. | ho- hw- (hwéé-): them, people. |
| 3i. | 'a-~'i- ('éé-): someone or something unspecified. | | |
| 3s. | ho-~hw-: space, area, impersonal "it". | | |

REFLEXIVE: 'ádi-: self, at self.
RECIPROCAL: 'ahi- ~ 'ałhi-: at each other, together, convergent, joining

P- serves to represent any prefix of Position Ia except 3a, 3i, 3s, Reflexive and Reciprocal

#### Position Ib

Three types: (1)Postpositional,(2)Adverbial-Thematic, (3)Nominal.

(1) Postpositional

-á-: for, on behalf of
'á-: for someone or something.
'ádá-: \ for self
P-á-: for P.

-a'-~'a-'- (a compound:< -a-~ -aa-, to + '[a]- unidentified): to (a recipient) on a temporary loan basis, lend to, borrow from.
'a'-: lending to someone.
'aha'- ~ 'ałha-: lending to each other.
P-a'-: lending to P.

-aa- ~ -a-: to, about, concerning, on, off, by (as in passing).
'aa- ~ 'a-: about, to, passing someone unspecified.
'ádaa- ~ 'áda-: about self, to self.
'ahaa-~'aha-~ 'ałhaa-~'ałha- about each other, to each other together (joining or concentrating - as objects in a pile or bunch).
P-aa- ~ P-a-: about, concerning, to, on, off, by P.

-ą- (< -ąą ~ 'ąą, beyond, over): over and resting on (as a rope thrown over a limb).
'ał'ą-: over each other.
P-'ą-: over P.
wó'ą-: over an edge, into a ditch.

-ą́ą́'- ~ -ání'- (a compound: -'ą́ < -ą́ąh, passing by + ná-ld[?] + '[a]-IV): uncovering (as in removing dirt or leaves from a buried object).
P-ą́ą́'- ~ P-ą́ní'-: uncover P.

-ba-: use up, exhaust (a supply of something, as food, water), move to completion, come to an end.
P-ba-: use up P, exhaust P, complete P.

-chá-: bunched, huddled, "hog-tied."
'áchá-: "self-bunched."
P-chá-: P is bunched together, "hog-tied."

chą́- (meaning obscure): crave, like be addicted to (?) (as tobacco, candy, liquor).
P-chą́-: crave P, like P.

-ch'o-: support, help.
'ałch'o-: help or support each other, be allies, partners, helpmates, spouses.
P-ch'o-: support or help each other, take P's side, be P's helpmate, ally, spouse or partner.

-da- (~ da-)_: cover or plug an opening. (Cf. -daa': lip, -dáá': edge, -dááh; in front of, meet.)
P-da-: cover or plug P.

-dá- (~dá-): block or obstruct an an opening (as by closing or plugging an entry or exit).(Cf. -dáá': edge, -daa': lip, -dááh: in front of, meeting.)
'ádá-: enclosing self (as by blocking an entry or exit, closing a door).
P-dá-: enclosing or blocking P, closing P in (as by plugging a hole, locking a door).

-dáá- (~dáá-)(= -dá +.ná-Id): block P (as an exit, by standing in the way).
P-dáá-: block P.

-éé- ~ -éná- (= -í- ~ -é- + ná-Id). (V. -í- ~ -é-.)

-éé-~-éná- (= -í-~-é- + ná$^{1}$-Ib) (V. -í-~-é-.)
-éé- ~ -éná- (= -í- ~ -é- + ná$^{4}$-Ib) (V. -í- ~ -é-.)

-í- ~ -é-: against, joining, reaching, contacting, overtaking.
'í- ~ 'é-: against, reaching, contacting something.
'ádí- ~ 'ádé-: against self, contacting self.
'ádéé- ~ 'ádéná- (= 'ádé- + ná-Id): back against self, about self.
'ádéé- ~ 'ádéná- (= 'ádé- + ná$^{4}$-Ib(2) ): onto self (as in piling objects on oneself).
'ádéé- ~ 'ádéná- (= 'ádé- + ná$^{1}$-Ib(2) ): around self, encircling self.
'ahí- ~ 'ałhí- ~ 'ahé- ~ 'ałhé-: against, contacting, reaching each other.
'ahéé- ~ 'ahéná- ~ 'ałhéé- ~ 'ałhéná- ('ahí- ~ 'ałhí- ~ 'ahé- ~ 'ałhé + ná$^{4}$-Ib[2]:' onto each other (as in piling objects onto each other).

'ahéé- ~ 'ahéná- ~ 'ałhé- ~ 'ałhéná- ('ahí- ~ 'ałhí- ~ 'ahé- ~ 'ałhé + ná$^{1}$-Ib(2):'around in a circle, around making a circuit.
'éé-~'éná- (= 'í-~'é- + ná-Id): back against something, about something.
'éé- ~ 'éná- (= 'í- ~ 'é- + ná$^{4}$-Ib[2]): onto something (as in piling objects).
P-éé-~P-éná- (= P-í-~P-é- + ná-Id): back against P, about P.
P-éé-~P-éná- (=P-í-~P-é- + ná$^{4}$-Ib[2]): onto P (as in piling objects onto P).
P-éé-~P-éná- (= P-í-~P-é- + ná$^{1}$-Ib[2]): around P, encircling P.
P-í-~P-é-: against P, contacting, reaching or overtaking P.
-gha- ~ -ha-: away from (by force or suasion), winning from (as in a footrace).
'agha-: away from someone (by force or suasion - as by robbery or argument).
'ałgha- ~ 'aha- ~ 'ałha- ~ 'ahiłgha-: away from each other, competing with each other (as in a footrace).
'ałgháá' ~ 'ałghaná'- ~ 'ałháá'- ~ 'ałhaná'-(= 'ałgha- ~ 'ałha- + ná-Id + '[a]-IV[?]): swap trade, exchange with each other.
P-gha-: away from P (by force or suasion (as in taking O away from P, convincing P by argument).

-ghá-: through, penetrating or piercing through.
'aghá-: through something or someone.
'ághá-~'ádígháá-: through self.
'ałghá-~'ahiłghá-: through each other.
P-ghá-: through P.

-gháá'- ~ -háá'-: V. -gha-.

-ká- ~ -ka- (~ há$^{1}$-Ib[2], ha$^{3}$-Ib[2]: for, after (to get or to find - as in going after water, searching for an object).
'áká-: for or after something.
'ádíká-: for or after self (as in helping oneself).
'áłká-~'ahiłká-: for or after each other (as in helping each other).
P-ká-~P-ka-: after P, for P (as in going for P/searching for P).

-k'eh-: overcome (as in a fight.
P-k'eh-: overcome P.

-k'i-~-k'e-~-k'ee-: on, on top of, off of.
'ak'i- 'ak'é- 'ak'ee-: on,, on top of, off of something.
'ák'i- ~ 'ák'e- = 'ák'ee-: on, on top of, off of self.
'ałk'i- ~ 'ałk'e- ~ 'ałk'ee-: on or off each other.
P-k'i-~P-k'e-~P-k'ee: on or off of P, on top of P.

-k'í-~-k'é- (probably a compound: -k'(i)- + -í-Ib(1)), against, contacting): onto.
'ak'í- ~ 'ak'é-: onto something or someone.
'ák'í- ~ 'ák'é-: onto self.
'ałk'í- ~ 'ałk'é-: onto each other.
P-k'í- ~ P-k'é-: onto P.

-lá- (< -lááh, beyond): ahead, in foremost position.
'alá-: ahead (as in a game), in the lead.

-na$^{1}$- ~ -naa- ~ -ni- ~ -n- ~ n- (~na$^{1}$-Ib[2]: around, around about, surrounding.
P-na- ~ P-naa- ~ P-ni- ~ P-n-: around P, surrounding P.

-na$^{2}$-: extending over (as over a limb, over one's shoulder).
'ána-: over self (as a bag slung over one's shoulder.
(P-nah, over P.)
-ná$^{1}$- ~ -ní- ~ -ń- (~ná$^{1}$-Ib[2]): around encircling, embracing.
'aná-: around something.
'áná- ~ 'ádíná- ~ 'ádéé-: around self.
'ahiná- ~ 'ałhiná- ~ 'ahéé- ~ 'ałhéé-: around each other,embracing each other.
P-ná-: around P, encircling P.

-ná$^{2}$-: beside. (~ -nah, beside)
'ałná-: in opposite directions back and forth (as in commuting), switching locations.
'ałnáná- ~ 'ałnáá- (= 'ałná- + ná-Id): to a location and back.
(P-nah, beside P.)

-ní-: penetrating the surface of (without piercing through - as in biting into an apple, digging into an arroyo bank).
P-ní-: into P's surface.

-níká-: through (an opening, as a window), through (penetrating).
'ádiníká-: through self, piercing through self.
'ahiníká- ~ 'ałhiníká-: through each other.
P-níká-: through P.

-niiłt'a'- ~ -niit'a'- (a compound: components uncertain. Cf. tséniit'aa: along the cliff; kiniit'aa: alongside the building, along the street): to a barrier or blockage.
'ahinii(ł)t'a- ~ 'ałhinii(ł)t'a-: blocking each other (as two person meeting on a ledge).
P-nii(ł)t'a-: blocking P's way (as a canyon, cliff).

-ta- ~ -taa- (~ta-Ib[2])(P-tah, among P): among, mix, miingle.
'ałta- ~ 'ałtaa-: among each other, intermingled, mixed.
P-ta- ~ P-taa-: among P, intermixed with P.

-tá-: grazing, barely touching, coming close (but missing), slipping (as one's grip).
'ałtá-: grazing each other; lengthwise (as in cutting a board or cloth).

-t'a- ~ t'aa- (P-tah, its pocket, niche): into a niche, pocket, recess, interior space, under covers.
'át'a- ~ 'át'aa-: under one's own cover (as under one's shirt).
'ałt'a- ~ 'ałt'aa- ~ 'ahiłt'a- ~ 'ahiłt'aa-: under the same covers with each other, close together (as in placing chairs together - lit. in each other's space).
P-t'a-~P-t'aa-: into P's cover, under P's cover, in bed with P.

-ts'á- (< P-ts'ą́ą́', away from P): away from, separating from, leaving, to the detriment of.
'ats'á-: separating from someone or something, apart, aside, separate.
'ats'áá- ~ 'ats'áná- (= 'ats'á- + ná-Id): back apart.
'áts'á-: separating from self, divesting self.
'ałts'á-: away from each other, separating from each other.
'ałts'áá- ~ 'ałts'áná- (= 'ałts'á- + ná-Id): separating back from each other, divorcing.
P-ts'á-: away from P, separating from P.
P-ts'áá- ~ P-ts'áná- (= P-ts'á- + ná-Id): back away from P, separating back from P.

-ya- (< P-yah, P-yaa, under P): under, beneath.
'aya-: under something.
P-ya-: under P, scooping out.

---

Position Ib

(2) Adverbial-Thematic

'a-~'e-~'i-~'ii-~'o-: away, away out of sight.
yah 'a- (góne' yah 'a-): into an enclosure (as a room, house, pasture, burrow, cave).

'á¹- (occurs in combination with ní¹-VIb): marks Comparative Aspect with Neuter Adjectivals.

'á²-: thus, that way. (Cf. 'áá-, there.)

'á³-: thematic with verbs of making, doing, awareness.
'áá- ~ 'áná- (= 'á- + ná-Id).
'áá- (= 'á- + yi-VII).

'á⁴-: thematic with dwindle, disappear. (Probably identical with 'á³-)
'áá- (= 'á- + yi-VII).

'ada- (~'adah, down)(~ bida- ~ hada-): downward from a height (as in descending, climbing down, unloading.

'ahá-: apart, in two. (Cf. postpositional 'ah-á-, for each other).

'ahi-: apart (as in chopping a piece of wood apart for firewood - possibly the null postposition 'ahi-: together, converging.)

'áko-: thus, that way. (Cf. ko-)

'aso- (thematic): suffer, bear.

'atí- ~ 'até- (thematic): harm, injury, suffering. (Cf. tí, tí'-.)

'atsí- ~ 'atsé- (thematic): mental concern, thought. (Cf. tsí-.)
'áá-: V. 'á³-, 'á⁴- above.

'ááł- ~ 'ááh-: signify, mean.

bida- (~bidah, down)(~'ada-~ hada-): downward from a height (as in descending, climbing down, unloading).

cha¹- (thematic): darkness.

cha²-: verb stem CHA, cry, used as a verb prefix.

chi- ~ cho- (thematic): usefulness use. (Occurs in compound form: chi- + [y]i2-VIa.)

ch'aa- (~ch'aa): travel, visit, go out of view.

ch'í- ~ ch'é-: out horizontally (as out a door), coming into view, starting.
ch'éé- (= ch'í- + ná-Id): back out, starting over.

da- (thematic): death (with reference to one subject).

da- (~ dah): up at an elevation, off (as in start off).

dá- (Cf. P-dá-Ib[1]): block, plug, obstruct (as an exit or entry).

dáá- (= dá- + ná-Id).

-de-: over, in excess of. (Cf. de, up; P-de, above P.)
'áde-: above self, beyond one's capacity (as in eating too much).

déé- = di-Ib(2) + ná-Id/ná-II.

di-: into or near fire. Cooccurs with di⁵-VIa, relates to fire.
déé-: (= di- + ná-Id) (as in rekindle a fire).
déé- (= di- + ná-II).

dzi- ~ ji-: away into space. (Cf. dzi-VIa, away into space or distance.

dzídza- ~ tsídza-: into the fire, into the flames.

ha¹-: up out, up vertically (as from an enclosed space, out of (as out of the mud, snow, water).
háá- (= ha- + ná-Id): back up out, back out, returning back out.

ha²-: up ascending, climbing (probably identical with ha¹-)
háá- (= ha- + ná-Id, back up, climbing back up.

ha³-: variant of postpositional -ká-, -ka-Ib(1) and há1-Ib[2]): for, after (to get - as in going for, searching for).

ha⁴- (thematic): with verbs of examine, inspect, watch.

ha⁵- (thematic): worn out, old.

ha⁶- (occurs in combination with di¹⁴-VIa = hadi-): all the way from one end to the other.

há¹-: for, after (to get). Variant of postpositional -ká-, -ka- and ha³-Ib(1). V. ha³- above.

há²: pointedness(?). Occurs as
háá-. Possibly ha- + ná-Id).
In verbs meaning make a point,
sharpen.

hada- (~ hadah, down)(~ 'ada- ~ bida-):
downward from a height (as in
descending, climbing down,
unloading).

hasht'e-~'asht'e-: in order, ready,
prepared.
hasht'éé- = hasht'e- + ná-Id: back
in order.

hatł'a- (a compound: components
uncertain): headlong, head over
heels (as in a sudden fall)

háá¹- = ha¹- + ná-Id: back up out

háá²- = ha²- + ná-Id: ascending back
up.

háá³- = há²- + ná-Id(?): sharpen to
a point.

hił- ~ hi-: darkness, dusk (Hił is often
imisidentified as hi¹-VIa + łi-.)

ka-: chronically ill, invalid.

kéé- (thematic): live, reside. (Cf. ké- of
kéyah, land.)

kí-: up an incline, lean, acend.

kó-: this way, thus, correctly. (cf. 'áko,
that way.)

ko-: this much, like this (demonstrating)
(Cf. ko- of kodi, here.)

k'a-~k'aa- (< k'aa', arrow), wound,
blemish.

k'e- (thematic): loosen, untie, take
down (a loom, one's hair)
k'éé- = k'e- + ná-Id: back down
(hair, loom), untie again, reloosen,
erase, rub back out.

k'é- (thematic): peace, friendliness,
amicable relations. (Cf. -k'éí,
kinsman, relative - lit. "friendly one").

k'éé¹- = k'i- + ná-Id. V. k'i-.

k'éé²- = k'í¹- + ná-Id. V. k'í¹-

k'éé³- = k'í²- +.ná-Id. V. k'í²-

k'i- (thematic): plant, farm.
k'éé- = k'i- + ná-Id: replant.
k'éé- = k'i- + ná -II: plant repeatedly.

k'í¹-~k'é-: straight, erect, outstretched
(as one's legs).
k'éé- = k'í- + ná-Id: straightened back
out, re-straightened (as a bent nail).

k'í²- ~ k'é-: in two, severed, cut off.

k'í³-: tipped, at the tip (as in "red-tipped").
(Cf. postpositional -k'i-/-k'í-.)

k'í⁴- (thematic): keep on, continue (an
activity despite a momentary interruption).

łí- (thematic): flattery, cajolery,
cheating.

na¹- ~ naa- ~ ni- ~ n-: around about, without defined direction. (Cf. postpositional -na¹-Ib(1): around, in the vicinity.)

na²-~ni- ~ n-: across, crosswise. (Cf. naa,
naanii, crosswise, across, over
- as "fall over").

na³-~naa- ~ ni- ~ n-: downward, down
from a height, descend.

ná¹- ~ ní- ~ń-: around encircling, embracing. (Cf. postpositional -ná¹-Ib[1]:
around encircling.)

ná²- (thematic) ~ ní- ~ ń-: with verbs
"skin/butcher", "smoke" and possibly
"sew").

ná³- (thematic) né- ~ ní- ~ ń-: fear, dread,
wild, untamed. (May be postpositional
- cf. P-ná-: fear P.)

ná⁴-~né-~ní-~ń-: upward, rising, up
from a surface, start.
dah ná-: get snagged, grounded,
caught up.
náá- = ní- + ná-Id: back up.

ná⁵-~né-~ní-~ń-: repetition.
(Ná-II and ná⁵- may be the same
prefix, although they cooccur.
Ná⁵- occurs most commonly in
the compound ná-ni-: repetitive
marker.)

naa¹-: V. na¹-Ib(2).

naa²-: V. na²-Ib (2).

naa³-: V. na³-Ib(2).

náá¹- = ná⁴-Ib(2) + ná-Id.

náá²-: occurs with a verb meaning "sacrifice."

naaná-~naané-~naaní-~naań- =
naa¹- + ná¹-: reversing direction
around to and fro.

ni- ~ nii- ~ n-: cessative-terminative:
end, stop, finish.

niki¹-~nihi-: start, begin.
nikéé- = niki- + ná-Id: start
back

niki²-~nihi-~nikee-~nikii-: on
a surface, to earth (as ""all
to earth"), on the ground (as
""and on the ground").
nikéé- = niki- + ná-Id: back to
a surface, back to earth.

nikí-~niké- (probably a compound
nik[i]- + -í-Ib[1] = against a
surface, on a surface).

nikéé¹-= niki¹- + ná-Id: start
back.

nikéé²- = niki²- + ná-Id: back to a
surface, back to earth.

ńłk'éé- (a compound: components
uncertain. -k'éé-probably includes ná¹-Ib(2)): spiralling
(as an eagle).

ntsi¹- (thematic): appears to relate to mental state, apprehen-
sion, worry.

ntsi²- (thematic): with verb meaning "kneel, genuflect."

ntsí- (a compound: na¹-Ib[2] + tsí-)~
ntsé-: mental process, thought.
(Cf. tsí-.)

ńtsí- (a compound: ná⁴-Ib[2] + tsi-) ~
ńtsé-: start a mental process,
start to think.

so- ~ tso- (thematic): prayer.

soh- (thematic): hardship.

shó¹- (thematic): excessively,
awfully, terribly (always in a
negative frame).

shó²-(thematic - always in combination with [y])²-VIa = shóí-)
acquire, get, obtain.

ta- (thematic -< -tah, among[?]):
scatter.

tá- (thematic - occurs in combination with di$^{14}$-VIa = tá-di-): here and there, wandering, traveling.

tí- ~ té- (thematic): injury, wound. (Cf. 'atí-, ti'-.)

ti'- (thematic): suffering.

tii- (~tiih): tackle, attack.

tsí$^{1}$-(thematic - usually in combination with na$^{1}$-Ib[2] or ná$^{4}$-Ib[2] = ntsí- / ńtsí-): mental process, thought.

tsí$^{2}$- (thematic): startle, fright.

tsi'-~tsí'-: aimlessly, zigzag.

tsístł'a-: cornered, trapped, blocked, baffled, into a cul-de-sac. (Cf. ńtsis-tł'ah: the recessed space under the poles on the west side of a forked stick hogan, and nástł'ah: inside corner, niche.)

wó'ą- ~ wó'ąą-: over an edge, into a ditch. (V. -'ą-Ib[1]).

ya$^{1}$- (< -ya$^{1}$-Ib[1]): under, beneath.

ya$^{2}$-: upward/downward, vertically, start abruptly.

yá$^{1}$-: up into the air. (Cf. yá, sky.)
yáá- ~ yání- = yá- + ná$^{4}$-Ib(2): up in the air.

yá$^{2}$- (thematic): talk.

yá$^{3}$- (thematic): suitable, good.

yá$^{4}$-: bashfulness, shame.

yaa$^{1}$- = ya$^{1}$- + (y)i$^{1}$-VIc: dump, spill.

yaa$^{2}$-: down. (Cf. postpositional, -yaa, under.)

yáá$^{1}$- = yá$^{1}$- + ná$^{4}$-Ib(2): up into the air.

yisdá- ~ 'asdá- ~ hasdá-: to safety, escaping from danger, rescue, save.

---

POSITION Ib

(3) Nominal

---

'áni- (a compound: 'á- = 'í-Ib[1]: against something + -ni- = ni', earth, ground): pin to the ground (a hide that is beng cured).

'a'ą́- (< 'a'áán: hole, burrow): into a hole or burrow.

dá'ák'e- ~ dá'ák'ee- (< dá'ák'eh, corn-field, field): into the field.

dį́- (< dį́į́': four) be(come) a group of four, a foursome.

dzíłts'á-:~tsíłts'á-: away from fire or water, out of the fire or out of the water. (V. tsíłts'á- below.)

jé- (< jéí, pleura, heart): carefully, (against the heart) (as in handling a fragile object.)

-kéłk'e- ~ -kéłk'ee- ~ -kék'e- ~ -kék'ee- (< -kék'eh, footprint, footstep).
'ałkéłk'e- ~ 'ałkéłk'ee-: in each other's footprints, in agreement with each other.

-lák'ee- (~ -ák'ee: hand, area of the hand): into hand.
'ahílák'ee- ~ 'ałhílák'ee- ~ 'ałhíłák'ee-: into each other's hands (as in "shaking" hands).
P-lák'ee-: into P's hand, hand to P.

-láta- (< -látah: tip, end, extremity): at the tip.
P-láta-: at P's tip.

łe- (< łeeh: into dirt or ashes, łeezh: dirt, soil): into the ashes (in order to to cook O).

-nák'ee- (< -nák'ee: ocular area, eye place): in(to) the eye, on the eye.
P-nák'ee-: in(to) P's eye.

naa- (< 'anaa': war): war, enemy.

ni- ~ n- (< naaki: two)(always in combin-ation with di$^{7}$-VIa + ni$^{6}$-VIb): a pair, a couple, two, by two's.

-niik'i- (< -nii': face + -k'i-Ib[1]: on): on the face.
P-niik'i-: (put on) a halter.

tá$^{1}$- (< táá': three): a group of three, a threesome.

tá$^{3}$- (= a combining form of tó, water).
táłts'á-: out of the water, to shore.
táá- ~ táná- = tá- + ná-Id.

tó- (= tó, water): water, fluid.

tózhą́-: watery.

tóó- (~ tó, water): into water. (Also as the derivational prefix in tóó'ásh'aah: hide the ball in the Moccasin Game.)

t'á-(< -t'á ~ -t'a': wing): wings.

tsíłts'á- ~ dzíłts'á- (< tsíł- ~ dzíł-: fire )?) + -ts'á-Ib[1]: away from): away from away from fire or water, out of the fire or out of the water. (Cf. tsídza- ~ dzídza-: into the fire.)

-tsą́- (< -tsá, belly): belly, in the belly (as in "kick in the belly"): food.
P-tsą́-: in P's belly.

-za- (a combining form of -zéé': mouth): into mouth.
'aza-: into a mouth.
'áza-: into own mouth.
'ałza-: into each other's mouth.
P-za-: into P's mouth.

-zá- (< -zéé': mouth, neck): neck, throat.
P-zá-: P's throat.

-zé- (< -zéé', mouth, neck): mouth, neck.
'ázéé- ~ 'ázéná- = 'ázé- + ná$^{1}$ Ib(2): around (one's) own neck.
P-zéé- ~ P-zéná- = -zé- + ná$^{1}$-Ib(2): around P's neck.

---

POSITION Ic

Reflexive

---

'á- (occurs in combination with di-IV: self.

POSITION Id

Reversionary

---

ná- ~ né- ~ ní- ~ ń-: returning back, reverting to a previous location, state or condition (often equivalent to English re-).

---

POSITION Ie

Semeliterative

---

náá- ~ nááná- ~ nááné- ~ nááni- ~ nááń-: one more time, repeat once again, again. In combination with ła': one, some, łanáá- = one more, another one, some more.

POSITION II

Iterative Mode

ná- ~ né- ~ ní- ~ ń-: serves to derive the Iterative Mode, a type of Frequentative, from the Usitative. Although ná-II and ná5-Ib(2) cooccur they are similar in meaning, and they may be identical morphemes. (ńánísts'in, I'm beating him with my fists/ níńánísts'įįh, I repeatedly beat him with my fists.

POSITION III

Distributive Plural

da- ~ de- ~ daa-: indicates that 3+ (3 or more) subjects or objects participate or are involved individually in the action, event, condition or state of being denoted by the verb base. Da- occurs as a distributive pluralizing agent with nouns, pronouns and postpositions, as well as with verbs, and also appears as an independent particle.

Da- marks the boundary between the DISJUNCT and the CONJUNCT verb prefix categories.

The Conjunct Prefixes

POSITION IV

Position IV contains the verb-incorporated pronominal prefixes that serve to represent the direct object. These have the following shape.

Singular
Person

1. shi-/sh-: me.
2. ni-/n-: you.
3. bi-/b-: him, her, it.
3o. yi-/-i-/yí-/-í-: him,her,it.
3a. ha-/ho-/hw-: him, her, one, a person
3s. ha-/ho-/hw-: space, area, impersonal "it/things". The 3s object pronoun frequently occurs as a thematic prefix, representing an impersonal 3rd person object including a sorrow, disease or event, or with an obscure semantic function.

3i. 'a-~'e-~'i-~'o-~'-: someone or something unspecified. Shape of the prefix is determined by the phonological environment. The 3i pronoun often functions as a thematic prefix, although in the verb bases involved it may have functioned historically as an indefinite object pronoun. (Cf. 'ashhosh, I'm asleep, 'ashhą́ą́', I'm snoring.)

Duoplural

1. nihi-/nih-: us.
2. nihi-/nih-: you.
3. bi-/b-: them.
3o. yi-/-i-/yí-/-í-: them.
3a. ha-/ho-/hw-: them, people.

REFLEXIVE: -di-/-dí-/-d-
('á-di-/'á-dí-/'á-d-): self.
RECIPROCAL: 'ahi-/'ah-: each other, one another.

Ø serves to represent any prefix of Position IV except the 3a, 3s, 3i, Reflexive and Reciprocal.

POSITION V

Subject Pronouns

The 3i and 3s pronouns of Positions V and IV share the same shapes and they are identical semantically except that those in Position V represent the subject of an intransitive verb while those in Position IV represent the direct object of a transitive verb. They cannot co-occur.

3a (or 4th person): ji- ~ dzi- ~ -zh- ~ -sh- ~ -z- ~ -i-: he,she, one, a person, people, they. (the 3a subject pronoun represents a person, in both a specific and an impersonal sense, or a personified animal. The shape of the morpheme is determined by the phonological environment.)

3s: ha-~ho-~hw-: space, area, impersonal "it/things," a sorrow, disease, event.

3i. 'a- ~ 'e- ~ 'i- ~ 'o- ~ '-: someone or something unspecified, a person, people. The shape of the morpheme is determined by environment.) The 3i subject pronoun represents a specific entity when it is a non-solid of the type gas, vapor,cloud, fog, smoke (as in k'os na'ajooł, a cloud is drifting about. Cf. naajooł it is drifting about, referring to a solid entity, as deenínínaajooł,the tumbleweed is drifting about.

Agentive: -'di-. Probably the 3i subject pronoun 'a- + -di-: person (reduced to -'di- because, as the marker of subject in Agentive Passive verbs the compound prefix is always preceded by a direct object pronoun. E.g. bi'diiłtsą́ = bi'adiiłtsą́, he/she/it was seen (i.e. unspecified subject saw him/her/it; yisdáshi'doodlóóz = yisdáshi'adoodlóóz, I was rescued, led to safety (i.e.unspecified subject led me to safety).

POSITION VI

Position VI is divided into 3 sub categories identified as Positions VIa, VIb and VIc.

POSITION VIa

Thematic and adverbial elements

'i- ~ '-: an unidentified morpheme that occurs in a few verb bases. (E.g. n'diiyá, he broke loose and got away; n'dii'ą́, I took it [SRO] down, picked it [as an apple]; na'iidįį'ą́, he took it down, picked it. ) Reduced to -'- this element appears to be a component in the compound prefix -'nii- that marks the Inchoatives. (E.g. bi'niiyą́ą́, I startedto eat it; 'i'niiyą́ą́, I started to eat; shi'niitih, I started to get old.)

di1- ~ d-: occurs as a component of verb bases that involve movement of the arms or legs.

di2- ~ d-: occurs as a component of verbs that involve relinquishment, relaxation, opening or closing and addition or reduction.

di3- ~ d-: appears as a component of some verb bases that involve an elongated object (cf. the di-generic prefix of Carrier dintsa: elongated object is big, contrasting with ntsa, object of unspecified shape is big). Di$^{3}$- also marks verb bases that describe extension into space or time, and bases that mark the inception of movement or activity that progresses along in space or time (i.e. "start along"). Di$^{3}$ and di$^{13}$- are probably identical.

dí$^{4}$- ~ d-: occurs as a component of bases that are concerned with refuge, relief, succour (probably cognate with or identical to di$^{6}$- and dí$^{2}$-).

di$^{5}$- ~ d-: occurs as a component of verb bases that are concerned with fire or light. Di$^{5}$- appears to be identical with the di- prefix of Position Ib(2), also concerned with fire, with which di$^{5}$- co-occurs. (Cf. didíí'ą́, I set it (SRO) on or near the and independent adverbial dih, into the fire.)

di$^{6}$- ~ d-: occurs as a component of verb bases concerned with the mouth, stomach, throat, oral action, food, smell, noise, speech. (Cf. di$^{12}$-VIa.)

di$^{7}$- ~ d-: occurs in combination with ni$^{6}$VIb in certain Neuter Imperfective Adjectivals. (Ni- deletes in 3rd person: e.g. dinishjool: I'm plump / dijool he, she, it is plump.)

di$^{8}$- ~ d-: occurs in verb bases concerned with pain, hurt.

di$^{9}$- ~ d-: occurs as a component of verb bases that involve holiness, faith, respect, immunity from the effects of a ceremony, prayer.

di$^{10}$- ~ d-: occurs in certain Active and Neuter verb bases that are concerned with color. (Cf.Chipewyan <u>de</u>elk'os : it is red,Carrier <u>du</u>lk'un, it is red, Hare dedele: it is red and Navajo dinilchíí': it is reddish or pink.)

di$^{11}$- ~ d-: occurs as a component of verb bases that involve tilting, slant,ing, placing on edge, leaning, dangling; and di$^{11}$ - is also probably the d- component of the compound verb prefix náhi<u>de</u>e-: turn over, capsize.

di$^{12}$- ~ d-: appears as a component of verb bases that involve sound, hearing. (Cf. di$^{6}$-above.)

di$^{13}$- ~ d-: probably identical with di$^{3}$- above. Di$^{13}$- is identified as the inceptive marker that, in combination with yi-VII (Progressive Mode marker), produces the Future paradigms. (Di$^{3}$- and di$^{13}$- may coocccur, as in dideeshááł, I'll start to go along.)

di$^{14}$- ~ d-: a "catch-all" for di- prefixes that, even speculatively, cannot be assigned to one of the foregoing categories.

dí$^{1}$- ~ dé-: occurs as a component of a few verb bases concerned with sight, vision.

dí$^{2}$- ~ dé-: occurs with bases that involve disablement, relief, assistance, boredom. Some bases also require the independent adverbial particle yah, as in yah déshdá, I sit waiting for aid. (Cf. di$^{4}$- above.)

dee-: a compound prefix, the components of which are not identifiable at present. (E.g. bídééyá: I brushed against him, náhidééłts'id: it turned over, capsized, na'ídééłkid: I inquired, dééłgizh: I cut a trench.)

dzi-~ji-~zh-~-z-~j-: away into space or idistance. Shape is determined by the phonological environment. (Cf. the dzi-prefix of Position Ib[2], of similar meaning.)

hi$^{1}$-~he-~ha-~hee-~haa-~h-~ yi-~-i-: the Seriative marker, denoting segmented verbal action as that involved in (1) hopping, skipping, writhing, (2) arriving, exiting, entering, ascending, descending, etc. in series - one after another in contradistinction to collective or group action and (3) handling or propelling objects one after another in contradistinction to handling (i.e. bringing, carrying, giving, picking up etc.) or propelling (i.e. tossing, throwing, dropping) them collectively. The number of subjects or objects must total at least 3. Prefix shape is determined by the phonological environment. When immediately preceded by dzi-VIa or by a prefix of Position IV or V hi$^{1}$- takes the alternant shape yi- ~-i-. (V. yi$^{3}$-VIc.) (V. also THE NAVAJO LANGUAGE, Revised Edition 1987, pp.83-85.)

hi$^{2}$-: occurs as a component of verb bases that involve dangling, hanging, extending partly in/partly out, over-, turning, wagering, bet.ting May be identical with hi$^{1}$-. (V. also yi$^{3}$-VIc.)

hí-~yi3-VIc: in bases with the meaning "lie in ambush, bet." (Probably identical with hi$^{2}$-)

ji-~dzi-~j-~dz-: occurs in bases that involve emotional states such as kind-generosity, hate, trust, confidence. Ji- appears in combination with (y)i$^{2}$-VIa with which it contracts to produce joo- in certain environments; with (y)i$^{2}$-VIa + ni$^{7}$-VIb, again contracting to produce joo- in certain environ-iments; and with (y)í$^{1}$-VIa + ni$^{7}$-VIb, contracting to produce jó- in certain environments. (V. THE NAVAJO LANGUAGE, Revised Edition 1987, p. 85.)

łi- ~ -l-: identified (Krauss:1969) as łi- = ł-classifier. Occurs in the guise of a thematic prefix, in combination with ni$^{6}$-VIb, in certain Neuter Imperfective adjectivals relating to color and certain other inherent qualities and attributes (flammability, obesity, sweetness, oiliness, spottedness, etc,) Łi- takes the shape -l- and shifts to the classifier slot (Position IX) when preceded by dzi-VIa, or by a prefix of Position III or V.

si1-~(y)i$^{5}$-VIc: occurs as a component of a verb meaning "kill one object." The alternant shape (y)i$^{5}$-VIc is required when si$^{1}$- is preceded by a prefix of Position IV or V. (E.g. séłhį́: I killed him/niyéłhį́: I killed you.)

si$^{2}$-~(y)i$^{6}$-VIc: relates to the movement, production, reception or existence of sound.

si$^{3}$-~shi-: occurs as a component of verb bases that relate to absorption or permeation of liquid or moisture.

shi-~-sh-: occurs as a component in a verb base meaning "scold," "be mean or fierce," where it sometimes appears to occupy the classifier slot (Position IX). (E.g. nich'a hodoo<u>sh</u>-keeł, he will scold you.)

yi¹-~-i-: occurs as a component of verbs that describe the passage of night and the coming of dawn. (Yi¹- is y-initial - not gh-initial.)

yi²- ~ -i- ~ woo- ~ -oo-: meaning uncertain. Occurs in verbs of the type wooshdlą́ ~ yinishdlą́: I believe it, wooshbįįh, I'm winning or earning it, yisékan: I hired him, and as a component of compound -jiini- ~ joo- in jiinishba' ~ jooshba', I'm kind, generous, choinish'į́ ~ choosh'į́: I use it, taoshnih: I'm mixing it.

yí- ~ -í-: directive, directed at. Occurs in combination with ni⁷-VIb, with which it contracts, in certain environments, to produce -ó-. (Cf. yíníshtą': I have hold of it/ shótą': he has hold of me.)

---

POSITION VIb

Thematic and adverbial elements.

---

ni¹-~n-: terminative. Describes verbal action of a type that is inherently terminal - a concept that it shares with ni-Ib(2): cessative-terminative, and with ni-VII: a modal prefix. All three, along with ni', earth, ground, may be cognates. Ni-terminal + di³-VIa: inceptive combine to produce compound dini- ~ díní- that marks the Prolongatives.

ni²- ~ n-: identified as a vestigial generic classifier that served historically to distinguish the subject or object of a verb as spherical in shape. A generic classifier of similar shape and meaning remains productive in manyNorthern Athapaskan languages, including Canadian Carrier and Alaskan Ahtna.

ni³-~n: occurs as a component of verb bases that relate to the mind and to mental processes. (Cf. yíní- ~ -ni': mind.)

ni⁴-n-: occurs as a component of verb bases concerned with sight and vision. Probably relatable to ní¹-VIc.

ni⁵- ~ n-(thematic): occurs as a component of verb bases that describe the subject as weak, incapacitated, sick, wounded or exhausted.

ni⁶-~n- (identified by Krauss as ni-VII, the modal prefix): occurs as a component of Neuter adjectivals that describe the physical attributes of the subject, including color, size, weight, taste, appearance or condition. Ni⁶- often occurs in combination with di⁷-VIa, di¹⁰-VIa and ł-VIa.

ni⁷- ~ n-: a category into which are placed sundry ni-prefixes that cannot be readily identified, even speculatively, with a particular positional slot. (Cf. di¹⁴-VIa.)

ní¹- ~ ń- (thematic): appears to relate to sight and vision. (Cf. ni⁴-VIb.)

ní²- ~ ń-: marks Comparative Aspect in Neuter adjectivals that describe size, shape, or distance. Occurs often in combination with 'á-Ib.

-'nii-: a compound prefix that serves to form the Inchoatives.

-nee-: a compound prefix of uncertain constituency, comparable to dee-VIa. (E.g. bíneeshdlį́, I'm interested in it, honééniid, there was fun, enjoyment.)

---

POSITION VIc

Adverbial-Thematic

---

yi¹-~ yii- ~ -i- ~ -ii- ~ wo- ~ -o-: Transitional Aspect marker. Initial y-/w- are peg elements.

yi²- ~ yii- ~ -i- ~ -ii- ~ wo- ~ -o-: Semelfactive Aspect marker. Initial y-/w- are peg elements.

yi³- ~ -i- ~ y-: the alternant of hi¹,²- in certain phonological environments. (V. hi¹- and hi²- above.)

yi⁴- ~ -i-~y-: alternant of si¹-VIa, kill one object.

yi⁵- ~ -i-: alternant of si²-VIa, relating to sound.

yí- ~ -í-: alternant of hí-VIa.

---

POSITION VII

Modal-Conjugation Markers

---

Ø (zero): absence of a Position VII prefix is treated positively since Ø serves to mark the Ø-Imperfective-Usitative Modes and the yi-Ø Imperfective-Usitative and yi-Ø Perfectives.

yi- (=ghi-): marks the yi-Perfective and the Progressive Modes.

ni-: marks the ni-Imperfective a,d ni-Perfective Modes. (V. also ni⁶-VIb.)

si- ~ -s- ~ -z-: marks the si-Imperfective-Usitative and the si-Perfective Modes.

wó- ~ -ó- ~ wo- ~ -o-: marks the Optative Mode.

Included here, although not a prefix of Position VII, is / ´ /, derived by n-absorption from a historical ni-prefix, an element that serves to mark the Perfective Mode. /'/ appears in some persons and paradigms, but not in all.

---

THE PEG ELEMENTS

---

A phonological rule requires that all syllables have the shape CV (consonant-vowel) or CVC.(consonant-vowel-consonant), but with exception of ni , the 2nd person singular subject pronoun, the prefixes of Position VIII are non-syllabic. To prevent a word from beginning with a vowel or with any other non-syllabic prefix (including the stem classifiers of Position IX) a peg yi- ~ y ~ w-(before a following -o-) is inserted. (Thus: yi-shcha prevents shcha*, I'm crying, y-iishtał prevents iishtał,* I'm giving it a kick, yi-lzhééh prevents lzhééh*, it's being mowed, and w-ohcha prevents ohcha*, you dpl are crying.)

---

POSITION VIII

The Verb-incorporated Subject Pronouns

---

The prefixes of Position VIII represent the subject of the verb in the Primary or Base Paradigms. Assimilation, contraction, reduction, elision, Mode, Aspect and other factors determine prefix shape and form in particular environments.

SINGULAR

1. -sh- ~ -s- ~ Ø: I.
2. ni- ~ /'/ ~ Ø: you.
3. Ø: he, she, it.

DUOPLURAL

1. -ii(d)- ~ -aa(d)- ~ -ee(d)- ~ -oo(d)-: we.
2. -oh- ~- o(h)- ~ -ooh- ~ -oo(h)- ~ -áh- ~ -á(h)- ~ -ah- ~ -a(h)- ~ -éh- ~ -é(h)-: you.
3. Ø: they.

The extended paradigms include the subject pronoun prefixes of Position V: 3a (or 4th person) ji-, 3i 'a- and 3s ha- ho-.

---

POSITION IX

The Classifiers

---

Position IX contains four non-syllabic prefixes long known as "stem classifiers," although they do not in fact serve to classify anything. All verb themes must include one (rarely two) of these elements. In some verb themes the classifier functions as a thematic prefix, while in others it serves to mark causative transitivity and passivity.

The classifiers are: Ø (zero), Ł, D and L.

---

POSITION X

The Stem

---

The final morpheme in the verb construction proper is the stem.

---

# III. THE VERB PREFIXES

<u>These include:</u>

1. The subject and direct object pronouns
2. The modal-aspectival conjugation markers
3. The marker of distributive plurality
4. The thematic and adverbial-derivational elements

<u>Prefix Position</u>: the verb prefixes usually appear in a relatively fixed syntactic order, a feature that permits their assignment to a total of 16 numbered positional slots.

<u>Prefix Classes</u>: The Verb Prefixes include two broad classes: (1) inflectional and (2) derivational-thematic; and these are distinguished in *Conjunct / Disjunct* - categories based on functional, phonological and positional criteria.

<u>1.The Inflectional Prefixes:</u> include the stem classifiers in Position 9, the verb-incorporated subject pronouns of Positions 8 and 5, the modal-aspectival conjugation markers of Position 7, the markers of Transitional and Semelfactive Aspect in Position 6c, the Seriative marker in Position 6a / c, the direct object pronouns in Position 4, the marker of distributive plurality in Position 3, the Iterative Mode marker in Position 2, the reflexive pronoun in Position 1c, and the pronominal prefixes of Positions 0 and 1a.

<u>2. The Derivational (Thematic-Adverbial) Prefixes</u> include the elements in Positions 1b, 1d, 1e, 6a, 6b, and 6c, exclusive of Seriative in Positions 6a / c and the yi- Aspect markers in 6c.

## 1. The Conjunct Prefixes

The Conjunct category contains the prefixes of Positions 4 - 9, including all of the primary inflectional elements (the classifier, subject pronouns, modal-aspectival conjugation markers, and direct object pronouns).

<u>Phonological Features:</u> With exception of the classifier prefixes of Position 9, which are non-syllabic, the spatial / 4th person pronoun and the indefinite subject / object pronoun of Positions 5 / 4, the Conjunct Prefixes are all composed of a consonant + the vowel [ i ] or [ í ]. (Many Athapaskanists treat the Conjunct prefixes as consonantal and the i-vowel as epenthetic.)

A few Conjunct prefixes are inherently high in tone, as:

yí-directive in yíníshtą': I have hold of it
ní- in haa nítdáás: how heavy is he? <u>ní</u>níł'į: you're looking at it
dí- in yik'id<u>é</u>ez'į́į' (dí- reduces to d- and the inherent high tone carries over to the following vowel): he watches over it

Most of the Conjunct prefixes are neutral in tone - i.e. generally low, but taking high tone by assimilation in particular phonological environments, as:

ni-: low in nidaah, he’s in the act of sitting down, but high in nánídaah, he’s in the act of sitting back down - by assimilation to the high tone of preceding ná-.

ni-: low in nishch’id, I’m scratching you, but high in níích’id (< ni- + (y)í- > níí-): I scratched you - by assimilation to the following high tone (y)í-.

A Conjunct prefix vowel generally elides before a vowel-initial prefix such as the subject pronouns -ii(d)-: we and -o(h) -oo-: you plural:

n(i)-4 + -iiltééł > niiltééł: we’re carrying you along
sh(i)-4 + -oołtééł > shoołtééł: you two are carrying me along
d(i)-6a + -iit’ash > diit’ash: we two will go
n(i)-7 + -oo’áázh > noo’áázh: you two went

However, the prefix vowel remains before (y)-í (= gh-í), Position 7 conjugation marker (yi-Perfective), in 1st, 2nd and 3rd person Ø/Ł-class and 2nd person sgl D/L-class verb constructions, as in:

díízhéé’ < di- + -(y)ízhéé’: I spit / he, she spit
díínízhéé’ < di- + -(y)ínízhéé’: you spit
biih díínílchid < di- + -(y)ínílchid: you stuck your hand into it

dííniid < di- + -(y)íniid: I / he, she said
díínínniid < di- + -(y)íníniid: you said

biih nííłkaad < biih ni- + -(y)íłkaad: I drove (herded) them into it
biih nííníłkaad < biih ni- + -(y)íníłkaad: you drove them into it
yiih yinííłkaad < yiih yi-ni- + ~ (y)íłkaad, he drove them into it

nííchʼid < ni- + -(y)ích’id: I scratched you / he, she scratched you
shííních’id < shi- + -(y)íních’id: you scratched me

The inherent high tone Conjunct Prefixes also reduce to their initial consonant before a following vowel-initial prefix, but the high tone is transferred to the following syllable, as:

n(í)- + -iildáás > níildáás: we two are comparatively heavy (haa níildáás, how heavy are we?)
n(í)- + -oł’į > nół’į́: you two are looking at it.
-d(´)- + -eez > -déez- in shik’idéez’į́į́’: he watches over me

## Position 9: The Stem Classifiers

A prefix category long identified as “the Stem Classifiers,” or simply as “the Classifiers,” occupies positional slot 9, immediately preceding the Verb Stem. The name is a misnomer inasmuch as the “Classifiers” do not indeed “classify” anything! They are four in number (including Ø); they are non-syllabic, and they are positioned immediately before the stem. All Verb Themes must include one (rarely two) Classifier prefixes. These elements function as thematic prefixes, without discernible meaning in some Verb Themes, while in others they perform an identifiable grammatical function. The Classifiers have the shape: Ø, Ł, D, L.

1. Ø-Classifier: appears in about 41% of the Verb Themes. Actually, Ø simply represents the absence of a prefix in Position 9, but it is convenient to treat Ø (zero) as a positive element.

naaØmaas: he's rolling around
neiØ'á: he's carrying it around (SRO)

2. Ł-Classifier occurs in about 28% of the Verb Themes, functioning as a thematic element in some; and as a causative-transitivizing agent in others, as:

yáłti': he's talking (ł-thematic)
neiłmaas: he's rolling it around (ł-causative: he's causing it to roll around)

Ł- deletes when preceded by [-s-] or [-sh-], as:

naashjid < naash(ł)jid: I'm carrying it around on my back.
yist'é < yis(ł)t'é: he roasted it

Ł- contracts with (devocalizes) stem-initial z- / zh-, as in:

désas < dé(ł)zas: I'm strewing it along
yiisį' < yii(ł)zį': I stood him up
yíshéé' < yí(ł)zhéé': I mowed it

Ł- devocalizes stem-initial l- / gh-, as in:

dííłid < dííłlid: I burned it
yíłhį́į́' < yíłyį́į́' (= yíłghį́į́'): I melted it
'ałhą́ą́' < 'ałghą́ą́': he's snoring

Ł- deletes the -h-component of preceding -oh-: 2nd person dpl subject pronoun: you dual / plural , as:

wołbéézh < wo(h)łbéézh: you two are boiling it

Ł- > L- under d-effect in 1st person dpl, Passive, Reflexive and Reciprocal verbs, as:

yiiltééł < y(i)-ii(d)-łtééł: we're carrying him along
taah yilteeh < yi-(d)--łteeh: it's being put in water
taah bi'dilteeh < bi'di-(d)--łteeh: he's being put in water
'ádílnaad < 'ádi-(d)--łnaad: it's licking itself
'ahilnaad < 'ahi-(d)--łnaad: they're licking each other

3. D-Classifier functions as a theme constituent in a small number (about 13%) of Verb Bases. It does not emerge as (d) - except perhaps as a component of dl/dz (written as digraphs) in Navajo. Rather, D-Classifier is manifested in the effect (d-effect) that it exerts on a following stem-initial consonant:

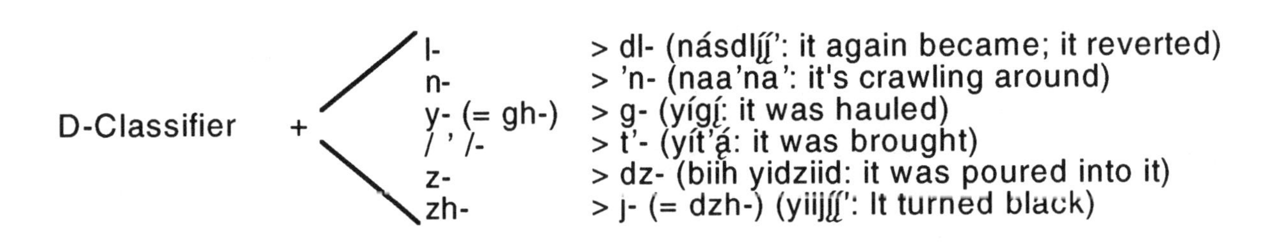


D-Classifier is not manifested before stem-initial: b-, ch-, ch'-, d-, dl-, dz-, t-, t'-, tł-, tł'-, ts-, ts'-, g-, k-, k'-. In these environments its presence is reflected indirectly (e.g. the Verb Theme [d]t'a': "fly" as in: ch'ídaast'a' not *ch'ídaazt'a': they flew out - if the Theme contained Ø-Classifier the lexical construction would take the form ch'ídaazt'a'. Similarly, the Theme (d)kai: "plural go" as in bił nisiskai not bił *nisékai: I accompanied them - nisékai would be the proper construction if the Theme were Økai).

D-class verbs are predominantly Passive, Mediopassive, Reflexive or Reciprocal derivatives from Ø-class verbs.

ní'ą́ (< -Ø'ą́: move SRO): (Active) I brought it
yít'ą́ (< -d'ą́ = -t'ą́: be moved SRO): (Passive) it was brought

biih yí'ą́ (< -Ø'ą́: move SRO): (Active) I put it into it
biih yit'ą́ (< -d'ą́ = -t'ą́: be moved SRO): it was put into it
biih neesht'ą́ (< -d'ą́ = -t'ą́: move own SRO): (Mediopassive) I put my head (i.e. my own SRO) into it

séloh (< -Øloh: lasso, snare): (Active) I lassoed it
yisdloh (< d-loh =-dloh: be lassoed, snared): (Passive) it was lassoed or snared
'ádeesdloh (< -d-loh) = -dloh: (Reflexive) he lassoed himself
'ahisdloh (< d-loh): (Reciprocal) they lassoed each other

4. L-Classifier, produced as the result of d-effect on Ł-Classifier, is a theme constituent in about 18% of Verb Bases. Like D-class Themes, those containing L- are predominantly Passive, Mediopassive, Reflexive or Reciprocal derivatives, but here stemming from Ł-class Themes.

níłtį́ (< łtį́: move AnO): (Active) I brought it
yíltį́ (< ltį́: be moved AnO): (Passive) it was brought

biih yíłne' (< łne': toss / propel SRO): (Active) I tossed it into it
yiih noolne' (< lne' toss / propel own SRO): (Mediopassive) he quickly stuck his head into it (i.e. propelled his own SRO into it)

'ázayoolne' (< lne'): (Reflexive) he tossed it (SRO) into his own mouth

'ałzayoolne' (< lne'): (Reciprocal) they tossed it (SRO) into each other's mouth

L- deletes when preceded by -s- / -sh-, as in:

yishdéél < yish(l)déél: I ate them (as berries)
ná'ádístsááh < ná'ádís(l)tsááh:I'm drying myself

Before stem-initial z- / zh- or gh- the presence of L-Classifier is reflected in failure of the stem-initial consonant to devoice, as:

bił 'ahisisził < 'ahisis(l)ził: I'm playing "grab" with him
yishghał < yish(l)ghał: I'm eating it (meat)
'ádíshzhééh < 'ádísh(l)zhééh: I'm shaving myself

L-Classifier is devoiced by the preceding -h-component of the 2nd person dpl subject pronoun -oh-, as in:

wołghał (< wo[h]lghał): you two are eating it (meat)

L-Classifier functions as a thematic prefix in a small number of Verb Themes, as in:

yil'is: he's stepping along
náldzid: he's afraid

A few Verb Themes appear to contain two classifiers, as:

yoołt'ááł < yoo-ł-d-'ááł: he's carrying it (fire/torch) along
yiyoołwoł < yiyoo-ł-(l)-woł: he's running it, causing it to run (the presence of L-Classifier is reflected by the fact that stem-initial w- does not devoice - it would take the shape -hoł if preceded by -ł- alone.)
nábidiił'na' < nábidii-ł-d-na': I stood it back up.

## Position 8: Subject Pronouns

Position 8 contains the verb-incorporated subject pronouns, the shape of which is determined by the phonological and / or grammatical environment in which this element appears in any given verb construction. (See The Verb Paradigms.)

The Verb-Incorporated Subject Pronouns are:

| | |
|---|---|
| -s-/-sh-/-Ø- = I | -ii(d)- /-aa(d)- / -ee(d)- /- oo(d)- = we |
| -ni-/ ´ / Ø = you sgl | -o(h)-/-oo(h)-/-oo- = you dpl |
| Ø = he,she,it | Ø = they |

yishcha: I'm crying / nisneez / yíØcha: I cried
nicha: you're crying / níneez: you're tall / yiiØgááh: you're turning white
yiØcha (< Øcha): he's crying / they're crying

yiicha: we're crying / hahaa'nil: we extracted them / ch'íhee'nil: we put them out / woodle': that we might become
wohcha: you're crying / hadoohdzih: you dpl will speak / soozį́: you dpl stand

## Position 7: Modal-Aspectival Conjugation Markers

Position 7 contains the modal-aspectival conjugation markers, including Ø. These, alone or in combination with particular stem shapes, serve to mark all Modes except the Iterative (which is marked by a Disjunct Prefix in Position 2), and the Future, which is a derivative of the Progressive.

The Modal-Aspectival Conjugation Markers are:

ni-: Imperfective and Perfective Modes
yi-: Progressive and Perfective Modes
Ø-: Imperfective/Usitative/Perfective Modes
-ó-/-o-: Optative Mode
si-: Imperfective/Usitative/Perfective Modes

## Position 6: Thematic, Derivational and Aspect Markers

For the most part the prefixes of Position 6 (the Jetté-Kari "Qualifier Class") share the shape di-, ni- or yi-. Semantic identification is often difficult and sometimes quite speculative. There are possibly 40 or more prefix constituents of Position 6, which are contained in three subcategories identified as 6c, 6b and 6a.

1. Position 6c includes a group of semantically distinct yi- (~ -i- ~ -ii-) prefixes: yi[1]- marks Transitional Aspect; yi[2]- marks Semelfactive Aspect and yi[3,4]- function as the allomorphs of hi-6a and si[2]-6a respectively.

yi[1]-: yiilch'iil (Transitional): it became curly, it curled
yi[1]-: yiishjį́į́' (Transitional): I turned black

yi[2]-: yiishtał (Semelfactive): I'm in the act of giving it a kick
yi[2]-: yiists'ǫs (Semelfactive): I'm in the act of giving her a kiss

hi-: yisdáhideesdzį́į́s (Seriative): I'll drag them to safety one after another, BUT
yi[3]-: yisdánihidiyeesdzį́į́s (Seriative): I'll drag you (plural) to safety one after another.
si[2]-: séłhį́: I killed it BUT
yi[4]-: yiyiisxį́: he killed it

2. Position 6b includes a group of semantically distinctive ni- (~ n-) prefixes. Of these ni[1]- marks verbal action as terminal, and ni[2]- is identified as a vestigial generic classifier for round shape (cognate with an element of similar meaning, used productively in many Northern Athapaskan languages).

ni[1]-: nidaah (terminal): he's in the act of sitting down

niilch'iil (terminal): he closed his eyes
ni$^{2}$-: hanoolne' (generic for roundness):it stuck its head up out (as a prairie dog from its burrow)
hanííbą́ą́z (generic for roundness): the full moon came up

3. Position 6a includes a group of di-, dzi-, hi-, ji-, 'i-, łi-, si- and yi-prefixes, many of which function as thematic elements.

di$^{1}$- is identified as a thematic constituent of Verb Themes concerned with movement of the arms (hands) and legs (feet), as in:

biih deeshnii': I reached into it, put my hand into it
biih deeshtáál: I stepped into it, put my foot into it

di$^{5}$- is identified as a thematic constituent of Verb Themes that are concerned with fire and light, as:

dííłid: I burned it
bigháḏi'nídíín: light shines through it
'aḏoołdlał: he's going along shining a light (as a lantern or flashlight)

di$^{6}$- is identified as a thematic constituent of Verb Themes that relate to stomach, food, oral noise, as:

díníza': you belched
dííniid: I / he said

'i- (~ -i-) is tentatively identified as a thematic constituent of a group of Verb Bases that are concerned with "downward movement to a state of freedom or detached independence." In this sense 'i- is complemented by na$^{3}$-Position 1b meaning "downward" + an unidentified di-prefix of Position 6a. Conjugated in a Transitional Aspect pattern, the prefix cluster na-'i-di-(y)i$^{1}$- ~ n'dii- functions as a derivational-semantic unit. Compare:

tł'ízí n'diiyá: the (tethered) goat broke loose and got away (got down to freedom)
ch'ah n'diilts'id: the hat came off (its peg) and fell
beeldléí bił n'diiyol: the blanket (hanging) was blown down by the wind
naa'ahóóhai bik'os n'diikal: I chopped off the chicken's head
łį́į́' biyéél shá na'iidii'ą́: he took down the (hanging or shelved) saddle for me
ch'ééh jiyání n'dii'ą́: I picked a watermelon

'i-: Position 6a may also be the '- component of -'nii-: marker of the Inchoative (see Transitional Aspect), and the -'- component of other Verb Bases:

bi'niidléézh (Inchoative): I started to paint it
ba'ní'ą́: I loaned it to him (SRO)

## The Seriative

The Seriative is marked by hi- in Position 6a, or by its yi-allomorph, assigned to Position 6c. Hi- appears variously as ha- ~ he-, by assimilation to a preceding prefix vowel, and the yi-allomorph appears variously as yi- ~ yii- ~ -i- ~ -ii-.

The Seriative is required in verbs of locomotion (go, run, fly, crawl) when three or more (3+) subjects act seriatim (one after another, in series) instead of collectively (in a body or unit group). Seriative constructions of this type usually include the distributive plural prefix da- of Position 3, reflecting the fact that each of the subjects is involved in the action denoted by the verb.

'áłchíní 'ólta' góne' yah 'adahaaskai: the 3+ children (each) entered the school (one after another, in series). (Cf. 'áłchíní 'ólta' yah 'eekai: the 3+ children entered the school - in a body, all at once)

jaa'abaní tsé'ą́ą́dę́ę́' ch'ídahaast'a': the 3+ bats flew out of the cave (in series). (Cf. jaa'abaní tsé'ą́ą́dę́ę́' ch'ídaast'a': the 3+ bats flew out of the cave in a body - all at once.)

In transitive constructions the Seriative describes the movement or processing of 3+ direct objects, one or one quantity after another in contradistinction to their movement or processing as a collective unit.

'ólta'dę́ę́' naaltsoos ch'éhéjaa': I carried the 3+ books out of the school one (or one quantity) after another. (Cf. 'ólta'dę́ę́' naaltsoos ch'íníjaa': I carried the books out of the school - in one armful.)

ts'in k'íhidéłdéél: I broke the 3+ bones in two one after another. (Cf. ts'in k'ídiníłdéél: I broke the bone in two.)

The yi-allomorph of hi- is required when hi- is immediately preceded by a direct object pronoun prefix of Position 4, by a deictic subject pronoun of Position 5, or by dzi-: Position 6a "away into space."

'áłchíní yisdáhádzį́į́z: I dragged the 3+ children to safety one after another (a 3rd person direct object is represented by Ø in Position 4, so the Seriative here is represented by hi-.)

tł'éédą́ą́' yisdánihiyédzį́į́z: last night I dragged you 3+ one after another to safety (-nihi- Position 4 requires the shift to Seriative yi-).

tł'éédą́ą́' 'áłchíní yisdájiizdzį́į́z (~ yisdádziizdzį́į́z): last night a person dragged the children to safety one after another (ji-Position 5 triggers the shift to Seriative yi-).

'adziyétáál: I let fly a series of kicks, I kicked away into space one time after another. (Cf. 'adzíítáál: I let fly a kick.)

Yi-4 + hi-/yi- Seriative + di-6a: When hi-Seriative and di-, both of Position 6a coocur in a Verb Base, hi- takes position to the left of di-, as in tsin hidéłnáá': I made the tree (start to) move

But when subject and direct object are both 3rd person yi-Position 4 is positioned to the left of di-, and Seriative yi- in Position 6c takes position to the right of di-6a, as in:

'ashkii tsin yidiyiisnáá' (< yi-4 + di-6a + yii-6c: Seriative + -snáá'): the boy made the tree (start to) move

Yi-4 + hi-/yi-Seriative + ni-Position 6b: When hi-Seriative and ni-6b co-occur in a Verb Base, hi- appears to the left of ni-, as in:

beeldléí k'íhinéłtah: I unrolled the blanket

But when the subject is also 3rd person the direct object must be represented by yi- in Position 4, triggering a shift of hi-Seriative to its yi-allomorph. However, yi-Seriative remains to the left of ni-, as in:

'ashkii beeldléí k'íineestah (< k'í-1b + [y]i-4 + [y]i-6: Seriative + -neestah): the boy unrolled the blanket

## Position 5: Deictic Subject Pronouns

Position 5 contains the "deictic" subject pronouns and the pronoun that functions as the subject of Agentive Passive Verbs, the shape of which is determined by the phonological environment in any given verb construction.

1. ji-/-zh-/-z-/-ii-: 3a or 4th person: he, she, one, they

| | |
|---|---|
| jicha: he's crying | dazhdííniid: they (3+) said |
| daznízin: they (3+) think | bił niizhníłhaal (dzi-6a + ji-5 > -ii-): he clubbed him |

2. 'a- / -'i- / -'- / -'e-: 3i person: someone/something unspecified

'acha: there is crying (literally: somone is crying)
'e'e'aah/'i'íí'ą: the sun is setting/set (lit. unspecified SRO moves away out of sight)
bíká 'i'doolwoł: he'll receive assistance (literally: someone unspecified will run after him = help him)

(Oddly, indefinite 'a- functions as subject in verbs derived with the Theme ØJOOL: NCM moves, when it represents a coreferential nominal of the type łid (smoke), 'áhí(fog), łeezh(dust), tł'id(stench), níłtsą́(rain-squall)

łid < na'ajooł: smoke drifts about
łid < ha'ajooł: smoke drifts up
łid < ch'é'éjooł: smoke drifts out

3. ho- / ha-/ hw-: 3s pronoun: space, area, impersonal "it / things"

| | |
|---|---|
| hóteel: area is broad | haleeh: area becomes |

hwiiná: area / place is lively

4. -'(a)di- (-'di-/-di'-): unspecified person as subject of Agentive Passive Verb

shi'deeltį: I was brought    shidi'dooltééł (< shi'didooltééł): I'll be brought

**Position 4: Direct Object Pronouns**

Position 4 contains the direct object pronouns. The 3i and 3s object pronouns of Position 4 and their subject pronoun correspondents in Position 5 are identical - if the verb construction in which either of these elements occurs is transitive the 3i/3s pronoun represents the direct object; but if the verb is intransitive the same pronoun represents the subject.

| | |
|---|---|
| 1. shi-: me | 1. nihi-: us |
| 2. ni-: you sgl | 2. nihi-: you dpl |
| 3. yi-(-i-) / bi-/ Ø: him / her / it | 3. yi-(-i-) / bi- / Ø: them |

3i. 'a-/-'i-/-'e-/-'-/ : something, someone unspecified
3s. ha-/ho-/hw-: space, area, impersonal "it / things"
3a (4). ha-/ho-: 3a (4th) person him, her, them, one

Reflexive: -di- ('á-di-): self
Reciprocal: 'ahi-/'ałhi-: each other

shich'id: he's scratching me
yich'id: he's scratching it
nihohch'id: you dpl are scratching us
'ayą́: he's eating (something)

nishch'id: I'm scratching you
nihiich'id: we're scratching you dpl
'íyą́ą́': he ate (something)

'e'eshch'iish: I'm making a notch or groove (literally: I'm filing away (something)
hodéłdláád: I plowed a furrow
hodiyoołhééł: he'll kill him (4th person)
'ádích'id: he's scratching himself
'ádinísh'į: I'm looking at myself
'ahiníil'į: we're looking at each other

ch'į'níłbą́ą́z: I drove out (in something = an unspecified car or wagon)
hałdééh: he's tidying up the place
'ahich'id: they're scratching each other

Prefix shape is determined by the phonological environment with reference to the 3i indefinite pronoun 'a- and spatial / 4th person ha-/ho-.

Ø (zero) represents the 3rd person direct object of a transitive verb when the subject is 1st or 2nd person, as:

Øséłhį (< Ø-4: it + séłhį): I killed it (cf. niyéłhį: I killed you)

Øńísh'į (< Ø-4: it + ńísh'į): I'm looking at it (cf. nińísh'į: I'm looking at you)
ńØdiiłtį (< ń- < ná-: up + Ø-4: it + -diiłtį): I picked it up (AnO)(cf. náshidiiłtį: he picked me up)

When both subject and direct object are 3rd person the Position 4 direct object pronoun prefix yi- (if the noun first mentioned is the subject), or bi- (if the noun first mentioned is the direct object) are required, as :

'ashkii mósí yinéł'į: the boy is looking at (it) the cat
shizhé'é bįįh yiyiisxį: my father killed (it) the deer
shizhé'é k'asdą́ą́' tó biisxį́: my father almost drowned (literally: water almost killed (him) my father)
'ashkii mósí néidiiłtį: the boy picked up (it) the cat
'ashkii mósí nábidiiłtį: the cat picked up (him) the boy
hastiin łį́į́' nabiyé: the man is riding horseback (literally: the horse is carrying (him) the man about)
hastiin łį́į́' neiyé: the man is carrying (it) the horse around

Exception: In Verb Bases in which the subject is represented as an agent who causes an object, usually animate, to perform an action, the object involved is represented by a null postposition in Position 1a. (See Position 1a.)

shicheii binéłdá: I seated my grandfather (i.e., I caused him to sit down)
chidí nibiníłtła: I stopped the car (i.e., I caused it to come to a halt)
'awéé' bidiyésa': I burped the baby (i.e., I caused it to emit a series of burps)

The 3i and 3s direct object pronouns as Thematic Prefixes: 'a- / 'e- / 'i- / -'- /: someone or something unspecified, and ha- / ho- / hw-: space, area, impersonal "it, things" often appear as thematic constituents in Verb Bases, where their original meaning is lost. Thus:

'ashhosh: I'm asleep
'ashzhish: I'm dancing
'ałhą́ą́': he's snoring
'eeshkǫ́ǫ́ł: I'm swimming along
yóó' 'e'ełkǫ́ǫ́h: it's swimming away
yóó' 'i'íítkǫ́ǫ́': it swam away

hashtaał: I'm singing
hodé'ą́: I suggested, made a suggestion
hashne': I'm telling
hweeshne': I told
honishchin: I smell like, have the odor of (something - as gasoline)

## 2. The Disjunct Prefixes

The Disjunct Prefixes occupy Positions 0-3, inclusive. They are composed of a consonant + vowel, but unlike the Conjunct Prefixes, the Disjunct class may include any of the four vowels. And again, unlike most of the Conjunct prefixes, the Disjunct elements (except those of Position 1a) *all* carry inherently low or high tone. The Disjunct Prefix vowel may have the shape:

a (ha-: up) / aa (naa-: around) / á (ná-: reversion) / áá (náá-: semeliterative)

ą (bi'ą-: over it) / ą́ą́ (bą́ą́-: uncover it) / ą́ (hastą́-: 6)

e (be- < bi-: at it) / ee (bee- < bi-: at it) / é (bé- < bí-: against it) / éé (béé-: about it)

i (ni-: stop) / í (bí-: against it) / į́ (dį́-: four)

o (ko-: thus ) / ó (kó-: thus)

Tone Assimilation: a low tone Disjunct prefix vowel may take high tone in certain environments, assimilating to that of a following prefix, as:

háá'á < ha- + (y)í'á: it protrudes, sticks out
yah 'íí'ą́ < yah 'i- + -(y)í'ą́: I carried it in (SRO)

The na-/ná-/ni-Disjunct prefixes take variable shape in particular phonological environments: (v = any vowel)

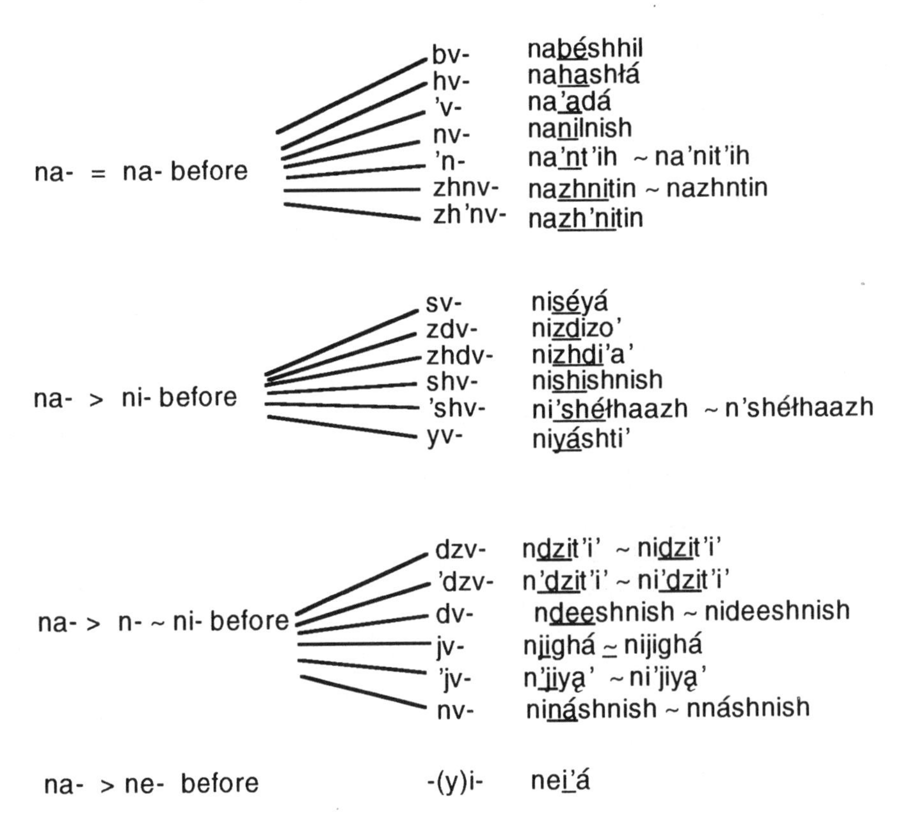

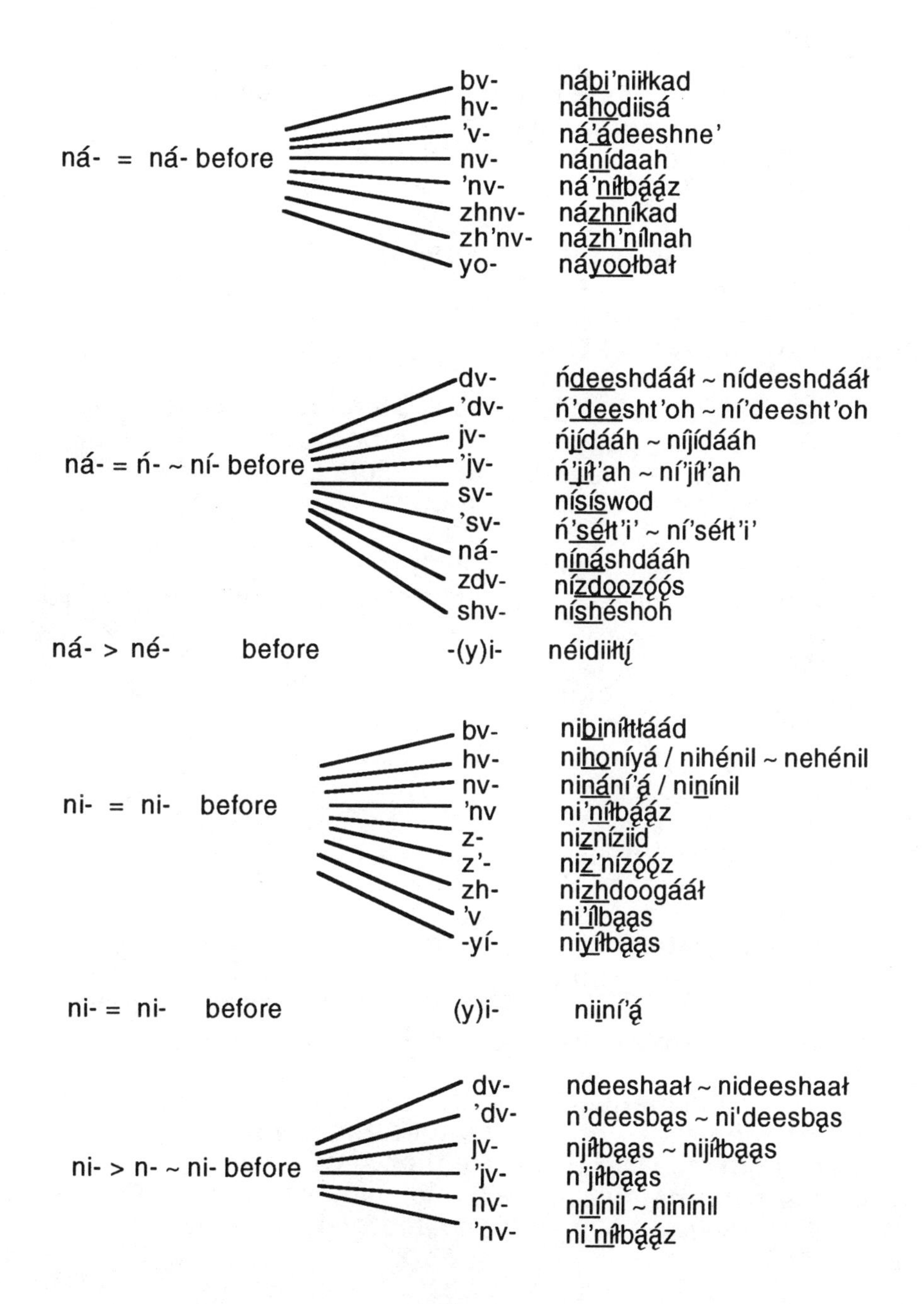


## Position 3: Distributive Plural Marker

Position 3: Distributive Plural Marker

Position 3 contains a single prefix with the shape da- (~ daa- ~ de-), which serves to mark the subject or the direct object of a verb as plural (3 or more), usually in a distributive sense (each of 3 or more). Most fully conjugated verbs include a distributive plural paradigm, produced by prefixing da- to the corresponding duoplural forms when the subject is distributive plural; or to any verb-incorporated subject or object pronoun in comitative and Distributive Aspectual constructions.

When da- functions as the conjugational determinant its behavior is similar to that of the Ca-prefixes (= consonant + -a-) of Position 1b, thus obviating the need to repeat a distributive plural paradigm for each conjugation.

Da- is usually required whenever the number of subjects is 3 or more, although the duoplural functions as a collective plural in some contexts. (See Number in the Verb - p. 60.)

'awéé' daacha: the 3+ babies are (each) crying (cf. 'awéé' yicha: the baby OR the 2 babies is/are crying.)
bił daniidzin: we 3+ are (each) sleepy
deiicha: we 3+ are (each) crying

Da- in Comitative Constructions: The Comitatives are constructed with the postposition P-ił: "in company with P" as a component of the Verb Base, as in shideezhí bił naashné: I'm playing with my little sister, but when the subject + companions totals 3 or more, da- is included in the verb. Thus:

'ashiiké bił ndaashné: I'm playing with the 2+ boys
Bilagáanaásh bił ndanilnish? do you work with White people? - are your 2+ fellow workers White? (Cf. Bilagáanaásh bił nanilnish? do you work with a White person - is your fellow-worker White?)
'áłchíní da'alzhishgo bił dahoneeni: the 3+ children have fun dancing
'áłchíní bił dahoneenigo da'alzhish: the 3+ children are having fun dancing
shizhé'é Bilagáana yił ndaalnish: my father works with 2+ White people - his fellow-workers are White

With Number-Specific Verbs: With verbs whose Stems mark number as singular da- describes an action or state in which a distributive plurality of subjects act individually; with Stems that mark the subject as dual (2) da- describes an action or state in which a distributive plurality of couples or pairs are involved; and if the Stem marks the subject as plural (3+) the distributive plurality injected by da- can be construed either as simply 3+ individuals, or it can be construed as 3+ groups of 3+ each. Thus:

béégashii ńdíshchííyaagi ndaaztį́: the 3+ cows are lying scattered singly under the pinetrees - one cow under each of 3+ pinetrees. (Cf. béégashii ńdíshchííyaagi naaztį́: the 3+ cows are lying about singly under the pinetree[s]; béégashii ńdíshchííyaagi sitį́: the cow is lying under the pinetree.) (TĮ́: single animate subject lies.)

béégashii ńdíshchííyaagi ndaazhtéézh: the cows are lying scattered in 3+ pairs under the pinetrees - one pair under each of 3+ pinetrees. (Cf. béégashii ńdíshchííyaagi naazhtéézh: the cows are lying about in 3+ pairs under the pinetrees; béégashii ńdíshchííyaagi shitéézh: the pair of cows are lying under the pinetree.) (TÉÉZH: 2 animate subjects lie)

béégashii ńdíshchííyaagi ndaazhjéé': the 3+ cows are lying scattered about under the pinetree(s) OR the cows are lying about in 3+ groups of 3+ cows each under the pinetrees. (Cf. béégashii ńdíshchííyaagi naazhjéé': the 3+ cows are lying under the pinetree[s] OR the cows are lying about in 3+ groups of 3+ cows each under the pinetrees; béégashii ńdíshchííyaagi shijéé': the 3+ cows are lying under the pinetree.) (JÉÉ': 3+ animate subjects lie) 'azee' yibézhí t'áálá'ígo tózis táá' biih dasé'ą́: I put one Alkaseltzer tablet into each of 3 glasses. (Cf. 'azee' yibézhí t'áálá'ígo tózis biih yí'ą́: I put one Alkaseltzer tablet into the glass.)

'azee' yibézhí naakigo tózis táá' biih dasénil: I put two Alkaseltzer tablets into each of 3 glasses. (Cf. 'azee' yibézhí naaki tózis biih yínil: I put two Alkaseltzer tablets into the glass.)

'ashiiké dóó at'ééké Naa'ahóóhaidi 'ałhíla' dayótą'go 'ahił ndaa'aash: 3+ couples of boys and girls are walking around hand in hand at the Fair. ('AASH: two subjects go)

siláo 'atiingóó ałkéé' deíkááh: the 3+ soldiers are walking along the road, one behind the other (single file).(KÁÁH: 3+ subjects go)

siláo 'atiingóó ałkéé' deí'aash: the soldiers are marching along the road in 3+ pairs - one pair behind the other (double file)

ashiiké 'ólta' góne' deílyeed: the boys are running, one at a time, into the school (YEED: one subject runs)

<u>The Distributive Aspectual Verbs</u> are distinguished by special Stem shape in the Imperfective and Optative Modes; they are transitive and constructions in this category usually include da-Position 3 distributive plural marker. Thus:

látsíní dįį́'go dootł'izhii t'áálá'ígo bikáa'gi dah daash'a': I'm putting one turquoise set on each of four bracelets (Cf. látsíní bikáa'gi dootł'izhii naakigo dah shishnííł: I'm putting two turquoise sets on the bracelet)
látsíní 'ashdla'go dootł'izhii naakigo bikáa'gi dah daashnííł: I'm putting two turquoise sets on each of five bracelets (Cf. látsíní bikáa'gi dootł'izhii t'áálá'í dah shish'aah: Im putting one turquoise set on the bracelet)

dah díníilghaazh 'ahádaashti': I'm breaking the fried bread into 3+ pieces OR I'm breaking the 3+ fried breads apart. (Cf. dah díníilghaazh 'aháníshtííh: I'm breaking the fried bread in two.)

shimá łeets'aa' ndeinil: my mother is setting the table (i.e. placing 3+ dishes about).

tł'oh 'ałch'į' be'estł'ónígíí łįį́' bá ndaash'a': I'm setting out 3+ bales of hay for the horses - one here and one there in 3+ locations / --- bá ndaashnil: I'm setting out 3+ bales, one or more in 3+ locations / --- táa'go łįį́' bá ndaashnil: I'm setting out 3+ bales in piles of 3 each here and there in 3+ locations

<u>Da- With Si-Perfective</u>: Although da- appears in the distributive plural paradigm of Yi- and Ni-Perfective conjugations, it more frequently requires a shift to Si-Perfective in these conjugations - especially in 3rd person forms. Thus: Yi-Perfective yisdáyíínil: he/they two rescued them, but Si-Perfective yisdádeiznil: they (3+) rescued them (not yisdádayíínil*); Ni-Perfective ch'ííní'ą́: he/they two carried it (SRO) out but Si-Perfective ch'ídeiz'ą́: they (3+) carried it (SRO) out (preferred over ch'ídeiní'ą́). Da- does not trigger a shift to Si-Perfective with Yi-Ø-Perfectives. (See Yi-Perfective and Yi-Ø-Perfective.)

Da- Occurs with Nouns, Pronouns and Postpositions as well as with verbs. Thus:

k'os: cloud / daak'os: distributive plural clouds
chą́shk'eh: wash, arroyo / chą́daashk'eh: distributive plural washes
bí: him/her/his/hers / daabí: they/theirs
bikáá': on it / dabikáá': on each of 3+
'éé': clothing / daa'éé': distributive plural articles of clothing

## Position 2: Iterative Mode

Position 2 contains a ná-prefix that serves to mark a verbal action or event as repetitive, usually in a frequentative sense. In conjunction with the Usitative stem and a Ø, yi-Ø or si-Imperfective conjugation pattern, ná- produces the Iterative Mode - the only Mode marked by a Disjunct Prefix. (Ná- is also identified as ná5-: Position lb: repetition.)

náshdlį́įh: I (repeatedly) drink it (as in t'áá 'ákwíí bíní gohwééh náshdlį́įh: I drink coffee every morning)
néishshį́įh: I (repeatedly) blacken O (as in t'áá 'ákwíįį́ shikee' néishshį́įh: I polish my black shoes every day)
dah níshíshbał: I put it up (as an awning)(shimá 'atł'óogo beeldléí bá dah níshíshbał: when my mother weaves I put up a blanket canopy for her

**Position 1:** Position 1 is divided into five subcategories, identified as Position 1a, 1b, 1c, 1d, 1e.

Position 1e contains the Semeliterative prefix náá- ~ náánáá-: once again; one more time; one more; another one.

Náá- appears before a consonant-initial prefix (exclusive of the non-syllabic form taken by si-: Position 7 in 3rd person and Passive Si-Perfective constructions: -s-, -z-, -sh-, -zh), as: .

náánísdzá: I again went
nááshédléézh: I painted it again
náásínídlį́į': you again became
ła' naa náádeesh'ááł: I'll give you another one of them (SRO)
náázhdoodááł: he will go again
ła' náázhní'ą́: he/she brought another one (SRO)

Náánáá- is required in all other phonological environments as:

náánásdlį́į': he again became
náánádzá: he again went
náánácha: it's again crying
hanáánáádzíí': he again spoke
ła' náánást'ą́: another one sits / lies (SRO)
taah náánéiiltį́: we put him into the water again
hanáánáodziih: that he might speak out again

Many Ø-class verbs require a shift to D-Classifier in the presence of the Semeliterative prefix; with some the shift is optional.

níyá: I went requires náánísdzá: I again went, but optionally
baa ní'ą́: I brought it (SRO) to him / baa náání'ą́ or baa náánísht'ą́: I brought it to him again (ła' baa náánísht'ą́: I brought him another one)

Position 1d contains the Reversionary prefix ná- (~ né- ~ ní- ~ ń-), indicating return to a previous location, state or condition. The shape taken by the Reversionary prefix is determined by the phonological environment. (See chart pp. 38-39. )

nádzá: he returned
ńdoodááł: he will return
nísísdlį́į́': I reverted, turned back into
nánídaah: sit back down!
taah néiiltį́: we put him back into the water

Ná-1d: Reversionary, ná-2: Iterative Mode, and ná[3]-1b: Thematic contract with certain Ca-/Cá- and Ci-/Cí- prefixes of Position 1a and 1b to produce Cáá-/Céé- respectively.

'ahi-1a: converging + ná-2 > 'ahéé-, as in bił 'ahéédiisht'ash: I repeatedly meet with him/her - rendezvous with him/her
bi-1a: at/contacting him/them + ná-2 > béé-, as in béé'áshniih: I repeatedly get word to them/notify them about it
bi-1a: at it/him/her + ná[3]-1b > béé-, as in béésísdzííd: I became afraid of it/him/her
ch'í-1b: out horizontally + ná-1d > ch'éé-, as in ch'éédoodááł: he'll go back out
dá-1b: close + ná-1d > dáá-, as in dáádétł'ǫ́: I closed it (a sack with a drawstring)
di-1b: fire, light + ná-1d > déé- as in déédííłjéé': I rekindled the fire (cf. didííłjéé': I made a fire).
ha-1b: up, up out = ná-1d > háá-, as in háájoo'na': he crawled back up
ná[4]-1b: upward + ná-1d > náá-, as in náádii'ą́: I picked it (SRO) back up, repossessed it (as a car)

Contractions of the type illustrated above are usually optional, although some have become crystallized, as ch'éénísdzid: I woke (back) up, reawakened (but ch'ínádzid: he reawakened, woke up - contraction is blocked in this phonological environment).

Contraction is blocked in phonological environments of the type:

ná- + -sh-8: hanáásh'na' (not háásh'na'*): I crawled back up out
ná- + (y)i-4: hanéídzį́į́s (not hááídzį́į́s*): he's pulling it back up
ná- + -ii(d)-8: hanéiidzį́į́s (not hááiidzį́į́s*): we're pulling it back up
ná- + -o(h)-8: hanáohdzį́į́s ~ hanáhdzį́į́s (not hááohdzį́į́s*): you two are pulling it back up
ná- + -o-7: hanáosh'nééh (not hááosh'nééh*): that I might crawl back out
ná- + -z-/-s-7: hanás'na' (not háás'na'*): it crawled back up

ná- + Theme (Position 7 and 8 vacant): ch'ínádzid (not ch'éédzid*): he woke up

Position 1c contains the reflexive pronominal constituent 'á- which, in combination with -di- in Position 4, produces the reflexive object pronoun prefix 'á-di-: self, as:

'ádíshzhééh: I'm shaving myself
'ádadiilzhééh: we (3+) are shaving ourselves
'ánáádílzhééh: he's shaving himself again

Position 1b contains a large number and variety of derivational-adverbial and thematic prefixes - 150 or more (depending on identification and count). Classed in four subcategories, these elements include:

1. Simple adverbials of the type:

'a- ~ 'e- ~ 'i-: away out of sight, as in yah 'adoogááł: he'll enter; 'i'íí'ą́: the sun set; 'e'e'aah: the sun is setting (i.e. something moves away out of sight)
ha-: up, up out, as in haséyá: I climbed up; hanoolne': it stuck its head up out (as from a hole)
'ahá-: apart, in half, in two, as in: 'ahánígizh: I cut it in two
'ada-: downward from a height, as in: 'adadeesháátł: I'll descend; bich'į' 'adáá'ą́: I lowered it (SRO) down to him
ch'í-: out horizontally, as in: tł'óó'góó ch'íníyá: I went outside; ch'íshiníłtį́: he carried me out.

A number of prefixes are similar in shape but distinct in meaning, as:

na1-: around, around about, as in: naaghá: he's walking around (here and there); nanishté: I'm carrying you around
na3-: downward, as in: dzi'izí bik'i náá́yá: I got down off the bicycle; tsé bich'į' náá'ą́: I lowered the rock down to him
ná1-: around encircling, as in: názt'i': it extends around in a circle (as a fence)
ná4-: up from a surface, as in : ńdii'na': he arose, got up

2. Thematic elements of the type:

da-: sgl die, as in dadootsaał: it will die
ná-: smoke (tobacco), as in ná'ásht'oh" I'm smoking
k'i-: plant, farm, as in k'i'dishłé: I'm farming, planting
tsí-: mental, as in ntséskees: I'm thinking; tsídeesyiz: I was amazed
tso ~ so-: pray, as in tsodilzin ~ sodilzin: he's praying
yá-: talk in yáłti': he's talking

3. Bound Postpositionals (normally occur in combination with an object pronoun of Position 0, here written as P- representing any person)

P-k'í-: onto P, as in bik'íséką́: I poured it onto him; tó shik'íízt̨ą́: he poured water onto me
P-í-: against, reaching, contacting P, as in tsé tó bélk'oł: water is lapping against the rock; bíníshwod: I overtook him running, I ran and caught up with him; 'anilí tsésǫ' béshjoł: I'm rubbing a rag on (against) the window
P-gha-: away from P by force, as in naaltsoos bighanisht'ą́: I took the book away from him
P-ghá-: through P, penetrating through P, as in géeso béésh bighánííłgeed: I stuck a knife through the cheese
P-a'-: to P on a loan basis, as in naaki béeso sha'nínil: he loaned me two dollars

4. Verb-incorporated nouns (generally in combination with a prefix of Position 0 representing the possessor. The Position 0 prefix is written P-, to represent any person. Some nouns take a special combining form when they appear as verb-incorporated elements)

P-za-: into P's mouth < P-zéé': P's mouth, as in bizáá'ą́: I put it into his mouth (a SRO)(< biza-+ [y]í'ą́)
'a-ą́-: into a hole or burrow < 'a'áán: hole, burrow, as in dlǫ́ǫ́' 'a'ą́ą́lwod: the prairie dog ran into its hole(< 'a'ą́-+ [yi]lwod)
dá'ák'e-: into a field < dá'ák'eh: field, cornfield, as in télii dá'ák'eelwod: the burro ran into the field (< dá'ák'e- + [yi]lwod)
P-íłák'e-: into P's hand or grasp < P-íłák'eh: P's hand, as in béésh bíłák'éé'ą́: I handed him the knife (< bíłák'e- + [y]í'ą́)

Position 1b Prefix Clusters are produced when two elements assigned to Position 1b cooccur in a Verb Base. In clusters of this type the relative position of each constituent is fixed, as in:

1. Two simple adverbial prefixes:

na[1]- ~ naa-: around about + ná[1]- ~ ní: around encircling = naaná- ~ naaní-: with the unit meaning "to and fro, reversing direction," as in naanááshwoł: I'm running about to and fro, running "all around;" naaníséyá: I turned around (while walking), I made a turn (as around a corner); naanísétbą́ą́z: I turned it around, made a turn with it (a car)
na[2]- ~ naa-: down, crosswise, across, over + 'a- ~ 'i-: away out of sight, as in naa'adeeshch'ish: I'll saw it down (as a tree); naa'íígo': I fell over

2. Simple adverbial + thematic:

na[1]- ~ ni- ~ n-: around about + -tsí-: thematic in verbs involving mental processes, thought, as in: ntséskees: I'm thinking

ni- ~ n-: terminative + -tsi-: thematic, as in ntsidinígo': I got down on my knees
na[1]- ~ ni-: around about + yá-: thematic in verbs of talking, as in niyáłti': he goes around making speeches, giving talks

3. Simple adverbial + bound postposition. Here the simple adverbial is always dominant and the bound postposition takes position to the right of the simple adverbial, as in:

'a-: away out of sight + P-í-: against P, as in yah 'abííyil: I pushed it inside (as a wheelbarrow); 'abídzíígo': I butted (away) against it
'ahá-: apart, in half + P-í-: against P, as in ahábízníłtáál: I kicked it in two, kicked it apart
ch'í-: out horizontally + P-í-: against P, as in ch'íbíníyil: I pushed it out (as a wheelbarrow)
ha-: up, up out + P-í-: against P, as in habí'ííshiizh: I gouged it out (as with a chisel)
na[1]-: around about + P-k'í-: onto P, as in nabik'éshłá: I'm prospecting for it (as oil, gold)

4. Bound Postpositional + thematic. Here the postposition is dominant, as:

P-í-: against P + yá-: thematic, as in łeeh bíyááłti': I cast a spell on him (i.e. I talked him into the grave)

5. Simple adverbial + bound postpositional + thematic

na[1]-: around about + P-k'í-: onto P + -tsí-: thematic, as in nabik'ítséskees: I'm considering it, pondering it
'a-: away out of sight + P-í-: against P + yá-: thematic, as in 'abíyááłti': I attracted it (goods, wealth, by "talking it away")
háá- < ha-: up out + ná-: reversionary + P-í: against him + yá-: thematic, as in háábíyáłti': I broke the spell on him (i.e. I talked him back up out of the grave)

6. Bound Postposition + Bound Postposition. Two such elements rarely cooccur, but appear in bighábíníyil < bighá-: through it + bí-: against it: I pushed it through it (as a wheelbarrow through a fence)

7. Bound Noun + Postpositional, as in:

P-nii- < P-nii': P's face + k'i-: on, as in biniik'idi'nisht'ą́: I put a halter on it (lit. I put something SRO on its face)
P-zá-: on P's mouth + k'í-: on, as in bizák'ídiilo': I strangled it (as with a cord)
P-zé- < P-zéé': P's mouth or neck + ná-: around encircling, as in: bizénáshnih: I'm embracing or hugging him (i.e. I'm putting my arm around his neck); bizéé- < bizé- + ná-: encircling, as in bizéésénih: I embraced or hugged him
(See also Position 1a below.)

<u>Position 1a</u> : the null postpositions (P-).

The null postpositions comprise a set of personal pronoun prefixes (including reflexive, reciprocal and spatial). Their base shapes are:

<u>Person</u>

| | | |
|---|---|---|
| 1. | shi- | (me) |
| 2. | ni- | (you) |
| 3. | bi- | (him, her, it, them) |
| 3a. | ho- | (him, her, them, people) |
| 3s. | ho- | (space, area, impersonal "it) |
| 3i. | 'a- ~ 'i- | (something or someone unspecified) |
| 1. | nihi- | (us) |
| 2. | nihi- | (you plural) |

| | | |
|---|---|---|
| Reflexive: | 'ádi- | (self) |
| Reciprocal: | 'ahi- ~ 'ałhi- | (together, joining, converging) |

The null postpositions function variously, depending on the Verb Base in which they occur.

I. In some Bases the null postpositions represent an indirect object, in the sense of "in the direction of, at," as in:

bineesdzin (< bi-1a: at him + -neesdzin: I directed mind / thought / desire): I hexed him, bewitched him, wished evil on him, cast a spell on him
binítsi (< bi-1a : contacting him + -nítsi: I moved a pointed object): I poked him with it
bidiił'á (< bi-1a: at him + -diił'á): I'm holding and pointing a rigid object): I'm holding it pointed at him (as a stick, rifle)
bidííchid (< bi-1a: contacting it + -dííchid: I relinquished by hand-movement): I let go of it, released it
shiidiitsi (< shi-:1a: at me + -[y]i-: it + -diitsi: he pointed): he pointed it at me
'ahiidiitsi (< 'ahi-1a: at each other + -[y]i-: it + -diitsi: they pointed): they pointed it at each other
beesh'į́ (< bi-1a + -sh'į́): I'm imitating him/it (lit. I do like it/him)

'Ádi-: at self, functions as a unit, in Position 1a:

'ádiidiitsi (< 'ádi-1a: at self + -[y]i-: it + -diitsi: he pointed): he pointed it at himself
'ádideidiitsi (< 'ádi-1a: at self + -da-: distributive plural marker + -(y)i-: them + -diitsi: they pointed): they pointed them at themselves (as guns)

'Ahi- ~ 'ałhi-: the null reciprocal has the meaning "at each other" in the sense of convergence in contexts of the type:
'ahidiilį́: they converge, flow together (as two streams)
'ahidadiilį́: they converge, flow together distributive plural (3+) streams
'ahinoolin: they look alike, converge in appearance (as two people).

'ahidanoolin: they (3+) resemble one another

A reciprocal prefix of similar shape but distinct meaning occurs also in Position 4, where it represents "each other" as a direct object. Compare:

'ahidoogą́ął: they two will kill each other
da'ahidoogą́ął: they 3+ will kill each other
'ahiníil'į́: we two are looking at each other

II. There is a transitive verb category in which the subject of the verb is represented as an agent who causes the object of the verb to (1) perform an activity (e.g., get up, halt, grow up, burp, talk, walk, run, dance, smile); (2) assume a posture (e.g. sit down, lie down, stand up, lean against something); (3) be in a position at rest (e.g. sit. lie, stand); or (4) ingest food or liquid (e.g. eat O, drink O - see Yi-Perfective: pp. 166-193. )

In verb constructions of these types the object is represented pronominally by a null postposition, which appears in all persons and numbers. If the action that the subject is caused to perform is itself transitive (i.e. eat, drink) the direct object is represented by a definite object pronoun of Position 4, or by 'a- (~ 'i-: something unspecified) if indefinite.

The several types are illustrated below.

1. Perform an Activity

ashkii ńdii'na': the boy got up / 'ashkii nábidiił'na': I got the boy up - set the boy on his feet; 'ashkii náshidiił'na': the boy got me up (i.e. he caused me to get up).

kǫ' na'ałbąąsii shá niiltła: the train stopped for me / kǫ' na'ałbąąsii ná nibiníłtła: I stopped the train for you (i.e. I caused it to stop for you).

Yootóodi néyą́: I grew up in Santa Fe / shiye' Yootóodi binésą́: I raised my son (caused him to grow up) in Santa Fe

bizhéé' hólóní ła' yishdlą́ą́'go déza': I burped when I drank a beer /'awéé' 'ííyą́ą́' dóó bidiyésa': when the baby ate I burped it (i.e. caused it to burp).

'ashkii yáłti'go sidá: the boy sits talking / 'awéé' yábiishti'go sédá: I sit getting the baby to talk (i.e. causing it to talk).

'ashkii yázhí ch'é'édą́ą'gi naaghá: the little boy is walking around in the dooryard / 'awéé' ch'é'édą́ą'gi nabiishłá: I'm walking the baby around in the dooryard (holding it while it walks about)(i.e. I'm causing it to walk about).

'ólta' doo 'ákót'éégóó yilwoł da: the school isn't running well / bá'ólta'í nizhónígo 'ólta' yiyoołwoł: the teacher runs the school nicely (a calque from English) (i.e. she causes it to run nicely).

'at'ééd yázhí bikáá'adání yikáa'gi alzhish: the little girl is dancing on the tabletop / 'awéé' bikáá'adání bikáa'gi bi'iishshish: I'm dancing the baby on the tabletop (i.e. I'm causing it to dance) 'awéé' ch'ídeeldlo': the baby smiled / 'awéé' ch'íbidiníłdlo': I made the baby smile (i.e. I caused it to smile)

2. Assume a Posture

bik'idah'asdáhí bikáa'gi dah nédá: I sat down on the chair / shicheii bik'idah'asdáhí bikáa'gi dah binéłdá: I seated my grandfather on a chair (i.e. caused him to sit down)

tsásk'eh bikáa'gi dah nétį́: I lay down on the bed / 'awéé' tsásk'eh bikáa'gi dah binéłtį́: I laid the baby on the bed (i.e. caused it to lie down)

bik'idah'asdáhí bikáa'gi dah yiizį': I stood up on the chair / 'ashkii yázhí bik'idah'asdáhí bikáa'gi dah biisį': I stood the little boy up on the chair (i.e. caused him to stand)

'awééshchíín ńdíshchíí' bíniidá / bíniitį́ / bíniizį́: the doll sits / lies / stands leaning against the pinetree / 'awééshchíín ńdíshchíí' bíbiniiłdá / bíbiniiłtį́ / bíbiniisį': I sat / laid / stood the doll leaning against the pinetree (i.e. I caused it to perform the action involved).

3. Neuter Positional

The Neuter positionals are distinguished in the several object classes (see the Classificatory Verbs: SRO, SSO, SFO, FFO), and an agent can cause any type of object to sit, lie or otherwise be in position.

However, the object classes include two distinctive categories: inanimate and animate. Inanimate things lack the ability to move under their own power, and if they are caused to assume a position (sit, lie, lean), it is the result of direct placement by an agent; similarly, if an agent elects to maintain an inanimate object in some positional status he does so by simply placing it and leaving it in position. Thus:

naaltsoos bikáá'adání bikáa'gi dah si'ą́: the book lies on the table
naaltsoos bikáá'adání bikáa'gi dah séł'ą́: I have / keep the book on the table (i.e. I cause it to lie on the table)
'at'ééd naaltsoos bikáá'adání yikáa'gi dah yis'ą́: the girl keeps the book on the table

In the foregoing transitive examples the direct object is represented by a prefix of Position 4 - Ø, if the subject of the verb is 1st or 2nd person, yi- when both subject and direct object are 3rd person.

An animate being has the capacity to move under its own power. If it is caused to assume or be in position by an agent its positional status is one that it assumes or maintains - it sits down, lies down or stands up, whether independently or at the direction of an agent, and it maintains a static position, whether independently or at the direction of an agent. Consequently, animate transitive positionals - whether Active or Neuter require representation of the object by a null postposition of Position 1a: the agent does not place the animate object in position in the same manner as he places an inanimate book - rather he causes it to perform the action involved in assuming a position; and if he causes an animate object to be in position, it is the object that maintains the posture involved. Compare:

shilééchąą'í kin yíighahgi sitį́: my dog is lying by the house / hooghandi łééchąą'í ła' bisétłį́: I have (keep) a dog (lying) at home

tsídiiłtsooí tsin bigaan yik'i dah sidá: the canary is sitting on the limb / hooghandi tsídiiłtsooí ła' biséłdá: I have a canary at home (i.e. I cause it to sit)

łį́į́' hooghan yíighahgi sizį́: the horse is standing beside the hogan / łį́į́' hooghandi ła' bisésį́: I have (keep) a horse at home (i.e. I cause it to stand)

shichidí hooghan bine'jí sizį́: my car stands behind the hogan / shichidí hooghan bine'jí bisésį́ (or optionally sésį́): I keep my car (standing) behind the hogan (a car has "legs" - its wheels, so it may be treated as though it were animate)

tł'óół chidí bii' silá: there's a length of rope in the car / tł'óół chidí bii' séłá: I keep a length of rope in the car / hooghandi tł'iish ła' biséłá: I keep a snake at home

(See Si-Perfective Neuter: p. 230 ff.)

4. Transitive Process

When one feeds or waters a person or an animal he acts in the capacity of an agent who causes it to perform the action involved in eating or drinking - action of a type that, in turn, involves an object. Consequently, "feed / water" verb constructions must include pronominal representation of two objects: (a) the person or animal that is caused to act and (b) the object upon which that person or animal acts.

(a) is represented by a null postposition in Position 1a, and (b) is represented by a direct object pronoun of Position 4. If the direct object is a definite thing, it is represented by Ø; and if it is "something unspecified" it is represented by 'a- in Position 4.

In addition, verb constructions of the type in reference include a yi-prefix, tentatively identified as the yi-allomorph of hi-seriative.

'ashkii yázhí géeso yiyą́: the little boy is eating cheese
'ashkii yázhí géeso biissą́: I'm feeding the little boy cheese
shimá 'ashkii yázhí géeso yiyiisą́: my mother is feeding the little boy cheese
The Stem and constituent prefixes are identified as follows:

yiyą́ (< yi-4 + Ø-7 + Ø-8 + Øyą́): he's eating it
biissą́ (< bi-1a + Ø-4 + [y]i-6c + Ø-7 + -s[h]-8 + -są́ = -ł-yą́): I'm causing him to eat it

yiyiisą́ (< yi-1a + yi-4 [y]i-6c + Ø-7 + Ø-8 + -są́): she's causing him to eat it

'ashkii yázhí géeso yiyííyą́ą́': the little boy ate cheese
'ashkii yázhí géeso biyíísą́ą́': I fed the little boy cheese
shimá 'ashkii yázhí géeso yiyíísą́ą́': my mother fed the little boy cheese

yiyííyą́ą́': (< yi-4 + yi-4 [duplicated] + [y]í-7 + Ø-8 + -Øyą́ą́'): he ate it
biyíísą́ą́':(< bi-1a + Ø-4 + yi-6c + yí-7 + Ø-8 + -są́ą́' = ł-yą́ą́'): I caused him to eat it
yiyíísą́ą́': (< yi-1a + Ø-4 + [y]i-6c + yí-7 + Ø-8 + -są́ą́' = ł-yą́ą́'): she caused him to eat it

'ashkii yázhí géeso yidooyį́įł: the little boy will eat cheese
'ashkii yázhí géeso bidiyeessį́įł: I'll feed the little boy cheese

yidooyį́įł (< yi-4 + d[i]-6a + yi- > -oo-7 + -Øyį́įł): he will eat it
bidiyeessį́įł (< bi-1a + Ø-4 + d[i]-6a + y[i]-6c + yi- > -ee-7 + -s[h]-8 + -sį́įł = -ł-yį́įł): I'll cause him to eat it

The object eaten is unspecified 'a-4 in:

'awéé' 'ayą́: the baby is eating
'awéé' bi'iissą́: I'm feeding the baby
shimá 'awéé' yi'iisą́: my mother is feeding the baby

'ayą́ (< 'a-4 + Ø-7 + Ø-8 + Øyą́): it's eating (something)
bi'iissą́ (< bi-1a + '[a]-4 + [y]ii-6c + Ø-7 + Ø-8 + -są́ = ł-yą́): I'm causing it to eat (something)
yi'iisą́ (< yi-1a + '[a]-4 + [y]ii-6c + Ø-7 + Ø-8 + -są́ = ł-yą́): she's causing it to eat (something)

'awéé' 'ííyą́ą́': the baby ate
'awéé' bi'iyíísą́ą́': I fed the baby
shimá 'awéé' yi'iyíísą́ą́': my mother fed the baby

'ííyą́ą́': (< 'i- ~ 'a-4 + [y]í-7 + Ø-8 + -Øyą́ą́'): the baby ate (something)
bi'iyíísą́ą́':(< bi-1a + 'i- ~ 'a-4 + yi-6c + yí-7 + Ø-8 + -są́ą́' = ł-yą́ą́'): I caused it to eat (something)
yi'iyíísą́ą́': (< yi-1a + 'i- ~ 'a-4 + yi-6c + yí-7 + Ø-8 + -są́ą́' = ł-yą́ą́'): she caused it to eat (something)

'awéé' 'adooyį́įł: the baby will eat
'awéé' bidi'yeessį́įł: I'll feed the baby
shimá 'awéé' yidi'yoosį́įł: my mother will feed the baby

'adooyį́įł (< 'a-4 + d[i]-6a + yi- > -oo-7 + -Øyį́įł): he will eat (something)
bidi'yeessį́įł (< bi-1a + d[i]-6a + 'a-4 + + y[i]-6c + yi- > -ee-7 + -s[h]-8 + -sį́įł = -ł-yį́įł): I'll cause it to eat (something)
yidi'yoosį́įł (< yi-1a + di-6a + 'a-4 + + y[i]-6c + yi- > -oo-7 + -s[h]-8 + -sį́įł = -ł-yį́įł): she'll cause it to eat (something)

(See also Yi-Ø-Imperfective and Yi-Ø-Perfective, Inchoative: pp. 152-153 & 267-268. )

In some constructions the null postposition is reinterpreted as the 3rd person direct object pronoun of Position 4. Thus:

'at'ééd bimósí géeso ła' yidiyoosį́į́ł: the girl will feed cheese to her cat. Yiidiyoosį́į́ł (< yi-1a + [y]i-4) would be expected, but yi- has been reinterpreted as the direct object pronoun.)

Yi-1a and yi-4 both appear as expected in:

sáanii ba'áłchíní 'atsį' yideidiyoosį́į́ł: the women (3+) will feed meat to their children

Similarly:

géeso ła' ná bidideeshgish: I'll cut a piece of cheese for you
shimá géeso ła' ná yididoogish: my mother will cut a piece of cheese for you
sáanii ba'áłchíní géeso ła' yá yideididoogish: the women will cut pieces of cheese for their children

III. The Inchoatives incorporate the null postpositions, which perform three functions (see also Inchoative, under Transitional Aspect, pp. 69-71).

1. In one type of intransitive the null postposition represents the subject, as in:

bi'niitin: it started to freeze
shi'niitsą́: I started to die (i.e. I fell ill)
hani'niitih: you started to get old

2. In one type of intransitive a 3i person form of the null postposition ('i-) functions as a thematic element, as in:

'i'niichxííł: it started to snow
'i'niicha: I/he started to cry
'in'nicha: you started to cry
'i'niilghą́ą́': we started to snore

3. Transitive Inchoatives employ the null postpositions to represent the direct object, as in:

bi'niiyą́ą́': I started to eat it
'i'niiyą́ą́': I/he started to eat
bida'niidą́ą́': we 3+ started to eat it
ła' yinááda'niiyą́ą́': they 3+ started to eat another one of them

**Position 0: Object Pronouns**

The personal pronoun prefixes that represent the object of a postposition are assigned to Position 0. They are illustrated below:

1. shi- / shí- / sh-
   shi-k'í-: onto me
   shí-ká-: after me
   sh-í-: against me

2. ni- / ní- / n-
   ni-k'í-: onto you
   ní-ká-: after you
   n-í-: against you

3. bi- / bí- / b-
   bi-k'í-: onto it
   bí-ká-: after him
   b-í-: against it

3o. yi- / yí- / y-
   yi-k'í-: onto it
   yí-ká-: after him
   y-í-: against it

1. nihi- / nihí- / nih-
   nihi-k'í-: onto us
   nihí-ká-: after us
   nih-í-: against us

2. nihi- / nihí- / nih-
   nihi-k'í-: onto you dpl
   nihí-ká-: after you dpl
   nih-í-: against you dpl

Reflexive: 'á- / 'ádí- / 'ád-
   'á-k'í-: onto self
   'ádí-ká-: after self
   'ád-í-: against self

Reciprocal: 'ał- / 'ałh- / 'ahíł-
   'ał-k'í-: onto each other
   'ahíł-ká-: after each other
   'ałh-í-: against each other

## IV. DERIVATIONAL LEVELS IN THE VERB

### 1. The Verb Theme

Following derivation of the Stems from the underlying Root, production of the Verb Theme constitutes the first derivational level in the process of creating a meaningful word.

The Verb Theme consists of a Stem + Classifier + Thematic Prefix (if any). E.g.:

<u>cha</u> is a Stem meaning "cry."

<u>Øcha</u> is the Theme upon which the lexical form yicha (= yi-Øcha): he's crying, is constructed.

<u>máász</u> is a (Perfective) Stem derived from a verbal Root meaning "globularity."
<u>Ømáász</u> is a Theme with the meaning "globularity moved (rolling)," as in taah yímáász (= yí-Ømáász): it / he rolled into the water.
<u>łmáász</u> is a causative-transitive Theme meaning "cause globularity to move (rolling)," as in taah yíłmáász (= yí-łmáász): I rolled it into the water (i.e. I caused it to roll into the water)
<u>ti'</u> is a Stem meaning "talk."
<u>yá-łti'</u>, including yá-thematic is the Theme for the lexical construction yáníłti' (= yá-ní-łti'): you're talking

<u>ne'</u> is a Stem with the meaning "propel a SRO."
<u>ni-lne'</u>, including ni-thematic (generic classifier for round shape) is the Theme for the lexical construction hanoolne' (= ha- 1b: up out + nool-ne': it "propelled" or quickly moved its own SRO ): it quickly stuck its head up out (as a prairie dog from its burrow)

## 2. The Verb Base

The Verb Base is the skeleton of a lexical form. The simplest possible Base lacks only the essential inflectional prefixes of Positions 8 and 7 (subject and modal-conjugation markers respectively) to function as a meaningful word. In the absence of a derivational prefix the Verb Theme alone functions as the Verb Base. Thus, the Themes Øcha: cry, and Øch'id: scratch function alone as Verb Bases in constructions such as:

nicha (< Ø-7 + ni-8: you + -Øcha): you are crying
yishch'id (< yi-peg element + Ø-7 +-sh-8: I + -Øch'id): I'm scratching it
yínícha (< -yí-7: Perfective Mode marker +ní-8: you + -Øcha): you cried

Derived Verb Bases include one or more adverbial modifiers of Positions 1, 3 or 6, pronominal elements from Position 4 functioning thematically or, in some Bases, independent adverbial modifiers. Thus:

ha-1b: start + Øchééh : cry = the Base ha#-(Ø)--Øchééh: start to cry, as in hanichééh: you start to cry
ha-1b: start + -náá-1e: again + Øchééh: cry = the Base ha-náá#-(Ø)--Øchééh: start to cry again, as in hanáánichééh: you again start to cry
ho-4: spatial, functioning thematically + Ølįįd: be = the Base ho-(ni)--Ølįįd: appear, arrive, come), as in honílįįd: I / he appeared / came
ch'í-lb: out horizontally + -'(a)-4: thematic + -lzhiizh: dance = the Base ch'í#-'(a)-(ni)--lzhiizh: come dancing out, as in ch'í'íínílzhiizh: you came dancing out
taah: into water + -łtį́: move AnO = the Base taah (Ø)--łtį́: put an AnO into the water, as in taah yíníłtį́': you put it into the water

Active verbs are conjugated in as many as 7 Modes: (I) Imperfective, (Usit.) Usitative, (It.) Iterative, (P) Perfective, (Prog.) Progressive, (F) Future and (O) Optative. Of these, the Imperfective and the Perfective are not readily predictable for all Verb Bases. The Imperfective may be variously marked by Ø, ni- or si- in Position 7, and the Perfective may be marked by Ø, yi- (= ghi-), ni- or si-; and both Modes may include a yi-aspect marker in Position 6c with Ø in Position 7. The Usitative differs from the corresponding Imperfective only in stem shape, and the Iterative employs the same stem as the Usitative, but it is derived with the addition of a ná-repetitive prefix to the corresponding Imperfective-Usitative Base (except that ni-Position 7 does not appear in the Usitative nor in the Iterative Modes – ni-Imperfectives are complemented by Ø-Usitative/ Iterative conjugations, and some Iterative Bases require a switch to D- in lieu of Ø-classifier, and to L- in place of Ł). In addition to these variables the components of the Stem Set required by the several Modes in which the Base is conjugated usually vary in shape.

A Verb Base can function quite adequately as a dictionary entry form, provided that the entry includes (1) identification of the required Imperfective/Perfective conjugations (the conjugation pattern for the remaining Modes is readily predictable), and (2) provided that the entry includes the Verb Theme in the stem forms that correspond to all of the Modes in which the Base is conjugated.

To illustrate: the Base for a verb construction meaning "extract a SRO" is composed of the adverbial prefix ha-Position 1b: (up) out + a "handle" Theme based on the Stem Set corresponding to the Momentaneous Aspect, and this derivative is conjugated as a Ø-Imperfective / yi-Perfective. The entry then takes the shape:

> ha-(Ø/yi)-: Ø'aah(I), Ø'ą́(P), Ø'ááh / t'ááh(Usit./It.), Ø'ááł(F/O): extract a SRO

The modal components of the Base entry would be reconstructed in lexical form (in 1st person sgl) as:

> haash'aah (I): I'm extracting it
> haash'ááh (Usit.): I usually extract it
> hanásht'ááh (It.): I repeatedly extract it (on repeated occasions)
> háá'ą́ (P): I extracted it
> hadeesh'ááł (F): I'll extract it
> haosh'ááł (O): that I might extract it

### 3. The Verb as a Lexical Unit

Normally, the simplest construction capable of functioning as a meaningful word must include:

> A Theme (= Stem + Classifier),
> A marker of subject in Position 8 or 5, and
> A modal-aspectival conjugation marker in Position 7.

However, with exception of the Stem, part or all of the required components may be Ø because:

Ø in Position 7 marks the Ø- and the Yi-Ø-Imperfective/Usitative Modes, as well as the Yi-Ø-Perfective; while Ø in Position 8 marks subject as 3rd person in all verbs. In addition, Ø in Position 8 marks subject in both 1st person sgl and 3rd person sgl/dpl in Ø/Ł-Class Perfective constructions.

> yishcha (< yi-peg element + Ø-7 + -sh-8 + Øcha): I'm crying
> yicha (< yi-peg element + Ø-7 + -Ø-8 + Øcha): it/he/she/they 2 is/are crying
> yiishgááh (< yi-6c Transitional + Ø-7 + -sh-8 + Øgááh): I'm turning white
> yiigááh: (< yi-6c Transitional + Ø-7 + -Ø-8 + Øgááh): it's turning white

yíyą́ą́': (< yí-7 + Ø-8 + Øyą́ą́'): I ate it
yícha: (<yí-7 + Ø-8 + Øcha): I cried; he/she/it/they 2 cried
yiyą́ (< yi-4: it + Ø-7 + Ø-8 + Øyą́): he's eating it
sidá (< si-7 + Ø-8 + Ødá): he's sitting
níyá (< ní-7 + Ø-8 + Øyá): I/he arrived

In a very few instances a naked Verb Theme functions as a word, as:

ní (Øní): he says (cf. dishní: I say)
lą'í (Ølą'í): (they are) many (cf. niidlą'í: we are many)

## V. SEMANTICS

The Derivational Process: Three major processes are utilized for the derivation of meaning in the Navajo verb: (1) the simple, straightforward modification of root/stem meaning by means of adverbial prefixal elements - often a transparent process in which the stems and the prefixes are used with their central or base meaning: (2) figurative extension of the base meaning of stems or prefixes, and (3) idiom - a process in which a verb or a phrase has a specialized, often metaphorical meaning that may not be clearly reflected by its constituents. Thus:

The Verbal Theme (Perfective Stem) Ø'Ą́ has the base meaning "move a solid roundish compact object (SRO)." Modified by the adverbial prefix ha-: up out, a lexical construction háá'ą́ is produced, with the meaning "I took it out, extracted it," as in ch'ah tsits'aa' bii'dę́ę́' háá'ą́: I took the hat out of the box." Similarly, the theme ØNII' (Perfective stem) has the meaning "act with the hands or arm; move the arm directionally." In combination with the prefixes ni-zé-ná-: your-neck-around, the lexical form nizénáznii' is produced, with the meaning "he/she put his/her arms around your neck, hugged you." The inherently punctual nature of movement "up-out" opens the way for figurative use of ha- to denote inception in some verbs that describe processes, as in hááchxííł: it started to snow; háácha: I/it started to cry; háághal: I/he started to look; háázil: it started to breathe/drew its first breath (a newborn child); hahóóyá: it started (an event, ceremony); ha'ííth'ǫ́: she started to weave.

Similarly, the compound prefix ńdii- (< ń- ~ ná: up + -di-: inceptive + -i-: Transitional Aspect marker) carries an inherent punctual connotation that permits its use as an inceptive with the meaning "start to." With "handle" verbs ńdii- derives constructions meaning "pick O up, lift O, find O, choose O (perhaps literally start to move O upward)," as in 'awéé' ńdiiłtį́: I picked the baby up; látsíní ńdiitą́: I picked up, found, chose the bracelet. And with "activity" verbs ńdii- marks beginning, as in ńdiibį́į́': I started to bathe; ńdiishnish: I started to work; ńdiine': I began to play; ńdiish'na': I got up (started to squirm upward).

Di- alone marks inception in constructions of the type dishááh: I'm in the act of starting to go along (as in: 'azee'íił'íní bich'į' dishááh: I'm going to see the doctor, and ni- alone marks an action as terminal, as in nishdaah: I'm in the act of sitting down. But di- and -ni- join to produce a compound prefix with unitary meaning: dini- marks an action as prolonged, as in chidí séí yiih dinoolwod: the car ran into the sand and remained (i.e. it terminatively started to run = got stuck).

With addition of ha-: up out / start, the combination hadini- marks an action that the subject commences, but which continues overlong. Thus: 'awéé' hadínéeshcha: the baby cried and cried (it started to cry prolongedly - it "prolonged the start")(cf. háácha: it began to cry); tł'éédą́ą́' hadí'néshzhiizh: I stayed too long at the dance last night (i.e. I started to dance and kept on and on)(cf. 'eeshzhiizh: I danced).

With the addition of Disjunct ni-cessative, the combination ndini- marks a terminal action as one that continues in effect. Thus Yootóodi ndininisdzá: I got stranded in Santa Fe (i.e. my arrival and stopping status there was prolonged). (Cf. niníyá: I went as far as [a stopping point], I stopped going, halted.)

And the inceptive phase of an action marked by compound ńdii- is cast into a prolonged state with the additiion of dini- (di is not replicated). Thus: ńdíníisdzá: I got a good start, got well underway - as in kintahgóó ńdíníisdzáago 'índa shibéeso bizis bénááshnii': I didn't remember my purse until I was well on my way to town - i.e. until I got into a prolonged state of starting to go. (Cf. baa ńdiisdzá: I started to do it - started to go about it.)

Root/Stem Polysemy: it is the verbal root itself, in the form of its derived stems, that becomes polysemantic as the result of extensions of meaning that, although often disparate, become crystallized with usage. Such extensions probably begin as metaphors.

The "run" verbs provide classic examples of crystallized metaphor.

"Singular-run" verbs are derived from a root WOD (Perfective Stem), the base meaning of which is "flex, bend." With Ø-Classifier the Verb Theme ØWOD is produced and this Theme, in combination with adverbial 'ahá-: apart, derives the Verb Base 'ahá-Øwod with the meaning "bend apart, become disjointed," as in shigaan 'ahááwod: my arm became disjointed (bent apart). With Ł-Classifier the "bend" theme is transitivized to acquire the meaning "cause to bend," and again in combination with 'ahá-: apart, the Verb Base 'ahá--łhod is generated, with the meaning "cause to bend or flex apart, break by flexing apart" as in béésh 'áłts'ózí 'ahááłhod: I bent or flexed the wire apart.

With L-Classifier the causative-transitive Theme becomes mediopassive, serving to derive constructions in which the subject and object are the same. LWOD and its Stem variants produce lexical constructions that describe the subject as "self-flexing" and this came to be used as a metaphor for "run," an action performed by flexing the legs. Thus 'ashkii 'ólta'dę́ę́' ch'élwod: the boy ran ("self-flexed") out of the school; 'ashkii 'ólta'di yílwod: the boy ran ("arrived self-flexing") to school; 'ashkii 'atiin góyaa yilwoł: the boy is running ("self-flexing") down the road.

The concept involved in running carries a connotation of "swift movement," a feature that opens the way to further extension of what began as a metaphoric mediopassive Theme. With the meaning "go swiftly" the "singular-run" verbs are applied to inanimate objects - contexts in which "self-flex" plays no part, as in chidí (dzi'izí, nááts'ó'oołdísii, kǫ' na'ałbąąsii) yilwoł: the car (bicycle, whirlwind, locomotive) is running along; k'aa' shighálwod: the arrow went through me.

Applied to conveyances, in Verb Bases that include the postposition P-ił: in company with P, the "transportation by fast vehicle" verbs are generated. Here the subject is the vehicle and the person transported is represented by the pronoun object of the postposition P-. Thus: chidí shił yilwoł: I'm riding along in the car (i.e. the car is running along with me; kintahdę́ę́' shił ná'oolwoł: I'm returning from town by (unspecified) fast moving vehicle (car, motorcycle) (literally, something unspecified is running back with me); Yootóodi shił 'íı̨́lwod, I arrived in Santa Fe (by unspecified fast moving vehicle). other modes of travel are distinguished by other verbal roots, as P-ił (d)t'a': fly; P-ił Ø'éél: go by boat; P-ił ldloozh: go by quadruped (horse, burro); P-ił (d)'na': go by slow-moving (crawling) vehicle (tractor, army tank, heavy truck).

"Run" is used idiomatically in expressions of the type: Pí-ká 'a--lwod: help P (literally "run away out of sight after P"), as in shimá bíká 'eeshwod: I helped (ran away after) my mother; Pí-lák'ee ha--lwod: escape from P, as in 'awáalyaaí shílák'ee haalwod: the prisoner escaped from me (literally "ran out of my hand"), 'éé' biih --lwod: dress hurriedly, as in 'éé' biih yishwod: I dressed quickly (literally "ran into my clothes").

And finally, the "singular-run" Theme appears as a calque from English, functioning with the meaning "operate," as in naalyéhé bá hooghan yiyoołwoł: he runs a trading post, he runs a store (literally: he causes it to be running along).

The "run" verbs employ three distinct Stems, distinguishing number as singular, dual and plural (1, 2 and 3+ subjects).

"Dual-run," like "singular-run," is derived somewhat deviously as a metaphor - but here one in which the two subjects are described literally as "chasing each other."

An intransitive Verb Theme NI-ØCHĄ́Ą́' (Perfective Stem) and its modal variants carry the meaning "flee," as in tsé'ą́ą́ góne' yah 'aníícháą́': I fled into the cave; siláo yik'ee noochééł: he's fleeing from the police. Ł-Classifier produces a causative-transitive Theme NI-ŁCHĄ́Ą́': chase (cause to flee), as in łééchąą'í shinoołchééł: the dog is chasing me (i.e. causing me to flee).

When the direct object of the causative-transitive Theme is reciprocal 'ahi-: each other, L-Classifier replaces Ł-, and the theme takes the shape 'ahi-NI-LCHĄ́Ą́': chase each other. It is this Theme that carries the figurative meaning "dual-run," as in 'ashiiké 'atiin góyaa 'ahinoolchééł: the two boys are running ("chasing each other") down the road.

If the Verb Base includes a Position 1 prefix such as ha-: up, 'a-: away, bighá-: through it, or ch'í-: out, it is positioned to the left of 'ahi-4. However, to better accomodate the 1b prefix, the 'a- of 'ahi- shifts to the right, producing -hi'(a), as in Yi-Perfective yah 'ahi'noolchą́ą́': they two ran inside ("chased each other"). Here the initial 'a- is the Position 1b prefix and -'- represents the shifted 'a- of 'ahi-4. In Ni-Perfective 1st and 2nd person the -'(a)- of 'ahi- shifts farther to the right, taking position between ni-6b: thematic and ni-7: conjugation marker, as in bigháhini'niilchą́ą́': we two ran (chased each other) through it; ch'íhini'noołchą́ą́': you two ran (chased each other) out.

Again, the connotation of "swift movement" permits extension of the "dual-run" verbs to include inanimate objects, as in chidí 'atiin góyaa 'ahinoolchééł: the two cars are running down the road; k'aa' naakigo shigháhi'neelchą́ą́': two arrows went through me (literally "chased each other through me"). And "dual-run" verbs are used idiomatically in contexts of the type 'at'ééké bimá yíká 'ahi'noolchą́ą́': the two girls helped their mother (literally "they ran away out of sight after her"), 'awáalyaaí shíłák'ee hahi'noolchą́ą́': the two prisoners escaped from me (literally "they chased each other out of my hand").

Language Growth is an important factor in the generation of vocabulary as new cultural acquisitions place new communicational demands on language. New verbal concepts require, as a first step in the generation of new terms, choice of an appropriate verbal root from the approximately 550-member repertoire, and choice must reflect some salient feature that can be used as a basis upon which to describe the new concept.

The generative process can be illustrated by the new vocabulary that followed acquisition of the horse early in the 18th century (or before), followed by the introduction of horse-drawn wheeled vehicles - wagons and buggies, and sometime later by other types of vehicles that entered the scene - cars, bicycles, boats.

A salient feature involved in the operation of a horse-drawn conveyance was the reins used by the driver to control the team of horses. An available Navajo verbal root LO'/LOH (Perfective Stems) describes action performed with a ropelike object or loop (including the handle on a purse or bucket, a lariat or snare). The root appears, with its base meaning, in contexts of the type: tó bee naakahí ch'íníło': I brought the bucket out; béégashii yáázh séloh: I lassoed the calf; łóó' háálo': I caught the fish (i.e. I pulled it out by means of a line).

The root LO' and its Stem variants were extended to describe the operation of a horse-drawn vehicle, where meaning focussed on the "ropelike objects" employed by the driver. However, the action performed by the reins resulted in the "guiding" of the conveyance - a connotation that superseded the original literal semantic focus, and led subsequently to application of the LO' derivatives to describe the operation of any guided vehicle - car, bicycle, motorboat. It soon came to mean simply "drive a vehicle," as in hastiin tsinaabąąs (chidí, dzi'izí) neilo': the man is driving the wagon (car, bicycle) around; 'ashkii tsinaabąąs (chidí) tséyi'dę́ę́' ch'ííníło': the boy drove the wagon (car) out of the canyon, and, with an indefinite object pronoun 'ashkii tséyi'dę́ę́' ch'í'nílo'": the boy drove out of the canyon (in an unspecified guided vehicle). (Cf. 'ashkii tó bee naakahí hooghandę́ę́' ch'ííníło': the boy carried the bucket out of the hogan by its handle.)

The reins were not the only feature to which the root LO' was applicable in the generation of new vocabulary surrounding the operation of a horse-drawn conveyance, for an early braking system depended, in part, on a rope. A loop of rope attached to a lever was used to bring the brake shoe into contact with a wagon wheel. Braking a wagon then came to be described by terms of the types bídiilo': I applied its brake (literally: I brought it into contact with something unspecified by means of a ropelike object), and bídííníshło'" I'm keeping its brake on (lit.: I'm holding it extended against it by means of a ropelike object).

The action involved resulted in slowing or stopping the vehicle, so the semantic focus soon moved beyond the "mechanics" involved in braking to a more general meaning "brake, put on the brake." The term was applied to the more elaborate braking systems installed on wagons at a later date, and in subsequent years the same LO' derivatives were applied to the braking system in any kind of vehicle - a "ropelike object" was no longer involved.

Again, the operation and braking of vehicles were not the only applications to which LO', with its historic focus on action performed with a ropelike object, was put. The primitive balance scales, as first introduced to Navajo culture, took the form of a pair of pans joined by a beam and suspended by a chain or cord. The salient feature involved in weighing appeared, to the observer, to be simply "suspension by means of a ropelike object." Dah hidiilo' has the base meaning I hung it up (by a cord or handle), as in: tó bee naakahí dah hidiilo': I hung the bucket up (as on a nail); 'iisxíinii dah bidi'diidlo': the murderer was hung. And 'aghaa' dah hidiilo', literally I hung up the fleece, but by extension I weighed the wool; 'awéé' dah hidiilo': I weighed the baby (literally I hung the baby); kintahdi dah 'ádiishdlo': I weighed (hung) myself in town. The semantic focus shifted away from suspension by a cord to include determination of weight.

On a par with language in general Navajo employs a variety of idiomatic extensions of meaning that are intelligible only to the initiated. The surface meaning of bik'ee 'anááłdéél is "I tossed a slender flexible object back away on account of it," but the message conveyed by this expression is "I was amazed or astounded by it," and bich'į' 'ák'eeshdlaad with the surface meaning "I roughly tore the cover off myself toward him" means "I was furious with him, enraged at him." When a leader is described as 'ayóo náhoolghał: literally "he's much given to flopping over and over," the intended meaning is "he waffles - he's indecisive," and when a resource such as water is developed (as a well) it is "tethered" - dah haastł'ǫ́, and finally when "broad horns flipped him up into the air" = deeteel yáábí'iisha', it means "he kicked off - died."

## VI. GRAMMATICAL CATEGORIES IN THE VERB

### A. General Categories

1. NUMBER: in the verb is distinguished as singular, dual/duoplural, and plural/distributive plural.

Subject number is marked as singular or duoplural by the pronominal prefixes of Position 8, and it is marked as distributive plural by da-Position 3 + the duoplural subject pronouns.

Third person subject is marked by Ø in Position 8, with the result that singular he/she/it and duoplural they are distinguished by context only.

'at'ééd nísh'į́: I'm looking at the girl
'at'ééd níil'į́: we two are looking at the girl
'at'ééd daníil'į́: we distributive plural (3+) are looking at the girl
'ashkii 'at'ééd yiníł'į́: the boy is looking at the girl
'ashiiké 'at'ééd yiníł'į́: the two boys are looking at the girl
'ashiiké 'at'ééd deiníł'į́: the 3+ boys are looking at the girl

A few locomotional and positional Stems are number specific, identifying the subject as singular, dual or plural:

GO
- sgl: (Theme: ØYÁ)
  ch'íníyá: I/he went out
- dual: (Theme: Ø'ÁÁZH)
  ch'íní'áázh: they 2 went out
- plural: (Theme: [D]KAI)
  ch'ékai: they 3+ went out

RUN
- sgl: (Theme: LWOD)
  ch'élwod: he ran out
- dual: (Theme: NI-LCHĄ́Ą́')
  ch'íhi'neelchą́ą́': they 2 ran out
- plural: (Theme: ØJÉÉ')
  ch'íníjéé': they 3+ ran out

SIT DOWN
- sgl: (Theme: ØDÁ)
  neezdá: he sat down
- dual: (Theme: ØKÉ)
  neezké: they 2 sat down
- plural: (Theme: ØBIN)
  dineezbin: they 3+ sat down

LIE DOWN
- sgl: (Theme: ØTĮ́)
  neeztį́: he lay down
- dual: (Theme: ØTÉÉZH)
  neezhtéézh: they 2 lay down
- plural: (Theme: ØJÉÉ')
  neezhjéé': they 3+ lay down

DIE
- sgl (Theme: DA-ØTSĄ́)
  daaztsą́: he died
- plural (Theme: NI-ØNÁ)
  neezná: they 2+ died

Seriative Plurality: Subject number is implicitly plural (3+) in intransitive verbs that include the Seriative prefix hi- ~ yi-Position 6a/6c. Here the subjects are performing the verbal action in sequence: one after another.

> mósí yázhí kin bitł'ááh góne' 'ahees'na' (or 'adahaas'na'): the kittens crawled one after another under the house

Collective Plurality is represented by the duoplural in contexts of the type:

Ch'osh t'óó ahayóigo silį́į́'go tsídii dó' t'óó 'ahayóí dooleeł (when it comes to be that insects are abundant, birds will also be plentiful). Díí tsídiiyígíí ch'osh 'ánéelt'e'ígíí yilááh noot'ą́ągo tsídiiyígíí t'áá bíni'ídii yaa kóńdoo'niił ch'oshígíí t'áá yił 'aheenéelt'e' (when the number of birds grows to exceed the number of insects, the number goes back down until their numbers are in balance with each other).

Diné'ałdó' t'áá 'ákót'éego nahasdzáán bikáá' hólǫ́ (Man exists on the earth in the same way) ndi dinéjí t'áadoo le'é tsídii bee 'ádinii bee hólǫ́ (but Man has something that the bird lacks)---

Hastą́ą́ shinááhaigo shiwoo' háánísą́ (my teeth grew back when I was six years old - i.e. I got my permanent teeth).

Distributive Plurality is marked by da-Position 3 (See Position 3).

Direct Object Number. A few Verb Stems distinguish object number as singular or plural. These include:

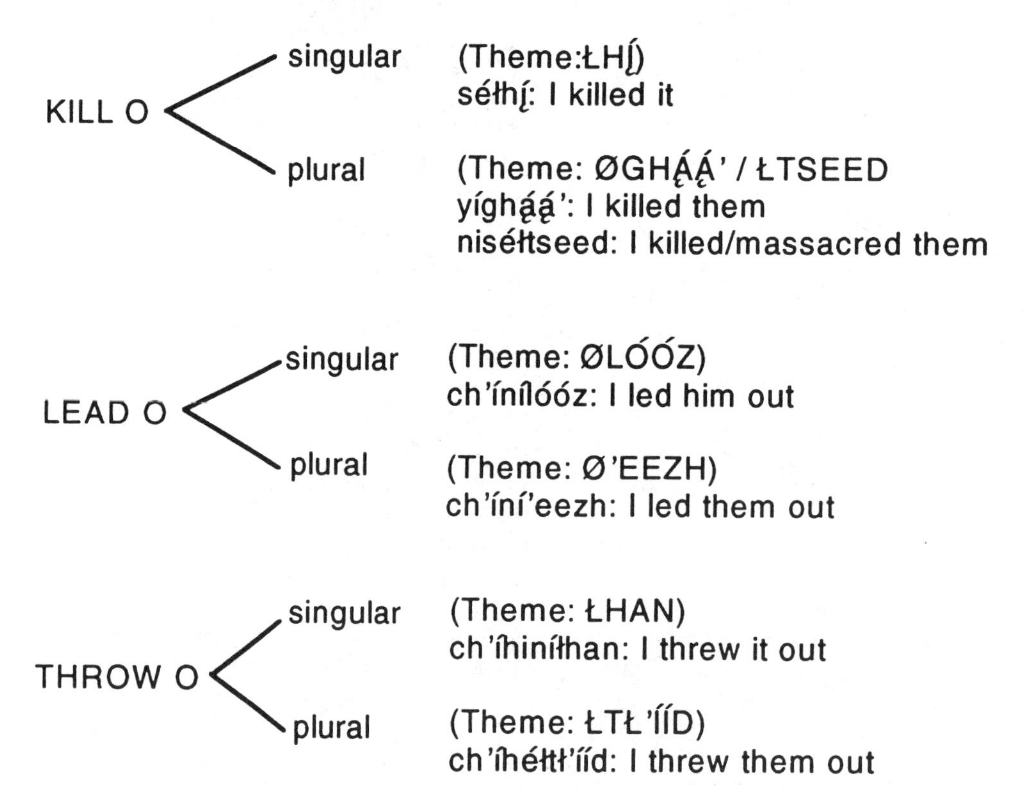


Distributive Plurality in Number-Specific Verbs of Locomotion: The GO/Run verbs distinguish singular and dual number, both of which may be marked as distributive plural.. Compare:

'ashkii kin góne' yah 'ííyá/yah 'eelwod: the boy went/ran into the house; 'ashiiké kin góne' yah 'adááyá/yah 'adaalwod: the 3+ boys went/ran into the house one at a time.

'ashiiké kin góne' yah 'íí'áázh/yah 'ahi'noolchą́ą́': the two boys went/ran into the house; 'ashiiké kin góne' yah 'adáá'áázh/yah 'adahi'noolchą́ą́': the 3+ boys went/ ran into the house two at a time

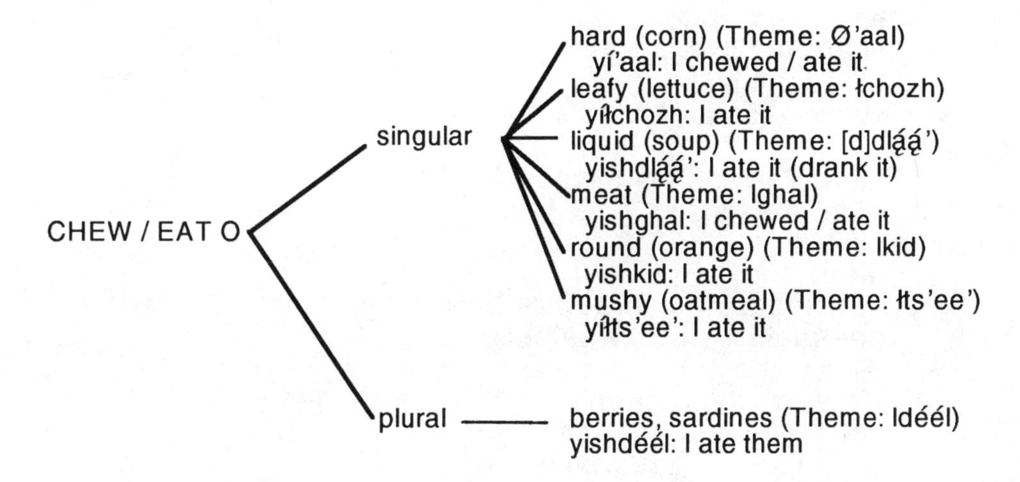


Distributive Plurality of the direct object is marked by incorporation of da-: Position 3, as in:

tsineheeshjíí' 'ahádashéch'iizh: I sawed the board into 3+ pieces or I sawed 3+ boards in half. (Cf. 'aháních'iizh: I sawed it in half.)
'ałk'ésdisí 'ałts'ádaséti': I broke the stick of candy into 3+ pieces or I broke 3+ pieces of candy apart. (Cf. 'ałts'ániti': I broke it apart.)

If the number of actors (subjects) is 3+ da- is not repeated, so:

tsineheeshjíí' 'ahádashiich'iizh = we two sawed the board into 3+ pieces / we two sawed 3+ boards in half / we 3+ sawed the board in half / we 3+ sawed 3+ boards in half / we 3+ sawed the board into 3+ pieces

The classsificatory "handle" verbs employ the Distributive Aspectual Stem Sets with da-, as:

łeets'aa' ndaashnil: I'm setting the table (i.e. I'm distributing 3+ dishes around here and there)
'áłchíní 'atoo' bá ndaashka': I'm setting out bowls of soup for the children.

2. OTHER CATEGORIES

The verb may be:

1. Active: describing an action or event, as

yish'ááł: I'm carrying it (SRO) along
ńdiiłtį́: I picked him up
naalnish: he's working
nahóółtą́: it rained

2. Neuter: describing an attribute, a state of being, a condition, or a position, as

łigai: it is white
łikan: it's sweet, tasty
nineez: it is long
shiláah 'ánííłnééz: he's taller than me

hiná: it lives, it is alive
hólǫ́: it exists
nilį́: he is
'át'é: it is
deesk'aaz: it's cold (weather)
deesdoii: it's hot (weather)
sik'az: it's cold (as water)
k'é'éltǫ': it's broken
sédá: I'm seated, I sit
si'ą́: it sits or lies (SRO - as a rock)
didíí'á: it extends into the fire (as a log)
náá'á: it hangs down (as an icicle)

3. Intransitive: Active or Neuter. Position 4 (the direct object pronoun) is vacant, as:

naalnish: he's working
yishwoł: I'm running along
bináshchid: I'm putting my arm around her
sínítį́: you are lying down, reclining
k'éz'á: it is erect, stands straight

4. Transitive: Active or Neuter. Position 4 is filled ( by Ø if the direct object is 3rd person and the subject is lst or 2nd person), as:

Øyish'ááł (Ø = it): I'm carrying it along (SRO)
Øyí'ááł (Ø = it): you're carrying it along
Øséł'ą́ (Ø = it): I keep it (SRO)

yoo'ááł (y- < yi- = it): he's carrying it along (SRO - as a book)
náshidiiłtį́ (-shi- = me): he picked me up
k'íyółdon (-y- < yi- = it): he's holding it straight out (as his leg)
yis'ą́: he keeps it (has it in position - a SRO, as a bottle)

5. Passive: Simple (3rd person only; non-human referents primarily); Agentive Passive (indefinite pronominal subject in Position 5; direct object pronoun in Position 4 - human referent), as:

shaa yít'ą́ (Simple): it was brought to me (a SRO - as a book)
ch'édzį́į́z: (Simple): it was dragged out
baa shi'deeltį́ (Agentive): I was given to him
ch'íshi'deedzį́į́z (Agentive): I was dragged out

6. Mediopassive: verbs in which the subject is, at the same time, the object or the recipient of his own action - but unlike the Reflexive verbs, the Mediopassives include no reflexive object pronoun, as:

ch'íninisht'ą́ (< ch'í-: out + -ni-: generic classifier for round shape + -nisht'ą́ = I moved my own round object [my head] out): I stuck my head out (as out a window)(cf . ch'íní'ą́: I moved or carried it (SRO) out)- as a book)
yooldéél: he ate them (literally: he tossed them into himself - as berries) (cf. biih yíłdéél: I tossed them into it - as a pair of shoes into a box)

7. Reflexive: the direct object is represented by the compound pronominal prefix 'á-di-: self, as:

'ádílzhééh: he's shaving himself
'ádílnaad: it's licking itself

8. Reciprocal: the direct object is represented by the reciprocal object pronoun prefix 'ahi- / 'ałhi-: each other, one another, as:

'ahiníl'į́: they're looking at each other
'ahilnaad: they're licking each other

## B. Mode and Aspect in the Verb

Active Verbs distinguish 7 Modes and at least 12 Aspects. Neuter Verbs are conjugated in a single Imperfective or Perfective modal paradigm

### A. The Modes

Mode serves to distinguish the manner in which a verbal action or event is conceived: whether incomplete, complete, ongoing, customary, prospective or potential (positively or negatively desired).

Mode is marked by special stem shape or by prefix (in Position 7 or 2), or by both. The 7 Modes are:

**1. The Imperfective Mode** usually describes an action or event as begun but incomplete. In this sense it is generally equivalent to an English present tense. The Imperfective is sometimes used in a Future context, and the 2nd person forms are used as immediate imperatives.

The Imperfective Mode is conjugated in 4 distinctive paradigms for Active Verbs. These are marked by Ø, ni- or si- in Position 7, and by yi-Position 6c + Ø-Position 7, and the Imperfective appears in all Aspects except the Cursive (although the Cursive Theme is based on the Momentaneous Imperfective Stem in the presence of da-distributive plural. See Progressive Mode.)

(1.) Ø-Imperfective is distinguished by a lack of modal-aspectival conjugation marker in Position 7, and consequently it functions semantically as a simple completive - i.e. the verbal action involved is not marked as terminative or stative in nature or effect.
'awoo' haash'aah (< ha-1b: out + Ø-7 + -sh-8 + Ø'aah: move SRO): I'm in the act of pulling the tooth

bilasáana yishą́ (< yi-: peg element + Ø-7 + -sh-8 + Ø(y)ą́ eat) : I'm eating the apple
'awéé' yicha (< yi-:peg element + Ø-7 + Ø-8 + Øcha: cry): the baby is crying
naaltsoos naash'á (< na-lb: around about + Ø-7 + -sh-8 + Ø'á: move SRO): I'm carrying the book around
hahgoshą' nádááh: when is he coming back (= when *will* he come back)?
ńdaah dóó 'íyą́: sit down and eat!
wóshdę́ę́' yah 'aninááh: come in!

An immediate negative imperative is produced with Ø-Imperfective + the frame t'áadoo ---í, for verbs that are continuant in Aspect. (See Continuative, Durative, Repetitive Aspect.)

t'áadoo nchaaí (< ncha: Durative): stop crying!
t'áadoo nanitazí (< nanitaz: Continuative): quit squirming around!
t'áadoo 'ádích'idí (< 'ádích'id: Repetitive): stop scratching yourself!

(2.) Ni-Imperfective is marked by ni-Position 7, identifying the verbal action as terminative: the subject finishes, arrives or otherwise reaches a goal. Ni-Imperfective is restricted to the Momentaneous Aspect because the action it describes takes place at a point in time.

t'ah doo yígháah da: he hasn't yet arrived
tł'iish léi' ch'é'néehgo yiiłtsą́, I saw a snake crawling out (i.e. as it was in the act of crawling out)
ch'ínílyeed: run out!
ch'ah shaa ní'aah: give me the hat!
yiską́ągo naa nánísht'ááh (naa ńdeesht'ááł): I'll give it (SRO) back to you tomorrow
'ałní'ní'ą́ądóó bik'ijį' naa náníshdááh (naa ńdeeshdááł): I'll come back to see you after noon
hahgoshą' nánídááh (ńdíínááł): when will you be (come) back?

(3.) Si-Imperfective is marked by the si-prefix of Position 7, identifying the verbal action as a type that has a stative-conclusive result upon completion. Si- does not appear in 3rd person and Passive forms; in these, the si-Imperfective paradigm switches to Ø-Imperfective.

naaltsoos bikáá'adání bikáa'gi dah sí'aah: set the book on the table!
tsin bąąh hasí'nééh: climb the tree!
tsin bąąh hashish'néehgo k'asdą́ą́' hadáátłizh: I nearly fell climbing the tree

*but* mósí tsin yąąh haa'néehgo yiiłtsą́: I saw the cat climbing the tree

(4.) Yi-Ø-Imperfective is derived with a yi-prefix of Position 6c that serves to mark Transitional and Semelfactive Aspect. It is marked by Ø in Position 7.

'at'ééd bitsii' yiyiiłch'ííłgo 'ádoodlid: the girl burned herself while curling her hair (Transitional)
k'adę́ę dah diisháahgo nikihoníłtą́: I was about to start off when it began to rain (Transitional)

jooł yéigo yiishtał ńt'éé' chą́ą́h dégo': I was giving the ball a swift kick when I fell flat on my face (Semelfactive)
tsitł'élí yiissohgo sits'ą́ą́' k'é'éltǫ': the match broke on me when I was scratching it (Semelfactive)

**2. The Usitative Mode:** describes a verbal action or event as one that is customarily performed. The Usitative is distinguished from the corresponding Ø- or si- Imperfective by stem shape - the Usitative takes a repetitive stem. Semelfactive Verbs usually use a single stem shape for all Modes. Ni-Position 7 modal-aspectival conjugation marker is restricted to the Momentaneous Aspect and consequently ni- does not appear in the Usitative Mode. Usitatives that correspond to ni-Imperfectives are conjugated in a Ø-Imperfective pattern.

1. Ø-Usitative corresponds to Ø- and ni-Imperfectives

'ahbínígo gohwééh yishdlį́įh łeh: I usually drink coffee in the morning (yishdlį́įh: Usitative = I usually drink it)
hastą́ądigo ńdiish'nah: I (usually) get up at six
'e'e'áahgo yah 'anishka'ii' 'atsą́ 'ádísh'įįh: in the evening I drive the sheep back in and prepare a meal (yah 'anishka': Usitative = I usually herd [them] in; 'ádísh'įįh: Usitative = I usually make it)
'e'e'áahgo Nááts'ózí dééh deidlį́įh: the Japanese (usually) drink tea in the evening

2. Si-Usitative corresponds to si-Imperfective

'awéé' tsásk'eh bikáa'gi dah shishtéehgo bitł'eestsooz bá 'ánáshdlééh, I (usually) lay the baby on the bed to change its diaper

3. Yi-Ø-Usitative corresponds to yi-Ø-Imperfective

shimósí bich'į' 'ahíshka'go niilk'oł łeh: my cat blinks (usually) when I (usually) clap my hands at him
'e'e'áahgo tó niissił dóó łeets'aa' tánásgis: in the evening I (usually) heat water and wash the dishes
'ahbínígo 'áłchíní ńdadiineeh: in the morning the children (usually) start to play

**3. The Iterative Mode** is a type of frequentative that describes a verbal action or event as one that takes place repeatedly (and customarily). The Iterative is marked by a Disjunct ná-prefix in Position 2, (probably identical with a Position lb prefix, identified as ná[5]-: repetition), and it employs the same stem as the corresponding Usitative. Ni-Position 7 modal-aspectival conjugation marker does not appear in the Iterative Mode; Ni-Imperfectives are complemented by Ná-Ø Iterative. Many Ø-class Verb Themes take D-classifier in the Iterative Mode.

1. Ná-Ø-Iterative

haigo łeejin baa náshgééh: I haul coal to him in the winter

'ahbínígo tł'óó'góó ch'ínáshdááh: I always (repeatedly) go outdoors in the morning
'ahbínígo gohwééh náshdlį́į́h: I drink coffee in the morning (repeatedly and customarily)
tł'ée'go mósí ch'ínásh'nił: at night I put the cats out

2. Ná-si-Iterative

t'áá 'ákwíí jį́ dííí tsin bąąh hanáshísh'nah (háashísh'nah): I climb this tree every day
'ahbínígo 'awéé' tsásk'eh bikáa'gi dah náshíshtééh: in the morning I lay the baby on the bed

3. Ná-yi-Ø-Iterative

naanishgóó dah ńdiishdáahgo she'esdzą́ą́ néists'ǫs: I give my wife a kiss when I leave for work
shį́į́go na'nishkaadgo néishjį́į́h: I get sunburned in the summer herding sheep
'ahbínígo shizhé'é bilį́į́' bá néishdloh: I rope my father's horse for him in the morning

**4. The Perfective Mode**, usually equivalent to a past tense in English, describes a verbal action or event as completed. The Perfective is marked by stem shape and, in Position 7, by yi-(= ghi-), ni-, si- or by Ø in 7 + yi- in Position 6c, for Transitional Aspect. It is conjugated in a total of 8 paradigms: Ø/Ł-Class Verb Themes and D/L-Class Themes take distinctive conjugation patterns (see The Verb Paradigms). The 1st, 2nd and 3rd person sgl forms of Ø/Ł-Class verbs and the 2nd person sgl of D / L-class Yi-, Ni- and Si-Perfective verbs include a high tone marker of Perfective Mode on the modal prefix.

Yi-Perfective describes a verbal action or event as simply completed, without a connotation of termination, conclusive or static sequel; Ni-Perfective describes a verbal action or event as terminative in sequel: finish, arrive or otherwise reach a goal; Si-Perfective describes a verbal action or event as one involving a static-durative sequel: the subject or object remains in the position or condition denoted by the stem; and Yi-Ø-Perfectives describe the subject or object as shifting from one state, condition or position to another.

(1.) Yi-Perfective - Ø/Ł-Class

biwoo' bá háá'ą́: I pulled his tooth for him
bilasáana yíyą́ą́': I ate the apple
'at'ééd bilasáana yiyííyą́ą́', the girl ate the apple
ha'át'íísha' biniiyé taah yíníyá: why did you go into the water?
'ashkii taah yíyá: the boy got into the water

Yi-Perfective - D/L-Class

'a'ą́ą́dę́ę́' haash'na': I crawled up out of the hole

dibé bitsį' ła' yishghal: I ate some mutton
'at'ééd dibé bitsį' ła' yoolghal: the girl ate some mutton
ha'át'íísh ą' biniiyé taah yíní'na': why did you crawl into the water?
'ashkii taah yi'na': the boy crawled into the water

*All verbs that are conjugated as Yi-Perfectives take Ø-Imperfective.

(2.) Ni-Perfective - Ø/Ł-Class

hádą́ą́'shą' yíníyá: when did you arrive?
táá' yiskánídą́ą́' níyá: I arrived three days ago
mósí tł'óó'góó ch'íníłt'e': I put the cat out
shimá mósí tł'óó'góó ch'íiníłt'e': my mother put the cat out
'ąą dinítą́ą́ dóó ch'íníyá: I opened the door and went out

Ni-Perfective - D/L-Class
hádą́ą́'shą' néínídzá: when did you return?
dibé bighangóó nishtł'á: I trotted to the sheep corral
táchééhdę́ę́' ch'íníshdloozh: I crawled out of the sweathouse
shizhé'é táchééhdę́ę́' ch'éldloozh: my father crawled out of the sweathouse
'ashkii bijáátah dinishtáál: I tripped the boy with my foot
'ashkii shijáátah deeltáál: the boy tripped me with his foot

*All verbs that are conjugated as Ni-Perfectives are also conjugated as Ni-Imperfectives.

(3.) Si-Perfective - Ø/Ł-Class

shikin łigaigo shédléézh: I painted my house white
shimá dibé bitsį' ła' shá yist'é: my mother roasted some mutton for me
tsásk'eh bikáa'gi dah nétį́į́ dóó 'iiłhaazh: I lay down on the bed and went to sleep
'ashkii tsásk'eh yikáa'gi dah neeztį́į́ dóó 'iiłhaazh: the boy lay down on the bed and went to sleep
'awéé' tsásk'eh bikáa'gi binéłtį́: I laid the baby down on the bed

Si-Perfective - D/L-Class

'awééts'áál bitis dah néshjį́į́d: I jumped over the babyboard
'ashkii 'awééts'áál yitis dah neeshjį́į́d: the boy jumped over the babyboard
'adą́ą́dą́ą́' yéigo nishishnish: I worked hard yesterday
'adą́ą́dą́ą́' shizhé'é bichidí yinaashnish: yesterday my father worked on his car
tsin bąąh hasis'na': I climbed the tree

*Most verbs that are conjugated as Si-Perfectives are conjugated as Ø-Imperfectives, except the Semelfactives, which are conjugated in a Yi-Ø-Imperfective paradigm, and the Si-Imperfectives.

(4.) Yi-Ø-Perfective - Ø/Ł-Class

mą'ii shiiłtsą́ągo yóó' 'íísaal: when the coyote saw me it ran away

shi'dééji'go yiizį': I stood up when my name was called
tł'éédą́ą' sho yiigaii: it frosted last night (i.e. last night frost whitened)
dah yiitįhí ch'il yikáa'gi dah yiitą́ągo yiiłtsą́: I saw a hummingbird hovering over a plant
diyogí ńdiiyį́į́ dóó kingóó dah diiyá: I picked up the rug and started off for the store

Yi-Ø-Perfective - D/L-Class

shį́įdą́ą' hado biyi' na'nishkaadgo yiishjį́į́': I got sunburned last summer herding in the heat (i.e. I turned black)
dah yiishdloozhgo 'awéé' bił nisénе': I got down on my hands and knees and played with the baby
diyogí shaa nahaaznii'go hooghangóó dah ńdiisdzá: I started back home when I sold the rug

*All verbs conjugated as Yi-Ø-Perfectives are also conjugated as Yi-Ø-Imperfectives.

**5. The Progressive Mode** describes a verbal action or event as one that is ongoing - along in a line in time or space. It is generally equivalent to a verb phrase composed of a present participle + a form of the verb "to be" in English. The Progressive is conjugated in two distinctive paradigms: (1) marked by a yi-(= ghi-) prefix in Position 7 + a distinctive stem, when the subject of the verb is sgl or dpl; and (2) marked by da-yí- + ni-7 + the stem of the Imperfective Mode when the subject of the verb is distributive plural.

1.Yi-Progressive

'atiingóó yishááł: I'm walking along the road
'ashkii naanáálwoł: the boy is running about to and fro
chidí bijáád nááshbał; I'm whirling the car wheel
'atiingóó yiikah: we (3+) are walking along the road in a group
'ashkii jooł yoołmas: the boy is rolling the ball along
'ashkii dibé kingóó yinoołkał: the boy is driving the herd of sheep to the store

Da-yí-ní-Progressive

'atiingóó deíníikááh: we (3+) are going along the road in a scattered group
Bilagáana léi' 'atiingóó łį́į́' deílóosgo yiiłtsą́: I saw some white men (3+) leading horses along the road

**6. The Future Mode** functions primarily as a tense form, to describe an action or event as prospective. It is a derived construction, consisting of di-inceptive + the Progressive. However, verbs that lack a Progressive nonetheless usually include a Future.

yiską́ągo kintahgóó deeshááł: I'll go to town tomorrow
'ałní'ní'ą́ągo naa ńdeeshdááł: I'll come back to see you at noon
yah 'adeeshááł dóó dínéeshdaał: I'll go inside and sit down

tł'óó'góó ch'ídeeshááł nisin: I want to go outdoors

**7. The Optative Mode** serves primarily to express a positive or a negative wish or desire. It is marked by an -ó/-o-prefix in Position 7.

nahółtin laanaa: I hope that it rains
nahółtin lágo: I hope it doesn't rain
'ashiiké ńjódle' daniidzin: we wish (i.e. one wishes) that we could turn back into boys

Secondarily, the 2nd person forms of the Optative are used to express a negative imperative for verbs that are punctual in Aspect, as:

tsásk'eh bikáa'gi dah nóótééł (lágo): don't lie down on the bed!
shinóół'į́į́' (lágo): don't look at me! (but Durative t'áadoo shinínił'íní: quit looking at me!)

## B. The Aspects

The Aspects serve to distinguish the *kind* of action or state that is expressed by a verb: whether punctual (occurring at a point in time), continuing, repetitive, occurring a single time, reversing direction, shifting from one state to another, or attempted.

Aspect is distinguished by distinctive stem shape, by special prefix, or by a combination of the two.

The Aspects crosscut the Modes - that is to say that a verbal action can be distinguished as Imperfective (incomplete) in Mode, but at the same time punctual, continuing or repetitive in Aspect. Thus:

ńdiists'in: I'm in the act of hitting him one time (with my fist) (= punctual)
nánísts'in: I'm beating him with my fists (= repetitive)
ńdiishbeeh: I'm starting to bathe (= punctual)
naashbé: I'm swimming about, bathing (= continuing)

Navajo distinguishes at least 12 Aspects for the Active Verbs. These are identified and illustrated below:

**1. The Momentaneous Aspect** describes a verbal action or event that takes place at a point in time - punctually. The Momentaneous is the most productive for lexical derivation - i.e. most lexical derivatives employ the Momentaneous Stem Sets, a circumstance that is reflected by the fact that many of the derivational prefixes of Positions 1 and 6 are restricted (for semantic reasons) to the Momentaneous Aspect. Thus, the Conjunct prefix di-: start, can only refer to an action that takes place at a point in time; and similarly, the Disjunct prefix ch'í-: horizontally out, connotes an action that is punctual - neither di-: start, nor ch'í-: out, can describe a verbal action that is continuative. *Start* and *exit* are not actions that occupy a span of time. Momentaneous in Aspect are verbs of the type:

hooghandi nánísdzá: I arrived back home
didzé ła' 'ázaasht'ą́: I put a berry into my mouth
łééchąą'í tł'óó'góó ch'élwod: the dog ran out
naaltsoos baa ní'ą́: I brought or gave him the book

Arrive, put, run out and bring all describe actions that occur at a point in time.

*All of the Imperfective / Perfective Conjugation markers of Position 7 occur with the Momentaneous Aspect.

**2. The Continuative Aspect** describes verbal action that (1) occupies an indefinite span of time and (2) that moves "around about" - without specified direction. It occurs with verbs of locomotion (go, fly, carry), and with verbs that describe certain types of processes (work, narrate, think). The Continuative is marked by special stem shape, especially in the Imperfective and Optative Modes (which usually use the same stem), and by special stem shape in other Modes in some verbs; and Continuative aspectual Verb Bases always include the Disjunct prefix na[1]-lb: around, about, here and there. Compare the Momentaneous and the Continuative Stem Sets:

máás(I.), mas(Iter.), mááz(P.), mas(F.), máás(O.) (Momentaneous): roll
maas(I.), mas(Iter.), mááz(P.), mas(Prog./F.), maas(O.) (Continuative): roll (about)

'aah(I.), 'ááh(Iter.), 'ą́(P.), 'ááł(F.), 'ááł(O), (Momentaneous): move a SRO
'á(I.), 'aah(Iter.), 'ą́(P.), 'aał(F.), 'aał(O.), (Continuative): move SRO (about)

The Continuative Aspect is illustrated below:

kintahdi naasháago 'i'íí'ą́: I spent the day (going about) in town
shimá na'niłkaadgo 'i'íí'ą́: my mother spent the day herding
shiłééchąą'í ndilchą́ą'go naanáálwoł: my dog is running around to and fro following a scent (ndilchą́ą' < nadilchą́ą': it is sniffing about)
níyolgo t'iis naha'ná: the cottonwood tree is moving in the wind
shizhé'é 'ólta'di naalnish: my father works (about) at the school

*The Continuative Aspect is always conjugated in a Ø-Imperfective / si-Perfective pattern.

**3. The Durative Aspect,** like the Continuative, describes verbal action of a type that occupies an indefinite span of time. However, the Durative does not occur with verbs of locomotion - it is restricted to processes in which verbal action takes the form of an uninterrupted continuum (as in eating, drinking, urinating, crying, talking; and including such repetitive actions as scratching, pecking, pounding, jerking).(See The Repetitive Aspect.)

Durative Aspect is marked primarily in the Imperfective / Optative Modes, by special stem form. Compare the Momentaneous and Durative Stem Sets:

chééh(I.), chah(Iter.), cha(P), chah(F.), chééh(O) (Momentaneous): cry
cha(I.), chah(Iter.), cha(P.), chah(F.), cha(O) (Durative): cry

Verbs of the type listed below are simple Duratives:

'ashkii bilasáana yiyą́ą́go sidá: the boy sits eating an apple
'awéé' yichago sitį́: the baby lies crying
ha'át'íishą' baa yáníłti': what are you talking about?

*The Simple Duratives take a Ø-Imperfective / Yi-Perfective conjugation pattern.

**4. The Repetitive Aspect** describes verbal action that involves a continuum of repetitive acts (tapping, scratching, jerking, pounding, rubbing, sprinkling), or a connected series of acts (as beating, slapping, kicking, throwing at). The Repetitives fall into several subtypes, as:

Simple Repetitive: derived with the Usitative / Iterative stem and conjugated in a Ø-Imperfective paradigm.

'anilí tsésǫ' béshjoł (< b-í-O-1b: against it + -shjoł): I'm rubbing a rag against the window
bésh'ááh: I'm rubbing it (SRO - as a bar of soap) against it
táláwosh tsé yíí'ááh (< y-í-O-1b + -(y)i-4 > yíí- + Ø'ááh): he's rubbing (a bar of) soap against the rock
béésh da'hólzha'í tsin bídíshdił (< b-í-O-lb: against it + di-6a + -shdił): I'm beating the chain against the tree
bee'ak'e'elchíhí nikídíshdiłgo sédá (< nik-1b:surface + -í-1b: against + -shdił): I sit bouncing a pencil

Durative Repetitive: constructed and conjugated like the Simple Duratives described in (3) above, and conjugated in Ø-Imperfective / yi-Perfective patterns.
'ashkii 'ásaa' yiłtązhgo sidá: the boy sits beating (lightly - tapping on) a drum
sitsiits'iin yihę́ęsgo biniinaa yishch'id: I'm scratching my head because it itches
'awéé' tsineheeshjíí' yitsidgo sidá: the baby sits pounding on a board

Yíní- Durative Repetitives: marked by the compound prefix yí-ni-: directed at, (yí-ni- > -ó- in the absence of a prefix of Position 8). The yíni-Repetitives are conjugated as Ø-Imperfectives, and they are constructed on the Momentaneous Imperfective stem of verbs that describe the propulsion of an object (including the fist in striking, the foot in kicking, the flat of the hand in slapping and the hand or paw in grabbing). (With the Perfective stems of non-motion verbs that describe a process, such as that involved in grasping, yí-ni- derives Neuters with the meaning "hold.")

yínísts'in: I'm striking or pawing at him (with my fist)

łééchąą'í ts'in yółts'in: the dog is digging for a bone
neii'néego sitsilí hashtł'ish bee yíníshtłeeh: I'm slinging mud at my little brother as we play
sitsilí hashtł'ish yee shótłeeh: my little brother is slinging mud at me

(Cf. Neuter yínístsa': I'm holding it grasped in my teeth)

Seriative (Consecutive) Repetitives describe verbal action that is Durative in the Imperfective Mode, but Conclusive in the Perfective (See Conclusive Aspect.) The Seriative Repetitive is marked by the compound prefix ná-ni- (< ná[5]-Position 1b: repetition + -ni[1]-Position 6b: terminative), and it is conjugated as a Ø-Imperfective / si-Perfective.

'ashkii léi' hááhgóóshįį́ náshineests'in: some boy really gave me a beating (i.e. a consecutive series of blows with his fist)
shiléécháą'í náníshkadgo sédá: I sit petting my dog (consecutive patting actions
'ił 'adaalkaałí tsé bee nánéłne', I pounded the nail with a rock (consecutive blows)

The Usitative and Iterative Modes are used as Simple Repetitives in contexts of the type:

Usitative:

tł'iish shich'į' dino'go sitį́: the snake lies flicking its tongue at me (Simple Repetitive)
naghái 'ashkii 'ayóo dino': that boy is always moistening his lips (Usitative)

Iterative:

ńdídáhí nihich'ą́ąh ńdídááh: the sentinel is walking back and forth in front of us (Simple Repetitive)
hastą́ądigo naanishgóó ńdíshdááh: I start for work at six (Iterative)

**5. The Conclusive Aspect** is a variant of the Durative, in which si-Perfective represents the verbal action as a type that terminates with a static sequel.

'aghaa' yisdiz: I'm spinning the wool / 'aghaa' sédiz: I have the wool spun
kin yishdleesh: I'm painting the house / kin shédléézh: I have the house painted
'ashłizh: I'm urinating / 'ashélizh: I've urinated

**6. The Semelfactive Aspect** stands in a complementary relationship to the Repetitive, serving to isolate a single act from a repetitive series. It occurs in three distinctive forms, identified as (1) the Simple Semelfactive, (2) the ńdi-Semelfactive, and (3) the yíní-directive Semelfactive.

(1) The Simple Semelfactive is a completive that serves to describe a verbal action as one that occurs a single time. It is derived with the yi-Semelfactive marker of Position 6c, in all Modes except the Future and the Perfective. It takes a Yi-Ø-Imperfective- Usitative - Iterative - Optative, and a Si-Perfective conjugational pattern, and most Simple Semelfactives employ a single stem shape for all Modes.

niishch'ił: I blink (one time); nániishch'ił: I blink on repeated occasions; néshch'ił: I blinked; dínéeshch'ił: I'll blink; nooshch'ił: that I might blink

yiists'ǫs (Imperfective): I'm in the act of giving him / her a kiss (cf. Iterative néists'ǫs: I repeatedly give him / her a kiss; Perfective séts'ǫs: I gave him / her a kiss)

(2) The ńdi-Semelfactives use the Momentaneous Stem Set. They take a Yi-Ø-conjugational pattern in the Imperfective-Usitative, Iterative and Optative Modes, but a Yi-Perfective conjugation. The ńdi-Semelfactives are restricted to verbs that describe a blow (as with fist, club, whip or hand).

ńdiists'in (< ń- < ná$^{4}$-: upward + di$^{13}$ -: 6a inceptive + -i-6c: Semelfactive Aspect marker + Ø-7 + -sts'in): I'm in the act of striking him a blow with my fist (but Perfective ńdííłts'in: I struck him with my fist)
nínádiists'įįh (< ní- < ná $^{4}$-: upward + + -ná$^{2}$- : Iterative Mode marker = repeatedly + di$^{13}$ - 6a inceptive + -i-6c: Semelfactive Aspect marker + -sts'įįh): I repeatedly hit him with my fist (i.e. on repeated occasions)
náshidííłts'in (< ná$^{4}$ - upward + -shi-4: me + di- - 6a + -íłts'in): he struck me with his fist
ńdoosts'in (< ń- < ná$^{4}$ -: upward + d- < di$^{13}$ - inception + -i-6c: Semelfactive + -o-7: Optative Mode marker + -sts'in): that I might strike him with my fist

(3) Yíní-Directive Semelfactives use the Momentaneous Stem Set and Yi-Ø- Imperfective, Perfective, Iterative and Optative conjugation patterns.

yíníishłeeh (< yíní-6a / 6b: directed at + -i-6c: Semelfactive + --shłeeh): I'm in the act of throwing a loop or noose at it
néíníishdloh (< né- < ná-2: Iterative Mode marker + -íní- 6a / 6b: directed at + -i-6c: Semelfactive + --shdloh): I repeatedly (i.e. on repeated occasions) throw a loop or noose at it
yíníilo' (< yíní-6a / 6b: directed at + -i-6c: Semelfactive + --lo'): I threw a noose or loop at it

**7. The Distributive Aspect** describes: (1) the distributive placement of objects in space; (2) the distribution of objects to recipients; or (3) the distributive performance of verbal actions. The Distributive is conjugated in a Ø-Imperfective / Si-Perfective pattern, and some verbs require distinctive stem shapes.

shilįį' tó bá ndaashka': I'm placing (3+ containers of) water about for my horses
shideezhí łeets'aa' ndeinilgo bíká 'anáshwo': I help my younger sister set the table (literally: I help my sister as she places 3+ dishes about)
'áłchíní naaltsoos bitaasénil: I passed out books to the children

'áłchíní t'ááłá'í béeso bitaash'a': I'm distributing dollars to the children - one to each recipient
ch'iyáán bá hooghan góne' ch'iyáán bitaa'ashchį́į́hgo tádísháah: I'm going around in the store sniffing (among) the food
ch'il 'ałtaas'áí bitaa'séłį́h: I sampled different plants (by tasting among them)

**8. The Diversative Aspect** describes movement : (1) that is distributed among things, or (2) movement that takes place here and there. The first type has much in common, both structurally and semantically, with the Distributive forms derived with postpositional bitaa-: among them, described above, and it is conjugated in a Ø-Imperfective / Si-Perfective pattern. And, again like the Distributive, the Diversatives derived with bitaa- may require a distinctive Stem Set.

'ałk'idą́ą́' Diné Naakaii yitaadaabaah ńt'éé': long ago the Navajos used to raid (among) the Mexicans.
haidą́ą́' tahoniigááh nihitaadaasnii': a flu epidemic spread among us last winter.

Diversatives of type (2) are derived with the compound prefix tá-di-, and they take the Momentaneous Stem Set, with a Ø-Imperfective / Yi-Perfective conjugation pattern.

kintahdi 'awéé' tádíshteehgo 'i'íí'ą́: I carried the baby around all day in town.
Hoozdodi tádíshnííshgo sheeshį́: I spent the summer doing odd jobs (itinerant labor) in Phoenix.

**9. The Reversative Aspect** describes a verbal action that results in a directional change - a turn or a reversal. The Reversative is derived with ná1-1b: around encircling, around making a turn, and with compound náhidi-: turn over. Some Reversative Verb Themes require a distinctive Stem Set, while others employ the Momentaneous stem shapes. The ná-Reversatives are conjugated in a Ø-Imperfective / Si-Perfective pattern, and the náhidi-Reversatives require a distinctive -ee-Imperfective / Perfective pattern.

náhínááh: turn around!
bikáá'adání shá náhí'ááh: turn the table around for me!
'ashkii yázhí tsé néítł'ingo naané: the little boy plays piling rocks in a circle
shimá binášhchid: I'm putting my arm around my mother
tł'éédą́ą́' shichidí shił náhidéélts'id: my car turned over with me last night

**10. The Conative Aspect** describes *attempted* verbal action. Durative Repetitives derived with postpositional -í-1b: against, function as Conatives with the "handle" verbs in certain contexts; and Verb Bases derived with postpositional -gha-1b: away from by force + a "handle" stem convey the concept "try to take O away from (someone)." The Conatives are conjugated as Ø-Imperfectives.

'ashkii léi' bizhéé' hólóní bésh'ááh ńt'éé' doo yinízin da: I offered a boy a beer but he didn't want it (literally: I rubbed a beer on him; cf. táláwosh sitsiits'iin bésh'ááh: I'm rubbing a bar of soap on my head)
sitsilí shinaaltsoos shighait'ááh: my little brother is trying to get my book away from me

**11. The Transitional Aspect** describes verbal action of a type that involves a shift from one state of being, form, condition or position to another. The Transitional is marked by the -i- ( ~ yi-) aspect marker of Position 6c, and conjugated in a Ø-Imperfective / Ø-Perfective pattern (Yi-Ø-Imperfective / Yi-Ø-Perfective). Most Transitionals use the Momentaneous Stem Set; a few Transitional Bases require a distinctive Stem Set.

shį́į́dą́ą́' na'nishkaadgo yiishjį́į́': I got sunburned herding sheep last summer (literally: I turned black) (łinishzhin: I am black)
t'ah doo tééh hóyání yiistséeh da: I've never seen a dolphin (literally: I haven't yet shifted from a state of not glimpsing to one of seeing) (yish'į́: I see it)
shiléécháą'í shiiłtsą́ągo bijaa' yayiitsi: when my dog saw me it pricked up its ears (literally: when it shifted to a state of glimpsing me it shifted its ears to a stick-up position) (bijaa' yaa'á: its ears stick up)
bee'eldǫǫh ńdiitą́ą́ dóó dziłgóó dah diiyá: I picked up the gun and set off for the mountain (I changed the position of the gun and, in starting off, I changed my own status) (déyá: I am on my way - in a state of having started)
hastą́ądigo ńdiish'na' dóó 'íįyą́ą́': I got up at six and ate

The Inchoative Inceptives are a distinctive derivative based on the Transitional. They are derived with a compound -'nii-prefix and conjugated in a yi-Ø pattern, except in the Future Mode where yi-marking Transitional Aspect is omitted. The Inchoative prefix complex usually includes a null postpositional (Position 1a). For some verbs the Inchoative is the only conjugation in which the Momentaneous/Transitional stem appears, in Imperfective/Optative Modes.

*The null postposition represents the direct object if the verb is transitive, and inflection follows a regular yi/Ø pattern.

| | | |
|---|---|---|
| Imperfective: | bi'niishbíísh | start to braid it |
| Perfective: | bi'niibizh | |
| Iterative: | biná'niishbish | |
| Future: | bidí'néeshbish | |
| Optative: | bi'nooshbíísh | |

shimá bitsii' yi'niibizh: my mother started to braid her hair

*The direct object is represented by 'i-: "something unspecified" in constructions of the type:

| | | |
|---|---|---|
| Imperfective: | 'i'niishtł'óóh | start to weave |
| Perfective: | 'i'niitł'ǫ́ | |
| Iterative: | 'i'ná'niishtł'óóh | |
| Future: | 'idí'néeshtł'óół | |
| Optative: | 'i'nooshtł'óóh | |

shimá 'i'niitł'ǫ́: my mother started to weave (something unspecified)

*The null postposition represents the subject in some types of intransitive construction, and inflection involves only the null postposition, as P-'niidlí: get cold (a person)

| | | |
|---|---|---|
| Imperfective: | P-'niidlóóh | (1.shi'niidlóóh, 2.ni'niidlóóh, 3.bi'niidlóóh, 3a.ho'niidlóóh, 1.nihi'niidlóóh, 2.nihi'niidlóóh) |
| Perfective: | P-'niidlí | (1.shi'niidlí, 2.ni'niidlí, 3.bi'niidlí, 3a.ho'niidlí, 1.nihi'niidlí, 2.nihi'niidlí) |
| Iterative: | P-ná'niidlóóh | (1.shiná'niidlóóh, 2.niná'niidlóóh ---) |
| Future: | P-dí'nóodlóół | (1.shidí'nóodlóół, 2.nidí'nóodlóół ---) |
| Optative: | P-'noodlóóh | (1.shi'noodlóóh, 2.ni'noodlóóh ---) |

na'nishkaadgo shi'niidlí: I got cold herding
'abe' bi'niichxǫ': the milk started to spoil
shi'niitsą́: I became ill (lit. I started to die)
ni'niits'iiní: you began to get skinny

* In some types of intransitive Inchoative verbs the indefinite (3i) null postposition occupies the position of the direct object, but appears to function as a thematic element: i.e. the combination 'i'nii- = simply "start to," as in:

| | | |
|---|---|---|
| Imperfective: | 'i'niishchééh | start to cry |
| Perfective: | 'i'niicha | |
| Iterative: | 'i'ná'niishchah | |
| Future: | 'idí'néeshchah | |
| Optative: | 'i'nooshchééh | |

'awéé' 'i'niicha: the baby started to cry
'i'niiłhą́ą́': I started to snore
'i'niihai: it became winter, winter started
'i'niichxíįł: it started to snow

* The relative positional slot occupied by the null postposition varies:

The null postposition appears to the right of a prefix of Position 1b:

'ábi'niishłaa ('á-1b: thematic): I started to make it
'ahábi'niiłdlááđ ('ahá-1b: apart): I started to rip it apart
habi'niiłchaad (ha-1b: up out): I started to card it
haho'niigeed (ha-1b: up out): I started to dig a hole

In constructions of the type illustrated above the null postposition takes position to the right of other Disjunct constituents of the prefix complex, as:

'áyi'niilaa ('á-1b: thematic): he started to make it / 'ánááyi'niilaa ('á-1b = náá-1e: semeliterative): he again started to make it, he started to make another one / 'ánáádayi'niilaa ('á-1b: thematic + náá-1e: semeliterative + da-3: distributive plural marker): they 3+ started to make another one

haho'niigeed (ha-1b): he started to dig a hoel / hanáádaho'niigeed (ha-1b + náá-1e + da-3): they 3+ started to dig another hole

mósí 'ádi'niilnáád ('á-di-: 1c-4: reflexive): the cat started to lick itself / mósí 'ánáádadi'niilnáád ('á-1c + náá-1e + da-3 + di-4): the 3+ cats started to lick themselves again

* In the presence of so- ~ tso-: Position 1b thematic prefix, the null postposition is omitted:

sodi'niiszin: I started to pray / sodin'nilzin: you started to pray

**12. The Cursive Aspect** describes verbal action of a type that progresses in a line through time or space. It appears in a single Mode: the Progressive. (See Progressive Mode.)

yishááł: I'm walking along
yishtééł: I'm carrying it along (AnO)
nááshdááł (< ná-1d: Reversionary + -á- < yi-7: Progressive Mode marker + -shdááł): I'm going along returning
naanááshwoł (< naa- < na[1]-1b: around about + -ná[1]-1b: around in a turn or circle + -á- < yi-7: Progressive` Mode marker + -shwoł): I'm running about to and fro
heeshááł (< hi-6a: Seriative marker + -ee- < yi-7: Progressive Mode marker + -shááł): I'm stepping or shuffling along
'anaa' náás yit'ih: the war continues (i.e. extends forward in a line)

With prepounded dah (up, up at an elevation) the Progressive describes a frozen but continuing static - "action along" = "status along."

'ásaa' yish'ááł: I'm carrying the jar along
'ásaa' dah yish'ááł: I'm holding the jar up
tsinaabąąs yisbąs: I'm driving the wagon along
tsinaabąąs dah yisbąs: I have the wagon parked
yishááł: I'm walking / going along

dah yisháál: I make my living

## VII. INFLECTIONAL MORPHOLOGY

Functionally, the Navajo verb is a system, in the classic sense that it is composed of varying numbers and types of interactive elements that, joined together, constitute a semantic unit.

The system involves two distinctive parts: the Theme (stem and classifier + thematic prefix, if any) and the Prefix Complex (all of the elements that join to mark person, number, direct object, mode and aspect, as well as all of those that function adverbially or as constituents of the Theme).

The system is further divided into distinctive parts in the form of several modes, which again take distinctive forms corresponding to the aspects that crosscut them.

Conjugation of the verb for person and number involves primarily the prefix complexes employed by the several distinctive subdivisions described above, where the incorporation of inflectional morphemes of variable shape triggers a variety of morphophonemic rules that govern prefix form in the changing phonological environment. Secondarily, conjugation involves changing shapes taken by adverbial and other constituents of the Prefix Complex as they come into variable juxtaposition with one another or with the inflectional morphemes.

The model paradigms that follow detail the changes in form, and reflect the pertinent rules that govern verb inflection for most types of Prefix Complex. Although the resulting multiple conjugational patterns may appear to be highly complicated, careful analysis will disclose the basic simplicity of the rules involved in the conjugational process.

The chart below outlines the usual relative syntactic order taken by the constituent Theme and prefixes in an inflected Verb Base.

| EXTENDED BASE PARADIGM | | |
|---|---|---|
| | BASE PARADIGM | THEME: 9-10<br>+<br>SUBJECT PRONOUN: 8<br>+<br>CONJUGATION MARKER: 7 |
| | Conjunct Prefixes | +<br>ASPECTUAL DERIVATIONAL THEMATIC : 6<br>+<br>DEICTIC SUBJECT PRONOUNS : 5<br>+<br>DIRECT OBJECT PRONOUNS : 4 |
| | Disjunct Prefixes | +<br>DISTRIBUTIVE PLURAL: 3<br>+<br>DERIVATIONAL-THEMATIC PRONOMINAL : 2, 1<br>+<br>POSTPOSITIONAL OBJECT PRONOUN : 0 |

The Base Paradigms constitute the primary conjugational pattern or patterns for each of the seven Modes, and they provide the underlying conjugational patterns for all derived Verb Bases. Composed of the Verb Theme in Positions 9-10 + the markers of subject in Position 8 + the modal-aspectual conjugation markers in Position 7, the Base Paradigms are the simplest conjugations possible for the several Modes.

The Extended Base Paradigm: The Base Paradigms are extended variously by the incorporation of pronominal, adverbial and/or thematic elements, and such extenson generates changes in the conjugational pattern that reflect the rules of juncture that come into play as various types and classes of prefix are linked to one another and to the Base forms.

The Extended Base Paradigms appear in three broad levels:

1. A primary level consisting of the Base Paradigm in combination with one or more prefixes of Positions 5, 4 and 3. These elements, representing deictic subject, direct object and distributive plural number respectively are shared, potentially, by all fully conjugated Verb Bases, limited only by constraints inherent in the nature of the Base (e.g. only transitive constructions incorporate the object pronoun prefixes of Position 4, and some verbs, such as <u>rain</u>, <u>snow</u> are not conjugated for person).

2. A second level consisting of the Base Paradigm in direct combination with an adverbial-derivational or thematic prefix of Position 6 or 1.

3. A third level includes the Extended Base Paradigms in which composite Verb Bases are conjugated - i.e. those in which the Base Paradigm is joined with any combination of multiple Conjunct and Disjunct prefixes of Positions 1, 2, 3, 4, 5, and 6, as in:

ch'ínáádeideeshdą́zh (< ch'í-1b + náá-1e + da-3 + [y]i-4 + d[i]-6a + -eeshdą́zh): they 3+ again jerked him out (as a recalcitrant person)

## The Conjugational Determinant

For the <u>Base</u> Paradigms the modal-aspectival conjugation markers in Position 7 determine the conjugational pattern for the paradigm, and for the <u>Extended</u> Base Paradigms the determinant is the pronominal, derivational or thematic prefix that is linked directly to the Base forms. In either case, linkage often results in morphological alterations stemming from contraction, reduction or other factors. Thus, for example, ni-7 takes the shape yí- in Imperfective and D/L-Class Perfective paradigms, in forms that lack a prefix in Position 8 (i.e. 3rd person and Simple Passive), as:

yílyeed: he's arriving at a run / yílwod: he arrived running
yíltsooz: it (FFO) was delivered

When the ni-Imperfective / ni-Perfective Base Paradigm is extended by incorporating a Ci-prefix of Position 1,4,5, or 6 the resulting shape assumed by the combination depends on the extending prefix and the environment:

Ci-1 + yí- > Cii, as in <u>nii</u>lyeed: he stops running / <u>nii</u>lwod: he stopped running
Cí-1 + yí- > Cé-, as in ch'élyeed: he runs out/ch'élwod: he ran out
Ci-4 + yí- > Cí, as in naa shíłteeh: he's giving me to you (no D/L-class transitives)
Ci-5 + yí- > Cí, as in jílyeed: he arrives running / jílwod: he arrived running
Ci-6 + yí- > Cee-, as in ch'ídeeldlóóh: he's in the act of smiling / ch'ídeeldlo': he smiled

However, irrespective of morphophonemic alterations affecting given prefix combinations, in any Extended Base Paradigm the primary conjugational Determinant remains the prefix that is directly linked to the Base Paradigm. Alterations of the types described above follow relatively simple rules, and derivational or pronominal elements that appear to the left of the Determinant usually do not affect the conjugational patterns proper, although these too may undergo alterations in shape as they come into juxtaposition. Thus a Ø-Imperfective Base Paradigm extended by incorporation of a di-prefix of Position 6a takes the shape:

Person

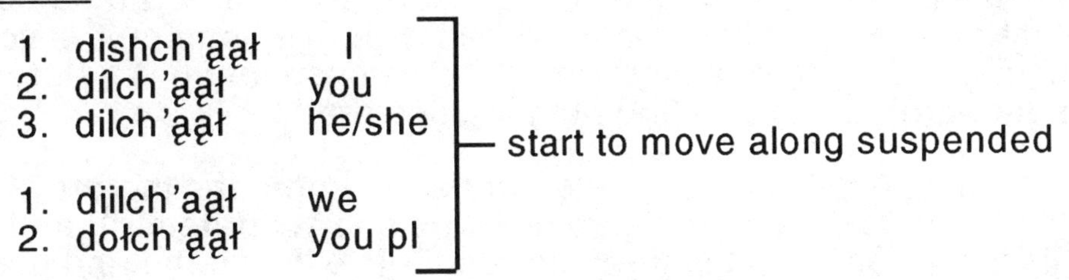

1. dishch'ąął — I
2. dílch'ąął — you
3. dilch'ąął — he/she

1. diilch'aął — we
2. dołch'ąął — you pl

— start to move along suspended

Di-6a is the Conjugational Determinant, and it continues to function in that capacity when the paradigm is further extended, as in:

Person

1. náá-díshch'ąął
2. náá-dílch'ąął
3. náá-dílch'ąął
3a. náázhdílch'ąął

— start to move along again suspended

| | |
|---|---|
| 1. náá-diilch'aął | (we two) |
| náá-da-diilch'ąął | (we 3+) |
| náá-da-hi-diilch'ąął | (we 3+ one after another) |
| 3a.náá-da-hi-zh-diilch'ąął | (they 3+ one after another) |

The conjugational pattern for verbs in which a Conjunct Prefix is in determinant position differs substantially from that of verbs in which the Conjugational Determinant is a Disjunct Prefix. The Conjunct elements are primarily Ci- in shape, with neutral tone, while the Disjunct class is CV in shape with inherent high or low tone, and the vowel component may be any vowel, long or short, oral or (for some) nasal.

The behavior of the Conjunct Ci- and the Disjunct CV prefixes in a simple Ø-Imperfective Extended Base Paradigm is contrasted below:

| Person | ni-6b | | Person | na-1b | |
|---|---|---|---|---|---|
| 1. Cish- | nishdaah | sit down | 1. CVVsh- | naash'na' | crawl around |
| 2. Cí- | nídaah | | 2. CVni- | nani'na' | |
| 3. Ci- | nidaah | | 3. CVV- | naa'na' | |
| 1. Cii(d)- | niikeeh | | 1. CVii(d)- | neii'na' | |
| 2. Co(h)- | nohkeeh | | 2. CVo(h)- | naoh'na' | |

The Conjunct ni-prefix retains its base form in 1st and 3rd person; in 2nd person sgl ni-8 (subject pronoun) is absorbed as a high tone on the vowel of ni-6b, producing ní-; and ni-6b reduces to its initial consonant (n-) before vowel initial -ii(d) and -o(h)- in 1st and 2nd person duoplural.

The Disjunct Prefix na-, on the other hand, lengthens the prefix vowel in 1st and 3rd person; it does not absorb ni-8 (the subject pronoun); and it does not reduce to its initial consonant before -ii(d) and -o(h)- in 1st and 2nd person duoplural.

## The Model Paradigms

The format chosen for presentation of the model verb paradigms is based on a progressive series of charts for each of the Modes, beginning with the Base Paradigm and following, in succession, with the Extended Base Paradigms. These, in turn, begin with the Conjunct Prefixes and include a series of levels: first, the “deictic” subject pronouns of Position 5 in their juncture with the 3rd person of the Base Paradigm; followed by the direct object pronouns of Position 4 in their juncture with the Base Paradigm; followed in turn by the derivational-thematic prefixes of Position 6 + the Base Paradigm; and finally by the Disjunct Prefixes of Position 3 and 1 as they join the Base forms. The format is an attempt to reflect the derivational process as lexical constructions are built by the incorporation of pronominal and adverbial elements with the Base.

Each Extended Paradigm chart repeats the Base, reflecting the form it takes when combined with the Extending prefixes.

The model paradigms include constructions derived with prefixes of Positions 1-6, inclusive. The elements involved comprise syllables composed of a consonant + a vowel, and since the consonant is variable it is represented by C- = any consonant. Thus Ca- = any consonant + the vowel -a- (as ha-, na-, da-, ’ada-): and Ci- = any consonant + the vowel -i- (as ni-, bi-, si-, hi-).

In addition, P- represents any object pronoun prefixed to a postpositional stem, and any possessive pronoun prefixed to a noun stem (as P-k’í-: onto me, nik’í-: onto you, bik’í-: onto him/her/it/them, etc., and P-za- = my mouth, your mouth, hi/her/its/their mouth, etc.).

# CHAPTER 2

# THE IMPERFECTIVE MODE

Imperfective Mode is distinguished by Stem shape for most Verb Bases, and Imperfective Stem shape often varies for Aspect. Thus:

Momentaneous: naashtįįh: I lower a SSO down
Continuative: naashtin: I'm carrying a SSO about
Distributive: ndaashtį': I'm setting SSO about
Repetitive: béshtį́įh: I'm rubbing SSO against it (as lipstick on lips)

The Imperfective Mode is conjugated in four basic patterns, distinguished by the Ø, ni- and si- conjugation markers, in Position 7, and yi-Ø (= Ø-7 + yi-6c) for the Semelfactive and Transitional Imperfectives.

<u>Active Verbs</u>: For Active Verbs the Imperfective Mode describes an action or event as incomplete and, although the time of occurrence is not a primary concern, the Imperfectives correspond, generally, to the present tense in English.

When Aspect is identified as punctual (Momentaneous, Semelfactive, Transitional, Reversative), the verbal action or event takes place at a point in time; the subject of the verb is *"in the act"* of performing an aspectually punctual action, as in:

taah yishááh (Momentaneous): I'm (in the act of) getting into the water
ńdiish'nééh (Transitional): I'm (in the act of) getting up
ńdiists'in (Semelfactive): I'm (in the act of) hitting him once with my fist
náháshááh (Reversative): I'm (in the act of) turning around

When Aspect is identified as continuant (Continuative, Durative, Repetitive), the Imperfective Mode describes verbal action as a type that occupies an indeterminate span of time - the subject is *"in the process"* of performing the verbal action, as:

naashá (Continuative): I'm (in the process of) going around (here and there)
'ashą́ (Durative): I'm (in the process of) eating
'ádíshch'id (Repetitive): I'm (in the process of) scratching myself

<u>Neuter Verb Bases,</u> conjugated in a single paradigm, include The Descriptive Adjectivals and the Existentials (verbs of being). They are marked by a ni-prefix formerly identified as ni[6] -: Position 6b, but here treated as ni-: Position 7, the conjugation marker of Ni-Imperfective/ Perfective Modes. On this premise the Imperfective Neuters in reference above are treated under Ni-Imperfective.

## 1. THE Ø-IMPERFECTIVE

The Ø-Imperfective is so designated because it is unmarked in Position 7. In the absence of a modal-aspectival conjugation marker it carries no connotation of ensuing durative or static effect - semantically it is a simple completive.

The Ø-Imperfective is the most highly productive of the several Imperfective conjugations.

The Base Paradigm of the Ø-Imperfective requires a peg-element to maintain syllable integrity, and to prevent the naked Verb Theme from appearing as a word. With exception of syllabic /n, ń/ an acceptable syllable has the shape CV (consonant + vowel) or CVC (consonant + vowel + consonant). Since there is no conjugation marker in Position 7 the 1st person sgl would have -sh- in Positiion 8 as the initial element: -shcha, I'm crying. Here CVC syllable integrity is attained by adding peg yi- to produce yishcha: I'm crying.

In 3rd person, Positions 7 and 8 are both Ø, and if the verb is intransitive Position 4 is also vacant, with the result that the Verb Theme (Stem) -Øcha would function as a word meaning "he / she is crying." This is unacceptable, so peg yi- fills the vacuum, to produce yicha: he / she is crying.

In 1st and 2nd persons dpl the Base constructions would begin with a vowel, as -iicha, we're crying; -ohcha, you dpl are crying so, to produce the necessary syllable peg y- is prefixed to -iicha, to produce yiicha, and peg w- is prefixed to -ohcha to produce wohcha, thus satisfying the requirement for syllable integrity.

### THE MODEL PARADIGMS

In the model paradigms that follow it is convenient to let C- (= Consonant) and Ci- (= Consonant + -i-) represent any Conjunct pronominal prefix of Position 4 (except the 3i and 3s object pronouns 'a- ~ 'i- ~ -'- and ha- ~ ho-) and any neutral tone derivational-thematic element from Position 6. The Position 4 yi-prefix, identified as 3o, that represents a 3rd person object when the subject of the verb is also 3rd person, is Ci- in composition. In the model paradigms 3o person is included individually because many transitive verbs take a 3rd person object exclusively (e.g. melt O, carry a flat flexible object, eat leafy O); and in the model paradigms the 3o derivative is entered as yi- rather than Ci-.

The -h-component of the 2nd person dpl subject pronoun is written in parentheses, indicating its deletion if the classifier is Ł or L, as in:

wołdééh (< wo(h)-łdééh): you dpl are wiping it off
'ádółzhééh (< 'ádó(h)-lzhééh): you dpl are shaving

The 1st person dpl subject pronoun, along with the Passives, the Reflexives and the Reciprocals, are written with a parenthetic (d), representing d-effect on the Verb Theme.

y-ii(d)-Øleeh > yiidleeh: we become

Lexical examples appended to each of the model paradigms are given in the form of Verb Bases, and the Position 7 conjugation marker is given in parentheses, as in:

(Ø)--Øleeh: become. Parenthetic (Ø) = Ø-Position 7
(ni)--łį́: bring AnO Parenthetic (ni) = Ni-Perfective
(si)--Ødiz: spin O (yarn) Parenthetic (si) = Si-Perfective

O = any object pronoun of Position 4
# = boundary marker between Conjunct / Disjunct

## Base Paradigm

Although many intransitive Verb Bases, derived with prefixes of Position 1 and/or 6, are conjugated as Ø-Imperfectives, there are relatively few intransitives that include no derivational element. The simple Verb Bases listed below are conjugated in the pattern outlined in the chart.

Table 1

| PERSON | Prefix Position | | | | | | | | |
|---|---|---|---|---|---|---|---|---|---|
| Sgl | 7 | Peg | + | 8 | + | 9-10-T | | | as in: |
| 1. | Ø | yi- | + | -sh- | + | Ø/leeh | > | yish- | yishłeeh |
| 2. | Ø | Ø | + | -ni- | + | Ø/leeh | > | -ni- | nileeh |
| 3. | Ø | yi- | + | Ø | + | Ø/leeh | > | Ø | yileeh |
| Dpl | | | | | | | | | |
| 1. | Ø | y- | + | -ii(d)- | + | Ø/leeh | > | yii(d)- | yiidleeh |
| 2. | Ø | w- | + | -o(h)- | + | Ø/leeh | > | wo(h)- | wohłeeh |

Øcha: weep; cry
(d)dlóóh: be cold
Øghááh, biih ---: get into it (sgl)
Ødziih; remain, be left
Øleeh: become
Øgeeh, biih ---: fall into it
(d)'nééh, biih ---: crawl into it
Ø'ees, keeh ---: put on shoes
Ømáás, biih ---: roll into it
Øtłíísh, biih ---: fall into it

## Extended Base Paradigms

### 1. Conjunct Prefixes

The Conjunct Derivatives of the Ø-Imperfective include all verb constructions in which a prefix of Position 6, 5 or 4 is linked directly to the Base, where it functions as the Conjugational Determinant.

Since Position 7 is vacant in the Ø-Imperfective, any derivational or pronominal element that is joined to the Base must be joined directly to the subject pronoun prefixes in Position 8. However, a 3rd person subject is represented by Ø in Position 8, so in 3rd person forms the derivational elements join directly with the Verb Theme and, if the Theme contains a Ø-Classifier, the juncture is with the Stem itself. Thus:

The prefixes of Position 4 are the direct object pronouns. One of these elements may be conjoined with any verb-incorporated subject pronoun in Ø-Imperfective constructions, as:

'a-4 + Ø-7 + -sh-8 + Øtł'ǫ > 'ashtł'ó: I'm weaving (something unspecified)
ni-4 + Ø-7 + -sh-8 + -Øch'id > nishch'id: I'm scratching you
shi-4 + Ø-7 + Ø-8 + -Øch'id > shich'id: he's scratching me
shi-4 + Ø-7 + \ ´ /-8 + Øch'id > shích'id: you're scratching me
nih(i)- + Ø-7 + -ii(d)-8 + -Øch'id > nihiich'id: we're scratching you dpl

The prefixes of Position 6 are, with exception of the yi-aspect marker of Position 6c, adverbial-thematic derivational elements. These also can be conjoined with any subject pronoun prefix of Position 8, as:

di-6a + Ø-7 + -sh-8 + -Ødzį́į́s > disdzį́į́s: I'm starting to drag it along
d(i)-6a + Ø-7 + -ii(d)-8 + -Ødzį́į́s > diidzį́į́s: we're starting to drag it along
di-6a + Ø-7 + \ ´ /-8 + -Øzééh > dízééh: you're in the act of belching.
ni-6b + Ø-7 + -sh-8 + -Ødaah > nishdaah: I'm in the act of sitting down
ni-6b + Ø-7 + Ø-8 + -Ødaah > nidaah: he's in the act of sitting down
ni-6b + Ø-7 + \ ´ /-8 + -Ødaah > nídaah: you're in the act of sitting down

The prefixes of Position 5 are the 3rd person deictic subject pronouns; these are, in effect, joined to the 3rd person Base form where they replace the Ø-marker of 3rd person subject. Thus, to 3rd person: yi-Peg + Ø-7 + Ø-8 + -Øleeh > yileeh: it is (in the act of ) becoming; delete peg-yi- and add:

ji-5 + Ø-7 + Ø-8 + -Øleeh > jileeh: he/she/one (= 3a/4th person) is (in the act of) becoming
'a-5 + Ø-7 + Ø-8 + -Øleeh >'aleeh: something or someone unspecified (3i person) is (in the act of) becoming (e.g. 'áłah 'aleeh: a meeting takes place = literally: unspecified people become together)
ha-5 + Ø-7 + Ø-8 + -Øleeh > haleeh: space, area (3s person) is (in the act of) becoming

-'(a)di-5 + Ø-7 + Ø-8 + -(d)ch'id > bi'dich'id: he's being scratched. (-'adi- = indefinite agent as subject in Agentive Passive constructions. (-a- always deletes because the agentive subject pronoun is always preceded by an object pronoun prefix of Position 4, thus creating a phonological environment in which the 'a-syllable reduces to \'/, its initial consonant.)

## Extended Base Paradigms

Position 5 prefixes + Base

Table 2

T = any Verb theme

| PERSON Sgl / Dpl | Prefix Position 5 | + | Base | | | as in: |
|---|---|---|---|---|---|---|
| 3a.(4) | ji- | + | (yi)-Ø-T | > | ji-T | jileeh |
| 3i. | 'a- | + | (yi)-Ø-T | > | 'a-T | 'aleeh |
| 3s. | ha- | + | (yi)-Ø-T | > | ha-T | haleeh |
| AP | -'adi- | + | (yi)(d)-Ø-T | > | O'di-T | O'dich'id |

In Table 2 the "deictic" subject pronoun prefixes of Position 5 replace the Peg Element in the 3rd person of Table 1, so the forms listed under "Base" in the Table above correspond, in each instance, to the 3rd person of the Base Paradigm. The Agentive Passive (AP) is restricted to transitive verbs. -'adi-, in Position 5, is a subject pronoun with the meaning "someone unspecified," and O represents any object pronoun prefix of Position 4. (shi'dich'id: I'm being scratched, ni'dich'id: you're being scratched, etc.).

Prefixes of Positions 4 and 5 + Base

Table 3

T = any Verb theme

| PERSON | Prefix Position | | | | | | |
|---|---|---|---|---|---|---|---|
| Sgl | 4 | + | 5 | + | Base | Ø-4 | Ci-4 |
| 1. | Ø/Ci- | + | --- | + | (yi)-sh-T | yishch'id | nishch'id |
| 2. | Ø/Ci- | + | --- | + | *ni-\ ´/-T | nich'id | shích'id |
| 3. | ---/Ci- | + | --- | + | (yi)-Ø-T | --- | shich'id |
| SP | Ø/--- | + | --- | + | (yi)-Ø(d)-T | yich'id | --- |
| 3o. | ---/yi- | + | --- | + | (yi)-Ø-T | --- | yich'id |
| 3a. | Ci- | + | -ji- | + | (yi)-Ø-T | jich'id | shijich'id |
| AP | O | + | -'(a)di- | + | (yi)-Ø-(d)-T | --- | bi'dich'id |
| Dpl | | | | | | | |
| 1. | Ø/Ci- | + | --- | + | (y)-ii(d)-T | yiich'id | nihiich'id |
| 2. | Ø/Ci- | + | --- | + | (w)-o(h)-T | wohch'id | nihohch'id |

* The 2nd person sgl subject pronoun is absorbed as a high tone on the vowel of a preceding low tone Conjunct Prefix

Table 3 describes a transitive Ø-Imperfective. When Position 4 is vacant - i.e. Ø, the direct object must be construed as 3rd person, and the paradigm then is identical in form to that of an intransitive Ø-Imperfective.The column identified as Ci- (consonant + -i-) represents the direct object pronoun prefixes: shi-: me, ni-: you, yi-: him/her/it/them, nihi-: us, and nihi-: you dpl.

When the 2nd person sgl subject pronoun ni-Position 8 is preceded by a Conjunct Prefix which has low (neutral) tone, ni-8 is absorbed as a high tone \ ´/ on the vowel of the preceding prefix. Thus:

shi-4: me + -ni-8: you + -Øch'id > shi-nich'id > shích'id: you're scratching me
ni[1]-6b + -ni-8: you + -Ødaah > ni-nidaah > nídaah: you're in the act of sitting down

In the absence of a preceding Conjunct Prefix, when the direct object is 3rd person, represented by Ø in Position 4, a 2nd person sgl subject is represented by ni- in Position 8, as in nich'id: you're scratching him / her / it.

Of the Subject Pronouns of Position 5, only 3a (4th person) ji- and Agentive -'adi- can take a direct object (represented by an object pronoun prefix of Position 4), as in:

shi-jich'id > shijich'id: he's scratching me
shi-'adich'id > shi'dich'id > I'm being scratched (by -'adi-: unspecified agent)

A large number of simple transitive Verb Bases are conjugated in the pattern outlined above, including those listed below:

(Ø)--Ødiz: spin O (yarn)
(Ø)--łdzééh: scrape O (hide)
(Ø)--Ø'iz: pedal O
(Ø)--łmaz: twirl O
(Ø)--Øzéés: singe O
(Ø)--łt'ees: roast / cook O
(Ø)--Øtsid: pound O
(Ø)--łts'il: crack O
(Ø)--łxiz: twirl O
(Ø)--łbéézh: boil O
(Ø)--Øbizh: braid O
(Ø)--łdééh: wipe O off
(Ø)--(d)dlą́: drink O
(Ø)--łdǫ': jerk
(Ø)--Øyą́: eat O
(Ø)--ldeeł: eat O (plural objects
(Ø)--łchozh: eat O (leafy matter)
(Ø)--Ø'ááł: eat O (hard matter)
(Ø)--lkeed: eat O (roundish thing)
(Ø)--łts'ééh: eat O (mushy matter)(Ø)
(Ø)--lghał: eat O (meat)
(Ø)--łhį́į́h: melt O
(Ø)--łhozh: tickle O
(Ø)--łjįzh: crush O
(Ø)--Øk'aash: grind O fine
(Ø)--ł(l)ą́ąh: increase O
(Ø)--Ønizh: pick O (plants)
(Ø)--lzhééh: shave (self)
(Ø)--Øti': break O off
(Ø)--łt'á: fletch O (arrow)
(Ø)--łtłah: smear O
(Ø)--Øch'iish: saw / file O
(Ø)--Ødzį́į́s, biih ---: pull O into it
(Ø)--Øk'ą́ąs: straighten O
(Ø)--Ølóós: biih ---: lead O into it
(Ø)--łmáás, biih ---: roll O into it
(Ø)--sį́į́h ( = łzį́į́h): bless O
(Ø)--łtł'is: harden O
(Ø)--Øts'i': pluck O
(Ø)--Øts'ǫǫs: suck on O
(Ø)--łbal: wave O (FFO, as a towel); flap O (wings)
(Ø)--łchin: smell O
(Ø)--łdlaad: husk O (corn)
(Ø)--Ødleesh: paint O
(Ø)--łgan: dry O
(Ø)--łháád: shake O
(Ø)--łhod: rock O
(Ø)--Øjeeh: grease O
(Ø)--Øk'á: grind O (grain)
(Ø)--'aał: eat O (hard O)
(Ø)--łnaad: lick O
(Ø)--shééh: (= łzhééh): mow O
(Ø)--łtązh: tap / peck
(Ø)--łtin: freeze O
(Ø)--Øt'eesh: blacken O
(Ø)--Øtł'ó: weave O

All verbs of locomotion, transitive and intransitive, include a simple Ø-Imperfective Base. However, simple verbs in this category, lacking a derivational prefix, require an independent adverbial directional marker, such as:

biih: into it    taah: into water    kį́į́h: into town

tł'iish taah yi'nééh: the snake is crawling into the water
jaa'abaní chidí yiih yit'ááh: the bat is flying into the car

Motion Verb Bases of the types listed below are all conjugated as simple Ø-Imperfectives.

| OBJECT CLASS | | HANDLE put O | PROPEL toss O | FLY fall |
|---|---|---|---|---|
| SRO | biih + | (Ø)--Ø'aah | (Ø)--łne' | (Ø)--lts'íííd |
| LPB | | (Ø)--Øyeeh | (Ø)--Øyeeh | (Ø)--łhęęzh |
| NCM | | (Ø)--łjooł | (Ø)--łjooł | (Ø)--Øjooł |
| SFO | | (Ø)--Ølé | (Ø)--łdeeł | (Ø)--Ødeeł |
| SSO | | (Ø)--Øtįįh | (Ø)--łt'e' | (Ø)--Økęęs |
| FFO | | (Ø)--łtsóós | (Ø)--Ø'áád | (Ø)--Ønééh |
| MM | | (Ø)--Øtłeeh | (Ø)--Øtleeh | (Ø)--łhę́ę́sh |
| PIO | | (Ø)--Øníìł | (Ø)--Øníìł | (Ø)--ni-Ødeeh |
| PIO | | (Ø)--Øjááh | (Ø)--łkaad | (Ø)--ni-Ødeeh |
| OC | | (Ø)--Økaah | (Ø)--łkaad | (Ø)--Økaad |
| AnO | | (Ø)--łteeh | (Ø)--łt'e' | (Ø)--Øtłíísh/Øgeeh |

E.g.
shich'ah tsits'aa' biih yish'aah: I'm putting my hat in the box
shich'ah taah yishne': I'm tossing my hat into the water
shich'ah k'adęę taah yilts'íííd: my hat is about to fall into the water

mósí yázhí taah yishteeh: I'm in the act of putting the kitten into the water
mósí yázhí taah yisht'e': I'm in the act of tossing the kitten into the water
mósí yázhí k'adęę taah yitłíísh: the kitten is about to fall into the water

Table 4 sketches the Ø-Imperfective conjugational pattern for Verb Bases that include a low (neutral) tone Ci-prefix of Position 6a or 6b (as di-, ni-, hi-)

Prefix of Positions 6a or 6b + Extended Base

Table 4

T = any Verb theme

| PERSON Sgl | Prefix Position 5 | + | 6a/6b | + | Base | | | as in: | |
|---|---|---|---|---|---|---|---|---|---|
| 1. | --- | + | Ci- | + | (yi)-sh-T | > | Cish-T | diskos | nishį́į́d |
| 2. | --- | + | Ci- | + | \ ´ /-T | > | Cí-T | dílkos | nílį́į́d |
| 3. | --- | + | Ci- | + | (yi)-Ø-T | > | Ci-T | dilkos | nilį́į́d |
| 3a. | ji- | + | Ci- | + | (yi)-Ø-T | > | ji-Ci-T | jidilkos | jinilį́į́d |
| 3i. | 'a- | + | Ci- | + | (yi)-Ø-T | > | 'a-Ci-T | 'adildlóósh | --- |
| 3s. | ho- | + | Ci- | + | (yi)-Ø-T | > | ho-Ci-T | hodileeh | --- |
| Dpl | | | | | | | | | |
| 1. | --- | + | C(i-) | + | (y)-ii(d)-T | > | Cii(d)-T | diilkos | niilį́į́d |
| 2. | --- | + | C(i)- | + | (w)-o(h)-T | > | Co(h)-T | dołkos | nołį́į́d |

di-(Ø)--Øzhah: spit repeatedly
di-(Ø)--lníísh: start to work
di-(Ø)--Øno': flick the tongue
di-(Ø)--(d)'ní: groan
di-(Ø)--ltaał, taah---: step into the water
di-(Ø)--Ø'is: kick feet in the air
ni-(Ø)--lį́į́d: squat down
ni-(Ø)--lghaał: throw self down

di-(Ø)--ldlóósh: start along on all four
di-(Ø)--Øyih: pant, puff, breathe hard
di-(Ø)--Øghaał: open the eyes
di-(Ø)--Øzééh: belch
di-(Ø)--Øchííd, bíká ---: reach for it
di-(Ø)--yóół: start to blow (wind)
ni-(Ø)--lch'ił: blink
ni-(Ø)--Ødaah: sit down (1 subject)
ni-(Ø)--lne', biih ---: stick head into it

Prefixes of Positions 4-6 + Extended Base

Table 5

T = any Verb theme

| PERSON Sgl | Prefix Position 4 | + | 5 | + | 6 | + | Base | Ø-4 + Ci-6 | Ci-4 + Ci-6 | Ø-4 + Ci-6 |
|---|---|---|---|---|---|---|---|---|---|---|
| 1. | Ø/Ci- | + | --- | + | Ci- | + | (yi)-sh-T | disłóós | nidisłóós | nistsééś |
| 2. | Ø/Ci- | + | --- | + | Ci- | + | \´/-T | díłóós | shidíłóós | níłtsééś |
| 3. | Ø/Ci- | + | --- | + | Ci- | + | (yi)-Ø-T | --- | shidilóós | (nitsééś) |
| SP | Ø/-- | + | --- | + | Ci- | + | (yi)-Ø-(d)-T | didlóós | --- | niltsééś |
| AP | --/O- | + | 'adi- | + | Ci- | + | (yi)-Ø-(d)-T | --- | bidi'didlóós | --- |
| 3o. | yi- | + | --- | + | Ci- | + | (yi)-Ø-T | --- | yidilóós | yiniłtsééś |
| 3a. | Ø/Ci- | + | ji-/-zh- | + | Ci- | + | jiCi-/CizhCi-T | jidilóós | shizhdilóós | jiniłtsééś |
| Dpl | | | | | | | | | | |
| 1. | Ø/Ci- | + | --- | + | C(i)- | + | (y)-ii(d)-T | diidlóós | nidiidlóós | niiltsééś |
| 2. | Ø/Ci- | + | --- | + | C(i)- | + | (w)-o(h)-T | dohłóós | shidohłóós | nołtsééś |

Verb Bases of the type listed below are conjugated in the pattern outlined in Table 5 above.

di-(Ø)--Ølóos: start to lead O
di-(Ø)--Øtsééh: point O (a gun)
di-(Ø)--łts'ǫǫd: stretch O
di-(Ø)--łhį́į́h: melt O (as snow)
di-(Ø)--ł(l)id: burn O
ni-(Ø)--łmas: roll O into a ball
ni-(Ø)--łkaad, biih ---: herd O into it
ni-(Ø)--Ø'įįh: steal O
ni-(Ø)--łk'e': cool O
ni-(Ø)--Øtsééś: fire goes out
di-(Ø)--sááś (= łzááś): start to dribble O
di-(Ø)--łtsóóś: start to carry O along (FFO)
di-(Ø)--łbaał: hang O (curtainlike)
di-(Ø)--łkáah: start to track O along
di-(Ø)--Øníił: scatter O along
ni-(Ø)--łtsééś: extinguish O (a fire)
ni-(Ø)--łk'ah: fatten O
ni-(Ø)-lneeh: choke on O
ni-(Ø)--Øt'eesh: blacken O (with charcoal)

## Irregular Ø-Imperfectives

### 1. Conjunct Prefixes

The Conjunct Prefix class includes a group of thematic and inflectional prefixes that appear in Verb Bases that are conjugated as Ø-Imperfectives, but in patterns that diverge from those described in the foregoing charts. The prefixes in reference are:

'a- ~ 'i- ~ -'-: Position 4 - the 3i direct object pronoun.
dzi- ~ ji- ~ -z- ~ -zh- ~ -i-: Position 6a - away into space
ha- ho- hw-: Position 4 - the 3s direct object pronoun.
hi- ~ (y)i-: Position 6a/c - the Seriative marker
ní-: Position 6b - thematic.
yi-ni-: Position 6a/b - thematic.
yí-ní-: Position 6a/b - directive.
si[1]- / (y)i-: Position 6a/c - thematic

'A- ~ 'i- ~ -'-: Position 4 + Extended Base

Table 6

| PERSON | Prefix Position | | | | | | | |
|---|---|---|---|---|---|---|---|---|
| Sgl | 4 | + | 5 | + | Base | | | as in: |
| 1. | 'a- | + | --- | + | (yi)-sh-T | > | 'ash-T | 'ashą́ |
| 2. | 'i- | + | --- | + | \ ´ /-T | > | 'í-T | 'íyą́ |
| 3. | 'a- | + | --- | + | (yi)-Ø-T | > | 'a-T | 'ayą́ |
| SP | 'a- | + | --- | + | (yi)-Ø-(d)-T | > | 'a-T | 'adą́ |
| 3a. | 'a- | + | ji- | + | (yi)-Ø-T | > | 'aji-T | 'ajiyą́ |
| Dpl | | | | | | | | |
| 1. | '- | + | --- | + | (y)-ii(d)-T | > | 'ii(d)-T | 'iidą́ |
| 2. | '- | + | --- | + | (w)-o(h)-T | > | 'o(h)-T | 'ohsą́ |

Verb Bases constructed with the (Position 4 ) 3i object pronoun are transitive but the direct object is "something unspecified." Constructions of this type are often comparable to those of English in which a direct object is not mentioned, but is simply understood, as in:

'ashą́: I'm eating (literally: I'm eating something unspecified)
'ashdlą́: I'm drinking (literally: I'm drinking something unspecified)
'ashtł'ó: I'm weaving (something unspecified)

'a-(Ø)-łdzééh: do hide scraping
'a-(Ø)-yą́: eat
'a-(Ø)-łchin: be able to smell
'a-(Ø)-d-ą́, 'áde---, overeat
'a-(Ø)-Øtł'ó: weave
'a-(Ø)-Øtsid: pound; do silversmithing
'a-(Ø)-łchí: give birth; have a child
'a-(Ø)-(d)dlą́: drink; be a drunkard
'a-(Ø)-Ødleesh: paint

In some Verb Bases 'a-4 functions as a thematic prefix, as in:

'ashhosh: I'm asleep
'ashhą́ą́': I'm snoring
'ashjił: I'm sexually promiscuous
'ashzhish: I'm dancing

The 3s pronominal prefix represents space or area primarily; secondarily it represents "impersonal it/things," and in some Verb Bases it functions as a thematic prefix. The 3s person functions as a direct object of Position 4 with transitive verbs, and with intransitive verbs it represents a 3s subject.

The 3s pronoun has variable shape. Depending on the phonological environment it appears variously as ha- ho- or hw-.

In transitive Ø-Imperfectives:

Ha- is the shape taken before the 1st person singular subject pronoun of Position 8, and in 3rd-person and Simple Passive constructions where Position 8 is vacant, as:

hashdééh: I'm clearing off an area
haldééh: an area is being cleared off
hałdééh: he's clearing off an area

Ho- is the shape taken before ni-, the 2nd person subject pronoun of Position 8, which deletes and appears as a high tone on ho-: ho- + ni-8 > hó-, as in:

hółdééh: you're clearing off an area

And the 3s object pronoun also takes the shape ho- before a consonant, as in:

hojiłdééh: he's clearing off an area

hw- is the shape taken before a vowel, as in:

hwiildééh: we're clearing off an area
hwołdééh (written hołdééh): you dpl are clearing off an area

Ha- ~ ho- ~ hw-: Position 4 + Extended Base

Table 7

T = any Verb theme

| PERSON Sgl | Prefix Position 4 | + | 5 | + | Base | | | as in: |
|---|---|---|---|---|---|---|---|---|
| 1. | ha- | + | --- | + | (yi)-sh-T | > | hash-T | hashdééh |
| 2. | ho- | + | --- | + | \ ´ /-T | > | hó-T | hółdééh |
| 3. | ha- | + | --- | + | (yi)-Ø-T | > | ha-T | hałdééh |
| SP | ha- | + | --- | + | (yi)-Ø-(d)-T | > | ha-T | haldééh |
| 3a. | ho- | + | ji- | + | (yi)-Ø-T | > | hoji-T | hojiłdééh |
| Dpl | | | | | | | | |
| 1. | hw- | + | --- | + | (y)-ii(d)-T | > | hwii(d)-T | hwiildééh |
| 2. | h- | + | --- | + | (w)-o(h)-T | > | ho(h)-T | hołdééh |

Verb Bases of the following types are conjugated in the pattern outlined in Table 7 above:

ha-(Ø)--łdééh: clear off an area
ha-(Ø)--Øzéés: burn off an area
ha-(Ø)--Øtaał: sing
ha-(Ø)--łbį́': build a hogan
ha-(Ø)--lne': tell
ha-(Ø)--sééh (< -łzééh), bijáátah ---, limber up the legs
ha-(Ø)--łchí, nooh ---: make a cache
ha-(Ø)--łchįįh, bá ---: make him angry
ha-(Ø)--Øniih, baa ---: praise him
ha-(Ø)--Ødleesh: paint area
ha-(Ø)--ł(l)eeh: cause to come into being
ha-(Ø)--(d)'niih, 'ádaa ---: brag about oneself

The Seriative

Seriative hi- (~ ha- ~ he-): Position 6a, has a yi- ~ yii- ~ -i- allomorph in Position 6c. The allomorph is required in the presence of an immediately preceding Conjunct prefix of Position 4 or 5, or dzi- ~ ji-: Position 6a "away into space."

The Seriative is a constituent of all Verb Bases in which the *Stem* connotes segmented action, such as that inherent in "hop, skip, move on one's rump, crawl on one's belly," as in:

> nahałtingo ch'ał ndahatleeh: the frogs are hopping around in the rain
> tsídii taah hit'e', the bird is (in the act of) hopping into the water

And it appears in verbs of motion in which:

(1) Three or more subjects move in succession - one after another -, in contradistinction to collective movement. Constructions of this type usually include the da- marker of distributive plurality, Position 3, as in:

> 'áłchíní t'áá 'ałkéé' chidíłtsooí yiih dahikááh (~ dahakááh), the children are entering the schoolbus one after another

(2) And in transitive verbs in which movement involves a succession of objects, as in:

> naaltsoos tsits'aa' biih hishnííł, I'm putting the books into the box (one after another, rather than all at once)

In forms (primarily 3rd person) where hi- is preceded by a Position 4 object pronoun, the yi-allomorph is required. Actually, in the absence of a derivational prefix, the 3o object pronoun yi- appears to be reduplicated, as in:

> 'ashkii tsé 'ásaa' yiih yiyiinííł, the boy is putting stones into the jar (one after another) (Cf. biih hishnííł: I'm putting them into it)
> hastiin ch'il yiyiinizh, the man is plucking herbs (one after another) (Cf. hishnizh: I'm plucking them)
> (And, although an unlikely utterance): t'áá 'ałkéé' taah nihiishnííł, I'm putting you one after another into the water

The simplest possible paradigm of the Ø-Imperfective, in Verb Bases that include seriative hi- ~ yi- is outlined in Table 8 below:

Hi- ~ yi-: Seriative + Extended Base

Table 8

T = any Verb theme

| PERSON | Prefix Position | | | | | | | | | | | |
|---|---|---|---|---|---|---|---|---|---|---|---|---|
| Sgl | 4 | + | 5 | + | 6a | / | 6c | + | Base | | | as in: |
| 1. | Ø | + | --- | + | hi- | | --- | + | (yi)-sh-T | > | hish-T | hishnííł |
| 2. | Ø | + | --- | + | hi- | | --- | + | \ ´/-T | > | hí-T | hínííł |
| 3. | Ø | + | --- | + | hi- | | --- | + | (yi)-Ø-T | > | hi-T | hit'e' |
| SP | Ø | + | --- | + | hi- | | --- | + | (yi)-Ø-(d)-T | > | hi-T | hi'nííł |
| 3o. | yi- | + | --- | + | -yii- | | --- | + | (yi)-Ø-T | > | yiyii-T | yiyiinííł |
| 3a. | Ø | | j(i)- | + | -ii- | | --- | + | (yi)-Ø-T | > | jii-T | jiinííł |
| Dpl | | | | | | | | | | | | |
| 1. | Ø | + | --- | + | h- | | --- | + | (y)-ii(d)-T | > | hi(d)-T | hii'nííł |
| 2. | Ø | + | --- | + | h- | | --- | + | (w)-o(h)-T | > | ho(h)-T | hohnííł |

Verb Bases of the following types are conjugated in the pattern outlined in Table 8 above:

hi-(Ø)--Øt'e', biih ---: hop into it
hi-(Ø)--Øníił, biih ---: put O into it
hi-(Ø)--łne', biih ---: toss O into it
hi-(Ø)--Øgéésh: cut O (by snipping)
hi-(Ø)--łhaał: cut or hack O (as with a scythe)
hi-(Ø)--Øt'ood: pull O apart, shred O
hi-(Ø)--Ønizh: pluck O (as herbs)
hi-(Ø)--tííh: snap O off (as icicles)
hi-(Ø)--łmáás, biih ---: roll O into it
hi-(Ø)--(d)'nééh, taah ---: crawl into the water (one after another)
hi-(Ø)--(d)kááh, biih ---: get into it (one after another - as into a car)

When preceded by a Conjunct Prefix of Position 4 or 5, or by dzi-: Position 6a "away into space" hi- is replaced by its yi-allomorph. Simple Seriative Bases that are fully conjugated with yi³-, the alternant of hi-, are not common, but derived bases occur, as in the following example.

Yi³-: Position 6c Seriative + Extended Base

Table 9

T = any Verb theme

| PERSON | Prefix Position | | | | | | | | | | | |
|---|---|---|---|---|---|---|---|---|---|---|---|---|
| Sgl | 4 | + | 5 | + | 6c | + | 7 | + | Base | | | as in: |
| 1. | C- | + | --- | + | -(y)ii- | + | Ø | + | (yi)-sh-T | > | Ciish-T | yisdánihiishnííł |
| 2. | Ci- | + | --- | + | -yi- | + | Ø | + | \ ´ /-T | > | Ciyí-T | yisdánihiyínííł |
| 3o. | y(i)- | + | --- | + | -ii- | + | Ø | + | (yi)-Ø-T | > | Ciyii-T | yisdáyiinííł |
| 3a. | Ci- | + | -j- | + | -ii- | + | Ø | + | (yi)-Ø-T | > | Cijii-T | yisdánihijiinííł |
| AP | O | + | -'(a)di- | + | -ii | + | Ø | + | (yi)-Ø(d)-T | > | Ci'dii-T | yisdánihi'dii'nííł |
| Dpl | | | | | | | | | | | | |
| 1. | Ci- | + | Ø | + | -y- | + | Ø | + | -ii(d)-T | > | Ciyii(d)-T | yisdánihiyii'nííł |
| 2. | Ci- | + | Ø | + | -y- | + | Ø | + | -o(h)-T | > | Ciyo(h)-T | yisdánihiyohnííł |

yisdá#-yi-(Ø)--Øníił: save PIO; rescue O (yisdánihiishnííł: I save you 3+ one after another; yisdánihiyínííł: you save us 3+ one after another)
ha#-yi-(Ø)--Ødzį́į́s: drag O out or up (hanihiisdzį́į́s: I'm dragging you 3+ out)
yah 'a#-yi-(Ø)--Ødzį́į́s: drag O inside (yah 'anihiisdzį́į́s: I'm dragging you 3+ inside)
ni#-yi-(Ø)--łgéésh: slice O, cut O into strips (niyiiłgéésh: he's slicing it, cutting it up)

## Ho- ~ hw-: Position 4 + Extended Base

A few Seriative Verbs are derived with the 3s object pronoun ho- ~ hw-: Position 4:

Table 10

T = any Verb theme

| PERSON | Prefix Position | | | | | | | Base | | | |
|---|---|---|---|---|---|---|---|---|---|---|---|
| Sgl | 4 | + | 5 | + | 6c | + | Base | | | as in: |
| 1. | hw- | + | --- | + | -ii- | + | (yi)-sh-T | > | hwiish-T | bitah hwiishgéésh |
| 2. | ho- | + | --- | + | -yi- | + | \\´/-T | > | hoyí-T | bitah hoyígéésh |
| 3 | hw- | + | --- | + | -ii- | + | (yi)Ø-T | > | hwii-T | yitah hwiigéésh |
| SP | hw- | + | --- | + | -ii- | + | (yi)Ø(d)-T | > | hwii-T | bitah hwiigéésh |
| 3a | ho- | + | -j- | + | -ii | + | (yi)Ø-T | > | hojii-T | bitah hojiigéésh |
| Dpl | | | | | | | | | | |
| 1. | hw- | + | Ø | + | --- | + | (y)ii(d)-T | > | hwii(d)-T | bitah hwiigéésh |
| 2. | ho- | + | Ø | + | --- | + | (w)o(h)-T | > | hoo(h)-T | bitah hoohgéésh |

bitah ho-yi-(Ø)--Øgéésh: cut off its limbs (tree, animal)
ná#-ho-yi- (Ø)--Øzíid: rake around an area (as around a house)
na#-ho-(Ø)--łná, bich'į' ---: cause him trouble (literally, move "things" toward him one time after another) (bich'į' nahwiishná: I'm causing him trouble, "giving him a hard time")

## 'A- ~ -'-: Position 4 + Yi-Seriative + Extended Base

Table 11

T = any Verb theme

| PERSON | Prefix Position | | | | | | | | | |
|---|---|---|---|---|---|---|---|---|---|---|
| Sgl | 4 | + | 5 | + | 6c | + | Base | | | as in: |
| 1. | -'- | + | --- | + | -ii- | + | (yi)-sh-T | > | 'iish-T | ná'iishłááh |
| 2. | -'i- | + | --- | + | -yi- | + | \\´/-T | > | 'iyí-T | ná'iyíłááh |
| 3 | -'- | + | --- | + | -ii- | + | (yi)-Ø-T | > | 'ii-T | ná'iiłááh |
| 3a | -'- | + | -j- | + | -ii | + | (yi)-Ø-T | > | 'jii-T | ń'jiiłááh |
| Dpl | | | | | | | | | | |
| 1. | -'- | + | --- | + | --- | + | -ii(d)-T | > | 'ii(d)-T | ná'iidlááh |
| 2. | -'o- | + | --- | + | --- | + | -o(h)-T | > | 'oo(h)-T | ná'oohłááh |

ná#-'(i)-(y)ii-(Ø)--Øłááh: pick pinyons (literally, gather unspecified objects one after another)(ná'iishłááh: I'm pinyon-picking)
na#-'(i)-(y)ii-(Ø)--łniih: trade, shop; make purchases (na'iishniih: I'm doing my shopping)
'a#-'(i)-(y)ii-(Ø)--Øníił: toss away unspecified O one after another (bik'iįį' 'adah 'i'iishníił: I'm dropping bombs on it)

## Ní-Thematic: Position 6b + Extended Base

Ní- is a Conjunct Thematic prefix of Position 6b that carries inherent high tone. It is a constituent of a Verb Base with the meaning "look at" and, although probably not the same element, a ní- Conjunct Prefix tentatively treated as a Ni-Imperfective, also marks the Comparative Aspect of Neuter Verbs that relate to quantity and dimension. (See Ni-Imperfective-Neuter)

Since ní- carries inherent high tone the 2nd person sgl subject pronoun retains its Base form (ni-); it cannot reduce to a high tone on the preceding vowel because the preceding vowel is already high.

Table 12

T = any Verb theme

| PERSON | Prefix Position | | | | | | | | | | |
|---|---|---|---|---|---|---|---|---|---|---|---|
| Sgl | 4 | + | 5 | + | 6b | + | Base | | | as in: | |
| 1. | Ø | + | --- | + | ní- | + | (yi)-sh-T | > | nísh-T | nísh'į́ | nísdáás |
| 2. | Ø | + | --- | + | ní- | + | ní-T | > | ní-T | níníł'į́ | nínííłdáás |
| 3. | Ø | + | --- | + | ní- | + | (yi)-Ø-T | > | ní-T | --- | nííłdáás |
| SP | Ø | + | --- | + | ní- | + | (yi)-Ø-(d)-T | > | ní-T | níl'į́ | --- |
| 3o. | yi- | + | --- | + | ní- | + | (yi)-Ø-T | > | ní-T | yiníł'į́ | --- |
| 3a. | Ø | + | ji- | + | ní- | + | (yi)-Ø-T | > | jiní-T | jiníł'į́ | jinííłdáás |
| AP | O | + | -di'<-'adi- | + | ní- | + | (yi)-Ø-T | > | bidi'ní-T | bidi'níl'į́ | --- |
| Dpl | | | | | | | | | | | |
| 1. | Ø | + | --- | + | n\ ´/* | + | (y)-ii(d)-T | > | nîi(d)-T | nîil'į́ | nîildáás |
| 2. | Ø | + | --- | + | n\ ´/* | + | (w)-o(h)-T | > | nó(h)-T | nół'į́ | nółdáás |

*The high tone prefix vowel deletes but its high tone carries over to the following vowel-initial prefix.

ní-(Ø)--ł'į́: look at it  ní-(Ø)--łdáás: be comparatively heavy

Some speakers substitute -é- for -í- in 1st and 3rd person, to produce nésh'į́: I'm looking at it, and yinéł'į́ / jinéł'į́: he's looking at it; and it should be noted that the Perfective Mode *does* have -é-, as nééł'į́į́': I looked at it.

## Yí-ní-:Position 6a/b + Extended Base

The compound Conjunct Prefix yí-ní- functions as a directive in many Verb Bases. It occurs both high and low in tone. In the absence of a prefix of Position 8, high tone yí-ní- takes the shape -ó- and yi-ni- becomes -oo-. Yí-ní- derives Neuter, as well as Active verbs, as illustrated below:

Table 13

T = any Verb theme

| PERSON | Prefix Position | | | | | | | | | |
|---|---|---|---|---|---|---|---|---|---|---|
| Sgl | 4 | + | 5 | + | 6a + 6b | + | Base | | | as in: |
| 1. | Ø | + | --- | + | yí- ni- | + | (yi)-sh-T | > | yínísh-T | yíníshdon |
| 2. | Ø | + | --- | + | yí- ni- | + | \ ´ /-T | > | yíní-T | yíníłdon |
| SP | Ø | + | --- | + | wó- | + | (yi)-Ø-(d)-T | > | wó-T | wóldon |
| 3o. | y(i)- | + | --- | + | -ó- | + | (yi)-Ø-T | > | yó-T | yółdon |
| 3a. | Ø | + | -j- | + | -ó- | + | (y)-Ø-T | > | jó-T | jółdon |
| Dpl | | + | | | | | | | | |
| 1. | Ø | + | --- | + | yí- n\ ´ / | + | (y)-ii(d)-T | > | yíníí(d)-T | yínííldon |
| 2. | Ø | + | --- | + | yí- n\ ´ / | + | (w)-o(h)-T | > | yínó(h)-T | yínółdon |

yí-ní-(Ø)--łdon: shoot at O; shell O
yí-ní-(Ø)--Øbé: pick O (as fruit); strip O off (as buttons)
yí-ní-(Ø)--łta': count O; read O
yí-ní-(Ø)--Økeed: ask for O; request O
yí-ní-(Ø)--(d)dziih: cuss at O
yí-ní-(Ø)--Øzhí: name O, call O by name
yí-ní-(Ø)--Øtą': hold onto O
yí-ní-(Ø)--Øtsa': hold O clenched in teeth

Yi-ni-: Position 6a/6b + Extended Base

Table 14

T = any Verb theme

| PERSON | Prefix Position | | | | | | | | | |
|---|---|---|---|---|---|---|---|---|---|---|
| Sgl | 4 | + | 5 | + | 6a - 6b | + | Base | | | as in: |
| 1. | Ø | + | --- | + | yi- ~ ni- | + | (yi)-sh-T | > | *woosh-T | *wooshdlą́ |
| 2. | Ø | + | --- | + | yi- ~ ni- | + | \ ´ /-T | > | yiní-T | yinídlą́ |
| 3o. | y(i)- | + | --- | + | -oo- | + | (yi)-Ø-T | > | yoo-T | yoodlą́ |
| 3a. | Ø | + | j(i)- | + | -oo- | + | (yi)-Ø-T | > | joo-T | joodlą́ |
| SP | Ø | + | --- | + | woo- | + | (yi)-Ø-(d)-T | > | woo-T | woodlą́ |
| AP | O | + | '(a)d- | + | -oo- | + | (yi)-Ø-(d)-T | > | O'doo-T | bi'doodlą́ |
| Dpl | | + | | | | | | | | |
| 1. | Ø | + | --- | + | yi- ~ n(i)- | + | (y)-ii(d)-T | > | yinii(d)-T | yiniidlą́ |
| 2. | Ø | + | --- | + | yi- ~ n(i)- | + | (w)-o(h)-T | > | yinoh-T | yinohdlą́ |

*Optionally as yinish-T: yinishdlą́

Low tone yi-ni- appears in Verb Bases of the type:

woo--łbį́į́h: win O; earn O          woo--(d)dlą́: believe O

The derived Verb Bases cho#-(y)ini-(Ø)--ł'į́į́h: "use O," and shó#-(y)ini-(Ø)--łt'eeh: "acquire O" include the Disjunct Thematic Prefixes cho- and shó-, but the Bases are conjugated in the manner summarized in the chart above.

choinish'į́į́h ~ choosh'į́į́h: I use O          shóinisht'eeh ~ shóosht'eeh: I acquire O

A number of Verb Bases, derived with the Disjunct Prefixes ná- and ta- (Position 1), + yi-(ni-) reduce the compound prefix to -o- throughout the paradigm of the Ø-Imperfective and, in the inflection of these Bases the 2nd person sgl subject pronoun (-ni- ~ ń ~ \ ´ /: Position 8) is omitted.

## Ta-/ná-: Position 1 + yi-ni-:Position 6a/6b + Extended Base

Table 15

T = any Verb Theme

| PERSON | Prefix Position | | | | | | | | | | |
|---|---|---|---|---|---|---|---|---|---|---|---|
| Sgl | 1b | + | 4 | + | 5 | + | yi-ni- | + | Base | as in: | |
| 1. | ta-/ná- | + | Ø | + | --- | + | -o- | + | (yi)-sh-T | taoshnih | náoshkąąh |
| 2. | ta-/ná- | + | Ø | + | --- | + | -o- | + | -- | taonih | náokąąh |
| 3. | ta-/ná- | + | Ø | + | --- | + | -o- | + | (yi)-Ø-T | taokááh | --- |
| SP | ta-/ná- | + | Ø | + | --- | + | -o- | + | (yi)-Ø-T | tao'nih | --- |
| 3o. | ta-/ná- | + | -y- | + | --- | + | -oo- | + | (yi)-Ø-T | tayoonih | náyookąąh |
| 3a. | ta-/ná- | + | Ø | + | -j- | + | -oo- | + | (yi)-Ø-T | tajoonih | ńjookąąh |
| Dpl | | | | | | | | | | | |
| 1. | ta-/ná- | + | Ø | + | --- | + | (-o-) | + | (y)oo(d)-T | taoo'nih | náookąąh |
| 2. | ta-/ná- | + | Ø | + | --- | + | (-o-) | + | (w)oo(h)-T | taoohnih | náoohkąąh |

ta#o-(Ø)--Ønih: mix O (dough)
ta#o-(Ø)--łchį́į́h: rile O (water)
ta#o-(Ø)--(d)kááh: plural subjects (a crowd) disperse
ná#-(Ø)--Økąąh: beg O, beseech for O
ná#-(Ø)--łtááď: undo O; unroll O
ná#-(Ø)--Ø'áád: untie O; untwist O

## Si- ~ yi-:Position 6a/6c + Extended Base

Si- is a Thematic Prefix that appears in a single Verb Base meaning "kill one object." Si- has a Position 6c allomorph with the shape yi- ~ -ii- that is required in the presence of a preceding prefix of Position 4 or 5. (Cf. Seriative hi-/yi-.)

Table 16

T = any Verb Theme

| PERSON | Prefix Position | | | | | | | | | |
|---|---|---|---|---|---|---|---|---|---|---|
| Sgl | 4 | + | 5 | + | 6a/6c | + | Base | | | as in: |
| 1. | Ø | + | ---- | + | si-/--- | + | (yi)-sh-T | > | sis-T | sisxé |
| 2. | Ø | + | ---- | + | si-/--- | + | \ ´/-T | > | sí-T | síłhé |
| SP | Ø | + | ---- | + | see-/--- | + | (yi)-Ø-(d)-T | > | see-T | seelyé |
| 3o. | yi- | + | ---- | + | ---/-yii- | + | (yi)-Ø-T | > | yiyii-T | yiyiiłhé |
| 3a. | Ø | + | j- | + | ---/-ii- | + | (yi)-Ø-T | > | jii-T | jiiłhé |
| AP | O | + | -'(a)d- | + | ---/-ii- | + | (yi)-Ø-T | > | O'dii-T | bi'diilyé |
| Dpl | | | | | | | | | | |
| 1. | Ø | + | ---- | + | s-/--- | + | (y)-ii(d)-T | > | sii(d)-T | siilyé |
| 2. | Ø | + | ---- | + | s-/--- | + | (w)-o(h)-T | > | so(h)-T | sołhé |

si-(Ø)--łhe : kill sgl O

The Verb Base P-ąąh '(i)-ii-Ø--łhé: "kill one of P's relatives" (literally: "kill someone unspecified alongside P") includes the 3i object pronoun 'a- ~ 'i- ~ '-, of Position 4, thus requiring the yi-allomorph throughout the paradigm, as:

| Sgl | Dpl |
|---|---|
| 1. P-ąąh 'iishhé | 1. P-ąąh 'ayiilyé |
| 2. P-ąąh 'iyíłhé | 2. P-ąąh 'ayoołhé |
| 3o. Y-ąąh 'iiłhé | AP P-ąąh 'i'diilyé |
| 3a. P-ąąh 'ajiiłhé | |

Dzi- ~ ji- ~ yi-: Position 6a + Extended Base

A prefix with the variable shape dzi- ~ ji- appears in a number of semantically disparate Verb Bases. As a Conjunct Prefix of Position 6a, and as a Disjunct Prefix of Position 1b it has the meaning "away into space." In Bases in which it cooccurs with yi-ni- and yí-ní- (Positions 6a + 6b) it appears to be concerned with emotions of hate, trust and kindness. It is illustrated in:

jishtaał: I'm in the act of delivering a kick away into space, in: bitsą́ jíshtaał: I'm in the act of kicking him in the belly
jíínísh łí ~ jóshłí, baa ---: I trust him; I have confidence in him
jiinishłá ~ jooshłá: I hate him

Ji- + yi-ni- contract to produce joo- in the absence of a prefix of Position 8, and the same contraction occurs optionally in 1st person sgl.

Similarly ji- ~ dzi- + yí-ní- contract to produce dzo- ~ jó-. See paradigms that follow below.

Table 17

| dzi- ~ ji- PERSON | ji- + yí-ní- PERSON | ji- + yi-ni- PERSON |
|---|---|---|
| Sgl | Sgl | Sgl |
| 1. jishtaał | 1. jíínísh łí ~ jóshłí | 1. jiinishłá ~ jooshłá |
| 2. dzítaał | 2. dzíínílí | 2. jiiniłá |
| 3. dzitaał | 3. dzólí | 3o.yijoołá |
| 3a.yijitaał | 3a. yijólí | 3a.jijoołá |
| | | AP.biji'doodlá |
| Dpl | Dpl | Dpl |
| 1. dziitaał | 1. dzíínîidlí | 1. jiiniidlá |
| 2. dzohtaał | 2. dzíínóhłí | 2.jiinohłá |

dzi-(Ø)--Øtaał: let fly a kick dzí-(y)í-ní-[ ~ dzó-]-(Ø)--Ølí: trust
dzi-(y)i-ni-[ ~ joo-]-(Ø)--ł(l)á (< -łá): hate O

## 2. Disjunct Prefixes

The Disjunct Prefixes function in two capacities as constituents of a Verb Base:

(1) They may function as Conjugational Determinants, joined directly to the Base, or

(2) They may function as components of a prefix complex, in which a Conjunct element of Position 4, 5 or 6 is the Conjugational Determinant.

<u>The Disjunct Prefixes as Conjugational Determinants</u> behave in a readily predictable manner, including:

(1) A low tone prefix vowel lengthens before the 1st person sgl subject pronoun prefix of Position 8 (-sh-), and in constructions in which Position 8 is vacant (3rd person and Simple Passive), as in:

ha-1b + Ø-7 + -sh-8 + -Øchééh > haashchééh: I start to cry
ha-1b + Ø-7 + Ø-8 + -Øchééh > haachééh: he starts to cry
ha-1b + Ø-7 + Ø-8 + -(d)dzį́į́s > haadzį́į́s: it is being dragged up out

bíłák'e-1b + Ø-7 + -sh-8 + -łtsóós > bíłák'eestsóós: I'm handing a FFO to him
bíłák'e-1b + Ø-7+ Ø-8 + ltsóós > bíłák'eeltsóós: a FFO is being handed to him

(2) A low tone -i-prefix vowel lengthens and takes the optional shape -ee- ~ -ii- before -sh-8 and in constructions in which Position 8 is vacant, as:

bik'i-1b + Ø-7 + -sh-8 + -Ødzį́į́s > bik'eesdzį́į́s ~ bik'iisdzį́į́s: I'm pulling it off of him
yi-1a + Ø-7 + Ø-8 + -l'į́ > yeel'į́: he's imitating it

An exception to this rule is the behavior of ni-1b, which lengthens the prefix vowel in the phonological environments described above, but the vowel retains its base shape, as in:

ni-1b + Ø-7 + -sh-8 + -ltłi' > niishtłi': I usually stop
ni-1b + Ø-7 + Ø-8 + -ltłi' > niiltłi': he usually stops

(3) A high tone -í-prefix vowel most commonly takes the shape -é- before -sh-8 and in constructions in which Position 8 is vacant, as:

bí-1b + Ø-7 + Ø-sh-8 + -(d)'nah > bésh'nah: I'm rubbing myself against it
yí-1b + Ø-7 + Ø-8 + -(d)'nah > yé'nah: it's rubbing itself against it
bik'í-1b + Ø-7 + -sh-8 + Ølish > bik'éshłish: I'm urinating on it
yik'í-1b + Ø-7 + Ø-8 + Ølish > yik'élish: he's urinating on it

Of the four Imperfective Mode categories the Ø-Imperfective is by far the most productive. A majority of the Disjunct derivational elements occur in Conjugational Determinant position, including those listed below. In addition, those marked with an asterisk (*) take a Ø-Imperfective conjugational pattern exclusively:

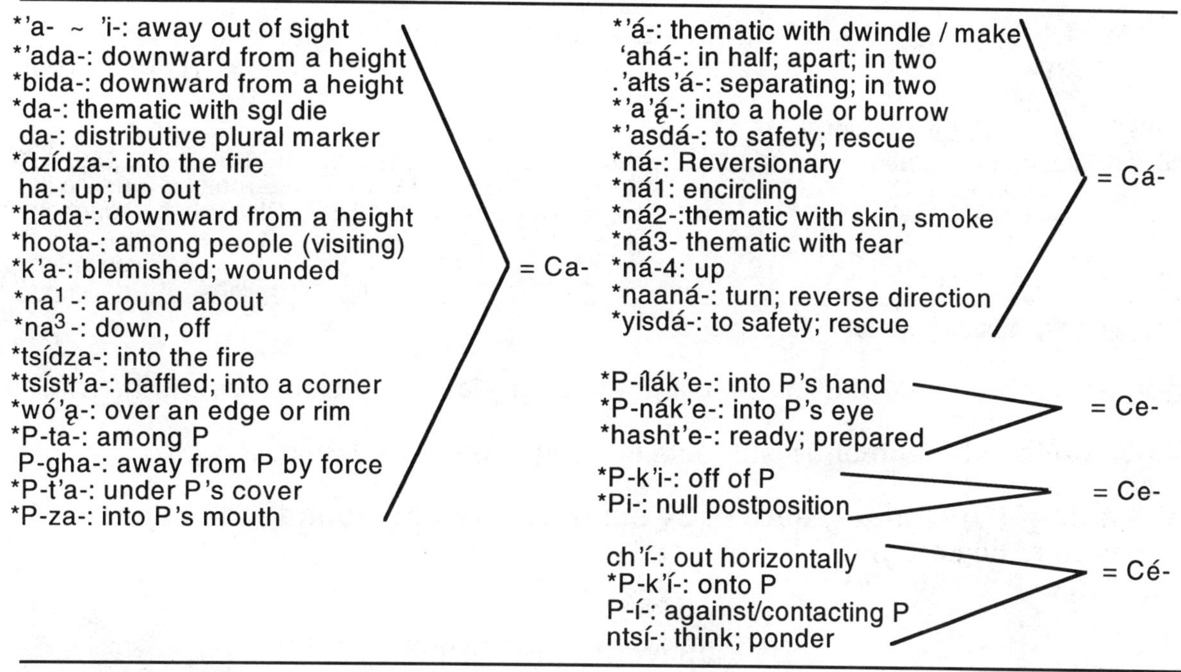


*P- = any pronominal prefix that represents the object of a postposition, or any possessive pronoun prefix attached to a verb-incorporated noun.

# marks Disjunct / Conjunct Boundary

## Da-Position 3 Marker of the Distributive Plural + Extended Base

Most fully conjugated Verb Bases include a Distributive Plural paradigm, marked by the Position 3 prefix da- "each of 3 or more subjects."

Da- behaves like the Ca-prefixes of Position 1b, both as a Conjugational Determinant and as a constituent of an Extended Base Paradigm. The consonant d is articulated in a forward position, a circumstance that results in assimilation of the vowel of da- when followed by -i-; da- + -i- > dei-.

deiicha: we 3+ are crying
daacha: they 3+ are crying

Da-3 also serves as a distributive pluralizing agent with reference to the direct object in certain Distributive aspectual verbs. Verb Bases derived with da-3 are conjugated in the pattern described for the Ca-prefixes of Position 1b, in Table 2 below.

łeets'aa' ndaashnil: I'm setting the table (i.e. I'm distributing dishes about)
béeso 'ałts'ádaashnil: I'm dividing up the money (in 3+ equal parts)

*Ø-Imperfective*

Table 1
Distributive Plural Subjects

T = any Verb Theme

| PERSON Dist. Plural | 3 | + | 4 | + | 5 | + | Base | | | as in: Intransitive | Transitive |
|---|---|---|---|---|---|---|---|---|---|---|---|
| 1. | de- | + | Ø | + | --- | + | (y)-ii(d)-T | > | deii(d)-T | deiicha | deiich'id |
| 2. | da- | + | Ø | + | --- | + | (w)-o(h)-T | > | *dao(h)-T | *daohcha | *daohch'id |
| 3. | daa- | + | Ø | + | --- | + | (yi)-Ø-T | > | daa-Ø-T | daacha | --- |
| 3o. | de- | + | -i- | + | --- | + | (yi)-Ø-T | > | dei-T | --- | deich'id |
| 3a | da | + | Ø | + | -ji- | + | (yi)-Ø-T | > | daji-T | dajicha | dajich'id |

*Or optionally as daa(h)-: daahcha / daahch'id

da#-(Ø)--Øcha: each of 3+ subjects cries (e.g. deiicha: we're crying; daacha: they're crying)

da#-(Ø)--Øch'id: each of 3+ subjects is scratching O (deich'id: they're scratching it)

na- ~ n-da-#-(Ø)--Ømaas: each of 3+ subjects is rolling around (ndaamaas: they're rolling around)

Distributive Plural Objects

| PERSON Sgl | 3 | + | 4 | + | 5 | + | Base | | Transitive | |
|---|---|---|---|---|---|---|---|---|---|---|
| 1. | daa- | + | Ø | + | ---- | + | (yi)-sh-T | > | daash-T | biih daashnil |
| 2. | da- | + | Ø | + | ---- | + | (yi)-ni-T | > | dani-T | biih daninil |
| SP | daa- | + | Ø | + | ---- | + | (yi)-Ø-(d)-T | > | daa-T | biih daa'nil |
| 3o. | de- | + | -i- | + | ---- | + | (yi)-Ø-T | > | dei-T | yiih deinil |
| 3a. | da- | + | Ø | + | ji- | + | (yi)-Ø-T | > | daji-T | biih dajinil |
| Dpl Dist. Pl | | | | | | | | | | |
| 1. | de- | + | Ø | + | ---- | + | (y)-ii(d)-T | > | deii(d)-T | biih deii'nil |
| 2. | da- | + | Ø | + | ---- | + | (w)-o(h)-T | > | dao(h)-T | biih daohnil ~ biih daahnil |
| 3o. | de- | + | -i- | + | ---- | + | (yi)-Ø-T | > | dei-T | yiih deinil |
| 3a. | da- | + | Ø | + | ji- | + | (yi)-Ø-T | > | daji-T | biih dajinil |

da#-(Ø)--Ønil, biih ---: put distributive plural O (as turquoise sets) in it (as in a ring)

na- ~ n--da#-(Ø)--ti': set distributive plural SSO (as legs) about here and there (ndaashti': I'm setting SSO about)

## Ca-: Position 1b + Extended Base

### Table 2

T- = any Verb Theme

| PERSON Sgl | Prefix Position 1b | + | 4 | + | 5 | + | Base | | | as in: Intransitive | Transitive |
|---|---|---|---|---|---|---|---|---|---|---|---|
| 1. | Caa- | + | Ø | + | ---- | + | (yi)-sh-T | > | Caash-T | haashchééh | haasdzį́į́s |
| 2. | Ca- | + | Ø | + | ---- | + | -ni-T | > | Cani-T | hanichééh | hanidzį́į́s |
| 3 | Caa- | + | Ø | + | ---- | + | (yi)-Ø-T | > | Caa-T | haachééh | -------- |
| SP | Caa- | + | Ø | + | ---- | + | (yi)-Ø-(d)-T | > | Caa(d)-T | --------- | haadzį́į́s |
| 3o. | Ca- | + | -i- | + | ---- | + | (yi)-Ø-T | > | Cai-T | --------- | haidzį́į́s |
| 3a. | Ca- | + | Ø | + | ji-/dzi- | + | (yi)-Ø-T | > | Caji-T | hajichééh | hadzidzį́į́s |
| 3i. | Ca- | + | --- | + | -'a- | + | (yi)-Ø-T | > | Ca'a-T | ha'achééh | -------- |
| AP | Ca- | + | O | + | '(a)di- | + | (yi)-Ø-(d)-T | > | CaO'di-T | --------- | habi'didzį́į́s |
| Dpl | | | | | | | | | | | |
| 1. | Ca- | + | Ø | + | ---- | + | (y)-ii(d)-T | > | Caii(d)-T | haiichééh | haiidzį́į́s |
| 2. | Ca- | + | Ø | + | ---- | + | (w)-o(h)-T | > | Cao(h)-T | *haohchééh | *haohdzį́į́s |

* Or optionally as haahchééh, haahdzį́į́s

ha#-(Ø)--Øchééh: start to cry
ha#-(Ø)--(d)dziih: exhale; speak
ha#-(Ø)--(d)'nééh: crawl up out
ha#-(Ø)--łgééd: stick O out (tongue)
da#-(Ø)--Øtsaah: become ill
P-t'a#-(Ø)--(d)'nééh: crawl under covers with P
P-ta#-(Ø)--Øjaah: distribute PIO to (among) P
na#-(Ø)--lnish: be working
na#-(Ø)--Øtįįh: lower a SSO
na#-(Ø)--Øtłíísh: fall downward
na#-(Ø)--Ø'á: carry a SRO around
P-za#-(Ø)--Ø'aah: put SRO in P's mouth

Note: The na-prefixes take variable shape in particular phonological environments. See chart on pages 30-31.

## Cá-:Position 1b + Extended Base

### Table 3

T = any Verb Theme

| PERSON Sgl | Prefix Position 1b | + | 4 | + | 5 | + | Base | | | as in: Intransitive | Transitive |
|---|---|---|---|---|---|---|---|---|---|---|---|
| 1. | Cá- | + | Ø | + | --- | + | (yi)-sh-T | > | Cásh-T | yáshti' | 'ahácshgéésh |
| 2. | Cá- | + | Ø | + | --- | + | -ni-T | > | Cání-T | yáníłti' | 'ahánígéésh |
| 3. | Cá- | + | Ø | + | --- | + | (yi)-Ø-T | > | Cá-T | yáłti' | --- |
| SP | Cá- | + | Ø | + | --- | + | (yi)-Ø-(d)-T | > | Cá-T | --- | 'ahágéésh |
| 3o. | Cá- | + | -í- | + | --- | + | (yi)-Ø-T | > | Cáí-T | --- | 'aháígéésh |
| 3a. | Cá- | + | Ø | + | -jí | + | (yi)-Ø-T | > | Cájí-T | yájíłti | 'ahájígéésh |
| 3i. | Cá- | + | Ø | + | -'á- | + | (yi)-Ø-T | > | Cá'á-T | yá'áti' | --- |
| 3s. | Cá- | + | Ø | + | -há- | + | (yi)-Ø-T | > | Cáhá-T | náhádleeh | --- |
| AP | Cá- | + | O | + | -'(a)di- | + | (yi)-Ø(d)-T | > | CáO'di-T | --- | 'ahábi'digéésh |
| Dpl | | | | | | | | | | | |
| 1. | Cá- | + | Ø | + | --- | + | (y)-ii(d)-T | > | Cáii(d)-T | yéiilti' | 'aháiigéésh |
| 2. | Cá- | + | Ø | + | --- | + | (w)-o(h)-T | > | Cáo(h)-T | yáołti' | 'aháohgéésh |

ná#-ha-(Ø)--(d)leeh: area reverts, again becomes

'á- ~ 'í- ~ \'/-(Ø)--Øłééh: make O ('áshłééh: I'm making it; 'íílééh: he's making it; 'íilnééh: we're making it)
yá#-(Ø)--łti': talk
háá-P-í-yá#-(Ø)--łtééh: break the spell on P
'a-P-í-yá#-(Ø)--łtééh: bring P in (as property - by talking or magic)
'ałná-ná#-(Ø)--łtééh: carry an AnO (as a baby) back and forth repeatedly (to a place and back - as to a clinic)
'ałts'á-da#-(Ø)--Øjaah: divide PlO up (as coins, seeds)
'ałts'á#-(Ø)--Øgéés: twist O apart
'a'ą́#-(Ø)--(d)'nééh: crawl into a hole or burrow
'ahá#-(Ø)--Øgéésh: cut O apart

Ce-:Position 1b + Extended Base

Table 4

T = any Verb Theme

| PERSON Sgl | 1b | + | 4 | + | 5 | + | Base | | | as in: Intransitive | Transitive |
|---|---|---|---|---|---|---|---|---|---|---|---|
| 1. | Cee- | + | Ø | + | ---- | + | (yi)-sh-T | > | Ceesh-T | dá'ák'eesh'nééh | bíłák'eesh'aah |
| 2. | Ce- | + | Ø | + | ---- | + | -ni-T | > | Ceni-T | dá'ák'eni'nééh | bíłák'eni'aah |
| 3. | Cee- | + | Ø | + | ---- | + | (yi)-Ø-T | > | Cee-Ø-T | dá'ák'ee'nééh | ----------- |
| SP | Cee- | + | Ø | + | ---- | + | (yi)-Ø-(d)-T | > | Cee-Ø-T | ---------- | bíłák'eet'aah |
| 3o. | Ce- | + | -i- | + | ---- | + | (yi)-Ø-T | > | Cei-T | ---------- | yíłák'ei'aah |
| 3a. | Ce- | + | Ø | + | -ji- | + | (yi)-Ø-T | > | Ceji-T | dá'ák'eji'nééh | bíłák'eji'aah |
| 3i. | Ce- | + | Ø | + | -'e- | + | (yi)-Ø-T | > | Ce'e-T | dá'ák'e'e'nééh | ----------- |
| Dpl | | | | | | | | | | | |
| 1. | Ce- | + | Ø | + | ---- | + | (y)-ii(d)-T | > | Ceii(d)-T | dá'ák'eii'nééh | bíłák'eiit'aah |
| 2. | Ce- | + | Ø | + | ---- | + | (w)-o(h)-T | > | Ceo(h)-T | dá'ák'eoh'nééh | bíłák'eoh'aah |

dá'ák'e#-(Ø)--(d)'nééh: crawl into the field
dá'ák'e#-(Ø)--lyeed: run into the field (sgl subject)
P-íłák'e#-(Ø)--Ø'aah: hand a SRO to P
P-íłák'e#-(Ø)--łtsóós: hand a FFO to P

Ci-:Position 1b + Extended Base

Table 5

T = any Verb Theme

| PERSON Sgl | 1b | + | 4 | + | 5 | + | Base | | | as in: Intransitive | Transitive |
|---|---|---|---|---|---|---|---|---|---|---|---|
| 1. | Cee- | + | Ø | + | --- | + | (yi)-sh-T | > | Ceesh-T | *bik'eesh'nééh | *bik'eesdzį́į́s |
| 2. | Ci- | + | Ø | + | --- | + | -ni-T | > | Cini-T | bik'ini'nééh | bik'inidzį́į́s |
| 3. | Cee- | + | Ø | + | --- | + | (yi)-Ø-T | > | Cee-Ø-T | *yik'ee'nééh | --- |
| SP | Cee- | + | Ø | + | --- | + | (yi)-Ø-(d)-T | > | Cee-Ø-T | --- | *bik'eedzį́į́s |
| 3o. | Ci- | + | -i- | + | --- | + | (yi)-Ø-T | > | Cii-T | --- | yik'iidzį́į́s |
| 3a. | Ci- | + | Ø | + | -ji- | + | (yi)-Ø-T | > | Ciji-T | bik'iji'nééh | bik'idzidzį́į́s |
| 3i. | Ce- | + | Ø | + | -'e- | + | (yi)-Ø-T | > | Ce'e-T | bik'e'e'nééh | --- |
| AP | Ci- | + | O | + | -'(a)di- | + | (yi)-Ø(d)-T | > | CiO'di-T | --- | bik'ibi'didzį́į́s |
| Dpl | | | | | | | | | | | |
| 1. | C- | + | Ø | + | --- | + | (y)-ii(d)-T | > | Cii(d)-T | bik'ii'nééh | bik'iidzį́į́s |
| 2. | Ci- | + | Ø | + | --- | + | (w)-o(h)-T | > | Cio(h)-T | bik'ioh'nééh | bik'iohdzį́į́s |

*optionally -k'ii-

P-ik'i#-(Ø)--(d)'nééh: crawl off of P (as off of a rug or blanket - not off an elevated surface)

P-k'i#-(Ø)--Ødzį́į́s: pull O off of P
Pi-#-(Ø)--l'į́: imitate Pi (as a bird)(Pi- represents the null postpositions of Position 1a)

Cí-Position 1b + Extended Base

Table 6

T = any Verb Theme

| PERSON | Prefix Position | | | | | | | | | as in: | |
|---|---|---|---|---|---|---|---|---|---|---|---|
| Sgl | 1b | + | 4 | + | 5 | + | Base | | | Intransitive | Transitive |
| 1. | Cé- | + | Ø | + | --- | + | (yi)-sh-T | > | Césh- | bésh'nah | béshjoł |
| 2. | Cí- | + | Ø | + | --- | + | -ni-T | > | Cíní-T | bíní'nah | bíníłjoł |
| 3. | Cé- | + | Ø | + | --- | + | (yi)-Ø-T | > | Cé-Ø-T | yé'nah | ------ |
| SP | Cé- | + | Ø | + | --- | + | (yi)-Ø-T | > | Cé-Ø(d)-T | ---- | béljoł |
| 3o. | Cí- | + | -í- | + | --- | + | (yi)-Ø-T | > | Cíí-T | ------ | yííłjoł |
| 3a. | Cí- | + | Ø | + | -jí- | + | (yi)-Ø-T | > | Cíjí-T | bíjí'nah | bíjíłjoł |
| 3i. | Cí- | + | Ø | + | -'í- | + | (yi)-Ø-T | > | Cí'í-T | bí'í'nah | ------ |
| Dpl | | | | | | | | | | | |
| 1. | Cí- | + | Ø | + | --- | + | (y)-ii(d)-T | > | Cíi(d)-T | bíi'nah | bíiljoł |
| 2. | Cí | + | Ø | + | --- | + | (w)-o(h)-T | > | Cío(h)-T | bóoh'nah | bóołjoł |

P-í#-(Ø)--(d)'nah: rub against P (as against a tree)
P-í#-(Ø)--łjoł: rub NCM against O (as a rag against a windowpane)
P-í#-(Ø)--Ø'ááh: rub SRO against O (as a bar of soap against one's head)
P-í#-(Ø)--łk'į́į́h: peel O (as potato with a knife)
'ád-í#-(Ø)--ljoł: rub NCM against self (as a towel against one's own body)
'ád-í#-(Ø)--t'ááh: rub SRO against self (as a bar of soap)
P-k'í#-(Ø)--Økaah: pour O on P (as water on a fire)
ch'í#-(Ø)--łmáás, 'adah ---: roll O over an edge (as a barrel over a precipice)

**Irregular Ø-Imperfectives**
2. Disjunct Prefixes

'A-Position 1b: "away out of sight," has an allomorph 'i-, that is required in certain phonological environments.

Similarly, the 3i object pronoun 'a-Position 4 has an allomorph 'i- required in particular environments, and 'a-1b + 'a-4 cooccur in a number of Verb Bases, taking variable shapes, depending on the phonological environment.

Similarly, P-í-Position 1b: "against P, in contact with P," takes the shape P-é- in certain environments, including constructions in which it cooccurs with 'a-4.

In each of the foregoing instances the resultant paradigms are divergent.

## 'A- ~ 'i-: Position Ib + Extended Base Paradigm

### Table 7

T = any VerbTheme

| PERSON | Prefix Position | | | | | | | | | as in: | |
|---|---|---|---|---|---|---|---|---|---|---|---|
| Sgl | 1b | + | 4 | + | 5 | + | Base | | | Intransitive | Transitive |
| 1. | 'ii- | + | Ø | + | --- | + | (yi)-sh-T | > | 'iish- | 'iish'nééh | 'iishteeh |
| 2. | 'a- | + | Ø | + | --- | + | -ni-T | > | 'ani-T | 'ani'nééh | 'aniłteeh |
| 3. | 'ii- | + | Ø | + | --- | + | (yi)-Ø-T | > | 'ii-Ø-T | 'ii'nééh | -------- |
| SP | 'ii- | + | Ø | + | --- | + | (yi)-Ø-(d)-T | > | 'ii-Ø(d)-T | ----- | 'iilteeh |
| 3o. | 'i- | + | -i- | + | --- | + | (yi)-Ø-T | > | 'ii-T | ----- | 'iiłteeh |
| 3a. | 'a- | + | Ø | + | -ji- | + | (yi)-Ø-T | > | 'aji-T | 'aji'nééh | 'ajiłteeh |
| 3i. | 'e- | + | Ø | + | -'e- | + | (yi)-Ø-T | > | 'e'e-T | 'e'e'nééh | -------- |
| AP | 'a- | + | O | + | -'(a)di- | + | (yi)-Ø(d)-T | > | 'aO'di-T | ----- | 'abi'dilteeh |
| Dpl | | | | | | | | | | | |
| 1. | '- | + | Ø | + | --- | + | (y)-ii(d)- | > | 'ii(d)- | 'ii'nééh | 'iilteeh |
| 2. | 'o- | + | Ø | + | --- | + | (w)-o(h)-T | > | 'oo(h)-T | 'ooh'nééh | 'oołteeh |

'a#-(Ø)--(d)'nééh: crawl away out of sight
'a#-(Ø)--łteeh: carry an AnO away out of sight
'a#-(Ø)--Øgéés: twist O away (as a screw); turn O off (a faucet); screw O in
'a#-(Ø)--Øzǫ́ǫ́s: rip O (as cloth; tear O (as paper)
'a#-(Ø)--Øts'ǫǫd, yah ---: lean into an enclosure (as through an open window)
'a#-(Ø)--łts'ǫǫd, yah ---: stretch O into an enclosure (as a rope into a building)
'a#-(Ø)--łkaał, bił ---: nail O to it
'a#-(Ø)--łt'ééh, baa ---: plug O into it (as an electric cord into an outlet)
'a#-(Ø)--lgééd, 'ádaa---: stick O into self (as a needle)

## 'A-: Position 1b + 'a-: Position 4 + Extended Base

### Table 8

T = any Verb Theme

| PERSON | Prefix Position | | | | | | | | | |
|---|---|---|---|---|---|---|---|---|---|---|
| Sgl | 1b | + | 4 | + | 5 | + | Base | | | as in: |
| 1. | 'e- | + | -'e- | + | ---- | + | (yi)-sh-T | > | 'e'esh-T | 'e'eshnííł |
| 2. | 'i- | + | -i- | + | ---- | + | \ ´/-T | > | 'i'í-T | 'i'íníił |
| 3. | 'e- | + | -'e- | + | ---- | + | (yi)-Ø-T | > | 'e'e-T | 'e'eníił |
| 3a. | 'i- | + | -'- | + | -ji- | + | (yi)-Ø-T | > | 'i'ji-T | 'i'jiníił |
| SP | 'e- | + | 'e | + | ---- | + | (yi)Ø(d)-T | > | 'e'e-(d)-T | 'e'e'nííł |
| Dpl | | | | | | | | | | |
| 1. | 'i- | + | -'- | + | ---- | + | (y)-ii(d)-T | > | 'i'ii(d)-T | 'i'ii'nííł |
| 2. | 'o- | + | -'- | + | ---- | + | (w)-o(h)-T | > | 'o'o(h)-T | 'o'ohnííł |

'a#-'a-(Ø)--Øníił: burrow; dig a hole or tunnel
'a#-'a-(Ø)--łkaał, bił ---: nail it down (literally: drive something unspecified away out of sight in company with it)
'a#-'a-(Ø)--łgééd, bíká ---: drill for it (as for oil or water)
'a#-'a-(Ø)--łkǫ́ǫ́h: swim away
'a#-'a-(Ø)--łne', hadah ---: drop a bomb (literally: cause an unspecified SRO to move abruptly away through the air downward)
'a#-'a-(Ø)--lgééd, 'ádaa ---: stab oneself
'a#-'a-(Ø)--Ø aah: the sun is setting ('e'e'aah)

## P-í-: Position 1b + 'a-Position 4 + Extended Base

Table 9

T = any Verb Theme

| PERSON Sgl | 1b | + | 4 | + | 5 | + | Base | | | as in: |
|---|---|---|---|---|---|---|---|---|---|---|
| 1. | P-é | + | -'e | + | --- | + | (yi)-sh-T | > | P-é'ésh-T | bé'éshjoł |
| 2. | P-í- | + | -'i- | + | --- | + | \ ´/-T | > | P-í'í-T | bí'íłjoł |
| SP | P-é- | + | -'é- | + | --- | + | (yi)-Ø-(d)-T | > | P-é'é-Ø-T | bé'éljoł |
| 3. | y-é- | + | -'é- | + | --- | + | (yi)-Ø-T | > | yé'é-Ø-T | yé'éłjoł |
| 3a. | P-í- | + | -'- | + | -jí- | + | (yi)-Ø-T | > | P-í'jí-T | bí'jíłjoł |
| Dpl | | | | | | | | | | |
| 1. | P-í- | + | -'- | + | --- | + | (y)-ii(d)-T | > | P-í'ii(d)-T | bí'iiljoł |
| 2. | P-í- | + | -'- | + | --- | + | (w)-o(h)-T | > | P-í'ó(h)-T | bí'ółjoł |

P-í#--'a-(Ø)--łjoł: wipe, rub, dust P with a rag (literally: rub unspecified NCM against P)
P-í#--'a-(Ø)--Øts'ih: pick on P (literally pinch something against P)

## Náá- ~ nááná-: Position 1e + Extended Base: Semeliterative

Náá(ná)-Position 1e is the Semeliterative marker, connoting a single repetition of the action or event denoted by the Verb Theme. It is generally equivalent to English "again," in a context of the type "he went out again;" but not in a reversionary context of the type "the sun came out again" if the meaning is "the sun came *back* out." Reversionary actions and events are marked distinctively by ná-, in Position 1d.

The reduplicated allomorph (nááná-) is required before the 1st person sgl subject pronoun (-sh-8). Likewise it is required in constructions in which Position 8 is vacant (3rd person and Simple Passive); and the reduplicated form is required before the vowel-initial 1st and 2nd person dpl subject pronouns. In transitive constructions náá- or nááná- are optional before the 3o direct object pronoun (yi- ~ -i-).

Table 10

T = any Verb Theme

| PERSON Sgl | 1e | + | 4 | + | 5 | + | Base | | | as in: Intransitive | Transitive |
|---|---|---|---|---|---|---|---|---|---|---|---|
| 1. | nááná- | + | Ø | + | --- | + | (yi)-sh-T | > | náánásh-T | náánáshcha | náánáshch'id |
| 2. | náá- | + | Ø | + | --- | + | -ní-T | > | náání-T | náánícha | nááních'id |
| 3. | nááná- | + | Ø | + | --- | + | (yi)-Ø-T | > | nááná-Ø-T | náánácha | --- |
| SP | nááná- | + | Ø | + | --- | + | (yi)-Ø-(d)-T | > | nááná-Ø-T | --- | náánách'id |
| 3o. | nááné- | + | -í- | + | --- | + | (yi)-Ø-T | > | náánéí-T | --- | náánéích'id |
| 3a. | náá- | + | Ø | + | -jí- | + | (yi)-Ø-T | > | náájí-T | náájícha | náájích'id |
| 3i | náá- | + | Ø | + | -'á- | + | (yi)-Ø-T | > | náá'á-T | náá'ácha | --- |
| 3s. | náá- | + | Ø | + | -há- | + | (yi)-Ø-T | > | nááhá-T | nááhádleeh | --- |
| AP | náá- | + | O | + | -'(a)di- | + | (yi)-Ø-(d)-T | > | nááO'di-T | --- | náábi'dich'id |
| Dpl | | | | | | | | | | | |
| 1. | nááné- | + | Ø | + | --- | + | (y)-ii(d)-T | > | náánéii-T | náánéiicha | náánéiich'id |
| 2. | nááná- | + | Ø | + | --- | + | (w)-o(h)-T | > | náánáo(h)-T | náánáohcha | náánáohch'id |

náá(ná)#-(Ø)--Øcha: be crying again
náá(ná)#-(Ø)--Øch'id: be scratching O again

náá#-há-(Ø)-d-leeh: area again becomes

## 'Á-di-:Position 1c / 4 + Extended Base

'Á-di- is the Reflexive object pronoun "self." It is a compound prefix, composed of 'á-: "self," in Position 1c + -di-: "person"(??) in Position 4.

'Á- is assigned the 1c slot in Position 1, although its position is variable. In the absence of a prefix or prefixes of intervening position the Reflexive is conjugated in the same pattern as other simple Ø-Imperfectives that include a prefix of Position 4. However, a prefix of Position 1e (Semeliterative) or Position 3 (Distributive Plural marker) takes an intervening position between 'á- and -di-; and the 3a subject pronoun of Position 5 undergoes metathesis, moving to the left of -di-4.

'ádích'id: he's scratching himself, **but:**
'á-náá-dích'id: he's again scratching himself
'á-da-dich'id: they (3+) are scratching themselves
'á-náá-da-dich'id: they (3+) are again scratching themselves.
'á-zh-dích'id: he (3a person) is scratching himself
'á-da--zh-dich'id: they (3+ 3a persons) are scratching themselves

The Reflexive requires D- or L-Classifier in Position 9. However, D-Classifier is actually manifest only if the stem-initial consonant is \'/, gh, z, zh, l or n, where:

D- + \'/ > t'-
D- + gh- > g-
D- + z- > d-z-
D- + zh- > j- [= d-zh]
D- + l- > d-l-
D- + n- > 'n-

Table 11

T = any Verb Theme

| PERSON | Prefix Position | | | | | | | | | |
|---|---|---|---|---|---|---|---|---|---|---|
| Sgl | 1c | + | 5 | + | 4 | + | Base | | | as in: |
| 1. | 'á- | + | --- | + | -dí- | + | (yi)-sh-T | > | 'ádísh-T | 'ádíshch'id |
| 2. | 'á- | + | --- | + | -dí- | + | [\ ´ /]-T | > | 'ádí-T | 'ádích'id |
| 3. | 'á- | + | --- | + | -dí- | + | (yi)-Ø-T | > | 'ádí-Ø-T | 'ádích'id |
| 3a. | 'á- | + | -zh- | + | -dí- | + | (yi)-Ø-T | > | 'ázhdí-T | 'ázhdích'id |
| Dp | | | | | | | | | | |
| 1. | 'á- | + | --- | + | -d- | + | (y)-ii(d)-T | > | 'ádii(d)-T | 'ádiich'id |
| 2. | 'á- | + | --- | + | -d- | + | (w)-ó(h)-T | > | 'ádó(h)-T | 'ádóhch'id |

'á#-dí--(Ø)--(d)ch'id: scratch self
'á#-dí-(Ø)--lzhééh: shave self
'á#-dí-(Ø)-(d)k'ąąs: stretch self
ná-'á#-dí-(Ø)--ltsaah: dry self
'á#-dí-(Ø)--d-lid: burn self
'á#-dí-(Ø)--lzhóóh: brush self
ná-'á#-di-ni-(Ø)--lts'in: beat self with fists
na-'á#dí-(Ø)--lts'ǫǫd: do calisthenics (i.e. stretch self around)

## RECAPITULATION

The conjugation patterns corresponding to the Base and to the various conjugational determinants can be recapitulated succinctly in the following form:

T = any Verb Theme
(d) = d-effect
O = any direct object pronoun in Position 4
P = any pronoun of Position 0 (object of a postposition or possessor of a noun)

## Ø-IMPERFECTIVE

### 1. Extended Base Paradigm

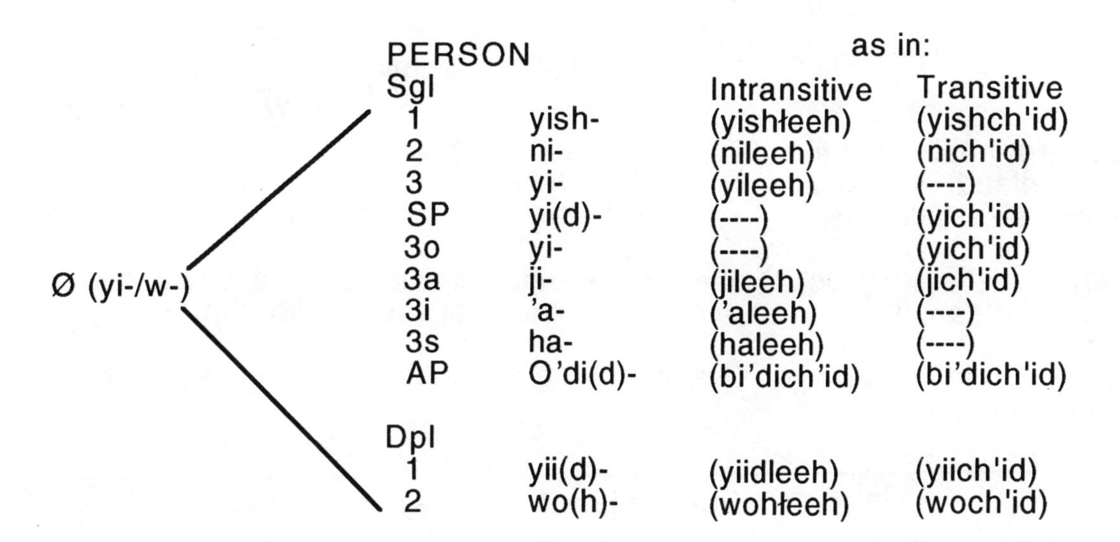

| | PERSON | | as in: Intransitive | Transitive |
|---|---|---|---|---|
| Ø (yi-/w-) | Sgl | | | |
| | 1 | yish- | (yishłeeh) | (yishch'id) |
| | 2 | ni- | (nileeh) | (nich'id) |
| | 3 | yi- | (yileeh) | (----) |
| | SP | yi(d)- | (----) | (yich'id) |
| | 3o | yi- | (----) | (yich'id) |
| | 3a | ji- | (jileeh) | (jich'id) |
| | 3i | 'a- | ('aleeh) | (----) |
| | 3s | ha- | (haleeh) | (----) |
| | AP | O'di(d)- | (bi'dich'id) | (bi'dich'id) |
| | Dpl | | | |
| | 1 | yii(d)- | (yiidleeh) | (yiich'id) |
| | 2 | wo(h)- | (wohłeeh) | (woch'id) |

(Ø)--Øleeh: become
(Ø)--Øch'id: scratch O (yishch'id)

## *CONJUNCT PREFIXES*

### 2. Ci-Conjunct + Extended Base

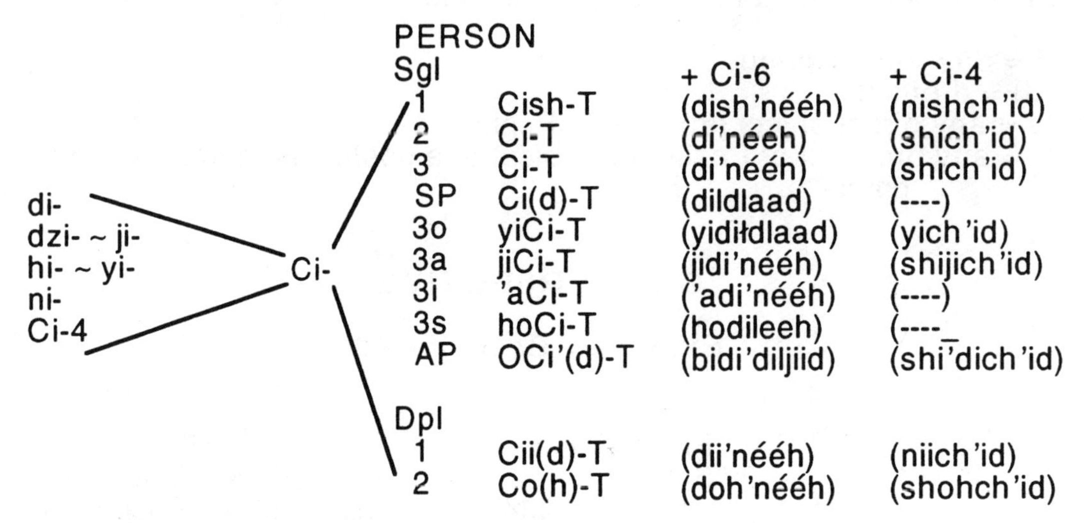


di-(Ø)--(d)'nééh: start to crawl along (dish'nééh)
di-(Ø)--łdlaad: start to plow a furrow (dishdlaad)
ji- ~ dzi- (Ø)--Øtaał, P-tsą̨ ---: kick P in the belly (bitsą̨ jíshtaał: I'm in the act of kicking him in the belly)
hi-(Ø)--Ønizh: pick/pluck O one after another (hishnizh: I'm plucking them)
ni-(Ø)--(d)t'aah, biih ---: put one's head into it (biih nisht'aah: I'm putting my head into it)
ni-(Ø)--Øch'id: scratch you (nishch'id: I'm scratching you; nich'id: he's scratching you)

### 3. 'A- / ho-Conjunct + Extended Base

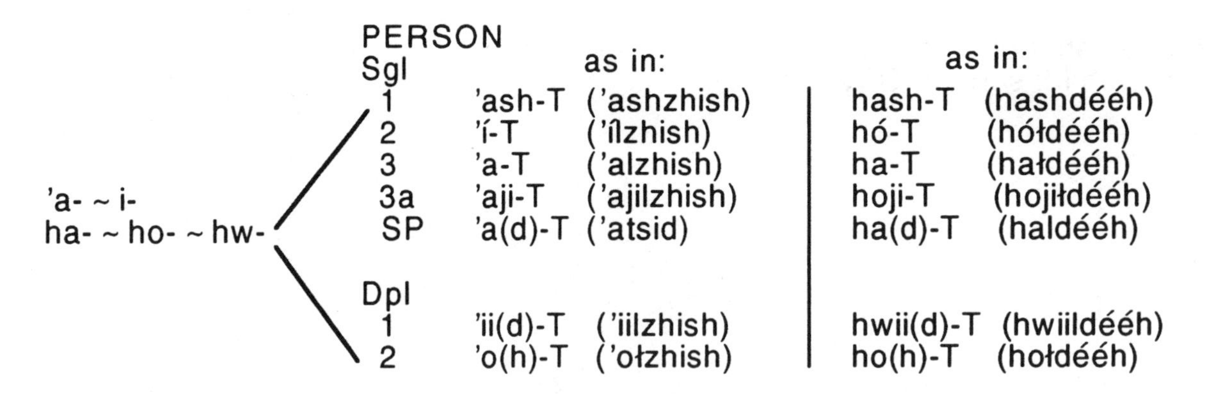


'a#(Ø)--lzhish: dance ('ashzhish: I'm dancing)
ha#-(Ø)--łdééh: clear an area (hółdééh: you're cleaning up the area)
ha#(Ø)--lne': tell (baa hashne': I'm telling about it)

## *DISJUNCT PREFIXES*

### 4. Ca-: Position 1b + Extended Base

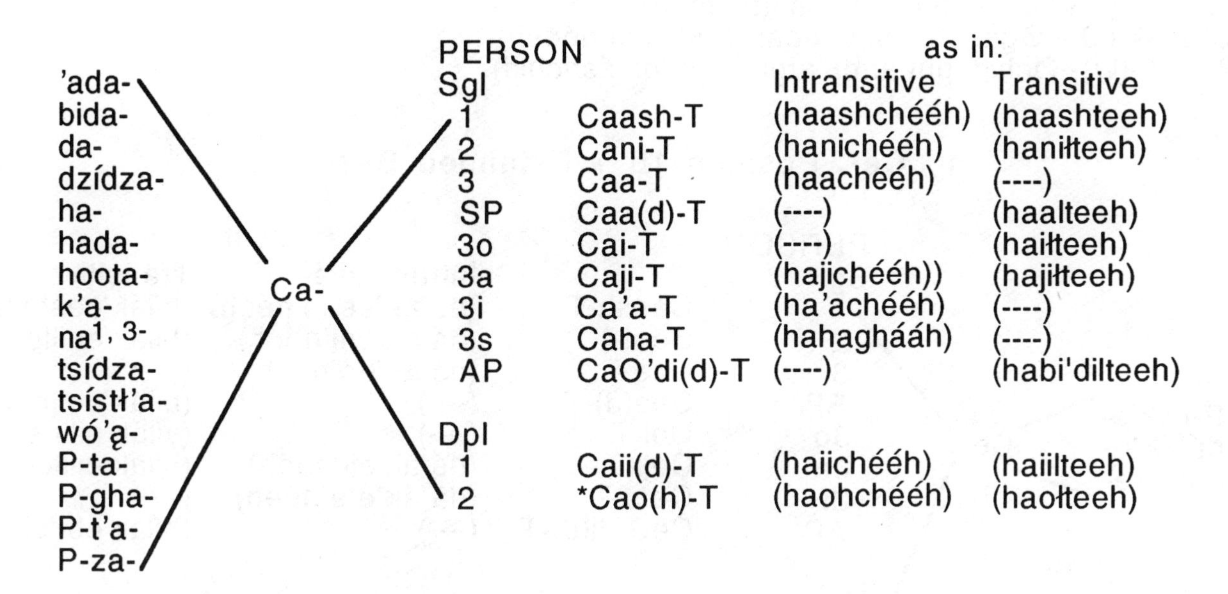


*optionally Caa(h)-T

ha#-(Ø)--łteeh:: take an AnO out (as from a box)
ha#-ha-(Ø)--Øgháah: an event starts
dzídza#-(Ø)--Ø'aah: put a SRO into the fire
P-za#-(Ø)--Ø'aah: put a SRO into P's mouth
na#-(Ø)--łté: carry an AnO about

### 5. Cá-: Position 1b + Extended Base

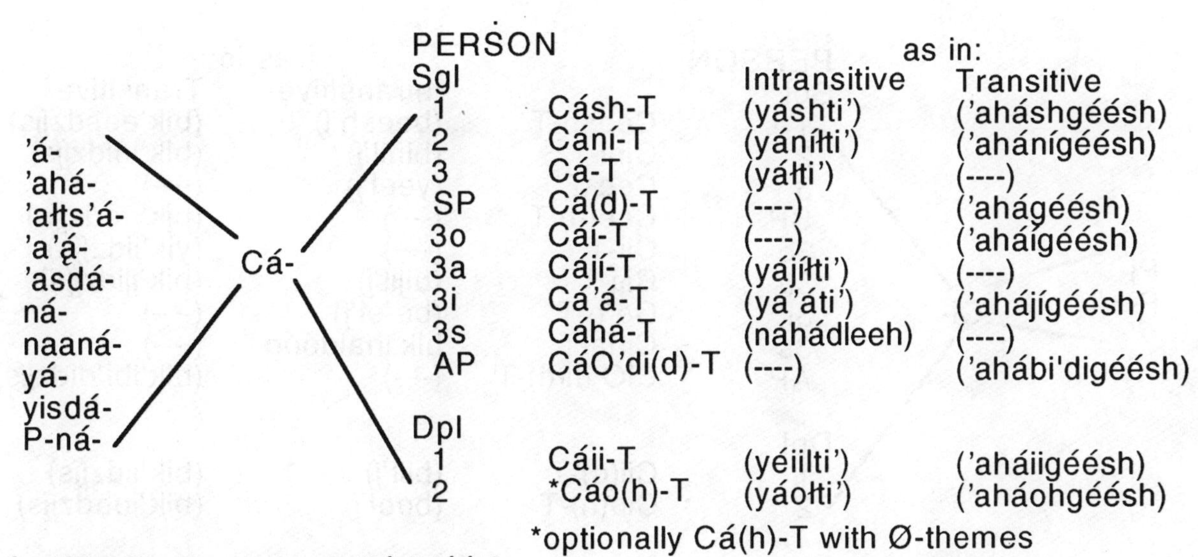


*optionally Cá(h)-T with Ø-themes

'á#-(Ø)--Øleeh: make O ('áshłééh)
yá-#(Ø)--łtį': talk

'ahá#(Ø)--(Ø)géésh: cut O in half ('ahá shgéésh)
'a'ą́#-(Ø)--Øtłíísh: fall into a hole ('a'ą́shtłíísh)
'iih ná#-(d)--(ł)teeh: put AnO back inside ('iih náshteeh)
yisdá-(Ø)--łteeh: rescue O (yisdáshteeh)
'ałts'á#-(Ø)--Øgéésh: cut O apart ('ałts'áshgéésh)
Pi-ná#-(Ø)--Øchid: put arms around P (bináshchid)

## 6. Ce-: Position 1b + Extended Base

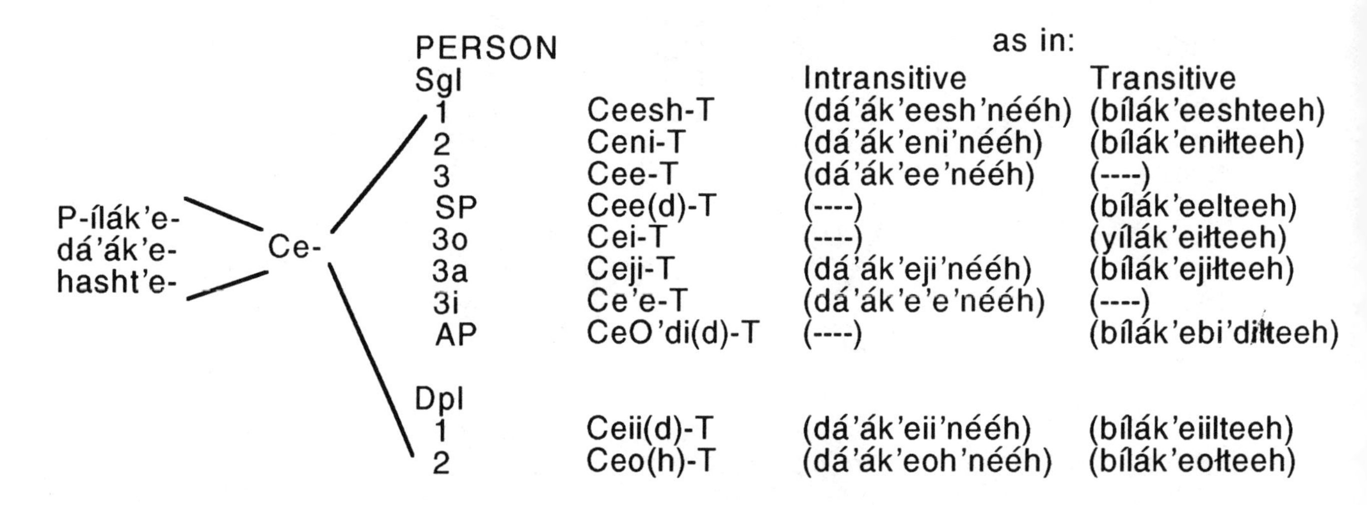


| PERSON | | as in: Intransitive | Transitive |
|---|---|---|---|
| Sgl | | | |
| 1 | Ceesh-T | (dá'ák'eesh'nééh) | (bíłák'eeshteeh) |
| 2 | Ceni-T | (dá'ák'eni'nééh) | (bíłák'eniłteeh) |
| 3 | Cee-T | (dá'ák'ee'nééh) | (----) |
| SP | Cee(d)-T | (----) | (bíłák'eelteeh) |
| 3o | Cei-T | (----) | (yíłák'eiłteeh) |
| 3a | Ceji-T | (dá'ák'eji'nééh) | (bíłák'ejiłteeh) |
| 3i | Ce'e-T | (dá'ák'e'e'nééh) | (----) |
| AP | CeO'di(d)-T | (----) | (bíłák'ebi'diłteeh) |
| Dpl | | | |
| 1 | Ceii(d)-T | (dá'ák'eii'nééh) | (bíłák'eiilteeh) |
| 2 | Ceo(h)-T | (dá'ák'eoh'nééh) | (bíłák'eołteeh) |

dá'ák'e#-(Ø)--(d)'nééh: crawl into a field (dá'ák'eesh'nééh)
bíłák'e#-(Ø)--lteeh: be handed to him (AnO)(bíłák'eelteeh)
hasht'e#-(Ø)--Øléé h: pack O; tidy O up (hasht'eeshłééh)

## 7. Ci-:1a/1b + Extended Base

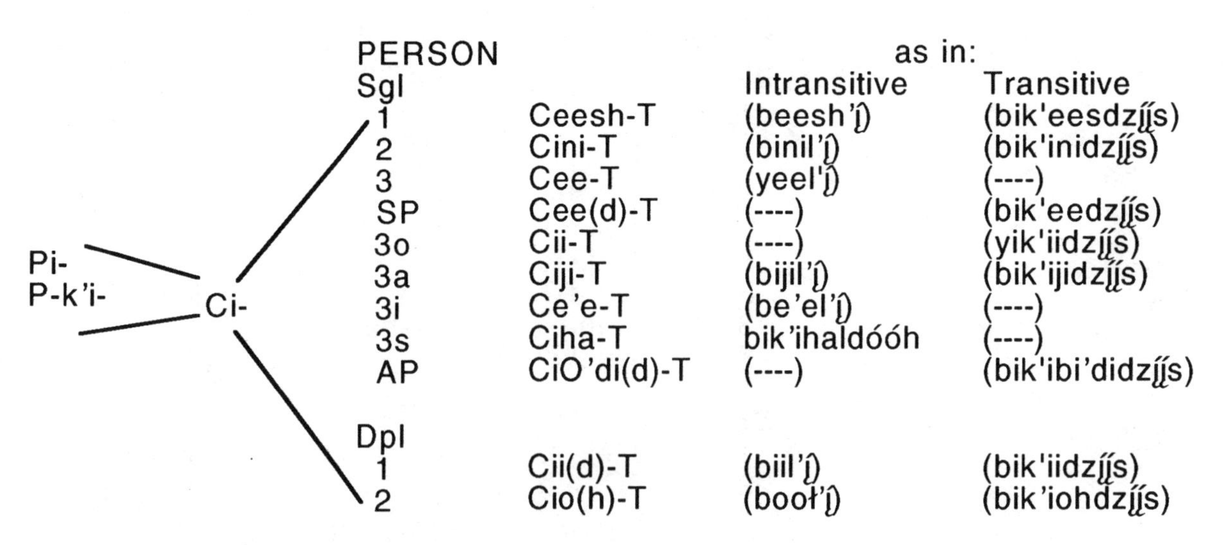


| PERSON | | as in: Intransitive | Transitive |
|---|---|---|---|
| Sgl | | | |
| 1 | Ceesh-T | (beesh'į́) | (bik'eesdzį́į́s) |
| 2 | Cini-T | (binil'į́) | (bik'inidzį́į́s) |
| 3 | Cee-T | (yeel'į́) | (----) |
| SP | Cee(d)-T | (----) | (bik'eedzį́į́s) |
| 3o | Cii-T | (----) | (yik'iidzį́į́s) |
| 3a | Ciji-T | (bijil'į́) | (bik'ijidzį́į́s) |
| 3i | Ce'e-T | (be'el'į́) | (----) |
| 3s | Ciha-T | bik'ihaldóóh | (----) |
| AP | CiO'di(d)-T | (----) | (bik'ibi'didzį́į́s) |
| Dpl | | | |
| 1 | Cii(d)-T | (biil'į́) | (bik'iidzį́į́s) |
| 2 | Cio(h)-T | (booł'į́) | (bik'iohdzį́į́s) |

bi#-(Ø)--l'į́: imitate it (yeel'į́: he imitates it)

bik'i#-(Ø)--(Ø)dzį́į́s: be pulled off of him; pull O off of him (shik'iidzį́į́s: he's pulling him off of me)
bik'i#-(Ø)--Øyóół: blow off of him
bik'i#-(Ø)--ha-ldóóh: feel relieved (lit. "things" waft off of him)

## 8. Cí-:1b + Extended Base

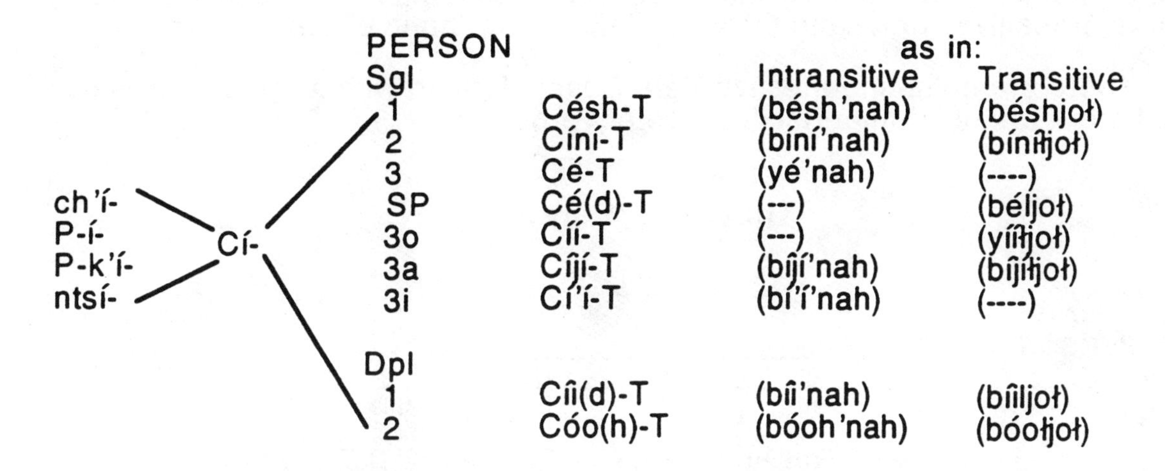


P-í#-(Ø)--(d)'nah: rub against it
P-í#-(Ø)--łjoł: rub NCM against it (béshjoł)
P-k'í-(Ø)--Økaah: pour O onto P (bik'éshkaah)
'adah ch'í#-(Ø)--(d)'nééh: crawl over an edge ('adah ch'ésh'nééh)

## Ø-IMPERFECTIVE NEUTER

There is a small number of verbs, conjugated in a Ø-Imperfective pattern, that function semantically after the fashion of Neuter Verbs. These describe characteristics, attributes or states of being with reference to the subject. They may take the form of the Base Paradigm, or they may take the form of Verb Bases derived with Conjunct 'a-: 3i object pronoun "something unspecified," or with Disjunct 'á-Thematic, and they may be intransitive or transitive.

(yi) - Øwozh: be ticklish (yiwozh: he's ticklish)
(yi) - Ødlee': be generous (baa yishdlee': I'm generous with it)
(yi) - Øt'į: be wealthy in it (property) (nit'į: you're wealthy in it (as in livestock)
'a-Øt'į: be wealthy ('at'į: he's wealthy)
'a-łhosh: be asleep ('ałhosh: he's asleep - probably metaphorical: "he's causing something to bubble").
'a-Ø'į: be fastidious ('ayóo 'a'į: s/he's very fastidious)
'á-Øt'į: be a "doer," be a certain person, guilty ('át'į: he is such and such person, he's to blame etc)l.
'á-ł'į: be a maker of it (kélchííh 'íít'į: he's a moccasinmaker; 'azee' 'íít'į: he's a medicine maker - a doctor)

# 2. THE SI-IMPERFECTIVE

Si-Imperfective describes a verbal action that is incomplete but which, upon completion, will have a static sequel. The si-modal-aspectival conjugation marker of Position 7 appears in 1st and 2nd person constructions exclusively; 3rd persons, along with Simple and Agentive Passives, switch to Ø-Imperfective.

Verb Bases that include a derivational prefix of Position 1(1b, 1d, 1e) occur both intransitive and transitive, but Bases that lack a Position 1 prefix occur as transitives only, and these all employ the “handle” stems.

There are no si-Imperfective Verb Bases derived with a prefix of Position 6, and there are no si-Imperfective Neuter verbs.

## The Base Paradigm

Table 1

| PERSON | Prefix Position | | | | | | | |
|---|---|---|---|---|---|---|---|---|
| Sgl | 7 | + | 8 | + | 9-10 | | | as in: |
| 1. | si- | + | -sh- | + | T | > | shish-T | shishteeh |
| 2. | si- | + | \ ´/- | + | T | > | sí-T | síłteeh |
| SP. | Ø | + | (yi)-Ø-(d)- | + | T | > | yi-Ø-T | yilteeh |
| Dpl | | | | | | | | |
| 1. | s- | + | -ii(d)- | + | T | > | sii(d)-T | siilteeh |
| 2. | s- | + | -o(h)- | + | T | > | so(h)-T | sołteeh |

dah (si)--łteeh: set an AnO up at rest (as a baby on a bed)
dah (si)--Ø’aah: set a SRO up at rest (as a jar on a table)

## The Extended Base Paradigms

### 1. Conjunct Prefixes

None of the pronominal prefixes of Position 5 – all of which are 3rd person – cooccur with si-7. The only Conjunct elements that can cooccur with si- are the direct object pronouns of Position 4. The Extended Base Paradigm is composed partly of Ø-Imperfective constructions, and partly of si-Imperfectives.

Ø/Ci-: Position 4 + Extended Base

Table 2

T = any "handle" Theme

Ø-4 = 3rd person object / 1st or 2nd person subject
Ci-4 = any Ci-prefix of Position 4

| PERSON | Prefix Position | | | | | | as in: | |
|---|---|---|---|---|---|---|---|---|
| Sgl | 4 | + | 5 | + | Base | | + Ø-4 | + Ci-4 |
| 1. | Ø/Ci- | + | ---- | + | -shish-T | > | dah shishteeh | dah nishishteeh |
| 2. | Ø/Ci- | + | ---- | + | -sí-T | > | dah sítteeh | dah shisítteeh |
| 3. | ---/Ci- | + | ---- | + | (yi)-Ø-T | > | ---------- | dah shiłteeh |
| SP | Ø/-- | + | --- | + | (yi)-Ø(d)-T | > | dah yilteeh | --- |
| 3o. | ---/yi- | + | ---- | + | (yi)-Ø-T | > | ---------- | dah yiłteeh |
| 3a. | Ø/Ci- | + | -ji- | + | (yi)-Ø-T | > | dah jiłteeh | dah shijiłteeh |
| AP. | ---/Ci | + | -'(a)di- | + | (yi)-Ø-(d)-T | > | ---------- | dah bi'dilteeh |
| Dpl | | | | | | | | |
| 1. | Ø/Ci- | + | ---- | + | sii(d)-T | > | dah siilteeh | dah nisiilteeh |
| 2. | Ø/Ci- | + | ---- | + | so(h)-T | > | dah sołteeh | dah shisołteeh |

dah (si)--łteeh: set an AnO up at rest (as on a bed or table) (dah nishishteeh: I'm setting you up at rest / dah shisíłteeh: you're setting me up at rest / dah shiłteeh: he's setting me up at rest / dah bi'dilteeh: he's being set up at rest)
dah (si)--Ø'aah: set a SRO up at rest (as a book on a shelf)
dah (si)--Økaah: set an open container and its contents up at rest (as a bowl of food on a table)

'A-: Position 4 + Extended Base

The 3i object pronoun 'a-: "something unspecified," occurs in several "idiomatic" Verb Bases.

Table 3

T = any Verb Theme

| PERSON | Prefix Position | | | Base | | | as in: |
|---|---|---|---|---|---|---|---|
| Sgl | 4 | + | 5 | | | | |
| 1. | 'a- | + | --- | -shish-T | > | 'ashish-T | bił dah 'ashish'aah |
| 2. | 'a- | + | --- | -sí-T | > | 'así-T | bił dah 'así'aah |
| 3. | 'a- | + | --- | (yi)-Ø-T | > | 'a-Ø-T | yił dah 'a'aah |
| SP. | 'a | | ----- | (yi)-Ø-(d)-T | > | 'a-Ø(d)-T | bił dah 'at'aah |
| 3a. | 'a | + | -ji- | (yi)-Ø-T | > | 'aji-T | bił dah 'aji'aah |
| Dpl | | | | | | | |
| 1. | 'a- | + | --- | -sii(d)-T | > | 'asii(d)-T | bił dah 'asiit'aah |
| 2. | 'a- | + | --- | -so(h)-T | > | 'aso(h)-T | bił dah 'asoh'aah |

bił dah 'a-(si)--Ø'aah: lock with a padlock (literally: place an unspecified SRO up at rest in company with it – "it" is the door)
dah 'a-(si)--łbaał: put up an awning (literally: place something fabric-like up at rest)

biɫ dah 'a-(si)--Øníɫ: button it up (as a shirt) (literally: place unspecified PIO up at rest in company with it - "it" is the garment buttoned)

The prefix vowel of 'a- deletes in the presence of a preceding prefix, as in:

dah da'siilbaaɫ (< dah da'(a)siilbaaɫ: we 3+ are putting up an awning)
biɫ dah ní'siit'aah (< ní'(a)siit'aah): we 3+ are relocking the door)

<u>Ho-: Position 4 + Extended Base</u>

The 3s object pronoun of Position 4 occurs, with the idiomatic meaning "trouble," in a single si-Imperfective Verb Base. It is conjugated in the pattern set forth below.

<u>Table 4</u>

T = any Verb Theme

| PERSON | Prefix Position | | | | | | |
|---|---|---|---|---|---|---|---|
| Sgl | 4 | + | 5 + | Base | | | as in: |
| 1. | ho- | + | --- | -shish-T | > | hoshish-T | 'ádą̨h dah hoshisht'aah |
| 2. | ho- | + | --- | -sí-T | > | hosí-T | 'ádą̨h dah hosít'aah |
| 3. | ha- | + | --- | (yi)-Ø-T | > | ha-Ø-T | 'ádą̨h dah hat'aah |
| 3a. | ho- | + | -ji- | (yi)-Ø-T | > | hoji-T | 'ádą̨h dah hojit'aah |
| Dpl | | | | | | | |
| 1. | ho | + | --- | -sii(d)- | > | hosii(d)-T | 'ádą̨h dah hosiit'aah |
| 2. | ho | + | --- | -so(h)-T | > | hoso(h)-T | 'ádą̨h dah hosoht'aah |

'ádą̨h dah ho-(si)--(d)t'aah: commit a crime; do a wrong, break the law (literally: place a trouble at rest up alongside self. Cf. 'ádą̨h dah shisht'aah: pin a SRO - as a brooch- on oneself.)

## 2. Disjunct Prefixes

Disjunct derivatives of the si-Imperfective are limited to da-Position 3, the marker of distributive plural number; ha-Position 1b: "up, up out;" ná-Position 1d: Reversionary "returning back (to a previous condition or location)," and Semeliterative náá-Position 1e: "once again."

The Disjunct derivatives occur in both intransitive and transitive Verb Bases.

## Da-Position 3 + Extended Base

### Table 1

T = any Verb Theme

| PERSON | Prefix Position | | | | | | | | | |
|---|---|---|---|---|---|---|---|---|---|---|
| Dist. Plur. | 3 | + | 4 | + | 5 | + | Base | | | as in: |
| 1. | da- | + | Ø | + | ---- | | -sii(d)-T | > | dasii(d)-T | dah dasiilteeh |
| 2. | da- | + | Ø | + | ---- | | -so(h)-T | > | daso(h)-T | dah dasołteeh |
| 3o. | de- | + | -i- | + | ---- | | -(yi)-Ø-T | > | dei-Ø-T | dah deiłteeh |
| 3a. | da- | + | Ø | + | -ji- | | -(yi)-Ø-T | > | daji-T | dah dajiłteeh |

dah da-(si)--łteeh: 3+ subjects set an AnO up at rest

## Ha-: Position 1b + Extended Base

### Table 2

T = any Verb Theme

| PERSON | Prefix Position | | | | | | | | | as in: | |
|---|---|---|---|---|---|---|---|---|---|---|---|
| Sgl | 1b | + | 4 | + | 5 | + | Base | | | Intransitive | Transitive |
| 1. | ha- | + | Ø | + | --- | + | -shish--T | > | hashish-T | hashish'nééh | hashishteeh |
| 2. | ha- | + | Ø | + | --- | + | -sí-T | > | hasí-T | hasí'nééh | hasíłteeh |
| 3. | haa- | + | --- | + | --- | + | (yi)-Ø-T | > | haa-Ø-T | haa'nééh | --------- |
| SP. | haa- | + | Ø | + | --- | + | (yi)-Ø-(d)-T | > | haa-Ø-T | --------- | haalteeh |
| 3o. | ha- | + | -i- | + | --- | + | (yi)-Ø-T | > | hai-T | --------- | haiłteeh |
| 3a. | ha- | + | Ø | + | -ji- | + | (yi)-Ø-T | > | haji-T | haji'nééh | hajiłteeh |
| 3i. | ha- | + | --- | + | -'a- | + | (yi)-Ø-T | > | ha'a-T | ha'a'nééh | --- |
| AP. | ha- | + | O | + | -'(a)di- | + | (yi)-Ø-T | > | haO'di-T | --- | habi'dilteeh |
| Dpl | | | | | | | | | | | |
| 1. | ha- | + | Ø | + | --- | + | -sii(d)-T | > | hasii(d)-T | hasii'nééh | hasiilteeh |
| 2. | ha- | + | Ø | + | --- | + | -so(h)-T | > | haso(h)-T | hasoh'nééh | hasołteeh |

bąąh ha-(si)--(d)'nééh: climb it (as a tree)
bąąh ha-(si)--łteeh: climb up carrying an AnO
ha-(si)--Øgháah: climb up (sgl subject - up a hill, ladder) (hashisháah: I'm climbing up; hasínááh: you're climbing up; haagháah: he's climbing up)

## Háá- ~ ha-ná-Position 1b + 1d + Extended Base

Ha-Position 1b contracts with Reversionary ná-Position 1d to produce háá-, and the contracted form appears in all constructions except in 3 and 3o persons and Simple Passive, where Position 8 is vacant. In these ná-reemerges.

Háá- ~ ha-ná- follows a pattern closely paralleling that of Semeliterative náá- ~ náá-ná-, in the paradigm.

<u>Table 3</u>

T = any Verb Theme

| PERSON | Prefix Position | | | | | | | | | as in: | |
|---|---|---|---|---|---|---|---|---|---|---|---|
| Sgl | 1b+1d | + | 4 | + | 5 | + | Base | | | Intransitive | Transitive |
| 1. | háá- | + | Ø | + | ---- | + | -shish-T | > | hááshísh-T | hááshísh'nééh | hááshíshteeh |
| 2 | háá- | + | Ø | + | ---- | + | -sí-T | > | háásí-T | háásí'nééh | háásíłteeh |
| 3. | ha-ná | + | --- | + | ---- | + | (yi)-Ø-T | > | haná-Ø-T | haná'nééh | --- |
| SP. | ha-ná- | + | Ø | + | ---- | + | (yi)-Ø-(d)-T | > | haná-Ø-T | --------- | hanálteeh |
| 3o. | ha-ná- | + | -í- | + | ---- | + | (yi)-Ø-T | > | hanéi- l | --------- | hanéíłteeh |
| 3a. | háá- | + | Ø | + | -jí- | + | (yi)-Ø-T | > | háájí-T | háájí'nééh | háájíłteeh |
| 3i. | háá- | + | --- | + | -'á- | + | (yi)-Ø-T | > | háá'ą́-T | háá'á'nééh | ---- |
| AP | háá- | + | O | + | -'(a)di- | + | (yi)-Ø-(d)-T | > | hááO'di-T | -------- | háábi'dilteeh |
| Dpl | | | | | | | | | | | |
| 1. | háá- | + | Ø | + | ---- | + | -sii(d)-T | > | háásii(d)-T | háásii'nééh | háásiilteeh |
| 2. | háá- | + | Ø | + | ---- | + | -so(h)-T | > | háásó(h)-T | háásóh'nééh | háásółteeh |

bąąh háá-(si)--(d)'nééh: climb back up it (as a tree)
bąąh háá-(si)--łteeh: climb back up carrying an AnO

## RECAPITULATION

### 1. Extended Base Paradigm

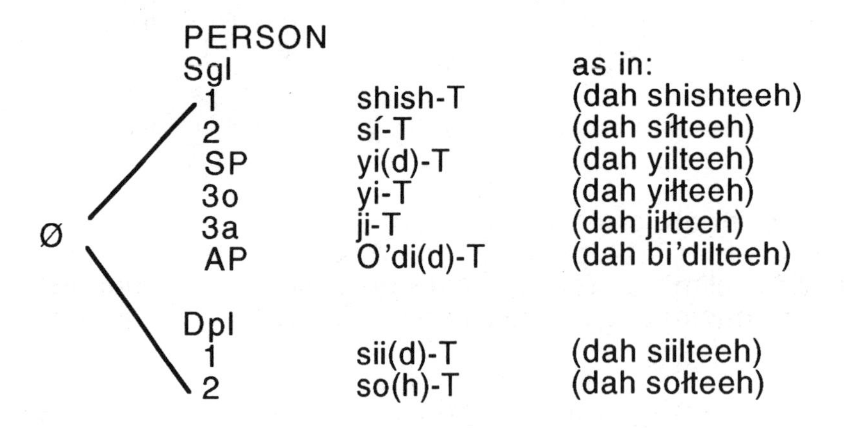


dah (si/Ø)--łteeh: set AnO up at rest (dah shishteeh)

## *CONJUNCT PREFIXES*

### 2. Conjunct + Extended Base

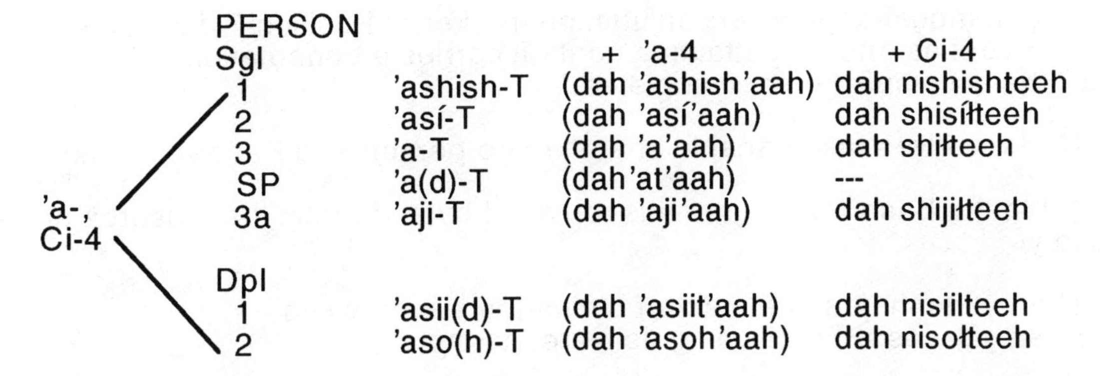

| | PERSON | | + 'a-4 | + Ci-4 |
|---|---|---|---|---|
| 'a-, Ci-4 | Sgl | | | |
| | 1 | 'ashish-T | (dah 'ashish'aah) | dah nishishteeh |
| | 2 | 'así-T | (dah 'así'aah) | dah shisíłteeh |
| | 3 | 'a-T | (dah 'a'aah) | dah shiłteeh |
| | SP | 'a(d)-T | (dah'at'aah) | --- |
| | 3a | 'aji-T | (dah 'aji'aah) | dah shijiłteeh |
| | Dpl | | | |
| | 1 | 'asii(d)-T | (dah 'asiit'aah) | dah nisiilteeh |
| | 2 | 'aso(h)-T | (dah 'asoh'aah) | dah nisołteeh |

bił dah 'a-(si/Ø)--Ø'aah: padlock it (a door - literally: place unspecified SRO up at rest in company with it)
dah ni-(si)--łteeh: set you up at rest (dah nishishteeh: I'm setting you up at rest)

## *DISJUNCT PREFIXES*

### 3. Ca- Prefixes + Extended Base

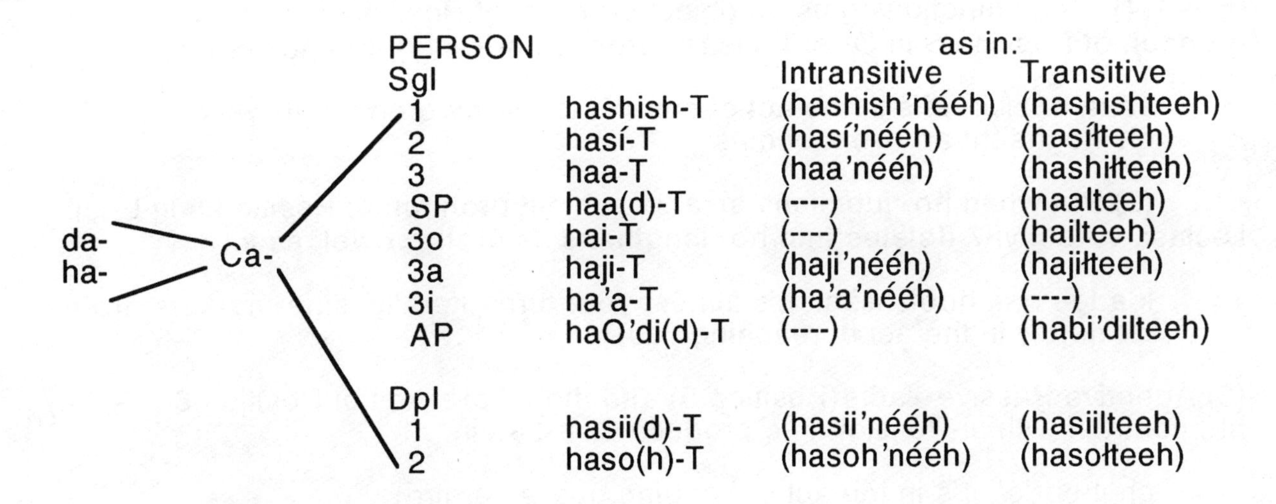

| | | PERSON | | as in: Intransitive | Transitive |
|---|---|---|---|---|---|
| da-, ha- | Ca- | Sgl | | | |
| | | 1 | hashish-T | (hashish'nééh) | (hashishteeh) |
| | | 2 | hasí-T | (hasí'nééh) | (hasíłteeh) |
| | | 3 | haa-T | (haa'nééh) | (hashiłteeh) |
| | | SP | haa(d)-T | (----) | (haalteeh) |
| | | 3o | hai-T | (----) | (hailteeh) |
| | | 3a | haji-T | (haji'nééh) | (hajiłteeh) |
| | | 3i | ha'a-T | (ha'a'nééh) | (----) |
| | | AP | haO'di(d)-T | (----) | (habi'dilteeh) |
| | | Dpl | | | |
| | | 1 | hasii(d)-T | (hasii'nééh) | (hasiilteeh) |
| | | 2 | haso(h)-T | (hasoh'nééh) | (hasołteeh) |

ha#-(si)--(d)'nééh: climb up
ha#-(si)--lteeh: be carried up (AnO)

# 3. THE NI-IMPERFECTIVE

## *ACTIVE VERBS*

The ni-modal-aspectival conjugation marker of Position 7 describes an action or event as one that attains a goal - it carries a connotation of "finish," "arrive," "be accomplished or completed."

Ni-derivatives take variable shape in 3rd person and Passive forms:

(1) In the Base Paradigm ni- is replaced by a yi-prefix that absorbs ni- to produce yí-.

shaa yí'nééh: it's in the act of coming to me crawling
shaa yíłtsóós: FFO is being delivered to me

(2) The Ci-prefixes of Position 4 delete the prefix vowel and take the form C-í- in combination with (y)-í-7.

naa sh-íłteeh: he's in the act of delivering me to you
shaa y-íłteeh: he's in the act of delivering it (an AnO) to me

(3) Similarly, the Position 5 prefixes 3a j-/ji- and 3i '-/'i- appear as j- and as '- respectively in combination with (y)í-7, as in:

shaa j-íłteeh: he's in the act of delivering an AnO to me
shił '-ílyeed: I'm in the act of arriving by unspecified fast moving vehicle (literally: something unspecified is in the act of arriving running with me)

(4) When functioning as an <u>object</u> pronoun of Position 4, or as a subject pronoun of Position 5 in Ø- or Ł-class verbs, 3s ho- + (y)í-7 > hó, as in:

shaa hóziíd: he's in the act of coming to me by groping his way
ch'íhógháah: an event begins

(5) But when ho- functions as a 3s <u>subject</u> pronoun of Position 5 in L- or D-class verbs, yí-7 deletes and ho- lengthens its prefix vowel, as in:

k'adę́ę naa hoolzhíísh: it's almost your turn (literally: time-markers are nearly in the act of reaching you)

(6) Agentive Passive -'adi- (Position 5) and the Ci-prefixes of Position 6 (di-, hi-, ni-) contract with ni-Position 7 to produce Cee-, as in:

ch'íheet'e': it's in the act of hopping out (as a bird)
shaa yidee'aah: he's relinquishing it to me (as land)
shaa deet'aah: it's being relinquished to me
ch'ídeeldlóóh: it's in the act of smiling
nineet'aah: he's in the act of putting his head down
ch'íbi'deelteeh: he's being carried out

## Base Paradigm

Table 1

T = any Verb Theme

| PERSON | Prefix Position | | | | | | | |
|---|---|---|---|---|---|---|---|---|
| Sgl | 7 | + | 8 | + | 9-10 | | | as in: |
| 1. | ni- | + | -sh- | + | T | > | nish-T | nish'nééh |
| 2. | ni- | + | \ ´ / | + | T | > | ní-T | ní'nééh |
| 3. | yí- | + | Ø | + | T | > | yí-T | yí'nééh |
| SP | yí- | + | Ø-(d)- | + | T | > | yí- | yíłtsóós |
| Dpl | | | | | | | | |
| 1. | n- | + | -ii(d)- | + | T | > | nii(d)-T | nii'nééh |
| 2. | n- | + | -o(h)- | + | T | > | no(h)-T | noh'nééh |

(ni)--(d)'nééh: arrive crawling
(ni)--Ø'eeł: arrive floating
(ni)--Ø'aah, P-aa --: give SRO to P
(ni)--łtsóós: arrive carrying a FFO
(ni)--łteeh: arrive carrying an AnO
(ni)--Ønééh: arrive moving with household
(ni)--łkááh: arrive tracking O
(SP yíłtsóós: FFO is being delivered)

## The Extended Base Paradigms

### 1. Conjunct Prefixes

The Conjunct derivatives of the Ni-Imperfective include all constructions in which a prefix of Position 4, 5 or 6 functions as the conjugational determinant. With the exceptions noted above with reference to 3rd person and Passive constructions, juncture of the Conjunct Prefixes with the Base Paradigm is quite straightforward.

Prefixes of Position 5 + Base

Table 2

T = any Verb Theme

| PERSON | Prefix Position | | | | | |
|---|---|---|---|---|---|---|
| Sgl | 5 | + | Base | | | as in: |
| 3a (4) | j- | + | (y)í-T | > | jí-T | jí'nééh |
| 3i | '- | + | (y)í-T | > | 'í-T | 'í'nééh |
| 3s | ho- | + | (y)í-T | > | hoo-T (-hó-T) | hoolzhíísh (ch'í#hóghááh) |
| AP | -'(a)d- | + | -ee-T | > | -'(a)dee-T | bi'deelteeh |

jí'nééh: he/she arrives crawling
'i'nééh: something arrives crawling (shił 'i'nééh: I arrive by slow vehicle)
baa hoolzhíísh: his turn is about to come
ch'íhóghááh: an event begins
shaa bi'deelteeh: he's being brought/given to me

## Ø/Ci- Prefixes of Positions 4 and 5 + Base

### Table 3

T = any Verb Theme

| PERSON | Prefix Position | | | | | | | |
|---|---|---|---|---|---|---|---|---|
| Sgl | 4 | + | 5 | + | Base | | Ø-4 | Ci-4 |
| 1. | Ø/Ci- | + | --- | + | -nish-T | > | nisłóós | ninisłóós |
| 2. | Ø/Ci- | + | --- | + | -ní-T | > | nílóós | shinílóós |
| SP | Ø/--- | + | --- | + | -yí-(d)-T | > | yídlóós | --- |
| 3. | ---/C(i)- | + | --- | + | (y)í-T | > | --- | shílóós |
| 3o | --/y(i)- | + | --- | + | -(y)í-T | > | --- | yílóós |
| 3a | Ø/Ci- | + | -j- | + | -(y)í-T | > | jílóós | shijílóós |
| AP | O | + | -'(a)d- | + | -ee-(d)-T | > | --- | bi'deedlóós |
| Dpl | | | | | | | | |
| 1. | Ø/Ci- | + | --- | + | -nii(d)-T | > | niidlóós | niniidlóós |
| 2. | Ø/Ci- | + | --- | + | -no(h)-T | > | nohłóós | shinohłóós |

(ni)--łteeh: arrive carrying an AnO; bring or give an AnO
(ni)--Ø'aah: arrive carrying a SRO; bring or give a SRO
(ni)--Ølóós: arrive leading one O; bring O by leading
(ni)--Ø'éésh: arrive leading PlO; bring PlO by leading
(ni)--łbą́ą́s: arrive driving O (car, wagon)

## Ci- Prefixes of Positions 6a/6b + Extended Base

The Ci-prefixes of Position 6 that appear in ni-Imperfective verbs include: di-, dzi-, hi-: Position 6a; and ni-Position 6b.

### Table 4

T = any Verb Theme

| PERSON | Prefix Position | | | | | | | | | as in: | |
|---|---|---|---|---|---|---|---|---|---|---|---|
| Sgl | 4 | + | 5 | + | 6a/b | + | Base | > | Intransitive | Transitive | |
| 1. | Ø/Ci- | + | ---- | + | Ci- | + | Cinish-T | > | dinishtaał | dinish'aah | ninissóód |
| 2. | Ø/Ci- | + | ---- | + | Ci- | + | Ciní-T | > | dinítaał | diní'aah | niníyóód |
| 3. | ---- | + | ---- | + | C- | + | Cee T | > | deeltaał | --- | --- |
| SP | Ø/--- | + | ---- | + | C- | + | Cee(d)-T | > | --- | deet'aah | needzóód |
| 3o | --yi- | + | ---- | + | C- | + | Cee-T | > | --- | yidee'aah | yineeyóód |
| 3a | Ø/Ci- | + | -j- | + | C- | + | Cee-T | > | jideeltaał | jidee'aah | jineeyóód |
| Dpl | | | | | | | | | | | |
| 1. | Ø/Ci- | + | ---- | + | Ci- | + | Cinii(d)-T | > | diniiltaał | diniit'aah | niniidzóód |
| 2. | Ø/Ci- | + | ---- | + | Ci- | + | Cino(h)-T | > | dinołtaał | dinoh'aah | ninohsóód |

di-(ni)--ltaał, P-jáátah ---: trip P with one's foot
di-(ni)--Ø'aah, P-aa ---: turn O over to P; relinquish O to P
di-(ni)--Øtį́į́h, 'ą́ą ---: open O (a door)
di-(ni)--łkeed, 'ą́ą- ---: open O, slide O open (window, pocket door)
ni-(ni)--Øyóód: drive O (a few animals or people) (yineeyóód: he drives them)
ni-(ni)--łkaad: drive O (a herd) (yineełkaad: he drives it)
Pi-#-di-(ni)--lnííh: touch, place hand on Pi-1a (bidinishnííh: I place my hand on it; yideelnííh: he places his hand on it)

ni#-di-(ni)--lchííd, bik'i ---: put hand down on it (yik'i ndeelchííd: he puts his hand down on it)
Pi-#-di-(ni)--lchííd: poke P with hand or finger (yideelchííd: he's in the act of poking him)

The complex constructions listed below are derived with the addition of a *Disjunct* Prefix, but they are conjugated in the pattern outlined above: # marks the Conjunct/Disjunct boundary.

ch'í#-di-(ni)--łdą́ą́sh: jerk O out (a recalcitrant animal or person) (ch'íideełdą́ą́sh: he jerks it out)
ch'í#-di-(ni)--Øzóóh: spit O out (ch'íideezóóh: he spits it out)
ch'í#-di-(ni)--lnííh: stick one's arm out (as out a window)
ch'í#-di-(ni)---Ø'aah: make O available for a purpose; appropriate O (as money) (ch'íidee'aah)
ch'í#-di-(ni)--ldlóóh: smile, chuckle ((ch'ídeeldlóóh: he chuckles, smiles)
n#-di-(ni)--Ø'aah: make O available for a purpose, appropriate O (as money); finish singing it (a song) (niidee'aah: he finishes it)
n#-di-(ni)--łtsóós, hasht'e'---: place FFO in readiness; store FFO (a document) (niideełtsóós)

## Dzi- ~ ji- ~ -z- ~ -zh-: Position 6a + Extended Base

Dzi-: Position 6a and its allomorphs: "away into space," appears in combination with ni-Position 1b: "cessative-terminative," in a group of Verb Bases that are conjugated as Ni-Imperfectives. # marks the Conjunct/Disjunct boundary.

The postposition -ił: "in company with," is a component of the Verb Base. Literally, the subject "strikes terminatively with fists away into space in company with P" (P is the victim, represented by the pronoun object of the postposition).

Table 5

T = any Verb Theme

| PERSON | Prefix Position | | | | | | | | | |
|---|---|---|---|---|---|---|---|---|---|---|
| Sgl | 1b | + | 5 | + | 6a | + | Base | > | | as in: |
| 1. | ni-# | + | ---- | + | -zh- | + | -nish-T | > | nizhnish-T | nizhnists'in |
| 2. | ni-# | + | ---- | + | -z- | + | ní-T | > | nizní-T | nizníłts'in |
| 3. | ni-# | + | ---- | + | dz- | + | (y)í T | > | ndzí-T | ndzíłts'in |
| 3a | n-# | + | -ii- | + | -j- | + | -(y)í-T | > | niijí-T | niijíłts'in |
| SP | n-# | + | ---- | + | dz- | + | -(y)-í-(d)-T | > | ndzí-T | ndzílts'in |
| Dpl | | | | | | | | | | |
| 1. | ni-# | + | ---- | + | -z- | + | -nii(d)-T | > | niznii(d)-T | nizniilts'in |
| 2. | ni-# | + | ---- | + | -z- | + | -no(h)-T | > | nizno(h)-T | niznołts'in |

ni#-dzi-(ni)--łts'in, P-ił ---: beat P up with one's fists; lay P out
ni#-dzi-(ni)--łhaał, P-ił ---: club P to death
ni#-dzi-(ni)--Øtaał, P-ił ---: give P a kicking; kick P to death
ni#-dzi-(ni)--łne', P-ił ---: stone P to death

Conjugated in a similar pattern are derived Verb bases of the type listed below:

'ahá-bí#-dzi-(ni)--łtaał: kick O apart (as a box)
bighá#-dzi-(ni)--łne': throw a SRO through it (as a stone through a window)
bighá#-dzi-(ni)--Øtaał: kick a hole in it
bighá#-dzi-(ni)--łhaał: bat a hole through it (with a club)

## Seriative hi-: Position 6a ~ yi-6c + Extended Base

Seriative hi- and its yi-allomorph of Position 6c, in ni-Imperfective constructions, appears primarily in Verb Bases in which the Stem describes inherently segmented action as in "hop, skip, move on one's rump or belly." The allomorph is required when hi- is preceded by a prefix of Position 5.

Table 6

T = any Verb Theme

| PERSON | Prefix Position | | | | | | | |
|---|---|---|---|---|---|---|---|---|
| Sgl | 5 | + | 6a/6c | + | Base | > | | as in: |
| 1. | ---- | + | hi-/--- | + | -nish-T | > | hinish-T | hinisht'e' |
| 2. | ---- | + | hi-/--- | + | ní-T | > | hiní-T | hiníťe' |
| 3. | ---- | + | h-/--- | + | -ee-T | > | hee-T | heet'e' |
| 3a | -ji- | + | ---/-y- | + | -ee-T | > | jiyeeT | jiyeet'e' |
| Dpl | | | | | | | | |
| 1. | ---- | + | hi/--- | + | -nii(d)-T | > | hinii(d)-T | hiniit'e' |
| 2. | ---- | + | hi/--- | + | -no(h)-T | > | hino(h)-T | hinoht'e' |

hi-(ni)--(d)t'e': arrive hopping

hi-(ni)-lghaał: arrive wriggling on belly

## 'A- ~ -'-: Position 4 + Base

The 3i object pronoun 'a-Position 4: "something unspecified," retains its base shape throughout the simple ni-Imperfective paradigm, except in 3rd person, where it reduces to its initial consonant -'- before (y)í-.

When 'a- is preceded by a Disjunct Prefix it reduces to -'- as in:

ch'í'nísbąąs (< ch'í-1b + '[a]-4 + -nisbąąs): I'm driving out (an unspecified vehicle - as out of a garage or canyon)
da'niilbąąs (< da-3 + '[a]-4 + -niilbaąs): we 3+ are in the act of arriving by unspecified wheeled vehicle

When the Verb Base includes a Disjunct Prefix + a Prefix of Position 6, 'a- reduces to -'- and moves to the right of the Position 6 element except in 3a (4th) person, as:

badi'nish'aah = ba-'adinish'aah: I'm giving him permission
bazh'dee'aah = ba-'ajidee'aah): he's giving him permission

ch'ídi'nishdlaad = ch'í-'adinishdlaad: I'm shining a light out (as out a doorway)
ch'ízh'deeɬdlaad = ch'í-'ajideeɬdlaad: he's shining a light out

Table 7

T = any Verb Theme

| PERSON Sgl | Prefix Position 4 | + | 5 | + | Base | > | | as in: |
|---|---|---|---|---|---|---|---|---|
| 1. | 'a- | + | --- | + | -nish-T | > | 'anish-T | 'anishkǫ́ǫ́h |
| 2. | 'a- | + | --- | + | ní-T | > | 'aní-T | 'aníɬkǫ́ǫ́h |
| 3. | '- | + | --- | + | (y)-í--T | > | 'í--T | 'íɬkǫ́ǫ́h |
| 3a | 'a- | + | -j- | + | (y)-í--T | > | 'ají-T | 'ajíɬkǫ́ǫ́h |
| Dpl | | | | | | | | |
| 1. | 'a- | + | --- | + | -nii(d)-T | > | 'anii(d)-T | 'aniilkǫ́ǫ́h |
| 2. | 'a- | + | --- | + | -no(h)-T | > | 'ano(h)-T | 'anoɬkǫ́ǫ́h |

'a-(ni)--ɬkǫǫh: arrive swimming
'a-(ni)-ɬbąąs: arrive driving (unspecified O)
'a-(ni)--ɬ'eeɬ: arrive by boat (i.e. by sailing or paddling unspecified O)
P-a#-'(a)-(ni)--Ø'aah: lend a SRO to P (ba'nish'aah: I lend O to him)
P-a#-di-'(a)-(ni)--Ø'aah (< P-a#-'a-di-[ni]--Ø'aah): permit P to do something. (Literally: relinquish unspecified SRO to P. Cf. baa dinish'aah: I relinquish it to him.)
ch'í#-di-'(a)-(ni)--Ø'aah (<ch'í#-'a-di-[ni]--Ø'aah): make an appropriation – setting aside unspecified O for a purpose. Cf. ch'í#-di-[ni]--Ø'aah: appropriate O)
ch'í#-di-'(a)-(ni)--ɬdlaad (< ch'í#-'a-di-[ni]--ɬdlaad): shine it out (a light).

## Ho-: Position 4 + Extended Base

Ho-Position 4, the 3s object pronoun + -(y)-í- in the 3rd person of ni-Imperfective constructions combine to produce hó-.

Table 8

T = any Verb Theme

| PERSON Sgl | Prefix Position 4 | + | 5 | + | Base | > | | as in: |
|---|---|---|---|---|---|---|---|---|
| 1. | ho- | + | --- | + | -nish-T | > | honish-T | honissííd |
| 2. | ho- | + | --- | + | ní-T | > | honí-T | honízííd |
| 3. | ho- | + | --- | + | (y)-í--T | > | hó-T | hózííd |
| 3a | ho- | + | -j- | + | (y)-í--T | > | hojí-T | hojízííd |
| Dpl | | | | | | | | |
| 1. | ho- | + | --- | + | -nii(d)-T | > | honii(d)-T | honiidzííd |
| 2. | ho- | + | --- | + | -no(h)-T | > | hono(h)-T | honohsííd |

ho-(ni)-Øzíid: go or arrive groping one's way
ho-(ni)-Ølį́į́h: come, arrive, appear

ch'í#-ho-(ni)-shóóh (<ɬzhóóh): sweep area out
ch'í#-ha-(ni)-lzhóóh: area is being swept out

## 2. Disjunct Prefixes

The Disjunct derivatives of the Ni-Imperfective include all verb constructions in which a derivational-thematic prefix of Position 1 or the marker of distributive plurality in Position 3 function as the conjugational determinant; secondarily, Verb Bases in which a prefix complex also includes a Conjunct element.

The tables that follow reflect the behavior of these elements in conjunction with prefixes of Positions 4 and 5, as well as in conjunction with those of the Base Paradigm proper.

Actually, the ni-modal-aspectival conjugation marker of Position 7 triggers few morphophonemic alternations in the ni-Imperfective Mode. Those that occur include:

(1) Yí-, representing ni-7 in 3rd person and Simple Passive constructions, deletes when it is immediately preceded by a prefix of Position 1. If the Position 1 prefix is low in tone, its vowel lengthens. Compare:

yílyeed: it's in the act of arriving running
shaa yíltsóós: FFO is being delivered to me

+ High tone prefix-

CV́-Position 1 + (yí-) = CV́, as:

nályeed (< ná-1d + [yí-]lyeed): it's in the act of returning at a run
ch'élteeh (< ch'í-1b + [yí-]lteeh): it (AnO is being carried out)
ch'élyeed (< ch'í-1b + [yí-]lyeed): it's in the act of running out

-but low tone prefix-

CV-Position 1 + (yí-) = CVV, as:
bighaat'aah (<bigha-1b + [yí-]t'aah: it (SRO) is being taken away from him
ni' niit'aah (< ni-1b + [yí-]t'aah): it (SRO) is being set down
niiltłáád (< ni-1b + [yí-]ltłáád): it's in the act of stopping

(2) Da-Position 3, the marker of distributive plural does not behave like a low tone Disjunct Prefix of Position 1b. In the presence of da-, (y)í-7 remains, and da- does not lengthen the prefix vowel. Thus:

ch'ídeí'nééh: they (3+) are crawling out
'ańt'i' yighádeí'nééh: they (3+) are crawling through the fence
ndeílníísh: they (3+) are in the act of quitting work

(3) A high tone -í-prefix vowel takes the shape -é- in 3rd person and Simple Passive constructions, where yí- deletes and Position 8 is vacant:

ch'é'nééh (<ch'í-1b + [yí-][d]'nééh)
k'égéésh (< k'í-1b + [yí-][d]géésh): it's being cut off

## Da-Position 3 + Extended Base

Da-Position 3 marks distributive plurality - each of 3 or more subjects. Da- > de- before a following -i- but otherwise, as the conjugational determinant, it is simply joined to the dpl forms of the ni-Imperfective paradigm.

### Table 1

T = any Verb Theme

| PERSON | Prefix Position | | | | | | | | | | |
|---|---|---|---|---|---|---|---|---|---|---|---|
| Dist. Pl. | 3 | + | 4 | + | 5 | + | Base | | | as in: | |
| 1. | da- | + | Ø | + | --- | + | -nii(d)-T | > | danii(d)-T | danii'nééh | daniilteeh |
| 2. | da- | + | Ø | + | --- | + | -no(h)-T | > | dano(h)-T | danoh'nééh | danołteeh |
| 3. | da- | + | Ø | + | --- | + | (y)-í--T | > | deí--T | deí'nééh | ---- |
| 3o | da- | + | (y)- | + | --- | + | (y)-í--T | > | de(y)íT | ---- | deíłteeh |
| 3a | da- | + | Ø | + | -j- | + | (y)-í--T | > | dají-T | dají'nééh | dajíłteeh |

da#-(ni)--łteeh: dist. pl. subjects carry an AnO
da#-(ni)---(d)'nééh: dist pl. subjects move (arrive crawling)

## Ca-:Position 1b + Extended Base

The only available Verb Bases that are derived with a Ca-Disjunct Prefix of Position 1b are those produced with the bound postpositional prefix P-gha-: "away from P by force." "Take O away from P," P-gha- always requires D- or L-classifier.

### Table 2

T = any Verb Theme

| PERSON | Prefix Position | | | | | | | | | |
|---|---|---|---|---|---|---|---|---|---|---|
| Sgl | 1b | + | 4 | + | 5 | + | Base | | | as in: |
| 1. | Ca- | + | Ø | + | --- | | -nish-T | > | Canish-T | bighanisht'aah |
| 2. | Ca- | + | Ø | + | --- | | -ní-T | > | Caní-T | bighanít'aah |
| SP | Caa- | + | Ø | + | --- | | Ø-T | > | Caa-T | bighaat'aah |
| 3o | Ca- | + | (-i-)- | + | --- | | (y)-í--T | > | Caí-T | yighaít'aah |
| 3a | Ca- | + | Ø | + | -j- | | (y)-í--T | > | Caji-T | bighajít'aah |
| AP | Ca- | + | O | + | -'(a)d- | | -ee-(d)-T | > | CaO'dee-T | bighabi'deelteeh |
| Dpl | | | | | | | | | | |
| 1. | Ca- | + | Ø | + | --- | | -nii(d)-T | > | Canii((d)-T | bighaniit'aah |
| 2. | Ca- | + | Ø | + | --- | | -no(h)-T | > | Cano(h)-T | bighanoht'aah |

P-gha#-(ni)--Øt'aah: take SRO away from P by force (as a book, knife)
P-gha#-(ni)--lteeh: take an AnO away from P by force

## Cá-Position 1b + Extended Base

### Table 3

In 3o. person y(i)-4 + (y)í-7 contract to appear as -í- (yigháíłgééd).

T – any Verb Theme as in:

| PERSON Sgl | 1b/1d | + | 4 | + | 5 | + | Base | | | Intransitive | Transitive |
|---|---|---|---|---|---|---|---|---|---|---|---|
| 1. | Cá- | + | --- | + | --- | + | -nish-T | > | Cánísh-T | bighánísh'nééh | bighánísh géé d |
| 2. | Cá- | + | --- | + | --- | + | -ní-T | > | Cání-T | bighání'nééh | bigháníłgééd |
| 3 | Cá- | + | --- | + | --- | + | Ø-T | > | Cá-T | yighá'nééh | --- |
| SP | Cá- | + | --- | + | --- | + | Ø-T | > | Cá-(d)-T | --- | bighálgééd |
| 3o | Cá- | + | (yi-) | + | --- | + | -(y)-í-T | > | Cáí-T | --- | yigháíłgééd |
| 3a | Cá- | + | --- | + | -j- | + | -(y)-í--T | > | Cájí-T | bighájí'nééh | bighájíłgééd |
| 3i | Cá- | + | --- | + | -'a- | + | Ø-T | > | Cá'á-T | bighá'á'nééh | --- |
| Dpl | | | | | | | | | | | |
| 1. | Cá- | + | --- | + | --- | + | -nii(d)-T | > | Cánii((d)-T | bighánii'nééh | bighániilgééd |
| 2. | Cá- | + | --- | + | --- | + | -nó(h)-T | > | Cánó(h)-T | bighánóh'nééh | bighánółgééd |

bighá#-(ni)---(d)'nééh: crawl through it (as a fence, a smoke cloud)
ná#-(ni)--(d)'nééh: return crawling; crawl back (nánísh'nééh)
P-ts'á#-(ni)-(d)nééh: crawl away from P (bits'ánísh'nééh)
biníká#-(ni)--(d)'nééh: crawl through it (binîkánísh'nééh)
bighá#-(ni)--łgééd: stab O through it (bighánísh gééd)

## Ci-: Position 1b + Extended Base

### Table 4

T = any Verb Theme

| PERSON Sgl | 1b | + 4 | + 5 | + Base | | | Intransitive | Transitive +Ø-4 | Transitive + Ci-4 |
|---|---|---|---|---|---|---|---|---|---|
| 1. | ni- | Ø/Ci- | ---- | -nish-T | > | ninish-T | ninish'nééh | ninishteeh | nininishteeh |
| 2. | ni- | Ø/Ci- | ---- | ní-T | > | niní-T | niní'nééh | niníłteeh | nishiníłteeh |
| 3. | nii- | ---- | ---- | Ø-T | > | nii-T | nii'nééh | --- | nishíłteeh |
| SP | nii- | ---- | ---- | Ø-(d)-T | > | nii(d)-T | --- | niilteeh | --- |
| 3o. | ni- | y- | --- | (y)í-T | > | niyí-T | --- | --- | niyíłteeh |
| 3a. | ni- | Ø/Ci- | -j- | -(y)-í-T | > | nijí-T | nijí'nééh | nijíłteeh | nishijíłteeh |
| 3i. | ni- | --- | -'- | -(y)í-T | > | ni'í-T | ni'í'nééh | --- | --- |
| AP | ni- | ---/O | '(a)d- | -ee(d)-T | > | niO'dee(d)-T | --- | --- | nishi'deelteeh |
| 3s. | ni- | --- | ho-/<br>hoo- | -(y)í-T | > | nihó-T<br>nihoo-T | nihóghááh*<br>nihoolzhíísh | --- | --- |
| Dpl | | | | | | | | | |
| 1. | ni- | Ø | ---- | -nii(d)-T | > | ninii((d)-T | ninii'nééh | niniilteeh | nininiilteeh |
| 2. | ni- | Ø | ---- | -no(h)-T | > | nino(h)-T | ninoh'nééh | ninołteeh | nishinołteeh |

*or nihooghááh
ni#-(ni)--(d)'nééh: crawl to a stopping point; stop crawling
ni#-(ni)--łteeh, ni' ---: set an AnO down (ni'nishiníłteeh: set me down)
ni#-ho-(ni)--Øghááh: event ends (nihóghááh ~ nihooghááh)
ni#-ho-(ni)--lzhíísh: era ends (nihoolzhíísh)

Cí-:Position 1b + Extended Base

Table 5

T = any Verb Theme

| PERSON | Prefix Position 1b | + | 4 | + | 5 | + | Base | > | | Intransitive | Transitive +Ø-4 | Transitive + Ci-4 |
|---|---|---|---|---|---|---|---|---|---|---|---|---|
| Sgl | | | | | | | | | | | | |
| 1. | Cí- | + | Ø/Ci- | + | --- | + | -nish-T | > | Cínish-T | ch'ínísh'nééh | ch'íníshteeh | ch'íninishteeh |
| 2. | Cí- | + | Ø/Ci- | + | --- | + | ní-T | > | Cíní-T | ch'íní'nééh | ch'íníłteeh | ch'íshiníłteeh |
| 3. | Cé- | + | Ø/Ci- | + | --- | + | -Ø-T | > | Cé-T | ch'é'nééh | --- | ch'íshíłteeh |
| SP | Cé- | + | Ø/-- | + | --- | + | Ø(d)-T | > | Cé-(d)-T | --- | ch'élteeh | ---- |
| 3o. | Cí- | + | y(i)- | + | --- | + | (y)-í-T | > | Cíyí-T | --- | ---- | ch'íyíłteeh |
| 3a. | Cí- | + | Ø/Ci- | + | -j(i)- | + | (y)-í-T | > | Cíjí-T | ch'íjí'nééh | ch'íjíłteeh | ch'íshijíłteeh |
| 3i. | Cí- | + | --- | + | -'(í)- | + | -(y)í-T | > | Ci'í-T | ch'í'í'nééh | --- | --- |
| 3s. | Cí- | + | ---/Ø | + | -ho-/ hoo- | + | \ ´ /Ø | > | Cíhó-/ Cíhoo | ch'íhóghaah/ ch'íhoolzhíísh | --- | --- |
| AP | Cí- | + | ---/O | + | -'(a)d- | | -ee(d)-T | > | CíO'dee-(d)-T | --- | --- | ch'íbi'deelteeh |
| Dpl | | | | | | | | | | | | |
| 1. | Cí- | + | Ø/Cí- | + | --- | + | -nii(d)-T | > | Cínii((d)-T | ch'ínii'nééh | ch'íniilteeh | ch'íniniilteeh |
| 2. | Cí- | + | Ø/Cí- | + | ---- | + | -no(h)-T | > | Cíno(h)-T | ch'ínoh'nééh | ch'ínołteeh | ch'íshinołteeh |

ch'í#(ni)--(d)'nééh: crawl out
P-í#-(ni)--(d)'nééh: overtake P crawling (bínísh'nééh)
P-k'í#-(ni)--(d)'nééh: come upon P crawling; discover P crawling (yik'é'nééh: he finds it)
ch'í#-(ni)--łteeh: carry AnO out

## *NEUTER VERBS*

A number of Neuter Verb Bases are derived with a Conjunct ni-prefix, here treated as the Ni-Imperfective/Perfective Conjugation marker of Position 7, but previously identified as a prefix of Position 6b. Krauss (1969) and Kari (1976) suggested identification of the verbs in reference as Ni-Imperfective Neuters. This suggestion is adopted tentatively, despite the fact that a ni-prefix also appears as a thematic element in a group of D/L-Class Yi-Perfective Neuter Verbs concerned with appearance. (See Yi-Perfective Neuter.)

The Verb Bases here identified as Ni-Imperfective Neuter are intransitive constructions that serve to describe the subject in terms of existence (the Existentials: be), or in terms of color, shape, texture, size, weight, appearance, taste (sweet/ bitter), quality (good/suitable), moisture content (wet/dry), oiliness, flammability and obesity. They are essentially adjectivals in which ni-7 deletes in 3rd person constructions in the presence of a preceding prefix. For example:

| | | |
|---|---|---|
| dibéésh: flinty | ditłéé': wet | nidaaz: heavy |
| dichił: glittering | diwol: rough, rutted | nilį́: he is |
| dích'íí': bitter, piquant | łikan sweet, tasty | nineez: long. tall |
| dich'íízh: rough, coarse | łik'aii: obese | nitsaa: big |
| dijool: round, plump | łiyin: oily | nizhóní: pretty |
| dilkǫǫh: smooth | łizhin: black | yá'át'ééh: good, suitable |

The adjectivals of dimension and mass occur in two aspects: Absolute and Comparative. The Comparative is marked by a ní-prefix of Position 6b (?), here included as with the Ni-Imperfectives. Compare:

Absolute: nineez: he's tall, it's long
Comparative: nííłnééz (haa nííłnééz: how tall is he?)
'ánííłnééz (shiláah 'ánííłnééz: he's taller than me)

The Ni-Imperfective Neuters are conjugated in two distinctive patterns, identified as type 1 and type 2.

Type 1 includes the Adjectivals of size, weight and color, and Type 2 includes an Existential Base and its adjectival derivatives.

Ni- deletes in 3rd person Adjectivals of Type 1, when it is preceded by a deictic subject pronoun of Position 5, or by a di[7]- prefix of Position 6a, and the ni-prefix appears as a high tone on the vowel of the preceding prefix, as in jíneez: he (3a person) is tall.

## *TYPE 1*

### Extended Base Paradigm

Table 1

T = any Verb Theme

| PERSON | Prefix Position | | | | | | | |
|---|---|---|---|---|---|---|---|---|
| Sgl | 5 | + | 7 | + | Base | | | as in: |
| 1. | ---- | + | ni- | + | -sh-T | > | nis(h)-T | nisneez |
| 2. | ---- | + | ni | + | \ ´ /-T | > | ní-T | níneez |
| 3. | ---- | + | ni- | + | Ø-T | > | ni-T | nineez |
| 3a. | j- | + | -í- | + | Ø-T | > | jí-T | jíneez |
| 3i. | '- | + | -í- | + | Ø-T | > | 'í-T | 'íneez |
| 3s. | ho- | + | - ´ - | + | Ø-T | > | hó-T | hóneez |
| Dpl | | | | | | | | |
| 1. | ---- | + | n- | + | -ii(d)-T | > | nii(d)-T | nii'neez |
| 2. | ---- | + | n- | + | -o(h)-T | > | no(h)-T | nohneez |

(ni)--Øneez: be long or tall
(ni)--Øtł'a: be left-handed
(ni)--Øzhóní: be pretty
(ni)--Øtł'iz: be hard
(ni)--Ølį́: be (a profession, class or clan)

(ni)--Ødaaz: be heavy
(ni)--Øteel: be wide, broad
(ni)--Øchį': be stingy
(ni)--łchxon: be stinking
dí-(ni)--lch'il > dííłch'il: be dense (vegetation)
dí-(ni)--Øch'íí' > dích'íí': be bitter, piquant

## Ho-: Position 4 + Extended Base

TwoVerb Bases, one an Existential, include the 3s prefix ho-Position 4, functioning as a thematic element. Ho- absorbs ni-7 to produce hó- in 3rd person.

### Table 2a

T= any Verb Theme

| PERSON | Prefix Position | | | | | | | |
|---|---|---|---|---|---|---|---|---|
| Sgl | 4 | + | 5 | + | Base | | | as in: |
| 1. | ho- | + | ---- | + | nish-T | > | honish-T | honishłǫ́ |
| 2. | ho- | + | ---- | + | ní-T | > | honí-T | honíłǫ́ |
| 3 | ho- | + | ---- | + | \ ´/-Ø-T | > | hó-T | hólǫ́ |
| 3a. | ho- | + | -j- | + | -í-Ø-T | > | hojí-T | hojíłǫ́ |
| Dpl | | | | | | | | |
| 1. | ho- | + | ---- | + | nii(d)-T | > | honii(d)-T | honiidlǫ́ |
| 2. | ho | + | ---- | + | no(h)-T | > | hono(h)-T | honohłǫ́ |

ho-(ni)--Ølǫ́: exist; be
ho-(ni)--ł'į́, P-k'eh ---: be obedient to P, obey P (shik'eh hół'į́: he obeys me)

(3rd person hólǫ́ is also equivalent to English "there is, there are" and, in combination with postpositional P-ee: "with P" the meaning "have, possess" is derived, as chidí shee hólǫ́: I have a car.)

### Table 2b

A variant of the ho-(ni)-Existential described in 2a above is composed of a Disjunct na-prefix (na[1]-Position 1b: around about??) + the Theme ho-lnin ~ ho-Ølin (in the latter form L-Classifier has been reinterpreted as the Stem-initial consonant. (See Yi-Perfective Neuter.)

| PERSON | | |
|---|---|---|
| Sgl | | |
| 1. | nahonishnin | (~ nahonishłin) |
| 2. | nahonílnin | (~ nahonílin) |
| 3 | nahalnin | (~ nahalin) |
| 3a. | nahojílnin | (~ nahojílin) |
| Dpl | | |
| 1. | nahoniilnin | (~ nahoniidlin) |
| 2. | nahonołnin | (~ nahonohłin) |

na#ho-(ni)--lnin ~ Ølin: appear, look like, resemble (shimósí náshdóí nahalnin ~ nahalin: my cat looks like a bobcat; nahodoołtį́į́ł t'óó nahalin: it looks like rain

## Di$^{10}$-: Position 6a + Extended Base

### Table 3

Di$^{10}$-Position 6a is a thematic prefix that relates to color. The conjugational pattern is divergent, in that ni-7 is not deleted with di$^{10}$ – as it is with di$^{7}$ – in 3rd person constructions. (See Table 5.)

T= any Verb Theme

| PERSON | Prefix Position | | | | | | | |
|---|---|---|---|---|---|---|---|---|
| Sgl | 5 | + | 6a | + | Base | | | as in: |
| 1. | ---- | + | di- | + | -nish-T | > | dinish-T | dinishzhin |
| 2. | ---- | + | di- | + | -ní-T | > | diní-T | dinílzhin |
| 3. | ---- | + | di- | + | -ni-T | > | dini-T | dinilzhin |
| 3a. | ji- | + | di- | + | -ni-T | > | *jidini-T | *jidinilzhin |
| 3s. | ho- | + | di- | + | -ni-T | > | hodini-T | hodinilzhin |
| Dpl | | | | | | | | |
| 1.. | ---- | + | di- | + | -nii(d)-T | > | dinii(d)-T | diniilzhin |
| 2. | ---- | + | di- | + | -no(h)-T | > | dino(h)-T | dinołzhin |

*or as dizhni-T / dizhnilzhin

di-(ni)--lzhin: be dark brown; bay
di-(ni)--lchíí': be reddish, pink
di-(ni)--lgai: be off-white, beige
di-(ni)--lbá: be grayish, light gray
di-(ni)--ltso: be yellowish, orange

## *TYPE 2*

## The Extended Base Paradigms

The Existential Theme (ni)--Øt'é: "be," is divergent, in that ni-7 does not appear in 3rd person constructions. In 3rd person a yi-prefix (a peg) appears, which deletes in the presence of a preceding prefix. A number of adjectivals, derived with di$^{7}$-, follow the conjugational pattern of ni--Øt'é.

## Ni-Position 7 + Extended Base

### Table 4

T = any Verb Theme

| PERSON | Prefix Position | | | | | | | |
|---|---|---|---|---|---|---|---|---|
| Sgl | 5 | + | 7 | + | 8 | | | as in: |
| 1. | ---- | + | ni- | + | -sh | > | nish-T | nisht'é |
| 2. | ---- | + | ni- | + | \´/ | > | ní-T | nít'é |
| 3. | ---- | + | yi- | + | Ø | > | yi-Ø-T | yit'é |
| 3a. | ji- | + | Ø | + | Ø | > | ji-Ø-T | jit'é |
| 3s | hoo- | + | Ø | + | Ø | > | hoo-T | hoot'e |
| Dpl | | | | | | | | |
| 1. | ---- | + | n- | + | -ii(d) | > | nii(d)-T | niit'é |
| 2. | ---- | + | n- | + | -o(h) | > | no(h)-T | noht'é |

(ni)--Øt'é: be (qualitatively, in condition, color, health, appearance) (See 'á#-(ni-)--Øt'é, under Disjunct Derivatives.) (Ninááʼshą' haa yit'é: what color are your eyes? Nichidíshą' haa yit'é: what color is your car? – Łichíí' daats'í – łitso daats'í? – red, yellow? Haash nít'é: how are you?)

## 1. Conjunct Prefixes

Di[7]- + Extended Base

On a par with (ni)--Øt'é Existential, the di-ni-derivatives delete ni-7 in all 3rd person constructions.

Table 5

T = any Verb Theme

| PERSON | Prefix Position | | | | | | | |
|---|---|---|---|---|---|---|---|---|
| Sgl | 5 | + | 6a | + | Base | | | as in: |
| 1. | ---- | + | di | + | nish-T | > | dinish-T | dinishjool |
| 2. | ---- | + | di- | + | -ní-T | > | diní-T | diníjool |
| 3. | ---- | + | di- | + | (yi)-T | > | di-Ø-T | dijool |
| 3a. | ji- | + | di- | + | (yi)-T | > | jidi-T | jidijool |
| 3i. | 'a- | + | di- | + | (yi)-T | > | 'adi-T | 'adijool |
| 3s. | ho- | + | di- | + | (yi)-t | > | hodi-T | hodijool |
| Dpl | | | | | | | | |
| 1. | ---- | + | di- | + | -nii(d)-T | > | dinii(d)-T | diniijool |
| 2. | ---- | + | di- | + | -no(h)-T | > | dino(h)-T | dinohjool |

di-(ni)--Øjool: be spherical, ball-like, plump
di-(ni)--Øjáád: be swift, fleet
di-(ni)--Ø'il: be hairy, hirsute
di-(ni)--Øtłéé': be wet
di-(ni)--Øtsiz: be shaky, tremulous
di-(ni)--lwo': be a fast runner
di-(ni)--Øyin: be holy, supernatural
di-(ni)--Øbid: be gluttonish
'a-di-(ni)--Øjool: something is ball-like (látah 'adijoolí: flax. Literally, there is something ball-like at the tip)

## Łi- + Extended Base

Krauss (l969) identified łi- as Ł-Classifier, in origin. In Ni-Imperfective adjectival derivatives łi- functions like a Conjunct Thematic Prefix of Position 6a, except in constructions that include a prefix of Position 5 or in the absence of a prefix of Position 8, da-3 as well; in these, łi- takes the shape -l- and appears in Position 9 - the Classifier slot.

### Table 6

T = any Verb Theme

PERSON Prefix Position

| Sgl | 5 | + | 6a | + | Base | + | 9 | | | as in: |
|---|---|---|---|---|---|---|---|---|---|---|
| 1. | ---- | + | łi- | + | -nish-T | + | Ø-T | > | łinish-T | łinishzhin |
| 2. | ---- | + | łi- | + | -ní-T | + | Ø-T | > | łiní-T | łinízhin |
| 3. | ---- | + | łi- | + | Ø-T | + | Ø-T | > | łi-Ø-T | łizhin |
| 3a | ji- | + | --- | + | --- | + | l-T | > | jil-T | jilzhin |
| 3i. | 'a- | + | --- | + | --- | + | l-T | > | 'al-T | 'alzhin |
| 3s. | ha- | + | --- | + | --- | + | l-T | > | hal-T | halzhin |
| Dpl | | | | | | | | | | |
| 1. | ---- | + | łi- | + | -nii(d)-T | + | Ø-T | > | łinii(d)-T | łiniijin |
| 2. | ---- | + | łi- | + | -no(h)- | + | Ø-T | > | łino(h)-T | łinohzhin |

Dist.Pl. Prefix Position

| | 3 | + | 5 | + | 6a | + | Base | + | 9 | | | as in: |
|---|---|---|---|---|---|---|---|---|---|---|---|---|
| 1. | da- | + | ---- | + | -łi- | + | -nii(d)- | + | Ø-T | > | dałinii(d)-T | dałiniijin |
| 2. | da- | + | ---- | + | -łi- | + | -no(h)- | + | Ø-T | > | dałino(h)-T | dałinohzhin |
| 3. | daa- | + | ---- | + | Ø | + | --- | + | l-T | > | daal-T | daalzhin |
| 3a. | da- | + | ji- | + | Ø | + | --- | + | l-T | > | dajil-T | dajilzhin |

łi-(ni)--Øzhin: be black
łi-(ni)--Øtso: be yellow
łi-(ni)--Øchíí': be red
łi-(ni)--Øk'aii: be obese, fat
łi-(ni)--Økon: be flammable

łi-(ni)--Øgai: be white
łi-(ni)--Øbá: be gray
łi-(ni)--Økizh: be spotted, dappled
łi-(ni)--Økan: be sweet, taste good
łi-(ni)--Øyin: be oily

## 2. Disjunct Prefixes

### 'Á-: Position 1b + Extended Base

The Position 1b Thematic Prefix 'á- combines with Existential (ni)--Øt'e to produce 'á#-(ni)--Øt'é: "be" (qualitatively - as in tsé 'át'é: it's a rock). Ni-7 deletes in all 3rd person constructions.

Table 1

T = any Verb Theme

| PERSON | Prefix Position | | | | | | | |
|---|---|---|---|---|---|---|---|---|
| Sgl | 1b | + | 5 | + | Base | | | as in: |
| 1. | 'á- | + | ---- | + | nísh-T | > | 'ánísh- | 'ánísht'é |
| 2. | 'á- | + | ---- | + | ní-T | > | 'ání-T | 'áníť'é |
| 3 | 'á | + | ---- | + | (yi)-T | > | 'á-Ø-T | 'át'é |
| 3a. | 'á | + | -jí- | + | (yi)-T | > | 'ájí-T | 'ájít'é |
| 3s. | 'á | + | -hoo- | + | (yi)-T | > | 'áhoo-T | 'áhoot'é |
| Dpl | | | | | | | | |
| 1. | 'á- | + | ---- | + | -nii(d)-T | > | 'ánii(d)-T | 'ániit'é |
| 2. | 'á- | + | ---- | + | -no(h)-T | > | 'ánó(h)-T | 'ánóht'é |

'á#-(ni)--Øt'é: be (qualitatively - tsé 'át'é: it's a rock)
'á#-(ni)--łts'ísí: be small, little
'á#-(ni)--łts'óózí: be slim, narrow, slender

### Yá-'á-:Position 1b + Extended Base

Table 2

T = any Verb Theme

| PERSON | Prefix Position | | | | | | | |
|---|---|---|---|---|---|---|---|---|
| Sgl | 1b | + | 5 | + | Base | | | as in: |
| 1. | yá-'á- | + | ---- | + | -nísh-T | > | yá'ánísh-T- | yá'ánísht'ééh |
| 2 | yá-'á- | + | ---- | + | -ní-T | > | yá'ání-T | yá'áníť'ééh |
| 3. | yá-'á- | + | ---- | + | (yi)-T | > | yá'á-Ø-T | yá'át'ééh |
| 3a. | yá-'á- | + | -ji- | + | (yi)-T | > | yá'ájí-T | yá'ájít'ééh |
| 3s. | yá-'á- | + | -hoo- | + | (yi)-T | > | yá'áhoo-T | yá'áhoot'ééh |
| Dpl | | | | | | | | |
| 1. | yá-'á- | + | ---- | + | -nii(d)-T | > | yá'ánii(d)-T | yá'ániit'ééh |
| 2. | yá-'á- | + | ---- | + | -no(h)-T | > | yá'ánó(h)-T | yá'ánóht'ééh |

yá'á#-(ni)--Øt'ééh: be good, suitable, well (in health)
yá'á#-(ni)--Øshǫ́ (< ł + zhǫ́?)*: be good

*But d-effect does not voice ł to produce lzh-: yá'ániishǫ́ - not yá'ániilzhǫ́*: we are good

Kó-: Position 1b + Extended Base

Table 3

T = any Verb Theme

| PERSON | Prefix Position | | | | | | | |
|---|---|---|---|---|---|---|---|---|
| Sgl | 1b | + | 5 | + | Base | | | as in: |
| 1. | kó- | + | ---- | + | -nísh-T | > | kónísh-T- | kónísht'é |
| 2. | kó- | + | ---- | + | -ní-T | > | kóní-T | kónít'é |
| 3. | kó- | + | ---- | + | (yi)-T | > | kó-Ø-T | kót'é |
| 3a. | kó- | + | -ji- | + | (yi)-T | > | kójí-T | kójít'é |
| 3s. | kó- | + | -hoo- | + | (yi)-T | > | kóhoo-T | kóhoot'é |
| Dpl | | | | | | | | |
| 1. | kó- | + | ---- | + | -nii(d)-T | > | kónii(d)-T | kóniit'é |
| 2. | kó- | + | ---- | + | -nó(h)-T | > | kónó(h)-T | kónóht'é |

kó#-(ni)--Øt'é: be thus; be this way.
(Similarly: 'á-kó#-(ni)--Øt'é: be that way; be correct.)

## *THE COMPARATIVE ADJECTIVALS*

The Neuter Comparative Adjectivals are marked by a ní-prefix in Position 6b (?). Ní- has inherent high tone. The Comparatives describe the subject as *comparatively* endowed with the size, weight or other attribute denoted by the Stem.

The 2nd person sgl subject pronoun ni-Position 8 remains, since it cannot be absorbed as a high tone on a morpheme that is already high; nor can ní-Position 6b be absorbed as a high tone on a preceding prefix of Position 5. Neuter Comparative Verb Themes usually carry high tone and include Ł-Classifier in Position 9.

The vowel [-í-] of the ní-prefix deletes in the 1st and 2nd persons dpl, and the high tone is carried over to the vowel of the subject pronoun prefix that follows.

The Comparatives appear in two distinctive Verb Bases, of which one is marked by the Disjunct Prefix 'á- in Position 1b.

The unmarked Comparatives serve to ask a question of the type "haa nínílnéez: how (comparatively) tall are you?" or to make a statement of the type "daa shį́į́ níshdíil sélį́į'go shi'éé' doo dashííghah da silį́į́': when I reached a certain (comparative size) my clothes wouldn't fit - i.e. I outgrew my clothes."

## Base Paradigm

Ní-: Position 6b + Extended Base

Table 1

T = any Comparative Verb Theme

| PERSON | Prefix Position | | | | | | | |
|---|---|---|---|---|---|---|---|---|
| Sgl | 5 | + | 6b | + | Base | | | as in: |
| 1. | --- | + | ní- | + | (yi)-sh-T | > | nísh-T | nísnééz |
| 2. | --- | + | ní- | + | -ní-T | > | níní-T | níníłnééz |
| 3. | --- | + | ní- | + | (yi)-Ø-T | > | ní-Ø-T | níłnééz |
| 3a. | ji- | + | -ní- | + | (yi)-Ø-T | > | jiní-T | jiníłnééz |
| 3s. | ho- | + | -ní- | + | (yi)-Ø-T | > | honí-T | honíłnééz |
| Dpl | | | | | | | | |
| 1. | --- | + | ní-* | + | (y)-ii(d)-T | > | nii(d)-T | níilnééz |
| 2. | --- | + | ní-* | + | (w)-o(h)-T | > | nó(h)-T | nółnééz |

* the prefix vowel -í- reduces to its high tone before a vowel-initial prefix, and the high tone appears on the following prefix vowel.

ní-(Ø)--łnééz: be comparatively tall or long
ní-(Ø)--łtsází: be comparatively lean
ní-(Ø)--ldííl: be comparatively large, corpulent
ní-(Ø)--łdáás: be comparatively heavy
ní-(Ø)--łtsoh: be comparatively big

## Disjunct Derivatives

Disjunct Derivatives are produced with the addition of 'á-, sho-, P-ee-, 'ahee-: Position 1b to the Comparative Base summarized in the chart above. The 'á-derivatives are required in the presence of a limiting adverb (e.g "very, more, less"), and they correspond roughly to English comparatives produced with the suffixes -er, -est. E.g.

díí tł'óół 'ayóo 'áníłnééz: this rope is very long
díí tł'óół 'aghá 'áníłnééz: this rope is the longest (literally: this rope is comparatively the farthest long)
shizhé'é bilááh 'ánísnééz: I'm taller than my father (literally: I am comparatively tall beyond my father)
shínaaí bi'oh 'ánísdáás: I'm not as heavy (I'm less heavy than) my older brother
doo sho-- da: excessively, too (doo shónísdáas da: I'm too heavy)
P-ee ---: as --- as (neenísnééz: I'm as tall as you)
P-ił 'ahee ---: the same, equally (bił 'aheenísnééz: I'm the same height as he is)
'aheeníildáás: we weigh the same
'aheehoníłtsxo: the areas are equal in size
'ayóo 'áníníłnééz: you're very tall
shi'oh 'áníníłnééz: you're shorter in stature than I

## 'Á-: Position 1b + Extended Base

### Table 2

T = any Comparative Verb Theme

| PERSON Sgl | 1b | + | 5 | + | 6b | + | Base | | | as in: |
|---|---|---|---|---|---|---|---|---|---|---|
| 1. | 'á- | + | ---- | + | -ní- | + | (yi)-sh- | > | 'ánísh-T | 'ánísnéez |
| 2. | 'á- | + | ---- | + | -ní- | + | -ní-T | > | 'áníní-T | 'ánínííłnééz |
| 3. | 'á- | + | ---- | + | -ní- | + | (yi)-)-T | > | 'ání-T | 'ánííłnééz |
| 3a. | 'á | + | -zh- | + | -ní- | + | (yi)-Ø-T | > | 'ázhní-T | 'ázhnííłnééz |
| 3s. | 'á- | + | -ho- | + | -ní- | + | (yi)-Ø-T | > | 'áhoní-T | 'áhonííłnééz |
| Dpl | | | | | | | | | | |
| 1. | 'á- | + | ---- | + | -ní- | + | (y)-ii(d)-T | > | 'áníí(d)-T | 'ánííłnééz |
| 2. | 'á- | + | ---- | + | -ní- | + | (w)-o(h)-T | > | 'ánó(h)-T | 'ánółnééz |

'á#-ní-(Ø)--łnééz: be comparatively long or tall
'á#-ní-(Ø)--ldííl: be comparatively big, stout, corpulent
'á#-ní-(Ø)--łdáás: be comparatively heavy
'á#-ní-(Ø)--łzólí: be comparatively light (ł- + stem-initial z- usually contract to produce s-; contraction fails to take place in the łzólí theme)

## RECAPITULATION

### 1. Extended Base Paradigm

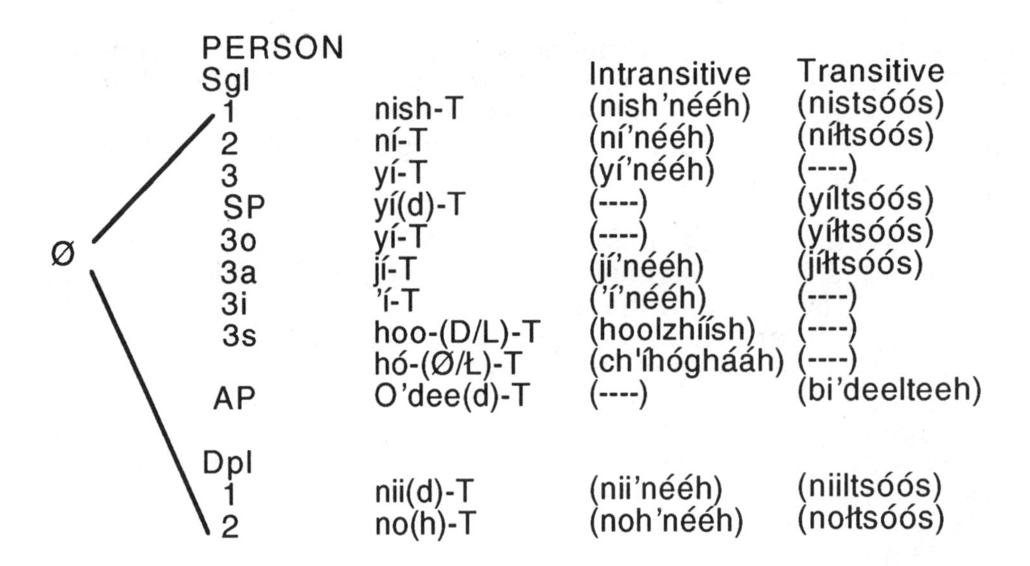

| PERSON | | Intransitive | Transitive |
|---|---|---|---|
| Sgl | | | |
| 1 | nish-T | (nish'nééh) | (nistsóós) |
| 2 | ní-T | (ní'nééh) | (níłtsóós) |
| 3 | yí-T | (yí'nééh) | (----) |
| SP | yí(d)-T | (----) | (yíltsóós) |
| 3o | yí-T | (----) | (yíłtsóós) |
| 3a | jí-T | (jí'nééh) | (jíłtsóós) |
| 3i | 'í-T | ('í'nééh) | (----) |
| 3s | hoo-(D/L)-T | (hoolzhíísh) | (----) |
| | hó-(Ø/Ł)-T | (ch'íhóghááh) | (----) |
| AP | O'dee(d)-T | (----) | (bi'deelteeh) |
| Dpl | | | |
| 1 | nii(d)-T | (nii'nééh) | (niiltsóós) |
| 2 | no(h)-T | (noh'nééh) | (nołtsóós) |

(ni)--(d)'nééh: arrive crawling
(ni)--łtsóós: handle a FFO (nistsóós)(bring. give)
(ni)--łteeh: handle an AnO (nishteeh)(bring. give)

## *CONJUNCT PREFIXES*

### 2. Ci- Prefixes of Position 6a/b + Extended Base

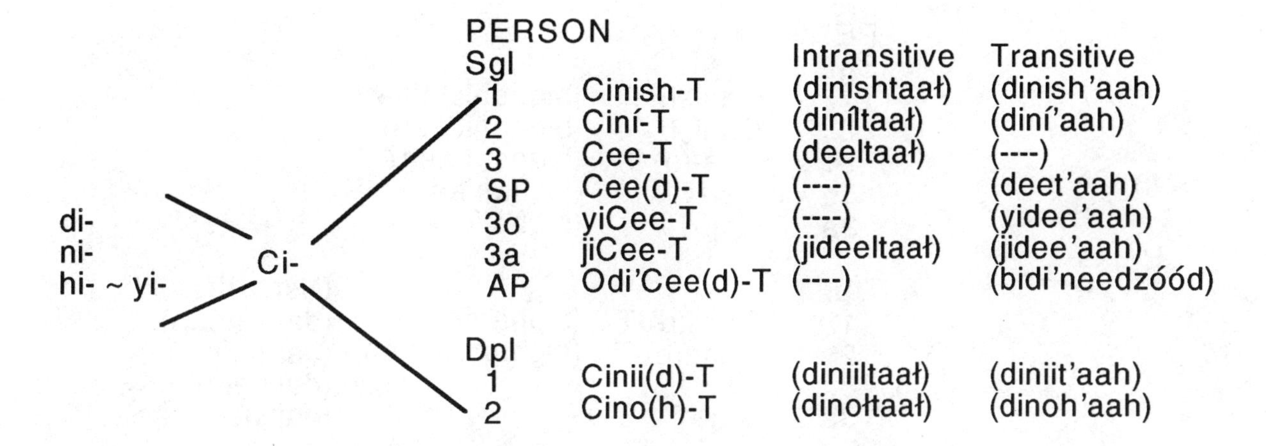


| PERSON | | Intransitive | Transitive |
|---|---|---|---|
| Sgl | | | |
| 1 | Cinish-T | (dinishtaał) | (dinish'aah) |
| 2 | Ciní-T | (diníłtaał) | (diní'aah) |
| 3 | Cee-T | (deeltaał) | (----) |
| SP | Cee(d)-T | (----) | (deet'aah) |
| 3o | yiCee-T | (----) | (yidee'aah) |
| 3a | jiCee-T | (jideeltaał) | (jidee'aah) |
| AP | Odi'Cee(d)-T | (----) | (bidi'needzóód) |
| Dpl | | | |
| 1 | Cinii(d)-T | (diniiltaał) | (diniit'aah) |
| 2 | Cino(h)-T | (dinołtaał) | (dinoh'aah) |

baa di-(ni)--Ø'aah: relinquish SRO to him
bijáátah di-(ni)--ltaał: trip him with one's foot (bijáátah dinishtaał)
(bidi'needzóód: several persons are driven)
ni#-zh-(ni)--łts'in:, P-ił ---: beat P with fists (bił nizhnists'in)
hi-(ni)--(d)t'e': arrive hopping (hinisht'e'; tsídii shaa heet'e': the bird comes hopping to me))

### 3. Ci- Prefixes of Position 4 + Extended Base

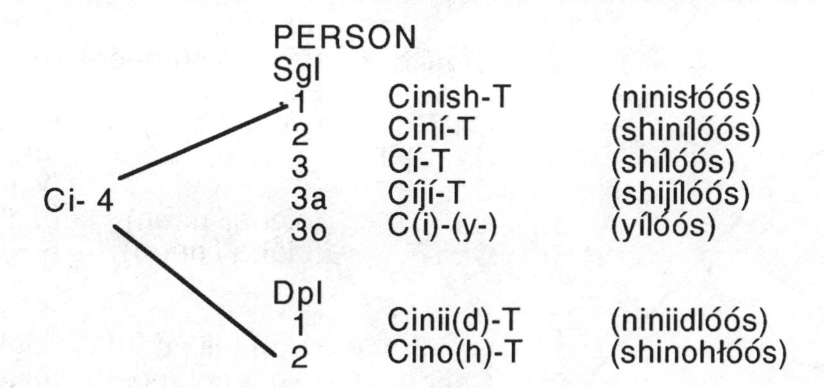


| PERSON | | |
|---|---|---|
| Sgl | | |
| 1 | Cinish-T | (ninisłóós) |
| 2 | Ciní-T | (shinílóós) |
| 3 | Cí-T | (shílóós) |
| 3a | Cíjí-T | (shijílóós) |
| 3o | C(i)-(y-) | (yílóós) |
| Dpl | | |
| 1 | Cinii(d)-T | (niniidlóós) |
| 2 | Cino(h)-T | (shinohłóós) |

(ni)--Ølóós: lead O (ninisłóós: I lead you; shinílóós: you lead me, etc.)

## *DISJUNCT PREFIXES*

### 4. Ca- Prefixes + Extended Base

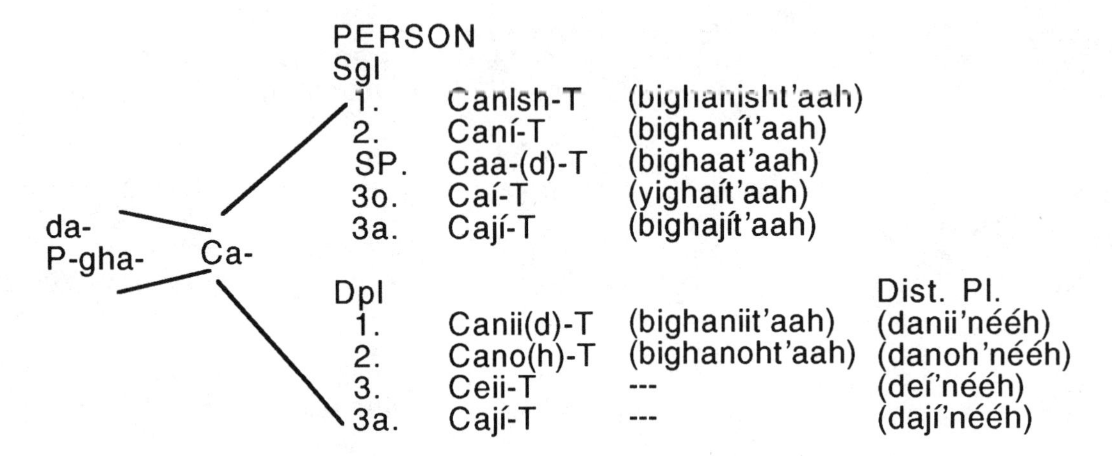


bigha#-(ni)--(d)t'aah: take a SRO away from him
da#-(ni)--(d)'nééh: 3+ subjects come/arrrive (deí'nééh)

### 5. Cá- Prefixes + Extended Base

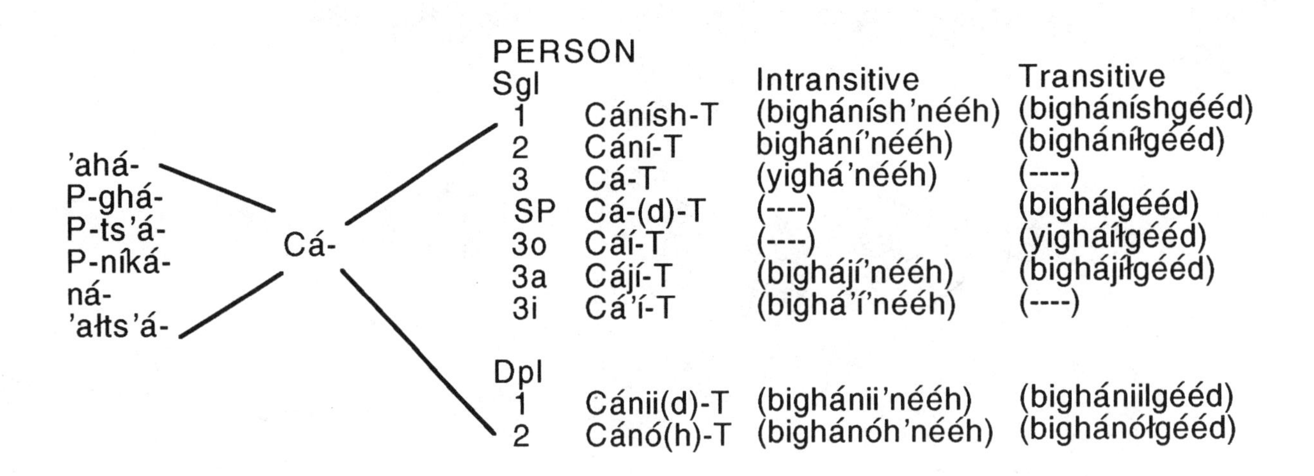


bighá#-(ni)--(d)'nééh: crawl through it (as a fence)(bighánísh'nééh)
bighá#-(ni)--łgééd: stick it through it (bighánísh géed)
P-ts'á#-(ni)--(d)'nééh: crawl away from P (bits'ánísh'nééh)
P-níká#-(ni)--(d)'nééh: crawl through P (an opening)(biníkánísh'nééh)
'ahá#-(ni)--Øgéésh: cut O in half ('ahánísh géésh)
ná#-(ni)--łteeh: bring an AnO back (nánísh teeh)

## 6. Ni- + Extended Base

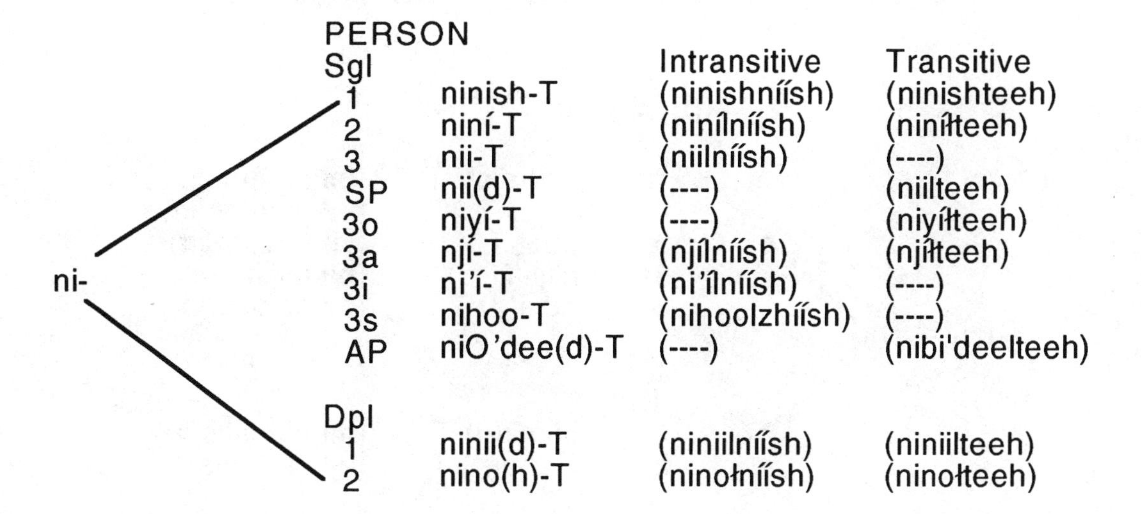

| PERSON | | Intransitive | Transitive |
|---|---|---|---|
| Sgl | | | |
| 1 | ninish-T | (ninishnííísh) | (ninishteeh) |
| 2 | niní-T | (niníłnííísh) | (niníłteeh) |
| 3 | nii-T | (niilnííísh) | (----) |
| SP | nii(d)-T | (----) | (niilteeh) |
| 3o | niyí-T | (----) | (niyíłteeh) |
| 3a | njí-T | (njíłnííísh) | (njíłteeh) |
| 3i | ni'í-T | (ni'íłnííísh) | (----) |
| 3s | nihoo-T | (nihoolzhííísh) | (----) |
| AP | niO'dee(d)-T | (----) | (nibi'deelteeh) |
| Dpl | | | |
| 1 | ninii(d)-T | (niniilnííísh) | (niniilteeh) |
| 2 | nino(h)-T | (ninołnííísh) | (ninołteeh) |

ni- (branching to all persons)

ni#-(ni)--lnííísh: stop working; quit work (ninishnííísh)
ni#-(ni)--łteeh: carry AnO as far as a stopping point (ninishteeh)
ni#-ho-(ni)--lzhííísh: time period ends
ni#-(ni)--ltłáád: stop, halt(ninishtłáád)

## 7. Cí- Prefixes + Extended Base

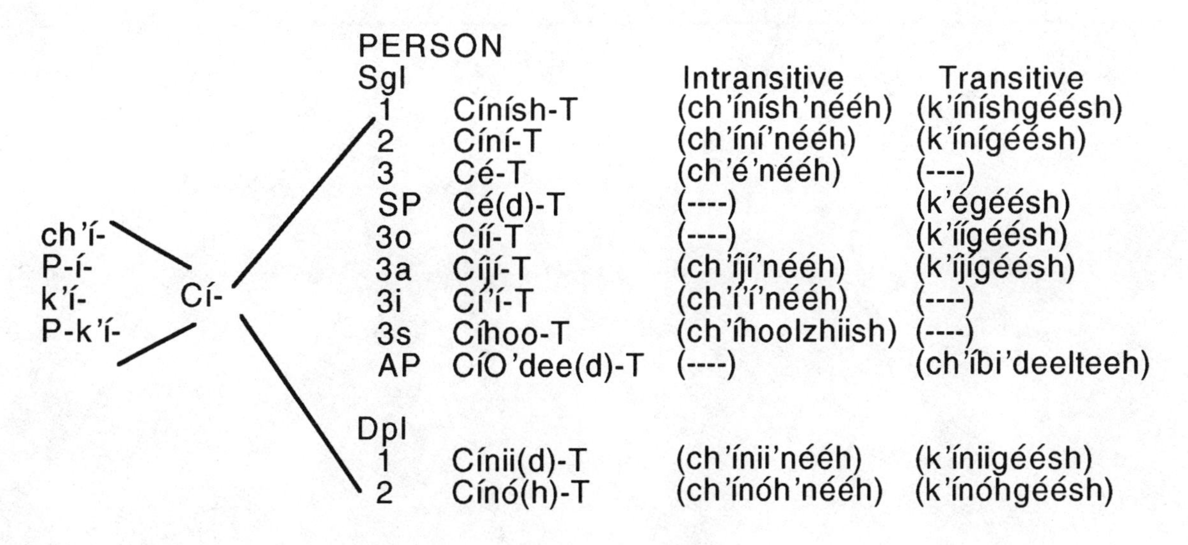

| PERSON | | Intransitive | Transitive |
|---|---|---|---|
| Sgl | | | |
| 1 | Cínísh-T | (ch'ínísh'nééh) | (k'íníshgéésh) |
| 2 | Cíní-T | (ch'íní'nééh) | (k'ínígéésh) |
| 3 | Cé-T | (ch'é'nééh) | (----) |
| SP | Cé(d)-T | (----) | (k'égéésh) |
| 3o | Cíí-T | (----) | (k'íígéésh) |
| 3a | Cíjí-T | (ch'íjí'nééh) | (k'íjígéésh) |
| 3i | Cí'í-T | (ch'í'í'nééh) | (----) |
| 3s | Cíhoo-T | (ch'íhoolzhiish) | (----) |
| AP | CíO'dee(d)-T | (----) | (ch'íbi'deelteeh) |
| Dpl | | | |
| 1 | Cínii(d)-T | (ch'ínii'nééh) | (k'íniigéésh) |
| 2 | Cínó(h)-T | (ch'ínóh'nééh) | (k'ínóhgéésh) |

ch'í-, P-í-, k'í-, P-k'í- → Cí-

k'í#-(ni)--Øgéésh; cut it in two; cut it off
ch'í#-ho-(ni)--lzhííísh: period of time starts
ch'í#-(ni)--lteeh: be carried out (AnO) (ch'íbi'deelteeh: he's being carried out)
P-k'í#-(ni)--lyeed: come upon P; find P (bik'íníshyeed)
P-í#-(ni)--łkááh: track P down; overtake P by tracking (bíníshkááh)
ch'í#-(ni)--(d)'nééh: crawl out horizontally

## IRREGULAR

### 8. Dzi- ~ -zh-: Position 6a + Extended Base

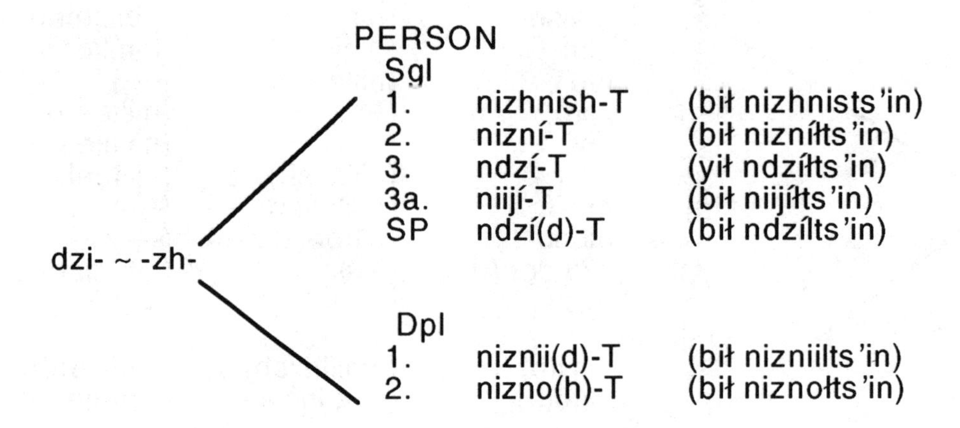


P-ił ni#-zh-(ni)--łts'in: beat P up with one's fists; knock P out (lit. strike away terminatively into space in company with P).

## 4. THE YI-Ø-IMPERFECTIVE

The Yi-Ø-Imperfectives are derived with a yi-aspect marker arbitrarily assigned to Position 6c, + Ø-Conjugation Marker in Position 7. For both the Transitional and the Semelfactive Aspects the Imperfective Mode is conjugated in the Yi-Ø- pattern.

The Transitional Aspect usually employs the Momentaneous Stem Set, while the Semelfactive Aspect usually employs a single repetitive stem (the Usitative-Iterative) for all Modes.

Transitional Aspect describes the subject of an intransitive verb, or the direct object of a transitive verb, as shifting from one state of being, form or status to another, as:

tó yiiłtooł: the water is clearing up (shifting from a turgid to a clear state)
yiishjį́į́h: I'm turning black (changing from one hue to another)
sitsii' yiishch'į́į́ł: I'm curling my hair (causing it to change form)
'at'ééd 'aghaa' yiyiiłgááh: the girl is whitening the wool

Semelfactive Aspect stands in a complementary relationship to the Repetitive Aspect, where it serves to isolate a single act from a repetitive series, as:

yiishtąsh: I'm giving it a tap or peck (cf. náníshtąsh: I'm giving it a consecutive series of taps or pecks
yiishhash: I'm giving it a bite (cf. náníshhash: I'm biting it - a consecutive series of bites)

The Transitional Aspect always has a Yi-Ø- conjugation pattern in the Perfective Mode, as well as in the Imperfective; but the Semelfactive takes a si-Perfective.

As the conjugation charts for the Base Paradigm and for the Conjunct and the Disjunct derivatives show:

(1) the yi-Aspect marker lengthens the prefix vowel (> -ii-) before the 1st person sgl subject pronoun -sh-, and in constructions in which Position 8 (the subject pronoun) is vacant.

(2) the initial y- / w-, a peg element in constructions that lack a preceding prefix, is required for syllable integrity; it deletes in the presence of a preceding prefix, except the 3o object pronoun yi- of Position 4, where yi-4 + yii-6c > yiyii-. In the presence of a preceding prefix, however, yi- 4 + yii-6c > yii-, as in:

yiyiishį́į́h: he's blackening it, but:

dayiishį́į́h: they (3+) are blackening it
náyiishį́į́h: he's reblackening it, polishing it (black shoe)

(3) yi- + -ii(d)-Position 8 > yii(d)-: yiigááh: we're turning white.

(4) yi- + -o(h)-Position 8 > woo(h)-: woohgááh: you dpl are turning white.

(5) the 2nd person sgl subject pronoun ni-Position 8 does not usually appear (although some speakers do include it).

## Base Paradigm

Table 1

T = any Verb Theme

| PERSON | Prefix Position | | | | | | | | | | |
|---|---|---|---|---|---|---|---|---|---|---|---|
| Sgl | 6c | + | 7 | + | 8 | + | 9-10 | | | as in: |
| 1. | yii- | + | Ø | + | -sh | + | T | > | yiish-T | yiishgááh |
| 2. | yii- | + | Ø | + | Ø | + | T | > | yii-T | yiigááh |
| 3. | yii- | + | Ø | + | Ø | + | T | > | yii-T | yiigááh |
| SP. | yii- | + | Ø | + | Ø-(d)- | + | T | > | yiil-T | yiilgááh |
| Dpl | | | | | | | | | | |
| 1. | y(i)- | + | Ø | + | -ii(d)- | + | T | > | yii(d)-T | yiigááh |
| 2. | wo- | + | Ø | + | -o(h)- | + | T | > | woo(h)-T | woohgááh |

yi-(Ø)--Øgááh: turn white
yi-(Ø)--jį́į́h (< d-zhį́į́h): turn black
yi-(Ø)--lgááh: be whitened
yi-(Ø)--łtooł: become clear (as water)

## The Extended Base Paradigms

### 1. Conjunct Prefixes

Position 5 Prefixes + Base

Table 2

T = any Verb Theme

| PERSON | Prefix Position | | | | | |
|---|---|---|---|---|---|---|
| Sgl /Dpl | 5 | + | Base | | | as in: |
| 3a(4) | j- | + | (y)-ii-T | > | jii-T | jiigááh |
| 3i. | '- | + | (y)-ii-T | > | 'ii-T | 'iigááh |
| 3s. | ho- | + | (y)-ii-T | > | hoo-T | hoogááh |
| AP. | -'(a)d- | + | (y)-ii-(d)-T | > | O'dii-T | bi'diilgááh |

yi-(Ø)--gááh: turn white (bi'diilgááh: he's being whitened)

## Prefixes of Positions 4 and 5 + Base

### Table 3

Ø-4 = a 3rd person direct object with a 1st or 2nd person subject.
Ci-4 = any direct object pronoun of Position 4 with Ci- shape.

T = any Verb Theme

| PERSON | Prefix Position | | | | | as in: | |
|---|---|---|---|---|---|---|---|
| Sgl | 4 | + | 5 | + | Base | Ø-4 | Ci-4 |
| 1. | Ø/C- | + | --- | + | (y)-iish-T | yiishgááh | niishgááh |
| 2. | Ø/C- | + | --- | + | (y)-ii-T | yiiłgááh | shiiłgááh |
| 3. | --/C- | + | --- | + | (y)-ii-T | --- | shiiłgááh |
| SP. | Ø/--- | + | --- | + | (y)-ii-(d)-T | yiilgááh | --- |
| 3o. | --/yi- | + | --- | + | yii-T | --- | yiyiiłgááh |
| 3a. | Ø/C- | + | -j(i)- | + | (y)-ii-T | jiiłgááh | shijiiłgááh |
| AP. | --/Ci- | + | -'(a)d- | + | (y)-ii-(d)-T | --- | bi'diilgááh |
| Dpl | | | | | | | |
| 1. | Ø/C- | + | --- | + | (y)-ii(d)-T | yiilgááh | niilgááh |
| 2. | Ø/C- | + | --- | + | (wo)-o(h)- | woołgááh | shoołgááh |

yi-(Ø)--Øgááh: turn white
yi-(Ø)--lyíísh: bend over, stoop
yi-(Ø)--Øloh: lasso O
yi-(Ø)--łgááh: whiten O
yi-(Ø)--łtsééh: catch sight of O
yi-(Ø)--Ønod: give O a lick

## Ho-: Position 4 in Extended Base

The 3s object pronoun prefix of Position 4 contracts with yi-: Position 6c to produce hoo- before -sh- in the 1st person sgl and in constructions that lack a prefix in Position 8 (2nd and 3rd sgl and Simple Passive). Ho- appears as hw- before -ii(d)- in the 1st person dpl; and before -oo(h)- in the 2nd person dpl (where it is written h-).

### Table 4

| PERSON Sgl | | | PERSON Dpl | | |
|---|---|---|---|---|---|
| 1. | hoosh- | hooshgááh | 1. | hwii(d)- | hwiilgááh |
| 2. | hoo- | hoołgááh | 2. | hoo(h)- | hoołgááh |
| 3. | hoo- | hoołgááh | | | |
| 3a. | hojii- | hojiiłgááh | | | |

ho-i-(Ø)--łgááh: whiten area (as in whitewashing a wall)
ho-i-(Ø)--ł'aah: make space (as in shá hooł'aah: he makes room for me)
bí#-ho-i-(Ø)--ł'aah: learn it (bíhoosh'aah: I'm learning it. Cf. bíbiyiish'aah: I teach it to him)

## 'A- ~ 'i- ~ '-: Position 4 in Extended Base

The 3i direct object pronoun of Position 4 takes the reduced form '- before -ii- in all persons. The paradigm takes the shape:

Table 5

| PERSON Sgl | | | PERSON Dpl | | |
|---|---|---|---|---|---|
| 1. | 'iish- | 'iishháásh | 1. | 'ii(d)- | 'iilgháásh |
| 2. | 'ii- | 'iiłháásh | 2. | 'oo(h)- | 'oołháásh |
| 3. | 'ii- | 'iiłháásh | | | |
| 3a. | 'ajii- | 'ajiiłháásh | | | |

'(i)-ii-(Ø)--łháásh: go to sleep
'(i)-ii-(Ø)--łtsóód: be a holder (of a parturient)

## Prefixes of Positions 6a / 6b + Extended Base

The Conjunct Prefix vowel elides before -ii-.

Table 6

T = any Verb Theme

| PERSON | Prefix Position | | | | | | | as in: Intransitive | | |
|---|---|---|---|---|---|---|---|---|---|---|
| Sgl | 5 | + | 6a/b | + | Base | | | | | |
| 1. | --- | + | -C- | + | (y)-iish-T | > | Ciish-T | diishch'ééh | niishch'ííł | náhiish'naah |
| 2. | --- | + | -C- | + | (y)-ii-T | > | Cii-T | diich'ééh | niilch'ííł | náhii'naah |
| 3. | --- | + | -C- | + | (y)-ii-T | > | Cii-T | diich'ééh | niilch'ííł | náhii'naah |
| 3a. | ji- | + | -C- | + | (y)-ii-T | > | jiCii-T | jidiich'ééh | jiniilch'ííł | náhijii'naah |
| 3i. | 'a- | + | -C- | + | (y)-ii-T | > | 'aCii-T | 'adiigááh | --- | ná'iyii'naah |
| 3s. | ho- | + | -C- | + | (y)-ii-T | > | hoCii-T | hodiiltłáád | honiigááh | --- |
| Dpl | | | | | | | | | | |
| 1. | --- | + | -C- | + | (y)-ii(d)-T | > | Cii(d)-T | diich'ééh | niilch'ííł | náhii'naah |
| 2. | --- | + | -C- | + | (w)-oo(h)-T | > | Coo(h)-T | doohch'ééh | noołch'ííł | náhooh'naah |

d(i)-ii-(Ø)--Øch'ééh: open mouth
d(i)-ii-(Ø)--ldǫǫh: it explodes, pops
n(i)-ii-(Ø)--lch'ííł: close the eyes
h(i)-ii-(Ø)--Ønaah: come to life
dah d(i)-ii-(Ø)--(d)'nééh: start off crawling
d(i)-ii-(Ø)--łheeł: become quiet, calm
n(i)-ii-(Ø)--lch'ił: blink one time
ho-d(i)-ii-(Ø)--ltłáád: area starts to burn
ho-n(i)-ii-(Ø)--Øgááh: weather becomes hot
'a-d(i)-ii-(Ø)--Øgááh: corn ripens (i.e. something turns white - the husks)
'a-d(i)-ii-(Ø)--lyeed: something starts off at a run (as in shił dah 'adiilyeed: I start off in a fast moving conveyance - "something" starts off running with me)
ná#-h(i)-ii-(Ø)--(d)'naah: regain consciousness, come back to life, resuscitate

## Prefixes of Positions 6a / 6b + Extended Base

### Table 7

T = any Verb Theme as in:

| PERSON | Prefix Position | | | | | | | | | Transitive | |
|---|---|---|---|---|---|---|---|---|---|---|---|
| Sgl | 4 | + | 5 | + | 6a/b | + | Base | | | | |
| 1. | Ø | + | --- | + | -C- | + | (y)-iish-T | > | Ciish-T | diishtłáád | niishgááh |
| 2. | Ø | + | --- | + | -C- | + | (y)-ii-T | > | Cii-T | diiłtłáád | niiłgááh |
| SP. | Ø | + | --- | + | -C- | + | (y)-ii-T | > | Cii(d)-T | diiltłáád | niilgááh |
| 3o. | yi- | + | --- | + | -C- | + | (y)-ii-T | > | yiCii-T | yidiiłtłáád | yiniiłgááh |
| 3a. | Ø | + | ji- | + | -C | + | (y)-ii-T | > | jiCii-T | jidiiłtłáád | jiniiłgááh |
| Dpl | | | | | | | | | | | |
| 1. | Ø | + | --- | + | -C- | + | (y)-ii(d)-T | > | Cii(d)-T | diiltłáád | niilgááh |
| 2. | Ø | + | --- | + | -Ci- | + | (w)-o(h)-T | > | Coo(h)-T | doołtłáád | noołgááh |

d(i)-ii-(Ø)--łtłáád: set O on fire

n(i)-ii-(Ø)--łgááh: heat O

## Ø/Ci-4 + hi-/yi-6a/6c Seriative + yi-6c Transitional + Extended Base

### Table 8

T = any Verb Theme

| PERSON | Prefix Position | | | | | | | | | Transitive | |
|---|---|---|---|---|---|---|---|---|---|---|---|
| Sgl | 4 | + | 5 | + | 6a/c | + | 6c | Intransitive | Ø-4 | Ci-4 | |
| 1. | Ø/Ci- | + | --- | + | hi-/yi- | + | -i- | hiishnaah | hiishnaah | niyiishnaah | |
| 2. | Ø/Ci- | + | --- | + | hi-/yi- | + | -i- | hiinaah | hiiłnaah | shiyiiłnaah | |
| 3. | Ø/Ci- | + | --- | + | hi-/yi- | + | -i- | hiinaah | --- | shiyiiłnaah | |
| SP. | Ø/-- | + | --- | + | hi-/-- | + | -i- | --- | hiilnaah | --- | |
| 3o. | --/yi- | + | --- | + | --/yi- | + | -i- | --- | --- | yiyiiłnaah | |
| 3a. | Ø/Ci- | + | ji-* | + | --/y- | + | -i- | hijiinaah | hijiiłnaah | shijiyiiłnaah | |
| AP. | --/O | + | -'(a)d- | + | --/yi- | + | -i- | --- | --- | bi'diilnaah | |
| Dpl | | | | | | | | | | | |
| 1. | Ø/Ci- | + | --- | + | h-/y- | + | (-i-) | hii'naah | hiilnaah | niyiilnaah | |
| 2. | Ø/Ci- | + | --- | + | h-/y- | + | -i- | hoohnaah | hoołnaah | shiyoołnaah | |

*Ji-3a follows hi-6a but precedes yi-6c

hi-6a + -i-6c-(Ø)--Ønaah: come to life (hiishnaah - as a newborn baby)
hi-6a + -i-6c-Ø-4-(Ø)--łnaah:bring O to life; generate O (electricity)
Ci-4 + yi-6c-Seriative + -i-6c-Transitional-(Ø)--łnaah: bring O to life; generate O
ná#-hi-/yi-i-(Ø)--łnaah: revive O; resuscitate O (náhiishnaah: I'm reviving him; náshiyiiłnaah: he's reviving me)

## Ø-4 + hi-: Position 6a Seriative + Extended Yi-Ø Base

### Table 9

T = any Verb Theme as in:

| PERSON Sgl | Prefix Position: 4 | + 6a | + 5 | + 6a | 6c | + Base | | | Transitive | Intransitive |
|---|---|---|---|---|---|---|---|---|---|---|
| 1. | Ø | + hi- | + --- | + -d(i)- | --- | -iish-T | > | hidiish-T | dah hidiishłeeh | dah hidiishch'ąął |
| 2. | Ø | + hi- | + --- | + -d(i)- | --- | -ii-T | > | hidii-T | dah hidiileeh | dah hidiilch'ąął |
| 3. | Ø | + hi- | + --- | + -d(i)- | --- | -ii-T | > | hidii-T | --- | dah hidiilch'ąął |
| 3o. | yi- | + yi- | + --- | + -d(i)- | --- | -ii-T | > | yidiyii-T | dah yidiyiileeh | --- |
| SP. | Ø | + hi- | + --- | + -d(i)- | --- | -ii-(d)-T | > | hidii(d)-T | dah hidiidleeh | --- |
| 3a. | Ø | + hi- | + -zh- | + -d(i)- | --- | -ii-T | > | hizhdii-T | dah hizhdiileeh | dah hizhdiilch'ąął |
| Dpl | | | | | | | | | | |
| 1. | Ø | + hi- | ---- | + -d(i) | --- | (y)-ii(d)-T | > | hidii(d)-T | dah hidiidleeh | dah hidiilch'ąął |
| 2. | Ø | + hi- | ---- | + -d(i) | --- | -oo(h)-T | > | hidoo(h)-T | dah hidoołeeh | dah hidoołch'ąął |

dah hi-d(i)-ii-(Ø)--Øleeh: hang O up by means of a cord, rope or looped handle
dah hi-d(i)-ii-(Ø)--łmáás: start off rolling O one after another (as barrels)
dah hi-d(i)-ii-(Ø)--(d)kááh: start off in succession (one after another – 3+ subjects)
dah hi-d(i)-ii-(Ø)--lch'ąął: dangle, hang suspended (tsin bigaan bąąh dah hidiishch'ąął: I'm dangling from a tree branch)

## Irregular Yi-Ø-Imperfectives

### 1. Hi-/yi-6 + di-6 + yi-Ø Imperfective

Seriative hi-Position 6a has a yi-allomorph in Position 6c, required in all constructions in which hi- is immediately preceded by a Prefix of Position 4 or 5.

A di-prefix of Position 6a cooccurs with hi-/yi-Seriative in a group of Verb Bases that also include the yi- (-ii-) Transitional Aspect marker of Position 6c. In Bases of this type two prefixes of Position 6a and two prefixes of Position 6c cooccur.

When the prefix of Position 4 is Ø, representing a 3rd person direct object in a verb whose subject is 1st or 2nd person, or in constructions in which a Seriative verb is intransitive, hi-6a takes position to the left of di-6a, as in:

dah hidiishłeeh (< Ø-4 = hi-6a + d(i)-6a + -ii-6c + (Ø) + -shłeeh: I'm in the act of hanging it up (as a bucket by its handle)

In the presence of a preceding prefix of Position 4 however, the yi-allomorph of hi- takes position to the right of di-, where it merges with -i- ~ (-ii-)-6c, marker of Transitional Aspect. In constructions of this type yi-6c Seriative + -i-Transitional> yii-, as in:

dah shidiyiileeh (< shi-4 + di-6a + yii-6c transitional + (Ø) + Øleeh: he's hanging me up; he's weighing me

3a (4th person ji-Position 5 is represented by its -zh-allomorph, which undergoes metathesis and appears to the right of hi-6a, if Position 4 is vacant, as in:

dah hizhdiileeh (< hi-6a + -zh-5 + d(i)-6a + -ii-6a + (Ø) + Øleeh: he's in the act of hanging him up; weighing him

But if Position 4 is filled by other than Ø the Seriative must be represented by its yi-allomorph, as in:

dah shizhdiyiileeh (< shi-4 + -zh-5 + di-6a + -yii-6c + (Ø)--Øleeh): he's in the act of hanging me up; weighing me

The Agentive Passive subject pronoun of Position 5 also triggers a shift to the yi-Seriative allomorph, as in:

dah bidi'diyiidleeh (< bi-4 + -di'-5 + di-6a + -yii-6c + (Ø) + d-leeh: he's being hung up; weighed

Ci-4 + yi-6c Seriative + yi-6c Transitional + Extended yi-Ø Base

Table 10

T = any Verb Theme

| PERSON | Prefix Position | | | | | | | | | | | | |
|---|---|---|---|---|---|---|---|---|---|---|---|---|---|
| Sgl | 4 | + | 5 | + | 6a | + | 6c | + | 6c | + Base | | as in: | |
| 1. | Ci- | + | --- | + | -di- | + | -y(i) | + | (-i-) | -iish-T | > | Cidiyiish-T | dah nidiyiishłeeh |
| 2. | Ci- | + | --- | + | -di- | + | -y(i) | + | (-i-) | -ii-T | > | Cidiyii-T | dah shidiyiileeh |
| 3o. | Ci- | + | --- | + | -di- | + | -y(i) | + | (-i-) | -ii-T | > | Cidiyii-T | dah yidiyiileeh |
| 3a. | Ci- | + | -zh- | + | -di- | + | -y(i) | + | (-i-) | -ii-T | > | Cizhdiyii-T | dah shizhdiyiileeh |
| AP. | O | + | di'- | + | -di- | + | -y(i) | + | (-i-) | -ii(d)- | > | Cidi'diyii(d)-T | dah shidi'diyiidleeh |
| Dpl | | | | | | | | | | | | | |
| 1. | Ci- | + | --- | + | -di- | + | -y(i) | + | (-i-) | -ii(d)-T | > | Cidiyii(d)-T | dah nidiyiidleeh |
| 2. | Ci- | + | --- | + | -di- | + | -y(i) | + | (-i-) | -oo(h)-T | > | Cidiyoo(h)-T | dah shidiyoohłeeh |

dah ni-di-yii-(Ø)--Øleeh: hang you (as by a rope)
dah shi-di-yii-(Ø)-Øleeh: hang me (as by a rope)
ná#-Ci-di-yii-(Ø)--níił: pick up PIO one after another (as in nánihidiyiishníił: I'm picking you 3+ up one after another)

## The Inchoative

The Inchoative is marked by the compound prefix -'nii-, usually preceded by a null postposition of Position 1a. The Inchoative includes 3 types: Type (1) - transitive verbs, in which the null postposition represents a direct object; Type (2) - a class of intransitive verbs in which the null postposition represents the subject; and Type (3) - a class of intransitive verbs in which an indefinite (3i) form of the null postposition ('i-) functions as a thematic prefix.

## Type (1) - Null Postposition = Direct Object

Table 11a

P = any person

| PERSON Sgl | | | Dist. Pl. |
|---|---|---|---|
| 1. | P-'niish-T | (bi'niishdleesh) | 1. P-da'niidleesh |
| 2. | P-nii-T | (bi'niidleesh) | 2. P-da'noohdleesh |
| 3o. | yi'nii-T | (yi'niidleesh) | 3. yida'niidleesh |
| 3a. | P-zh'nii-T | (bizh'niidleesh) | 3a. bidazh'niidleesh |
| Dpl | | | |
| 1. | P-'nii(d)-T | (bi'niidleesh) | |
| 2. | P-'noo(h)-T | (bi'noohdleesh) | |

bi'niishdleesh: I start to paint it
'ábi'niishłééh: I start to make it
'ádi'niishzhéeh: I start to shave myself
'i'niishį́į́h: I start to eat
bi'niishbíísh: I start to boil it

## Type (2) - Null Postposition = Subject

Table 11b

| PERSON Sgl | | Dist. Pl. |
|---|---|---|
| 1. | (shi'niits'iiní) | 1. nihida'niits'iiní |
| 2. | (ni'niits'iiní | 2. nihida'niits'iiní |
| 3. | (bi'niits'iiní) | 3. bida'niits'iiní |
| 3a. | (ho'niits'iiní) | 3a. hoda'niits'iiní |
| Dpl | | |
| 1. | (nihi'niits'iiní) | |
| 2. | (nihi'niits'iiní) | |

shi'niits'iiní: start to get skinny
ni'niitsaah: you become sick (lit. start to die)
nihi'niinééh: we become sick (lit. start to die)
habi'niitííh: it starts to wear out or get old
'abe' bi'niichxǫǫh: the milk starts to spoil

## Type (3) - Null Postposition = Thematic

Table 11c

| PERSON | | | Dist. Pl. |
|---|---|---|---|
| Sgl | | | |
| 1. | 'i'niish-T | ('i'niishchééh) | 1. ('ida'niichééh) |
| 2. | 'i'nii-T | ('i'niichééh) | 2. ('ida'noohchééh) |
| 3o. | 'i'nii-T | ('i'niichééh) | 3. (('ida'niichééh) |
| 3a. | 'izh'nii-T | ('izh'niichééh) | 3a. ('idazh'niichééh) |
| Dpl | | | |
| 1. | 'i'nii(d)-T | ('i'niichééh) | |
| 2. | 'i'noo(h)-T | ('i'noohchééh) | |

'i'niishchééh; I start to cry
'i'niilíísh: you/he/they start to urinate
'i'niistsą̨ah: I start to become pregnant
'i'niichxííł: it starts to snow

## N'di- (< na$^3$-1b + -'i-6a + di=6a) + Transitional

Na$^3$-Position 1b : down combines with an unidentified -'i- ~ -'- prefix assigned to Position 6a + a di-prefix of Position 6a to produce Transitional derivatives with the meaning "take O down, break loose and fall, pick O - as a melon."

Table 12

| PERSON | | | + Seriative hi-/yi- | |
|---|---|---|---|---|
| Sgl | | | | |
| 1. | n'diish-T | (n'diish'aah) | nahi'diish-T | (nahi'diish'aah) |
| 2. | n'dii-T | (n'dii'aah) | nahi'dii-T | (nahi'dii'aah) |
| 3. | n'dii-T | (n'diighááh) | nahi'dii-T | (nahi'diikááh) |
| SP. | n'dii(d)-T | (n'diit'aah) | nahi'dii(d)-T | (nahi'diit'aah) |
| 3o. | na'iidii-T | (na'iidii'aah) | neidi'yii-T | (neidi'yii'aah) |
| 3a. | nizh'dii-T | (nizh'dii'aah) | nahizh'dii-T | (nahizh'dii'aah) |
| Dpl | | | | |
| 1. | n'dii(d)-T | (n'diit'aah) | nahi'dii(d)-T | (nahi'diit'aah) |
| 2. | n'doo(h)-T | (n'dooh'aah) | nahi'doo(h)-T | (nahi'dooh'aah) |

n'diish'aah: take SRO down (hat from a peg, book from a shelf); pick SRO (a melon); unfasten SRO (a button)
n'diighááh: it breaks loose and gets away (as a tethered dog)
n'diilts'ííd: it breaks loose and falls (a bucket from a nail in the wall)
na'iidii'aah: he takes a SRO down (a book from a shelf); he picks SRO (a melon)
neidi'yii'aah: he takes SRO down one after another (books); he picks them (melons)
nahi'diikááh: they break loose and get away one after another (as tethered dogs)

## 2. Disjunct Prefixes

A relative few of the Disjunct Prefixes serve as derivational elements, in determinant position, with the Yi-Ø-Imperfective. Those that appear in this capacity include:

da-: Position 3: distributive plural makrer
ya-: Position 1b: up/down vertical
ya-ná-: Position 1b compound: up into the air
kí: Position 1b: up an incline
P-k'i-:Position 1b: on P
ná-: Position 1d: reversionary
P-í-: Position 1d: against P
P-'ą-: over P (as a limb)

Ca-Prefix + Extended Base

Ca- + yi- > Caa- before the 1st person sgl subject pronoun -sh- and in 2nd and 3rd persons and Simple Passive, where there is no intervening Conjunct Prefix of Position 8.

Table 1

T = any Verb Theme

PERSON Prefix Position

| Sgl | 1b | + | 4 | + | 5 | + | Base | | | Intransitive | Transitive |
|---|---|---|---|---|---|---|---|---|---|---|---|
| 1. | Caa- | + | Ø | + | --- | + | -(yii)sh-T | > | Caash-T | yaashtaał | yaashheeh |
| 2. | Caa- | + | Ø | + | --- | + | -(yii)-T | > | Caa-T | yaaltaał | yaayeeh |
| 3. | Caa- | + | Ø | + | --- | + | -(yii)-T | > | Caa-T | yaaltaał | ---- |
| SP. | Caa- | + | Ø | + | --- | + | -(yii)(d)-T | > | Caa(d)-T | ---- | yaageeh |
| 3o. | Ca- | + | y(i)- | + | --- | + | -ii-T | > | Cayii-T | ---- | yayiiyeeh |
| 3a. | Ca- | + | Ø | + | -j(i)- | + | -ii-T | > | Cajii-T | yajiiltaał | yajiiyeeh |
| AP. | Ca- | + | O | + | '(a)d(i)- | + | -ii(d)-T | > | CaO'dii(d)-T | ---- | yabi'diikaah |
| Dpl | | | | | | | | | | | |
| 1. | Ce- | + | Ø | + | --- | + | (y)-ii(d)-T | > | Ceii(d)-T | yeiiltaał | yeiigeeh |
| 2. | Ca- | + | Ø | + | --- | + | (w)-oo(h)-T | > | Caoo(h)-T | yaoołtaał | yaoohheeh |

Dist. Pl

| Sgl | 1b | + | 3 | + | 4 | + | 5 | + | Base | | | Intransitive | Transitive |
|---|---|---|---|---|---|---|---|---|---|---|---|---|---|
| 1. | Ca- | + | de- | + | Ø | + | --- | + | (y)ii(d)-T | > | Cadeii(d)-T | yadeiiltaał | yadeiigeeh |
| 2. | Ca- | + | da- | + | --- | + | --- | + | (w)oo(h)-T | > | Cadoo(h)-T | yadaoołtaał | yadaoohheeh |
| 3. | Ca- | + | daa- | + | --- | + | --- | + | -(yii)-T | > | Cadaa-T | yadaaltaał | yadaaltaał |
| 3o. | Ca- | + | da- | + | y(i)- | + | --- | + | -ii-T | > | Cadayii-T | ---- | yadayiiyeeh |
| 3a. | Ca- | + | da- | + | Ø | + | -j(i)- | + | -ii-T | > | Cadajii-T | yadajiiltaał | yadajiiyeeh |

ya#-yi-(Ø)--Øyeeh: dump O (a load) (yaashheeh)
ya#-yi-(Ø)--ltaał: dash off (yaashtaał)
ya#-yi-(Ø)--Økaah: dump (human) contents of an open container (as a coffin) (yayiikaah)
ya-da#-yi-(Ø)--Øyeeh: 3+ subjects dump O (yadayiiyeeh)

## Cą-Prefix + Extended Base

Postpositional bi'ą- is reduced from bi'ąą-: beyond it. As a verb prefix it carries the meaning "over it" (as "over but lying <u>on</u> a limb" - a rope tossed over a limb). It is loosely joined to the Verb Base, as:

Table 2

T = any Verb Theme

| PERSON | Sgl | | PERSON | Dpl | |
|---|---|---|---|---|---|
| 1. | bi'ąish-T | (bi'ąishdeeł) | 1. | bi'ąiil-T | (bi'ąiildeeł) |
| 2. | bi'ąi-T | (bi'ąiłdeeł) | 2. | bi'ąooł-T | (bi'ąoołdeeł) |
| SP. | bi'ąi(d)-T | (bi'ąildeeł) | | | |
| 3o. | yi'ąyii-T | (yi'ąyiiłdeeł) | | | |
| 3a. | bi'ąjii-T | (bi'ąjiiłdeeł) | | | |

bi'ą#-yi-(Ø)--łdeeł: toss a SFO over it (as a rope over a limb)
bi'ą#-yi-(Ø)--Ø'áád: toss a FFO over it (as a blanket over a clothesline)

## Cá-Prefix + Extended Base

Ná-: Position 1d: reversionary, náá(ná)-: Position 1e: semeliterative and -ná⁴-: Position 1b (in the compound ya-ná-): up into the air, occur as Disjunct determinants in the Yi-Ø-Imperfective. Ná⁴-1d and ya-ná-1b behave differently, as illustrated below. (See Table 4.)

Table 3

T = any Verb Theme

| PERSON | Prefix Position | | | | | | | | | |
|---|---|---|---|---|---|---|---|---|---|---|
| Sgl | 1d | + | 4 | + | 5 | + | Base | | | as in: |
| 1. | né- | + | Ø | + | --- | + | (y)iish-T | > | *néish-T | néishshį́į́h |
| 2. | né- | + | Ø | + | --- | + | (y)ii-T | > | néi-T | néishį́į́h |
| 3. | né- | + | Ø | + | --- | + | (y)ii-T | > | néi-T | néijį́į́h |
| SP. | né- | + | Ø | + | --- | + | (y)ii(d)-T | > | néi(d)-T | néilzhį́į́h |
| 3o. | ná- | + | y(i)- | + | --- | + | -ii-T | > | náyii-T | náyiishį́į́h |
| 3a. | ń- | + | Ø | + | -j(i)- | + | -ii-T | > | ńjii-T | ńjiishį́į́h |
| AP. | ná-- | + | O | + | '(a)d(i)- | + | -ii(d)-T | > | náO'dii(d)-T | nábi'diilzhį́į́h |
| Dpl | | | | | | | | | | |
| 1. | né- | + | Ø | + | --- | + | (y)-ii(d)-T | > | néii(d)-T | néiilzhį́į́h |
| 2. | ná- | + | Ø | + | --- | + | (w)-oo(h)-T | > | náoo(h)-T | náoohshį́į́h |

*written néish- = néiish-

ná#-yi-(Ø)--shį́į́h(< -łzhį́į́h): reblacken it, polish them (black shoes)
ná#-yi-(Ø)--(d)jį́į́h (< d-zhį́į́h): turn black again (i.e. revert to black)

## Ya-ná-1b + Extended Base

The compound prefix ya-ná- of Position 1b takes the shape yanáa- in contraction with yi-6c before the 1st person sgl subject pronoun -sh- and in the 2nd and 3rd person and Simple Passive, where Position 8 is vacant.

Table 4

T = any Verb Theme

| PERSON | Prefix Position | | | | | | | | | |
|---|---|---|---|---|---|---|---|---|---|---|
| Sgl | 1b | + | 4 | + | 5 | + | Base | | | as in: |
| 1. | yanáa- | + | Ø | + | --- | + | (yii)sh-T | > | yanáash-T | yanáashne' |
| 2. | yanáa- | + | Ø | + | --- | + | (yii)-T | > | yanáa-T | yanáałne' |
| 3. | yanáa- | + | Ø | + | --- | + | (yii)-T | > | yanáa-T | yanáatłíísh |
| SP. | yanáa- | + | Ø | + | --- | + | (yii)(d)-T | > | yanáa(d)-T | yanáalne' |
| 3o. | yaná- | + | y(i)- | + | --- | + | -ii-T | > | yanáyii-T | yanáyiiłne' |
| 3a. | yań- | + | Ø | + | -j(i)- | + | -ii-T | > | yańjii-T | yańjiiłne' |
| AP. | yaná- | + | O | + | '(a)d(i)- | + | -ii(d)-T | > | yanáO'dii(d)-T | yanábi'diilt'e' |
| Dpl | | | | | | | | | | |
| 1. | yané- | + | Ø | + | --- | + | -ii(d)-T | > | yanéii(d)-T | yanéiilne' |
| 2. | yaná- | + | Ø | + | --- | + | -oo(h)-T | > | yanáoo(h)-T | yanáoołne' |

ya-ná#-yi-(Ø)--łne': toss a SRO up into the air
ya-ná#-yi-(Ø)--Øtłíísh: animate subject bounces up into the air
ya-ná#-yi-(Ø)--łt'e': toss a SSO or an AnO up into the air

## Ci-Prefix + Extended Base

The only Ci- prefix of Position 1b that appears in determinant position is the loosely joined postposition P-k'i-: on P.

Table 5

T = any Verb Theme

| PERSON | Prefix Position | | | | | | | | | |
|---|---|---|---|---|---|---|---|---|---|---|
| Sgl | 1b | + | 4 | + | 5 | + | Base | | | as in: |
| 1. | C(i)- | + | Ø | + | --- | + | -(y)iish-T | > | Ciish-T | bik'iishne' |
| 2. | C(i)- | + | Ø | + | --- | + | -(y)ii-T | > | Cii-T | bik'iiłne' |
| 3. | C(i)- | + | Ø | + | --- | + | -(y)ii-T | > | Cii-T | yik'iilyeed |
| SP. | C(i)- | + | Ø | + | --- | + | -(y)ii(d)-T | > | Cii(d)-T | bik'iilne' |
| 3o. | Ci- | + | y(i)- | + | --- | + | -ii-T | > | Ciyii-T | yik'iyiiłne' |
| 3a. | Ci- | + | Ø | + | -j(i)- | + | -ii-T | > | Cijii-T | bik'ijiiłne' |
| Dpl | | | | | | | | | | |
| 1. | C- | + | Ø | + | --- | + | (y)ii(d)-T | > | Cii(d)-T | bik'iilne' |
| 2. | Ci- | + | Ø | + | --- | + | (w)oo(h)-T | > | Cioo(h)-T | bikioołne' |

P-k'i#-yi-(Ø)--łne': drop a SRO onto P (as a stone down onto one's foot)
P-k'i#-yi-(Ø)--lyeed: jump P, assail or attack P

Cí-Prefix + Extended Base

Table 6

T = any Verb Theme

| PERSON Sgl | Prefix Position 1b | + | 4 | + | 5 | + | Base | | | as in: | |
|---|---|---|---|---|---|---|---|---|---|---|---|
| 1. | Cí- | + | Ø | + | --- | + | -ish-T | > | Cíísh-T | kííshjiid | bííshtł'in |
| 2. | Cí- | + | Ø | + | --- | + | -i-T | > | Cíí-T | kííłjiid | bíítł'in |
| 3. | Cí- | + | Ø | + | --- | + | -i-T | > | Cíí-T | kíílyeed | yíílyeed |
| SP. | Cí- | + | Ø | + | --- | + | -i(d)-T | > | Cíí(d)-T | kííljiid | bíítł'in |
| 3o. | Cí- | + | y(i)- | + | --- | + | -ii-T | > | Cíyii-T | kíyiiłjiid | yíyiitł'in |
| 3a. | Cí- | + | Ø | + | -j(i)- | + | -ii-T | > | Cíjii-T | kíjiiłjiid | bíjiitl'in |
| AP. | Cí- | + | O | + | '(a)d(i)-+ | | -ii(d)-T | > | CíO'dii(d)-T | kíbi'diiljiid | --- |
| Dpl | | | | | | | | | | | |
| 1. | Cí- | + | Ø | + | --- | + | (y)ii(d)-T | > | Cíí(d)-T | kííljiid | bíítł'in |
| 2. | Cí- | + | Ø | + | --- | + | (w)oo(h)-T | > | Cíoo(h)-T | kíoołjiid | bóohtł'in |

kí#-yi-(Ø)--łjiid: lug O up an incline on one's back (kííshjiid)
kí#-yi-(Ø)--lyeed: run up an incline (as upstairs - one subject) (kííshyeed)
bí#-yi-(Ø)--Øtł'in: pile O against it (as logs against a wall) (bííshtł'in)
bí#-yi-(Ø)--lyeed: run up it (one subject - as up a ladder; get on one - as a spider) (bííshyeed)

## RECAPITULATION

## YI-Ø-IMPERFECTIVE

### 1. Base Paradigm

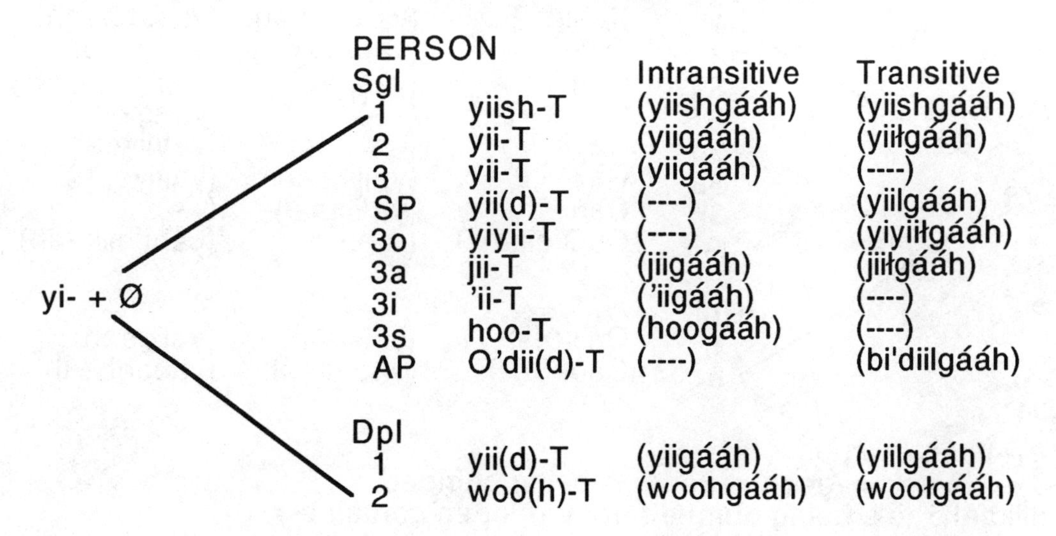


yi-i-(Ø)--Øgááh: turn white
yi-i-(Ø)--łgááh: whiten O

## *CONJUNCT PREFIXES*

### 2. Ci- Prefix + Extended Base

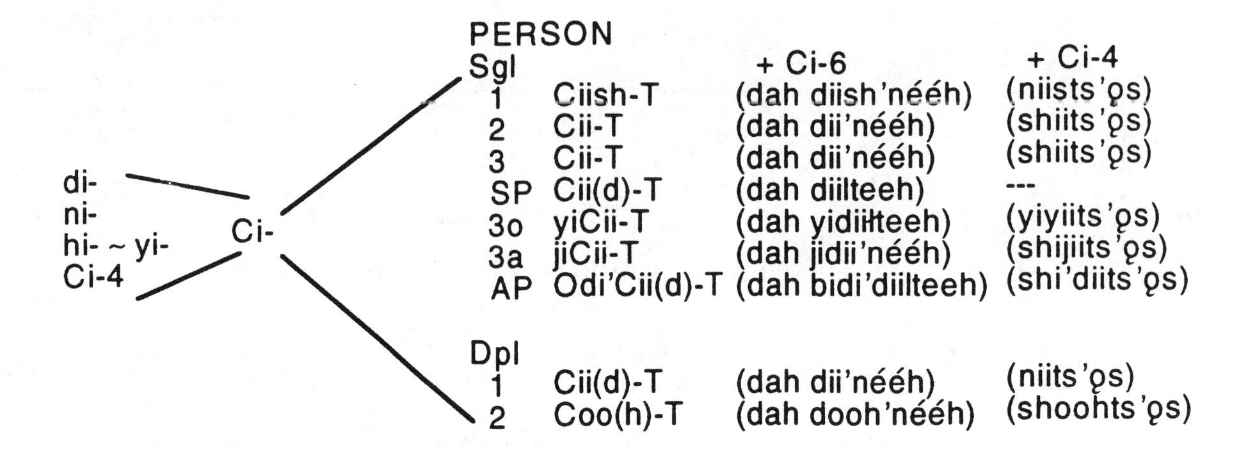

di- / ni- / hi- ~ yi- / Ci-4 → Ci-

| PERSON | | + Ci-6 | + Ci-4 |
|---|---|---|---|
| Sgl | | | |
| 1 | Ciish-T | (dah diish'nééh) | (niists'ǫs) |
| 2 | Cii-T | (dah dii'nééh) | (shiits'ǫs) |
| 3 | Cii-T | (dah dii'nééh) | (shiits'ǫs) |
| SP | Cii(d)-T | (dah diilteeh) | --- |
| 3o | yiCii-T | (dah yidiiłteeh) | (yiyiits'ǫs) |
| 3a | jiCii-T | (dah jidii'nééh) | (shijiits'ǫs) |
| AP | Odi'Cii(d)-T | (dah bidi'diilteeh) | (shi'diits'ǫs) |
| Dpl | | | |
| 1 | Cii(d)-T | (dah dii'nééh) | (niits'ǫs) |
| 2 | Coo(h)-T | (dah dooh'nééh) | (shoohts'ǫs) |

d(i)-ii-(Ø)--(d)'nééh, dah---: start off crawling
n(i)-ii-(Ø)--łgááh: heat O (niishgááh)
n(i)-ii-(Ø)--Øts'ǫs: give you a kiss (niists'ǫs)

## *DISJUNCT PREFIXES*

### 4. Ca- Prefix + Extended Base

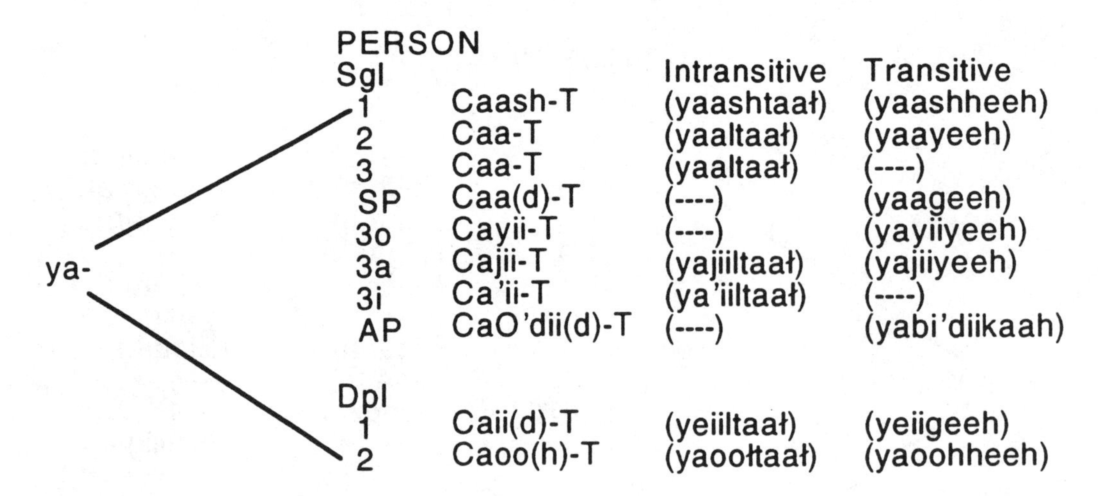

ya-

| PERSON | | Intransitive | Transitive |
|---|---|---|---|
| Sgl | | | |
| 1 | Caash-T | (yaashtaał) | (yaashheeh) |
| 2 | Caa-T | (yaaltaał) | (yaayeeh) |
| 3 | Caa-T | (yaaltaał) | (----) |
| SP | Caa(d)-T | (----) | (yaageeh) |
| 3o | Cayii-T | (----) | (yayiiyeeh) |
| 3a | Cajii-T | (yajiiltaał) | (yajiiyeeh) |
| 3i | Ca'ii-T | (ya'iiltaał) | (----) |
| AP | CaO'dii(d)-T | (----) | (yabi'diikaah) |
| Dpl | | | |
| 1 | Caii(d)-T | (yeiiltaał) | (yeiigeeh) |
| 2 | Caoo(h)-T | (yaoołtaał) | (yaoohheeh) |

ya-i-(Ø)--ltaał: dash off
ya-i-(Ø)--(d)yeeh < -geeh: it (load) is being dumped
(yabi'diikaah: he's being dumped from an open container)

## 5. Cá- Prefix + Extended Base

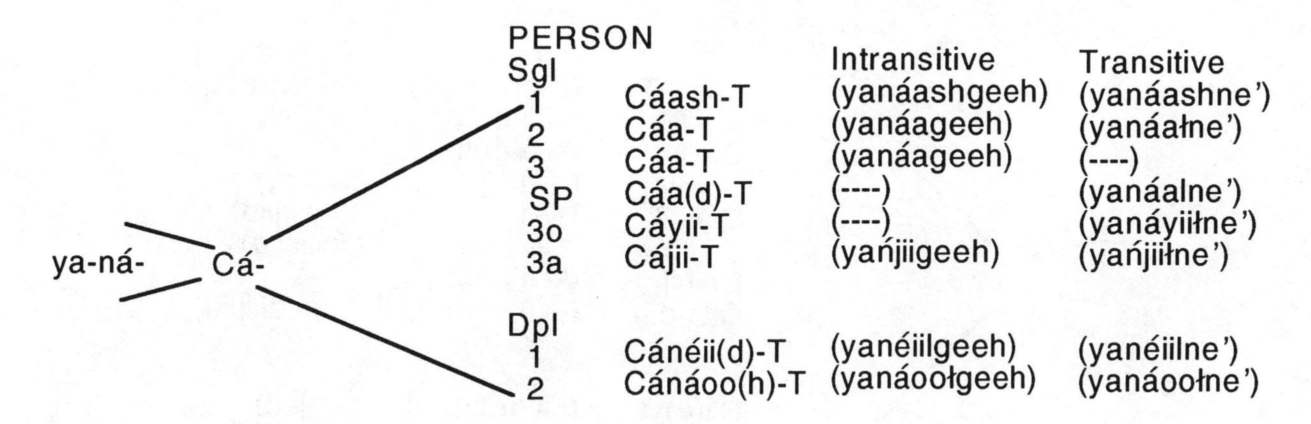


| PERSON | | Intransitive | Transitive |
|---|---|---|---|
| Sgl | | | |
| 1 | Cáash-T | (yanáashgeeh) | (yanáashne') |
| 2 | Cáa-T | (yanáageeh) | (yanáałne') |
| 3 | Cáa-T | (yanáageeh) | (----) |
| SP | Cáa(d)-T | (----) | (yanáalne') |
| 3o | Cáyii-T | (----) | (yanáyiiłne') |
| 3a | Cájii-T | (yańjiigeeh) | (yańjiiłne') |
| Dpl | | | |
| 1 | Cánéii(d)-T | (yanéiilgeeh) | (yanéiilne') |
| 2 | Cánáoo(h)-T | (yanáoołgeeh) | (yanáoołne') |

ya-ná#-i-(Ø)--Øgeeh: bounce up into the air
ya-ná#-i-(Ø)--łne': toss SRO up into the air (yanáashne')

## 6. Ci- Prefix + Extended Base

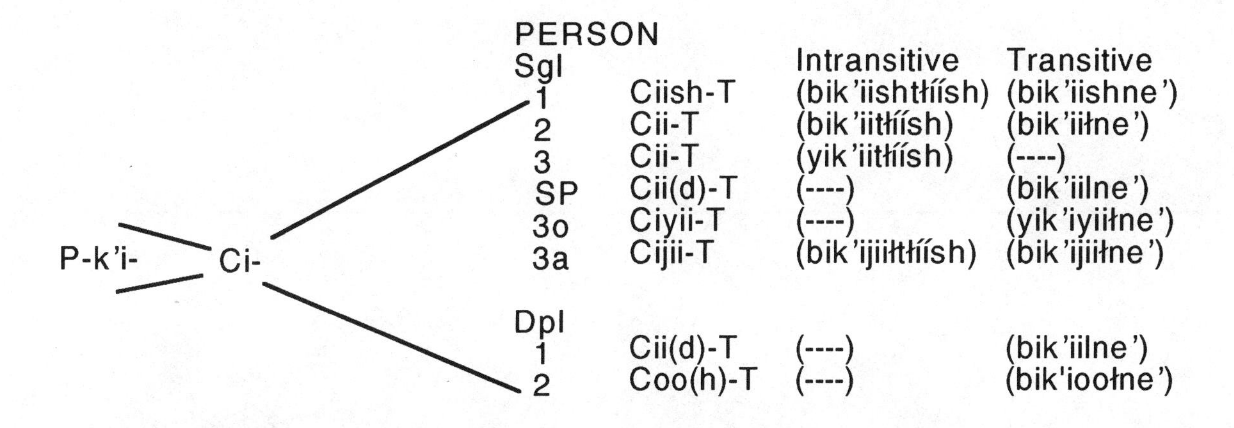


| PERSON | | Intransitive | Transitive |
|---|---|---|---|
| Sgl | | | |
| 1 | Ciish-T | (bik'iishtłíísh) | (bik'iishne') |
| 2 | Cii-T | (bik'iitłíísh) | (bik'iiłne') |
| 3 | Cii-T | (yik'iitłíísh) | (----) |
| SP | Cii(d)-T | (----) | (bik'iilne') |
| 3o | Ciyii-T | (----) | (yik'iyiiłne') |
| 3a | Cijii-T | (bik'ijiiłtłíísh) | (bik'ijiiłne') |
| Dpl | | | |
| 1 | Cii(d)-T | (----) | (bik'iilne') |
| 2 | Coo(h)-T | (----) | (bik'ioołne') |

P-k'i#-i-(Ø)--łne': drop a SRO on P
P-k'i#-i-(Ø)--Øtłíísh: fall on P (single subject)

## 7. Cí- Prefix + Extended Base

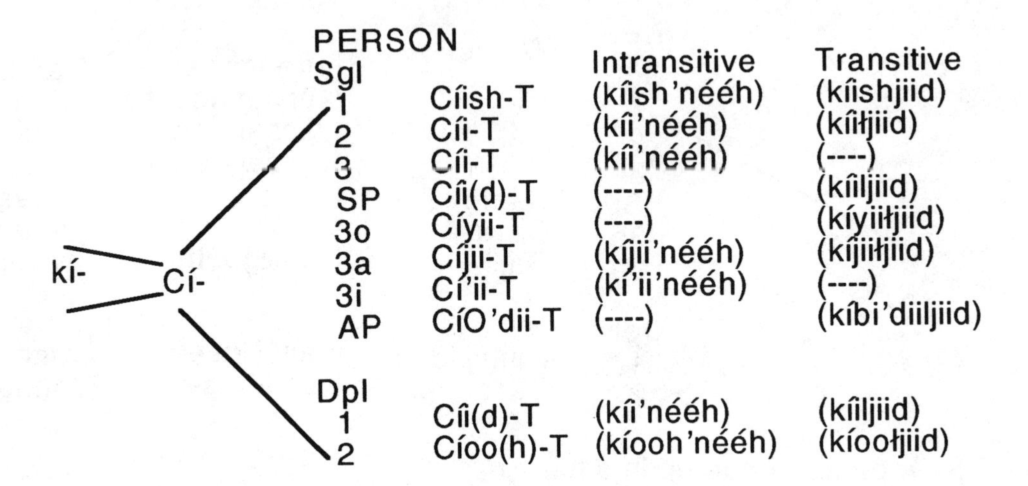


| PERSON | | Intransitive | Transitive |
|---|---|---|---|
| Sgl | | | |
| 1 | Cíísh-T | (kíísh'nééh) | (kííshjiid) |
| 2 | Cíí-T | (kíí'nééh) | (kííłjiid) |
| 3 | Cíí-T | (kíí'nééh) | (----) |
| SP | Cíí(d)-T | (----) | (kíílјiid) |
| 3o | Cíyii-T | (----) | (kíyiiłjiid) |
| 3a | Cíjii-T | (kíjii'nééh) | (kíjiiłjiid) |
| 3i | Cí'ii-T | (kí'ii'nééh) | (----) |
| AP | CíO'dii-T | (----) | (kíbi'diiljiid) |
| Dpl | | | |
| 1 | Cíí(d)-T | (kíí'nééh) | (kííljiid) |
| 2 | Cíoo(h)-T | (kíooh'nééh) | (kíoołjiid) |

kí#-i-(Ø)--(d)'nééh: crawl up an incline
kí#-i-(Ø)--łjiid: lug O up an incline on one's back (kííshjiid)

# CHAPTER 3:

# THE USITATIVE AND ITERATIVE MODES

## THE USITATIVE MODE

The Usitative Mode describes actions or events that are performed, or that take place, repeatedly and usually, customarily. The Usitative is marked by stem shape alone. It is conjugated in the same pattern as the corresponding Imperfective. The Usitative stem is Repetitive while the corresponding Imperfective is punctual or continuant in aspect.

The Ø-, Yi-Ø and Si-Imperfectives may have a corresponding Usitative, but ni-Position 7 marker of ni-Imperfective never occurs in the Usitative Mode - Ni-Imperfective is complemented by Ø-Usitative.

Compare:

1. Ø-Imperfective / Usitative

| | |
|---|---|
| Ø-Imperfective: | 'e'e'aah, the sun is (in the act of) going down |
| Usitative: | 'e'e'ááh, the sun usually goes down |
| Ø-Imperfective: | gohwééh yishdlą́, I'm drinking coffee |
| Usitative: | gohwééh yishdlį́į́h, I usually drink coffee |
| Ø-Imperfective: | bíłák'eestsóós, I'm handing a FFO to him |
| Usitative: | bíłák'eestsos, I usually hand a FFO to him |

2. Ni-Imperfective / Ø-Usitative

| | |
|---|---|
| Ni-Imperfective: | tł'óó'góó ch'íníshááh, I'm (in the act of) going outside |
| Ø-Usitative: | tł'óó'góó ch'éshááh, I usually go outside |
| Ni-Imperfective: | baa nish'aah, I'm (in the act of) giving him a SRO |
| Ø-Usitative: | baa yish'ááh, I usually give him a SRO |

3. Si-Imperfective / Usitative

| | |
|---|---|
| Si-Imperfective: | dah shishłé, I'm (in the act of) setting them up at rest (as a pair of shoes on a chair) |
| Si-Usitative: | dah shishłééh, I usually set them up at rest |

4. Yi-Ø- Imperfective / Usitative

| | |
|---|---|
| Yi-Ø-Imperfective: | ńdiish'nééh, I'm (in the act of) getting up |
| Yi-Ø-Usitative: | ńdiish'nah, I usually get up |
| Yi-Ø-Imperfective: | niishch'íił, I'm (in the act of) blinking |
| Yi-Ø-Usitative: | niishch'ił, I usually blink |

## THE ITERATIVE MODE

A type of frequentative, the Iterative serves to describe an action or event that is performed or that takes place on repeated occasions. The Iterative is based on the same Repetitive stem as the Usitative, but with the addition of a Disjunct ná- ~ ní- ~ ń- prefix assigned to Position 2. The ná-Iterative marker is probably identical with ná[5]-: Position 1b, which also marks action as Repetitive.

The Iterative Mode is conjugated as a Ø-, Si- or Yi-Ø Imperfective. The ni-conjugation marker of Position 7 does not appear in the Iterative Mode — Ni-Imperfectives are complemented by Ø-Iteratives.

Many Ø-Verb Themes shift to D-classifier in the Iterative Mode, and some Ł-class Verb Themes shift to L- under D-effect.

Compare:

1. Ø-Imperfective / Iterative

Ø-Imperfective: 'e'e'aah, the sun is (in the act of) going down
Ø-Usitative: 'e'e'ááh, the sun usually goes down
Ø-Iterative: 'aná'át'ááh, the sun repeatedly goes down (i.e. on repeated occasions)

Ø-Imperfective: taah yilyeed, it's (in the act of) running into the water
Ø-Usitative: taah yilwo', it usually runs into the water
Ø-Iterative: taah nálwo', it repeatedly runs into the water (i.e. on repeated occasions)

2. Ni-Imperfective / Ø-Iterative

Ni-Imperfective: tł'óó'góó ch'íníshááh, I'm (in the act of) going outside
Ø-Usitative: tł'óó'góó ch'éshááh, I usually go outside
Ø-Iterative: tł'óó'góó ch'ínáshdááh, I repeatedly go outside (i.e. on repeated occasions)

3. Si-Imperfective / Si-Iterative

Si-Imperfective: tsin bąąh hashish'nééh, I'm (in the act of) climbing the tree
Si-Iterative: tsin bąąh háášhísh'nah, I repeatedly climb the tree (i.e. on repeated occasions). (Háá- < a contraction of ha-: Position 1b, "up," + -ná-Position 2)

4. Yi-Ø-Imperfective / Yi-Ø-Iterative

yi-Ø-Imperfective: sitsii' yiishch'įįł, I'm (in the act of) curling my hair
yi-Ø-Iterative: sitsii' néishch'ił, I repeatedly curl my hair (i.e. on repeated occasions)

yi-Ø-Imperfective: yiishtał, I'm (in the act of) giving him a kick
yi-Ø-Iterative: néishtał, I repeatedly give him a kick (i.e. on repeated occasions)

All fully conjugated verbs generally include the Iterative Mode, so ná-Position 2, the Iterative Mode marker, occurs both as the conjugational determinant and as an inflectional element separated by intervening pronominal or derivational prefixes from the Base. Thus:

1. Ø-Imperfective / Ø-Iterative

Ø-Imperfective: yishdleesh, I'm painting it
Ø-Iterative: náshdlish, I repeatedly paint it (i.e. on repeated occasions)
(ná- = conjugational determinant)

Ø-Imperfective: dishníísh, I'm (in the act of) starting to work
Ø-Iterative: ńdíshnish, I repeatedly start to work (i.e. on repeated occasions)
(-di- = conjugational determinant)

Ø-Imperfective: nishdaah, I'm (in the act of) sitting down
Ø-Iterative: náníshdaah, I repeatedly sit down (i.e. on repeated occasions)
(-ni- = conjugational determinant)

Ø-Imperfective: nahałtin, it's raining
Ø-Iterative: nináháłtį́į́h, it repeatedly rains (i.e. on repeated occasions)
(-ha- = conjugational determinant)

2. Yi-Ø-Imperfective / Yi-Ø-Iterative

yi-Ø-Imperfective: yiishgááh, I'm whitening it
yi-Ø-Iterative: néishgah (~ néiishgah), I repeatedly whiten it (i.e. on repeated occasions)
(ná- = conjugational determinant)

yi-Ø-Imperfective: ńdiish'nééh, I'm (in the act of) getting up
yi-Ø-Iterative: nínádiish'nah (~ náádiish'nah), I repeatedly get up (i.e. on repeated occasions)
(-di- = conjugational determinant)

yi-Ø-Imperfective: niishgááh, I'm heating it
yi-Ø-Iterative: náníishgah, I repeatedly heat it (i.e. on repeated occasions)
(-ni- = conjugational determinant)

Lacking distinctive stem shape, the Imperfective Reversionary (marked by ná-1d) and the Iterative (marked by ná-2) are homophonous, as:

náníshdaah: I sit back down; I repeatedly sit down
nádleeh: it is changing back; it repeatedly changes
néistséėh: I'm seeing it again - "re-seeing it"/I repeatedly catch sight of it
néishshį́į́h: I'm re-blackening it; I repeatedly blacken it

Compare:

| PERSON | | | | | | as in: Imperfective | Iterative |
|---|---|---|---|---|---|---|---|
| Sgl | 2 + | | Base | | | ná-1d | ná-2 |
| 1. | ná- | + | (yi)-sh-T | > | nász-T | 'iih násh'nééh | 'iih násh'nah |
| 2. | ná- | + | -ni-T | > | nání-T | 'iih nání'nééh | 'iih nání'nah |
| 3. | ná- | + | (yi)-Ø-T | > | ná-T | 'iih ná'nééh | 'iih ná'nah |
| Dpl | | | | | | | |
| 1. | ná- | + | (y)-ii(d)-T | > | néii(d)-T | 'iih néii'nééh | 'iih néii'nah |
| *2. | ná- | + | (w)o(h)-T | > | ná(h)-T | 'iih náh'nééh | 'iih náh'nah |

*or optionally náoh'nééh/ náohnah

'iih ná-(Ø)--(d)'nééh: crawl back inside
'iih ná-(Ø)--(d)'nah: repeatedly crawl inside, crawl in on repeated occasions

Ná-Position 2 + 6a/6b Prefixes + Ø-Base

| PERSON | Prefix Position | | | | | + di-6a | + ni-6b |
|---|---|---|---|---|---|---|---|
| Sgl | 2* + | Ø-4 | 5 | 6a/6b | Base | Intransitive | Transitive |
| 1. | ná-/ní-/ń- | --- | --- | -Ci- | (yi)-sh-T | ńdíshníísh | nánístsis |
| 2. | ná-/ní-/ń- | --- | --- | -Ci- | -ni-T | ńdílníísh | nánítsis |
| 3. | ná-/ní-/ń- | --- | --- | -Ci- | (yi)-Ø-T | ńdílníísh | --- |
| 3i. | ná-/ní-/ń- | --- | -'a- | -Ci- | (yi)-Ø-T | ń'diilnííish | --- |
| 3o. | né- | -i- | --- | -Ci- | (yi)-Ø-T | --- | **néiniłtsis** |
| 3a. | ná-/ní- | --- | -zh- | -Ci- | (yi)-Ø-T | nízhdílnííish | názhníłtsis |
| 3s. | ná- | --- | -ho- | -Ci- | (yi)-Ø-T | náhodilzhish | --- |
| Dpl | | | | | | | |
| 1. | ná-/ní-/ń- | | --- | -Ci- | (y)-ii(d)-T | ńdiilnííish | náníiltsis |
| *2. | ná-/ní-/ń-+ | | --- | -Ci- | (w)o(h)-T | ńdółnííish | nánóołtsis |

* The ná-prefixes take variable shape. See chart, pages 30-31.

ná-di-(Ø)--lnííish: start to work, commence working (on repeated occasions)
ná-ni-(Ø)--łtsis: extinguish it (fire) (on repeated occasions)
ná-ho-di-(Ø)--lzhish: it repeatedly starts (as an era or season)

# CHAPTER 4:

# THE PERFECTIVE MODE

The Perfective Mode is distinguished by Stem shape for most Verb Bases, and a single Perfective Stem shape usually appears, irrespective of Aspect. Thus:

| | | |
|---|---|---|
| Momentaneous: | náát̲ą́: | I lowered a SSO down |
| Continuative: | nisét̲ą́: | I carried a SSO about - made a round trip with it |
| Distributive: | ndasét̲ą́: | I set SSO about |
| Transitional: | ńdiit̲ą́: | I picked a SSO up |

Conjugation markers: The Perfective is marked by yi- (= ghi-), ni-, si- or Ø in Position 7. The Ø-Perfective is derived with a yi-prefix of Position 6c that serves to mark Transitional Aspect. In addition a high tone, derived from an underlying n̲ marks Perfective Mode in some constructions.

Perfective Verbs are

1. *Active:* intransitive or transitive; passive, mediopassive or reflexive; describe an action or event.

2. *Neuter:* intransitive or transitive; passive, mediopassive or reflexive. Neuter Perfectives describe the subject or direct object as being in a state of rest (the Positionals and Extensionals) or they are concerned with features of status (distance, visibility, texture, number).

   Each Neuter Perfective Verb Base is conjugated in a single paradigm.

Conjugational Patterns: The Perfective Mode is conjugated in two distinctive paradigms for each of the four modal-aspectival Conjugation markers – a total of eight patterns.

Of these, one pattern corresponds to Ø/Ł-class Verb Themes (i.e. Themes that include a Ø- or Ł-classifier); and the other corresponds to D/L-class Verb Themes.

The high tone marker of the Perfective Mode appears in the 1st and 2nd persons singular and 3rd persons singular/duoplural of Ø/Ł-class verbs, but in the 2nd person singular alone for D/L-class verbs.

# 1. THE YI-PERFECTIVE

## *ACTIVE VERBS*

The Base Paradigms are composed of a Theme (Stem and Classifier Prefix) in Positions 9-10, a subject pronoun in Position 8, which may be Ø, and the Conjugation Marker in Position 7.

The Base Paradigms of the Ø/Ł-class and D/L-class Perfectives are described below:

### The Base Paradigm

Table 1

T = any Verb Theme

| PERSON | Ø/Ł-Class | | | | | | | | D/L-Class | | | | | | | | |
|---|---|---|---|---|---|---|---|---|---|---|---|---|---|---|---|---|---|
| Sgl | 7 | + | 8 | + | T | | | as in: | 7 | + | 8 | + | T | | | as in: |
| 1 | yí- | + | Ø | + | T | > | yí-T | yícha | yi- | + | -sh- | + | T | > | yish-T | taah yish'na' |
| 2 | yí- | + | -ní- | + | T | > | yíní-T | yínícha | yí- | + | -ní- | + | T | > | yíní-T | taah yíní'na' |
| 3 | yí- | + | Ø | + | T | > | yí-T | yícha | yi- | + | Ø | + | T | > | yi-T | taah yi'na' |
| Dpl | | | | | | | | | | | | | | | | |
| 1 | y- | + | -ii(d) | + | T | > | yii(d)-T | yiicha | y- | + | -ii(d)- | + | T | > | yii(d)-T | taah yii'na' |
| 2 | w- | + | -oo- | + | T | > | woo-T | woocha | w- | + | -oo(h) | + | T | > | woo(h)-T | taah wooh'na' |

(yi)--Øcha: cry

taah (yi)--(d)'na': crawl into water

### The Extended Base Paradigms

#### 1. Conjunct Prefixes

The primary extension of the Base Paradigm is that produced by incorporating the subject pronouns of Position 5 and/or the direct object pronouns of Position 4 with the Base. These, as well as the derivational-thematic prefixes of Position 6, behave in distinctive manners, depending on the composition of the Verb Theme: themes produced with Ø/Ł-classifiers behave differently in some constructions from those that contain D/L-classifiers.

With Ø/Ł-Class verbs the Conjunct Prefixes are simply combined with the Base, with assimilative raising of prefix tone where the Base morpheme is high.

With D/L-Class Verbs, on the other hand, the Yi-conjugation marker of Position 7 appears as -ee- in 1st person sgl and as -oo- in 3rd person, Agentive Passive, Reflexive and Reciprocal constructions in the presence of a Conjunct Prefix of Position 4, 5 or 6.

## Prefixes of Position 5 + Base

### Table 2

T = any Verb Theme

| PERSON | Ø/Ł-Class | | | | | D/L-Class | | | | |
|---|---|---|---|---|---|---|---|---|---|---|
| Sgl/Dpl | 5 | + Base | | | as in: | 5 | + Base | | | as in: |
| 3a. | ji- | (y)í- | > | jíí-T | (jíícha) | j- | -oo- | > | joo-T | joo'na' |
| 3i. | 'i- | (y)í- | > | 'íí-T | ('íícha) | '- | -oo- | > | 'oo-T | 'oo'na' |
| 3s. | ho- | (y)í- | > | hóó--T | (hóózhǫǫd) | h- | -oo- | > | hoo-T | hoodzą́ |
| AP | --- | --- | | --- | --- | '(a)d- | -oo- | > | -'(a)doo-T | bi'dooch'id |

Ø/Ł

jíícha: he/she wept
'íícha: there was weeping
hóózhǫǫd: conditions became peaceful

D/L

taah joo'na': he/she crawled into the water
taah 'oo'na': something crawled into the water
(shił taah 'oo'na': I rode into the water on a tractor or other unspecified crawling vehicle)
bii' hoodzą́: it's hollow
bi'dooch'id: he was scratched

## Ci- Prefixes of Position 4 + Extended Base

### Table 3A
### Ø/Ł-Class Verbs

The Ci-prefixes of Position 4 are those composed of a consonant + the vowel -i-. The object pronoun prefixes of Position 4 include the divergent forms 'a- ~ i- ~ '-: 3i (something / someone unspecified) and ha- ~ ho- ~ hw-: 3s (the pronoun of space / area), also functioning as the object pronoun representing 3a (4th) person. 'A- and ha- are treated separately.

In 3rd person (where a 3rd person direct object is represented by yi- in Position 4 and the subject is also 3rd person), the 3o pronoun appears to be reduplicated in the absence of a preceding prefix, as:

> yiyíích'id (< yi-3o + yí-3o + [y]ích'id: he scratched him (Cf. shíích'id (< shí + [y]ích'id, he scratched me); hayíích'id (< ha#- + yi- + [y]ích'id): he scratched it out)

Ø in Position 4 represents a third person direct object when the subject of the verb is 1st or 2nd person, an environment in which the intransitive and transitive paradigms converge in shape.

T = any Verb Theme

| Sgl | PERSON 4 | + | Prefix Position 5 | + | Base | | Intransitive | Transitive + Ø-4 | + Ci-4 |
|---|---|---|---|---|---|---|---|---|---|
| 1. | Ø/Ci- | + | --- | + | (y)í-T | > | yícha | taah yíł́óóz | nííł́óóz |
| 2. | Ø/Ci- | + | --- | + | (y)íní-T | > | yínícha | taah yíníł́óóz | shííníł́óóz |
| 3. | ---/Ci- | + | --- | + | yí-T | > | yícha | --- | shííł́óóz |
| 3o. | *yiyi- | + | --- | + | (y)í-T | > | --- | --- | yiyííł́óóz |
| 3a. | Ø/Ci- | + | ji- | + | (y)í-T | > | jíícha | taah jííł́óóz | shijííł́óóz |
| Dpl | | | | | | | | | |
| 1. | Ø/C(i)- | + | --- | + | (y)ii(d)-T | > | yiicha | taah yiidlóóz | niidlóóz |
| 2. | Ø/C(i)- | + | --- | + | (w)oo-T | > | woocha | taah woolóóz | shoolóóz |

(yí)--Øcha: cry

(yí)--Ølóóz, taah ---: lead O to water

## Table 3B
## D/L Class Verbs

A Ci- prefix of Position 4 + yi-7 combine to take the shape C-ee- in 1st person singular, and C-oo- in 3rd person and Agentive Passive.

There are few simple transitive D/L class verbs.

T = any Verb Theme

| Sgl | PERSON 4 | + | Prefix Position 5 | + | Base | as in: Ø-4 | + Ci-4 |
|---|---|---|---|---|---|---|---|
| 1. | Ø/C(i)- | + | --- | + | yish-/-eesh-T | yishghal | neeshghal |
| 2. | Ø/C(i)- | + | --- | + | yíní-T | yíníł́ghal | shííníł́ghal |
| 3. | --/C(i)- | + | --- | + | yi-T/-oo-T | --- | shoolghal |
| SP | Ø/-- | + | --- | + | yi(d)-T | yidlóóz | --- |
| 3o. | y- | + | --- | + | -oo-T | --- | yoolghal |
| 3a. | Ø/Ci- | + | -j- | + | -oo-T | joolghal | shijoolghal |
| AP | O | + | -'(a)d- | + | -oo-T | --- | bi'doolghal |
| Dpl | | | | | | | |
| 1. | Ø/C(i)- | + | --- | + | (y)ii(d)-T | yiilghal | niilghal |
| 2. | Ø/C(i)- | + | --- | + | (w)oo(h)-T | woołghal | shoołghal |

(yi)--lghal: eat O (meat) (yishghal: I ate it; neeshghal: I ate you; shííníł́ghal: you ate me; shoolghal: it ate me; niilghal, we ate you, etc.)
(yi)--ldlóóz, taah ---: it was led to water

Note: the Verb Base (yi)--lghal: eat O (meat) is a Mediopassive type of construction, and it does not permit a Simple Passive.

All verbs of locomotion, transitive and intransitive, include a simple yi-Perfective. However, simple verbs in this category, lacking a derivational-directional prefix, require an independent adverbial directional marker, such as:

biih: into it     taah: into water     kįįh: into town

Motion Verbs of the types listed below are all conjugated as simple Yi-Perfectives:

| OBJECT CLASS | HANDLE put O | PROPEL toss/drop O | FLY fall |
|---|---|---|---|
| SRO | (yi)--Ø'ą́ | (yi)--łne' | (yi)--lts'id |
| LPB | (yi)--Øyį́ | (yi)--Øyį́ | (yi)--łhęęzh |
| NCM | (yi)--łjool | (yi)--łjool | (yi)--Øjool |
| SFO | (yi)--Ølá | (yi)--łdéél | (yi)--Ødéél |
| SSO | (yi)--Øtą́ | (yi)--łt'e' | (yi)--0kę́ę́z |
| FFO | (yi)--łtsooz | (yi)--Ø'ah | (yi)--Øna' |
| MM | (yi)--Øtłéé' | (yi)--Øtłéé' | (yi)--łhęézh |
| PLO | (yi)--Ønil | (yi)--Ønil | (yi)--ni-Ødee' |
| PLO | (yi)--Øjaa' | (yi)--łkaad | (yi)--ni-Ødee' |
| OC | (yi)--Øką́ | (yi)--łkaad | (yi)--Økaad |
| AnO | (yi)----łtį́ | (yi)--łt'e' | (yi)--Øtłizh/Øgo' |

E.g.
shich'ah tsits'aa' biih yí'ą́: I put my hat into the box
shich'ah taah yíłne': I tossed/dropped my hat into the water
shich'ah k'asdą́ą́' taah yílts'id: my hat nearly fell into the water

mósí yázhí taah yíłtį́: I put the kitten into the water
mósí yázhí taah yíłt'e': I tossed/dropped the kitten into the water
mósí yázhí k'asdą́ą́' taah yítłizh: the kitten nearly fell into the water

## 'A- ~ 'i- ~ '-: Position 4 + Extended Base

### Table 4A
### Ø/Ł Class Verbs

The 3i object pronoun of Position 4 "someone/something unspecified" appears as 'a- before a consonant; it combines with (y)i-7 in 1st and 2nd person sgl and 3rd person sgl/dpl in the form of its 'i- allomorph, and it reduces to its initial consonant before a vowel in 1st and 2nd persons dpl.

In some Verb Bases 'a- (~ i-) functions as a thematic prefix: 'a-(yi)--łhą́ą́': snore; 'a- (yi)--łkǫ́ǫ́': swim; 'a-/(yi)--lzhiizh: dance.

T = any Verb Theme

| PERSON Sgl | Prefix Position 4 | + | 5 | + | Base | | | as in: |
|---|---|---|---|---|---|---|---|---|
| 1. | 'i- | + | --- | + | (y)í-T | > | 'íí-T | 'ííłhą́ą́' |
| 2. | 'i- | + | --- | + | (y)íní-T | > | 'ííní-T | 'ííníłhą́ą́' |
| 3. | 'i- | + | --- | + | (y)í-T | > | 'íí-T | 'ííłhą́ą́' |
| 3a. | 'a- | + | ji- | + | (y)í-T | > | 'ajíí-T | 'ajííłhą́ą́' |
| Dpl | | | | | | | | |
| 1. | '- | + | --- | + | (y)ii(d)-T | > | 'ii(d)-T | 'iilghą́ą́' |
| 2. | '- | + | --- | + | (w)oo-T | > | 'oo-T | 'oołhą́ą́' |

'a-(yi)--łhą́ą́': snore
'a-(yi)--Ø'aal: chew something hard ('íí'aal)
'a-(yi)--łkǫ́ǫ́', biih ---: swim into it (a sunken ship)(biih'ííłkǫ́ǫ́')

Table 4B
D/L Class Verbs

'A-Position 4 reduces to '- before a vowel and, like other Position 4 prefixes, it triggers a shift to -ee in 1st person sgl and to -oo- in 3rd persons.

T = any Verb Theme

| PERSON Sgl | Prefix Position 4 | + | 5 | + | Base | | | as in: |
|---|---|---|---|---|---|---|---|---|
| 1. | '- | + | --- | + | -eesh-T | > | 'eesh-T | 'eeshghal |
| 2. | 'i- | + | --- | + | (y)íní-T | > | 'íiní-T | 'íinílghal |
| 3. | '- | + | --- | + | -oo-T | > | 'oo-T | 'oolghal |
| 3a. | 'a- | + | -j- | + | -oo-T | > | 'ajoo-T | 'ajoolghal |
| Dpl | | | | | | | | |
| 1. | '- | + | --- | + | (y)ii(d)-T | > | 'ii(d)-T | 'iilghal |
| 2. | '- | + | --- | + | (w)oo(h)-T | > | 'oo(h)-T | 'oołghal |

'a-(yi)--lghal: eat (meat)('oolghal)
'a-(yi)--lzhiizh: dance ('oolzhiizh)
'a-(yi)--(d)dlą́ą́': drink ('oodlą́ą́')

Ho- ~ hw-: Position 4 + Extended Base

Table 5A
Ø/Ł Class Verbs

The 3s object pronoun of Position 4 represents space or area in some Verb Bases, while in others it represents a 3a (4th) person as direct object, or impersonal "it/things." And in some contexts it functions as a thematic prefix.

Ho- appears before a consonant; hwi- before -(y)íní- in 2nd person sgl; and hw-/h- before a vowel in 1st and 2nd person dpl.

T = any Verb Theme

| PERSON Sgl | Prefix Position 4 | + | 5 | + | Base | | | as in: |
|---|---|---|---|---|---|---|---|---|
| 1. | ho- | + | --- | + | (y)í-T | > | hóó-T | hóółdee' |
| 2. | hwi- | + | --- | + | (y)íní-T | > | hwííní-T | hwíínítdee' |
| 3. | ho- | + | --- | + | (y)í-T | > | hóó-T | hóółdee' |
| 3a. | ho- | + | ji- | + | (y)í-T | > | hojíí-T | hojíítdee' |
| Dpl | | | | | | | | |
| 1. | hw- | + | --- | + | (y)ii(d)-T | > | hwii(d)-T | hwiildee' |
| 2. | h(w)- | + | --- | + | (w)oo-T | > | hoo-T | hoołdee' |

ho-(yi)--łdee': clean up an area
ho-(yi)--łchį', bá ---: make him angry (bá hóółchį')
ho-(yi)--Øtáál: sing (hóótáál)
ho-(yi)--Øzéez: burn off an area (hóózéez)

## Table 5B
## D/L Class Verbs

On a par with other Position 4 prefixes, ho- ~ hw- + yi-7 > hwee- in 1st person sgl and hoo- in 3rd person.

T = any Verb Theme

| PERSON | Prefix Position | | | | | | | |
|---|---|---|---|---|---|---|---|---|
| Sgl | 4 | + | 5 | + | Base | | | as in: |
| 1. | hw- | + | --- | + | -eesh-T | > | hweesh-T | hweeshne' |
| 2. | hwi- | + | --- | + | (y)íní-T | > | hwííní-T | hwíínílne' |
| 3. | h(w)- | + | --- | + | -oo-T | > | hoo-T | hoolne' |
| 3a. | ho- | + | -j- | + | -oo-T | > | hojoo-T | hojoolne' |
| SP | h(w)- | + | --- | + | -oo(d)-T | > | hoo-T | hooldee' |
| Dpl | | | | | | | | |
| 1. | hw- | + | --- | + | (y)ii(d)-T | > | hwii(d)-T | hwiilne' |
| 2. | h(w)- | + | --- | + | (w)oo(h)-T | > | hoo(h)-T | hoołne' |

hw-(yi)--lne': tell

ho-(yi)--ldee': area was cleared

## Ci-Prefixes of Positions 6a/6b + Extended Base

## Table 6A
## Ø/Ł Class Verbs

There are several derivational-thematic prefixes with the shape di- and ni- in Position 6. Of these some take yi-Perfective, including 6a: di-[1], di-[2], di-[5], di-[6], di-[11] and di-[13]; and 6b: ni-[2], ni-[4]. Likewise, dzi- ~ ji-: Position 6a: "away into space" occurs in yi-Perfective.

T = any Verb Theme

| PERSON | Prefix Position | | | | | | | | |
|---|---|---|---|---|---|---|---|---|---|
| Sgl | 4 | + | 5 | + | 6a/6b | + | Base | Intransitive | Transitive |
| 1. | Ø | + | --- | + | Ci- | + | (y)í-T | díízhéé' | biih níł'į́į́' |
| 2. | Ø | + | --- | + | Ci- | + | (y)íní-T | díínízhéé' | biih nííníł'į́į́' |
| 3. | --- | + | --- | + | Ci- | + | (y)í-T | díízhéé' | --- |
| SP | Ø | + | --- | ~ | C- | + | -oo(d)-T | --- | biih noolkaad |
| 3o | yi- | + | --- | + | Ci- | + | (y)í-T | --- | biih yiníł'į́į́' |
| 3a. | --- | + | ji- | + | Ci- | + | (y)í-T | jidíízhéé' | biih jiníł'į́į́' |
| AP | O | + | -di'- | + | C- | + | -oo(d)-T | --- | biih bidi'noolkaad |
| Dpl | | | | | | | | | |
| 1. | Ø | + | --- | + | C- | + | (y)ii(d)-T | diijéé' | biih niil'į́į́' |
| 2. | Ø | + | --- | + | C- | + | (w)oo-T | doozhéé' | biih nooł'į́į́' |

di-(yi)--Øzhéé', biih ---: spit into it (díízhéé')
di-(yi)--Øniid: say (it - to him)(dííniid)
di-(yi)--Øyį́į́d: become holy (dííyį́į́d)
di-(yi)--łzéí > séí: dribble O (dííséí)
di-(yi)--łdą́zh, biih ---: pull O into it (biih díítdą́zh)
di-(yi)--łhį́į́': melt O (dííłhį́į́')
dzi-(yi)--łne', taah ---: hit the water (taah dzííłne')
dzi-(yi)--łhaal, biiih ---: tumble into it (biih dzííłhaal)
dzi-(yi)--Øtáál, bitsą́ --: kick him in the bellv (bitsą́ dzíítáál)
ni -(yi) -- ł'į́į́', biih --- : sneak O into it

ni-(yi)--ł'į́į́', biih ---: slip O into it unobserved (biih nííł'į́į́')
ni-(yi)--Øyood, biih ---: drive O into it (biih nííyood)
ni-(yi)--łkaad, biih ---: drive O (a herd) into it (biih nííłkaad)

## Table 6B
## D/L Class Verbs

The Position 6a/6b prefixes trigger the same contractions in 1st and 3rd person as those of Position 4 (yi-7 > -ee/-oo-).

T = any Verb Theme

| PERSON | Prefix Position | | | | | | | | | | |
|---|---|---|---|---|---|---|---|---|---|---|---|
| Sgl | 4 | + | 5 | + | 6a/6b | + | Base | | Intransitive | | Transitive |
| 1. | Ø | + | --- | + | C- | + | -eesh-T | > | deeshchid | neeshne' | bí-deesht'ą́ą́' |
| 2. | Ø | + | --- | + | Ci- | + | -íní-T | > | dííniĺchid | nííniĺne' | bí-dííníť'ą́ą́' |
| 3. | Ø | + | --- | + | C- | + | -oo-T | > | doolchid | noolne' | --- |
| 3o. | -i- | + | --- | + | C- | + | -oo-T | > | --- | --- | yí-idoot'ą́ą́' |
| 3a. | --- | + | ji-/-zh- | + | C- | + | -oo-T | > | jidoolchid | jinoolne' | bí-zhdoot'ą́ą́' |
| Dpl | | | | | | | | | | | |
| 1. | Ø | + | --- | + | C- | + | -ii(d)-T | > | diilchid | niilne' | bí-diit'ą́ą́' |
| 2. | Ø | + | --- | + | C- | + | -oo(h)-T | > | doołchid | noołne' | bí-dooht'ą́ą́' |

Transitive D/L Class verbs are uncommon; the only available examples for transitive Bases derived with prefixes of Position 6 are those that include certain Disjunct Prefixes of Position 1, as:

bí#-di-(yi)--(d)t'ą́ą́': eat meat off the bone
di-(yi)--lchid, biih---: stick hand into it (biih deeshchid)
di-(yi)--ltáál, taah ---: stick foot into the water (taah deeshtáál)
'ána#-di-(yi)--(d)tą́: throw it over shoulder (as gun, pole)('ánadeeshtą́)
nááa#-di-(yi)--(d)'niid: say (it) again (náádeesh'niid)
ni- (yi)--lne', biih ---: stick head quickly into it (biih neeshne')
'a#-ni-(yi)--lyil: doze, nearly go to sleep ('aneeshyil: I dozed off)

### Seriative (?)yi$^{3}$-: Position 6c + Extended Base

A small group of yi-Perfectives are derived with a yi-prefix of uncertain identity, that behaves like the yi-allomorph of Seriative hi-. (Hi-/yi-Seriatives usually take Si-Perfective.) Verb Bases derived with this element represent the subject (in Position 8) as an agent who causes an (indirect) object, represented by a null postposition (of Position 1a) to perform an action. If the action thus caused is, in turn, transitive the person represented by the postposition becomes functionally the subject whose action affects a direct object represented by a prefix of Position 4: 'i- (~ 'a-) "something unspecified" if the direct object is not a definite thing, Ø if a definite thing. (See Position 4: Exception.)

chidí habiyííłchxa: I honked the car horn (one time)(literally, I made the car cry out. Cf. háách xa: it cried out, started to cry; Future habidiyeeshchxah; Progressive biyiishchxa: I'm honking it)

'awéé' bi'iyíísą́ą́' (< bi-1a: it + -'i-4: something unspecified + yi-seriative [?] + -[y]í-Perfective + -są́ą́' < -łzą́ą́': cause to eat): I fed the baby (i.e. I caused it to eat something. Cf. 'ííyą́ą́': it ate; bidi'yeessį́į́ł: I'll feed it)
'awéé' 'atsį' biyíísą́ą́' (< bi-1a: it + Ø-4: it + yi-seriative [?] + -[y]í-Perfective + -są́ą́'): I fed meat to the baby - I caused the baby to eat it (meat).

The positional slot filled by the null postposition is variable in some environments, as:

hiłiijį́į́hgo nihe'awéé' <u>bi</u>ńda'iyiilzįį́h: we (3+) feed our babies in the evening (bi- in Position 1a slot), but
t'áá 'áníiltso nihe'awéé' 'atsį' ńda<u>bi</u>yiilzį́į́h: we (3+) all feed our babies meat (bi- in Position 4 slot)

(Cf. Si-Perfective déza': I burped / bidiyésa': I made it burp)

<u>Table 7</u>

PERSON

| Sgl | 1a + 'i-4 | | 1a + Ø-4 | |
|---|---|---|---|---|
| 1. | bi'iyíí- | bi'iyíísą́ą́' | biyíí- | biyíísą́ą́' |
| 2. | bi'iyííní- | bi'iyíínísą́ą́' | biyííní- | biyíínísą́ą́' |
| 3. | yi'iyíí- | yi'iyíísą́ą́' | --- | --- |
| SP | bi'iyoo(d)- | bi'iyoolzą́ą́' | biyoo(d)- | biyoolzą́ą́' |
| 3o. | --- | --- | yiiyíí- | yiiyíísą́ą́' |
| 3a. | bi'jiyíí- | bi'jiyíísą́ą́' | bijiyíí- | bijiyíísą́ą́' |
| Dpl | | | | |
| 1. | bi'iyii(d)- | bi'iyiilzą́ą́' | biyii(d)- | biyiilzą́ą́' |
| 2. | bi'iyoo- | bi'iyoosą́ą́' | biyoo- | biyoosą́ą́' |
| Dist Pl | | | | |
| 1. | bida'iyii(d)- | bida'iyiilzą́ą́' | bidayii(d)- | bidayiilzą́ą́' |
| 2. | bida'iyoo- | bida'iyoosą́ą́' | bidayoo- | bidayoosą́ą́' |
| 3. | yida'iyíí- | yida'iyíísą́ą́' | --- | --- |
| 3o. | --- | --- | yideiyíí- | yideiyíísą́ą́' |
| 3a. | bida'jiyíí- | bida'jiyíísą́ą́' | bidajiyíí- | bidajiyíísą́ą́' |

bi#-'i-(y)i-(yí)--są́ą́' < łzą́ą́': feed him (something) (bi'iyíísą́ą́': I fed him)
bi#-'i-(y)i-(yí)--łdlą́ą́': feed him liquid; water it (biyííłdlą́ą́': I fed it it - as soup)
bi#-'i-(y)i-(yí)--shiizh < łzhiizh: make it dance; bounce it (bi'iyííshiizh: I danced it up and down - as a baby)
bi#-'i-(y)i-(yí)--łt'óód: nurse it (cause it to suckle)(bi'iyííłt'óód: I nursed it - as a baby)

## 2. The Disjunct Prefixes

The Disjunct derivational, thematic and inflectional prefixes are those of Positions 1-3, inclusive.

The ná-prefix of Position 2 derives the Iterative Mode, and this is treated separately under the heading **The Iterative Mode**.

The Disjunct derivatives of the Yi-Perfective include: (1) verb constructions in which an inflectional, derivational or thematic prefix of Position 1 or 3 functions as the Conjugational Determinant, and (2) verb constructions in which a derivational-thematic prefix of Position 1 is joined to an Extended Base. In these, and in many Verb Bases that include a complex of multiple Disjunct / Conjunct Prefixes, the element farthest to the right (a Conjunct Prefix) is the Conjugational Determinant.

The tables that follow describe the behavior of the Disjunct Prefixes in combination with the Extended Base (= Positions 1 or 3 + Positions 4,5,7,9-10).

Da-: Position 3: Distributive Plural

Da- marks subject number as distributive plural (= each of 3 or more). Yi-Perfective verbs of motion generally shift to Si-Perfective in 3rd person in the presence of da-, and some derivatives (those with 'a-: Position 1b, away out of sight, for example) prefer Si-Perfective throughout the Perfective paradigm with da-. Compare:

| yi-/Si-Perfective | Si-Perfective |
|---|---|
| taah deiiltį́: we 3+ put AnO into water | yah 'adasiiltį́: we 3+ carried AnO in |
| taah daoołtį́: you 3+ put AnO into water | yah 'adasoołtį́: you 3+ carried AnO in |
| taah deistį́: they 3+ put AnO into water | yah 'adeistį́: they 3+ carried AnO in |
| taah dajistį́: they 3+ put AnO into water | yah 'adajistį́: they 3+ carried AnO in |

However, Kari's Operative (Durative and Repetititve) and Successive Theme categories do not shift to Si-Perfective in the Distributive Plural paradigm - these remain Yi-Perfective. An illustrative list of Yi-Perfective Verb Bases that do not shift to Si-, (or that occur both as Yi- and Si-Perfective) is appended below:

(yi)--ł'aad: send O, direct O (dayíił'aad)
(yi)--Ø'aal: chew/eat hard O (dayíí'aal)
(yi)--Øcha: cry (dáácha)
(yi)--łchozh: eat O (leafy O) (dayííłchozh)
(yi)--Øchxǫ': become ruined (dááchxǫ')
(yi)--łchxǫ': ruin O (dayííłchxǫ')
(yi)--łch'al: lap O up (dayííłch'al)
(yi)--Øch'id: scratch O(dayíích'id)
(yi)--Øch'iizh: scrub/file O (dayíích'iizh)
ni-(yi)--Ødee', biih ---: plural S fall into it (biih/yiih daníídee')
(yi)--łdee': wipe O off (dayííłdee')
(yi)--ldéél: eat PlO (dayooldéél)
(yi)--łdon, 'ásaa' ---: beat a drum ('ásaa' dayííłdon)
(yi)--łdláád: husk O (corn) (dayííłdláád

(yi)--(d)dlą́ą́':: drink O (dayoodlą́ą́')
(yi)--łdzą́: scrape O (hide) (dayííłdzą́)
(yi)--łdzid: shake O (in pan)(dayííłdzid)
(yi)--lghal: chew/eat O (meat) (dayoolghal)
(yi)--Øghaz, tsiih ---: lacerate O (with claws) (tsiih dayííghaz)
(yi)--Øgháád: shake O (dayíígháád)
(yi)--Øgháázh: gnaw O (dayííghéázh)
(yi)--Øghą́ą́': kill plural O (dayííghą́ą́')
(yi)--łhaal: shell O (corn)(dayííłhaal)
(yi)--Øhęęz: itch (dááhęęz)
(yi)--łhį́į́': melt O (dayííłhį́į́')
(yi)--łhod: rock O (baby); pump O (dayííłhod)
(yi)--łhozh: tickle O (dayííłhozh)
ha-(yi)--Øcha: start to cry (hadáácha)
ho-(yi)--Øchįįd, bá ---: get angry (bá dahóóchįįd)
ho-(yi)--łchįįd, bá ---: make them angry (bá dahóółchįįd or bá dahashchįįd)
ha-(yi)--ł'éél, yąąh ---: strain O (milk)(yąąh hadayííł'éél or hadeis'éél)
ha-(yi)--sid: inspect O (hadayíísid)
ho-(yi)--lne': tell (dahoolne')
ho-(yi)--Øts'íid, bitah doo --- da: feel sick, nauseated (bitah doo dahóóts'íid da)
(yi)--Økad, bidaa' ---: whoop (bidaa' dayííkad)
(yi)--lkid: eat round O (orange) (dayoolkid)
(yi)--Øk'ą́: grind O (dayíík'ą́)
(yi)--Øk'ą́ą́z: straighten O (dayíík'ą́ą́z)
ha-(yi)--Øk'ęę': notch O (sheep's ear) (hadayíík'ęę' or hadeizk'ęę')
(yi)--Øląąd: become many, multiply (dááląąd)
(yi)--ł(l)ąąd: increase O (dayííłąąd)
(yi)--łnáád: lick O (dayííłnáád)
(yi)--Ønii': hear about O (dayíínii')
(yi)--są́: tan O (hide)(dayíísą́)
(yi)--sį́į́': bless O (dayíísį́į́')
(yi)--shéé': mow O (dayííshéé')
(yi)--shóó': brush O (dayííshóó')
(yi)--shǫǫd: tame O (dayííshǫǫd)
(yi)--łta': count/read O (dayííłta')
(yi)--łtązh: peck/tap on O (dayííłtązh)
(yi)--Øtáál, ké yiih ---: put on shoes quickly (ké yiih dáátáál)
yá-(yi)--łti': talk (yádááłti')
(yi)--Øti': break (brittle O)(dayííti')
(yi)--Øt'óód: wipe O (dayíít'óód)
(yi)--łtłis: harden O (dayííłtł'is)
(yi)--łtsih: cut O (green corn) off(dayííłtsih)
(yi)--łts'ee': eat O (mushy O) (dayííłts'ee')
(yi)--Øts'i': pluck O (dayííts'i')
(yi)--łts'il: crack O (nut)(dayííłts'il)
(yi)--Øts'ǫ́ǫ́z: suck on O (dayííts'ǫ́ǫ́z)
(yi)--Øyą́ą́': eat O (dayííyą́ą́')
(yi)--Øyį́į́': melt (dááyį́į́')
(yi)--Øzeez: singe O (dayíízeez)
(yi)--Øziid, yiih ---: pour O into it (yiih dayííziid)
(yi)--Øzhi': call O (dayíízhi')

## Da-: Position 3 + Extended Base

### Table 1A
### Ø/Ł-Class Verbs

T = any Verb Theme

| PERSON | Prefix Position | | | | | | | | as in | |
|---|---|---|---|---|---|---|---|---|---|---|
| Dist. Pl | 3 + | 4 | + | 5 | + | Base | | | Intransitive | Transitive |
| 1. | de- | Ø/C(i)- | + | --- | + | -ii(d)-T | > | deii(d)-T | deiicha | deiich'id |
| 2. | da- | Ø/C(i)- | + | --- | + | -oo-T | > | daoo-T | daoocha | daooch'id |
| 3. | da- | Ø/Ci- | + | --- | + | -(y)í-T | > | dáá-T | dáácha | --- |
| 3o. | da- | --/-yi- | + | -- | | -(y)í-T | > | dayíí-T | --- | dayíích'id |
| 3a. | da- | - Ø/Ci- | + | -ji- | + | -(y)í-T | > | dajíí-T | dajíícha | dajíích'id |

(yi)--Øcha: cry

(yi)--Øch'id: scratch

### Table 1B
### D/L Class Verbs

| PERSON | Prefix Position | | | | | | | | as in | |
|---|---|---|---|---|---|---|---|---|---|---|
| Dist. Pl | 3 + | 4 | + | 5 | + | Base | | | Intransitive | Transitive |
| 1 | de- | Ø/C(i)- | + | --- | + | -ii(d)-T | > | deii(d)-T | deiilnóód | deiilghal |
| 2 | da- | Ø/C(i)- | + | --- | + | -oo(h)-T | > | daoo(h)-T | daoołnóód | daoołghal |
| 3. | daa- | --- | + | --- | + | (yi)-T | > | daa-T | daasnóód | --- |
| 3o. | da- | --/-y(i)- | + | -- | + | -oo-T | > | dayoo-T | --- | dayoolghal |
| 3a. | da- | - Ø/Ci- | + | -j- | + | -oo-T | > | dajoo-T | dajisnóód | dajoolghal |

(yi)--lghal: chew/eat O (meat)
(yi)--ldéél: eat PlO (as berries)

taah da-(yi)--lnóód: dive into the water

## Ca-: Position 1b + Extended Base

### Table 2A
### Ø/L-Class Verbs

Ca-1b + yi-7 generally contract to produce Cáá- when the derivational prefix is in determinant position, in 1st and 3rd person sgl, although Cáí- is sometimes heard. The tone of the prefix vowel is inherently low, but it assimilates to the high tone of the following yí-prefix of Position 7.

T = any Verb Theme

| PERSON | Prefix Position | | | | | | | | | | | Transitive | |
|---|---|---|---|---|---|---|---|---|---|---|---|---|---|
| Sgl | 1b | + | 4 | + | 5 | + | Base | | | Intransitive | +Ø-4 | +Ci-4 |
| 1 | Ca- | + | Ø/Ci- | + | --- | + | (y)í-T | > | Cáá-T | háácha | háátłį́ | haníítłį́ |
| 2 | Ca- | + | Ø/Ci- | + | --- | + | (y)íní-T | > | Cáíní-T | háínícha | háínítłį́ | hashííníítłį́ |
| 3 | Ca- | + | --/Ci- | + | --- | + | (y)í-T | > | Cáá-T | háácha | --- | hashíítłį́ |
| 3o. | Ca- | + | --/-yi- | + | -- | + | (y)í-T | > | Cayíí-T | --- | --- | hayíítłį́ |
| 3a. | Ca- | + | Ø/Ci- | + | -ji- | + | (y)í-T | > | Cajíí-T | hajíícha | hajíítłį́ | hashijíítłį́ |
| 3i | Ca- | + | -- | + | -'i- | + | (y)í-T | > | Ca'íí-T | ha'íícha | --- | --- |
| Dpl | | | | | | | | | | | | |
| 1 | Ca- | + | Ø/C(i)-+ | | --- | + | (y)ii(d)-T | > | Caii(d)-T | haiicha | haiiltį́ | haniiltį́ |
| 2 | Ca- | + | Ø/C(i)- + | | --- | + | (w)oo-T | > | Caoo-T | haoocha | haoołtį́ | hashoołtį́ |

ha#-(yi)--Øcha: start to cry
ha#-(yi)--łtį́: take AnO out (as from a box)(haníítłį́: I took you out; hashííníítłį́: you took me out; hashíítłį́: he took me out, etc.)
'ahá#-(yi)--Øgizh: cut O apart ('aháágizh)

## Table 2B
## D/L Class Verbs

Ca-1b + yi-7 contract to produce Caa- in 1st and 3rd persons sgl and Simple Passive, when the derivational prefix is in determinant position.

Transitive D/L-Class verbs derived with Disjunct Ca-1b are not available.

T = any Verb Theme

| PERSON | Prefix Position | | | | | | | | | | |
|---|---|---|---|---|---|---|---|---|---|---|---|
| Sgl | 1b | + | 4 | + | 5 | + | Base | | | Intransitive | Transitive |
| 1 | Ca- | + | --- | + | --- | + | (y)ish-T | > | Caash-T | haash'na' | --- |
| 2 | Ca- | + | --- | + | --- | + | (y)íní-T | > | Cáíní-T | háíní'na' | --- |
| 3 | Ca- | + | --- | + | --- | + | (yi)-T | > | Caa-T | haa'na' | --- |
| SP | Ca- | + | Ø | + | -- | + | (yi)-T | > | Caa(d)T | --- | haaltį́ |
| 3a. | Ca- | + | --- | + | -j- | + | -oo-T | > | Cajoo-T | hajoo'na' | --- |
| 3i | Ca- | + | --- | + | -'- | + | -oo-T | > | Ca'oo-T | ha'oo'na' | --- |
| AP | Ca- | + | O | + | -'(a)d- | + | -oo-T | > | CaO'doo-T | --- | habi'dooltį́ |
| Dpl | | | | | | | | | | | |
| 1 | Ca- | + | Ø/C(i)-+ | | --- | + | (y)ii(d)-T | > | Caii(d)-T | haii'na' | --- |
| 2 | Ca- | + | Ø/C(i)-+ | | --- | + | (w)oo-T | > | Caoo(h)-T | haooh'na' | --- |

ha#-(yi)--(d)'na': crawl up out
ha#-(yi)--ltį́: AnO was taken out (Simple Passive corresponding to ha#-[yi]--łtį́: take an AnO out)
ha#-O'di-(yi)--ltį́: person was taken out or carried up (habi'dooltį́)(Agentive Passive corresponding to ha#-[yi]--łtį́: take an AnO out)
ha#-'(a)-(yi)--(d)'na': something unspecified climbed/crawled up out (shił ha'oo'na': I rode up out/climbed up in a slow-moving vehicle, as in an army tank)

## Cá-: Position 1b + Extended Base

### Table 3A
### Ø/Ł-Class Verbs

Cá-1b + yi-7 contract to produce Cáá- in 1st and 3rd persons sgl, when the derivational prefix is in determinant position.

T= any Verb Theme

| PERSON | Prefix Position | | | | | | | | | Intransitive | Transitive |
|---|---|---|---|---|---|---|---|---|---|---|---|
| Sgl | 1b | + | 4 | + | 5 | + | Base | | | | +Ø-4 |
| 1 | Cá- | + | Ø/Ci- | + | --- | + | (y)í-T | > | Cáá-T | yááłti' | yisdááłtį |
| 2 | Cá- | + | Ø/Ci- | + | --- | + | (y)íní-T | > | Cáíní-T | yéíníłti' | yisdéíníłtį́ |
| 3 | Cá- | + | Ø/Ci- | + | --- | + | (y)í-T | > | Cáá-T | yááłti' | --- |
| 3o | Cá- | + | --/yi- | + | -- | + | (y)í-T | > | Cáyíí-T | --- | yisdáyííłtį́ |
| 3a. | Cá- | + | Ø/Ci- | + | -ji- | + | (y)í-T | > | Cájíí-T | yájííłti' | yisdájííłtį́ |
| Dpl | | | | | | | | | | | |
| 1 | Cá- | + | Ø/C- | + | --- | + | (y)ii(d)-T | > | Cáii(d)-T | yéiilti' | yisdéiiltį́ |
| 2 | Cá- | + | Ø/C-- | + | --- | + | (w)oo-T | > | Cáoo-T | yáoołti' | yisdáoołtį́ |

yá#-(yi)--łti': talk
ná#-(yi)--Ø'ą́, taah ---: put SRO back into the water
'ahá#-(yi)--Øgizh: cut O apart
yisdá#-(yi)--łtį́: carry AnO to safety (yisdáníííłtį́: I saved you; yisdáshííłtį́: he saved me, etc.)

### Table 3B
### D/L-Class Verbs

Cá- + yi-T contract to produce Cáá- in 1st and 3rd person sgl and in Simple Passives, when the derivational prefix is in determinant position.

T = any Verb Theme

| PERSON | Prefix Position | | | | | | | | | Intransitive | Transitive |
|---|---|---|---|---|---|---|---|---|---|---|---|
| Sgl | 1b | + | 4 | + | 5 | + | Base | | | | +Ø-4 |
| 1 | Cáá- | + | Ø | + | --- | + | (yi)sh-T | > | Cáásh-T | náásh'na' | náásh'nil |
| 2 | Cá- | + | Ø | + | --- | + | (y)íní-T | > | Cáíní-T | néíní'na' | néíní'nil |
| 3 | Cáá- | + | Ø | + | --- | + | (yi)-T | > | Cáá-T | náá'na' | --- |
| SP | Cáá- | + | Ø/-- | + | -- | + | (yi)-T | > | Cáá(d)T | --- | náá'nil |
| 3o | Cá- | + | --/-y- | + | --- | + | -oo-T | > | Cáyoo-T | --- | náyoo'nil |
| 3a. | Cá- | + | Ø | + | -j- | + | -oo-T | > | Cájoo-T | ńjoo'na' | ńjoo'nil |
| AP | Cá- | + | O | + | -'(a)d- | + | -oo-T | > | CáO'doo-T | --- | --- |
| Dpl | | | | | | | | | | | |
| 1 | Cá- | + | Ø | + | --- | + | (y)ii(d)-T | > | Cáii(d)-T | néii'na' | néii'nil |
| 2 | Cá- | + | Ø | + | --- | + | (w)oo(h)-T | > | Cáoo(h)-T | náooh'na' | náooh'nil |

taah ná#-(yi)--(d)'na': crawl back into the water
kééh ná#-(yi)--(d)t'eez: put shoes back on; step back into shoes (keeh náást'eez)
'ahiih ná#-(yi)--(d)'nil: put O back together ('ahiih náásh'nil)
yisdá#-(yi)--(d)'na': crawl to safety (yisdáásh'na')

## Ce-: Position 1b + Extended Base

### Table 4A
### Ø/Ł-Class Verbs

Ce-1b + yi-7 contract to produce Céé- in 1st and 3rd persons sgl when the derivational prefix is in determinant position.

T = any Verb Theme

| PERSON | Prefix Position | | | | | | | | | |
|---|---|---|---|---|---|---|---|---|---|---|
| Sgl | 1b | + | 4 | + | 5 | + | Base | | | |
| 1 | Ce- | + | Ø | + | --- | + | (y)í-T | > | Céé-T | bílák'ééłtsooz |
| 2 | Ce- | + | Ø | + | --- | + | (y)íní-T | > | Céíní-T | bílák'éíníłtsooz |
| 3o | Ce- | + | yi- | + | -- | + | (y)í-T | > | Ceyíí-T | yílák'eyííłtsooz |
| 3a. | Ce- | + | --- | + | -ji- | + | (y)í-T | > | Cejíí-T | bílák'ejííłtsooz |
| Dpl | | | | | | | | | | |
| 1 | Ce- | + | Ø | + | --- | + | (y)ii(d)-T | > | Ceii(d)-T | bílák'eiiltsooz |
| 2 | Ce- | + | Ø | + | --- | + | (w)oo-T | > | Ceoo-T | bílák'eoołtsooz |

P-ílák'e#-(yi)--łtsooz: hand a FFO to him (< P-lák'e- P's hand-place + yíłtsooz: I put it = I put it into [his] hand)

### Table 4B

Ce-1b + yi-7 Contract to produce Cee- in 1st and 2nd person sgl verbs, when the derivational prefix is in determinant position.

### D/L-Class Verbs

T = any Verb Theme

| PERSON | Prefix Position | | | | | | | |
|---|---|---|---|---|---|---|---|---|
| Sgl | 1b | + | 5 | + | Base | | | as in: |
| 1 | Cee- | + | --- | + | (-yi)sh-T | > | Ceesh-T | dá'ák'eesh'na' |
| 2 | Ce- | + | --- | + | -(y)íní-T | > | Céíní-T | dá'ák'éíní'na' |
| 3 | Cee- | + | --- | + | (-yi)-T | > | Cee-T | dá'ák'ee'na' |
| SP | Cee- | + | -- | + | (-yi(d))-T | > | Cee(d)T | bílák'eeltsooz |
| 3a. | Ce- | + | -j- | + | -oo-T | > | Cejoo-T | dá'ák'ejoo'na' |
| 3i | Ce- | + | -'i- | + | -oo-T | > | Ce'oo-T | dá'ák'e'oo'na' |
| Dpl | | | | | | | | |
| 1 | Ce- | + | --- | + | (y)ii(d)-T | > | Ceii(d)-T | dá'ák'eii'na' |
| 2 | Ce- | + | --- | + | (w)oo(h)-T | > | Ceoo(h)-T | dá'ák'eooh'na' |

dá'ák'e#-(yi)--(d)'na': crawl into a field (< dá'ák'eh: field + -yish'na': I crawled)
P-ílák'e#-(yi)--ltsooz: FFO was handed to P

## Ci-: Position 1b + Extended Base

### Table 5A
### Ø/Ł-Class Verbs

Ci-1b + yi-7 contract to produce Céé- (or optionally Cíí-) in 1st and 3rd persons sgl, when the derivational prefix is in determinant postion.

T = any Verb Theme

| PERSON Sgl | 1b | + | 4 | + | 5 | + | Base | | | Intransitive | Transitive + Ø-4 | + Ci-4 |
|---|---|---|---|---|---|---|---|---|---|---|---|---|
| 1 | Ce- | + | Ø/Ci- | + | --- | + | (y)í-T | > | Céé-T | --- | bik'éédzį́į́z | bik'i níídzį́į́z |
| 2 | Ci- | + | Ø/Ci- | + | --- | + | (y)íní-T | > | Cííní-T | --- | bik'íínídzį́į́z | bik'ishíínidzį́į́z |
| 3 | Ce- | + | Ø/Ci- | + | --- | + | (y)í-T | > | Céé-T | bik'ééyol | --- | yik'ishíídzį́į́z |
| 3o | Ci- | + | --/-yi- | + | --- | + | (y)í-T | > | Ciyíí-T | --- | yik'iyíídzį́į́z | yik'iyíídzį́į́z |
| 3a. | Ci- | + | Ø/Ci- | + | -ji- | + | (y)í-T | > | Cijíí-T | --- | bik'ijíídzį́į́z | bik'ishijíídzį́į́z |
| Dpl | | | | | | | | | | | | |
| 1 | C(i)- | + | Ø/C(i)- | + | --- | + | (y)ii(d)-T | > | Cii(d)-T | --- | bik'iidzį́į́z | bik'iniidzį́į́z |
| 2 | Ci- | + | Ø/C(i)-- | + | --- | + | (w)oo-T | > | Cioo(h)-T | --- | bik'ioodzį́į́z | bik'ishoodzį́į́z |

P-k'i#-(yi)--Ødzį́į́z: pull O off of P (as a dog off a man)(yik'ishíídzį́į́z)
P-k'i#-(yi)--Øyol: blow off P (bik'ééyol ~ bik'ííyol: it blew off of him - as his hat)
P-k'i#-(yi)--Øzǫ́ǫ́z: peel O; skin O (bik'éézǫ́ǫ́z ~ bik'íízǫ́ǫ́z)
P-k'i#-(yi)--Ø'ą́: take O off of P (as P's hat)(bik'éé'ą́ ~ bik'íí'á)

### Table 5B
### D/L Class

Ci-1b + yi-7 contract to produce Cee- in 1st and 3rd persons sgl and in Simple Passive, when the derivational prefix is in determinant position.

T = any Verb Theme

| PERSON Sgl | 1b | + | 5 | + | Base | | | as in: |
|---|---|---|---|---|---|---|---|---|
| 1 | Cee- | + | --- | + | (-yi)sh-T | > | Ceesh-T | bik'eesh'na' |
| 2 | Ci- | + | --- | + | -(y)íní-T | > | Cííní-T | bik'ííní'na' |
| 3 | Cee- | + | --- | + | (-yi)-T | > | Cee-T | yik'ee'na' |
| SP | Cee- | + | -- | + | (-yi(d))-T | > | Cee(d)T | bik'eelmááz |
| 3a. | Ci- | + | -j- | + | -oo-T | > | Cijoo-T | bik'ijoo'na' |
| AP | Ci- | + | -'(a)d- | + | -oo-T | > | CiO'doo-T | bik'ibi'doodzį́į́z |
| Dpl | | | | | | | | |
| 1 | C- | + | --- | + | (y)ii(d)-T | > | Cii(d)-T | bik'ii'na' |
| 2 | Ci- | + | --- | + | (w)oo(h)-T | > | Cioo(h)-T | bik'iooh'na' |

bik'i#-(yi)--(d)'na': crawl off of it (as off a blanket on the floor - not from a height)(bik'ibi'doodzį́į́z: Agentive Passive: he was dragged off of him - as an attacker)

## Cí-: Position 1b + Extended Base

### Table 6A
### Ø/Ł-Class Verbs

Cí-1b + yí-7 contract to produce Céé- or optionally Cíí- in 1st and 3rd persons when the derivational prefix is in determinant postion.

In 3o person Cí- + (y)i-4 + -(y)í-7 > Cíí- and in 1st person dpl Cí- + -ii(d)- > Cîi(d)-.

T = any Verb Theme

| PERSON | Prefix Position | | | | | | | | | | |
|---|---|---|---|---|---|---|---|---|---|---|---|
| Sgl | 1b | + | 4 | + | 5 | + | Base | | | Intransitive | Transitive |
| 1 | Cé-~Cí | + | Ø | + | --- | + | (y)í-T | > | Céé-/Cíí-T | ch'ééyá | béézǫ́ǫ́z |
| 2 | Cí- | + | Ø | + | --- | + | (y)íní-T | > | Cííní-T | ch'ííníyá | bííníz ǫ́ǫ́z |
| 3 | Cé- | + | --- | + | --- | + | (y)í-T | > | Céé-T | ch'ééyá | --- |
| 3o | Cí- | + | -yi- | + | --- | + | (y)í-T | > | Cíyíí-T | --- | yíyíízǫ́ǫ́z |
| 3a. | Cí- | + | Ø- | + | -ji- | + | (y)í-T | > | Cį́jíí-T | ch'į́jííyá | bį́jíízǫ́ǫ́z |
| Dpl | | | | | | | | | | | |
| 1 | C(í)- | + | Ø | + | --- | + | (y)ii(d)-T | > | Cîi(d)-T | ch'îit'áázh | bîidǫ́ǫz |
| 2 | Cí- | + | Ø | + | --- | + | (w)oo-T | > | Cíoo(h)-T | ch'íoo'áázh | bíoozǫ́ǫ́z |

'adah ch'í#-(yi)--Øyá: one subject walks over an edge
'adah ch'í#-(yi)--Ø'áázh: two subjects walk over an edge('adah ch'éé'áázh)
'adah ch'í#-(yi)--łmááz: roll O over an edge ('adah ch'íyííłmááz)
bí#-(yi)--Øzǫ́ǫ́z: peel O; skin O
'atí#-(yi)--Øt'įįd: harm O ('atéét'įįd ~ 'atíít'įįd)

### Table 6B
### D/L-Class Verbs

Cí- + yi-7 > Céé- in 1st and 3rd persons sgl and Simple Passive, when the derivational prefix is in determinant position.

T = any Verb Theme

| PERSON | Prefix Position | | | | | | |
|---|---|---|---|---|---|---|---|
| Sgl | 1b | + | 5 | + | Base | | as in: |
| 1 | Céé- | + | --- | + | (-yi)sh-T | > Céésh-T | ch'éésh'na' |
| 2 | Cí- | + | --- | + | -(y)íní-T | > Cííní-T | ch'ííní'na' |
| 3 | Céé- | + | --- | + | (-yi)-T | > Céé-T | ch'éé'na' |
| SP | Céé- | + | -- | + | (-yi(d))-T | > Céé(d)T | ch'éélmááz |
| 3a. | Cí- | + | -j- | + | -oo-T | > Cį́joo-T | ch'į́joo'na' |
| AP | Cí- | + | -'(a)d- | + | -oo-T | > CíO'doo-T | ch'íbi'doolmááz |
| Dpl | | | | | | | |
| 1 | C(í)- | + | --- | + | (y)ii(d)-T | > Cîi(d)-T | ch'îi'na' |
| 2 | Cí- | + | --- | + | (w)oo(h)-T | > Cíoo(h)-T | ch'íooh'na' |

'adah ch'í#-(yi)--(d)'na': crawl over an edge
'adah ch'í#-(yi)--lmááz: be rolled over an edge
'adah ch'í#-O'doo--lmááz: be rolled over an edge (a person)

## 'A- ~ 'i-: Position 1b + Extended Base

### Table 7A
### Ø/Ł-Class Verbs

In determinant position, in 1st and 2nd person sgl and 3rd person sgl/dpl, 'a-Position 1b: away out of sight appears in the form of its 'i-allomorph, assimilating to the high tone of a following yí–7; 'a-1b reduces to its initial consonant ('-) before vowel-initial -ii(d)- and -oo- in 1st and 2nd persons dpl.

In the presence of distributive plural da-Position 3, the paradigm shifts to Si-Perfective.

T = any Verb Theme

| PERSON | Prefix Position | | | | | | | | | Intransitive | Transitive | |
|---|---|---|---|---|---|---|---|---|---|---|---|---|
| Sgl | 1b | + | 4 | + | 5 | + | Base | | | | +Ø-4 | +Ci-4 |
| 1 | 'i- | + | Ø/Ci- | + | --- | + | (y)í-T | > | 'íí-T | 'ííná | 'ííłtį́ | 'aníííłtį́ |
| 2 | 'i- | + | Ø/Ci- | + | --- | + | (y)íní-T | > | 'ííní-T | 'ííníná | 'íínííłtį́ | 'ashííníłtį́ |
| 3 | 'i- | + | --- | + | --- | + | (y)í-T | > | 'íí-T | 'ííná | --- | 'ashííłtį́ |
| 3o | 'a- | + | -yi- | + | --- | + | (y)í-T | > | 'ayíí-T | --- | --- | 'ayííłtį́ |
| 3a. | 'a- | + | Ø/Ci- | + | -ji- | + | (y)í-T | > | 'ajíí-T | 'ajííná | 'ajííłtį́ | 'ashijííłtį́ |
| 3i | 'i- | + | --- | + | -'i- | | (y)í-T | > | 'i'íí-T | 'i'íít'i' | --- | --- |
| 3s | 'a- | + | --- | + | -ho- | | (y)í-T | > | 'ahóó-T | 'ahóót'i' | --- | --- |
| Dpl | | | | | | | | | | | | |
| 1 | '(i)- | + | Ø/C(i)- | + | --- | + | (y)ii(d)-T | > | 'ii(d)-T | 'ii'ná | 'iiłtį́ | 'aniiłtį́ |
| 2 | '(i)- | + | Ø/C(i)- | + | --- | + | (w)oo-T | > | 'oo-T | 'ooná | 'oołtį́ | 'ashoołtį́ |

'a#-(yi)--łtį́: carry an AnO away out of sight
('aníííłtį́: I carried you away; 'ashííníłtį́; you carried me away; 'ashííłtį́: he carried me away ,etc.
'a#-(yi)---ná: move away with household (yóó' 'ííná: I/he moved away)
'i'íít'i' something extends away
'ahóót'i': area extends away

## Table 7B
## D/L-Class Verbs

'A- ~ 'i-: Position 1 + yi-7 > 'ee- in 1st and 3rd person intransitives and in Simple Passive (there are few transitives). Before a vowel in 1st and 2nd persons dpl, the derivational prefix reduces to its initial consonant ('-).

With distributive plural da-Position 3, a shift to si-Perfective is mandatory. Thus:

yah 'ii'na': we two crawled in
yah 'adasii'na': we 3+ crawled in

T = any Verb Theme

| PERSON | Prefix Position | | | | | | | | | | Transitive | |
|---|---|---|---|---|---|---|---|---|---|---|---|---|
| Sgl | 1b | + | 4 | + | 5 | + | Base | | | Intransitive | +Ø-4 | +Ci-4 |
| 1 | '- | + | Ø/C- | + | --- | + | -yish-T | > | 'eesh-T | 'eesh'na' | 'eeshtį́ | 'aneeshtį́ |
| 2 | 'i- | + | Ø/C- | + | --- | + | -(y)íní-T | > | 'ííní-T | 'ííní'na' | 'íínííltį́ | 'ashíínííltį́ |
| 3 | 'i- | + | Ø/C- | + | --- | + | -yi-T | > | 'ee-T | 'ee'na' | --- | 'ashooltį́ |
| SP | 'i- | + | Ø/-- | + | --- | + | -yi(d)-T | > | 'ee(d)T | --- | 'eeltį́ | --- |
| 3o | 'a- | + | -y- | + | --- | + | -oo-T | > | 'ayoo-T | --- | --- | 'ayooltį́ |
| 3a. | 'a- | + | Ø/C- | + | -j- | + | -oo-T | > | 'ajoo-T | 'ajoo'na' | 'ajooltį́ | 'ashijooltį́ |
| Dpl | | | | | | | | | | | | |
| 1 | '- | + | Ø/C- | + | --- | + | (y)ii(d)-T | > | 'ii(d)-T | 'ii'na' | 'iiltį́ | 'aniiltį́ |
| 2 | '- | + | Ø/C- | + | --- | + | (w)oo(h)-T | > | 'oo(h)-T | 'ooh'na' | 'oołtį́ | 'ashoołtį́ |

'a#-(yi)--(d)'na': crawl away out of sight
'áyaa 'a#-(yi)--ltį́: place an AnO under oneself; take charge of AnO ('áyaa 'aneeshtį́: I took charge of you; 'áyaa 'ashooltį́; he took charge of me, 'áyaa 'eeshtį́: I took charge of him, etc.)

### 'A- ~ 'i-: Position 1b + 'a- ~ 'i-: Position 4 + Extended Base

## Table 8A
## Ø/Ł Class Verbs

'A- ~ 'i-: Position 1b and the indefinite object pronoun 'a- ~ 'i-: Position 4, cooccur in a number of Verb Bases. 'A-4 represents the subject if the verb is intransitive, the direct object if it is transitive.

A shift to si-Perfective is mandatory in 3rd person distributive plural constructions. Thus:

yóó' 'i'íiłkǫ́ǫ́': he swam away and disappeared
yóó' 'ada'askǫ́ǫ́': they (3+ ) swam away and disappeared

T = any Verb Theme

| PERSON | Prefix Position | | | | | | | | | |
|---|---|---|---|---|---|---|---|---|---|---|
| Sgl | 1b | + | 4 | + | 5 | + | Base | | | as in: |
| 1 | 'i- | + | -'i- | + | --- | + | (y)í-T | > | 'i'íí-T | 'i'ííjaa' |
| 2 | 'i- | + | -'i- | + | --- | + | (y)íní-T | > | 'i'ííní-T | 'i'íínííjaa' |
| 3 | 'i- | + | -'i- | + | --- | + | (y)í-T | > | 'i'íí-T | 'i'ííjaa' / 'i'íí'ą́ |
| 3a. | 'i- | + | -'- | + | -ji- | + | (y)í-T | > | 'i'jíí-T | 'i'jííjaa' |
| Dpl | | | | | | | | | | |
| 1 | 'i- | + | -'- | + | --- | + | (y)ii(d)-T | > | 'i'ii(d)-T | 'i'iijaa' |
| 2 | 'o- | + | -'- | + | --- | + | (w)oo-T | > | 'o'oo-T | 'o'oojaa' |

'a#-'a-(yi)--Øjaa': scatter unspecified PIO (as grain for chickens)(naa'ahóóhai bá 'i'ííjaa': I fed the chickens)
bił 'a#-'a-(yi)--łkaal: nail it (i.e. pound something away out of sight in company with it)(tsineheeshjíí' bił 'i'ííłkaal: I nailed the board)
'a#-'a-(yi)--łkǫ́ǫ́': swim away out of sight (yóó'i'ííłkǫ́ǫ́': it swam away)
'a#-'a-(yi)--Ø'ą́: the sun set (i.e. something solid and round moved away out of sight)

## Irregular Paradigms

The verbs of making and doing are highly irregular. The Perfective stems for each semantic category are derived from the same suppletive source, but for the verbs of making, the Perfective stem appears with the alternant shapes laa/yaa while for the verbs of doing the Perfective stem appears as dzaa. (See Krauss-Leer 1981: 142-145; Young and Morgan 1991: 682.)

Themes for both categories occur with and without the Disjunct Thematic Prefix 'á-: Position 1b.

Table 1

| PERSON | MAKE | | DO | |
|---|---|---|---|---|
| Sgl | | + 'á- ~ 'í-1b | | + 'á- ~ 'í-1b |
| 1. | yishłaa | 'áshłaa ~ 'íishłaa | yisdzaa | 'ásdzaa |
| 2. | yinilaa | 'íinilaa | yinidzaa | 'íinidzaa |
| 3. | --- | --- | yidzaa | 'ádzaa |
| SP. | yilyaa | 'ályaa | --- | --- |
| 3o | yiyiilaa | 'áyiilaa | --- | --- |
| 3a. | jiilaa | 'ájiilaa | dziidzaa | 'ádziidzaa |
| 3s. | --- | --- | hoodza | 'áhoodzaa |
| Dpl | | | | |
| 1. | yiilyaa | 'íilyaa | yiidzaa | 'íidzaa |
| 2. | woohłaa | 'óohłaa | woohdzaa | 'óohdzaa |

ła' (yi)--Ølaa: accomplish it, complete it (ła'iyiilaa: he completed it)
'á#-(yi)--Ølaa: make O ('áyiilaa: he made it)
(yi)--(d)dzaa: do, happen (haalá yinidzaa: what happened to you?)
'á#-(yi)--(d)dzaa: do thus (yaa 'ádzaa: he bent down)

## Céé-Prefixes of Position 6 + Extended Base

### Table 2

Déé-/néé- are tentatively identified as contractions of unidentified di-/ni-6a/6b + unidentified ni-6b. Derivatives remain Yi-Perfective in the presence of da-3: Distributive plural.

| PERSON | | Ø/Ł | | D/L | | |
|---|---|---|---|---|---|---|
| Sgl | 6 | Intransitive | Transitive | | Intransitive | Transitive |
| 1. | -Céé-T | bídééyá | bízéédééłtsooz | -Céésh-T | bínééshdlįįd | |
| 2. | -Cííní-T | bídííníyá | bízéédííníłtsooz | -Cííní-T | bínííánídlįįd | |
| 3. | -Céé-T | yídééyá | --- | -Céé-T | yínéédlįįd | |
| 3o | -iCéé-T | --- | yízéidééłtsooz | --- | --- | |
| 3a. | -zhCéé-T | bízhdééyá | bízéézdéełtsooz | --- | bízhnéédlįįd | |
| Dpl | | | | | | |
| 1. | -Cee(d)-T | bídeet'áázh | bízéédéeltsooz | -Cee(d)-T | bíneedlįįd | |
| 2. | -Coo-T | bídoo'áázh | bízéédóołtsooz | -Coo(h)-T | bínoohdlįįd | |

P-í#-déé-(yi)--Øyá: accidentally brush against P (shídééyá: he brushed against me; bídeet'áázh: we two brushed against him)
P-í#-déé-(yi)--lchid: accidentally touch P, brush P with hand (shídéélchid: he accidentally touched me)
P-zéé#-déé-(yi)--łtsooz: put FFO (scarf) around P's neck (sizéidééłtsooz: he put O around my neck)
bí#-néé-(yi)--(d)dlįįd: become interested in it (bínééshdlįįd: I became interested in it)
bí#-néé-(yi)--l'ąąd: become capable of it, able to afford it (bínéésh'ąąd: I became capable of it)

## YI-PERFECTIVE NEUTER

The Yi-Perfective Neuter Verbs are primarily concerned with the directional extension of a subject or object into time or space.

Ø/Ł-Class Yi-Perfective Neuters occur intransitive and transitive, but D/L-Class Bases occur intransitive only. Some verbs identified as D/L-Class Neuters describe attributes of the subject, as:

yilcháázh: it's soft, cushiony
yilzhólí: it's soft, fluffy, downy
hoolzhólí: the place is soft, padded
hoodzą́: it's perforated, has a cavity
hool'in: there is daylight (i.e. space/area has visibility)
noolin ~ noolnin: it looks like, has the appearance of

The Ø/Ł-Class Neuter Extensional Verb Bases generally require an independent adverbial component to mark direction if the Verb Base does not include a directional prefix component. Thus, yít'i' is a simple Completive "extended in a line;" it cannot occur independently. The Base, transitive or intransitive must include an adverbial direction marker such as:

biih: into it - biih yít'i': it extends into it (as a wick into a lamp)
biih yíłt'i': I caused it to extend into it; I have it extending into it

taah: into water - taah yít'i': it extends into the water

Simple Intransitive Yi-Perfective Neuters (i.e. those that lack an adverbial derivational prefix)occur in 3rd person only, while corresponding transitive Bases are conjugated in the same pattern as Active Yi-Perfectives of similar composition.

## Base Paradigm

| PERSON Sgl | Ø/Ł | Intransitive | Transitive | D/L | Intransitive |
|---|---|---|---|---|---|
| 1 | yí-T | --- | yíłt'i' | --- | --- |
| 2 | yíní-T | --- | yíníłt'i' | --- | --- |
| 3 | yí-T | yít'i' | --- | yi-T | yilzhólí |
| 3o | yiyíí-T | --- | yiyííłt'i'. | --- | --- |
| 3a. | jíí-T | --- | jííłt'i' | --- | --- |
| 3s | hóó-T | | hóót'i' | hoo-T | hoolzhólí |
| Dpl | | | | | |
| 1 | yii(d)-T | --- | yiilt'i' | --- | --- |
| 2 | woo-T | --- | woołt'i' | --- | --- |

biih (yi)--Øt'i': extend into it (biih yít'i': it extends into it)
biih (yi)--łt'i': cause O to extend into it (biih yíłt'i': I have it extending into it)
(yi)--lzhólí: be soft, fluffy (yilzhólí: it's soft and fluffy)
(yi)--lcháázh: be cushiony, soft (yilcháázh: it's cushiony)
ho-(yi)--l'in: be daylight (i.e. space/area/"things" have visibility)(hool'in: it's daylight)

Verb Bases derived with Conjunct Prefixes in determinant position include:

di[5]-: Position 6a - fire + di-1b: fire, light
di#-di-(yi)--Ø'á: extend into the fire (didíí'á: it extends into the fire
dzi-: Position 6a: away into space
ha#-dzi-(yi)--Øá: protrude (as a lump or bump)(hadzíí'á: it protrudes)
ho-(yi)--l'á: space/time extend (hool'á)
ni[6](?)-(yi)-Ølin ~ lnin: look like, have the appearance of

Verb Bases derived with Disjunct Prefixes in determinant position include:

'a-: Position 1b - away out of sight
yah 'a#-(yi)--Øt'i': extend in a line into an enclosure (as a telephone line)(yah 'íít'i': it extends into it)
yah 'a#-(yi)--łt'i': cause it to extend in a line into an enclosure (yah 'ííłt'i': I cause it to extend into it)
'a#-(yi)--lkid: it (a hilly ridge) extends away ('eelk'id: it extends away)

ha-: Position 1b - up out; protruding
ha#-(yi)--Ø'á: extend up out, protrude (háá'á: it protrudes)

ha#-(yi)--ł'á:; cause it to extend out (háál'á: I have it extended out; I cause it to be protruding)

dzídza- ~ tsídza-: Position 1b - into the fire

dzídza#-(yi)--ł'á: extend into the fire (dzídzáá'á ~ tsídzáá'á: it extends into the fire)

dzídza#- (~ tsídza-)(yi)--ł'á: cause it to extend into the fire (dzídzááł'á ~ tsídzááł'á: I make it extend into the fire)

na³-: Position 1b - downward

na#-(yi)--Ø'á: hang (extend) down (náá'á: it hangs down)

na#-(yi)--ł'á: cause it to extend down (nááł'á: I cause it to extend down)

Ni⁶-(?)-Position 6b + Extended Neuter Base

There is a set of Verb Bases, concerned with physical appearance, that are derived with a ni-prefix tentatively assigned to Position 6b, and conjugated as D/L-Class Yi-Perfectives (or as D/L-class Ni-Perfective Neuters?).

The members of this group are all based on the Stem LNIN ~ ØLIN. (Krauss-Leer [1981:143] explain ØLIN as an allomorphic variant in which the L-Classifier has been reinterpreted as the Stem-initial consonant.) (Compare also Ni-Imperfective Neuter na#-ho-[n]-LNIN ~ ØLIN: look like, resemble.)

| PERSON | | | + P-1a | | + 'á-1b | |
|---|---|---|---|---|---|---|
| Sgl | | | | | | |
| 1. | neeshnin | (~ neeshłin) | bineeshnin | (~ bineeshłin) | 'áneeshnin | (~ 'áneeshłin) |
| 2. | níínílnin | (~ níínílin) | biníínílnin | (~ biníínílin) | 'áníínílnin | (~ 'áníínílin) |
| 3. | noolnin | (~ noolin) | yinoolnin | (~ yinoolin) | 'ánoolnin | (~ 'ánoolin) |
| 3a. | jinoolnin | (~ jinoolin) | bizhnoolnin | (~ bizhnoolin) | 'ázhnoolnin | (~ 'ázhnoolin) |
| 3s. | honoolnin | (~ honoolin) | ----- | ----- | 'áhonoolnin | (~ 'áhonoolin) |
| Dpl | | | | | | |
| 1. | niilnin | (~ niidlin) | biniilnin | (~ biniidlin) | 'ániilnin | (~ 'ániidlin) |
| 2. | noołnin | (~ noohłin) | binoołnin | (~ binoohłin) | 'ánoołnin | (~ 'ánoohłin) |

ni-(yi)--lnin ~ Ølin: look like, have the appearance of (haa noolnin ~ noolin: what does it look like?)

bi-1a (null postposition)#-(yi)--lnin ~ Ølin: look like him/her/it (shizhé'é bineeshnin ~ bineeshłin: I resemble my father)

kó-1b (this way, thus)#-(yi)--lnin ~ Ølin: look like this ('ashkii nishłínę́ędą́ą́' kóneeshnin ~ kóneeshłin ńt'éé': I looked like this when I was a boy)

'á-1b (comparative marker)#-(yi)--lnin ~ Ølin, 'ayóí ---: be handsome, pretty, good-looking ('ayóí 'áníínílnin: you're good-looking; nilááh 'áneeshnin: I'm better looking than you)

ni-(yi)--(d)dǫ́ǫ́z: be striped, look striped (neesdǫ́ǫ́z: I'm striped; noodǫ́ǫ́z: it/he is striped)

ni-(yi)--(d)jí: be corrugated, rippled, rough-surfaced (neeshjí: I'm rippled [as when one lies on a rippled surface that leaves its imprint]; noojí: it's rippled, rough)

di-ni-(yi--ltł'izh: be greenish or bluish (dineeshtł'izh: I'm sort of greenish; dinooltł'izh: it's greenish)

## RECAPITULATION

The conjugational pattern corresponding to the Base Paradigm of the Yi-Perfective, the Extended Base Paradigms and the Conjunct/Disjunct derivatives can be recapitulated succinctly in the following form:

T = any Verb Theme
(d) = D-effect
O = any direct object pronoun of Position 4

### Yi-Perfective

### 1. Extended Base Paradigm

PERSON

| | | Ø/Ł | | | D/L | |
|---|---|---|---|---|---|---|
| Sgl | | Intransitive | | Transitive | Intransitive | Transitive |
| yi- | 1. | yí-T | (yícha) | (yích'id) | (biih yish'na') | (yishghal) |
| | 2. | yíní-T | (yínícha) | (yíních'id) | (biih yíní'na') | (yíníłghal) |
| | 3. | yí-T | (yícha) | --- | (yiih yi'na') | --- |
| | SP | --- | --- | --- | --- | (yich'id)[1] |
| | 3o. | yiyíí-T | --- | (yiyíích'id) | --- | (yoolghal) |
| | 3a. | jíí-T | (jíícha) | (jíích'id) | (biih joo'na') | (joolghal) |
| | 3i. | 'íí-T | ('íícha | --- | (biih 'oo'na') | --- |
| | 3s. | hóó-T | (hóółtseii) | --- | (hoodzą́) | --- |
| | AP | --- | --- | | --- | (bi'doolghal)<br>(bi'dooch'id) |
| | Dpl | | | | | |
| | 1. | yii(d)-T | (yiicha) | (yiich'id) | (biih yii'na') | (yiilghal) |
| | 2. | woo-T | (woocha) | (wooch'id) | (biih wooh'na') | (woołghal) |

(yi)--Øcha: cry
(yi)--Øch'id: scratch O
(yi)--(d)'na', biih ---: crawl into it (biih yish'na')
(yi)--lghal: eat O (meat)
ho-(yi)--dzą́: perforated, has a cavity (hoodzą́)

(1) (yi)--lghal: eat meat, is a Mediopassive construction, and the Mediopassives cannot take a Simple Passive. 'Atsį' yoolghal: he ate the meat, and dzidzé yooldéél: he ate the berries, but not Simple Passive 'atsį' yilghal/dzidzé yildéél: the meat/berries was (were) eaten. Where meaning permits, the Mediopassives may take an Agentive Passive- a construction in which - 'adi- functions as an indefinite 3rd person subject pronoun (someone) as bi'doolghal: he was eaten. The noun Tązhii Daaghał : Thanksgiving Day, circumvents the foregoing rule by deleting the L-Classifier, leaving only the(Usitative) Stem-ghał: meat-eating (usually), and this is modified by the distributive marker da-, producing tązhii: turkey + daaghał: distributive plural meat-eating takes place usually = "distributive plural turkey-meat-eating-usually-takes-place" = Thanksgiving Day

## *CONJUNCT PREFIXES*

### 2. Ci-: Position 6/4 + Extended Base

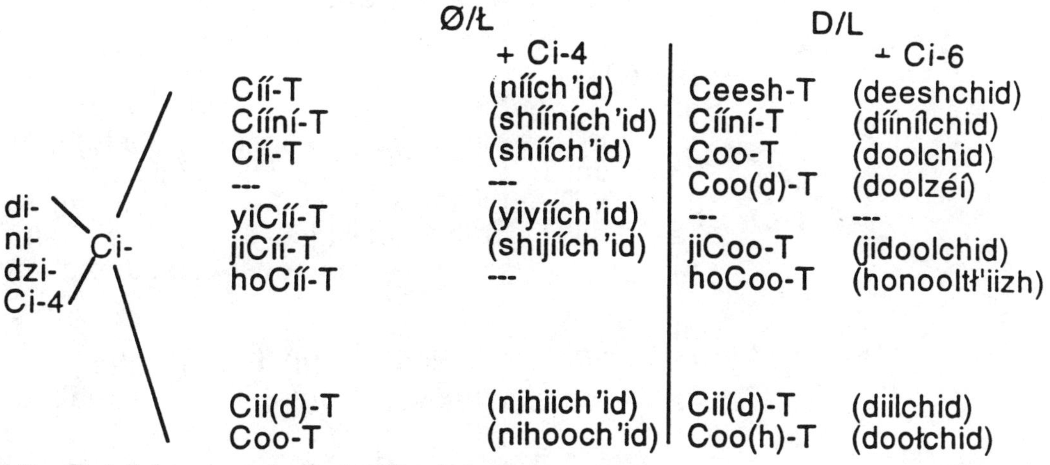


Ci-4-(yi)--Øchʼid: scratch O (shííchʼid: he scratched me)
di-(yi)--ł(l)id: burn O
di-(yi)--Ølid: burn (díílid)
di-(yi)--lchid. biih---: stick hand into it (biih deeshchid)
ni-(yi)--tʼą́, biih---: stick head (slowly) into it (biih neeshtʼą́: I stuck my head into it)
di-(yi)--lzéé: be crumbled (SP)
ni-(yi)--ltłʼiizh: be serpentine (nooltłʼiizh)
ni-(yi)--lneʼ, biih ---: stick head into it quickly (biih neeshneʼ)
ʼa#-dzi-(yi)--Øtáál: let fly a kick (ʼadzíítáál)
ʼa#-ji-(yi)--lghaal, ʼádee ---: throw self down (ʼádee ʼajeeshghaal)

### 3. Cí-: Position 6a + Extended Base

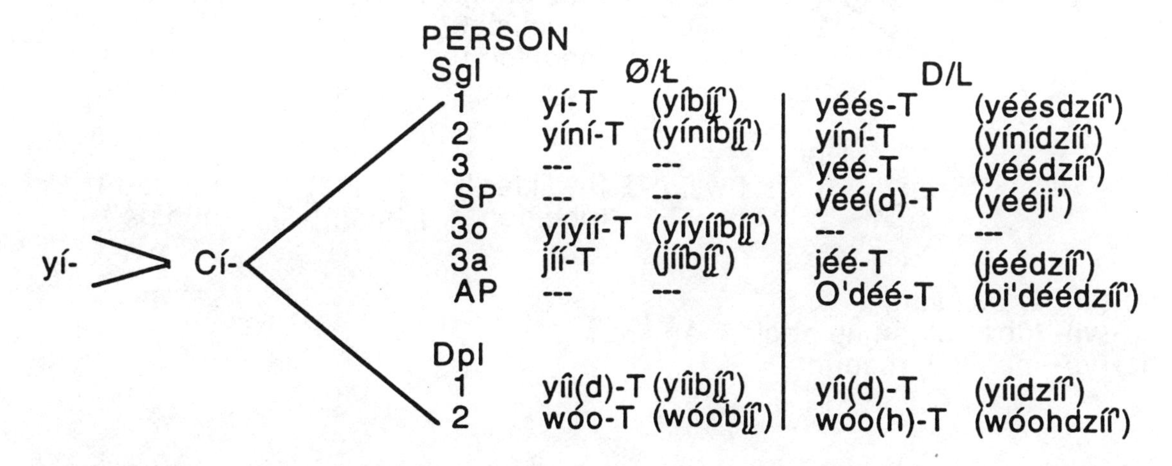


yí-(yi)--Øbį́į́ʼ: pick O (as berries)
bí#-(y)í-(yi)--Økeed: ask him for it (bííkeed: I asked him for it)
yí-(yi)--(d)dzííʼ: curse him (biʼdeedzííʼ: he was cursed)
yí-(yi)--Øzhiʼ: name O, call O by name (yééjiʼ: it was named; biʼdééjiʼ: he was named)

### 4. 'A- ~ 'i-: Position 4 + Extended Base

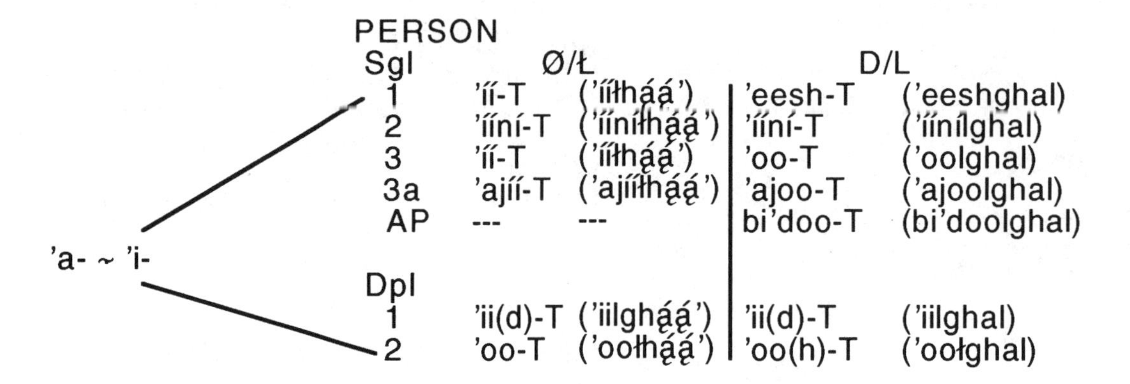

'a- ~ 'i-

| PERSON | Ø/Ł | | D/L | |
|---|---|---|---|---|
| Sgl | | | | |
| 1 | 'íí-T | ('ííłhą́ą́') | 'eesh-T | ('eeshghal) |
| 2 | 'ííní-T | ('ííníłhą́ą́') | 'ííní-T | ('íínílghal) |
| 3 | 'íí-T | ('ííłhą́ą́') | 'oo-T | ('oolghal) |
| 3a | 'ajíí-T | ('ajííłhą́ą́') | 'ajoo-T | ('ajoolghal) |
| AP | --- | --- | bi'doo-T | (bi'doolghal) |
| Dpl | | | | |
| 1 | 'ii(d)-T | ('iilghą́ą́') | 'ii(d)-T | ('iilghal) |
| 2 | 'oo-T | ('oołhą́ą́') | 'oo(h)-T | ('oołghal) |

'a-(yi)--łhą́ą́': snore
'a-(yi)--lghal: eat unspecified O (meat)('eeshghal: I ate; bi'doolghal: he was eaten)

### 5. Ho- ~ hw-: Position 4 + Extended Base

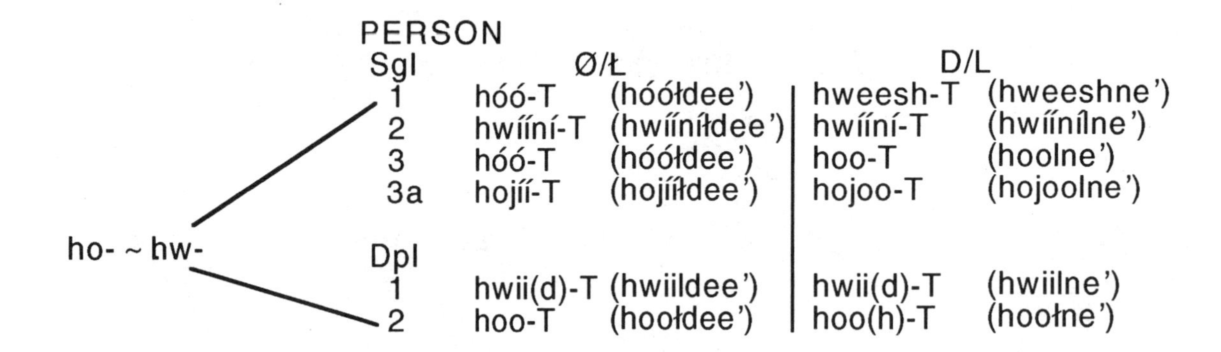

ho- ~ hw-

| PERSON | Ø/Ł | | D/L | |
|---|---|---|---|---|
| Sgl | | | | |
| 1 | hóó-T | (hóółdee') | hweesh-T | (hweeshne') |
| 2 | hwííní-T | (hwííníłdee') | hwííní-T | (hwíínílne') |
| 3 | hóó-T | (hóółdee') | hoo-T | (hoolne') |
| 3a | hojíí-T | (hojííłdee') | hojoo-T | (hojoolne') |
| Dpl | | | | |
| 1 | hwii(d)-T | (hwiildee') | hwii(d)-T | (hwiilne') |
| 2 | hoo-T | (hoołdee') | hoo(h)-T | (hoołne') |

ho-(yi)--Øtáál: sing
ho-(yi)--łdee': clean up or clear an area
ho-(yi)--lne': tell, recount

## *DISJUNCT PREFIXES*

### 6. Ca-: Position 1b + Extended Base

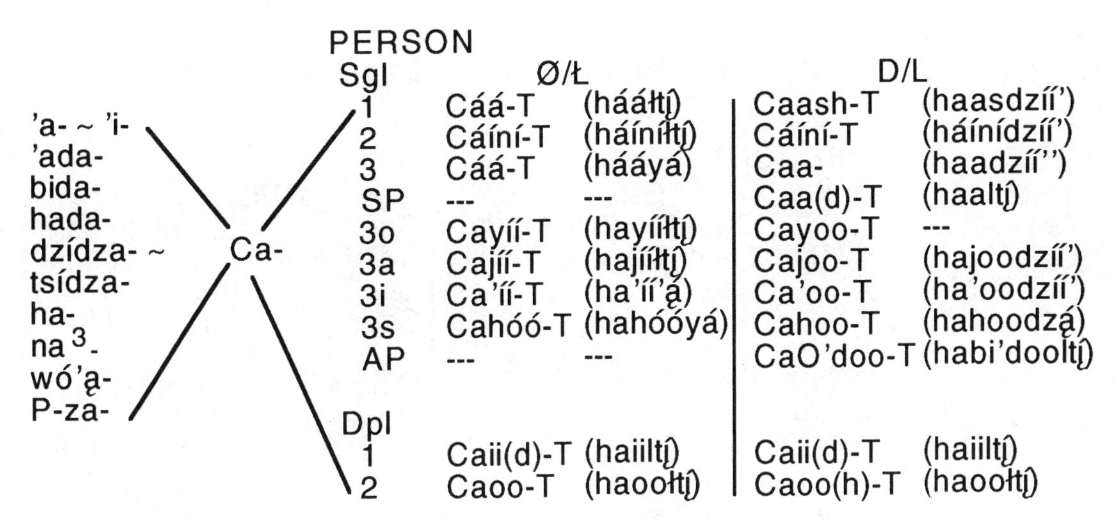

'a- ~ 'i-, 'ada-, bida-, hada-, dzídza- ~ tsídza-, ha-, na$^3$-, wó'ą-, P-za- → Ca-

| PERSON | Ø/Ł | | D/L | |
|---|---|---|---|---|
| Sgl | | | | |
| 1 | Cáá-T | (háátį́) | Caash-T | (haasdzíí') |
| 2 | Cáíní-T | (háínítį́) | Cáíní-T | (háínídzíí') |
| 3 | Cáá-T | (hááyá) | Caa- | (haadzíí'') |
| SP | --- | --- | Caa(d)-T | (haaltį́) |
| 3o | Cayíí-T | (hayííłtį́) | Cayoo-T | --- |
| 3a | Cajíí-T | (hajííłtį́) | Cajoo-T | (hajoodzíí') |
| 3i | Ca'íí-T | (ha'íí'ą́) | Ca'oo-T | (ha'oodzíí') |
| 3s | Cahóó-T | (hahóóyá) | Cahoo-T | (hahoodzą́) |
| AP | --- | --- | CaO'doo-T | (habi'dooltį́) |
| Dpl | | | | |
| 1 | Caii(d)-T | (haiiltį́) | Caii(d)-T | (haiiltį́) |
| 2 | Caoo-T | (haooɫtį́) | Caoo(h)-T | (haooɫtį́) |

'a- ~ 'i-#-(yi)--łtį́: carry an AnO <u>away</u> out of sight ('ííłtį́)
ha#-(yi)--łtį́: take an AnO <u>out</u> (as from a box)(háátį́)
ha#-(yi)--Øyá: one actor emerged, got <u>up out</u> (hááyá)
ha#-ho-(yi)--Øyá: an event began (hahóóyá)
ha#-ho-(yi)--dzą́: there is an exit hole
ha#-(yi)--(d)dzíí': speak (haasdzíí')
ha#-(yi)--Øcha: start to cry (háácha)
na$^3$#-(yi)--Ø'ą́: lower SRO <u>down</u> (náá'ą́)
dzídza- ~ tsídza#-(yi)--Ø'ą́: put SRO into fire (dzídzáá'ą́ ~ tsídzáá'ą́)
wo'ą#-(yi)--(d)'na': crawl <u>over an edge</u> (wó'ąąsh'na')
P-za#-(yi)--Ø'ą́: put SRO <u>into P's mouth</u> (bizáá'ą́)
ha#-'a-5-(yi)--Ø'ą́: the sun came up (i.e. something round moved up)

### 7. Cá-: Position 1 + Extended Base

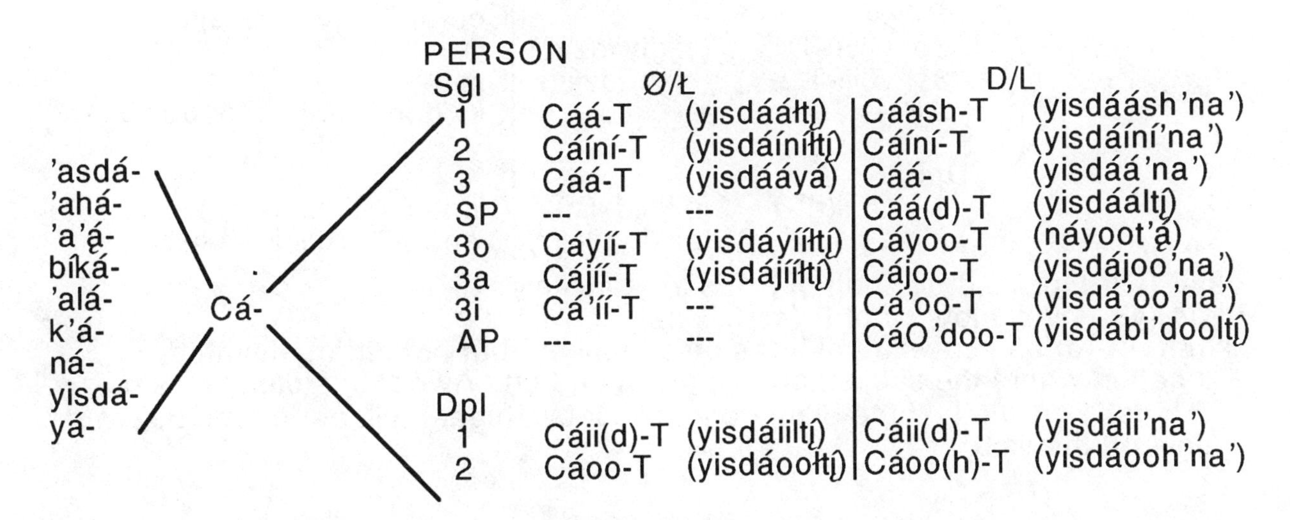

'asdá-, 'ahá-, 'a'ą́-, bíká-, 'alá-, k'á-, ná-, yisdá-, yá- → Cá-

| PERSON | Ø/Ł | | D/L | |
|---|---|---|---|---|
| Sgl | | | | |
| 1 | Cáá-T | (yisdáátį́) | Cáásh-T | (yisdáásh'na') |
| 2 | Cáíní-T | (yisdáínítį́) | Cáíní-T | (yisdáíní'na') |
| 3 | Cáá-T | (yisdááyá) | Cáá- | (yisdáá'na') |
| SP | --- | --- | Cáá(d)-T | (yisdáálį́) |
| 3o | Cáyíí-T | (yisdáyííłtį́) | Cáyoo-T | (náyoot'ą́) |
| 3a | Cájíí-T | (yisdájííłtį́) | Cájoo-T | (yisdájoo'na') |
| 3i | Cá'íí-T | --- | Cá'oo-T | (yisdá'oo'na') |
| AP | --- | --- | CáO'doo-T | (yisdábi'dooltį́) |
| Dpl | | | | |
| 1 | Cáii(d)-T | (yisdáiiltį́) | Cáii(d)-T | (yisdáii'na') |
| 2 | Cáoo-T | (yisdáooɫtį́) | Cáoo(h)-T | (yisdáooh'na') |

yisdá#-(yi)--łtį́: carry an AnO <u>to safety</u>, rescue O

yisdá#-(yi)--Øyá: reach safety
yisdá#-(yi)--(d)'na': crawl to safety
ná#-(yi)--(d)t'ą́, biih ---: put SRO back into it

## 8. Ce-: Position 1b + Base

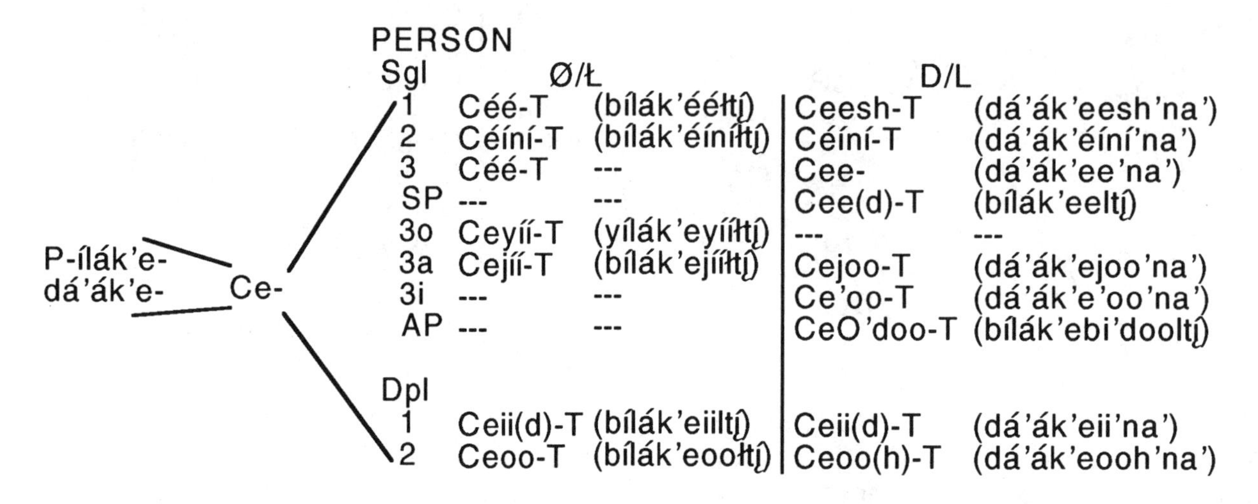


P-íłák'e#-(yi)--łtį́: hand an AnO to P
dá'ák'e#-(yi)--(d)'na': crawl into the field

## 9. Ci-: Position 1b + Extended Base

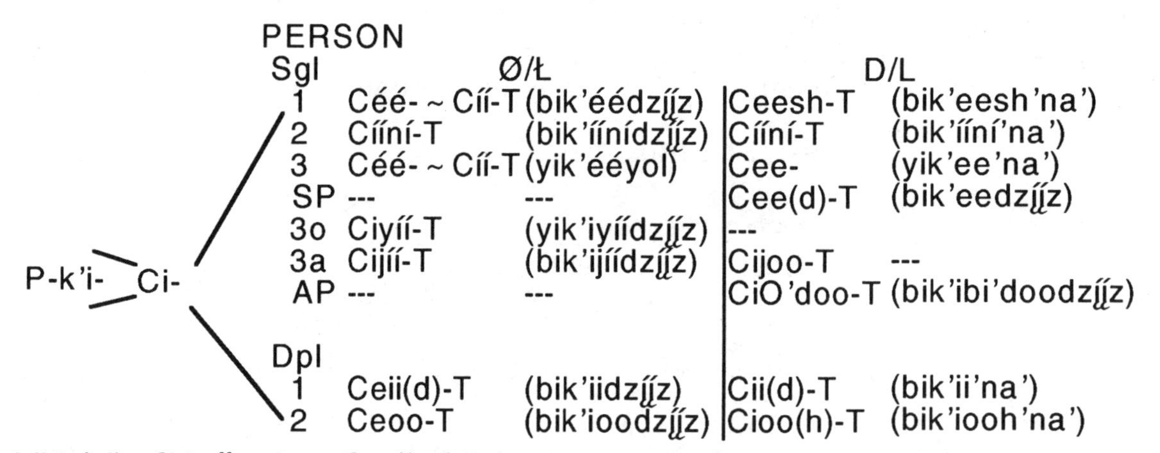


P-k'i#-(yi)--Ødzį́į́z: drag O off of P (as an attacker)
P-k'i#-(yi)--Øyol: blow off of P (as P's hat)
bik'i#-(yi)--(d)'na': crawl off of it (as off a blanket - but not off an elevated location where the subject moves down and off. 'Awéé' beeldléí yik'ee'na': the baby crawled off the blanket; jeeshóó' tsin bigaan yik'eet'a': the buzzard flew off the limb)

## 10. Cí-: Position 1b + Extended Base

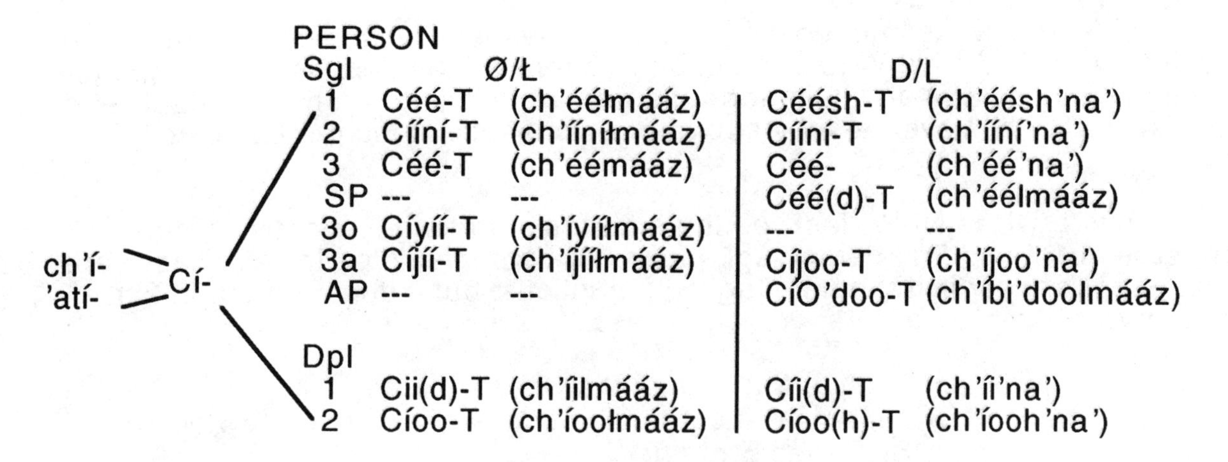

ch'í- / 'atí- → Cí-

| PERSON | Ø/Ł | | D/L | |
|---|---|---|---|---|
| Sgl | | | | |
| 1 | Céé-T | (ch'ééłmááz) | Céésh-T | (ch'éésh'na') |
| 2 | Cííní-T | (ch'ííníłmááz) | Cííní-T | (ch'ííní'na') |
| 3 | Céé-T | (ch'éémááz) | Céé- | (ch'éé'na') |
| SP | --- | --- | Céé(d)-T | (ch'éélmááz) |
| 3o | Cíyíí-T | (ch'íyííłmááz) | --- | --- |
| 3a | Cíjíí-T | (ch'íjííłmááz) | Cíjoo-T | (ch'íjoo'na') |
| AP | --- | --- | CíO'doo-T | (ch'íbi'doolmááz) |
| Dpl | | | | |
| 1 | Cii(d)-T | (ch'íilmááz) | Cíi(d)-T | (ch'íi'na') |
| 2 | Cíoo-T | (ch'íoołmááz) | Cíoo(h)-T | (ch'íooh'na') |

'adah ch'í#-(yi)--łmááz: roll O down over the edge
'adah ch'í#-(yi)--Ømááz: roll down over the edge
'atí#-(yi)--(d)t'įįd: undergo privation ('atéét'įįd ~ 'atíít'įįd)
'adah ch'í#-(yi)--(d)'na': crawl over the edge (as over a precipice)

## 2. NI-PERFECTIVE

Ni-Perfective is marked by the ni-modal-aspectival conjugation marker of Position 7. With Active Verbs an action or event is identified as one completed terminally, as by arrival, attainment of a goal or finishing. With Ni-Perfective Neuter Verbs, however, a subject or a direct object is described as extending in a line.

In Ø/Ł-Class Ni-Perfectives the high tone marking Perfective Mode appears in 1st and 2nd person sgl and in 3rd person sgl/dpl. In D/L-Class verbs it does not appear in 1st person sgl constructions, but it does appear in 2nd person and Simple Passive.

Ø/Ł: ní̲yá: I/he came; yí̲níyá: you came
D/L: nish'na': I came crawling; yí̲ní'na': you crawled; yí̲t'ą́: SRO was brought

Ni-7 is replaced by a yí-allomorph in the 3rd person and Simple Passive of D/L-Class verbs - provided that the Verb Base does not include a derivational prefix of Position 1, in which event yí- deletes.

yílwod: he arrived running
yíltsooz: FFO was brought/delivered

but

náltsooz (= ná- + (yí)-ltsooz): it (FFO) was returned
ch'élwod (= ch'í- + (yí)-lwod): he ran out

Third person distributive plural forms generallly require a shift to Si-Perfective, although some speakers retain Ni-Perfective.

shaa yinídzį́į́z; he dragged it to me
shaa deizdzį́į́z: they 3+ dragged it to me
jinídzį́į́z: he/she (4th person) came dragging it
dadzizdzį́į́z: they (4th person) came dragging it

### *ACTIVE VERBS*

#### Base Paradigm

Table 1

T = any Verb Theme

| PERSON | Ø/Ł | | | | | | D/L | | | | | |
|---|---|---|---|---|---|---|---|---|---|---|---|---|
| Sgl | 7 | + | 8 | | | as in: | 7 | + | 8 | | | as in : |
| 1. | ní- | + | Ø | > | ní-T | níná | ni- | + | -sh- | > | nish-T | nish'na' |
| 2. | yí- | + | -ní- | > | yíní-T | yíníná | yí- | + | -ní- | > | yíní-T | yíní'na' |
| 3. | ní- | + | Ø | > | ní-T | níná | yí- | + | Ø | > | yí-T | yí'na' |
| SP. | --- | + | --- | > | --- | --- | yí(d)- | + | Ø | > | yí(d)-T | yíltsooz |
| Dpl | | | | | | | | | | | | |
| 1. | n- | + | -ii d)- | > | nii(d)-T | nii'ná | n- | + | -ii(d)- | > | nii(d)-T | nii'na' |
| 2. | n- | + | -oo- | > | noo-T | nooná | n- | + | -oo(h)- | > | noo(h)-T | nooh'na' |

(ni)--Øná: arrive moving with household
(ni)--(d)'na': arrive crawling
(yi)--ltsooz: be brought (FFO)(shaa yíltsooz: it was given/brought/delivered to me)

## The Extended Base Paradigms

### 1. Conjunct Prefixes

Prefixes of Position 5 + Base

Table 2

In D/L-Class verbs the 3a and 3i deictic subject pronouns of Position 5 elide the prefix vowel and join (y)í-, the ni-7 allomorph.

j(i)- + (y)í- > jí-
'(a)- + (y)í- > 'í-

In the same environment 3s ho- lengthens the prefix vowel and yí- elides:

ho- + (yi)- > hoo-

And -'(a)di-, representing the agentive subject, behaves like a prefix of Position 6 in combination with yí-:

-'(a)di- + (yí) > -'(a)dee-

T = any Verb Theme

| PERSON | Ø/Ł-Class | | | | | | | D/L-Class | | | | | |
|---|---|---|---|---|---|---|---|---|---|---|---|---|---|
| Sgl | 5 | + | Base | | | as in: | 5 | + | Base | | | as in: |
| 3a. | ji- | + | -ní- | > | jiní-T | jiníná | j- | + | (y)í- | > | jí-T | jí'na' |
| 3i. | 'a-- | + | -ní- | > | 'aní-T | 'aníná | '- | + | (y)í- | > | 'í-T | 'í'na' |
| 3s. | ho- | + | -ní- | > | honí-T | honít'i' | hoo- | + | Ø | > | hoo-T | hoolzhiizh |
| AP | --- | + | --- | > | --- | --- | -'(a)d- | + | -ee- | > | -'(a)dee(d)-T | bi'deeltį́ |

(ni)--Øná: move with household (jiníná: he/she moved; shił 'aníná: I moved as a member of a family - lit. someone unspecified moved in company with me)
(ni)--Øt'i': extend in a thin line (honít'i': area extends in a line)
ho-(ni)--lzhiizh: time moves; an era arrives (baa hoolzhiizh: it became his turn - lit. a time period moved to him)
(ni)--łtį́: arrive carrying an AnO (Agentive Passive bi'deeltį́: he/she was given; shaa bi'deeltį́: he/she was given to me)

## Ci-Prefixes of Position 4 + Extended Base

### Table 3A
### Ø/Ł-Class Verbs

The Ci-Prefixes of Position 4 are the direct object pronouns. If the subject of the verb is 1st or 2nd person and the direct object is 3rd person, the object is represented by Ø; if both the subject and the object are 3rd person the object is represented by the 3o pronoun yi- (or bi- if subject and object are inverted).

The Transitive and Intransitive Paradigms converge in shape when the direct object is represented by Ø.

Ni-Perfective usually shifts to Si-Perfective in all 3rd persons in the distributive plural paradigm, derived with da-:Position 3.

T = any Verb Theme

| PERSON | Prefix Position | | | | | | | | Transitive | |
|---|---|---|---|---|---|---|---|---|---|---|
| Sgl | 4 | + | 5 | + | Base | | | Intransitive | + Ø-4 | + Ci-4 |
| 1 | Ø/Ci- | + | ---- | + | ní-T | > | ní-T | níná | níłtį́ | niníłtį́ |
| 2 | Ø/Ci-- | + | --- | + | (y)íní-T | > | yíní-T | yíníná | yíníłtį́ | shííníłtį́ |
| 3 | Ø/Ci- | + | --- | + | ní-T | > | ní-T | níná | --- | shiníłtį́ |
| 3o. | --/yi- | + | - | + | ní-T | > | yiní-T | --- | --- | yiníłtį́ |
| 3a. | Ø/Ci- | + | -ji-/zh- | + | ní-T | > | jiní-T | jiníná | jiníłtį́ | shizhníłtį́ |
| Dpl | | | | | | | | | | |
| 1 | Ø/Ci- | + | --- | + | nii(d)-T | > | nii(d)-T | nii'ná | niiltį́ | niniiltį́ |
| 2 | Ø/Ci- | + | --- | + | noo-T | > | noo-T | nooná | noołtį́ | shinoołtį́ |

(ni)--łtį́: bring AnO (baa shííníłtį́: you brought/gave me to him; yaa shiníłtį́: he brought/gave me to him, etc.)
(ni)--Øná: arrive moving with household

### D/L-Class Verbs

There are apparently no simple transitive Ni-Perfective D/L-Class Verb Bases - i.e. none that appear without a ná-Reversionary prefix of Position 1d. The simple paradigm includes only the Simple and Agentive Passives corresponding to the transitive paradigm.

*Simple Passive* converges in form with the 3rd person of a D/L-Class Ni-Perfective, as:

shaa yílwod: he came running to me
shaa yíltsooz: it (FFO) was given to me

*Agentive Passive* is derived with the Position 5 indefinite subject pronoun -'adi-: "unspecified person." The -di- component behaves like a derivational-thematic prefix of Position 6, in that the ni- (~ yí-) conjugation marker of Position 7 takes the shape -ee- in combination with -di-, as in:

shaa bi'deeltį́ (< bi-4 + -'(a)d-5 + -ee-7 + -ltį́): AnO was given to me

## Derivational-Thematic Prefixes of Position 6 + Extended Base

The Derivational-Thematic Prefixes of Position 6 (6a/6b/6c) have the shape Ci- (di-, ni-, dzi-, hi- ~ yi-). These combine with the Extended Ni-Perfective Base in a straightforward manner except in the 3rd person of D/L-Class Verbs, and in the Passives, where ni- (~ yí)-7 takes the shape -ee-.

### Ci-: Position 6a/6b + Extended Base

Table 4A
Ø/Ł Class Verbs

T = any Verb Theme

| PERSON | Prefix Position | | | | | | | | | | |
|---|---|---|---|---|---|---|---|---|---|---|---|
| Sgl | 4 | + | 5 | + | 6a/6b | + | Base | | | as in: | |
| 1 | Ø/Ci- | + | ---- | + | -Ci- | + | ní-T | > | ní-T | diní'ą́ | niníyood |
| 2 | Ø/Ci-- | + | --- | + | -Ci- | + | (y)íní-T | > | yíní-T | dííní'ą́ | niníníyood |
| 3 | --/Ci- | + | --- | + | -Ci- | + | ní-T | > | ní-T | (ntsidinígo') | --- |
| 3o. | --/yi- | + | - | + | -Ci- | + | ní-T | > | yiní-T | yidiní'ą́ | yininíyood |
| 3a. | Ø/Ci- | + | -ji-/-zh- | + | -Ci- | + | ní-T | > | jiní-T | jidiní'ą́ | jininíyood |
| Dpl | | | | | | | | | | | |
| 1 | Ø/Ci- | + | --- | + | -Ci- | + | nii(d)-T | > | nii(d)-T | diniit'ą́ | niniidzood |
| 2 | Ø/Ci- | + | --- | + | -Ci- | + | noo-T | > | noo-T | dinoo'ą́ | ninooyood |

P-aa ni-(ni)--Øyood: drive O to P (a few sheep)
P-aa di-(ni)--Ø'ą́: relinquish O (SRO) to P (kéyah baa diní'ą́: I turned the land over to him)
'ąą di-(ni)--Øtą́: open O (a door)('ąą dinítą́)
k'í#-di-(ni)--łdéél: break SSO in two (k'ídiníłdéél)
'ałts'á#-di-(ni)--łk'ą́ą́': burn O in two ('ałts'ádiníłk'ą́ą́')
ntsi#-di-(ni)--Øgo': kneel down (ntsidinígo')

Table 4B
D/L Class Verbs

D/L-Class Verb Bases derived with prefixes of Position 6 alone are uncommon; most Position 6a/6b derivatives include a Disjunct Prefix of Position 1b.

T = any Verb Theme

| PERSON | Prefix Position | | | | | | | | | | |
|---|---|---|---|---|---|---|---|---|---|---|---|
| Sgl | 4 | + | 5 | + | 6a/6b | + | Base | | | as in: | |
| 1 | --- | + | ---- | + | Ci- | + | -nish-T | > | Cinish-T | dinishtáál | (ni)-ninisht'ą́ |
| 2 | --- | + | --- | + | Ci- | + | -(y)íní-T | > | Cííní-T | dííníltáál | (ni)-nííníṫ'ą́ |
| 3 | --- | + | --- | + | C- | + | -ee-T | > | Cee-T | deeltáál | (ni)-neet'ą́ |
| SP. | --- | + | - | + | C- | + | -ee(d)-T | > | Cee(d)-T | deet'ą́ | needzood |
| 3a. | --- | + | -ji-/-zh- | + | C- | + | -ee-T | > | jiCee-T | jideeltáál | (ni)-zhneet'ą́ |
| AP | O | + | -'(a)d- ~-di'(a)-* | + | C- | + | -ee(d)-T | > | Odi'Cee(d)-T | --- | bidi'needzood |
| Dpl | | | | | | | | | | | |
| 1 | --- | + | --- | + | Ci- | + | nii(d)-T | > | nii(d)-T | diniiltáál | (ni)-niit'ą́ |
| 2 | --- | + | --- | + | Ci- | + | noo-T | > | noo-T | dinoołtáál | (ni)-nooht'ą́ |

* The Agentive Subject pronoun: Position 5 undergoes metathesis: -'(a)di- > -di'(a)-.

ni#-di-(ni)--lchid, bik'i ---: put hand down on it, thumbprint it (yik'i ndeelchid: he put his hand down on it)
bijáátah di-(ni)--ltáál: trip him (by placing one's foot between his legs as he walks)(shijáátah deeltáál) he tripped me)
ni#-ni-(ni)--(d)t'ą́: lay one's head down (ni#: Position 1b)(łééchąą'í sitsék'eegi nineet'ą́: the dog laid its head in my lap)
ch'í#-di-(ni)--(d)dza': stagger out (ch'ídinisdza')
ch'í#-di-(ni)--lnii': stick one's arm out (as out a window) (ch'ídinishnii': I stuck my arm out; ch'ídeelnii': he stuck his arm out))
P-aa deet'ą́: it was turned over to P, relinquished to P
P-aa bidi'needzood: they were driven to P (as a few sheep)

## 'A- ~ 'i- ~ '-: Position 4 + Extended Base

### Table 5A
### Ø/Ł Class Verbs

'A- (~ 'i- ~ '), the 3i subject/object pronoun of Positions 5/6: "something/someone unspecified," is a common component of Ni-Perfective verbs. 'A- reduces to its initial consonant ('-) before a following vowel-initial morpheme, and in environments that include a preceding prefix. If the latter is a Conjunct element of Position 6, '- takes position to its right. Compare:

shił 'íłwod: I arrived (i.e. an unspecified vehicle arrived running with me)
'aníłbą́ą́z: I arrived (i.e. came driving an unspecified wheeled vehicle)
ni'níłbą́ą́z: I parked (an unspecified wheeled vehicle)
badi'ní'ą́ (< ba'diní'ą́): I permitted (i.e. I relinquished something unspecified to him on a temporary basis. Cf. ba'ní'ą́: I loaned SRO to him; baa diní'ą́: I relinquished SRO to him))

In 2nd person sgl forms 'a- appears in the form of its 'i- allomorph, and in Bases that include a Disjunct Prefix, 'a- appears to the right of -zh-, the 3a (4th person) subject pronoun of Position 5.

T = any Verb Theme

| PERSON | Sgl | as in: | + Conjunct-6 | as in: | + Disjunct-1b | as in: |
|---|---|---|---|---|---|---|
| 1 | 'aní-T | ('aníłkǫ́ǫ́') | -di'ní-T | (badi'ní'ą́) | ni-'ní-T | (ni'nínil) |
| 2 | 'ííní-T | ('ííníłkǫ́ǫ́') | -'dííní-T | (ba'dííní'ą́) | ni--'ííní-T | (ni'íínínil) |
| 3 | 'aní-T | ('aníłkǫ́ǫ́') | -di'ní-T | (yadi'ní'ą́) | ni--'ní-T | (ni'nínil) |
| 3a. | 'azhní-T | ('azhníłkǫ́ǫ́') | -zhdi'ní-T | (bazhdi'ní'ą́) | ni--zh'ní-T | (nizh'nínil) |
| | Dpl | | Dpl | | Dpl | |
| 1 | 'anii(d)-T | ('aniilkǫ́ǫ́') | -di'nii(d)-T | (badi'niit'ą́) | ni--'nii(d)-T | (ni'nii'nil) |
| 2 | 'anoo-T | ('anoołkǫ́ǫ́') | -di'noo-T | (badi'noo'ą́) | ni--'noo-T | (ni'noonil) |
| | Dist. Pl | | Dist. Pl | | Dist.Pl | |
| 1 | da'nii(d)-T | (da'niilkǫ́ǫ́') | -dadi'nii(d)-T | (badadi'niit'ą́) | nda'nii(d)-T | (nda'nii'nil) |
| 2 | da'noo-T | (da'noołkǫ́ǫ́') | -dadi'noo-T | (badadi'noo'ą́) | nda'noo-T | (nda'noonil) |
| 3 | da'ní-T | (da'níłkǫ́ǫ́') | -dadi'ní-T | (yadadi'ní'ą́) | nda'ní-T | nda'nínil) |
| 3a | dazh'ní-T | (dazh'níłkǫ́ǫ́') | -dazhdi'ní-T | (badazhdi'ní'ą́) | ndazh'ní-T | (ndazh'nínil) |

'a-(ni)--łkǫ́ǫ́'): arrive swimming (da'níłkǫ́ǫ́': they 3+ came swimming)
P-a#-di'(a)-(ni)--Ø'ą́: permit P (badi'ní'ą́: I permitted him - literally: I relinquished something unspecified to him)

P-a#-'(a)-(ni)--Ø'ą́: loan a SRO to P (ba'ní'ą́: I loaned it to him)
ch'í#-'(a)-(ni)--łdlą́ą́d: shine a light out (as out a door)(ch'ídi'níłdlą́ą́d: I shined it out)
ch'í#-'(a)-(ni)--łkǫ́ǫ́': swim out (ch'í'níłkǫ́ǫ́': I swam out)
ni#-'(a)-(ni)--Øgizh: cock (a gun); put in gear (a car). (ni'nígizh: I cocked/shifted it)
ni#-'(a)-(ni)--łtła: stop, come to a halt. (ni'níłtła: I made a stop - as in a car - literally: I caused something to halt; bá ni'níłtła: I stopped for him)
ni#-'(a)-(ni)--Ønil, bíłátsíín ---: handcuff him (shíłátsíín ni'nínil: he handcuffed me; literally: he placed unspecified PIO on my wrists)
ni#-'(a)-(ni)--Ø'ą́, bąąh ---: put a cast on it (as on a broken limb) (shijáád yąąh ni'ní'ą́: he put a cast on my leg)
P-í#-'(a)-(ni)--Øbą́ą́z, p-ił ---: P overtook p (shił bí'níbą́ą́z: I overtook him, riding in an unspecified vehicle - literally: something arrived rolling in company with me to a point of contact with him)

## Table 5B
## D/L Class Verbs

D/LClass Ni-Perfectives that include 'a- are uncommon. The only available examples are Bases derived with prefixes of Position 1b.

| PERSON | Sgl | as in: | |
|---|---|---|---|
| 1 | -'nishT | ch'í'níshzhiizh | ni'nishzhiizh |
| 2 | -'íiní-T | ch'í'íinílzhiizh | ni'íinílzhiizh |
| 3 | -'í-T | ch'í'ílzhiizh | ni'ílzhiizh |
| 3a. | -'jí-T | ch'í'jílzhiizh | ni'jílzhiizh |
| SP | -'í(d)-T | --- | ni'í'nil |
| | Dpl | Dpl | Dpl |
| 1 | -'nii(d)-T | ch'í'niilzhiizh | ni'niilzhiizh |
| 2 | -'noo(h)-T | ch'í'noołzhiizh | ni'noołzhiizh |

ch'í#-'(a)-(ni)--lzhiizh: come out dancing (ch'í'níshzhiizh: I came out dancing)
ni#-'(a)-(ni)--lzhiizh: stop dancing (ni'nishzhiizh: I stopped dancing)
ni#-'(a)-(ni)--(d)nil, bíłátsíín ----: be handcuffed (shíłátsíín ni'í'nil: I was handcuffed)

## Ho-: Position 4 + Extended Base

### Table 6

Ho: Position 4 "space, area" occurs as a thematic prefix in a few *Simple* Active Verb Bases that are conjugated as Ni-Perfectives, and in others it represents 3a (4th) person as direct object. Most Bases that include ho- also contain a Disjunct derivational Prefix of Position 1.

Ho- appears in the form of its hw-allomorph before a vowel, in 2nd person sgl constructions; and takes the shape hoo- in 3rd person sgl/dpl D/L-Class Verbs and in Simple Passives, where yi-7 deletes.

T = any Verb Theme

| | Ø/Ł | | D/L |
|---|---|---|---|
| PERSON | Sgl | Sgl | Sgl |
| 1 | honíziid | ch'íhoní'ą́ | nihonishne' |
| 2 | hwíínízid | ch'íhwííní'ą́ | nihwíínílne' |
| 3 | honíziid | ch'íhoní'ą́ | nihoolne' |
| 3a. | hoznízid | ch'íhozhní'ą́ | nihojoolne' |
| SP | --- | --- | nihoot'ą́ |
| | Dpl | Dpl | Dpl |
| 1 | honiidziid | ch'íhoniit'ą́ | nihoniilne' |
| 2 | honooziid | ch'íhonoo'ą́ | nihonoołne' |

ho-(ni)--Øziid: arrive groping the way (shaa honíziid: he came groping his way to me)
ch'í#-ho-(ni)--Ø'ą́: make a statement (ch'íhoní'ą́: I made a statement)
ni#-ho-(ni)--lne': finish a narration (nihoolne': he finished telling)
P-á ni#-ho-(ni)--Ø'ą́: sentence P; set a date or period of time for P (bá nihoot'ą́: he was sentenced)

## Hi- ~ yi-: Seriative - Position 6a/6c

Verb Bases whose themes involve segmental action (hop, skip, move on rump, throw an O) require the seriative marker. Hi- appears in the form of its (y)i-6c allomorph when it is preceded by a prefix of Position 4 and, with D/L Class verbs, when preceded by the 3a subject pronoun ji-: Position 5.

### Table 7A
### Ø/Ł Class Verbs

T = any Verb Theme

| PERSON | Prefix Position | | | | | | | | | | |
|---|---|---|---|---|---|---|---|---|---|---|---|
| Sgl | 4 | + | 5 | + | 6a | 6c | + | Base | + Ø-4 | + Ci-4 |
| 1 | Ø/Ci- | + | ---- | + | -hi- | -i- | + | -ní-T | ch'íhinííłhan | ch'íniinííłhan |
| 2 | Ø/Ci-- | + | --- | + | -hi- | -í- | + | -íní-T | ch'íhíínííłhan | ch'íshíínííłhan |
| 3 | --/Ci- | + | --- | + | --- | -i- | + | -iní-T | --- | ch'íshiinííłhan |
| 3o. | --/i- | + | - | + | --- | -i- | + | -iní-T | --- | ch'íínííłhan |
| 3a. | Ø/Ci- | + | -ji /zh- | + | --- | -i- | + | -ní-T | ch'íhizhnííłhan | ch'íshijiinííłhan |
| Dpl | | | | | | | | | | |
| 1 | Ø/Ci- | + | --- | + | -hi- | -i- | + | nii(d)-T | ch'íhiniilghan | ch'íniiniilghan |
| 2 | Ø/Ci- | + | --- | + | -hi- | -i- | + | noo--T | ch'íhinoołhan | ch'íshiinoołhan |

ch'í#-hi-(ni)---łhan: throw O out (ch'íniiníłhan: I threw you out; ch'íshííníłhan: you threw me out; ch'íshiiníłhan: he threw me out, etc.)
bighá#-hi-(ni)--łhan: throw O through it (as through a doorway or glass window)
biníká#-hi-(ni)--łhan: throw O through it (an opening - as a doorway)

Table 7B
D/L Class Verbs

T = any Verb Theme

| PERSON | Prefix Position | | | | | | | | | |
|---|---|---|---|---|---|---|---|---|---|---|
| Sgl | 4 | + | 5 | + | 6a 6c | + | Base | | | as in: |
| 1 | --- | + | ---- | + | -hi- --- | + | nish-T | > | hinish-T | hinishghal |
| 2 | --- | + | --- | + | -hi- --- | + | -íní-T | > | hííní-T | hííníghal |
| 3 | --- | + | --- | + | -h- --- | + | -ee-T | > | hee-T | heelghal |
| SP | --- | + | --- | + | -h- --- | + | -ee(d)-T | > | hee(d)-T | heelghan |
| 3a. | --- | + | -ji | + | -- -y- | + | -ee-T | > | jiyee-T | jiyeelghal |
| AP | O | + | --- | + | -- -di'y- | + | -ee(d)-T | > | Odi'yee-T | ch'íbidi'yeelghan |
| Dpl | | | | | | | | | | |
| 1 | --- | + | --- | + | -hi- -- | + | -nii(d)-T | > | hinii(d)-T | hiniilghal |
| 2 | --- | + | --- | + | -hi- -- | + | -noo--T | > | hinoo-T | hinoołghal |

hi-(ni)--lghal: arrive crawling on belly or back
ch'í#-yi-(ni)--lghan: toss O out (ch'íbidi'yeelghan: he was tossed out)

Dzi- ~ -zh- ~ -z-: Position 6a + Extended Base

Dzi- and its allomorphs: Position 6a- "away into space" occur in a few Verb Bases derived with a Disjunct Prefix or prefixes of Position 1.

Table 8

| PERSON | | | | |
|---|---|---|---|---|
| Sgl | | | Dpl | |
| 1 -zní- | (nizníłts'in) | | 1. -znii(d)- | (nizniilts'in) |
| 2 -dzííní- | (ndzííníłts'in) | | 2. -znoo- | (niznoołts'in) |
| 3 -zní- | (nizníłts'in) | | | |
| 3a. -izhní- | (niizhníłts'in) | | | |

P-ił ni#-dzi-(ni)--łts'in: strike P terminatively with fist; knock P out (literally strike away terminatively into space in company with P)
P-ił ni#-dzi-(ni)--łne': stone P (to death)(bił ndzííníłne': you stoned it)
P-ił ni#-dzi-(ni)--łhaal: beat P with a club (yił nizníłts'in: he beat him)
bighá#-dzi-(ni)--łts'in: ram fist through it (bigháznííłts'in: I rammed my fist through it)
bighá#-dzi-(ni)--Øtáál: kick a hole in it (yigháznítáál: he kicked a hole in it)

## 2. Disjunct Prefixes

Da-: Position 3 - Distributive Plural

A switch to Si-Perfective in 3rd person distributive plural is generally preferred - it is mandatory for intransitive verbs. Retention of Ni-Perfective in the 3rd person distributive plural of "handle" verbs is acceptable to some speakers.

Table 1

T = any Verb Theme

| PERSON | Prefix Position | | | | | | | as in: | |
|---|---|---|---|---|---|---|---|---|---|
| Dist Pl | 3 | + | 4 | + | Base | | | Intransitive | Transitive |
| 1 | da- | + | Ø | + | -nii(d)-T | > | danii(d)-T | danii'ná | daniiltį́ |
| 2 | da- | + | Ø | + | -noo-T | > | danoo-T | danooná | danoołtį́ |
| 3 | da- | + | --- | + | -z-/-s-T | > | daaz-/-s--T | daazná | --- |
| 3o | de- | + | -i- | + | -z-/-s-T | > | deiz-T | --- | deistį́ |
| | de- | | -i- | | -ní-T | > | deiní-T | --- | deinííłtį́ |
| 3a. | da- | + | Ø | + | -jiz-/-s- | > | dajiz-/-s-T | dajizná | dajistį́ |
| | da- | + | Ø | + | -zhní- | > | dazhní-T | --- | dazhnííłtį́ |

da#-(ni)--Øná: move with household
da#-(ni)--łtį́: arrive carrying an AnO (shaa deistį́: they brought an AnO to me)
da#-(ni)--(d)'na': arrive crawling (baa danii'na': we went crawling to him)

## The Derivational Prefixes of Position 1

The Ni-Perfective conjugation marker (yí-7) deletes in 3rd person of D/L-Class Verbs, and in Simple Passive, in the presence of a prefix of Position 1b, 1d or 1e. Low tone derivational prefixes lengthen the prefix vowel in these environments:

niiltła (< ni-1b + [yí-] + ltła): he stopped, halted. (Cf. ninishtla: I stopped, halted.)
bighaat'ą́ (< bigha-1b + [yí-] + (d)t'ą́: a SRO was taken away from him (Cf. bighanisht'ą́: I took it away from him)
ch'é'na' (< ch'í-1b + [yí-] + [d]'na': it crawled out (Cf. ch'ínísh'na': I crawled out)
nádzá (< ná-1d + [yí-] + [d]dzá: he returned (Cf. nánísdzá: I returned)
ch'ínáánádzá (< ch'í-1b + nááná-1e + [yí-] + [d]dzá: he again went out (Cf. ch'ínáánísdzá: I again went out)

## Ca-: Position 1b + Extended Base

Postpositional P-gha-: "away from P by force" appears to be the only Ca- prefix of Position 1b that can take Ni-Perfective, and it requires a D/L-Class Verb Theme.

### Table 2

T = any Verb Theme

| PERSON | Prefix Position | | | | | | | | | |
|---|---|---|---|---|---|---|---|---|---|---|
| Sgl | 1b | + | 4 | + | 5 | + | Base | | | as in: |
| 1 | Ca- | + | Ø | + | --- | + | -nish-T | > | Canish-T | bighanisht'ą́ |
| 2 | Ca- | + | Ø | + | --- | + | (y)íní-T | > | Cáíní-T | bigháínít'ą́ |
| SP | Caa- | | Ø | + | --- | + | (yi)-T | > | Caa(d)-T | bighaat'ą́ |
| 3o | Ca- | + | -i- | + | --- | + | (yi)-T | > | Cáí-T | yigháít'ą́ |
| 3a. | Ca- | + | Ø | + | -j- | + | (y)í-T | > | Cají-T | bighajít'ą́ |
| AP | Ca- | + | O | + | -'(a)d- | + | -ee-T | > | CaO'dee(d)-T | bighabi'deeltį́ |
| Dpl | | | | | | | | | | |
| 1 | Ca- | + | Ø | + | --- | + | -nii(d)-T | > | Canii(d)-T | bighaniit'ą́ |
| 2 | Ca- | + | Ø | + | ---- | + | -noo(h)-T | > | Canoo(h)-T | bighanooht'ą́ |

P-gha#-(ni)--(d)t'ą́: take a SRO away from P
P-gha#-(ni)--ltį́: take an AnO away from P ('awéé' shighaaltį́: the baby was taken away from me; 'awéé' nishłínę́ędą́ą́' 'ánihwii'aahii léi' nighashíltį́: when I was a baby a judge took me away from you)

## Cá-: Position 1b + Extended Base

### Table 3A
### Ø/Ł-Class Verbs

The Cá-1 prefixes remain essentially unchanged throughout the paradigms in which they function as determinants.

T = any Verb Theme

| PERSON | Prefix Position | | | | | | | | | Intransitive | Transitive |
|---|---|---|---|---|---|---|---|---|---|---|---|
| Sgl | 1b | + | 4 | + | 5 | + | Base | | | Intransitive | Transitive |
| 1 | Cá- | + | Ø | + | --- | + | -ní-T | > | Cání-T | bits'ánínά | bits'ánítį́ |
| 2 | Cé- | + | Ø | + | --- | + | -(y)íní-T | > | Céíní-T | bits'éíníná | bits'áínítį́ |
| 3 | Cá- | + | Ø | + | --- | + | -ní-T | > | Cání-T | yits'ánínά | --- |
| 3o. | Cá- | + | -i- | + | --- | + | -ní-T | > | Cáiní-T | --- | yits'áinítį́ |
| 3a. | Cá- | + | Ø | + | -zh- | + | -ní-T | > | Cázhní-T | bits'ázhnínά | bits'ázhnítį́ |
| 3i | Cá- | + | --- | + | -'- | + | -ní-T | > | Cá'ní-T | bits'á'nínά | --- |
| 3s | Cá- | + | --- | + | -ho- | + | -ní-T | > | Cáhoní-T | bits'áhoníyéé' | --- |
| Dpl | | | | | | | | | | | |
| 1 | Cá- | + | Ø | + | --- | + | nii(d)-T | > | Cánii(d)-T | bits'ánii'ná | bits'ániiltį́ |
| 2 | Cá- | + | Ø | + | --- | + | noo--T | > | Cánoo-T | bits'ánooná | bits'ánoołtį́ |

P-ts'á#-(ni)--Øná: move away from P (with household)
P-ts'á#-(ni)--łtį́: take AnO away from P; separate AnO from P
P-ts'á#-ho-(ni)--Øyéé': scare it away from P

P-ts'á#-'(a)-(ni)--Øná: someone moves away from P with household (shił bits'á'níná: I moved away from it - with my family. Literally: someone / people moved away from it in company with me)
P-ghá#-(ni)--łtį́: carry AnO through P (as a fence, fog)(bigháninííłtį́: I carried you through it)
P-níká#-(ni)--łtį́: carry AnO through it (as a doorway)(biníkáshííníłtį́: you carried me through it)

Table 3B
D/L-Class Verbs

T = any Verb Theme

| PERSON Sgl | Prefix Position 1b | + | 4 | + | 5 | + | Base | | | as in: |
|---|---|---|---|---|---|---|---|---|---|---|
| 1 | Cá- | + | --- | + | --- | + | -nish-T | > | Cánísh-T | bits'ánísh'na' |
| 2 | Cé- | + | --- | + | --- | + | -(y)íní-T | > | Céíní-T | bits'éíní'na' |
| 3 | Cá- | + | --- | + | --- | + | Ø-T | > | Cá-T | yits'á'na' |
| SP | Cá- | + | --- | + | --- | + | Ø-T | > | Cá-T | bits'áltį |
| 3a. | Cá- | + | --- | + | -j- | + | -í-T | > | Cáji-T | bits'ájí'na' |
| 3i | Cá- | + | --- | + | -'- | + | -í-T | > | Cá'í-T | bits'á'í'na' |
| AP | Cá- | + | O | + | -ho- | + | -ee-T | > | CáO'dee-T | bits'ábi'deeltį |
| Dpl | | | | | | | | | | |
| 1 | Cá- | + | --- | + | --- | + | -nii(d)-T | > | Cánii(d)-T | bits'ánii'na' |
| 2 | Cá- | + | --- | + | --- | + | -noo(h)-T | > | Cánoo(h)-T | bits'ánooh'na' |

P-ts'á-#-(ni)--(d)'na': crawl away from P
P-ts'á-#-(ni)--lwod: run away from P (one subject)(sits'álwod: it ran away from me)
P-ghá#(ni)--)d)'na': crawl through P (as a fence) (yighá'na': he crawled through it)
ná#-(ni)--(d)'na': crawl back; return crawling (nánísh'na': I crawled back; ná'na': it crawled back)
P-níká#-(ni)--(d)'na': crawl through P (as a doorway)
P-ts'á#-(ni)--ltį́: an AnO was separated from P (bits'ábi'deeltį́: he was separated from them)

## Ci-: Position 1b + Extended Base

Cessative-Terminative ni- and inceptive niki- occur in Ni-Perfective Bases.

### Table 4A
### Ø/Ł-Class Verbs

T = any Verb Theme

| PERSON | Prefix Position | | | | | | | | | | Transitive | |
|---|---|---|---|---|---|---|---|---|---|---|---|---|
| Sgl | 1b | + | 4 | + | 5 | + | Base | | | Intransitive | + Ø/4 | + Ci-4 |
| 1 | Ci- | + | Ø/Ci- | + | --- | + | -ní-T | > | Ciní-T | nikinítłizh | niníłtį́ | nininíłtį́ |
| 2 | Ci- | + | Ø/Ci- | + | --- | + | -(y)íní-T | > | Cííní-T | nikíínítłizh | nííníłtį́ | nishííníłtį́ |
| 3 | Ci- | + | Ø/Ci- | + | --- | + | -ní-T | > | Ciní-T | nikinítłizh | --- | nishiníłtį́ |
| 3o. | Ci- | + | --/-i- | + | --- | + | -ní-T | > | Ciiní-T | --- | --- | niiníłtį́ |
| 3a. | Ci- | + | Ø/Ci- | + | -zh- | + | -ní-T | > | Cizhní-T | nikizhnítłizh | nizhníłtį́ | nishizhníłtį́ |
| 3i | Ci- | + | --- | + | -'- | + | -ní-T | > | Ci'ní-T | ni'níkę́ę́z | --- | --- |
| 3s | Ci- | + | --- | + | -ho- | + | -ní-T | > | Cihoní-T | nihoníyá | --- | --- |
| Dpl | | | | | | | | | | | | |
| 1 | Ci- | + | Ø/Ci- | + | --- | + | nii(d)-T | > | Cinii(d)-T | nikiniidee' | niniiltį́ | nininiiltį́ |
| 2 | Ci- | + | Ø/Ci- | + | --- | + | noo-T | > | Cinoo-T | nikinoodee' | ninoołtį́ | nishinoołtį́ |

niki#(ni)--Øtłizh: fall to earth (1 animate subject)(-Ødee': plural subjects)
niki#(ni)--łjid: start home packing O on one's back(nikiníłjid)
ni#-(ni)--łtį́: stop carrying AnO (ni'niníłtį́: I set AnO down; ni'nininíłtį́: I set you down; ni'nishiníłtį́: he set me down etc.)
ni#-'(a)-(ni)--Økę́ę́z: SSO falls and comes to rest (bikáá' ni'níkę́ę́z: a scab formed on it)
ni#-ho-(ni)--Øyá: an event ends (nihoníyá)

### Table 4B
### D/L-Class Verbs

T = any Verb Theme

| PERSON | Prefix Position | | | | | | | | | |
|---|---|---|---|---|---|---|---|---|---|---|
| Sgl | 1b | + | 4 | + | 5 | + | Base | | | as in: |
| 1 | ni- | + | --- | + | --- | + | -nish-T | > | ninish-T | ninishtła |
| 2 | ni- | + | --- | + | --- | + | -(y)íní-T | > | nííní-T | nííníltła |
| 3 | nii- | + | --- | + | --- | + | -Ø-T | > | nii-T | niiltła |
| SP | nii- | + | --- | + | --- | + | Ø-T | > | nii(d)-T | niiltį́ |
| 3a. | ni- | + | --- | + | -j- | + | -í-T | > | nijí-T | nijíltła |
| 3i | ni- | + | --- | + | -'- | + | -í-T | > | ni'í-T | ni'íltła |
| 3s | ni- | + | --- | + | -hoo- | + | Ø-T | > | nihoo-T | nihoolzhiizh |
| AP | ni- | + | O | + | -'(a)d- | + | -ee-T | > | niO'dee(d)-T | nibi'deeltį́ |
| Dpl | | | | | | | | | | |
| 1 | ni- | + | --- | + | --- | + | nii(d)-T | > | ninii(d)-T | niniiltła |
| 2 | ni- | + | --- | + | --- | + | noo-T | > | ninoo-T | ninoołtła |

ni#-(ni)--ltła: stop, halt (shił ni'íltła: I made a stop - a passenger; literally something unspecified stopped in company with me).
ni#-ho-(ni)--lzhiizh: era, period of time ends

## Cí-: Position 1b + Extended Base

### Table 5A
### Ø/Ł-Class Verbs

T = any Verb Theme

| PERSON | Prefix Position | | | | | | Base | | | | Transitive | |
|---|---|---|---|---|---|---|---|---|---|---|---|---|
| Sgl | 1b | + | 4 | + | 5 | + | Base | | | Intransitive | + Ø/4 | + Ci-4 |
| 1 | Cí- | + | Ø/Ci- | + | --- | + | -ní-T | > | Cíní-T | ch'íníná | ch'íníłtį́ | ch'íniníłtį́ |
| 2 | Cí- | + | Ø/Ci- | + | --- | + | -(y)íní-T | > | Cííní-T | ch'ííníná | ch'ííníłtį́ | ch'ishiiníłtį́ |
| 3 | Cí- | + | Ø/Ci- | + | --- | + | -ní-T | > | Cíní-T | ch'íníná | --- | --- |
| 3o. | Cí- | + | --/-i- | + | --- | + | -ní-T | > | Cííní-T | --- | --- | ch'ííníłtį́ |
| 3a. | Cí- | + | Ø/Ci- | + | -zh- | + | -ní-T | > | Cízhní-T | ch'ízhníná | ch'ízhníłtį́ | ch'íshizhníłtį́ |
| 3i | Cí- | + | --- | + | -'- | + | -ní-T | > | Cí'ní-T | ch'í'níná | --- | --- |
| 3s | Cí- | + | --- | + | -ho- | + | -ní-T | > | Cíhoní-T | ch'íhoníyá | --- | --- |
| Dpl | | | | | | | | | | | | |
| 1 | Cí- | + | Ø/Ci- | + | --- | + | nii(d)-T | > | Cínii(d)-T | ch'ínii'ná | ch'íniiltį́ | ch'íniniiltį́ |
| 2 | Cí- | + | Ø/Ci- | + | --- | + | noo-T | > | Cínoo-T | ch'ínooná | ch'ínoołtį́ | ch'íshinoołtį́ |

ch'í#-(ni)--Øná: move out with household (shił ch'í'níná: I moved out as a member of a group - Literally unspecified people moved out in company with me)
ch'í#-ho-(ni)--Øyá: an event commenced (ch'íhoníyá)
P-í#-'(a)-(ni)--Øbą́ą́z: something unspecified (as a wagon) overtakes P. (Shił bí'níbą́ą́z: I caught up with him [in an unspecified wheeled vehicle])
P-í#-(ni)--łbą́ą́z: catch up with P driving it (as a wagon)(yíiníłbą́ą́z: he caught up with him driving it)

### Table 5B
### D/L-Class Verbs

T = any Verb Theme

| PERSON | Prefix Position | | | | | | Base | | | as in: |
|---|---|---|---|---|---|---|---|---|---|---|
| Sgl | 1b | + | 4 | + | 5 | + | Base | | | |
| 1 | Cí- | + | --- | + | --- | + | -nísh-T | > | Cínísh-T | ch'ínísh'na' |
| 2 | Cí- | + | --- | + | --- | + | -(y)íní-T | > | Cííní-T | ch'ííní'na' |
| 3 | Cé- | + | --- | + | --- | + | Ø | > | Cé-T | ch'é'na' |
| SP | Cé- | + | --- | + | --- | + | Ø | > | Cé(d)-T | ch'éltį́ |
| 3a. | Cí- | + | --- | + | -j- | + | -í-T | > | Cíjí-T | ch'íjí'na' |
| 3i | Cí- | + | --- | + | -'- | + | -í-T | > | Cí'í-T | bí'íldloozh |
| 3s | Cí- | + | --- | + | -hoo- | + | Ø | > | Cíhoo-T | ch'íhoolzhiizh |
| AP | Cí- | + | O | + | -'(a)d- | + | -ee- | > | CíO'dee(d)-T | ch'íbi'deeltį́ |
| Dpl | | | | | | | | | | |
| 1 | Cí- | + | --- | + | --- | + | nii(d)-T | > | Cínii(d)-T | ch'íniiltį́ |
| 2 | Cí- | + | --- | + | --- | + | noo(h)-T | > | Cínoo(h)-T | ch'ínoołtį́ |

ch'í#-(ni)--(d)'na': crawl out (horizontally)
P-í#-'(a)-(ni)--ldloozh: something unspecified overtakes P while moving on all four. (Shił bí'íldloozh: I caught up with him while riding a horse; i.e. something overtook him on all four in company with me)
P-í#-(ni)--lwod: overtake P running (bíníshwod: I ran and caught up with him; shélwod: he ran and caught up with me, etc.)
bik'í#-(ni)--lwod: come upon it, find it (bik'íníshwod: I came upon it, found it; yik'élwod: he found it))
ch'í#-(ni)--łtį́: carry an AnO out (ch'íníłtį́: I carried an AnO out; ch'íbi'deeltį́ : AnO was carried out)

## Céé- ~ Cíná-: Position 1b/1d + Extended Base

The Position 1b prefixes P-í-: against, reaching to P, ch'í-: out horizontally, and niki-: start (for home) contract with Reversionary ná-: Position 1d in certain environments to produce P-éé-, ch'éé-, nikéé-, as in béénítkáá': I tracked it down, caught back up with it (by tracking); ch'éénísdzá: I went back outside; nikéénìshzhee': I started back home from hunting.

The contraction appears throughout the paradigm except in those constructions (3rd person and Simple Passive) in which Positions 7 and 8 are vacant (before yi-4 contraction is optional)

ch'éénísdzá (< ch'í- + ná- + -nisdzá): I went back out
ch'éénítłį́ (< ch'í- + ná- + -níłtį́): I carried AnO back out

but ná- reemerges in :

ch'ínádzá: he went back out
ch'ínáltį́: AnO was carried back out
ch'ééyiníłtį́ ~ ch'ínéiníłtį́: he carried AnO back out

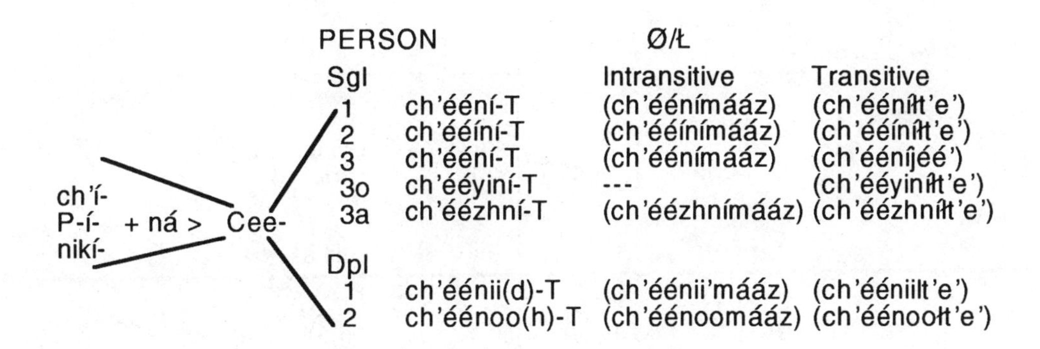

ch'í- / P-í- / nikí- + ná > Cee-

| PERSON | | Ø/Ł Intransitive | Transitive |
|---|---|---|---|
| Sgl | | | |
| 1 | ch'ééní-T | (ch'éénímáázh) | (ch'ééníłt'e') |
| 2 | ch'ééíní-T | (ch'ééínímáázh) | (ch'ééíníłt'e') |
| 3 | ch'ééní-T | (ch'éénímáázh) | (ch'ééníjéé') |
| 3o | ch'ééyiní-T | --- | (ch'ééyiníłt'e') |
| 3a | ch'éézhní-T | (ch'éézhnímáázh) | (ch'éézhníłt'e') |
| Dpl | | | |
| 1 | ch'éénii(d)-T | (ch'éénii'máázh) | (ch'ééniilt'e') |
| 2 | ch'éénoo(h)-T | (ch'éénoomáázh) | (ch'éénooht'e') |

ch'í- / P-í- / nikí- + ná > Cee-

| PERSON | | D/L Intransitive | Transitive |
|---|---|---|---|
| Sgl | | | |
| 1 | ch'éénísh-T | (ch'éénísh'na') | (ch'éénísh'nil) |
| 2 | ch'ééíní-T | (ch'ééíní'na') | (ch'ééíní'nil) |
| 3 | ch'íná-T | (ch'íná'na') | --- |
| SP | ch'íná(d)-T | (ch'ínált'e') | (ch'íná'nil) |
| 3o | --- | --- | (ch'ééyi'nil) |
| 3a | ch'ééjí-T | (ch'ééjíłt'e') | (ch'ééjí'nil) |
| AP | ch'ééO'dee(d)-T | --- | (ch'éébi'dee'nil) |
| Dpl | | | |
| 1 | ch'éénii(d)-T | (ch'éénii'na') | (ch'éénii'nil) |
| 2 | ch'éénoo(h)-T | (ch'éénooh'na') | (ch'éénooh'nil) |

ch'ééníłt'e': I set it free; released it/him
ch'éénísh'na': I crawled back out
nikééníshzhee': I started back home (or to camp) while hunting
ch'éénísdzid: I awakened, woke back up
ch'éénímáázh: I/he rolled back out
béénítkáá': I caught back up with him (by tracking)

béénínshwod: I caught back up with him running

## *NI-PERFECTIVE NEUTER VERBS*

Simple Ni-Perfective Neuters (i.e. those Verb Bases that lack a derivational prefix) occur as intransitive constructions serving to describe a subject or subjects as *extending* into space (a mountain range or ranges, a line of trees or houses, a row of people), as:

dził ní'á: the mountain (range) lies extending
dził daní'á: the 3+ mountain ranges lie extending
tooh nílį́: the river extends flowing; the river flows along (in a line)
t'áá 'ałkéé' niidzį́: we stand in a line (row or series) one behind the other

The conjugational pattern is similar to that of the simple Active Ni-Perfective:

### Base Paradigm

| PERSON | | | |
|---|---|---|---|
| Sgl | Ø/Ł | D/L | |
| 1. --- | --- | --- | --- |
| 2. --- | --- | --- | --- |
| 3. ní-T | (nít'i') | yí-T | (yíl'á) |
| 3s. honí-T | (honít'i') | hoo-T | (hool'á) |
| Dpl | | | |
| 1. nii(d)-T | (niit'i') | nii(d)-T | (niil'á) |
| 2. noo-T | (noot'i') | noo(h)-T | (nooł'á) |
| 3. ní-T | (nít'i') | yí-T | (yíl'á) |
| 3a. jiní-T | (jinít'i') | jí-T | (jíl'á) |

(ni)--Øt'i'): extend in a slender line or row (as a telephone line)(nít'i')
(ni)--Øzį́: stand extending in a line or row (t'áá 'ałkéé' niidzį́: we're in a line)
(ni)--l'á: extend in a line (yíl'á)
(ni)--lk'id: subject extends "humping" in a line (yílk'id: hill extends in a line)

### 1. Conjunct Derivatives

An unidentified di-prefix of Position 6a contracts with ni-: Position 7 to produce dé- in a group of 3rd person Ni-Perfective Neuter verbs based on the "handle" and certain other stems. These describe an object of a specified class as being in a dangling/hanging position. Thus:

dé'ą́: SRO sits dangling or hanging
ch'ah ntł'izí bik'i dé'ą́: he has on a hard hat
t'ááłá'í béeso sitsiist'ah dé'ą́: I have one dollar on my person (lit. I have one dollar hanging from my belt)

déłtsooz: FFO sits or lies dangling or hanging
shi'éétsoh shik'i déłtsoozgo sédá: I'm sitting with my overcoat draped over my shoulders
t'ááłá'í béeso t'éiya sitsiist'ah déłtsooz: I only have one dollar bill on me

dézhóód: huge object sits (hanging)
Naakai bich'ah shik'i dézhóódgo 'ashi'doolkid: I had my picture taken with a huge Mexican hat on

The prefix cluster hi-di- + (y)i-Transitional: Position 6a/c appears in active constructions that describe the act of hanging or suspending an object, as in:

dah hidiilo' (< hi-di-i-Ølo'): I hung it up by a cord or loop; I weighed it
dah 'ádiidlo' (< 'ád-i-i-[d]lo'): he hung / weighed himself

The Active Transitional is complemented by a Ni-Perfective Neuter derived with hi-di-, but conjugated in a pattern that more closely resembles Ni-Imperfective than Ni-Perfective.

Di-ni- contracts to produce -dé- in 3rd person constructions, where Position 8 is vacant.

| PERSON | | |
|---|---|---|
| Sgl | | |
| 1. | hidíníſh-T | (dah hidíníshtį) |
| 2. | hidíní-T | (dah hidínítį) |
| 3. | hidé-T | (dah hidétį) |
| 3a. | hizhdé-T | (dah hizhdétį) |
| Dpl | | |
| 1. | hidíníî(d)-T | (dah hidíníîtéézh) |
| 2. | hidínóo-T | (dah hidínóotéézh) |

dah hi-di-(ni)--Øtį́: AnO hangs dangling (as from a rope)
dah hi-di-(ni)--Ø'ą́: SRO hangs (as a hat - dah hidé'ą́)
dah hi-di-(ni)--(d)lo': weigh (neeznáá dah hidédlo': it weighs 10 pounds; dah hidíníshdlo': I weigh ---)

The Disjunct Prefixes ch'í-: "out horizontally" and bina-: "draped over it" + Ni-Perfective Neuter dé-T derive constructions of the type ch'íhidélá: it dangles out (as a string from one's pocket); binahidélá: it hangs over it (as a belt over the back of a chair).

(Cf. Yi-Perfective Neuter -hí-í- required in constructions derived with the Disjunct Prefixes 'a-: "away out of sight," ha-: "up out," and na-: " downward," as in 'ahíílá: "it arches [as a rainbow]," hahíílá: "it hangs or dangles up out," and nahíílá: "it hangs down [as a rope from a limb"].)

Hi-yi³-6a/6c occurs, in combination with an unidentified yi-prefix of Position 6, to produce a group of Verb Bases that carry the meanings "dangle, lean, extend from a point (as from a hole, limb, pocket)."

Hi- appears in the form of its yi³-allomorph when preceded by a Conjunct Prefix (as ji-5).

| PERSON | | |
|---|---|---|
| Sgl | | as in: |
| 1 | hííńísh-T | biih hííníshtį́ |
| 2 | hííní-T | biih hííníłtį́ |
| 3 | híí-T | yiih híítłį́ |
| 3a | jiyíí-T | biih jiyííłtį́ |
| Dpl | | |
| 1 | hííníí(d)-T | biih hííníiltéézh |
| 2 | hííńóo-T | biih hííńóołtéézh |

biih hi-(y)í-ni-(yi)--łtį́: be extending partly into it/partly out (taah hííníshtį́: I'm lying partly in/partly out of the water)

Similarly:

híí'ą́: (SRO, as a land area lies dangling [a continent or peninsula on a map])
biih hííłtsooz: FFO lies dangling (as partly out of a pocket)
biih híínil: PIO dangle into it/from it
biih híílá: SFO (as a string) dangles into/from it

Several Verb Bases are derived with Disjunct Prefixes and conjugated in the pattern summarized in the model paradigm above, including:

yah 'ahííníshtį́ (< yah: enclosure + 'a-: Position 1b: away out of sight + -hííníshtį́): lie partly in/partly out of an enclosure
hahííníshtį́ (< ha-: Position 1b: up out + -hííníshtį́): lie protruding up out
nahííníshtį́ (< na-: downward: Position 1b + -hííníshtį́): dangle downward
ch'íhííníshtį́ (< ch'í-: Position 1b: out horizontally + -hííníshtį́): lie extending out (as out a window).

## 2. Disjunct Derivatives

The Ni-Perfective Neuter, unlike its Active correspondent, does not always switch to Si-Perfective in the distributive plural – it usually remains ni-Perfective, as:

| PERSON | | | | |
|---|---|---|---|---|
| Sgl | Ø/Ł | | D/L | |
| 1. | danii(d)-T | (daniit'i') | danii(d)-T | (daniil'á) |
| 2. | danoo-T | danoot'i') | danoo(h)-T | (danooł'á) |
| 3. | daní-T | (daníť'i') | deí-T | (deíl'á) |
| 3a. | dazhní-T | (dazhníť'i') | dají-T | (dajíl'á) |

da#-(ni)--Øt'i': extend in a line (as a wire or rope)
da#-(ni)--l'á: extend in a line (as a line of trees or houses)
**but**
da#-(si)--lk'id: 3+ hills or ridges extend (sgl: yílk'id / dist. pl: daask'id)

<u>Prefixes of Position 1b + Extended Base</u>

Ni-Perfective Neuter Verb Bases derived with prefixes of Position 1b occur both intransitive and transitive. Again, the conjugational pattern is identical to that of Active Ni-Perfectives of similar composition, and like these the Ni-Perfective Neuters switch to Si-Perfective in 3rd persons of the distributive plural. Thus:

| PERSON | +ch'í-:1b | | + ni-:1b | |
|---|---|---|---|---|
| Sgl | Ø/Ł | D/L | Ø/Ł | D/L |
| 1. | ch'íníł'á | --- | niníł'á | --- |
| 2. | ch'ííníł'á | --- | nííníł'á | --- |
| 3. | chíní'á | ch'élk'id | niní'á | niilk'id |
| SP | --- | ch'él'á | --- | niil'á |
| 3o. | ch'íiníł'á | --- | niiníł'á | --- |
| 3a. | ch'ízhníł'á | --- | nizhníł'á | --- |
| Dpl | | | | |
| 1. | ch'íniil'á | --- | niniil'á | --- |
| 2. | ch'ínooł'á | --- | ninooł'á | --- |
| Dist. Pl | | | | |
| 1. | ch'ídaniil'á | --- | ndaniil'á | --- |
| 2. | ch'ídanooł'á | --- | ndanooł'á | --- |
| 3. | ch'ídaaz'á | ch'ídaask'id | ndaaz'á | ndaask'id |
| 3o. | ch'ídeis'á | --- | ndeis'á | --- |
| 3a. | ch'ídajis'á | --- | ndajis'á | --- |

ch'í#-(ni)--ł'á: hold O extending out (as a pole out a window)
ch'í#-(ni)--Ø'á: extend out (as a pole out a window)
ni#-(ni)--ł'á: hold O so that it extends as far as a stopping point
ch'í#-(ni)--lk'id: hill or ridge extends out (ch'élk'id: hill or ridge extends out)
ni#-(ni)--lk'id: hill or ridge extends as far as a stopping point (ndaask'id: dist. pl. hills extend as far as a stopping point)
'ahéé#-(ni) -- Øzį: stand in a circle ('ahééniidzį: we're standing in a circle)

## RECAPITULATION

### 1. Extended Base Paradigm

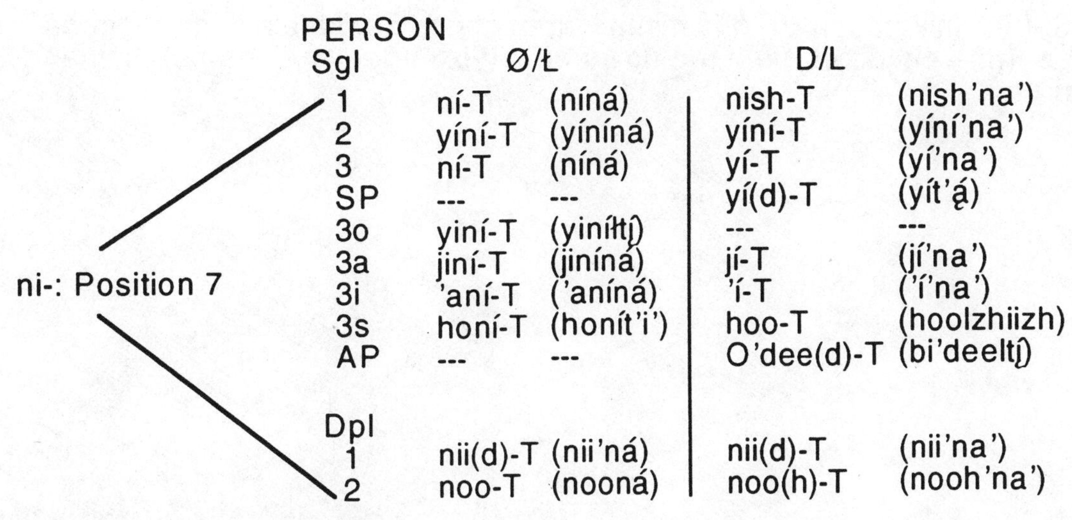

| PERSON | Ø/Ł | | D/L | |
|---|---|---|---|---|
| Sgl | | | | |
| 1 | ní-T | (níná) | nish-T | (nish'na') |
| 2 | yíní-T | (yíníná) | yíní-T | (yíní'na') |
| 3 | ní-T | (níná) | yí-T | (yí'na') |
| SP | --- | --- | yí(d)-T | (yít'ą́) |
| 3o | yiní-T | (yiníłtį́) | --- | --- |
| 3a | jiní-T | (jiníná) | jí-T | (jí'na') |
| 3i | 'aní-T | ('aníná) | 'í-T | ('í'na') |
| 3s | honí-T | (honít'i') | hoo-T | (hoolzhiizh) |
| AP | --- | --- | O'dee(d)-T | (bi'deeltį́) |
| Dpl | | | | |
| 1 | nii(d)-T | (nii'ná) | nii(d)-T | (nii'na') |
| 2 | noo-T | (nooná) | noo(h)-T | (nooh'na') |



(ni)--Øná: arrive moving with household
ho-(ni)--Øt'i': area extends

(ni)--(d)'na': arrive crawling
(ni)--(d)t'ą́: be brought
baa ho-(ni)--lzhiizh: become his turn (i.e. time moved to him)
shaa bi'deeltį́: he was given to me
baa (ni)--łtį́: bring/give AnO to him

## *CONJUNCT PREFIXES*

### 2. Ci-Prefixes of Positions 6, 4 + Extended Base

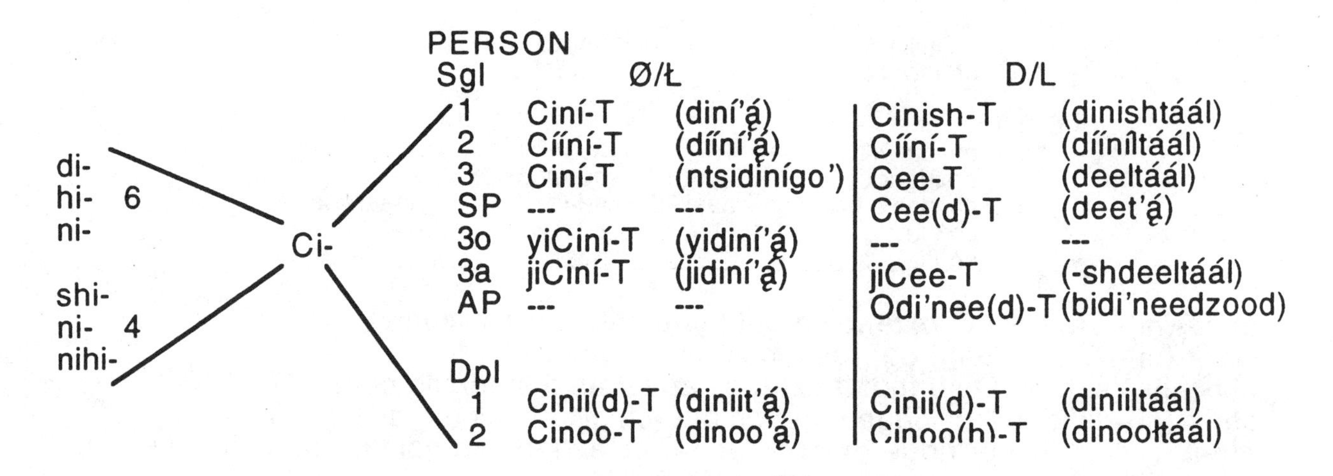


baa di-(ni)--Ø'ą́: relinquish O to him (baa diní'ą́: I relinquished it to him [as land]; baa deet'ą́: it was relinquished to him)
di-(ni)--ltáál: trip with one's foot (bijáátah dinishtáál: I tripped him with my foot)
di-(ni)--(d)dzood: drive them to him (baa bidi'needzood: they were driven to him)
hi-(ni)--lghal; crawl or wriggle on the belly (baa hinishghal: I crawled to him on my belly)
(ni)--Ølóóz: lead (baa shííníłóóz: you led me to him; shaa niníłóóz: he led you to me)
Pi-1a#-di-(ni)--lnii': touch Pi- (bidinishnii': I touched it; shideelnii': he touched me)
bik'i ni#-di-(ni)--lchid: put the hand down on it (yik'i ndeelchid; he put his hand down on it)

### 3. 'A-/ho-: Position 4 + Extended Base Ø/Ł-Class Verbs only

| PERSON | Ø/Ł | | Ø/Ł | |
|---|---|---|---|---|
| Sgl | | | | |
| 1 | 'aní-T | ('aníłbą́ą́z) | honí-T | (honíziid) |
| 2 | 'íiní-T | ('íiníłbą́ą́z) | hwíiní-T | (hwíiníziid) |
| 3 | 'aní-T | ('aníłbą́ą́z) | honí-T | (honíziid) |
| 3a | 'azhní-T | ('azhníłbą́ą́z) | hozhní-T | (hozhníziid) |
| Dpl | | | | |
| 1 | 'anii(d)-T | ('aniilbą́ą́z) | honii(d)-T | (honiidziid) |
| 2 | 'anoo-T | ('anoołbą́ą́z) | honoo-T | (honooziid) |

('a- / ho-)

'a-(ni)---łbą́ą́z: arrive driving ('aníłbą́ą́z: I arrived driving [an unspecified wheeled vehicle])
ho-(ni)--Øziid: arrive groping one's way (honíziid: I/he came groping my/his way)

## *DISJUNCT PREFIXES*

### 4. Ca-: Positions 3/1b

| PERSON | | Ø/Ł Intransitive | Ø/Ł Transitive | D/L | D/L Transitive |
|---|---|---|---|---|---|
| Sgl | | | | | |
| 1. | Caní-T | --- | --- | Canish-T | (bighanisht'ą́) |
| 2. | Caíní-T | --- | --- | Caíní-T | (bighaíníł't'ą́) |
| 3. | Caní-T | --- | --- | --- | --- |
| SP. | --- | --- | --- | Caa-T | (bighaat'ą́) |
| 3o. | Caíní-T | --- | --- | Caí-T | (yighaít'ą́) |
| 3a. | Cazhní-T | | | Cají-T | (bighajít'ą́) |
| Dpl | | | | | |
| 1. | Canii(d)-T | --- | --- | Canii(d)-T | (bighaniit'ą́) |
| 2. | Canoo-T | --- | --- | Canoo(h)-T | (bighanooht'ą́) |
| Dist Pl | | | | | |
| 1. | Canii(d)-T | (danii'ná) | (daniit'ą́) | Canii(d)-T | (bighadaniit'ą́) |
| 2. | Canoo-T | (danooná) | (danoo'ą́) | Canoo(h)-T | (bighadanooht'ą́) |
| 3. | Caní-T | (daní'á)* | --- | --- | --- |
| | Caaz-/s-T | (daazná) | --- | --- | --- |
| 3o. | Ceiní-T | --- | (deiní'ą́) | --- | --- |
| | Ceiz-T | --- | (deiz'ą́) | Ceis-T | (yighadeist'ą́) |
| 3a. | Cazhní-T | --- | (dazhní'ą́) | --- | --- |
| | Cajiz-/s-T | (dajizná) | (dajiz'ą́) | Cajis-T | (bighadajist'ą́) |

(da- / P-gha- — Ca-)

*Neuter Perfective only

da#-(ni)--Øná: arrive moving with household
*da#-(ni)--Ø'á: they 3+ extend (as mountain ranges, hills)
da#-(ni)--Ø'ą́: bring, arrive carrying a SRO
bigha#-(ni)--(d)t'ą́: take a SRO away from him

## 5. Cá-: Position 1 + Extended Base

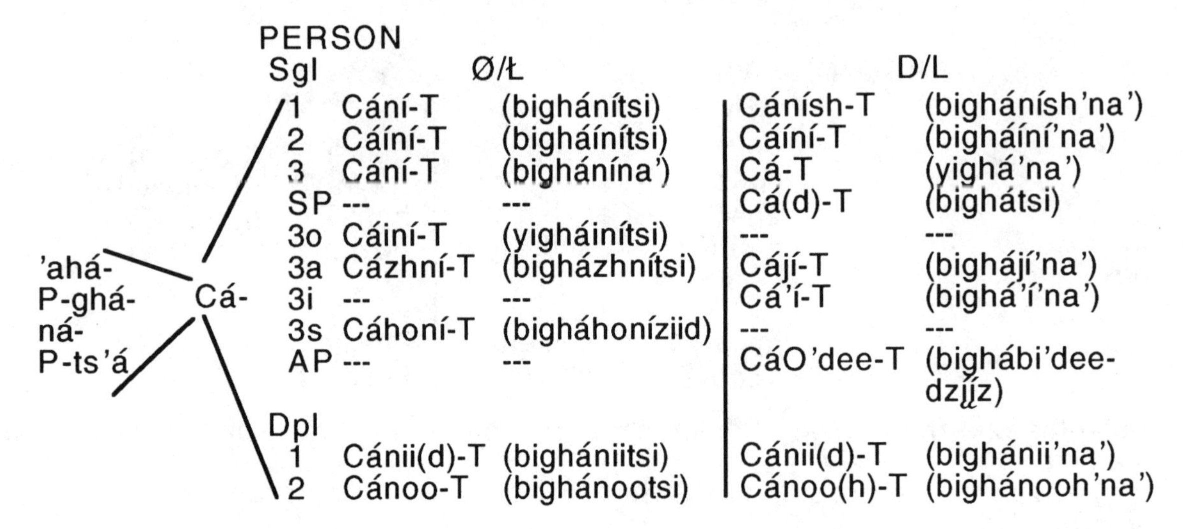

'ahá-, P-ghá-, ná-, P-ts'á → Cá-

| PERSON | Ø/Ł | | D/L | |
|---|---|---|---|---|
| Sgl | | | | |
| 1 | Cání-T | (bighánítsi) | Cánísh-T | (bighánísh'na') |
| 2 | Cáíní-T | (bigháínítsi) | Cáíní-T | (bigháíní'na') |
| 3 | Cání-T | (bighánína') | Cá-T | (yighá'na') |
| SP | --- | --- | Cá(d)-T | (bighátsi) |
| 3o | Cáiní-T | (yigháinítsi) | --- | --- |
| 3a | Cázhní-T | (bigházhnítsi) | Cájí-T | (bighájí'na') |
| 3i | --- | --- | Cá'í-T | (bighá'í'na') |
| 3s | Cáhoní-T | (bigháhoníziid) | --- | --- |
| AP | --- | --- | CáO'dee-T | (bighábi'dee-dzį́į́z) |
| Dpl | | | | |
| 1 | Cánii(d)-T | (bighániitsi) | Cánii(d)-T | (bighánii'na') |
| 2 | Cánoo-T | (bighánootsi) | Cánoo(h)-T | (bighánooh'na') |

bighá#-(ni)--Øtsi: stick it through it (bighánítsi: I stuck it through it ([as a stick through paper])
bighá#-(ni)--Øna': soak through it (bighánína': it leaked [soaked, flowed] through it)
(bighábi'deedzį́į́z: he was pulled through it - as through a fence)
bighá#-ho-(ni)--Øziid: it physicked him (bigháhoníziid)
'ahá#-(ni)--Øgizh: cut it in two ('ahánígizh: I cut it in two)
ná#-(ni)--(d)'na': crawl back (shaa ná'na': it crawled back to me)
bits'á#-(ni)--(d)'na': crawl away from it (bits'ánísh'na')
'ałts'á#-(ni)--Øgiz: twist O apart ('ałts'ánígiz)

## 6. Ci-: Position 1 + Extended Base

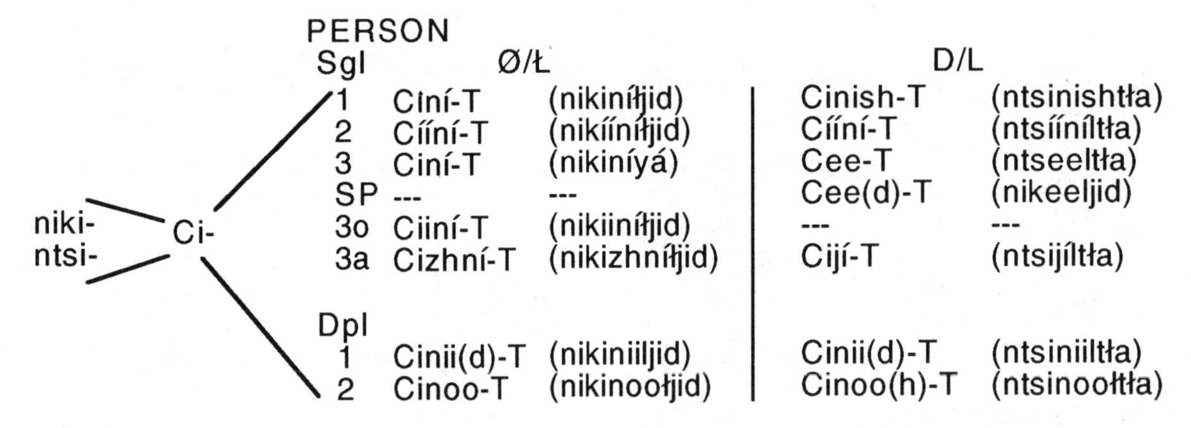

niki-, ntsi- → Ci-

| PERSON | Ø/Ł | | D/L | |
|---|---|---|---|---|
| Sgl | | | | |
| 1 | Ciní-T | (nikiníłjid) | Cinish-T | (ntsinishtła) |
| 2 | Cííní-T | (nikííníłjid) | Cííní-T | (ntsííníltła) |
| 3 | Ciní-T | (nikiníyá) | Cee-T | (ntseeltła) |
| SP | --- | --- | Cee(d)-T | (nikeeljid) |
| 3o | Ciiní-T | (nikiiníłjid) | --- | --- |
| 3a | Cizhní-T | (nikizhníłjid) | Cijí-T | (ntsijíltła) |
| Dpl | | | | |
| 1 | Cinii(d)-T | (nikiniiljid) | Cinii(d)-T | (ntsiniiltła) |
| 2 | Cinoo-T | (nikinoołjid) | Cinoo(h)-T | (ntsinoołtła) |

niki#-(ni)--Øyá: start for home (one subject)(nikiníyá: I started for home)
niki#-(ni)--łjid: start for home packing O on one's back (nikiníłjid: I started for home with it on my back)
ntsi#-(ni)--ltła: get nervous, apprehensive (ntsinishtła: I got nervous/ apprehensive)

### 7. Cí-: Position 1b + Extended Base

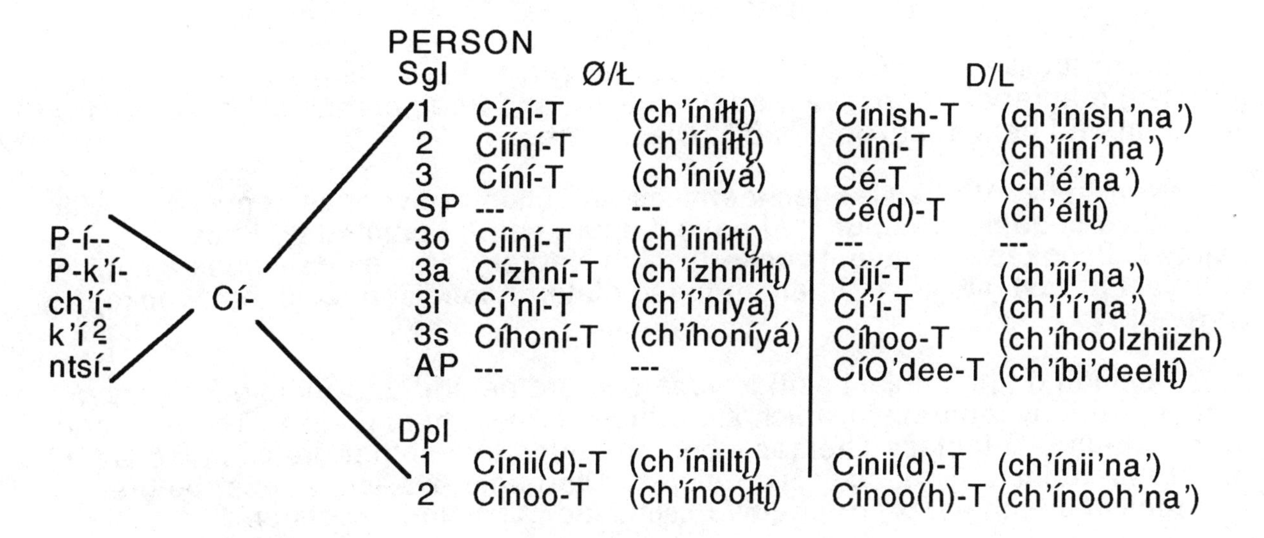

P-í--, P-k'í-, ch'í-, k'í[2], ntsí- → Cí-

| PERSON | Ø/Ł | | D/L | |
|---|---|---|---|---|
| **Sgl** | | | | |
| 1 | Cíní-T | (ch'íníłtį́) | Cínish-T | (ch'ínísh'na') |
| 2 | Cííní-T | (ch'ííníłtį́) | Cííní-T | (ch'ííní'na') |
| 3 | Cíní-T | (ch'íníyá) | Cé-T | (ch'é'na') |
| SP | --- | --- | Cé(d)-T | (ch'éltį́) |
| 3o | Cíiní-T | (ch'íiníłtį́) | --- | --- |
| 3a | Cízhní-T | (ch'ízhníłtį́) | Cíjí-T | (ch'íjí'na') |
| 3i | Cí'ní-T | (ch'í'níyá) | Cí'í-T | (ch'í'í'na') |
| 3s | Cíhoní-T | (ch'íhoníyá) | Cíhoo-T | (ch'íhoolzhiizh) |
| AP | --- | --- | CíO'dee-T | (ch'íbi'deeltį́) |
| **Dpl** | | | | |
| 1 | Cínii(d)-T | (ch'íniiltį́) | Cínii(d)-T | (ch'ínii'na') |
| 2 | Cínoo-T | (ch'ínoołtį́) | Cínoo(h)-T | (ch'ínooh'na') |

ch'í#-(ni)--łtį́: carry AnO out horizontally (ch'íníłtį́: I carried AnO out [as out the door])(ch'íbi'deeltį́: he was carried out)
ch'í#-(ni)--Øyá: go out (1 subject) (ch'íníyá: I went out)
ch'í#-ho-(ni)--Øyá: event starts (ch'íhoníyá: an event started [as a ceremony])
ch'í#-(ni)--(d)'na': crawl out (ch'ínísh'na': I crawled out; shił ch'í'í'na': I rode out [on an unspecified crawling vehicle - as a tractor])
ch'í#-ho-(ni)--lzhiizh: time period starts (ch'íhoolzhiizh: era or time period began)
P-í#-(ni)--sá (< łzá): catch up with P walking (bínísá: I caught up with him, overtook him [walking])
P-í#-(ni)--łbą́ą́z: overtake P while driving it (bíníłbą́ą́z: I caught up with him while driving it [a wheeled vehicle = wagon, car])
k'í#-(ni)--Øgizh: cut O off/in two (k'ínígizh: I cut it off or in two)
ntsí-#-(ni)--Økéez: reach a decision on it (bee hasht'e' ntsíníkéez: I reached a decision on it)

## 3. SI-PERFECTIVE

Si-Perfective is marked by si-modal-aspectival in Position 7 and by the high tone (-í-) marker of Perfective Mode in the 1st and 2nd persons sgl of Ø/Ł-Class verbs; in 2nd person sgl only of D/L-Class verbs.

With Active Verbs si- often identifies an action or event as conclusive, with a durative sequel (I've spun it / I have it spun [yarn]; I painted it / I have it painted; I cooked it /I have it cooked). With Neuter Verbs si- describes a subject or object at rest (sit, lie) or in an enduring state or condition (cold, hot, cooked, warped).

Position 8 (the subject slot) is vacant in 3rd person and Simple Passives, creating an environment in which si- reduces to -z-/-zh- in Ø-class Themes, and to -s-/-sh- in Ł-D-L-class Themes when preceded by another prefix. In the latter environment the Ł-/D-/L-classifier deletes. Alternants -zh-/-sh- appear before stem-initial ch-/ch'-/j-/zh- or sh-, by assimilation, or stem-final -zh/-sh

The only phonological clue to the presence of D-classifier in si-Perfective is often the devoiced form of the si-prefix, as in Active: yizdiz / Passive yisdiz (= yis(d)diz)(she spun it/it was spun).

An exception is the deletion of si- before a Øy- (Ø-classifier + a stem-initial y-) Theme, or substitution of -h- as an allomorph of si- before ly-.

Theme: Ødiz / (d)diz
yizdiz: she spun it (yarn) / yisdiz: it was spun
Theme: Øbizh / (d)bizh
yizhbizh: she braided it / yishbizh: it was braided
Theme: łįįzh / lįįzh
yishįįzh (< yish-łįįzh): he squeezed it / yishįįzh (< yish-lįįzh): it was squeezed
Theme: Øyá
naa(z)yá > naayá: he made a round trip
Theme: lya'
bíhoos(l)ya' > bíhoohya': he was missed (found to be absent)
Theme: lya'
binahoos(l)ya' > binahoohya': he was attacked with weapons

### *ACTIVE VERBS*

Si-Perfectives based on Ø/Ł-class Themes are almost exclusively Active Verbs, while those based on D/L-class Themes are predominantly Passive, Mediopassive, Reflexive or Reciprocal constructions. Active si-Perfectives are predominantly transitive. Consequently, there are few Active si-Perfective intransitive Base Paradigms comparable to the simple yi-/ni-Perfectives of the type níyá: I/he came, yícha: I/he wept. Si-Perfective sélį́į́'/silį́į́': I/he became, is an exception that converges in shape with the Neuter Base forms.

Active Transitive D/L-class si-Perfectives are largely confined to Verb Bases in which a Reversionary or Semeliterative prefix requires a shift from Ø- to D-classifier, or from Ł- to L-, or to Reflexive, Mediopassive, or Reciprocal constructions.

In the absence of a preceding prefix, 3rd person and Simple Passive D-L-class si-Perfectives require a "dummy" yi-prefix (Kari: 1976), as in yishjool: (yi-s-(l)jool): he sits huddled; yisdiz (yi-s-(d)diz): it was twisted, spun (yarn).

## Base Paradigms

### Table 1A
### Ø/Ł-Class Verbs

T = any Verb Theme

| PERSON | Prefix Position | | | | | | |
|---|---|---|---|---|---|---|---|
| Sgl | 7 | + | 8 | > | Base | Active | Neuter |
| 1. | sé- | + | Ø | > | sé-T (sí-T) * | sélį́į́' (sílį́į́') * | sézį́ (sízį́) * |
| 2. | sí- | + | -ní- | > | síní-T | sínílį́į́' | sínízį́ |
| 3. | si- | + | Ø | > | si-T | silį́į́' | sizį́ |
| Dpl | | | | | | | |
| 1. | s- | + | -ii(d) | > | sii(d)-T | siidlį́į́' | siidzį́ |
| 2. | s- | + | -oo- | > | soo-T | soolį́į́' | soozį́ |

* Some speakers retain sí- in 1st person sgl

(si)--Øzį́: be in a standing position (A Neuter Verb)

(si)--Ølį́į́: become

### Table 1B
### D/L-Class Verbs

T = any Verb Theme

| PERSON | Prefix Position | | | | | | |
|---|---|---|---|---|---|---|---|
| Sgl | 7 | + | 8 | | | Neuter | |
| 1. | si- | + | -s- | > | sis-T | sistin | shishjool |
| 2. | sí- | + | -ní- | > | síní-T | sínítin | shíníljool |
| 3. | yis- | + | Ø | > | yis-T | yistin | yishjool |
| SP | yis- | + | Ø | > | yis(d)-T | yistin | yishdléézh |
| Dpl | | | | | | | |
| 1. | s- | + | -ii(d) | > | sii(d)-T | siitin | shiiljool |
| 2. | s- | + | -oo- | > | soo(h)-T | soohtin | shoołjool |

(si)--(d)tin: be frozen (yistin)
(si)--ljool: cower; huddle (yishjool)
(si)--(d)dléézh: be painted (yishdléézh) (Simple Passive)

## Extended Base Paradigms

## 1. Conjunct Prefixes

### Position 5 Prefixes + Base

Table 2

T = any Verb theme

| PERSON Sgl/Dpl | 5 | + | Ø/Ł-Class Base | | 5 | + | D/L-Class Base | |
|---|---|---|---|---|---|---|---|---|
| 3a. | ji- | + | -z- > jiz-T | jizlíí' | ji- | + | -s-T > jis(h)-T | jishjool |
| 3i. | 'a- | + | -z- > 'az-T | 'azlíí' | 'a- | + | -s-T > 'as-T | 'asdá |
| 3s. | ha- | + | -z- > haz-T | hazlíí' | ha- | + | -s-T > has-T | haszee' |
| AP | --- | | --- --- | --- | -(a)di(d)- | + | -s-T > bi'dis(h)-T | bi'dishdléézh |

(si)--Ølíí': become (jizlíí': he/she became)
'a-(si)--Ølíí': unspecified "it" became ('áłah 'azlíí': there was a meeting - a coming together; Késhmish 'azlíí': it became Christmas; díkwíishą' 'azlíí': what time it it? - how many has it become?)
'a-(si)--Ødá: sit ('asdá: someone sits)
ha-(si)--Ølíí': impersonal "it," "things became ('awéé' hazlíí': a baby was born - came into existence; 'anaa' hazlíí': war broke out; biyaa hazlíí': he grew up - i.e. there came to be space under him)
ha-(si)--lzee': "it" became quiet, peaceful
(si)--(d)dléézh: be smeared, painted (bi'dishdléézh: he was daubed, smeared, painted)

### Prefixes of Positions 4 + 5 + Base

Table 3A
Ø/Ł Class Verbs

The intransitive paradigm is included to facilitate ready comparison.

T = any Verb Theme

| PERSON | Prefix Position 4 | + | 5 | + | Base | Intransitive | Transitive + Ø-4 | Transitive + Ci-4 |
|---|---|---|---|---|---|---|---|---|
| Sgl | | | | | | | | |
| 1. | Ø/Ci- | + | --- | + | sé-T | sélíí' | sétał | nisétał |
| 2. | Ø/Ci- | + | --- | + | síní-T | sínílíí' | sínítał | shisínítał |
| 3. | --/Ci- | + | --- | + | si/-z-/-s-T | silíí' | --- | shiztał |
| 3o. | yi- | + | --- | + | -z-/-s-T | --- | --- | yiztał |
| 3a. | Ø/Ci- | + | ji- | + | -z-/-s--T | jizlíí' | jiztał | shijiztał |
| Dpl | | | | | | | | |
| 1. | Ø/Ci- | + | --- | + | sii(d)-T | siidlíí' | siitał | nisiitał |
| 2. | Ø/Ci- | + | --- | + | soo-T | soolíí' | sootał | shisootał |

(si)--Ølíí': become
(si)--Øtał: give O a kick (nisétał: I gave you a kick; shisínítał: you gave me a kick; shiztał: he gave me a kick, etc.)

(si)--Øhash: give O a bite (shishhash: it bit me; nishhash: it bit you; nishéłhash: I bit you, etc.)
(si)--Øts'ǫs: give O a kiss (sizts'ǫs: she gave me a kiss; nisétsʼǫs: I gave you a kiss, etc.)

Table 3B
D/L-Class Verbs

T = any Verb Theme

| PERSON | Prefix Position | | | | | |
|---|---|---|---|---|---|---|
| Sgl | 4 | + | 5 | + | Base | as in: |
| 1. | --- | + | --- | + | sis-T | sistin |
| 2. | --- | + | --- | + | síní-T | sínítin |
| 3. | --- | + | --- | + | yis-T | yistin |
| SP | --- | + | --- | + | yis(d)-T | yistin |
| 3a. | --- | + | ji- | + | jis-T | jistin |
| 3i. | --- | + | 'a- | + | -s-T | 'astin |
| 3s. | --- | + | ha- | + | -s-T | hastin |
| AP | O | + | -'(a)di- | + | -s(d)-T | bi'distin |
| Dpl | | | | | | |
| 1. | --- | + | --- | + | sii(d)-T | siitin |
| 2. | --- | + | --- | + | soo(h)-T | soohtin |

(si)--(d)tin: freeze (hastin: area is frozen)(bi'distin: he was frozen)
(si)--(d)dá: sit (one subject) ('asdá: unspecified person sits, as in 'awáalya 'asdá: jail term = literally: person sits in jail)
(si)--łtin: freeze O (yistin: it was frozen)

## 'A- ~ -'-: Position 4 + Extended Base

### Table 4

The 3i direct object pronoun of Position 4 poses no problem in the paradigms of the Si-Perfective, where it retains its base shape in all constructions except those in which it is preceded by another prefix - da-: distributive plural, for example where 'a- reduces to -'-.

| PERSON | Ø/Ł-Class Verbs | | D/L-Class Verbs | |
|---|---|---|---|---|
| Sgl | | | | |
| 1 | 'asé-T | 'asédiz | 'asis-T | 'asist'įįd |
| 2 | 'asíní-T | 'asínídiz | 'asíní-T | 'asínít'įįd |
| 3 | 'az-/s-T | 'azdiz | 'as-T | 'ast'įįd |
| 3a | 'ajiz-/s-T | 'ajizdiz | 'ajis-T | 'ajist'įįd |
| Dpl | | | | |
| 1 | 'asii(d)-T | 'asiidiz | 'asii(d)-T | 'asiit''iįd |
| 2 | 'asoo-T | 'asoodiz | 'asoo(h)-T | 'asooht'įįd |
| Dist. Pl. | | | | |
| 1 | da'sii(d)-T | da'siidiz | da'sii(d)-T | da'siit'įįd |
| 2 | da'soo-T | da'soodiz | da'soo(h)-T | da'sooht'įįd |
| 3 | da'az-/s-T | da'azdiz | da'as-T | da'ast'įįd |
| 3a | da'jiz-/s-T | da'jizdiz | da'jis-T | da'jist'įįd |

'a-(si)--Ødiz: spin O (yarn)
'a-(si)--(d)t'įįd: become wealthy (in something unspecified. Cf. sét'įįd ~ sist'įįd = become rich in it - as in livestock)
na#-'(a)-(si)--(d)dlą': go bar-hopping; drink around here and there (ni'sisdlą': I went bar-hopping)

## The Prefixes of Position 6 + Extended Base

With Yi-, Ni- and Yi-Ø Perfective the prefixes of Position 4 as well as 6 are simply joined to the Base when in determinant position. However, when the same prefixes are combined with the Si-Perfective Base their behavior is divergent:

The Position 4 prefixes with the exception of -di-: reflexive component, follow the same pattern of juncture with Si-Perfective as they do with Yi-, Ni- and Yi-Ø - i.e. they simply join with the Base, and, in 3rd person, si- reduces to -z-/-zh- before Ø-classifier, -s-/-sh- before D, L or Ł-classifier. (<u>ni</u>sétal / <u>si</u>ztał: I kicked <u>you</u> / he kicked <u>me</u>.)

But the Position 6 pattern is distinctive. Here:

1. Si- is usually represented by -é- in 1st person sgl, and it deletes in 2nd sgl (déłkáá': I've started to track him; díníłkáá': you have started to track him)

2. Di-, hi-: Position 6a and ni-: Position 6b take the shape dee-, hee-, nee- in juncture with the reduced form of si-, in 3rd persons and Simple Passive, but

yi-[3]: the Position 6c allomorph of hi-: Seriative takes the shape yii- before -z-/-zh- or -s-/-sh- in 3rd and 3o persons. The 1st person dpl subject pronoun appears as -ee(d)- and si is often deleted in 2nd person dpl. (deelkáá': we've started to trail him; heelghaal: we hacked it [with a scythe]; neeké: we two sat down; yiyiishhaal: he hacked it [with a scythe].)

3. Yi[2]-: Position 6c takes the shape yoo- before Si-Perfective -z-/-zh- or -s-/-sh- in 3rd persons and Passives. (yisékan: I hired him / yooskan: he hired him.)

4. The yi[3]-6c alternant of hi-6a seriative lengthens its vowel when preceded by a prefix of Pos. 4 or by dzi-6a: yiih yiyiiznil/'adziiztáál, he put them into it/he let fly a series of kicks.

5. The compound derivational prefix di-ni- (< di[11]-6a + ni[2]-6b) takes high/falling tone in Si-Perfective, as in yaa dínésht'ą́: I hung my head; yaa dínéest'ą́: he hung his head.

6. The di-component of the compound reflexive pronoun 'á-di-, assigned to Position 4, behaves like a prefix of Position 6 in most Si-Perfective paradigms: 'ádéshtłah: I greased myself / 'ádeestłah: he greased himself (put on cold cream, etc.), but 'ádisisził: I grabbed myself / 'ádeesził: he grabbed himself.

## Ci- Prefixes of Positions 6a/6b

## Di-6a / ni-6b + Extended Base

## Table 5A
## Ø/Ł-Class Verbs

T = any Verb Theme

| PERSON | Prefix Position | | | | | | | Intransitive | Transitive | |
|---|---|---|---|---|---|---|---|---|---|---|
| Sgl | 4 | + | 5 | + | 6a/6b | + | Base | | +Ø-4 | + Ci-4 |
| 1. | Ø/Ci | + | --- | + | -C- | + | -é-T | déná | néłtsiz | nidélóóz |
| 2. | Ø/Ci | + | --- | + | -C- | + | -íní-T | díníná | níníłtsiz | shidíníłóóz |
| 3. | --/Ci | + | --- | + | -Cee- | + | -z-/-s-T | deezná | --- | shideezlóóz |
| 3o | yi- | + | --- | + | -Cee- | + | -z-/-s-T | --- | yineestsiz | yideezlóóz |
| 3a. | Ø/Ci | + | ji-/-zh- | + | -Cee- | + | -z-/-s-T | jideezná | jineestsiz | shizhdeezlóóz |
| 3i. | --- | + | 'a-/-'- | + | -Cee- | + | -z-/-s-T | 'adeezná | --- | --- |
| 3s. | --- | + | ho- | + | -Cee- | + | -z-/-s-T | hodeezlį́į́' | honeezná | --- |
| Dpl | | | | | | | | | | |
| 1. | Ø/Ci | + | --- | + | -C- | +- | -ee(d)-T | dee'ná | neeltsiz | nideedlóóz |
| 2. | Ø/Ci- | + | --- | + | -Ci- | + | -soo-T | disooná | nisoołtsiz | shidisoolóóz |

di-(si)--Øná: to have started to move with household (déná: I've started to move; I'm on my way moving)
ni-(si)--łtsiz: extinguish it (fire; put it out (néłtsiz: I put out the fire)
ni-(si)--Øtsiz: go out (fire)(neeztsiz: it went out)
di-(si)--Ølóóz: lead O (nidélóóz: I'm on the way leading you)
ho-di-(si)--Ølį́į́': start to come into being, start to-- (hodeezlį́į́': it started to become)

ho-ni-(si)--Øná: “ho” won (shaa honeezná: I lost - gambling; i.e. “ho” won from me)
’a-di-(si)--Øná: person(s) unspecified have started to move (shił ’adeezná: I’ve started to move as a member of the family)

## Table 5B
## D/L-Class Verbs

D/L-Class Si-Perfectives derived with a di-prefix of Position 6a or a ni-prefix of Position 6b are all intransitive. (The Agentive Passive is an impersonal derivative of a Ø/Ł-Class Verb.)

In 2nd person dpl ni-6b and si-7 switch slots: si-n-oo- in lieu of ni-s-oo-, and 1st person dpl dee- sometimes appears as disii-.

T = any Verb Theme

| PERSON | Prefix Position | | | | | | | | | | | | |
|---|---|---|---|---|---|---|---|---|---|---|---|---|---|
| Sgl | 4 | + | 5 | + | 6a/6b | + | 7 | + | 8 | > | Base | as in: | |
| 1. | --- | + | --- | + | -C- | + | -é- | + | Ø | > | Cé-T | désh’na’ | néshjį́į́d |
| 2. | --- | + | --- | + | -Cí- | + | Ø | + | ní- | > | Cíní-T | díní’na’ | nínílį́į́d |
| 3. | --- | + | --- | + | -Cee- | + | -s- | + | Ø | > | Cee-s-T | dees’na’ | neeshjį́į́d |
| SP | --- | + | --- | + | -Cee- | +- | -s- | + | Ø | > | Cee-s(d)-T | deesdlóóz | neestsiz |
| 3a. | --- | + | ji-/-zh- | + | -Cee- | + | -s- | + | Ø | > | Cee-s-T | jidees’na’ | jineeshjį́į́d |
| 3i. | --- | + | ’a-/-’- | + | -Cee- | + | -s- | + | Ø | > | Cee-s-T | ’adees’na’ | --- |
| 3s. | --- | + | ho- | + | -Cee- | + | -s- | + | Ø | > | Cee-s-T | hodees’á | --- |
| AP | O | + | -di’- | + | -Cee- | + | -s- | + | Ø | > | Cees(d)-T | bidi’deesdlóóz | --- |
| Dpl | | | | | | | | | | | | | |
| 1. | --- | + | --- | + | -C- | + | Ø | + | -ee(d) | > | Cee(d)-T | dee’na’ | neelį́į́d |
| 2. | --- | + | --- | + | -Ci- | + | -s- | + | -oo(h) | > | -Cisoo(h)-T | disooh’na’ | --- |
| | | | | | (si) | | (C-) | | -oo(h) | ~ | siCoo(h)-T | --- | sinoołį́į́d |

di-(si)--Ølóóz: lead it/him (bi’dideesdlóóz ~ bidi’deesdlóóz: he has started to be led along)
di-(si)--(d)’na’: to have started to crawl along (désh’na’: I’ve started to crawl along; I’m on my way crawling; shił ’adees’na’: I’ve started to ride along on an unspecified crawling vehicle, as a tractor. Lit. something has started to crawl along with me)
ho-di-(si)--l’á: there is extension (hastą́ą́dóó deigo hodees’áago --: above six - as six years, horses, books)
ni-(si)--ljį́į́d: squat (néshjį́į́d: I squatted down)

## Dí-ní: Compound prefix + Extended Base

### Table 6A
### Ø/Ł-Class Verbs

Di-Position 6a + ni-: Position 6b occur as a compound prefix in a number of Verb Bases that are conjugated as Si-Perfectives. In compound form di-ni- acquire high tone, appearing as dí-ní-. Thus:

di[13]-: position 6a: inception, start + ni[7]-: Position 6b thematic > díní- in dínéłkaad: I've started to drive it along (a herd).
di[11]-: Position 6a: slant + ni[2]-: Position 6b: generic classifier for round shape, as in yaa dínésht'ą́: I hung my head

T = any Verb Theme

| PERSON | Prefix Position | | | | | | | | | | |
|---|---|---|---|---|---|---|---|---|---|---|---|
| Sgl | 4 | + | 5 | + | 6a/6b | + | 7 | + | 8 | > | Base | as in: |
| 1. | Ø | + | --- | + | dín- | + | -é- | + | Ø | > | díné-T | dínéłkaad |
| 2. | Ø | + | --- | + | díní- | + | --- | + | ní- | > | díníní-T | díníníłkaad |
| 3. | --- | + | --- | + | dínée- | + | -z-/-s- | + | Ø | > | dínéez-/-s-T | dínéezhchą́ą́' |
| 3o. | yi- | + | --- | + | dínée- | + | -z-/-s- | + | Ø | > | yidínéez-/-s-T | yidínéeskaad |
| 3a. | Ø | + | ji-/-zh-+ | | dínée- | + | -z-/-s- | + | Ø | > | jidínéez-/-s-T | jidínéeskaad |
| Dpl | | | | | | | | | | | | |
| 1. | Ø | + | --- | + | dín(í)- | + | --- | + | -ée(d) | > | dínée(d)-T | dínéelkaad |
| 2 | Ø | + | --- | + | dín(í) | + | --- | + | -óo-T | | dínóo-T | dínóołkaad |

dí-ní-(si)--łkaad: start to drive a herd (dínéłkaad: I started to drive it)
dí-ní-(si)--Øchą́ą́': flee (dínéchą́ą́': I fled)
ha#dí-ní-(si)--Øtą́ą́': start out in search of it (hadínétą́ą́': I started out looking for it)

### Table 6B
### D/L-Class Verbs

For D/L-Class Verbs, si- appears in 2nd person dpl, but switches positional slots with ni-, taking position between the components of the compound dí-ní-.

Ní[2]-: Position 6b: generic classifier and ni[1]-: Position 6b: terminative behave differently in 2nd person sgl. Cf. yaa dí<u>níní</u>t'ą́: you hung your head, but hadí<u>nííní</u>cha: you cried and cried.

T = any Verb Theme

| PERSON | Prefix Position | | | | | | | | | | | |
|---|---|---|---|---|---|---|---|---|---|---|---|---|
| Sgl | 4 | + | 5 | + | 6a/6b | + | 7 | + | 8 | > | Base | as in: |
| 1. | Ø | + | --- | + | dín- | + | -é- | + | -sh- | > | dínésh-T | dínésht'ą́ |
| 2. | Ø | + | --- | + | díní- | + | --- | + | -ní- | > | díníní-T | díníníť'ą́ |
| 3. | Ø | + | --- | + | dínée- | + | -s- | + | Ø | > | dínées-T | dínéest'ą́ |
| 3o. | -i- | + | --- | + | dínée- | + | -s- | + | Ø | > | -idínées-T | haidínéesgį́ |
| 3a. | Ø | + | ji-/-zh-+ | | dínée- | + | --s- | + | Ø | > | jidínées-T | jidínéest'ą́ |
| Dpl | | | | | | | | | | | | |
| 1. | Ø | + | --- | + | dín(í)- | + | --- | + | -ee(d) | > | dínée(d)-T | dínéet'ą́ |
| 2 | Ø | + | --- | + | dín- | + | -si- | + | -óo(h)- | > | dísínóo(h)-T | dísínóoht'ą́ |

yaa dí-ní-(si)--(d)t'ą́: hang one's head
ha#-dí-ní-(si)--(d)cha: cry and cry (hadínéshcha: I cried and cried; 2nd sgl hadíníínícha: you cried and cried; hadínéeshcha: it cried and cried)
ha#-dí-ní-(si)--(d)gį́: haul O too far (beyond where it was to be hauled)(hadínéshgį́: I hauled it too far; haidínéesgį́: he hauled it too far)
ha#-dí-'(a)-ní-(si)--lzhiizh: dance too long; stay too long at a dance (hadí'néshzhiizh: I danced too long; hadi'níníłzhiizh: you danced too long (Cf. 'ashzhish: I'm dancing)

## Di-Reflexive: Position 4

### Table 7

The reflexive pronoun 'á-di- is a compound prefix in which di-, in determinant position, behaves like a di-prefix of Position 6a, in the Si-Perfective paradigm.

In distributive plural, da-: Position 3, takes position between 'á- and -di-.

In the paradigm below 'á- and -da- are identified as Disjunct Prefixes by the boundary marker #.

T = any Verb Theme

| PERSON | | |
|---|---|---|
| Sgl | | as in: |
| 1 | 'á#-désh-T | 'ádéshch'iizh |
| 2. | 'á#-díní-T | 'ádíních'iizh |
| 3. | 'á#-dees-T | 'ádeeshch'iizh |
| 3a. | 'á#-zhdees-T | 'ázhdeeshch'iizh |
| Dpl | | |
| 1. | 'á#-dee(d)-T | 'ádeech'iizh |
| 2 | 'á#-disoo(h)-T | 'ádisoohch'iizh |
| Dist Pl | | |
| 1 | 'áda#-dee(d)-T | 'ádadeech'iizh |
| 2 | 'áda#-disoo(h)-T | 'ádadisoohch'iizh |
| 3 | 'áda#-dees-T | 'ádadeeshch'iizh |
| 3a | 'áda#-zhdees-T | 'ádazhdeeshch'iizh |

'á#-di-(si)--(d)ch'iizh: scrub oneself ('ádéshch'iizh: I scrubbed myself [with a brush])
'á#-di-(si)--(d)lid: burn oneself ('ádéshdlid: I burned myself)

## Distributive Plural + Hi-/yi- Seriative + Extended Base

### Table 8A
### Ø/Ł-Class Verbs
### Intransitive

T = any Verb Theme

| PERSON | Prefix Position | | | | | | | | | |
|---|---|---|---|---|---|---|---|---|---|---|
| Pl | 3 | + | 5 | + | hi-/yi | + | Base | | | as in: |
| 1. | da- | + | --- | + | -h-/-- | + | -ee(d)-T | > | dahaa(d)-T | dahaa'mááz |
| 2. | da- | + | --- | + | -hi-/-- | + | -soo-T | > | dahisoo-T | dahisoomááz |
| 3. | da- | + | --- | + | -hee-/-- | + | -z-/-s-T | > | dahaaz-/-s-T | dahaazmááz |
| 3a. | da- | + | -ji- | + | --/-i- | + | -z-/-s-T | > | dajiiz-/-s-T | dajiizmááz |

taah da#-hi-(si)--Ømááz: roll one after another into the water (t'áá 'ałkéé' taah dahaazmááz: one after another they rolled into the water)

### Table 8B
### D/L-Class Verbs
### Intransitive

T = any Verb Theme

| PERSON | Prefix Position | | | | | | | | | |
|---|---|---|---|---|---|---|---|---|---|---|
| Sgl | 3 | + | 5 | + | hi-/yi | + | Base | | | as in: |
| 1. | da- | + | --- | + | -h-/-- | + | -ee(d)-T | > | dahaa(d)-T | dahaakai |
| 2. | da- | + | --- | + | -hi-/-- | + | -soo(h)-T | > | dahisoo(h)-T | dahisoohkai |
| 3. | da- | + | --- | + | -hee-/-- | + | -s-T | > | dahaas-T | dahaaskai |
| 3a. | da- | + | -ji- | + | --/-i- | + | -s-T | > | dajiis-T | dajiiskai |

biih da#-hi-(si)--(d)kai: get into it one after another (as into a vehicle)('áłchíní chidíłtsxoii yiih dahaaskai: the children got into the school bus one after another)

Verb Bases derived with Disjunct Prefixes of the following types are conjugated in the same pattern as the simple constructions outlined in the foregoing charts:

'a-: Position 1b: away out of sight
    yah 'a-dahaaskai: they (3+) entered seriatim

'ada-: Position 1b: downward from a height
    'ada-dahaaskai: they descended seriatim

ha-: Position 1b: up, up out
    ha-dahaaskai: they climbed up (out) seriatim

ch'í-: Position 1b: out horizontally
    ch'í-dahaaskai: they went out seriatim

ná-: Position 1d: Reversionary
    ń-dahaaskai: they went back seriatim

ni-: Position 1b: cessative
    ---jį' neheeskai: they went as far as ---

## Hi-yi- Seriative + Extended Base

With Ø in Position 4 (3rd person direct object), the transitive and the intransitive paradigms converge in shape – i.e. hi- represents the Seriative; but in the presence of a prefix of Position 4 or 5, hi- is replaced by its yi-allomorph.

In 3o person yi- is duplicated in the absence of a preceding prefix. It can be analyzed either as yi-4 + yii-6c, or as yi-4 + yi-4 + -ii-6c. Thus yiyiizhnizh: he plucked them one after another, but dayiizhnizh (< da-3 + y[i]-4 + -ii-6c): they 3+ plucked them)

### Table 9A
### Ø/Ł-Class Verbs
### Transitive

| PERSON Sgl | 4 | 5 | hi-6a | + Ø-4 | yi-6c | + Ci-4 | as in: |
|---|---|---|---|---|---|---|---|
| 1 | Ø/Ci- | --- | hé-T | hénil | yé-T | Ciyé-T | biih nihiyénil |
| 2 | Ø/Ci- | --- | híní-T | hínínil | yíní-T | Ciyíní-T | biih nihiyínínil |
| 3 | --/Ci- | --- | hee-T | --- | yiiz-/s-T | Ciyiiz-/s-T | yiih nihiyiiznil |
| 3o | --/yi- | --- | --- | --- | yiiz-/s-T | Ciyiiz-/s-T | yiih yiyiiznil |
| 3a | Ø/Ci- | j- | --- | jiiznil | -jiiz-/s-T | Cijiiz-/s-T | biih nihijiiznil |
| Dpl | | | | | | | |
| 1 | Ø/Ci- | --- | hee(d)-T | hee'nil | yee(d)-T | Ciyee(d)-T | biih nihiyee'nil |
| 2 | Ø/Ci- | --- | hisoo-T | hisoonil | yoo(h)-T | Ciyoo-T | biih nihiyoonil |

biih hi-(si)--Ønil: put 3+ O into it in series (biih hénil: I put them into it one after another; biih nihiyénil: I put you 3+ into it one after another; yiih nihiyiiznil: he put us into it one after another; yiih yiyiiznil: he put them 3+ into it one after another)

yisdá#-nihi-yi-(si)--Ønil: rescue (you) 3+ (yisdánihiyénil: I rescued you 3+ one after another; yisdánihiyiiznil: he rescued us one after another)

taah hi-(si)--łmááz: roll O into the water one after another (taah yiyiismááz: he rolled them into the water in series)

### Table 9B
### D/L-Class Verbs

There are no (available) D/L-Class transitive Seriative Verbs, so Table 10B contains only the Simple and Agentive Passives corresponding to Ø/Ł-Class transitive Verbs.

| PERSON | Prefix Position 4 | + | 5 | + | hi-Base | as in: | + yi-Base | as in: |
|---|---|---|---|---|---|---|---|---|
| SP | Ø | + | --- | + | hees-T | biih hees'nil | --- | --- |
| AP | O | + | -'(a)d- | + | --- | --- | -iis-T | biih bi'diis'nil |

biih hi-(si)--(d)'nil: be put into it one after another (naaltsoos tsits'aa' biih hees'nil: the books were put into the box; tídaalyaaígíí chidítsoh biih bi'diis'nil: the wounded were put into the truck)

## 'A-: Position 4 + Extended Yi-Seriative Base

### Table 10

Third person indefinite (3i) 'a-: Position 4: something/someone unspecified represents the direct object in several Seriative Verb Bases derived with Disjunct Prefixes of Position 1b or with the Position 3 marker of Distributive Plural.

In paradigms of this type 'a- takes its alternant shape 'i- before Seriative yi-, except in the 3rd person. There -'i- reduces to -'- and yi-Seriative elides its initial consonant, lengthening its vowel before -z-/-s-. The combination then contracts to produce -'iiz-/-s-.

Similarly, the 3a subject pronoun j(i)-: Position 5: he, she, they + (y)iiz-/s- contract to produce -jiiz-/-s-.

'I- reduces to -'- before ji-5 in the presence of a preceding prefix.

T = any Verb Theme

| PERSON | Prefix Position | | | | | | | | | |
|---|---|---|---|---|---|---|---|---|---|---|
| Sgl | 3 | + | 4 | + | 5 | + | yi -Base | | | as in: |
| 1. | --- | + | -'i- | + | --- | + | -yé- | > | -'iyé-T | ná'iyéláá' |
| 2. | --- | + | -'i- | + | --- | + | -yíní- | > | -'íyíní-T | ná'iyíníłáá' |
| 3. | --- | + | -'- | + | --- | + | -iiz-/-s- | > | -'iiz-/-s-T | ná'iizláá' |
| 3a. | --- | + | -'- | + | -j- | + | -iiz-/-s- | > | -'jiiiz-/-s-T | ná'jiizláá' ~ ń'jiizláá' |
| Dpl | | | | | | | | | | |
| 1 | --- | + | -'i- | + | --- | + | -yee(d)- | > | -'iyee(d)-T | ná'iyeedláá' |
| 2 | --- | + | -'i- | + | --- | + | -yoo- | > | -'iyoo-T | ná'iyooláá' |
| Dist. Pl. | | | | | | | | | | |
| 1 | da- | + | -'i- | + | --- | + | yee(d)- | > | da'iyee(d)-T | ńda'iyeedláá' |
| 2 | da- | + | -'i- | + | --- | + | yoo- | > | da'iyoo-T | ńda'iyooláá' |
| 3 | da- | + | -'- | + | --- | + | iiz-/-s- | > | da'iiz/-s-T | ńda'iizláá' |
| 3a | da- | + | -'- | + | -j- | + | jiiz-/-s- | > | da'jiiz-/-s-T | ńda'jiiizláá' |

ná#-'i-yi-(si)--Øláá': pick pinyon nuts (literally, gather unspecified objects) (ná'iyéláá': I went pinyon-picking. Cf. náháláá': I gathered them)

na#-'-yi-(si)--łnii': do shopping; trade; sell; make purchases (Literally, buy or sell unspecified things)(na'iyéłnii': I did my shopping. Cf. naháłnii': I bought it)

'a-#-'i-yi-(si)--nil: toss away unspecified plural objects one after another)(bik'ijį' 'adah 'i'yee'nil: we dropped bombs on them, or 'adah 'ida'yee'nil: we [dist. pl] dropped 3+ bombs on them one after another)

## Ho-: Position 4 + Extended Yi-Seriative Base

### Table 11

The 3rd person direct object ho- (3s): Position 4 representing space, area in some constructions and functioning as a thematic prefix in others, occurs in several transitive Seriative Verb Bases. For the most part these are derived with a prefix of Position 1b.

Ho- is replaced by its hw- alternant in 3rd person, where hw- + (y)iiz-/-s- > hwiiz-/-s-.

T = any Verb Theme

| PERSON | Prefix Position | | | | | | | |
|---|---|---|---|---|---|---|---|---|
| Sgl | 4 | + | 5 | + | yi -Base | | | as in: |
| 1. | ho- | + | --- | + | -yé- | > | hoyé-T | bitah hoyégizh |
| 2. | ho- | + | --- | + | -yíní- | > | hoyíní-T | bitah hoyínígizh |
| 3. | hw- | + | --- | + | -iiz-/-s- | > | hwiiz-/-s-T | yitah hwiizhgizh |
| 3a. | ho- | + | -j- | + | -iiz-/-s- | > | hojiiz-/-s-T | bitah hojiizhgizh |
| Dpl | | | | | | | | |
| 1 | ho- | + | --- | + | -yee(d)- | > | hoyee(d)-T | bitah hoyeegizh |
| 2 | ho- | + | --- | + | -yoo- | > | hoyoo-T | bitah hoyoogizh |

bitah ho-yi-(si)--Øgizh: cut off its limbs (bitah hoyégizh: I cut off its limbs)
bitah ho-yi-(si)--Øch'iizh: saw off its limbs (bitah hoyéch'iizh: I sawed off its limbs)
ha#-ho-yi--(si)--Øgeed: dig a hole or pit (hahoyégeed: I dug a hole; hahwiizgeed: he dug a hole)
na#-ho-yi-(si)--łdláád: plow (nahoyéłdláád ~ nihoyéłdláád: I plowed the area; nahwiisdláád: he plowed the area. Literally, he ripped furrows around on an area)

## Dzi-: Position 6a + Yi³- Seriative: Position 6c + Extended Base

### Table 12

Dzi-: Position 6a, away into space requires the shift from hi- to yi- in the Seriative. The paradigm closely resembles that summarized in Table 10A, except that the 3a subject pronoun of Position 5 takes the shape -ii-.

Dzi- Bases require a Disjunct 'a-: away out of sight.

T = any Verb Theme

| PERSON | Prefix Position | | | | | | | |
|---|---|---|---|---|---|---|---|---|
| Sgl | 5 | + | 6a | + | yi -Base | | | as in: |
| 1. | --- | + | -dzi- | + | -yé-T | > | -dziyé-T | 'adziyétáál |
| 2. | --- | + | -dzi- | + | -yíní-T | > | -dziyíní-T | 'adziyínítáál |
| 3. | --- | + | -dz(i)- | + | -iiz-/-s-T | > | -dziiz-/-s-T | 'adziiztáál |
| 3a. | -ii- | + | -j- | + | -iiz-/-s-T | > | -iijiiz-/-s-T | 'iijiiztáál |
| Dpl | | | | | | | | |
| 1 | --- | + | -dzi- | + | -yee(d)-T | > | -dziyee(d)-T | 'adziyiitáál |
| 2 | --- | + | -dzi- | + | -yoo-T | > | -dziyoo-T | 'adziyootáál |

'a#-dzi-yi-(si)--Øtáál: let fly a series of kicks ('adziyétáál: I let fly a series of kicks)(Cf. Yi-Perfective 'adzíítáál: I let fly a single kick.)

## Yi²-: Position 6a + Extended Base

### Table 13 A
### Ø/Ł-Class Verbs

Yi²-: Position 6a is (tentatively) identified as the directive, cognate with PA *u̲. In two types of Ø-Imperfective yi- occurs in combination with a ni-prefix of Position 6b, as in:

(1) yinishdlą́: I believe him

In many Imperfectives it occurs high in tone, combined with -ni-, as yíní-in:

(2) yíníshdon: I'm shooting at it

In both instances yini-/yíní- appear as (w)oo-/(w)ó- in particular environments.

wooshdlą́ ~ yinishdlą́: I believe it
yółdon: he's shooting at it

A number of Verb Bases, conjugated as Si-Perfectives, are derived with yi- – alone or in combination with derivational-thematic elements of Positions 6 or 1b. And again, in particular environments (before 1st person sgl - sh-8, and in 3rd person and Passive constructions), yi- appears as -oo-.

T = any Verb Theme

| PERSON Sgl | Prefix Position 4 | + | 5 | + | 6a | + | Base | | | +Ø-4 | + Ci-4 |
|---|---|---|---|---|---|---|---|---|---|---|---|
| 1. | Ø/Ci- | + | --- | + | yi- | + | -sé- | > | yisé-T | yisékan | niisékan |
| 2. | Ø/Ci- | + | --- | + | yi- | + | -síní- | > | yisíní-T | yisíníkan | shiisíníkan |
| 3. | Ø/Ci- | + | --- | + | -oo- | + | -z-/-s- | > | ooz-/-s-T | --- | shoozkan |
| 3o. | y- | + | --- | + | -oo- | + | -z-/-s- | > | yooz-T | --- | yoozkan |
| 3a. | Ø/Ci- | + | -j- | + | -oo- | + | -z-/-s- | > | jooz-/-s-T | joozkan | shijoozkan |
| Dpl | | | | | | | | | | | |
| 1 | Ø/Ci- | + | --- | + | yi- | + | -sii(d)- | > | yisii(d)-T | yisiikan | niisiikan |
| 2 | Ø/Ci- | + | --- | + | yi- | + | -soo- | > | yisoo-T | yisookan | shiisookan |

yi-(si)--Økan: hire O (lawyer, medicine man, technician)(shoozkan: he hired me)
na#-(y)i-(si)--Ø'ah: untwist O, untie O (neisé'ah)
shó#-(y)i-(si)--łt'e': acquire O, come to possess O (shóiséłt'e': I acquired it, came to possess it; shóyoost'e': he acquired it)

## Table 13B
## D/L-Class Verbs

T = any Verb Theme

| PERSON Sgl | Prefix Position 4 | + | 5 | + | 6a | + | Base | | | as in: |
|---|---|---|---|---|---|---|---|---|---|---|
| 1. | Ø | + | --- | + | yl- | + | -sis-T | > | yisis-T | yisisdląąd |
| 2. | Ø | + | --- | + | yi- | + | -síní-T | > | yisíní-T | yisínídląąd |
| 3o. | y- | + | --- | + | -oo- | + | -s-T | > | yoos-T | yoosdląąd |
| SP | Ø | + | --- | + | woo- | + | -s(d)-T | > | woos-T | woosdląąd |
| 3a. | Ø | + | -j- | + | -oo- | + | -s-T | > | joos-T | joosdląąd |
| AP | O | + | -'(a)d- | + | -oo- | + | -s(d)-T | > | O'doos-(a)-T | bi'doosdląąd |
| Dpl | | | | | | | | | | |
| 1 | Ø | + | --- | + | yi- | + | -sii(d)-T | > | yisii(d)-T | yisiidląąd |
| 2 | Ø | + | --- | + | yi- | + | -soo-T | > | yisoo(h)-T | yisoohdląąd |

yi-(si)--(d)ląąd: come to believe O (yisisdląąd: I came to believe it)
ná#-(y)i-(si)--(d)kan: beg for O; implore or beseech (néisiskan: I begged for it; náyooskan; he begged for it; nániiskan: I begged you for it; náshooskan; he begged me)
ná#-(y)i-(si)--(d)'nil: take O down (a structure - as a corral)(néisis'nil: I took it down; náyoos'nil: he took it down)

When the direct object is 3i person 'a- ~ 'i-, the object pronoun takes the shape 'i- and 'i- + (y)i- > 'ii-, as in ná'iisiskan: I begged; ná'ooskan: he begged.

### 2. Disjunct Prefixes

A relatively small number of Disjunct Prefixes occur in determinant position with Si-Perfective Verb Bases. These include:

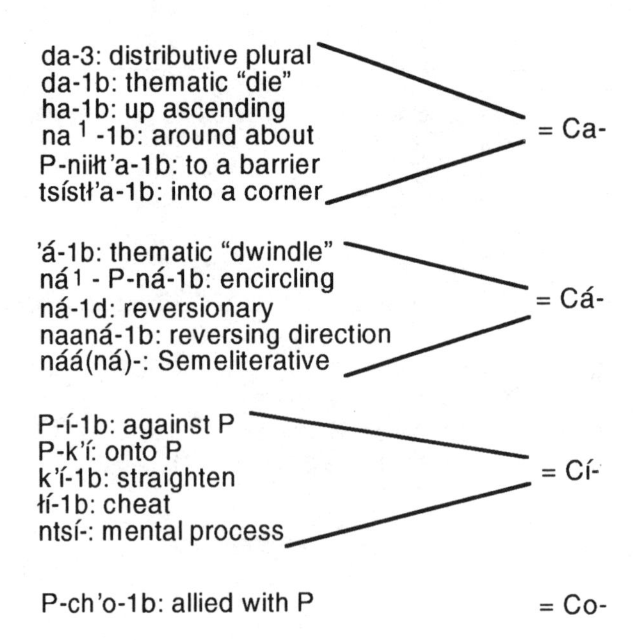

## Ca-: Position 1b + Extended Base

### Table 1A
### Ø/Ł-Class Verbs

With the exception of na$^{1}$- ~ ne- ~ ni- ~ n-1b, which takes variable shapes depending on the environment, the Ca- (= consonant + -a-) prefixes generally retain their base shape throughout the Si-Perfective paradigms. Ca- lengthens its vowel before -z-/-s- in 3rd person.

T = any Verb Theme

| PERSON | Prefix Position | | | | | | | | | Transitive | |
|---|---|---|---|---|---|---|---|---|---|---|---|
| Sgl | 1b/3 | + 4 + | 5 | + | Base | | | Intrans. | + Ø-4 | + Ci-4 |
| 1. | Ca- | + Ø/Ci- + | --- | + | -sé-T | > | Casé-T | haséná | haséłtį́ | haniséłtį́ |
| 2. | Ca- | + Ø/Ci- + | --- | + | -síní-T | > | Casíní-T | hasíníná | hasíníłtį́ | hashisíníłtį́ |
| 3. | Caa- | + --/Ci- + | --- | + | -z-/-s-T | > | Caaz-/s-T | haazná | --- | hashistį́ |
| 3o. | Ca- | + -i- + | --- | + | -z-/-s-T | > | Caiz-/s-T | --- | --- | haistį́ |
| 3a. | Ca- | + Ø/Ci- + | -j- | + | -z-/-s-T | > | Cajiz-/s-T | hajizná | hajistį́ | hanijistį́ |
| 3i. | Ca- | + --- + | -'a- | + | -z-/-s-T | > | Ca'az-/s-T | ha'azná | --- | --- |
| Dpl | | | | | | | | | | |
| 1 | Ca- | + Ø/Ci- + | --- | + | -sii(d)-T | > | Casii(d)-T | hasii'ná | hasiiltį́ | hanisiiltį́ |
| 2 | Ca- | + Ø/Ci- + | --- | + | -soo-T | > | Casoo-T | hasooná | hasoołtį́ | hashisoołtį́ |

ha#-(si)--Øná: move up with household (as up onto a mountain)
ha#-(si)--Øyá: climb up; ascend walking (1 subject)(haséyá: I climbed up; haayá: he climbed up)
ha#-(si)--łtį́: climb up carrying AnO (haniséłtį́: I carried you up; hashisíníłtį́: you carried me up, etc.)
da#-(si)--Øtsą́: die (1 subject)(daaztsą́: he died)
da#-(si)--Ønil, biih ---: set 3+ objects in it (as sets in a ring (biih dasénil: I set them in it)
tsístł'a#-(si)--Øyá: get cornered, into a cul-de-sac; be frustrated trying to solve a problem (1 subject) (tsístł'aséyá: I got cornered; tsístł'aayá: he got cornered)
P-niiłt'a#-(si)--Øyá: reach a barrier (1 subject) ('ańt'i' biniiłt'aséyá: I came to a fence barrier)(yiniiłt'aayá: he reached a barrier)

## Table 1B
## D/L-Class Verbs

Ca- lengthens the prefix vowel before -z-/-s- in 3rd person and Simple Passive.

T = any Verb Theme

| PERSON Sgl | Prefix Position 1b/3 | + | 4 | + | 5 | + | Base | | | as in: |
|---|---|---|---|---|---|---|---|---|---|---|
| 1. | Ca- | + | --- | + | --- | + | -sis-T | > | Casis-T | hasis'na' |
| 2. | Ca- | + | --- | + | --- | + | -síní-T | > | Casíní-T | hasíní'na' |
| 3. | Caa- | + | --- | + | --- | + | -s-T | > | Caas-T | haas'na' |
| SP. | Caa- | + | --- | + | --- | + | -s(d)-T | > | Caas(d)-T | haastį́ |
| 3a. | Ca- | + | --- | + | -ji- | + | -s-T | > | Cajis-T | hajis'na' |
| 3i. | Ca- | + | --- | + | -'a- | + | -s-T | > | Ca'as-T | ha'as'na' |
| AP | Ca | + | O | + | -'(a)di- | + | -s- | > | CaO'is(d)-T | habi'distį́ |
| Dpl | | | | | | | | | | |
| 1. | Ca- | + | --- | + | --- | + | -sii(d)-T | > | Casii(d)-T | hasii'na' |
| 2. | Ca- | + | --- | + | --- | + | -soo-T | > | Casoo-T | hasooh'na' |

ha#-(si)--(d)'na': climb up (tsin bą́ąh hasis'na': I climbed a tree)

tsístł'a#-(si)--(d)'na': crawl and get cornered (tsístł'asis'na': I crawled and got cornered)

P-niiłt'a#-(si)--(d)'na': come to a barrier crawling (tsé biniiłt'asis'na': I came to a a rock barrier crawling)

(habi'distį́ - Agentive Passive: he was carried up; haastį́ - Simple Passive: it AnO was taken up or out)

## Na- ~ ni-: Position 1b + Extended Base

### Table 2A
### Ø/Ł-Class Verbs

Na- takes variable shape, depending on the environment (ni- ~ naa- ~ ne- ~ n-). (See chart on pages 30-31.)

T = any Verb Theme

| PERSON Sgl | Prefix Position 1 | + | 4 | + | 5 | + | Base | | | Intrans. | + Ø-4 | Transitive + Ci-4 |
|---|---|---|---|---|---|---|---|---|---|---|---|---|
| 1. | ni- | + | Ø/Ci- | + | --- | + | -sé-T | > | nisé-T | nisébį́į́' | niséłtį́ | naniséłtį́ |
| 2. | ni- | + | Ø/Ci- | + | --- | + | -síní-T | > | nisíní-T | nisíníbį́į́' | nisíníłtį́ | nashisíníłtį́ |
| 3. | naa- | + | --/Ci- | + | --- | + | -z-/-s-T | > | naaz-/-s-T | naazbį́į́' | --- | nashistį́ |
| 3o. | ne- | + | -i- | + | --- | + | -z-/-s-T | > | neiz-/-s-T | --- | --- | neistį́ |
| 3a. | n- ~ ni- | + | Ø/Ci- | + | -ji- | + | -z-/-s-T | > | njiz-/-s-T | njizbį́į́' | njistį́ | nanijistį́ |
| 3i. | na- | + | --- | + | -'a- | + | -z-/-s-T | > | na'az-/-s-T | na'azbį́į́' | --- | --- |
| 3s | na- | + | --- | + | -ha- | + | -z-/-s-T | > | nahaz-/-s-T | nahazne' | --- | --- |
| Dpl | | | | | | | | | | | | |
| 1. | ni- | + | Ø/Ci- | + | --- | + | -sii(d)-T | > | nisii(d)-T | nisiibį́į́' | nisiiltį́ | nanisiiltį́ |
| 2. | ni- | + | Ø/Ci- | + | --- | + | -soo-T | > | nisoo-T | nisoobį́į́' | nisoołtį́ | nashisoołtį́ |

na#-(si)--Øbį́į́': bathe, swim about
na#-(si)--Øghal: look around (niséghal: I looked around; naazghal: he looked around)
na#-(si)--łtį́: carry an AnO about; make a round trip carrying an AnO (nashisíníłtį́: you carried me around; naniséłtį́: I carried you around)
na#-(si)--Øne', baa ---: it was told ("ha" told about it. From baa nahosisne': tell about it)

### Table 2B
### D/L-Class Verbs

T = any Verb Theme

| PERSON Sgl | Prefix Position 1 | + | 4 | + | 5 | + | Base | | | as in: |
|---|---|---|---|---|---|---|---|---|---|---|
| 1. | ni- | + | --- | + | --- | + | -sis-T | > | nisis-T | nisis'na' |
| 2. | ni- | + | --- | + | --- | + | -síní-T | > | nisíní-T | nisíní'na' |
| 3. | naa- | + | --- | + | --- | + | -s-T | > | naas-T | naas'na' |
| SP. | naa- | + | --- | + | --- | + | -s(d)-T | > | naas(d)-T | naast'ą́ |
| 3a. | n- | + | --- | + | -ji- | + | -s-T | > | njis-T | njis'na' |
| 3i. | na- | + | --- | + | -'a- | + | -s-T | > | na'as-T | na'as'na' |
| AP | na | + | O | + | -'(a)di- | + | -s(d)- | > | naO'dis(d)-T | nabi'distį́ |
| Dpl | | | | | | | | | | |
| 1 | ni- | + | --- | + | --- | + | -sii(d)-T | > | nisii(d)-T | nisii'na' |
| 2 | ni- | + | --- | + | --- | + | -soo(h)-T | > | nisoo-T | nisooh'na'í |

na#-(si)--(d)'na': crawl about, make a round trip crawling
na#(si)--(d)kai, bił ---: accompany them about; go about with them (companions) (bił nisiskai: I went about with them; yił naaskai: they went around with him)

## Cá-: Position 1b + Extended Base

### Table 3

The Thematic Prefix ’á- ~ ’í-: Position 1b, that appears in a Verb Base meaning “dwindle, become none, vanish, become extinct” retains its base shape throughout the Si-Perfective paradigm except in 3o person, where the ’í- allomorph is required before the following -i-: Position 4.

T = any Verb Theme

| PERSON Sgl | Prefix Position 1b | + | 4 | + | 5 | + | Base | | | as in: |
|---|---|---|---|---|---|---|---|---|---|---|
| 1. | ’á- | + | Ø | + | --- | + | -sé-T | > | ’ásé-T | ’ásé-łdįįd |
| 2. | ’á- | + | Ø | + | --- | + | -síní-T | > | ’ásíní-T | ’ásíníłdįįd |
| 3. | ’á- | + | --- | + | --- | + | -s-T | > | ’ás-T | ’ásdįįd |
| 3o. | ’í- | + | -i- | + | --- | + | -s-T | > | ’íis-T | ’íisdįįd |
| 3a. | ’á- | + | Ø | + | -jí- | + | -s-T | > | ’ájis-T | ’ájísdįįd |
| Dpl | | | | | | | | | | |
| 1 | ’á- | | --- | + | --- | + | -sii(d)-T | > | ’ásii(d)-T | ’ásiildįįd |
| 2 | ’á- | + | --- | + | --- | + | -soo-T | > | ’ásoo-T | ’ásoołdįįd |

’á#-(si)--łdįįd: get rid of O; use O all up (’ásé-łdįįd: I used it all up)
’á#-(si)--(d)dįįd: become extinct, nonexistent, used up (chidí bitoo’ ’ásdįįd: the gasoline ran out, was all used up)

## Ná- ~ ní-: Position 1b/1d + Extended Base

### Table 4A

Aside from ’á-: Position 1b, the only Cá- Disjunct Prefixes that occur with Si-Perfective are ná[1]-1b and ná-1d. Like ná[1]-1b the high tone prefixes take variable shape, depending on the environment. They appear as ná- ~ ní- ~ né- ~ ń-. (See na-prefix chart on pp. 38-39. )

### Ø/Ł-Class Verbs

T = any Verb Theme

| PERSON Sgl | Prefix Position 1 | + | 4 | + | 5 | + | Base | | | Intrans. | Transitive + Ø-4 | Transitive + Ci-4 |
|---|---|---|---|---|---|---|---|---|---|---|---|---|
| 1. | ní- | + | Ø/Ci- | + | --- | + | -sé-T | > | nísé-T | níséyiz | nísé-łhiz | nánisé-łhiz |
| 2. | ní- | + | Ø/Ci- | + | --- | + | -síní-T | > | nísíní-T | nísíníyiz | nísíníłhiz | náshisíníłhiz |
| 3. | ná- | + | --/Ci- | + | --- | + | -z-/-s-T | > | náz-/s-T | názyiz | --- | náshísxiz |
| 3o. | né- | + | -i- | + | --- | + | -z-/-s-T | > | néiz-/s-T | --- | --- | néísxiz |
| 3a. | ń- | + | Ø/Ci- | + | -ji- | + | -z-/-s-T | > | ńjíz/s-T | ńjízyiz | ńjísxiz | náshijisxiz |
| 3i | ná- | + | --- | + | -’á- | + | -z-/-s-T | > | ná’áz-/s-T | ná’ázyiz | --- | --- |
| 3s | ná- | + | --- | + | -há- | + | -z-/-s-T | > | náház-/s-T | náházyiz | --- | --- |
| Dpl | | | | | | | | | | | | |
| 1 | ní- | + | Ø/Ci- | + | --- | + | -sii(d)-T | > | nísii(d)-T | nísiigiz | nísiilyiz | nánisiilyiz |
| 2 | ní- | + | Ø/Ci- | + | --- | + | -soo-T | > | nísoo-T | nísooyiz | nísoołhiz | náshisoołhiz |

ná#-(si)--Øyiz: turn around
ná#-(si)--łhiz: turn O around

P-ná#-(si)--Øchid: put arms around P (binínshéchid: I put my arms around her)
naaná#-(si)--łbą́ą́z: make a turn driving O (car, wagon)(chidí naanísé łbą́ą́z: I turned the car around)

Table 4B
D/L-Class Verbs

T = any Verb Theme

| PERSON | Prefix Position | | | | | | | | | |
|---|---|---|---|---|---|---|---|---|---|---|
| Sgl | 1 | + | 4 | + | 5 | + | Base | | | as in: |
| 1. | ní- | + | --- | + | --- | + | -sís-T | > | nísís-T | nísísdlį́į́' |
| 2. | ní- | + | --- | + | --- | + | -síní-T | > | nísíní-T | nísínídlį́į́' |
| 3. | ná- | + | --- | + | --- | + | -s-T | > | nás-T | násdlį́į́' |
| SP. | ná- | + | --- | + | --- | + | -s-T | > | nás(d)-T | násyiz |
| 3a. | ń- | + | --- | + | -ji- | + | -s-T | > | ńjís-T | ńjísdlį́į́' |
| 3i | ná- | + | --- | + | -'á- | + | -s-T | > | ná'as-T | ná'ásdlį́į́' |
| 3s | ná- | + | --- | + | -há- | + | -s-T | > | náhás-T | náhásdlį́į́' |
| AP | ná- | + | O | + | -'(a)di- | + | -s-T | > | náO'dis-T | nábi'disyiz |
| Dpl | | | | | | | | | | |
| 1 | ní- | + | --- | + | --- | + | -sii(d)-T | > | nísii(d)-T | nísiidlį́į́' |
| 2 | ní- | + | --- | + | --- | + | -soo-T | > | nísoo-T | nísoohdlį́į́' |

ná#-(si)--(d)lį́į́': revert; become again; return to a previous state (yá'át'ééh nísísdlį́į́': I got well)
ná#-(si)--łtłéé': get wet (nástłéé': he got wet)

Ha-: Position 1b + ná: Position 1d

Table 5

Ha-1b: up ascending and ná-1d: reversionary contract to produce háá-. The contracted form remains throughout the paradigm, except in the 3rd person and Simple Passive constructions, where ná- reemerges. Thus:

| PERSON | D/L-Class | | Ø/Ł-Class | | |
|---|---|---|---|---|---|
| Sgl | | Dpl | Sgl | | Dpl |
| 1 | háásis'na' | háásii'na' | 1 | háásé łtį́ | háásiiłtį́ |
| 2 | háásíní'na' | háásooh'na' | 2 | háásíníłtį́ | háásoołtį́ |
| 3 | hanás'na' | | 3 | hanéístį́ | |
| 3a | háájís'na' | | 3a | háájístį́ | |
| 3i | háá'ás'na' | | 3i | --- | |

Háá- ~ haná#-(si)--(d)'na': climb back up (tsin bąąh háásís'na': I climbed back up the tree)

Ha- + ná- > háá- before a prefix of Position 6, before the distributive plural marker of Position 3 and before another prefix of Position 1b.

hááníísą́ (< ha-ná-ni-6b + (y)ísą́): they grew back (as one's teeth, after the baby teeth)
háádasii'na' (<ha-ná-da-3 + -sii'na'): we 3+ climbed back up

háásiiltį́ (<ha-ná-+ -siiltį́): we carried him back up (hanéístį́: he carried him back up)
háábíyáátti' ( < ha-ná-bí-yá- (y) íłti' = prefix sequence: ha-1b + ná- 1d + b- O + -í- 1b + yá- 1b + -(y) íłti'): I broke the spell on him (lit. I talked him back up out)

## Cí-: Position 1b + Extended Base

### Table 6A
### Ø/Ł-Class Verbs

The Cí- prefixes of Position 1b include P-í-: against P; P-k'í-:onto P; łí-: cheat; k'í-: straighten; continue, keep right on (performing the action denoted by the stem); ntsí-: think; ponder.

Beyond the fact that Cí- takes the shape Cé- in 3rd person and Simple Passives (where the following prefix is -z-/-s- and Position 8 is vacant), it is quite regular in determinant position.

T = any Verb Theme

| PERSON | Prefix Position | | | | | | | | Intrans. | Transitive | |
|---|---|---|---|---|---|---|---|---|---|---|---|
| Sgl | 1 | + | 4 | + | 5 + | Base | | | | + Ø-4 | + Ci-4 |
| 1. | Cí- | + | Ø/Ci- | + | --- + | -sé-T | > | Císé-T | k'ísédǫǫd | łíshécháázh | łínishécháázh |
| 2. | Cí- | + | Ø/Ci- | + | --- + | -síní-T | > | Císíní-T | k'ísínídǫǫd | łíshínícháázh | łíshishínícháázh |
| 3. | Cé- | + | --/Ci- | + | --- + | -z-/-s-T | > | Céz-/s-T | k'ézdǫǫd | --- | łíshízhcháázh |
| 3o. | Cí- | + | -í- | + | --- + | -z-/-s-T | > | Cíiz-/s-T | --- | --- | łíizhcháázh |
| 3a. | Cí- | + | Ø/Ci- | + | -ji- + | -z-/-s-T | > | Cíjíz/s-T | k'íjízdǫǫd | łíjízhcháázh | łíshijizhcháázh |
| Dpl | | | | | | | | | | | |
| 1 | Cí- | + | Ø/Ci- | + | --- + | -sii(d)-T | > | Císii(d)-T | k'ísiidǫǫd | łíshiicháázh | łínishiicháázh |
| 2 | Cí- | + | Ø/Ci- | + | --- + | -soo-T | > | Císoo-T | k'ísoodǫǫd | łíshoocháázh | łíshishoocháázh |

k'í#-(si)--Ødǫǫd: straighten up, become erect
k'í#-(si)--łdǫǫd: straighten O (as a bent nail)(k'íísdǫǫd: he straightened it)
łí#-(si)--Øcháázh: cheat O; shortchange O; take unfair advantage of O (łínishécháázh: I cheated you; łíshízhcháázh: he cheated me)
P-í#-(si)--Ø'ą́: rub a SRO against P (as a bar of soap)(bísé'ą́: I rubbed it against it; yíízʼą́: he rubbed it against it)
P-k'í#-(si)--Øziid: pour O on P (as water)(bik'íséziid: I poured it on him; shik'íízziid: he poured it on me
ntsí#-(si)--Økééz: think (baa ntsísékééz: I thought about it)
bik'í#-(si)--Ølizh: urinate on it (yik'ézhlizh: he urinated on it)

## Table 6B
## D/L-Class Verbs

T = any Verb Theme

| PERSON Sgl | Prefix Position 1 | + | 4 | + | 5 | + | Base | | | as in: |
|---|---|---|---|---|---|---|---|---|---|---|
| 1. | Cí- | + | --- | + | --- | + | -sís-T | > | Císís-T | bísís'na' |
| 2. | Cí- | + | --- | + | --- | + | -síní-T | > | Císíní-T | bísíní'na' |
| 3. | Cé- | + | --- | + | --- | + | -s-T | > | Cés-T | yés'na' |
| SP. | Cé- | + | --- | + | --- | + | -s(d)-T | > | Cés(d)-T | bik'ésdziid |
| 3a. | Cí- | + | --- | + | -ji- | + | -s-T | > | Cíjís-T | bíjís'na' |
| 3i | Cé- | + | --- | + | -'á- | + | -s-T | > | Cé'és-T | bé'és'na' |
| AP | Cí- | + | O | + | -'(a)di- | + | -s(d)-T | > | CíO'dis(d)-T | łíbi'dishcháázh |
| Dpl | | | | | | | | | | |
| 1 | Cí- | + | --- | + | --- | + | -sii(d)-T | > | Císii(d)-T | bísii'na' |
| 2 | Cí- | + | --- | + | --- | + | -soo(h)-T | > | Císoo(h)-T | bísooh'na' |

P-í#-(si)--(d)'na': rub against P (as against a tree) (yés'na': he rubbed against it; shés'na': it rubbed against me - as a cat)
k'í#-(si)--lwod: keep right on running (as after stumbling and falling)(k'ísíswod: I kept right on running)
k'í#-(si)--(d)t'a': keep right on flying (as a wounded bird) (k'ést'a')

## Céé- ~ Cíná-: Contraction 1b + 1d

## Table 7

The Cí- prefixes (P-í-, k'í-, ch'í-) commonly contract with ná-: Position 1d, Reversionary marker. The contracted form remains throughout the paradigm, except in the 3rd person and Simple Passive constructions, where ná- reemerges.

| PERSON Sgl | | Sgl | Sgl |
|---|---|---|---|
| 1 | k'ééséłdǫǫd | béésískwii | béésé'ą́ |
| 2 | k'éésíníłdǫǫd | béésíníłkwii | béésíní'ą́ |
| 3 | k'ínásdǫǫd | yénáskwii | --- |
| SP | k'ínásdǫǫd | --- | bénást'ą́ |
| 3o | k'ínéísdǫǫd | --- | yénéíz'ą́ |
| 3a | k'ééjísdǫǫd | bééjískwii | bééjíz'ą́ |
| Dpl | | Dpl | Dpl |
| 1 | k'éésiildǫǫd | béésiilkwii | béésiit'ą́ |
| 2 | k'éésoołdǫǫd | béésoołkwii | béésoo'ą́ |

k'éé- ~ k'íná#-(si)--łdǫǫd: restraighten O
k'éé- ~ k'íná#-(si)--Ødǫǫd: resume erect posture
béé- ~ béná#-(si)--lkwii: vomit (it) up
béé- ~ béná#-(si)--Ø'ą́: dip/dunk a SRO in it (as a doughnut in coffee)

The contraction also occurs before a prefix of Position 6 and before the distributive plural marker da-, as in:

k'éédasiildǫǫd: we 3+ restraightened it
bééhéttł'in: I piled them (3+ O) onto it one after another

## *NEUTER VERBS*

The Si-Perfective Neuter Verbs include two broad stative theme categories:

(1) The Positionals, and
(2) The Conditionals

(1) The **Positionals** occur intransitive and causative-transitive, Passive and Mediopassive. They describe a subject as an entity in an enduring state of rest resulting from cessation of motion, including "handling" and terminal action.

Simple Si-Perfective Neuters derived from the "handle" stems are equivalent to "sit, lie, be in position" with reference to the object classes, while those derived from posture stems reflect the terminal result of action performed by the subject or the object in assuming the posture (sit down, be seated, sit; lie down, be in a reclining position, lie; be kept in a reclining position). In addition, a few simple Si-Perfective Neuter Positionals are metaphorical derivatives of particular motion stems, the connotations of which imply an object that possesses particular physical characterisitics: e.g. zhóód: heavy bulky object moves . Neuter Positional shizhóód: heavy bulky object sits – as a boulder.

The several types of simple Positionals are illustrated below:

(a) The "handle" stems classifiy subject or object on the basis of physical characteristics, animacy or number:

SRO: si'ą́ / séł'ą́: it sits / I have or keep it sitting
'Ásaa' bikáá'adání bikáa'gi dah si'ą́: the pot is on the table
'Ásaa' bikáá'adání bikáa'gi dah séł'ą́: I keep the pot on the table

OC: siką́ / sétką́: it sits in an open container / I keep an open container and its contents
Tó béésh bii'kǫ'í bikáa'gi dah siką́: the open container of water is on the stove
Tó béésh bii'kǫ'í bikáa'gi dah sétką́: I keep an open container of water on the stove

Similarly:

SFO: silá / sélá (belt, rope, anything in pairs)
SSO: sitą́ / séłtą́ (pencil, rifle, pole)
LPB: siyį́ / séłhį́ (load, pack, bulky object)
MM: sitłéé' / séłtłéé' (mud, mush, putty)
NCM: shijool / shéłjool (tuft of wool, wig)
FFO: siłtsooz / séłtsooz (sheet of paper, shirt)
AnO: sitį́ / biséłtį́ (dog, cat, baby)
PIO sinil / sélnil (several objects)
PIO shijaa' / shéłjaa' (profusion of objects)

Huge: shizhóód / shéshóód: it sits / I have it sitting (a big heavy object – something which moves or is moved in a heavy dragging manner – as a boulder)

Streaming: siziid / sésiid: it lies / I have it lying (sand, gravel, liquid – something moved by streaming or pouring)
Spreading: sikaad / (bi)séłkaad: it lies / I keep it (a bush or plant – something that moves or lies spreading, as falling marbles, a brick wall, water - or that is characterized by spreading shape, as a bush or tree)
Draping: sibaal / séłbaal: it hangs / I keep it hanging (as an awning – something that moves curtainlike, swaying, as a curtain, tarpaulin, tent, awning)

(b) The "Posture" stems describe a subject or object, primarily animate, in a sitting, reclining or standing position. Si-Perfective Neuters "be sitting / be lying" result from the *terminal* action involved in sitting or lying down, while "be standing" results from the Transitional action involved in standing up – i.e. changing from a sitting, reclining or other posture to one in which the subject or object is on his feet. In each instance it is the subject or the object who performs the action involved – if in the capacity of object, the action is caused by an agent, but performed by the object. When transitivized, sit / lie / stand verbs require an object pronoun, here represented by a null postposition of Position 1a, irrespective of subject, to represent the animate object that the agent caused to perform the act. (See Position 1a.) Compare:

neezdá: he sat down ('ashkii tsásk'eh yikáa'gi dah neezdá: the boy sat down on the bed)
binéłdá: I seated him (caused him to sit down)('ashkii tsásk'eh yikáa'gi dah binéłdá: I seated the boy on the bed)
sidá: he is sitting ('ashkii tsásk'eh yikáa'gi dah sidá: the boy is sitting on the bed)
biséłdá: I have him seated (cause him to be in a seated position)('awéé' tsásk'eh bikáa'gi dah biséłdá: I'm holding the baby in a sitting position on the bed; tsésǫ'gi tsídiiłtsooí biséłdá: I keep a canary in my window)

Similarly:

neeztį́: he lay down
binéłtį́: I made him lie down
sitį́: he's lying down
biséłtį́: I have him in a reclining position ('awéé' bikáá'adání bikáa'gi dah biséłtį́: I'm holding the baby in a reclining position on the table; łééchąą'í hooghandi biséłtį́: I keep a dog at home)

neezhtéézh: they two lay down
binéłtéézh: I made them (2) lie down
shitéézh: they two are lying
bishéłtéézh: I have two of them in a reclining position (hooghandi łééchąą'í naaki bishéłtéézh: I keep two dogs at home)

But:

yiizį': he stood up
biisį́' (< biiłzį́'): I stood him up
sizį́: he's standing
bisésį́: I have it standing, hold it in a standing position (shichidí hooghan bine'jí bisésį́: I keep my car behind the hogan – a car's wheels are referred to as bijáád: its legs, so it is treated as though it were animate

in bisésį: I cause it to be in a standing position. 'Awéé' bikáá'adání bikáa'gi dah bisésį: I'm holding the baby in a standing position on the table)

(2) The **Conditional Si-Perfective Neuter Verbs** describe the status of the subject, as:

sido: it (a thing) is hot
sik'az: it (a thing) is cold)
sit'é: it is cooked, roasted, done
shibéézh: it is boiled
sigan: it is withered, dried up\
siłkid: it is adjusted (as a gunsight)
shiyish: it is bowed, arched, warped

Many Si-Perfective Neuter Verbs are fully conjugated for person — the only constraint in this regard is semantic.

The \ ´/-Perfective Mode marker appears on the 1st and 2nd person sgl of Ø/L-class verbs, and in the 2nd person sgl of D/L-class verbs; it is absent in 3rd person.

When preceded by another prefix, si- reduces to -z- ~ -zh- /-s- ~ -sh- in the absence of a prefix of Position 8 (i.e. in the 3rd person and Passive constructions). -Z- or -zh- represents si- if the Verb Theme contains a Ø-classifier; it takes the shape -s- or -sh- in the presence of any other classifier (-zh-/-sh- result from assimilation to a stem-initial consonant j, zh, or sh).

The sgl and dpl paradigms of the Si-Perfective Neuter follow a simple inflectional pattern with the exception of the 3rd person of D/L-class verbs, which, like the Simple Passive of Ø/Ł-class verbs, requires a "dummy" yi-prefix.

dah yishdloozh: he is stooped over

Si-Perfective Neuter

## Base Paradigm

Table 1

| | Ø/Ł-Class | | D/L-Class | |
|---|---|---|---|---|
| 1 | sé-T | sézį́ | sis-T | sistin |
| 2 | síní-T | sínízį́ | síní-T | sínítin |
| 3 | si- | sizį́ | yis-T | yistin |
| Dpl | | | | |
| 1 | sii(d)-T | siidzį́ | sii(d)-T | siitin |
| 2 | soo-T | soozį́ | soo(h)-T | soohtin |

(si)--Øzį́: be in a standing position
(si)--Økwii: feel nauseated (sékwii: I feel nauseated)
(si)--Øk'ai': be spread-legged (sék'ai': I have my legs spread)
kéé' (si)--Ø'eez: have shoes on (kéé' si'eez: he has shoes on)
(shi)--ljool: be huddled, hunched; cower(shishjool: I sit huddled or hunched; yishjool: he sits huddled)
dah (shi)--ljįįd: be on haunches, squat (dah shishjįįd: I'm squatting on my haunches; dah yishjįįd: he's on his haunches)

## Extended Base Paradigms

### 1. Conjunct Prefixes

Prefixes of Position 5 + Base

Table 2

| PERSON | Ø/Ł-Class 5 | Base | | as in: | D/L-Class 5 | Base | | as in: |
|---|---|---|---|---|---|---|---|---|
| 3a | ji- | -z-T | >. jiz-T | jizzį́ | ji- | -s-T | > jis-T | jishjool |
| 3i | 'a- | -z-T | > 'az-T | 'aztą́ | 'a- | -s-T | > 'as-T | 'asdá |
| 3s | ha- | -z-T | > haz-T | haz'ą́ | ha- | -s-T | > has-T | haszéé' |
| AP | --- | --- | --- | --- | O'di(d)- | -s-T | > O'dis-T | bi'dishdléézh |

ji-(-z-)--Øzį́: he's standing
'a-(-z-)--Øtą́: something slender/rigid lies (shich'ijí 'aztą́: I'm lucky; I have a lucky streak - literally, something slender/rigid lies on my side)
ha-(-z-)--Ø'ą́: area lies (haz'ą́: area lies/misfortune lies, as in shąąh dah haz'ą́: I'm sick - literally, a misfortune lies up alongside me)
ji-(-s-)--ljool: he sits huddled
'a-(-s-)--(d)-dá: someone (a person) sits ('awáalya 'asdá: jail sentence; literally, a person sits in jail)(The theme for [si]--Ødá: sgl sits has Ø-classifier except in 3i person where 'asdá implies d-classifier.)
ha-(s-)--(d)tin: area is frozen (Cf. sistin: I'm frozen)

ha-(s-)--(d)tin: area is frozen (Cf. sistin: I'm frozen)
ha-(-s-)--(l)zéé': it's quiet, calm, peaceful

<u>Prefixes of Position 4 + Extended Base</u>

<u>Table 3</u>

Semantically, the line of demarcation between simple Si-Perfective Neuter and simple Si-Perfective Active (Conclusive) Verbs is blurred in the sense that, in both such constructions a subject has completed a process and <u>he is</u> as a sequel or <u>he has it</u> in a completed status. Thus:

'aghaa' sédiz: I spun the wool (I have it in spun status)
hooghandi 'aghaa' ła' shéłjool: I keep some wool at home (I have it in location at home)

(But cf. dah sé'ą́/dah sétą́: I set SRO/SSO - as a book/rifle - in position up at an elevation. Naaltsoos/bee'eldǫǫh tsásk'eh bikáa'gi dah sé'ą́/sétą́.)

If the direct object is inanimate it is represented in the simple Si-Perfective Neuter Verbs by a direct object pronoun of Position 4. The object has no independent control over its placement or status but is moved into or maintained in position by an agent, the subject.

<u>Inanimate O</u>

| PERSON | Prefix Position | | | | | | | |
|---|---|---|---|---|---|---|---|---|
| Sgl | 4 | + | 5 | + | Base | | | as in: |
| 1. | Ø | + | --- | + | sé- | > | sé-T | séł'ą́ |
| 2. | Ø | + | --- | + | síní- | > | síní-T | sínił'ą́ |
| 3o. | yi- | + | --- | + | -z-/-s- | > | yiz-/yis-T | yis'ą́ |
| 3a. | Ø | + | -ji- | + | -z-/-s- | > | jiz-/jis-T | jis'ą́ |
| Dpl | | | | | | | | |
| 1. | Ø | + | --- | + | sii(d)- | > | sii(d)-T | siil'ą́ |
| 2 | Ø | + | --- | + | soo- | > | soo-T | sooł'ą́ |

(si)--ł'ą́: have a SRO in position, keep O (SRO)(as a book, bottle)
(si)--tą́: have a SSO in position, keep O (SSO - as a gun)

## Animate O

When the object maintained in position is animate it is represented by a null postposition of Position 1a because, although an agent (the subject) causes the object to maintain a posture, the actual posture (as reclining, sitting, standing) is a status assumed and maintained by the object, utilizing its own powers. (See Position 1a.)

PERSON Prefix Position

| Sgl | 1a | + | 5 | + | Base | | | as in: |
|---|---|---|---|---|---|---|---|---|
| 1. | Ci- | + | --- | + | sé- | > | Cisé-T | biséłtį́ |
| 2. | Ci- | + | --- | + | síní- | > | Cisíní-T | bisíníłtį́ |
| 3o. | yi- | + | --- | + | yiis- | > | yiyiis-T | yiyiistį́* |
| 3a. | Ci | + | -j- | + | -iis- | > | Cijiis-T | bijiistį́* |
| Dpl | | | | | | | | |
| 1. | Ci- | + | --- | + | sii(d)- | > | Cisii(d)-T | bisiiltį́ |
| 2 | Ci- | + | --- | + | soo- | > | Cisoo-T | bisoołtį́ |

*The reason for which the prefix vowel lengthens before -s- in 3 and 3a persons is not apparent. In 3rd person yiyiis-T the null postposition appears to be duplicated.

(Ci-si)--łtį́: have an AnO in reclining position, keep an AnO (that reclines, as a dog)(łééchąą'í biséłtį́: I keep a dog)
Ci-(si)--łdá: have an AnO in sitting position, keep an AnO (that sits, as a caged bird)(tsídii biséłdá: I keep a bird)
Ci-(si)--łtéézh: Keep two AnO in reclining position, have two AnO that recline (łééchąą'í naaki bishéłtéézh: I keep a pair of dogs)

## Prefixes of Position 6 + Extended Base

A number of Si-Perfective Neuter Verb Bases are derived with prefixes of Positions 6a/6b, including:

dí³- extension/inception
dí²- disablement
ni²-: generic for roundness
ni¹ terminal

Di³- extension occurs in verbs that describe an object or a geographical feature that extends along to a point: a pole, a ridge, a mountain range.

tsé, dził, tsin, deez'á: a rock, mountain, pole extends out to a point
tsé deesgai: rock ridge extends white
tsé deeshchii': rock ridge extends red
tsé deeshjin: rock ridge extends black

A Base derived with di³- + the Theme ł'á: cause a rigid object to extend is conjugated in the same pattern as the Active di³- derivatives, as:

Table 4

| PERSON Sgl | PERSON Dpl |
|---|---|
| 1 déł'á | 1 deel'á |
| 2 díníł'á | 2 disooł'á |
| 3o yidees'á | |
| 3a jidees'á | |

di-(si)--ł'á: cause a rigid object to extend to a point = hold O so it extends or sticks out to a point (as a pole)

Table 5

Dí[2]- disablement, has inherent high tone.

| PERSON Sgl | PERSON Dpl | PERSON Pl (3+) |
|---|---|---|
| 1 yah déshdá | 1 yah déeké | yah déetą́ |
| 2 yah dínídá | 2 yah dóoké | yah dóotą́ |
| 3 yah déesdá | 3 yah déeské | yah déestą́ |
| 3a yah jidéesdá | 3a yah jidéeské | yah jidéestą́ |

dí-(si)--(d)dá: sit waiting for aid (1 subject)
dí-(si)--Økė: sit waiting for aid (2 subjects)
dí-(si)--Øtą́: sit waiting for aid (3+ subjects)

Table 6

Ni[2]- generic classifier for round shape appears high in tone as the derivational agent in a Si-Perfective Neuter Mediopassive meaning "have one's head (i.e. subject's own round object) in position:" ni[2]- elides its vowel but retains the high tone before a vowel. (Cf. nininisht'ą́: I laid my head down.)

| PERSON Sgl | PERSON Dpl |
|---|---|
| 1 nésh'ą́ | 1 néel'ą́ |
| 2 nínił'ą́ | 2 nóoł'ą́ |
| 3o nées'ą́ | |
| 3a jinées'ą́ | |

(As in mósí sitsék'eegi nées'ą́: the cat has its head in my lap.)(Cf. mósí sitsék'eegi nineet'ą́: the cat laid its head in my lap.)

Ni[1]- terminative appears in derivatives of the type:

neezgai: it hurts, it is painful (literally, it is hot)
neezzílí: it is tepid, warm (as water)
neestin: it hangs (a cloud of mist, smoke, dust)

## Prolongative Neuter

There is a Neuter Verb category, here arbitrarily treated as Si-Perfective, that is conjugated in part like a yí-ní-directive, in part like a Si-Perfective. Verbs of this type take a Perfective stem and a compound Conjunct Prefix (dí-ní-, dí-[y]í-ní, hí-ní) which may be further modified by the addition of Disjunct (Position 1b) adverbial elements. Identity of the Position 6 prefixes is uncertain.

First person sgl subject is represented by -sh-: Position 8, and 2nd person dpl subject is represented by -o(h)-. Si- (-z-/-s-) appears only in 3rd person.

dí-ní- (= dí-: Position 6a + ni-:Position 6b) or optionally:

dí-í-ní- (= dí-6a + [y]í-6a directive[?] + ni-6b), or again optionally, in 1st person sgl, as dé-.

A speculative analysis of dí-ní- suggests the possibility that dí- < d(i)- + (y)í- + ni-; and for dí-í-ní- < di- + (y)í- + ní. (2nd person sgl: díní-T)

Hí- appears to be a syllabic Conjunct Prefix with inherent high tone. (2nd person sgl: hííní-T)

Again, di$^{3}$-6a: inception + ni$^{1}$-6b: termination are identifiable as the elements that combine to produce the dini-Prolongatives, as Yi-Perfective biih dineestsi: I stuck it in and got it stuck (as a key); biih dinees'eez: I stepped into it and got my foot stuck; and with díní- (high in tone) hadínéshcha: I cried and cried; hadínéshgį́: I hauled it too far. Possibly, the díní- of Neuter dííshch'a: I'm holding my mouth open, déezhch'a: he's holding his mouth open, is the same Prolongative marker as that of hadínéshcha and hadínéshgį́.

Individual speakers vary in their choice of forms in 1st person sgl and dpl, and in 2nd person sgl.

The paradigms that follow illustrate this class of Neuter Perfectives.

Table 7

| PERSON Sgl | | as in: | |
|---|---|---|---|
| 1 | dínísh-T<br>dííním-T<br>désh-T | dínishch'a<br>déshch'a | k'ídíníshnii'<br>k'ídííníshnii'<br>k'ídéshnii' |
| 2 | díní-T<br>dííní-T | díních'a | k'ídííníłnii' |
| 3 | dées-/-z-T | déezhch'a | k'ídéesnii' |
| 3o | -idées-T | --- | k'íidées'á |
| 3a | jidéez-/-s-T | jidéezhch'a | k'ízhdéesnii' |
| Dpl | | | |
| 1 | díníí(d)-T<br>dííníí(d)-T | díníích'a | k'ídííníílnii' |
| 2 | dínó(h)-T | dínóhch'a | k ídíínółnii" |

dí-í-ní- ~ díní-(si)--Øch'a: hold mouth open (Corresponds to Active Transitional diich'ee': I opened my mouth)

dí-ní-(si)--l'eez: hold foot in position (tsídzi' díníś'eez ~ dés'eez: I'm holding my foot in the fire (Corresponds to Active Yi-Perfective dees'eez, as in tsídza dees'eez: I put my foot in the fire)

dí-ní-(si)--lnii': hold hand in position (tsídzi' díníshnii' ~ déshnii': I'm holding my hand in the fire)( Corresponds to Active Yi-Perfective deeshnii', as in tsídza deeshnii': I put my hand into the fire)

dí-ní-(si)--łhéél: be quiet, still, calm (díníshhéél: I'm quiet, still; déesxéél: he's quiet)(Corresponds to Active Transitional diiłheel: I became quiet, calm)

k'í#-dí-ní- ~ k'í#-dí-í-ní-(si)--ł'á: hold O (rigid object) out straight (as a stick, pencil)(k'ídínísh'á ~ k'ídíínísh'á: I'm holding it straight out)

k'í#-dí-ní- ~ k'í#-dí-í-ní-(si)--lnii': have arms outstretched (k'ídíníshnii' ~ k'ídííníshnii' ~ k'ídéshnii': I have my arms outstretched; k'ídéesnii': he has his arms outstretched)

dá#-dí-ní- ~ dí-í-ní-(si)--tsxa: have the mouth clamped shut; have lockjaw (dádínístsxa ~ dádíínístsxa ~ dádéstsxa: I have my mouth clamped shut)

bí#-díní- ~ bí#-dí-í-ní-(si)--ł(l)o': have the brake on it; keep the brake on it (bídíníshło' ~ bídííníshło': I'm holding the brake on; yídéesło': he's holding the brake on)

P-zák'í#-dí-í-ní-(si)--ł(l)o': have a stranglehold on P with a cord (bizák'ídííníshło': I have a stranglehold on him; yizák'ídéesło': he has a stranglehold on him)

dáá#-dí-í-ní- ~ díní- ~ dé- (si)--lnii': hold a hand over it closing it (as a mouth)(bizéé' dáádíníshnii': I have my hand over its mouth, closing it)

dáá#-dí-í-ní-(si)--Øzį́: stand blocking an opening – as a gate or exit (dáádííníssį́: I stand blocking the way; dáádéezzį́: he stands blocking the way)
ntsi#-dí-í-ní-(si)--lgo': be on one's knees; be kneeling (ntsidííníshgo': I'm on my knees; ntsidéesgo': he's on his knees)
ya#-dí-í-ní-(si)--lnii': hold one's hands up (yadííníshnii': I have my hands up; yadéesnii'; he has his hands up)

<u>Hí-ni-: Position 6a/b + Extended Base</u>

<u>Table 8</u>

| PERSON | | as in: | |
|---|---|---|---|
| Sgl | híní- | Sgl | Pl (3+) |
| 1. | hínísh-T | hínísht̨į́ | héejéé' |
| 2. | hííní-T | híínítí̧ | híshóojéé' |
| 3. | hées-T | héestį́ | héeshjéé' |
| 3a. | jíís-T | jíístį́ | jíishjéé' |
| Dpl | | Dual | Dist. Pl |
| 1. | hée(d)-T | héetéézh | daháajéé' |
| 2. | híshóo-T | híshóotéézh | dahíshóojéé' |
| 3. | hées-T | héeshtéézh | daháashjéé' |
| 3a. | jíís-T | jíishtéézh | dajíishjéé' |

baa hí-ní-(si)--Øtį́: waylay him; lie in ambush for him (one subject)
baa hí-ní-(si)--Øtéézh: lie in ambush for him (two subjects)(baa héetéézh: we 2 lie in ambush for him
baa hí-ní-(si)--Øjéé': lie in ambush for him (three subjects)(baa héejéé': we 3+ lie in ambush for him; baa daháajéé': we 3+ individually lie in ambush for him)

## 2. Disjunct Prefixes

<u>Prefixes of Position 1 + Extended Base</u>

P-í-: against, in contact with P; ha- < ´ká- ~ ´ka-: after (to get); and Semeliterative náá- ~ nááná-: once again, another, occur with Si-Perfective Neuter. And the distributive plural for the Positionals is formed with na[1]-1b: around about , plus or minus da-: Position 3, distributive plural marker. (See Pluralization of Si-Perfective Neuter Positionals, pp. 249-250. )

P-í-: Position 1b + Extended Base

Table 1A
Ø/Ł-Class Verbs

| PERSON | | | | | | |
|---|---|---|---|---|---|---|
| Sgl | | | Base | | | as in: |
| 1. | bí- | + | -sé-T | > | bísé-T | bísésį́ |
| 2. | bí- | + | -síní-T | > | bísíní-T | bísínísį́ |
| 3. | yé- | + | -z-/-s-T | > | yéz-/s/-T | yéssį́ |
| 3a. | bíjí | + | -z-/-s-T | > | bíjíz-/-s-T | bíjíssį́ |
| Dpl | | | | | | |
| 1. | bí- | + | -sii(d)-T | > | bísii(d)-T | bísiilzį́ |
| 2. | bí- | + | -soo-T | > | bísoo-T | bísoosį́ |

bí-(si)--łsį́ (< łzį́): stand guarding it; stand waiting for him
bí-(si)--łdá: sit guarding it; sit waiting for him (1 subject)
bí-(si)--łké: sit guarding it; sit waiting for him (2 subjects)

Table 1B
D/L-Class Verbs

| PERSON | | | | | | |
|---|---|---|---|---|---|---|
| Sgl | | | Base | | | as in: |
| 1. | P-í- | + | -shish-T | > | P-íshísh-T | bíshíshjéé' |
| 2. | P-í- | + | -shíní-T | > | P-íshíní-T | bíshíníljéé' |
| 3. | P-é- | + | -zh-/-sh-T | > | P-ésh-T | yéshjéé' |
| 3a. | P-í- | + | -zh-/-sh-T | > | P-íjísh-T | bíjíshjéé' |
| Dpl | | | | | | |
| 1. | P-í- | + | -shii(d)-T | > | P-íshii(d)-T | bíshiiljéé' |
| 2. | P-í- | + | -shoo(h)-T- | > | P-íshoo(h)-T | bíshooɫjéé' |

P-í-(si)--ljéé': snuggle up to him/her; sit or lie close against him/her/it; sit or lie hugging him/her/it ('awéé' bimá yéshjée'go yił shitéézh: the baby lies snuggled close to its mother)

Ha-: Position 1b + Extended Base

Table 2

Verb Bases constructed with ha- (< ´ká- ~ ´ka-): after O (to get it) are conjugated in the same patterns as Active Si-Perfective Verb Bases produced with a Disjunct Ca-prefix of Position 1b (as ha-: up; up out).

The direct object, in transitive Verb Bases of this type, is not the thing that the subject goes after but the instrument or intermediary that he uses for the purpose. Thus:

haséł'a': I sent him after (it) (As in 'adą́ą́dą́ą́' shiye' dziłgóó chizh haséł'a': yesterday I sent my son to the mountain for firewood – he has completed the mission and is now back home)

haséyá: I went for it (making a round trip)
ha'séłbą́ą́z: I drove after (it)(in an unspecified wagon or car)(as in 'adą́ą́dą́ą́' dziłgóó chizh ha'séłbą́ą́z: I drove to the mountain for firewood yesterday – and I am now back, having completed the mission)

T = any Verb Theme

| PERSON | Prefix Position | | | | | | | Transitive | | Intransitive |
|---|---|---|---|---|---|---|---|---|---|---|
| Sgl | 1b | + | 4 | + | Base | | | +'(a)-4 | + Ø-4 | |
| 1. | ha- | + | '(a)-/Ø | + | sé-T | > | ha'sé-T | ha'séłbą́ą́z | hasééł'a' | haséyá |
| 2. | ha- | + | '(a)-/Ø | + | síní-T | > | ha'síní-T | ha'síníłbą́ą́z | hasíníł'a' | hasíníyá |
| 3 | ha- | + | 'a-/-- | + | -z-/-s-T | > | ha'az-/s-T | ha'asbą́ą́z | --- | haayá |
| 3o | ha- | + | -i- | + | -z-/-s-T | > | haiz-/s-T | --- | hais'a' | --- |
| 3a. | ha- | + | '(a)-/Ø | + | jiz-/-s-T | > | ha'jiz-/-s-T | ha'jisbą́ą́z | hajis'a' | hajiyá |
| AP | ha- | + | O | + | -'dis-T | > | haO'dis-T | --- | habi'dis'a' | --- |
| Dpl | | | | | | | | | | |
| 1. | ha- | + | '(a)-/Ø | + | -sii(d)-T | > | ha'sii(d)-T | ha'siilbą́ą́z | hasiil'a' | hashiit'áázh |
| 2 | ha- | + | '(a)-/Ø | + | -soo-T | > | ha'soo-T | ha'soołbą́ą́z | hasooł'a' | hashoo'áázh |

ha#-'a-(si)--łbą́ą́z: drive to get (it)(in an unspecified vehicle)
ha#-'a-(si)--ł'éél: go after (it) (in an unspecified floating vehicle – a boat)
ha#-'a-(si)--łt'a': fly after (it)(in an unspecified flying vehicle – a plane)
ha#-'a-(si)--ł'a': send O after (it)

Semeliterative náá- ~ nááná- combines with a Si-Perfective Positional to convey the meaning "another (one sits)," as:

kéyah si'ą́: a land or country lies
kéyah náánást'ą́: another land or country lies

## Distributive Pluralization of Si-Perfective Neuter Positionals

The Si-Perfective Neuter Positionals are pluralized to specify 3+ subjects by adding na[1]-: Position 1b: around about, here and there, or na[1]- + da-: Position 3: distributive plural marker, to the Base. (Some Positionals – those involving posture – have number-specific stems, marking sgl, dual and plural.) Compare:

'atiin bąąhgi tózis ła' si'ą́: there's a bottle lying beside the road / 'atiin bąąhgi tózis t'óó ahayóí naaz'ą́: there are many bottles lying about beside the road

béégashii bináníigi sitį́: the cow is lying on the hillside / béégashii bináníigi shitéézh: two cows are lying on the hillside / béégashii bináníigi shijéé': the 3+ cows are lying on the hillside (in a group), but béégashii bináníigi naazhjéé': the 3+ cows are lying on the hillside (individually or in scattered groups of 3 or more subjects in each)

With a stem that marks dual number na- pluralizes pairs, as in béégashii bináníigi naazhtéézh: the cows are lying in 3+ scattered pairs on the hillside.

And if the stem is sgl na- pluralizes individual subjects, as: béégashii bináníigi naaztį́: the 3+ cows are lying about singly on the hillside - one here, one there.

The Yi-Perfective Neuter Extensionals and the derived Ni-Perfective Neuter Extensionals shift to Si-Perfective when distributive plurality is marked by da-: Position 3, as:

Yi-Perfective: tsin ła' 'íí'á: a tree stands / tsin t'óó ahayóí 'adaaz'á: many trees stand

bitsee' 'a'ą́ą́dęę́' háá'á: its tail sticks up out of the hole / bitsee' 'a'ą́ą́dęę́' hadaaz'á: their 3+ tails stick up out of the hole

Ni-Perfective: tsah naaltsoos bighání'á: the awl sticks through the paper / tsah naaltsoos bighádaaz'á: the 3+ awls stick through the paper

tsin tsésǫ'dęę́' ch'íní'á: a pole sticks out the window / tsin tsésǫ'dęę́' ch'ídaaz'á: 3+ poles stick out the window

but

dził ní'á: a mountain range lies, extends; dził daní'á: mountain ranges lie/extend

## RECAPITULATION

The inflection of Active and Neuter Si-Perfective Verbs is recapitulated in succinct form in the paradigms that follow.

### 1. Extended Base Paradigm

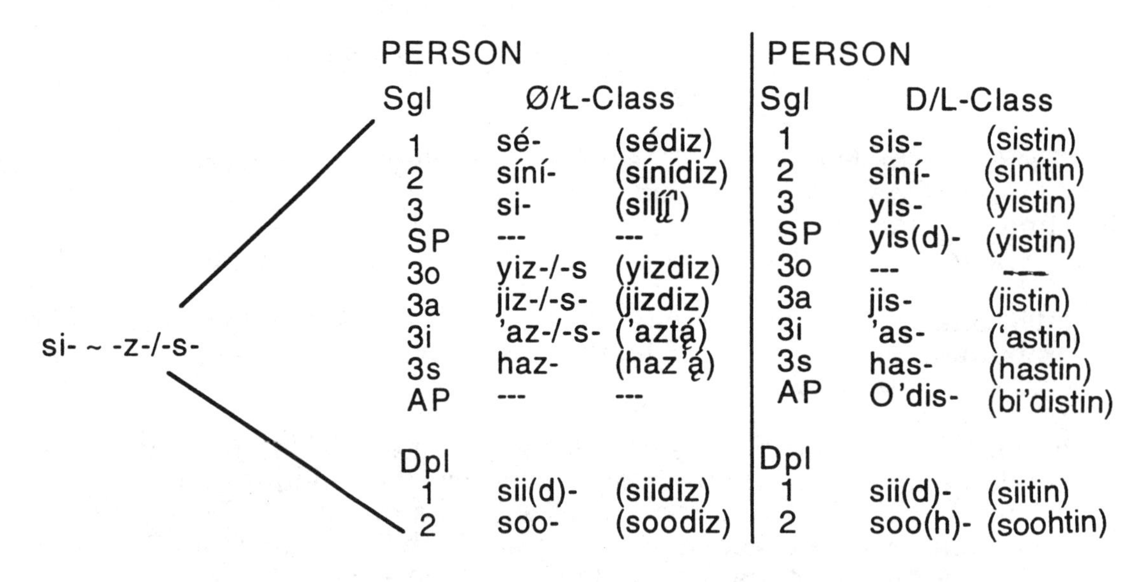

si- ~ -z-/-s-

| PERSON Sgl | Ø/Ł-Class | | PERSON Sgl | D/L-Class | |
|---|---|---|---|---|---|
| 1 | sé- | (sédiz) | 1 | sis- | (sistin) |
| 2 | síní- | (sínídiz) | 2 | síní- | (sínítin) |
| 3 | si- | (silį́į́') | 3 | yis- | (yistin) |
| SP | --- | --- | SP | yis(d)- | (yistin) |
| 3o | yiz-/-s | (yizdiz) | 3o | --- | --- |
| 3a | jiz-/-s- | (jizdiz) | 3a | jis- | (jistin) |
| 3i | 'az-/-s- | ('aztą́) | 3i | 'as- | ('astin) |
| 3s | haz- | (haz'ą́) | 3s | has- | (hastin) |
| AP | --- | --- | AP | O'dis- | (bi'distin) |
| Dpl | | | Dpl | | |
| 1 | sii(d)- | (siidiz) | 1 | sii(d)- | (siitin) |
| 2 | soo- | (soodiz) | 2 | soo(h)- | (soohtin) |

(si)--Ødiz: spin O (yarn)
(si)--Ø'ą́: SRO sits/lies
(si)--Ødá: 1 subject sits
(si)--Øtą́: SSO sits/lies

(si)--(d)tin: freeze
(si)--ljool: lie huddled
(si)--Ølį́į́': become

## *CONJUNCT PREFIXES*

### 2. Ci-Prefixes of Position 4 + Extended Base

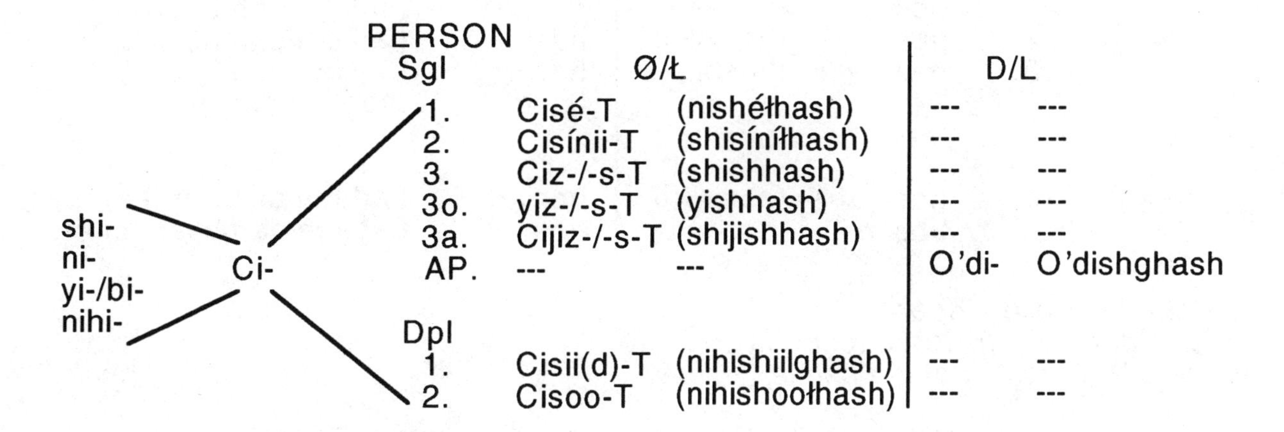

shi- / ni- / yi-/bi- / nihi- → Ci-

| PERSON | Ø/Ł | | D/L | |
|---|---|---|---|---|
| Sgl | | | | |
| 1. | Cisé-T | (nishéłhash) | --- | --- |
| 2. | Cisínii-T | (shisíníłhash) | --- | --- |
| 3. | Ciz-/-s-T | (shishhash) | --- | --- |
| 3o. | yiz-/-s-T | (yishhash) | --- | --- |
| 3a. | Cijiz-/-s-T | (shijishhash) | --- | --- |
| AP. | --- | --- | O'di- | O'dishghash |
| Dpl | | | | |
| 1. | Cisii(d)-T | (nihishiilghash) | --- | --- |
| 2. | Cisoo-T | (nihishoołhash) | --- | --- |

ni-(si)--łhash: bite you (nishéłhash: I bit you; shishhash: it bit me)

### 3. 'A-: Position 4 + Extended Base

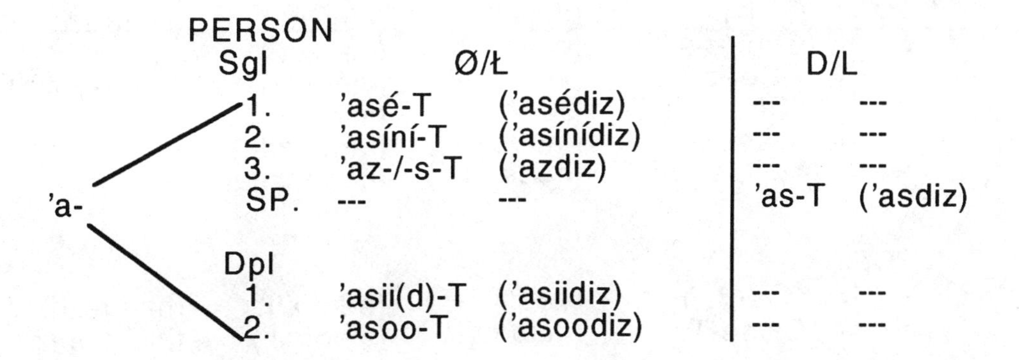

'a-

| PERSON | Ø/Ł | | D/L | |
|---|---|---|---|---|
| Sgl | | | | |
| 1. | 'asé-T | ('asédiz) | --- | --- |
| 2. | 'asíní-T | ('asínídiz) | --- | --- |
| 3. | 'az-/-s-T | ('azdiz) | --- | --- |
| SP. | --- | --- | 'as-T | ('asdiz) |
| Dpl | | | | |
| 1. | 'asii(d)-T | ('asiidiz) | --- | --- |
| 2. | 'asoo-T | ('asoodiz) | --- | --- |

'a-(si)--Ødiz: spin (yarn); do the spinning ('azdiz: she did the spinning)

## 4. Ho-: Position 4 + Extended Base

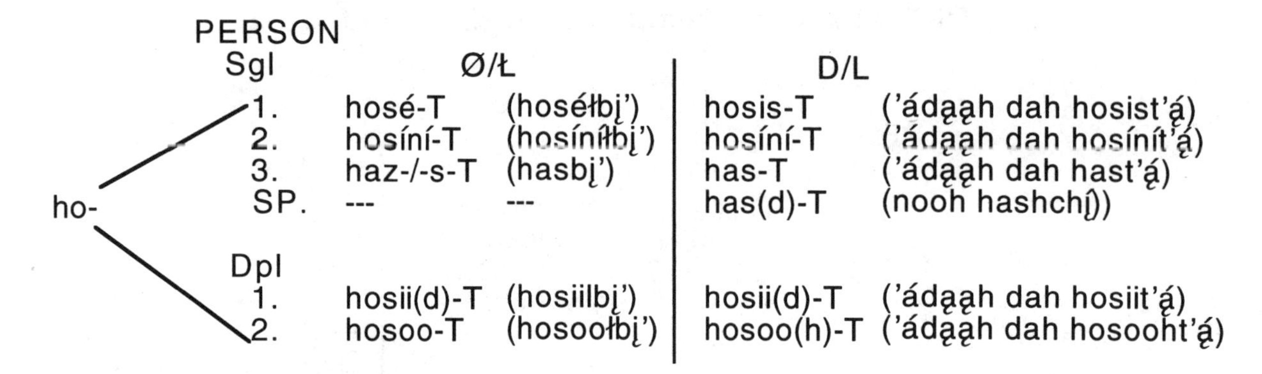

| PERSON | | Ø/Ł | | D/L | |
|---|---|---|---|---|---|
| ho- | Sgl | | | | |
| | 1. | hosé-T | (hoséłbį') | hosis-T | ('ádąąh dah hosist'ą́) |
| | 2. | hosíní-T | (hosíníłbį') | hosíní-T | ('ádąąh dah hosínít'ą́) |
| | 3. | haz-/-s-T | (hasbį') | has-T | ('ádąąh dah hast'ą́) |
| | SP. | --- | --- | has(d)-T | (nooh hashchį́) |
| | Dpl | | | | |
| | 1. | hosii(d)-T | (hosiilbį') | hosii(d)-T | ('ádąąh dah hosiit'ą́) |
| | 2. | hosoo-T | (hosoołbį') | hosoo(h)-T | ('ádąąh dah hosooht'ą́) |

ho-(si)--łbį': build a hogan
'ádąąh dah ho-(si)--(d)t'ą́: commit a crime
nooh ho-(si)--łchį́: make a cache

## 5. Prefixes of Position 6 + Extended Base

In 2nd person dpl si- usually moves to the left of ni-. Hi-Seriative appears as its yi-allomorph when preceded by a Conjunct Prefix.

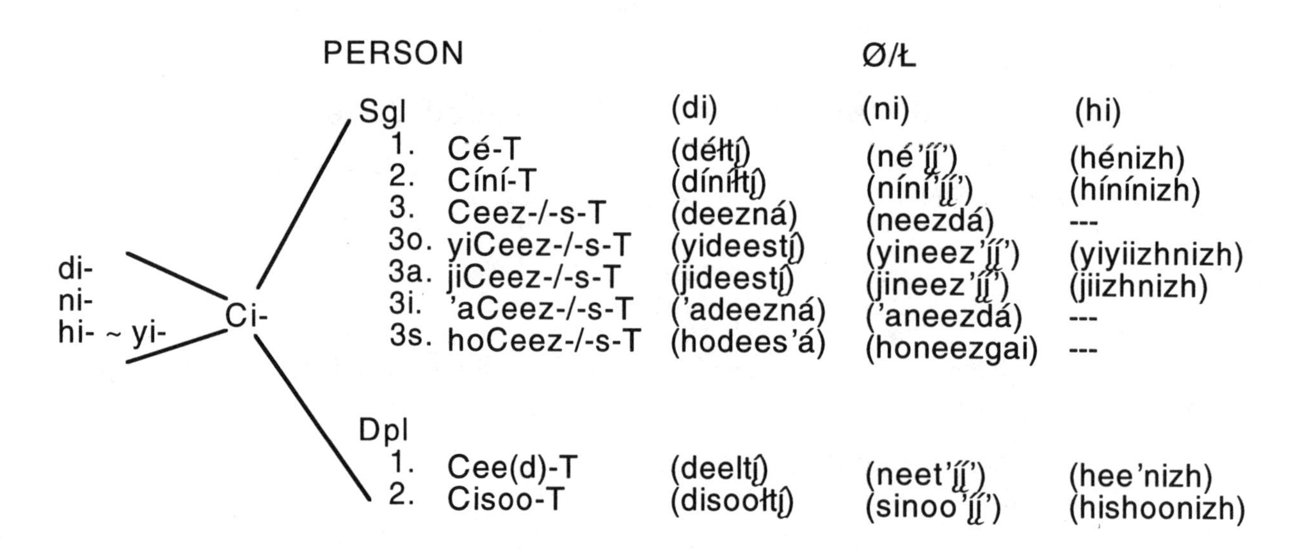

| | PERSON | | | Ø/Ł | |
|---|---|---|---|---|---|
| di- / ni- / hi- ~ yi- → Ci- | Sgl | | (di) | (ni) | (hi) |
| | 1. | Cé-T | (déłtį́) | (né'į́į́') | (hénizh) |
| | 2. | Cíní-T | (díníłtį́) | (níní'į́į́') | (hínínizh) |
| | 3. | Ceez-/-s-T | (deezná) | (neezdá) | --- |
| | 3o. | yiCeez-/-s-T | (yideestį́) | (yineez'į́į́') | (yiyiizhnizh) |
| | 3a. | jiCeez-/-s-T | (jideestį́) | (jineez'į́į́') | (jiizhnizh) |
| | 3i. | 'aCeez-/-s-T | ('adeezná) | ('aneezdá) | --- |
| | 3s. | hoCeez-/-s-T | (hodees'á) | (honeezgai) | --- |
| | Dpl | | | | |
| | 1. | Cee(d)-T | (deeltį́) | (neet'į́į́') | (hee'nizh) |
| | 2. | Cisoo-T | (disoołtį́) | (sinoo'į́į́') | (hishoonizh) |

di-(si)--Øná: to have started on the way moving with household (shił 'adeezná: I'm moving as a member of the household - literally unspecified subject is/are moving in company with me)
di-(si)--łtį́: to have started to carry an AnO along
ni-(si)--łtsiz: extinguish O (a fire)(kǫ' néłtsiz: I put the fire out)
ni-(si)--lį́į́d: squat down (neeshį́į́d: he squatted down)
hi-(si)--łhaal: hack with a scythe (héłhaal: I hacked O down; jiisxaal: he[3a subject] hacked them down - as weeds)
di-(si)--Ø'á: it extends out to a point, as a mountain or ridge (deez'á)
di-(si)--ł'á: be holding a rigid object so it extends out (as a pole)(déł'á)
ho-di-(si)--l'á: it extends (as a number or an area)(hodees'á)

ni-(si)--Ø'į́': steal O
ni-(si)--Ødá: sit down (1 subject)(shił 'aneezdá: I landed (in a plane); literally, something sat down with me; nédá: I sat down)
ho-ni-(si)--Øgai: be hot, painful(honeezgai)
hi-(si)--Ønizh: pick or pluck O (herbs, flowers)(hénizh)

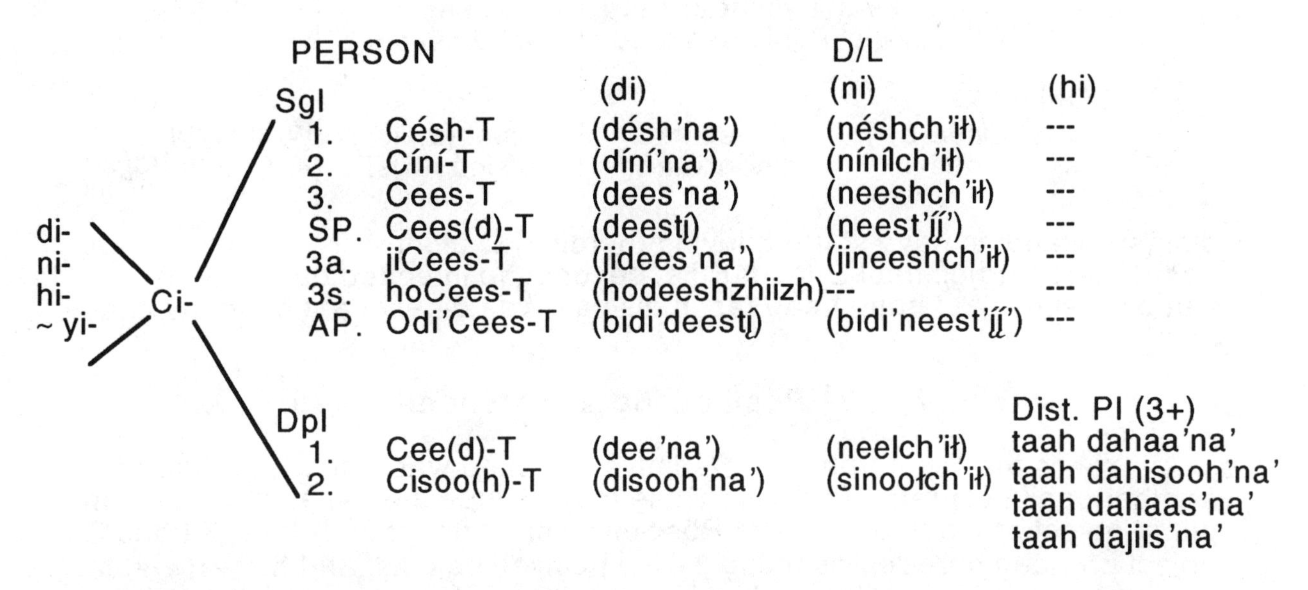


di-(si)--(d)'na': to have started on the way crawling (taah da-hi-di-[si]--[d]'na' > taah dahidee'na': crawl into the water one after another)
di-(si)--(d)'į́': be stolen (neest'į́')
di-(si)--ltį́: start to be carried along (an AnO)(deestį́)
ho-di-(si)--lzhiizh: period of time starts, era begins (hodeeshzhiizh)
ni-(si)--lch'ił: blink (néshch'ił)

### 6. Compound Di-ni-Prefix + Extended Base

Di[3]-6a and ni[7]-6b, low in tone when they occur singly, take high tone when functioning together as a compound prefix: <u>di</u>shdlaad: I start a furrow / biih <u>ni</u>shkaad: I drive them into it, but <u>díní</u>shkaad: I start to drive (herd) them along. (Di-6a + ni-6b + yi-7 > dínée-/dínóo- in Future Mode. Nishdaah: I sit down / dínéeshdaał: I'll sit down)

| PERSON Sgl | Ø/Ł-Class | | D/L-Class | |
|---|---|---|---|---|
| 1 | díné-T | dínéłkaad | dínésh-T | ha-dínéshgį́ |
| 2 | díníní-T | díníníłkaad | díníní-T | ha-díníníg į́ |
| 3 | dínéez-/-s-T | dínéezhchą́ą́' | dínées-T | yaa dínéest'ą́ |
| 3o. | yidínéez-/-s-T | yidínéeskaad | -idínées-T | ha-idínéesgį́ |
| 3a. | jidínéez-/-s-T | jidínéeskaad | -zhdínées-T | ha-zhdínéesgį́ |
| Dpl | | | | |
| 1 | dínée(d)-T | dínéelkaad | dínée(d)-T | ha-dínéegį́ |
| 2 | dínóo-T | dínóołkaad | dísínóo(h)-T | ha-dísínóohgį́ |

díní-(si)--łkaad: to have started driving (herding) O along
ha#-dí-ní-(si)--(d)gį́: haul O too far (i.e. beyond the intended destination)
yaa díní-(si)--(d)t'ą́: hang head (as in dismay)(yaa dínésht'ą́: I hung my head)

## 7. Yi3-Position 6c + Extended Base

Yi3- is the allomorph of hi-Seriative, required when hi- is preceded by another conjunct prefix. The Verb Base may include the 1st and 2nd person plural object pronoun prefixes of Position 4 (nihi-: us; you pl),'a- ~ 'i-4: the 3i object pronoun here representing 3+ unspecified objects; and ho- ~ hw-4: the 3s object pronoun in Verb Bases in which action involving 3+ objects takes place over an area. The Verb Base may include any Disjunct Prefix of Position 1, limited only by semantic constraints.

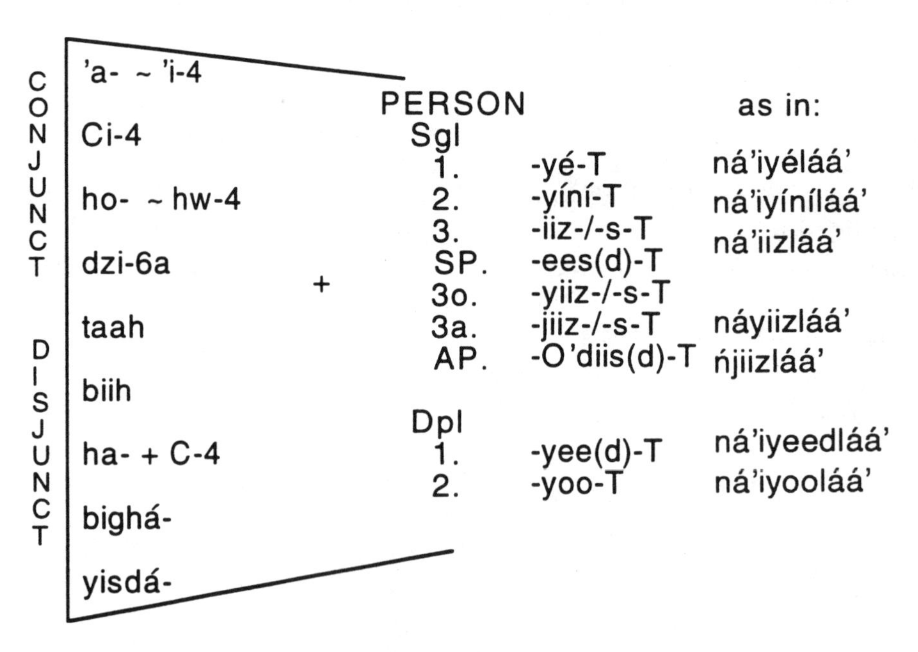


na'iyéláá' (< na-1b + 'i-4 + yéláá'): I picked pinyon nuts (literally, I gathered unspecified objects one after another)

bá 'i'iis'nil (< 'i- ~ 'a-1b + '(i)-4 + -iis'nil): he received votes (literally unspecified PIO were tossed away out of sight one after another for him)
nahoyéziid (< na--1b + ho-4 + -yéziid): I raked (around on) an area (nahwiizziid: he raked an area; nahwiidziid: we raked an area)
'adziyétáál (< 'a-1b + dzi-6a + -yétáál): I let fly a series of kicks
taah nihiizdzį́į́z(< taah: into water + nih[i]-4 + -iizdzį́į́z): he dragged us (3+) into the water one after another
hanihiishjid (< ha-1b + nih[i]-4 + -iishjid): he carried us (3+) up one after another on his back
yisdánánihiizdzį́į́z (<yisdá-1b + ná-1d + nih[i]-4 + -iizdzį́į́z): he dragged you/us (3+) back to safety one after another
háánihiyédzį́į́z: I pulled you plural back out one after another (as táyi'dę́ę́': from the water)

## 8. Yi²- ~ -oo²-: Position 6a + Extended Base

An unidentified yi- prefix of Position 6a takes the alternant shape -oo- when preceded by another Conjunct Prefix and followed by -z-/-s-.

| PERSON | | Ø/Ł | | D/L | |
|---|---|---|---|---|---|
| | Sgl | | | | |
| | 1. | yisé-T | (yisékan) | yisis-T | (yisisdląąd) |
| | 2. | yisíní-T | (yisíníkan) | yisíní-T | (yisínídląąd) |
| | 3. | --- | --- | --- | --- |
| | SP. | --- | --- | woos-T | (woosdląąd/wooskan) |
| yi- | 3o. | yooz-/-s-T | (yoozkan) | yoos-T | (yoosdląąd) |
| | 3a. | jooz-/-s-T | (joozkan) | joos-T | (joosdląąd) |
| | AP. | --- | --- | O'doos-T | (bi'doosdląąd) (bi'dooskan) |
| | Dpl | | | | |
| | 1. | yisii(d)-T | (yisiikan) | yisii(d)-T | (yisiidląąd) |
| | 2. | yisoo-T | (yisookan) | yisoo(h)-T | (yisoohdląąd) |

yi-(si)--Økan: hire O
shó#-(y)i-(si)--łt'e': acquire O (shóyoost'e': he acquired it; shóisélt'e': I acquired it)
baa yi-(si)--Ønah: forget about it (yaa yooznah: he forgot about it; baa yisénah: I forgot t))
ji-(y)i-(si)--Ølá': come to hate O (jiisélá': I came to hate O; yijooslá': he came to hate it)

## *DISJUNCT PREFIXES*

### 9. Ca-: Position 1b + Extended Base

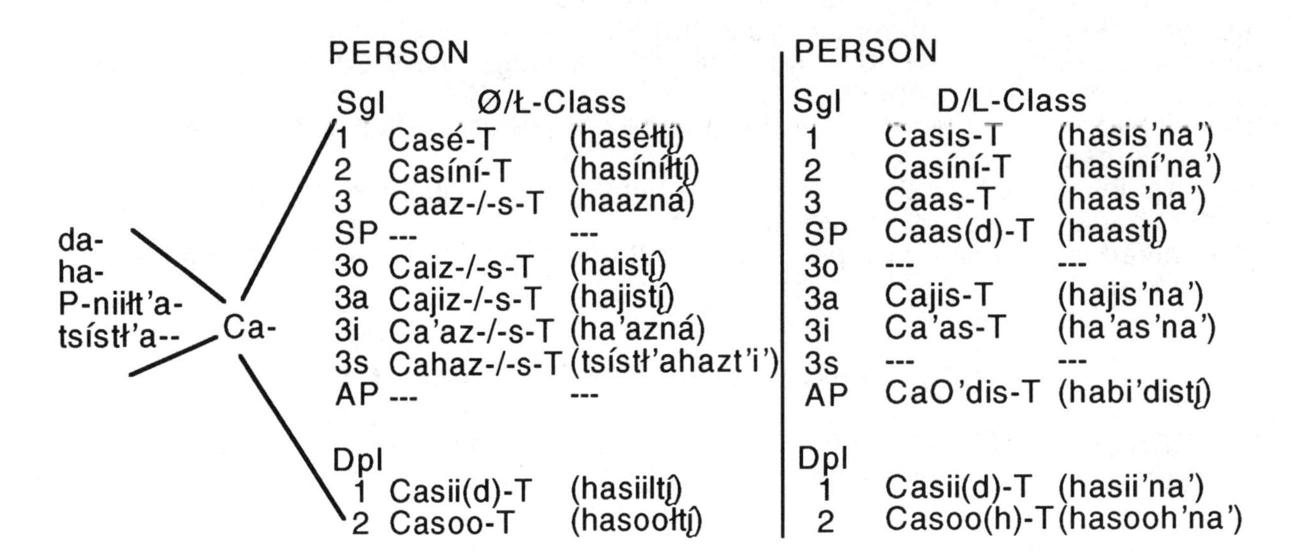


| PERSON | | | PERSON | | |
|---|---|---|---|---|---|
| Sgl | Ø/Ł-Class | | Sgl | D/L-Class | |
| 1 | Casé-T | (haséłtį) | 1 | Casis-T | (hasis'na') |
| 2 | Casíní-T | (hasíníłtį) | 2 | Casíní-T | (hasíní'na') |
| 3 | Caaz-/-s-T | (haazná) | 3 | Caas-T | (haas'na') |
| SP | --- | --- | SP | Caas(d)-T | (haastį) |
| 3o | Caiz-/-s-T | (haistį) | 3o | --- | --- |
| 3a | Cajiz-/-s-T | (hajistį) | 3a | Cajis-T | (hajis'na') |
| 3i | Ca'az-/-s-T | (ha'azná) | 3i | Ca'as-T | (ha'as'na') |
| 3s | Cahaz-/-s-T | (tsístł'ahazt'i') | 3s | --- | --- |
| AP | --- | --- | AP | CaO'dis-T | (habi'distį) |
| Dpl | | | Dpl | | |
| 1 | Casii(d)-T | (hasiiltį) | 1 | Casii(d)-T | (hasii'na') |
| 2 | Casoo-T | (hasoołtį) | 2 | Casoo(h)-T | (hasooh'na') |

ha#-(si)--łtį́: climb up carrying an AnO
ha#-(si)--Øná: move up with household (as up a mountain)
ha#-(si)--(d)'na': climb up (as up a tree)(tsin bąąh hasis'na': I climbed the tree)
da#-(si)--Øtsą́: die (sgl subject)(daaztsą́: it died, it's dead)
P-niiłt'a#-(si)--(d)'na': come to a barrier while crawling (as in a cave)(tsé biniiłt'asis'na': I came to a rock that barred the way while crawling)
tsístł'a#-(si)--lwod: run into a cul-de-sac and get cornered (sgl subject) (tsístł'asiswod: I ran into a cul-de-sac and got cornered)
tsístł'a#-ha-(si)--Øt'i': it's a dead end (as a street or canyon - lit. area extends into a corner or cul-de-sac)(tsístł'ahazt'i')

### 10. Na- ~ ni- ~ ne- ~ n-: Position 1b + Extended Base

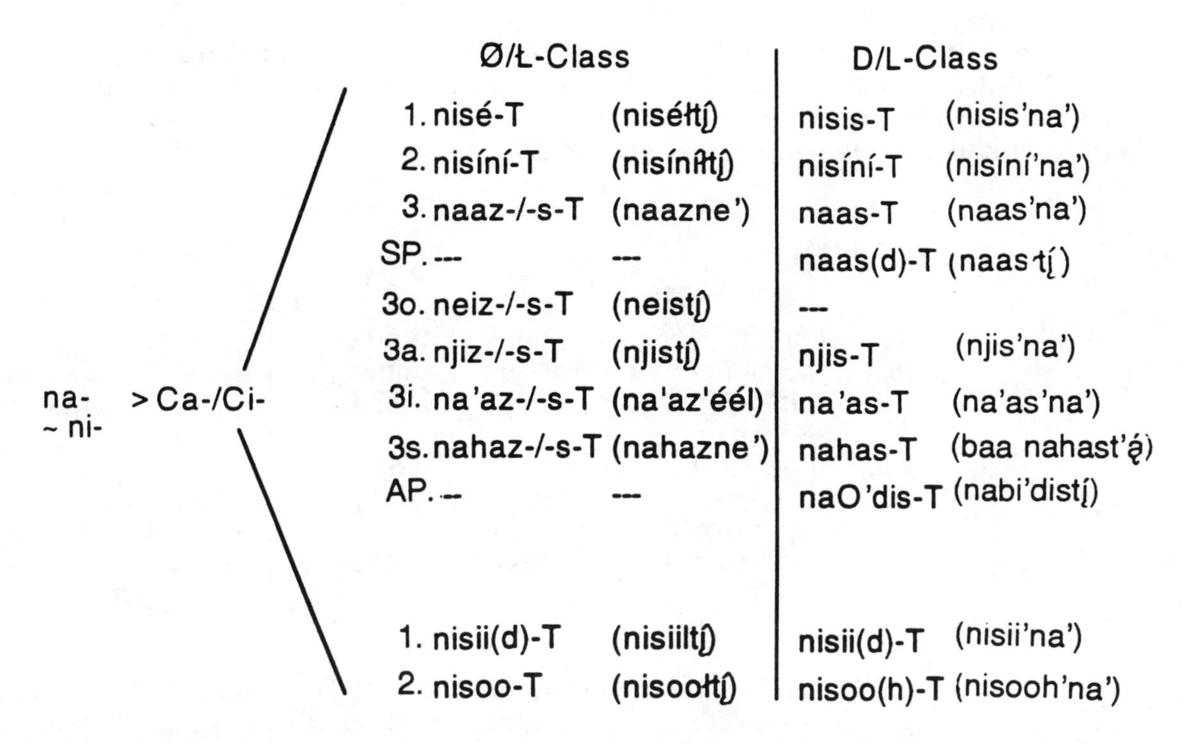

na- ~ ni- > Ca-/Ci-

| | Ø/Ł-Class | | D/L-Class | |
|---|---|---|---|---|
| 1. | nisé-T | (nisééłtį) | nisis-T | (nisis'na') |
| 2. | nisíní-T | (nisínííłtį) | nisíní-T | (nisíní'na') |
| 3. | naaz-/-s-T | (naazne') | naas-T | (naas'na') |
| SP. | --- | --- | naas(d)-T | (naastį) |
| 3o. | neiz-/-s-T | (neistį) | --- | |
| 3a. | njiz-/-s-T | (njistį) | njis-T | (njis'na') |
| 3i. | na'az-/-s-T | (na'az'éél) | na'as-T | (na'as'na') |
| 3s. | nahaz-/-s-T | (nahazne') | nahas-T | (baa nahast'ą́) |
| AP. | --- | --- | naO'dis-T | (nabi'distį) |
| 1. | nisii(d)-T | (nisiiltį) | nisii(d)-T | (nisii'na') |
| 2. | nisoo-T | (nisoołtį) | nisoo(h)-T | (nisooh'na') |

na#-(si)--łtį́: carry AnO about; make a round trip carrying AnO (nisééłtį)
na#-(si)--Øne': play (naazne': he played; niséne': I played)
na#-ha-(si)--Øne', baa ---: it was recounted, told (a story or account)(baa nahazne'; baa nahosisne': I told about it)
na#-(si)--(d)'na': crawl around; make a round trip crawling (naas'na': it/he crawled around)
na#-(si)--Ø'éél: something floated about or to a destination and back (shił na'az'éél: 2 made a round trip by boat
na-ho-(si)--Ø'ą́, baa ---: plan it (baa nahast'ą́: it was planned)

---

NOTE: Pluralization of si-Perfective Neuter Positionals. Constructions of this type are derived, in most instances, with the Classificatory Verb Stems. 3+random plurality is marked by adding the Disjunct Pos.1b prefix na-: around about, to the Verb Base, with or without the Distributive pluralizing prefix da-Pos. 3. The resulting form describes 3+objects in random distribution "here and there."

tózis si'ą́: the bottle lies/tózis naaz'ą́: bottles lie (about)

Similarly the number-specific positional verbs, as

shich'é'édą́ą́'gi, in my dooryard: mósí ła' sitį, a single cat lies; mósí naaztį (individual focus), 3+cats lie about singly; mósí shitéézh, a pair of cats lie; mósí naazhtéézh, 3+pairs of cats lie about; mósí shijéé' 3+cats lie (collective focus - either in a cluster or scattered): mósí naazhjéé', 3+cats lie about (either singly or in plural clustered groups).

## 11. Cá- (~ Cí-) + Extended Base

'Á- ~ í-: Position 1b and ná-1b/1d are the only Cá- prefixes that occur in determinant position in the Si-Perfective. 'Á- appears as 'í- before -(y)i- in 3o person, and ná- has variable shape (ná- ~ né- ~ ní- ~ ń- ) depending on the phonological environment. (See pp. 38-39. )

ná- / 'á- → Cá-

| PERSON | Ø/Ł | | | D/L | |
|---|---|---|---|---|---|
| **Sgl** | | | | | |
| 1. | nísé-T | (níséłhiz) | ('áséłdįįd) | nísís-T | (nísísdlį́į́') |
| 2. | nísíní-T | nísíníłhiz) | ('asíníłdįįd) | nísíní-T | (nísínídlį́į́') |
| 3. | náz-/-s-T | (názyiz) | ('ásdįįd) | nás-T | (násdlį́į́') |
| SP. | --- | --- | --- | nás-T | (násyiz) |
| 3o. | néiz-/-s-T | (néísxiz) | ('íísdįįd) | --- | --- |
| 3a. | ńjiz-/-s-T | (ńjísxiz) | ('ájísdįįd) | ńjís-T | (ńjísdlį́į́') |
| 3i. | ná'áz-/-s-T | (ná'ázyiz) | --- | ná'ás-T | (ná'ásdlį́į́') |
| 3s. | náház-/-s-T | (náházyiz) | ('áhásdįįd) | náhás-T | (náhásdlį́į́') |
| AP | --- | --- | --- | náO'dis-T | (nábi'disyiz) |
| **Dpl** | | | | | |
| 1. | nísii(d)-T | (nísiilyiz) | ('ásiildįįd) | nísii(d)-T | (nísiidlį́į́') |
| 2. | nísoo-T | (nísoołhiz) | ('ásoołdįįd) | nísoo(h)-T | (nísoohdlį́į́') |

ná#-(si)--łhiz: turn O around
ná#-(si)--Øyiz: turn around (názyiz: he turned around)
ná#-(si)--(d)lį́į́': revert, become (back) again)
'á#-(si)--łdįįd: get rid of it ('íísdįįd: he got rid of it)
á#-(si)--(d)dįįd: become extinct; run out (a supply)(shibéeso 'ásdįįd: my money ran out)
'á#-(si)--łdįįd: cause O to disappear, get rid of O ('áséłdįįd: I did away with it)

## 12. Cí-: Position 1b + Extended Base

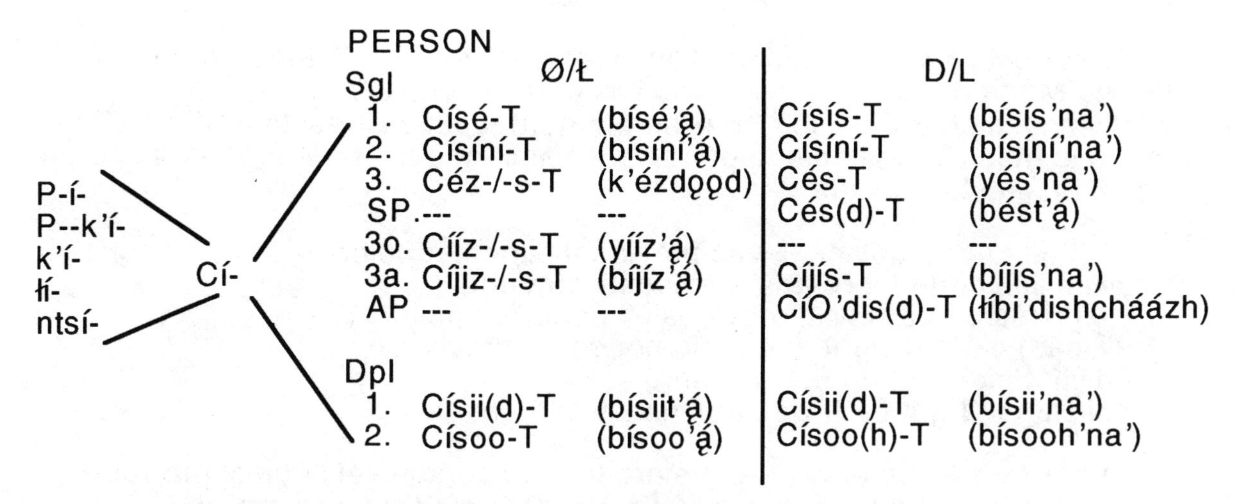


bí#-(si)--Ø'ą́: rub a SRO against it (e.g. a bar of soap)
bí#-(si)--(d)'na': rub against it
k'í#-(si)--Ødǫǫd: become erect (k'ézdǫǫd: it became erect, straight)
bik'í#-(si)--Øką́: pour it onto it (as water onto a fire, from an open container)
łí#-(si)--Øchaazh: cheat O, defraud O (łíshéchaazh: I cheated him;
łíbi'dishchaazh: he was cheated)

## YI-Ø-PERFECTIVE

### *ACTIVE VERBS*

Ø-Perfective lacks a conjugation marker in Position 7; the \ ´ / marker of Perfective Mode does not appear, and it is derived with a yi- (~ ii-) prefix arbitrarily assigned to Position 6c + the Momentaneous Perfective Stem. Yi- serves to identify Transitional Aspect: i.e. subject or object undergoes a change in condition, status, color or form, as:

yiishjį́į́': I turned black (I was previously another color)
yiiłch'iil: I curled it (it was previously straight)
yiizį': I stood up (I was previously in another position)
yiiłtsą́: I caught sight of it (I did not see it previously)
ńdiiłtį́: I picked it up (it was lying)
ńdiish'na': I got up (I was previously sitting or lying)

Yi- takes the shape yii- ~ -ii- before the 1st person sgl subject pronoun (-sh-) in D/L-Class Verbs, and in all inflectional forms that lack a prefix in Position 8.

Y- is a peg element required to maintain CV syllable integrity. It takes the shape w- before -oo-: 2nd person dpl subject pronoun; y- / w- elide in the presence of a preceding prefix, as in:

niiłtsą́ (< ni- + [y]iiłtsą́): I caught sight of you
shoołtsą́ (< shi- + [w]oołtsą́): you dpl caught sight of me

Yi- merges with the 1st and 2nd person dpl subject pronouns -ii(d)- / -oo- to produce y(i)- + -ii(d)- > y-ii(d)- and y(i)- + -oo- > w-oo-.

yiiltsą́ (< yi-iiltsą́): we caught sight of it
woołtsą́ (yi-oołtsą́): you dpl caught sight of it

#### Base Paradigm

Table 1A
Ø/Ł-Class

T = any Verb Theme

| PERSON | Prefix Position | | | | | | | | | |
|---|---|---|---|---|---|---|---|---|---|---|
| Sgl | 6c | + | 7 | + | 8 | + | T | | | as in: |
| 1. | yii- | + | Ø | + | Ø | + | T | > | yii-T | yiizį' |
| 2. | yi- | + | Ø | + | -ni- | + | T | > | yini-T | yinizį' |
| 3. | yii | + | Ø | + | Ø | + | T | > | yii-T | yiizį' |
| Dpl | | | | | | | | | | |
| 1. | y- | + | Ø | + | -ii(d) | + | T | > | yii(d)-T | yiidzį' |
| 2. | w- | + | Ø | + | -oo- | + | T | > | woo-T | woozį' |

yi-(Ø)--Øzį': stand up (yiizį': I/he stood up)
yi-(Ø)--Øgaii: turn white (yiigaii: I/he turned white)

yaa yi-(Ø)--Øtaaz: become stooped (as with age)(yaa yinitaaz: you became stooped

Table 1B
D/L-Class

T = any Verb Theme

| PERSON | Prefix Position | | | | | | | | | |
|---|---|---|---|---|---|---|---|---|---|---|
| Sgl | 6c | + | 7 | + | 8 | + | T | | | as in: |
| 1. | yii- | + | Ø | + | -sh- | + | T | > | yiish-T | yiishį́į́' |
| 2. | yi- | + | Ø | + | -ni- | + | T | > | yini-T | yinijį́į́' |
| 3. | yii | + | Ø | + | Ø | + | T | > | yii-T | yiijį́į́' |
| SP. | yii- | + | Ø | + | Ø | + | T | > | yii(d)-T | yiilzhį́į́' |
| Dpl | | | | | | | | | | |
| 1. | y- | + | Ø | + | -ii(d) | + | T | > | yii(d)-T | yiijį́į́' |
| 2. | w- | + | Ø | + | -oo(h)- | + | T | > | woo(h)-T | woohjį́į́' |

yi-(Ø)--(d)jį́į́' (= zhį́į́'): turn black
yi-(Ø)--lzhį́į́': be blackened (yiishį́į́' < yii-ł-zhį́į́': blacken it)
yi-(Ø)--lyiizh: stoop over, get on all four

## 1. Conjunct Prefixes

Prefixes of Position 5 + Base

Table 2

The prefix vowel (i) deletes in 3a, 3i, and AP constructions, and 3s ho- + -ii- > hoo- or hwii-.

T = any Verb Theme

| PERSON Prefix Position | | | | | | | Ø/Ł-Class | D/L-Class |
|---|---|---|---|---|---|---|---|---|
| Sgl | 4 | + | 5 | + | Base | | | |
| 1. | --- | + | -j- | + | -ii-T > | jii-T | jiigaii | jiijį́į́' |
| 2. | --- | + | -'(i)- | + | -ii-T > | 'ii-T | 'iigaii | 'iijį́į́' |
| 3. | --- | + | -ho- | + | -ii-T > | hoo-T | hoogaii | hoojį́į́' |
| AP. | O- | + | -'(a)d- | + | -ii-T > | O'(a)dii(d)-T | --- | bi'diilzhį́į́' |

hw-ii-(Ø)--łtsą́: see a place (hwiiłtsą́: I saw the place, visited it [as a country])
yi-(Ø)--Øgaii: turn white
yi-(Ø)--jį́į́' (< d-zhį́į́'): turn black (hoojį́į́': area turned black; bi'diilzhį́į́': he was blackened)

Ø/Ci-Prefixes of Position 4 + Extended Base
Table 3
Ø/Ł-D/L-Class

In 2nd person sgl the prefixes of Position 4, unlike those of Position 5 and 6, retain the prefix vowel (-i-), as shiiniłtsą́ (< shi-4 + -(y) iniłtsą́): you saw me; but niniłgaii

(< n(i)-6 + -(y)iniłgaii: you heated it. However, in the charts that follow, the Position 4 object pronouns will be shown with elided vowel, except in 2nd sgl.

In the Reflexive Transitional paradigm the di- of 'á-di-: self, behaves like a prefix of Position 6a/b, deleting the prefix vowel in 2nd person sgl constructions, as 'ádinilgaii (not 'ádiinilgaii*): you whitened yourself.

T = any Verb Theme

| PERSON | Ø/Ł-Class Prefix Position | | | | | | | D/L-Class |
|---|---|---|---|---|---|---|---|---|
| Sgl | 4 | + | 5 | + | Base | + Ø-4 | + Ci-4 | (Refl.) |
| 1. | Ø/C(i)- | + | Ø | + | (y)ii-T | yiiłgaii | niiłgaii | 'ádiishzhį́į́' |
| 2. | Ø/Ci- | + | Ø | + | (y)ini-T | yiniłgaii | shiiniłgaii | 'ádinilzhį́į́' |
| 3. | --/C(i)- | + | Ø | + | (y)ii-T | --- | shiiłgaii | 'ádiilzhį́į́' |
| SP. | Ø/-- | + | --- | + | (y)ii(d)-T | --- | --- | yiilzhį́į́' |
| 3o. | --/yi- | + | --- | + | (y)ii-T | --- | yiyiiłgaii | --- |
| 3a. | Ø/C(i)- | + | -j- | + | (y)ii-T | jiiłgaii | shijiiłgaii | 'ázhdiilzhį́į́' |
| AP. | C | + | -'(a)d- | + | (y)ii-T | --- | | bi'diilzhį́į́' |
| Dpl | | | | | | | | |
| 1. | Ø/C(i)- | + | Ø | + | (y)ii(d)-T | yiilgaii | niilgaii | 'ádiilzhį́į́' |
| 2. | Ø/C(i)- | + | Ø | + | (w)oo-T | woołgaii | shoołgaii | 'ádoołzhį́į́' |

yi-(Ø)--łgaii: whiten O; whitewash O; turn O white (niiłgaii: I whitened you; shiiłgaii: he whitened me)
yi-(Ø)--shį́į́' (< łzhį́į́'): blacken O ; dye O black (yiyiishį́į́': he dyed it black; yiilzhį́į́': it was dyed black)
'ád-ii--lzhį́į́': blacken oneself ('ádiishzhį́į́': I blackened myself)
'ah- ~ 'ałh-ii-lzhį́į́': blacken each other ('ahiilzhį́į́' ~ 'ałhiilzhį́į́': we blackened each other; they blackened each other)

'A- ~ 'i- ~ -'-: Position 4 + Extended Base

Table 4

Like other Conjunct Prefixes 'a-~'i-3i: someone/something unspecified, is here represented as eliding its prefix vowel although it is retained in the 2nd person sgl - a circumstance that suggests the possibility that the prefixes of Position 4 behave in a distinctive manner.

| PERSON | Prefix Position | | | | | | | |
|---|---|---|---|---|---|---|---|---|
| Sgl | 4 | + | 5 | + | Base | > | | as in: |
| 1. | '(i)- | + | --- | + | -ii-T | > | 'ii-T | 'iiłhaazh |
| 2. | '(i)- | + | --- | + | -ii-ni-T | > | 'iini-T | 'iiniłhaazh |
| 3. | '(i)- | + | --- | + | -ii-T | > | 'ii-T | 'iiłhaazh |
| 3a.. | 'a- | + | -j- | + | -ii-T | > | 'ajii-T | 'ajiilhaazh |
| Dpl | | | | | | | | |
| 1. | '(i)- | + | --- | + | -ii(d)-T | > | 'ii(d)-T | 'iilghaazh |
| 2. | '(i)- | + | --- | + | -oo-T | > | 'oo-T | 'oołhaazh |

'i-i-(Ø)--łhaazh: go to sleep
P-kétł'á 'i-i-(Ø--Øyil: boost P up (bikétł'á 'iiyil: I boosted him up; shikétł'á 'iiyil: he boosted me up)
P-aa 'i-i-(Ø)--łtsą́: see P's genitals (literally, see something about P)(shaa 'iiłtsą́: he saw my genitals)

## Ho- ~ hwi- ~ hw-: Position 4 + Extended Base

### Table 5

T = any Verb Theme

| PERSON | Prefix Position | | | | | | | |
|---|---|---|---|---|---|---|---|---|
| Sgl | 4 | + | 5 | + | Base | | | as in: |
| 1. | ho- | + | --- | + | (y)ii-T | > | hoo-T | hooł'a' |
| 2. | hwi- | + | --- | + | (y)ini-T | > | hwiini-T | hwiinił'a' |
| 3. | ho- | + | --- | + | (y)ii-T | > | hoo-T | hooł'a' |
| 3a. | ho- | + | -j- | + | (y)ii-T | > | hojii-T | hojiił'a' |
| Dpl | | | | | | | | |
| 1. | hw- | + | --- | + | (y)ii(d)-T | > | hwii(d)-T | hwiil'a' |
| 2. | h(w)- | + | --- | + | (w)oo-T | > | hoo-T | hooł'a' |

ho-i-(Ø)--ł'a': make space (bá hooł'a': I made room for him)
ho-i-(Ø)--łgaii: whiten an area; whitewash it (as a wall)
bí#-ho-i-(Ø)--ł'ą́ą́': learn it (bíhooł'ą́ą́': I learned it)

## Ci-Prefixes of Position 6a / 6b + Extended Base

The di- and ni- prefixes of Positions 6a/6b appear to elide the prefix vowel before yi- (-ii-) Position 6c, producing dii-/nii- in Transitional derivatives. However, hi-seriative and its yi-allomorph, in Positions 6a and 6c respectively, retain the prefix vowel (like also the prefixes of Position 4) before -i- -ii- Transitional, in 2nd sgl.

A number of prefix clusters and compounds, with unit meanings, include thematic or derivational elements from Position 6a / 6b, in determinant position. These combinations may include Disjunct derivational elements from Position 1b. The Position 6 elements include:

di[13]-6a: inceptive
di[2]-6a: relinquishment
di[10]-6a: color (possibly)
ni[7]-6b: thematic
hi-6a / yi[3]-6c: Seriative

## Di/ni/dzi-Prefixes of Position 6a/b + Extended Base

### Table 6A

### Ø/Ł-Class Verbs

The di/ni/dzi-prefixes retain the prefix vowel before a following consonant, but elide it before a vowel, including (y)ii-6c Transitional.

T = any Verb Theme

| PERSON | Prefix Position | | | | | | | Intransitive | | Transitive | |
|---|---|---|---|---|---|---|---|---|---|---|---|
| Sgl | 4 | + | 5 | + | 6a/b | + | Base | | | + Ø-4 | + Ci-4 |
| 1. | Ø/Ci- | + | --- | + | C(i)- | + | -ii-T | dah diisaal | dah diilóóz | niiłgaii | dah nidiilóóz |
| 2. | Ø/Ci- | + | --- | + | C(i)- | + | -ini-T | dah dinisaal | dah dinilóóz | niniłgaii | dah shidinilóóz |
| 3. | --/Ci- | + | --- | + | C(i)- | + | -ii-T | dah diisaal | --- | niigaii | dah shidiilóóz |
| 3o. | (y)i- | + | --- | + | C(i)- | + | -ii-T | --- | --- | yiniiłgaii | dah yidiilóóz |
| 3a. | Ø/Ci- | + | -ji-/-zh- | + | C(i)- | + | -ii-T | dah jidiisaal | *dah jidiilóóz | jiniiłgaii | dah shizhdiilóóz |
| 3i. | --- | + | 'a- | + | C(i)- | + | -ii-T | --- | dah 'adiiyá | | --- --- |
| 3s. | --- | + | ho- | + | C(i)- | + | -ii-T | honiidoii | --- | --- | --- |
| Dpl | | | | | | | | | | | |
| 1. | Ø/Ci- | + | --- | + | C(i)- | + | -ii(d)-T | dah diilzaal | dah diidlóóz | niilgaii | dah nidiidlóóz |
| 2. | Ø/Ci- | + | --- | + | C(i)- | + | -oo-T | dah doosaal | dah doołóóz | noołgaii | dah shidoolóóz |

* or dashdiilóóz

dah d(i)-ii-(Ø)--saal (< łzaal): rush off (dah diisaal)
dah d(i)-ii-(Ø)--Ølóóz: start off leading it/him (dah shidinilóóz: you started off leading me)
n(i)-ii-(Ø)--Øgaii: get hot (an object)
n(i)-ii-(Ø)--łgaii: heat O
ná- ~ ń#-d(i)-ii-(Ø)--Øbį́į́': start to bathe (ńdiibį́į́')
bíyah n(i)-ii-(Ø)--Øzį' (~ Øzį́): stand under it and hold it up (as a tent) (bíyah niizį')
bí#-n(i)-ii-(Ø)--Øzį': stand and lean against it (bíniizį')
bí#-n(i)-ii-(Ø)--Ødá: sit down leaning against it (bíniidá)
bí-Pi#-n(i)-ii-(Ø)--łdá: sit Pi- down leaning against it (Pi = any null postpositional pronoun prefix of Position 1a, representing the AnO who is caused to perform the act of sitting down by the subject, acting as agent) (bíbiniiłdá: I sat him down leaning against it; bíshininiłdá: you sat me down leaning against it; yíiniiłdá ~ yíniniiłdá: he sat him down leaning against it)
di[10]-n(i)-ii-(Ø)--łtsxoii: scorch O; turn O brown; toast O (bread) (diniiłtsxoii)
di[2]-n(i)-ii-(Ø)--łtłóó': slacken O: loosen O (as a taut wire) (diniiłtłóó')
ná- ~ ń#-dí[3]-'(a)-n(i)-ii-(Ø)--Øyą́ą́': just get a good start eating, when---: literally, I attained a state of prolongedly beginning to eat. The 3i. direct object pronoun of Position 4 appears between di-ni, and di-ni takes high tone. The combination ńdíníí- is the prolongative corresponding to ńdii-: start, as in ńdiibį́į́': I started to bathe.) (ńdí'níiyą́ą́')
niki#-'(a)-d(i)-ii-(Ø)--łbą́ą́z: start to drive (as a learner who starts his driving career) (niki'diiłbą́ą́z)
hi-i-(Ø)--łna': bring O to life; generate O (electric power) (hiiłna')
dah hi-d(i)-ii-(Ø)--Ø'ą́: hang a SRO up (as a hat) (dah hidii'ą́: I hung it)

## Table 6B

## D/L-Class Verbs

D/L-Class Verbs derived with Ci-prefixes of Position 6 in determinant position occur transitive only in Prolongative derivatives (i.e. those containing di-n(i)-+ -ii-: dinii- and dí-n(í)-ii-: dínî-).

T = any Verb Theme

| PERSON | Prefix Position | | | | | | | | |
|---|---|---|---|---|---|---|---|---|---|
| Sgl | 4 | + | 5 | + | 6a/b | + | Base | as in: | |
| 1. | --- | + | --- | + | C(i)- | + | -iish-T | dah diish'na' | niishch'iil |
| 2. | --- | + | --- | + | C(i)- | + | -ini-T | dah dini'na' | ninilch'iil |
| 3. | --- | + | --- | + | C(i)- | + | -ii-T | dah dii'na' | niilch'iil |
| SP. | --- | + | --- | + | C(i)- | + | -ii(d)-T | dah diidlóóz | --- |
| 3a. | --- | + | -ji-/-zh- | + | C(i)- | + | -ii-T | dashdii'na' | jiniilch'iil |
| 3i. | --- | + | 'a- | + | C(i)- | + | -ii-T | dah 'adii'na' | --- |
| 3s. | --- | + | ho- | + | C(i)- | + | -ii-T | hodiiyeel | --- |
| AP. | O | + | '(a)di- | + | C(i)- | + | -ii(d)-T | dah bidi'diidlóóz | --- |
| Dpl | | | | | | | | | |
| 1. | --- | + | --- | + | C(i)- | + | -ii(d)-T | dah dii'na' | niilch'iil |
| 2. | --- | + | --- | + | C(i)- | + | -oo(h)-T | dah dooh'na' | noołch'iil |

dah d(i)-ii-Ø)--(d)'na': start off crawling
ho-d(i)-ii-(Ø)--Øyeel: it /"things" (impersonal) became quiet; quiet descended
dah hi-d(i)-ii-(Ø)--lghal: start off crawling on back or belly; wriggle off
ná- ~ ń#-d(i)-ii-(Ø)--(d)'na': get up, rise
ná- ~ ń#-d(i)-ii-(Ø)--lnish: start to work
n(i)-ii-(Ø)--lch'iil: close eyes
di-n(i)-ii-(Ø)--łtsood: grab O and hang on (as a dog)(Prolongative corresponding to shiiłtsood: it grabbed me)
ná- ~ ń#-dín(i)-ii-(Ø)--lnish: just get a good start working, when an interruption occurs (Prolongative Inceptive corresponding to ńdiishnish: I started to work)
niki#-dí-n(i)-ii-(Ø)--lbą́ą́z, P-ts'ą́ą́' ---: borrow a vehicle and keep it (literally, prolongedly start to drive O to P's disadvantage)

## IRREGULAR YI-Ø-PERFECTIVES

Seriative hi-Position 6a has a yi-allomorph in Position 6c, required in all constructions in which hi- is preceded by a prefix of Position 4 or 5.

A di-prefix of Position 6a cooccurs with hi-/yi-Seriative in a group of Verb Bases that also include the yi- (-ii-) Transitional Aspect marker of Position 6c. Thus, in Bases of this type two prefixes of Position 6a or two prefixes of Position 6c cooccur.

When the prefix of Position 4 is Ø, representing a 3rd person direct object in a verb whose subject is 1st or 2nd person, or in constructions in which a Seriative verb is intransitive, hi-6a takes position to the left of di-6a, as in:

dah hidiilo' (< hi-6a + d(i)-6a + -ii-6c + Ølo'): I hung it up (as a bucket by its handle)

In the presence of a preceding prefix of Position 4 however, the yi-allomorph of hi- takes position to the right of di-, where it merges with -i- (-ii-) 6c, the marker of Transitional Aspect. In constructions of this type yi-6c Seriative + (y)i-Transitional > yii-, as in:

dah shidiyiilo' (< shi-4 + di-6a + yi-6c + -i-6c + Ølo'): he hung me (by a cord or rope); he weighed me

3a (4th) person ji-Position 5 is represented by its -zh- allomorph, which undergoes metathesis and appears to the right of hi-6a, if Position 4 is vacant, as in:

dah hizhdiilo' (< hi-6a + -zh-5 + d(i)-6a + -ii-6c + Ølo'): he hung him

But if Position 4 is filled by other than Ø-4 the Seriative must be represented by its yi-allomorph, as in:

dah shizhdiyiilo' (< shi-4 + -zh-5 + di-6a + yi-6c + -i-6c + Ølo'): he hung me

The Agentive Passive subject pronoun of Position 5 triggers a shift to the yi-Seriative allomorph, as in:

dah bidi'diyiidlo' (< bi-4 + di'-5 + di-6a + yi-6c + -i- + d-lo'): he was hung

## Hi-/yi-Seriative + Extended Base

### Table 8

Seriative hi- and its yi-allomorph behave like the prefixes of Position 4 in the Yi-Ø-Perfective paradigm, retaining the prefix vowel in 2nd person sgl. Thus, náhiiniłna': you brought it back to life / náshiyiiniłna': you brought me back to life (not náhiniłna / náshiyiniłna'*...)

T = any Verb Theme

| PERSON | Prefix Position | | | | | | | | | |
|---|---|---|---|---|---|---|---|---|---|---|
| Sgl | 4 | + | 5 | + | 6a/c | + | Base | | + Ø-4 | + Ci-4 |
| 1. | Ø/Ci- | + | --- | + | hi-/yi- | + | (y)ii-T | hii-/-yii-T | náhiiłna' | nániyiiłna' |
| 2. | Ø/Ci- | + | --- | + | hi-/yi- | + | (y)ini-T | hiini-/yiini-T | náhiiniłna' | náshiyiiniłna' |
| 3. | Ø/Ci- | + | --- | + | --/yi- | + | (y)ii-T | hii-T | --- | náshiyiiłna' |
| SP. | Ø | + | --- | + | hi-/-- | + | (y)ii(d)-T | hii(d)-T | náhiilna' | --- |
| 3o. | --/yi- | + | --- | + | --/yi- | + | (y)ii-T | --- --- | náyiyiiłna' | |
| 3a. | Ø/Ci- | + | ji- | + | --/yi- | + | (y)ii-T | jiyii-T | ńjiyiiłna' | náshijiyiiłna' |
| AP. | --/O | + | '(a)d- | + | --/(y)ii- | + | (y)ii(d)-T | --- | --- | nábi'diilna' |
| Dpl | | | | | | | | | | |
| 1. | Ø/Ci- | + | --- | + | h(i)-/y(i)-+(y)ii(d)-T | | | hii(d)-/yii(d)-T | náhiiłna' | nánihiyiilna' |
| 2. | Ø/Ci- | + | --- | + | h(i)-/y(i)-+(w)oo(h)-T | | | hoo-/yoo-T | náhoołna' | nánihiyoołna' |

ná#-hi-/yi-i-(Ø)--łna': revive O, bring O back to life, recharge O (a battery) (náhiiłna': I revived him; náshiyiiłna': he revived me, retored me to life)
hi-i-(Ø)--łna': bring O to life; generate O (electricity) (Cf. hiina': he came to life)

## The Inchoatives

The Inchoative is marked by the compound prefix -'nii-, usually preceded by a null postposition of Position 1a. The Inchoative includes 3 types: Type (1) - Transitive Verbs, in which the null postposition represents a direct object; Type (2) - a class of intransitive verbs in which the null postposition represents the subject; and Type (3) - a class of intransitive verbs in which an indefinite (3i) form of the null postposition ('i-) functions as a thematic prefix.

Table 9a

Type (1) - Null Postposition = Direct Object

T = any Verb Theme

| PERSON | | | | | |
|---|---|---|---|---|---|
| Sgl | | Ø/Ł | | D/L | |
| 1. | P-'nii-T | (bi'niidléézh) | P-'niish-T | (bi'niishdéél) | ('ádi'niishzhéé') |
| 2. | P-n'ni-T | (bin'nidléézh) | P-n'ni-T | (bin'nildéél) | ('ádin'nilzhéé') |
| 3. | P-'nii-T | --- | P-'nii-T | --- | ('ádi'niilzhéé') |
| 3o. | yi'nii-T | (yi'niidléézh) | yi-'nii-T | (yi'niildéél) | --- |
| 3a. | P-zh'nii-T | (bizh'niidléézh) | P-zh'nii-T | (bizh'niildéél) | ('ádizh'niilzhéé') |
| Dpl | | | | | |
| 1. | P-'nii(d)-T | (bi'niidléézh) | P-'nii(d)-T | (bi'niildéél) | ('ádi'niilzhéé') |
| 2. | P-'noo-T | (bi'noodléézh) | P-'noo(h)-T | (bi'noołdéél) | ('ádi'noołzhéé') |
| Dist Plural | | | | | |
| 1. | P-da'nii-T | (bida'niidléézh) | P-da'nii(d)-T | (bida'niildéél) | ('ádadi'niilzhéé') |
| 2. | P-da'noo-T | (bida'noodléézh) | P-da'noo(h)-T | (bida'noołdéél) | ('ádadi'noołzhéé') |
| 3. | P-da'nii-T | --- | P-da'nii-T | --- | ('ádadi'niilzhéé') |
| 3o. | yida'nii-T | (yida'niidléézh) | yida'nii-T | (yida'niildéél) | --- |
| 3a. | P-dazh'nii-T | (bidazh'niidléézh) | P-dazh'nii-T | (bidazh'niildéél) | ('ádadizh'niilzhéé') |

bi'niidléézh: I started to paint it
bi'niishdéél: I started to eat them (as berries)
'ádi'niishzhéé': I started to shave
'i'niiyą́ą́': I started to eat (something)

## Table 9b

### Type (2) - Null Postposition = Subject

| PERSON | | | |
|---|---|---|---|
| Sgl | | Dist Plural | |
| 1. | shi'niidlí | 1. | nihida'niidlí |
| 2. | ni'niidlí | 2. | nihida'niidlí |
| 3. | bi'niidlí | 3. | bida'niidlí |
| 3a. | ho'niidlí | 3a. | hoda'niidlí |
| Dpl | | | |
| 1. | nihi'niidlí | | |
| 2. | nihi'niidlí | | |

shi'niidlí: I got cold (started to freeze)
ni'niidlí: you got cold
bi'niidlí: he got cold

## Table 9c

### Type (3) - Null Postposition = Thematic

| PERSON | | | | |
|---|---|---|---|---|
| Sgl | Ø/Ł | | D/L | |
| 1. | 'i'nii-T | ('i'niicha) | 'i'niish-T | ('i'niistsąąd) |
| 2. | 'in'ni-T | ('in'nicha) | 'in'ni-T | ('in'niltsąąd) |
| 3. | 'i'nii-T | ('i'niicha) | 'i'nii-T | ('i'niiltsąąd) |
| 3a. | 'izh'nii-T | ('izh'niicha) | 'izh'nii-T | ('izh'niiltsąąd) |
| Dpl | | | | |
| 1. | 'i'nii(d)-T | ('i'niicha) | 'i'nii(d)-T | ('i'niiltsąąd) |
| 2. | 'i'noo-T | ('i'noocha) | 'i'noo(h)-T | ('i'noołtsąąd) |
| Dist Plural | | | | |
| 1. | 'ida'nii-T | ('ida'niicha) | 'ida'nii(d)-T | ('ida'niiltsąąd) |
| 2. | 'ida'noo-T | ('ida'noocha) | 'ida'noo(h)-T | ('ida'noołtsąąd) |
| 3. | 'ida'nii-T | ('ida'niicha) | 'ida'nii-T --- | ('i'da'niiltsąąd) |
| 3a. | 'idazh'nii-T | ('idazh'niicha) | 'idazh'nii-T | ('idazh'niiltsąąd) |

'i'niicha: I/he started to cry
'i'niiłhą́ą́': I/he started to snore
'i'niistsąąd: I became pregnant
'i'niichxííl: it started to snow
'i'niihai: it started to be winter
'i'niishzhiizh: I started to dance ('in'nilzhiizh: you started to dance)

N'd(i)-(< na[3]-1b + -'i-6a + di-6a)

Na[3]: Position 1b + unidentified -i- ~ -'-: Position 6a (?) + di-Position 6a + Transitional is a prefix cluster with the unitary meaning break loose or become detached and get free; take O down, pick O (as a melon). The '(i)-prefix is unidentified and is arbitrarily assigned to Position 6a.

Table 10

| PERSON | | | + hi-~ (y) i-Seriative | |
|---|---|---|---|---|
| Sgl | | | | |
| 1. | n'dii-T | (n'dii'ą́) | nahi'dii-T | (nahi'dii'ą́) |
| 2. | ndin'ni-T | (ndin'ni'ą́) | nahidin'ni-T | (nahidin'ni'ą́) |
| 3. | n'dii-T | (n'diiyá) | nahi'dii-T | (nahi'diikai) |
| SP. | n'dii(d)-T | (n'diit'ą́) | nahi'dii(d)-T | (nahi'diit'ą́) |
| 3o. | na'iidii-T | (na'iidii'ą́) | neidi'yii-T | (neidi'yii'ą́) |
| 3a. | nizh'dii-T | (nizh'dii'ą́) | nahizh'dii-T | (nahizh'dii'ą́) |
| Dpl | | | | |
| 1. | n'dii(d)-T | (n'diit'ą́) | nahi'dii(d)-T | (nahi'diit'ą́) |
| 2. | n'doo-T | (n'doo'ą́) | nahi'doo(h)-T | (nahi'doo'ą́) |

n'dii'ą́: take a SRO down (hat from peg, book from shelf); pick a SRO (melon); unfasten SRO (a button)
n'diiyá: it broke loose and got away (a tethered dog)
n'diilts'id: it broke loose and fell (bucket from a nail in the wall)
na'iidii'ą́: he took SRO down (book); he picked SRO (melon)
neidi'yii'ą́: he took SRO down one after another; he picked SRO (melons)
nahi'diikai: they got loose and got away one after another (as tethered dogs)

## 2. Disjunct Prefixes

The only Disjunct Prefixes that function as conjugational determinants jointly with Yi-Ø-Perfective are:

da-3: distributive plural marker
ya-1b: down
-ná-1b: up
-k'i-1b: on
-kí-1b: up an incline
P-í-1b: against P
ná-1d: reversionary (returning back)
náá- ~ nááná-1e: semeliterative (again)

## Da-: Position 3 + Extended Base

The distributive plural marker combines with the dpl forms without complication of any kind beyond taking the shape de- before -i-, and elision of the duplicate yi-4 prefix (See Base Paradigm).

Table 1

T = any Verb Theme

| PERSON | Prefix Position | | | | | | | | | |
|---|---|---|---|---|---|---|---|---|---|---|
| Dist. Pl. | 3 | + | 4 | + | 5 | + | Base | | | as in: |
| 1. | de- | + | Ø | + | --- | + | -ii(d)-T | > | deii(d)-T | deiiltsą́ |
| 2. | da- | + | Ø | + | --- | + | -oo-T | > | daoo-T | daoołtsą́ |
| 3. | de- | + | Ø | + | --- | + | -ii-T | > | deii-T | deiigaii |
| 3o. | da- | + | y- | + | --- | + | -ii-T | > | dayii-T | dayiiłtsą́ |
| 3a. | da- | + | Ø | + | j- | + | -ii-T | > | dajii-T | dajiiłtsą́ |

da#-(y)i-(Ø)--łtsą́: catch sight of O
da#-(y)i-(Ø)--Øgaii: turn white

## Ya-: Position 1b + Extended Base

Ya-1b + yi-6c > yaa- before the 1st person sgl subject pronoun (-sh-) and in constructions that lack a prefix in Position 8.

Table 2

T = any Verb Theme

| PERSON | Prefix Position | | | | | | Base | | as in: | |
|---|---|---|---|---|---|---|---|---|---|---|
| Sgl | 1b | + | 4 | + | 5 | + | Ø/Ł | D/L | Ø/Ł | D/L |
| 1. | yaa- | + | Ø | + | --- | + | (-ii)-T | (-ii)sh-T | yaayį́ | yaashtáál |
| 2. | ye- | + | Ø | + | --- | + | -ini-T | -ini-T | yeiniyį́ | yeiniltáál |
| 3. | yaa- | + | Ø | + | --- | + | (-ii-)T | (-ii-)-T | yaatsi | yaaltáál |
| SP. | yaa- | + | --- | + | --- | + | (-ii)(d)-T | (-ii)(d)-T | --- | yaagį́ |
| 3o. | ya- | + | yi- | + | --- | + | -i-T | --- | yayiiyį́ | 'ádá yayiidzíid |
| 3a. | ya- | + | Ø | + | ji- | + | -i-T | -ii-T | yajiiyį́ | yajiiltáál |
| 3i. | ya- | + | --- | + | 'i- | + | -i-T | -ii-T | --- | ya'iiltáál |
| Dpl | | | | | | | | | | |
| 1. | ye- | + | Ø | + | --- | + | -ii(d)-T | -ii(d)-T | yeiigį́ | yeiiltáál |
| 2. | ya- | + | Ø | + | --- | + | -oo-T | -oo(h)-T | yaooyį́ | yaoołtáál |

ya#-i-(Ø)--Øyį́: dump O (a load) (yaayį́)
ya#-i-(Ø)--Øtsi: stick O up into the air (as a pole) (yaatsi)
'ádá ya#-i-(Ø)--Øziid: pour O for oneself ('ádá yaasdziid)
'ádii' ya#-i-(Ø)--(d)t'ą́: gulp O down ('ádii' yaasht'ą́)
ya#-i-(Ø)--ltáál: rush, accelerate (yaashtáál)(shił ya'iiltáál: I speeded up, dashed - in a vehicle- literally, something dashed off with me)

## Ná$^{4}$-: Position 1b + Extended Base

### Table 3

Ná$^{4}$-1b: up, upward is a component of the compound prefix ya-ná-: up into the air. Ya-ná- + yi-6c Transitional > yanáa- in the absence of a following prefix of Position 4 or 5.

T = any Verb Theme as in:

| PERSON | Prefix Position | | | | | | | | | | | |
|---|---|---|---|---|---|---|---|---|---|---|---|---|
| Sgl | 1b | + | 4 | + | 5 | + | Base | | Intransitive | | Transitive |
| 1. | yanáa- | + | Ø | + | --- | + | (-ii)-T | > | yanáa-T | yanáago' | yanáałne' |
| 2. | yané- | + | Ø | + | --- | + | -ini-T | > | yanéini-T | yanéinigo' | yanéiniłne' |
| 3. | yanáa- | + | Ø | + | --- | + | (-ii-)T | > | yanáa-T | yanáago' | --- |
| SP. | yanáa- | + | Ø | + | --- | + | (-ii)(d)-T | > | yanáa(d)-T | --- | yanáalne' |
| 3o. | yaná- | + | yi- | + | --- | + | -i-T | > | yanáyii-T | --- | yanáyiiłne' |
| 3a. | yań- | + | Ø | + | ji- | + | -i-T | > | yańjii-T | yańjiigo' | yańjiiłne' |
| Dpl | | | | | | | | | | | |
| 1. | yané- | + | Ø | + | --- | + | -ii(d)-T | > | yanéii(d)-T | yanéiigo' | yanéiilne' |
| 2. | yaná- | + | Ø | + | --- | + | -oo-T | > | yanáoo-T | yanáoogo' | yanáoołne' |

ya-ná#-i-(Ø)--Øgo': go flying up into the air (as a rider thrown off a bucking horse)
ya-ná#-i-(Ø)--Økę́ę́z: SSO bounced up into the air (as a pole that fell and bounced up)
ya-ná# -i-(Ø) --łne': toss SRO into the air

## Ná-: Position 1d: Reversionary + Extended Base

### Table 4

Ná- + -ii- is written néi-.

T = any Verb Theme as in:

| PERSON | Prefix Position | | | | | | | | | | | |
|---|---|---|---|---|---|---|---|---|---|---|---|---|
| Sgl | 1d | + | 4 | + | 5 | + | Ø/Ł | D/L | | | Ø/Ł | D/L |
| 1. | né- | + | Ø | + | --- | + | -i-T | --- | > | néi-T | néiłgaii | --- |
| 2. | né- | + | Ø | + | --- | + | -ini-T | --- | > | néini-T | néiniłgaii | --- |
| SP. | né- | + | Ø | + | --- | + | --- | -i(d)-T | > | --- | --- | néilgaii |
| 3o. | ná- | + | y- | + | --- | + | -ii-T | --- | > | náyii-T | náyiiłgaii | --- |
| 3a. | ń- | + | Ø | + | j- | + | -ii-T | --- | > | ńjii-T | ńjiiłgaii | --- |
| Dpl | | | | | | | | | | | | |
| 1. | né- | + | Ø | + | --- | + | -ii(d)-T | --- | > | néii(d)-T | néiilgaii | --- |
| 2. | ná- | + | Ø | + | --- | + | -oo-T | --- | > | náoo-T | náoołgaii | --- |

ná#-i-(Ø)--łgaii: rewhiten O (as white shoes)
ná#-i-(Ø)--shį́į́' (< łzhį́į́'): reblacken O (as in polishing black shoes)

## Ci-: Position 1b + Extended Base

### Table 5

The only Ci-prefix of Position 1b that cooccurs with yi[1]-6c: Transitional is loosely joined P-k'i-: on P.

T = any Verb Theme

| PERSON | Prefix Position | | | | | | | | | as in: | |
|---|---|---|---|---|---|---|---|---|---|---|---|
| Sgl | 1b | + | 4 | + | 5 | + | Base | | | Intransitive | Transitive |
| 1. | P-k'(i)- | + | Ø | + | --- | + | -ii-T | > | P-k'ii-T | bik'iitłizh | bik'iiłne' |
| | | | | | | | | | P-k'iish-T* | bik'iishwod | --- |
| 2. | P-k'i- | + | Ø | + | --- | + | -ini-T | > | P-k'iini-T | bik'iinitłizh | bik'iiniłne' |
| 3. | P-k;'(i) | + | Ø | + | --- | + | -ii-T | > | P-k'ii-T | yik'iitłizh | --- |
| 3o. | P-k'(i)- | + | y- | + | --- | + | -ii-T | > | yi-k'iyii-T | --- | yik'iyiiłne' |
| 3a. | P-k'(i)- | + | Ø | + | j- | + | -ii-T | > | P-k'ijii-T | bik'ijiitłizh | bik'ijiiłne' |
| Dpl | | | | | | | | | | | |
| 1. | P-k'(i)- | + | Ø | + | --- | + | -ii(d)-T | > | P-k'ii(d)-T | --- | bik'iilne' |
| 2. | P-k'i- | + | Ø | + | --- | + | -oo-T | > | P-k'ioo- | --- | bik'ioołne' |

*D/L-class verbs

P-k'(i)#-ii-(Ø)--Øtłizh: fall down onto it
P-k'(i)#-ii-(Ø)--lwod: attack P, jump P
P-k'i#-i-(Ø)--łne': drop SRO on P (tsé shik'iyiiłne': he dropped a rock on me)

## Cí-: Position 1b + Extended Base

### Table 6

The only Cí-prefixes of Position 1b that cooccur with yi[1]-: Transitional are kí-1b: up an incline and postpositional P-í-1a: against P, contacting or joining P.

T = any Verb Theme

| PERSON | Prefix Position | | | | | | | | | Intransitive | | |
|---|---|---|---|---|---|---|---|---|---|---|---|---|
| Sgl | 1b | + | 4 | + | 5 | + | Base | | | Ø/Ł | D/L | Transitive |
| 1. | kí- | + | Ø | + | --- | + | -ii-T | > | kí-T | kîiyá | kîish'na' | kîiłjid |
| 2. | kí- | + | Ø | + | --- | + | -ini-T | > | kîini-T | kîiniyá | kîini'na' | kîiniłjid |
| 3. | kí- | + | --- | + | --- | + | -ii-T | > | kîi-T | kîiyá | kîi'na' | --- |
| SP. | kí- | + | Ø | + | --- | + | -ii(d)-T | > | kîi(d)-T | --- | kîiljid | --- |
| 3o. | kí- | + | yi- | + | --- | + | -ii-T | > | kíyii-T | --- | --- | kíyiiłjid |
| 3a. | kí- | + | Ø | + | ji- | + | -ii-T | > | kíjii-T | kîjiiyá | kîjii'na' | kíjiiłjid |
| Dpl | | | | | | | | | | | | |
| 1. | kí- | + | Ø | + | --- | + | -ii(d)-T | > | kîi(d)-T | kîit'áázh | kîi'na' | kîiljid |
| 2. | kí- | + | Ø | + | --- | + | -oo-T | > | kíoo-T | kíoołjid | kíoo'na' | kíoołjid |

kí#-i-(Ø)--łjid: lug O up (an incline) on one's back
kí#-i-(Ø)--Øyá: go up an incline (up a hill, upstairs)(one subject)
kí#-i-(Ø)--Ø'áázh: go up an incline (2 subjects)
kí#-i-(Ø)--(d)'na': crawl up an incline
P-í#-i-(Ø)--Øyá: join P (as a political party)
P-í#-i-(Ø)-- tł'in: pile O against it (as logs against a wall)
P-í#-i-(Ø)--lwod: run up P (as up a hill); get on P (as a spider on one)(one actor)

## The Positional Transitionals

### Ci-Position 1a + Extended Base

The null postpositions of Position 1a appear in a few Transitional verbs in which the subject is represented as a causative agent and Ci- represents an animate object that is caused to perform an action. Of the positionals, "be caused to sit or lie (down)" are conjugated as Ø-Imperfective/Si-Perfective, but "be caused to stand up (be put on one's feet, as after a fall)" is conjugated as a Transitional Imperfective/Perfective.

Table 7

T = any Verb Theme

| PERSON | Prefix Position | | | | | | | |
|---|---|---|---|---|---|---|---|---|
| Sgl | 1a | + | 5 | + | Base | | | as in: |
| 1. | Ci- | + | --- | + | -ii-T | > | Cii-T | biisį' |
| 2. | Ci- | + | --- | + | -ini-T | > | Ciini-T | biinisį' |
| SP. | Ci- | + | --- | + | -ii(d)-T | > | Cii(d)-T | biilzį' |
| 3o. | yi- | + | --- | + | -yii-T | > | yiyii-T | yiyiisį' |
| 3a. | Ci- | + | ji- | + | -ii-T | > | Cijii-T | jiisį' |
| AP. | Ci- | + | -'(a)d- | + | -ii(d)-T | > | Ci'dii(d)-T | bi'diilzį' |
| Dpl | | | | | | | | |
| 1. | C(i)- | + | --- | + | -ii(d)-T | > | Cii(d)-T | biilzį' |
| 2. | C(i)- | + | --- | + | -oo-T | > | Coo-T | boosį' |

bi#-i-(Ø)--sį' = łzį': stand it up, put it on its feet, right it (chidí náhidéélts'id léi' bideiilzį': we 3+ righted an overturned car)
ná-bi#-i-(Ø)--sį'= -łzį': stand him back up, put him/it back on his/its feet (łį́į́' ni'góó sitį́į́ léi' ńdabiilzį': we 3+ stood a horse that was lying on the ground back on its feet)
bi#-i---łda': leave him/her behind to guard the place (biiłda')(Cf. yiishda': I stayed behind to guard the place.)

## *NEUTER VERBS*

### Conjunct Derivatives

A few Yi-Ø-Perfective Neuter Verbs are derived with Conjunct Prefixes such as di-6a and ni-6b in determinant position, including prefix clusters with Disjunct elements. These may be transitive or intransitive, as:

di[3]-6a: extension
bidii'á (< bi-1a: null postposition + -dii'á): long rigid subject lies pointing at it / him (as a rifle on a table)
bidiił'á: I have O pointed at it (as a rifle)
shiidiił'á: he has O pointed at me
nikidii'á (<niki-1b: start + -dii'á): it slopes (as a mountain that slopes in a particular direction)
bi'diił'á: it worries him (lit. it holds an elongated object pointed at him)

ni[1]-6b: terminal
bíyah nii'á: it extends under it holding it up (as a support beam under a house)
bíyah niishdá: I'm sitting under it holding it up (as under a tent)
bíniishdá (< b-í-1b: against it + -niishdá): I'm sitting leaning against it

Ci-Prefixes of Positions 6a / 6b + Extended Base

Table 1A
Ø/Ł-Class Verbs

T = any Verb Theme

| PERSON | Prefix Position | | | | | | | | | | | |
|---|---|---|---|---|---|---|---|---|---|---|---|---|
| Sgl | 1e | + | 4 | + | 5 | + | 6a / 6b | + | Base | | | as in: |
| 1. | Pi- | + | Ø | + | --- | + | C(i)- | + | -ii-T | > | Cii-T | bidiił'á |
| 2. | Pi- | + | Ø | + | --- | + | C(i)- | + | -ini-T | > | Cini-T | bidinił'á |
| 3. | Pi- | + | --- | + | --- | + | C(i)- | + | -ii-T | > | Cii-T | bidii'á |
| 3o. | yi- | + | (y)i- | + | --- | + | C(i)- | + | -ii-T | > | yiiCii-T | yiidiił'á |
| 3a. | --- | + | Ø | + | -j-/zh- | + | C(i)- | + | -ii-T | > | jiCii-T | bizhdiił'á |
| 3i. | --- | + | --- | + | 'a- | + | C(i)- | + | -ii-T | > | 'aCii-T | bíyah 'anii'á |
| Dpl | | | | | | | | | | | | |
| 1. | Pi- | Ø | + | + | --- | + | C(i)- | + | -ii(d)-T | > | Cii(d)-T | bidiil'á |
| 2. | Pi- | Ø | + | + | --- | + | C(i)- | + | -oo-T | > | Coo-T | bidooł'á |

Pi#-d(i)-ii-Ø)--ł'á: hold a long rigid O pointed at Pi- (Pi- = any inflected form of the null postposition in Position 1a) (shiidiił'á: he's holding it pointed at me)
Pi#-d(i)-ii-(Ø)--Ø'á: a long rigid object lies pointed at it

Table 1B
D/L-Class Verbs

T = any Verb Theme

| PERSON Sgl | Prefix Position 5 | + | 6b | + | Base | | | as in: | |
|---|---|---|---|---|---|---|---|---|---|
| 1. | --- | + | C(i)- | + | -iish-T | > | Ciish-T | bíyah niishdá | bíniishdá |
| 2. | --- | + | C(i)- | + | -ini-T | > | Cini-T | bíyah ninidá | bíninidá |
| 3. | --- | + | C(i)- | + | -ii-T | > | Cii-T | yíyah niidá | yíniidá |
| 3a. | ji-/-zh | + | C(i)- | + | -ii-T | > | jiCii-T | bíyah jiniidá | bízhniidá |
| | -sh- | + | C(i)- | + | -ii-T | | | ~ bíyashniidá | |
| Dpl | | | | | | | | | |
| 1. | --- | + | C(i)- | + | -ii(d)-T | > | Cii(d)-T | bíyah niiké | bíniiké |
| 2. | --- | + | C(i)- | + | -oo(h)-T | > | Coo-T | bíyah noohké | bínoohké |

bíyah n(i)-ii-(Ø)--(d)dá: sit under it holding it up (1 subject)
bíyah n(i)-ii-(Ø)--(d)ké: sit under it holding it up (2 subjects)
bí#-n(i)-ii-(Ø)--(d)dá: sit leaning against it (1 subject)

## RECAPITULATION

### 1. Base Paradigm

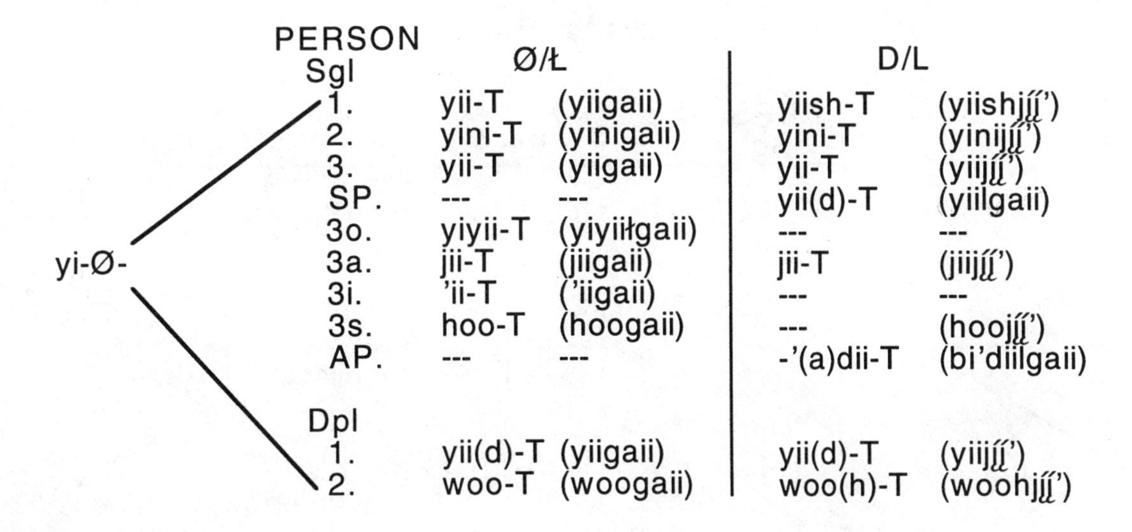

| | PERSON | Ø/Ł | | D/L | |
|---|---|---|---|---|---|
| yi-Ø- | Sgl | | | | |
| | 1. | yii-T | (yiigaii) | yiish-T | (yiishjįį́') |
| | 2. | yini-T | (yinigaii) | yini-T | (yinijįį́') |
| | 3. | yii-T | (yiigaii) | yii-T | (yiijįį́') |
| | SP. | --- | --- | yii(d)-T | (yiilgaii) |
| | 3o. | yiyii-T | (yiyiiłgaii) | --- | --- |
| | 3a. | jii-T | (jiigaii) | jii-T | (jiijįį́') |
| | 3i. | 'ii-T | ('iigaii) | --- | --- |
| | 3s. | hoo-T | (hoogaii) | --- | (hoojįį́') |
| | AP. | --- | --- | -'(a)dii-T | (bi'diilgaii) |
| | Dpl | | | | |
| | 1. | yii(d)-T | (yiigaii) | yii(d)-T | (yiijįį́') |
| | 2. | woo-T | (woogaii) | woo(h)-T | (woohjįį́') |

yi-(Ø)--Øgaii: turn white
yi-(Ø)--łgaii: whiten O
yi-(Ø)--jįį́' (< d-zhįį́'): turn black, be sunburned
yi-(Ø)--łch'iil: curl O

## Conjunct Prefixes

### 2. Ci-Prefixes of Position 4 and 6 + Extended Base

Di-6a, dzi-6a, hi-6a/yi-6c and ni-6b function as conjugational determinants with yi-Ø-Perfective, singly and as determinant constituents of prefix clusters and compounds.

The Ci-prefixes of Position 4 (direct object pronouns) and Seriative hi-yi- retain the prefix vowel, while di- and ni-(6a/6b) delete the prefix vowel. Cf:

| | |
|---|---|
| Base: | yinishį́į́': you sgl blackened it |
| + Ci-4: | shiinishį́į́': you blackened me |
| + hi-6a: | hiiniłna': you brought it to life |
| + yi-6c: | náshiyiiniłna': you resuscitated me |

but

| | |
|---|---|
| + d(i)-6a: | dah diniyá (< d[i]- + [y]iniyá): you started off |
| + n(i)-6b: | niniłgaii (< n[i]- + [y]iniłgaii): you heated it |

## Ø/Ł-Class Verbs

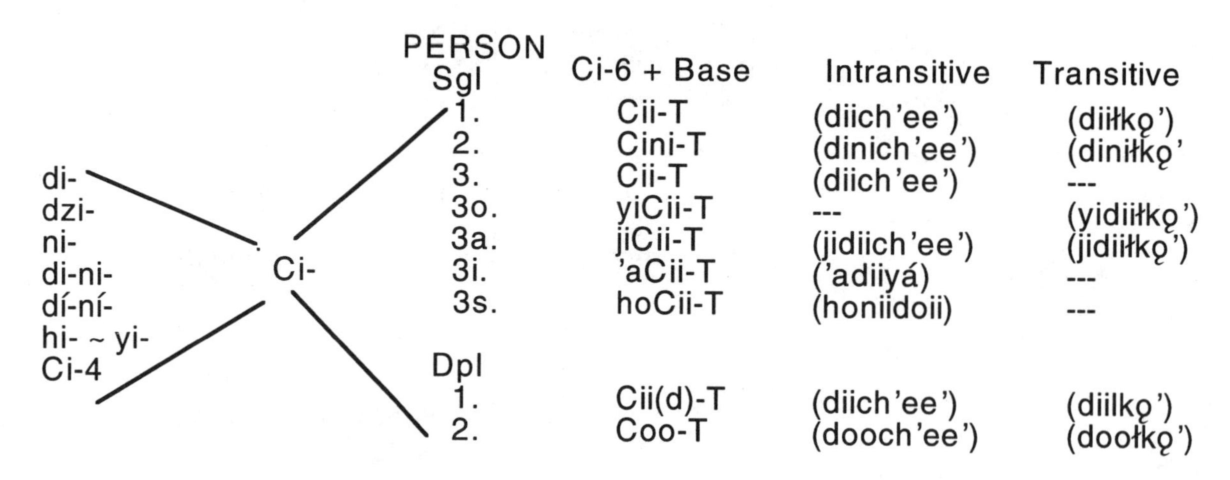


| PERSON | Ci-6 + Base | Intransitive | Transitive |
|---|---|---|---|
| Sgl | | | |
| 1. | Cii-T | (diich'ee') | (diiłkǫ') |
| 2. | Cini-T | (dinich'ee') | (diniłkǫ' |
| 3. | Cii-T | (diich'ee') | --- |
| 3o. | yiCii-T | --- | (yidiiłkǫ') |
| 3a. | jiCii-T | (jidiich'ee') | (jidiiłkǫ') |
| 3i. | 'aCii-T | ('adiiyá) | --- |
| 3s. | hoCii-T | (honiidoii) | --- |
| Dpl | | | |
| 1. | Cii(d)-T | (diich'ee') | (diilkǫ') |
| 2. | Coo-T | (dooch'ee') | (doołkǫ') |

d(i)-ii-(Ø)--Øch'ee': open mouth (diich'ee': I opened my mouth)
d(i)-ii-(Ø)--łkǫ': make O smooth; plane O (diiłkǫ': I planed it)
ná- ~ ń-#d(i)-ii-(Ø)--łtį́: pick an AnO up (ńdiiłtį́: I picked it up; I chose it)
ná- ~ ń-#d(i)-ii-(Ø)--Øbį́į́': start to bathe (ńdiibį́į́': I / he started to bathe)
dah d(i)-ii-(Ø)--łtį́: start off carrying an AnO (dah shidiiłtį́: he started off carrying me)
dah d(i)-ii-(Ø)--Øyá: start off; start to go (1 subject) (dah diiyá: I / he started off)
niki#-d(i)-ii-(Ø)--yá: start to walk (a baby) (nikidiiyá: it began to walk)
dah hi-d(i)-ii-(Ø)--Ø'ą́: hang a SRO up (as a hat) (dah hidii'ą́: I hung it up)

dah Ci-di-y(i)-ii--łtį́: hang Ci-4 up (dah shidiyiiłtį́: he hung me; dah yidiyiiłtį́: he hung it - an AnO)
P-k'i dah dz(i)-ii-(Ø)--Øgaii: P came into view (bik'i dah dziigaii: he came into view)
hi-i-(Ø)--łna': bring O to life; generate O (electricity)(hiiłna': I brought it to life)
Ci-yi-i-(Ø)--łna': bring Ci-4 to life (shiyiiniłna': you brought me to life)
n(i)-ii-(Ø)--Øgaii: become very hot (as a horseshoe)(niigaii: it got very hot)
n(i)-ii-(Ø)--łgaii: heat O very hot (yiniiłgaii: he heated it)
ho-n(i)-ii-Ødoii: get warm (weather, or a room)(honiidoii: it got warm)
di-n(i)-ii-(Ø)--łtłóó': slacken O (as a taut wire)(yidiniiłtłóó': he slackened it)
dah dí-n(í)-ii-(Ø)--łkaad: start off driving O (a herd)(dah díníiłkaad: I started off driving it)
ná- ~ ń-dí-'(a)-ní-i-(Ø)--Øyą́ą́': just get a good start eating (when an interruption occurs)(ńdí'níiyą́ą́': I just got a good start eating, when---)
Ci-4-i-(Ø)--łtsą́: catch sight of Ci-4 (niiłtsą́: I caught sight of you)

## D/L-Class Verbs

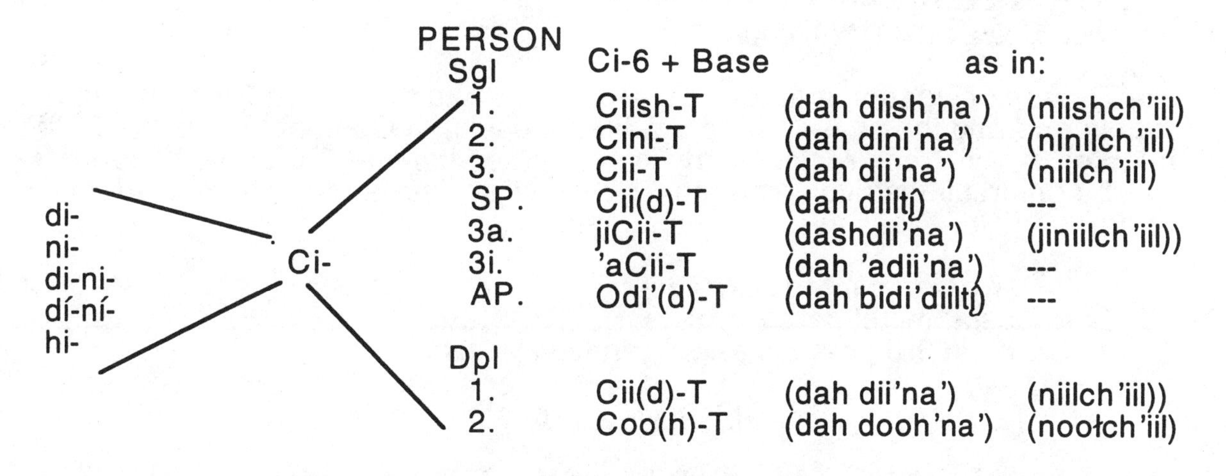


| PERSON | Ci-6 + Base | as in: | |
|---|---|---|---|
| Sgl | | | |
| 1. | Ciish-T | (dah diish'na') | (niishch'iil) |
| 2. | Cini-T | (dah dini'na') | (ninilch'iil) |
| 3. | Cii-T | (dah dii'na') | (niilch'iil) |
| SP. | Cii(d)-T | (dah diiltį́) | --- |
| 3a. | jiCii-T | (dashdii'na') | (jiniilch'iil)) |
| 3i. | 'aCii-T | (dah 'adii'na') | --- |
| AP. | Odi'(d)-T | (dah bidi'diiltį́) | --- |
| Dpl | | | |
| 1. | Cii(d)-T | (dah dii'na') | (niilch'iil)) |
| 2. | Coo(h)-T | (dah dooh'na') | (noołch'iil) |

ni-i-(Ø)--lch'iil: close eyes (niilch'iil: he closed his eyes)
bíyah ni-i-(Ø)--lkaal: support it from beneath - by pushing up
ni-i-(Ø)--lyool: bloat
di-ni-i-(Ø)--ltsood: grab O and hang on (shidiniiltsood: it grabbed me and hung on)
niki#-dí-ní-i-(Ø)--lbą́ą́z: borrow O (as a car) and keep it (chidí bits'ą́ą́' nikidíníisbą́ą́z: I borrowed his car and kept it)

## Disjunct Prefixes

See Tables on pages 269-273, inclusive.

# CHAPTER 5: THE PROGRESSIVE

The Progressive Mode describes an action or event as ongoing, without reference to beginning or end. It is conjugated in two distinctive patterns, of which one is marked by a yi- (= ghi-) prefix in Position 7 + a special stem, and the other by the distributive plural prefix of Position 3 (da-) + an unidentified yí- prefix of Position 6 with conjugation in a Ni-Imperfective pattern. These can be identified as the Yi-Progressive and the Da-yí-(ni)-Progressive.

## 1. THE YI-PROGRESSIVE

The Yi-Progressive is generally restricted to singular and duoplural number, with the exception of verbs based on number-specific stems. Thus:

yiltł'ééł: he is trotting along; they (two) are trotting along
yiiltł'ééł: we (two) are trotting along
but number-specific
yigááł: he is walking along
yiit'ash: we two are walking along
yiikah: we 3+ are walking along

The yi-conjugation marker of Yi-Perfective and that of the Progressive are probably one and the same. In determinant position a Conjunct Prefix (of Position 4,5 or 6) + yi-7 contract similarly in 1st person sgl and 3rd person Progressive verb constructions (including the Agentive Passive) and in the Yi-Perfective paradigms of D/L-Class verbs. In both instances:

C(i)(= any Conjunct Prefix) + yi- >
C-eesh-: in 1st person sgl
C-oo-: in 3rd persons and Agentive Passive

C(i)- + yi- > C-eesh-:

Progressive: ni$^7$-6a + yi- > neeshkał: I'm driving O (a herd) along

Perfective: ni$^2$-6b + yi- > biih neeshne': I stuck my head into it

Progressive: di$^5$-6a + yi- > deesht'ááł: I'm carrying it along (fire or torch)

Perfective: di$^1$-6a + yi- . biih deeshchid: I stuck my hand into it

Progressive: '(a)-4 + yi- > 'eesbą̨s: I'm driving along (an unspecified vehicle)

Perfective: '(a)-4 + yi- > 'eeshghal: I ate (unspecified meat)

Progressive: ni-4 + yi- > neeshchééł: I'm chasing you along

Perfective: ni-4 + yi- > neeshghal: I ate you

C(i)- + yi- > C-oo-:

Progressive: ni$^{7}$-6b + yi- > noochééł: he/they are fleeing

Perfective: ni$^{2}$-6b + + yi- > yiih noolne': he stuck his head into it
Progressive: di$^{6}$-6a + yi- > doolchį́į́ł: it's going along following a scent

Perfective: di$^{1}$-6a + yi- > yiih doolchid: he stuck his hand into it

Progressive: j(i)-5 + yi > joogááł: he (3a) is walking along

Perfective: (j(i)-5 + + yi- > joolghal: he (3a) ate it (meat)

Progressive: '(a)-4 + yi- > 'oołbąs: he's driving (something) along (a vehicle)

Perfective: '(a)-4 + yi- > 'oolghal: he ate (meat)

Progressive: y(i)-4 + yi- > yoołtééł: he's carrying an AnO along

Perfective: y(i)-4 + yi- > yoolghal: he ate it (meat)

Progressive: sh(i)-4 + yi-- > shoołtééł: he's carrying me along

Perfective: sh(i)-4 + yi- > shoolghal: he ate me

Agentive Passive Progressive: bi'dooltééł: he's being carried along

Agentive Passive Perfective: bi'doolghal: he was eaten

## Base Paradigm

Table 1

T = any Verb Theme

| PERSON | | | Prefix Position | | | | | |
|---|---|---|---|---|---|---|---|---|
| Sgl | 7 | + | 8 | + | 9-10 | | | as in: |
| 1. | yi- | + | -sh- | + | T- | > | yish-T | yishłeeł |
| 2. | yi- | + | \´/ | + | T- | > | yí-T | yíleeł |
| 3. | yi- | + | Ø | + | T- | > | yi-T d | yileeł |
| Dpl | | | | | | | | |
| 1. | y(i)- | + | -ii(d)- | + | T- | > | yii(d)-T | yiidleeł |
| 2. | wi- | + | -o(h)- | + | T- | > | woo(h)-T | woołeeł |

(yi)--Øleeł: be (in the process of) becoming (yá'át'ééh yileeł: he's getting well [a lifelong invalid])
(yi)--ltł'ééł: be jogging or trotting along (yiltł'ééł: he's jogging along)
(yi)--Ønééł: be in the process of moving residence (yinééł: he's on his way moving)

## Extended Base Paradigms

### 1. Conjunct Prefixes

Position 5 Prefixes + Base

Table 2

T = any Verb Theme

| PERSON Sgl/Dpl | Prefix Position 4 | + | 5 | + | Base | | | as in: |
|---|---|---|---|---|---|---|---|---|
| 3a. | --- | + | -j(i)- | + | -oo-T | > | joo-T | jooleeł |
| 3i. | --- | + | -'(a)- | + | -oo-T | > | 'oo-T | 'oogááł |
| 3s. | --- | + | -h(w)- | + | -oo-T | > | hoo-T | hooleeł |
| AP | O | + | -'(a)d(i)- | + | -oo-T | > | O'(a)doo-T | bi'dooltééł |

(yi)--Øleeł: be becoming (jooleeł: he/she/they is/are becoming [3a person]; hooleeł: area/space/things are becoming))
'(a)-(yi)--lkił: something is gliding along slowly (the hour hand on a clock)('oolkił)
O'd(i)-(yi)--ltééł: be carried along (a person)(shi'dooltééł: I'm being carried along)
(yi)--łtł'ééł: be jogging or trotting along (jooltl'ééł: he's jogging along)
(yi)--Øgááł: be walking/going along (1 subject) (joogááł: he/s walking along; 'oogááł: someone unspecified is going along; hoogááł: an event is progressing along)

Ci-Prefixes of Position 4 + Extended Base

Table 3

The Ci- direct object pronouns of Position 4 are added to the Extended Base (i.e. the Base + the subject pronoun prefixes of Position 5). When the direct object is 3rd person and the subject is 1st or 2nd person, the object is represented by Ø in Position 4. But when a direct object is represented by a Ci-prefix of Position 4, yi-7 takes the shape -ee- in 1st person sgl and -oo- in 3rd person, and the Position 4 object pronoun prefix retains its vowel in 2nd person sgl.

T = any Verb Theme

| PERSON Sgl | Prefix Position 4 | + | 5 | + | Base + Ø-4 | Base + Ci-4 | as in: Ø-4 | as in: Ci-4 |
|---|---|---|---|---|---|---|---|---|
| 1. | Ø/Ci- | + | --- | + | yish-T | C-eesh-T | yishtééł | neeshtééł |
| 2. | Ø/Ci- | + | --- | + | yí-T | Cí-í-T | yíłtééł | shííłtééł |
| 3. | --/C(i)- | + | --- | + | --- | C-oo-T | --- | shoołtééł |
| SP | Ø/-- | + | --- | + | yi(d)-T | --- | yiltééł | --- |
| 3o. | y(i)- | + | --- | + | --- | y-oo-T | --- | yoołteeł |
| 3a. | Ø/Ci- | + | j- | + | -oo-T | j-oo-T | joołtééł | shijoołtééł |
| AP | O | + | -'(a)d- | + | -oo(d)-T | O'd-oo(d)-T | --- | bi'dooltééł |
| Dpl | | | | | | | | |
| 1. | Ø/C(i)- | + | --- | + | -ii(d)-T | C-ii(d)-T | yiiltééł | niiltééł |
| 2. | Ø/C(i)- | + | --- | + | -oo(h)-T | C-oo(h)-T | woołtééł | shoołtééł |

(yi)--łtééł: be carrying an AnO along (yiltééł: it's being carried along [as a lamb]; shííłtééł: you're carrying me along; neeshtééł: I'm carrying you along; yoołtééł; he's carrying him/her/it along; bi'dooltééł: he's being carried along)

(Dah: up + Progressive > a static: be holding O up, as in: 'awéé' dah yoołtééł: she's holding the baby up; shich'ah dah yish'ááł: I'm holding my hat up; naanish bee dah yisháááł: I make my living from work - a job - i.e. I maintain myself in ambulatory status by work)

'A- ~ 'i- :Position 4 + Extended Base

Table 4

The 3i direct object pronoun of Position 4: something/someone, takes variable shape, depending on the phonological environment.

T = any Verb Theme

| PERSON | Prefix Position | | | | | | |
|---|---|---|---|---|---|---|---|
| Sgl | 4 | + | 5 | + | Base | | as in: |
| 1. | '(a)- | + | --- | + | -eesh-T | > 'eesh-T | 'eesbąs |
| 2. | 'í- | + | --- | + | -í-T | > 'íí-T | 'ííłbąs |
| 3. | '(a)- | + | --- | + | -oo-T | > 'oo-T | 'oołbąs |
| SP | '(a)- | + | --- | + | -oo(d)-T | > 'oo(d)-T | 'oot'į́ |
| 3a. | 'a- | + | -j- | + | -oo-T | > 'ajoo-T | 'ajoołbąs |
| Dpl | | | | | | | |
| 1. | '(a)- | + | --- | + | -ii(d)-T | > 'ii(d)-T | 'iilbąs |
| 2. | '(a)- | + | --- | + | -oo(h)-T | > 'oo(h)-T | 'oołbąs |

'a-(yi)--łbąs: be driving along (in an unspecified wheeled vehicle - literally: be causing something hoop-like to roll along)
'a-(yi)--łkǫ́ǫ́ł: be swimming along('eeshkǫ́ǫ́ł: I'm swimming along [literally, be smoothing something??])
'a-(yi)--Ø'į́: be seeing; see something ('eesh'į́: I can see; 'oot'į́ = noun "vision" - literally, something is seen)

## Ho- ~ hw- ~ h(w)-: Position 4 + Extended Base

### Table 5

The 3s direct object pronoun of Position 4: space, area, impersonal "it / things" takes variable shape, depending on the phonological environment.

T = any Verb Theme

| PERSON | Prefix Position | | | | | | |
|---|---|---|---|---|---|---|---|
| Sgl | 4 | + | 5 | + | Base | | as in: |
| 1. | hw- | + | --- | + | -eesh-T | > hweesh-T | hweesh'áál |
| 2. | hwí- | + | --- | + | 'í-T | > hwíí-T | hwíí'áál |
| 3. | h(w)- | + | --- | + | -oo-T | > hoo-T | hoo'áál |
| SP | h(w)- | + | --- | + | -oo(d)-T | > hoo(d)-T | hoot'áál |
| 3a. | ho- | + | -j- | + | -oo-T | > hojoo-T | hojoo'áál |
| Dpl | | | | | | | |
| 1. | hw- | + | --- | + | -ii(d)-T | > hwii(d)-T | hwiit'áál |
| 2. | h(w)- | + | --- | + | -oo(h)-T | > hoo(h)-T | hooh'áál |

ho-(yi)-Øááł: carry on planning; administer affairs (bá hweesh'ááł: I'm planning for them, administering their affairs(t'óó bee náás hweesh'ááł: I'm procrastinating on it - literally, moving "things" forward with it)
ho-(yi)--łdlał: plow a furrow (hoołdlał: he's plowing a furrow – literally, he's roughly ripping an area)

## Ci-Prefixes of Position 6 + Extended Base

Eleven of the 46 derivational-thematic prefixes of Position 6 (as listed in the Analytical Lexicon, pages 851-853) appear in Yi-Progressive Verb Bases, including:

di[1]-thematic: movement involving arms or legs
 dah doolnih: he's holding his hand up
 dah dool'is: he's holding his foot up
di[4]-thematic: refuge, succour, relief
 yah deeshdááł: I'm on a borrowing mission
di[5]-thematic: fire; light
 yidoołt'ááł: he's going along carrying a torch
 dook'ą́ął: a fire is moving along (as a grass fire)
di[6]-thematic: mouth, stomach, oral noise, food
 dah yidoozoh: he's holding a mouthful of it
hi[1]-Seriative: segmental action
 hoot'eeł: it's hopping along (a bird, rabbit)
 heesh'ááł: I'm moving a SRO along by applying a succession of tugs
yi[3]-allomorph of hi[1]-: Seriative: segmental action (required in the presence of a preceding Conjunct Prefix)
 yiyoo'ááł: he's moving a SRO along with a succession of tugs
dzi- ~ ji-derivational: away into space
 dzoot'ih: it's scampering long (as a squirrel on a limb)
 bíjeeshtał: I'm kicking it along (as a tin can)(bídzííłtał: you're kicking it along; yídzoołtał: he's kicking it along; bíjoołtał: he [3a person] is kicking it along)

si[2]-thematic: relates to the movement of sound
hosoolts'ǫ́ǫ́ł: a sound is moving along
ni[2]-thematic: generic classifier for round shape
dah noot'ááł: he holds his head up (as with pride)
ni[7]-thematic: meaning uncertain
yinoołkał: he's driving O (a herd) along
bízhneeshtał: I'm going along kicking (spurring) it (as a rider who spurs his mount)(yíznootał: he [3a person] is going along spurring)

With the Ci-Prefixes of Position 6 the Progressive paradigms follow the same pattern as that described in Table 3 above (Position 4 Prefixes + Extended Base).

Table 6

T = any Verb Theme

| PERSON | Prefix Position | | | | | | | | | | as in: | |
|---|---|---|---|---|---|---|---|---|---|---|---|---|
| Sgl | 4 | + | 5 | + | 6 | + | Base | | | | | |
| 1. | Ø/Ci- | + | --- | + | C(i)- | + | -eesh-T | > | Ceesh-T | | deeshdą́sh | neeshkał |
| 2. | Ø/Ci- | + | --- | + | Cí- | + | -í-T | > | Cíí-T | | dííłdą́sh | nííłkał |
| 3. | --/C(i)- | + | --- | + | C(i)- | + | -oo-T | > | Coo-T | | dook'ą́ą́ł | nooltǫ́ǫ́ł |
| SP | Ø/-- | + | --- | + | C(i)- | + | -oo(d)-T | > | Coo(d)-T | | dooldą́sh | noolkał |
| 3o. | --/y- | + | --- | + | C(i)- | + | -oo-T | > | yiCoo-T | | yidoołdą́sh | yinoołkał |
| 3a. | Ø/Ci- | + | j- | + | C(i)- | + | -oo-T | > | jiCoo-T | | jidoołdą́sh | jinoołkał |
| 3i. | --- | + | 'a- | + | C(i)- | + | -oo-T | > | 'aCoo-T | | 'adoo'nííł | 'anooltǫ́ǫ́ł |
| 3s. | --- | + | ho- | + | C(i)- | + | -oo-T | > | hoCoo-T | | hodook'ą́ą́ł | honoochał |
| AP | O | + | di'(a)d- | + | C(i)- | + | -oo(d)-T | > | Odi'Coo(d)-T | | bidi'dooldą́sh | bidi'noolchééł |
| Dpl | | | | | | | | | | | | |
| 1. | Ø/C(i)- | + | --- | + | C(i)- | + | -ii(d)-T | > | -ii(d)-T | | diildą́sh | niilkał |
| 2. | Ø/C(i)- | + | --- | + | C(i)- | + | -oo(h)-T | > | -oo(h)-T | | doołdą́sh | noołkał |

di-(yi)--łdą́sh: be jerking O along (a recalcitrant)(deeshdą́sh: I'm jerking him along; shidííłdą́sh: you're jerking me along)
di-(yi)--Øk'ą́ą́ł: it's burning along (a fire)(dook'ą́ą́ł: a fire is moving along)
'a-di-(yi)--(d)'nííł: peal of thunder rumbles along ('adoo'nííł: a peal of thunder rumbles by)
ho-di-(yi)--Øk'ą́ą́ł: area of fire is burning along; a forest fire is moving along (hodook'ą́ą́ł)
ni-(yi)--ltǫ́ǫ́ł: be galloping along (a horse)(shił nooltǫ́ǫ́ł: I'm riding it along at a gallop - literally, it's galloping along with me)
'a-ni-(yi)--ltǫ́ǫ́ł: something is galloping along (shił 'anooltǫ́ǫ́ł: I'm riding along at a gallop)
ni-(yi)--łkał: be driving O (a herd) along (dibé nííłkał: you're driving the herd of sheep along)
dah honoochał: area is in disorder; area is a mess

## Hi- / yi[3]-6a/6c: Seriative + Extended Base

The Seriative prefix hi- has a yi-allomorph that is required in the presence of a preceding Conjunct Prefix.

T = any Verb Theme

| PERSON Sgl | 4 | + | 5 | + | 6a | / 6c | + | Base | Ø 4 | + Ci-4 |
|---|---|---|---|---|---|---|---|---|---|---|
| 1. | Ø/Ci- | + | --- | + | h- | y- | + | -eesh-T | heeshtééł | niyeeshtééł |
| 2. | Ø/Ci- | + | --- | + | hí- | yí- | + | -í-T | hííłtééł | shiyííłtééł |
| 3. | --/C(i)- | + | --- | + | --- | y- | + | -oo-T | --- | shiyoołtééł |
| 3o. | --/yi- | + | --- | + | --- | y- | + | -oo-T | --- | yiyoołtééł |
| 3a. | Ø/Ci- | + | ji- | + | --- | y- | + | -oo-T | --- | jiyoołtééł |
| AP | O | + | di'(a)- | + | --- | y- | + | -oo-T | --- | shidi'yooltééł |
| Dpl | | | | | | | | | | |
| 1. | Ø/C(i)- | + | --- | + | h- | y- | + | -ii(d)-T | hiiltééł | niyiiltééł |
| 2. | Ø/C(i)- | + | --- | + | h- | y- | + | -oo(h)-T | hoołtééł | shiyoołtééł |

hi/yi-(yi)--łtééł: tug an AnO along (as by pulling first on one side, then on the other)(heeshtééł: I'm tugging him along; niyeeshtééł: I'm tugging you along; shiyoołtééł: he's tugging me along

## 2. Disjunct Prefixes

### The Prefixes of Position 1 + Extended Base

Of the many derivational-thematic prefixes assigned to Position 1, a relative few occur as determinant constituents of Progressive Verb Bases, and these produce few lexical derivatives.

'á-thematic: with verbs of making, doing, dwindling
'ááshnííł: be doing
'áádįįł: it is progressively vanishing
'áyoolííł: he's making it (along)
kw- ~ ko-derivational-thematic: thus
'ąą kwáániił: he's increasing in size, expanding
P-í-postpositional-derivational: against P
bééshhił: I'm pushing (against) O along (wheelbarrow)
bíká- ~ há-derivational: after it (to get it, as firewood, water)
bíkááshááł ~ hááshááł: I'm on my way going along after it
ná[1]-derivational: around in a circle; around making a turn
nááshbał: I'm whirling it around (as a wheel)
naanáálwoł: it's running about to and fro
bináashwoł: I'm running around it
ná-reversionary: returning back; reverting
nááshdááł: I'm on the way walking back
náyoołtééł: he's on the way bringing/taking an AnO back
náá(ná)-Semeliterative: once again; another one
nááhoołtįįł: another squall is moving along
náánááshtééł: I'm again going along carrying an AnO; I'm carrying another AnO along
yá-thematic: with verbs of talking

yááłtih: he's going along talking
P-k'i-postpositional: on
bik'iisdził: support them (one's family)
'ák'iisdził: support self; be self-supporting

## Cá-Prefixes of Position 1 + Extended Base

### Table 8

Cá- + yi-7 contract to produce Cáá- in 1st person sgl, 3rd person sgl/dpl and Simple Passive; and Cá- + yí-(< yi- + ni-8) contract to appear as Cáá- in 2nd person sgl.

T = any Verb Theme

| PERSON | Prefix Position | | | | | | | | | as in: | |
|---|---|---|---|---|---|---|---|---|---|---|---|
| Sgl | 1 | + | 4 | + | 5 | + | Base | | | + Ø-4 | + Ci-4 |
| 1. | Cáá- | + | Ø/Ci- | + | --- | + | (yi)sh-T | > | Cáásh-T | nááshtééł | náneeshtééł |
| 2. | Cáá- | + | Ø/Ci- | + | --- | + | (yí)-T | > | Cáá-T | náátééł | náshíítééł |
| 3. | Cáá- | + | Ø/Ci- | + | --- | + | (yi)-T | > | Cáá-T | náádááł | (náshooɫtééł) |
| SP | Cáá- | + | Ø/-- | + | --- | + | (yi[d])-T | > | Cáá(d)-T | nááltééł | --- |
| 3o. | Cá- | + | --/y- | + | --- | + | -oo-T | > | Cáyoo-T | --- | náyooɫtééł |
| 3a. | Cá- | + | Ø/Ci- | + | -j- | + | -oo-T | > | Cájoo-T | ńjooɫtééł | náshijooɫtééł |
| 3i. | Cá- | + | --- | + | -'- | + | -oo-T | > | Cá'oo-T | ná'oolwoł | --- |
| 3s. | Cá- | + | --- | + | h(w)- | + | -oo-T | > | Cáhoo-T | 'áhooníłł | --- |
| AP | Cá- | + | O | + | '(a)d- | + | -oo-T | > | CáO'doo-T | --- | nábi'dooltééł |
| Dpl | | | | | | | | | | | |
| 1. | Cá- | + | Ø/Ci- | + | --- | + | (y)ii(d)-T | > | Cáii(d)-T | néiiltééł | nániiltééł |
| 2. | Cá- | + | Ø/C(i)-+ | | --- | + | -a(h)-T | > | Cáá(h)-T | náátééł | náshooɫtééł |

ná-#-(yi)--ɫtééł: be carrying an AnO back (náneeshtééł: I'm carrying you back; náshooɫtééł: he's carrying me back/you two are carrying me back)
ná-#-(yi)--(d)dááł: be going along back (1 subject)(náádááł: he's going along back returning)
ná-#-'(a)-(yi)--lwoł: something unspecified is running along returning (as in shił ná'oolwoł: I'm on my way back by fast moving conveyance - literally something is running along returning in company with me)
'á#-ho-(yi)--Øníłł: an event is happening ('ádahooníłł: 3+ events are taking place; 'ádahooníłłígíí: current events)
ná-#-(yi)--ɫhis: be turning O around in a circle, be cranking or winding O (náásxis: I'm turning it around; nááɫhis: you're turning it around)
ná-#-(yi)--Øyis: be turning around (náásxis: I'm turning around; nááyis: you/he are/is turning around)

## Ci-: Position 1b + Extended Base

### Table 9

Postpositional -k'i-: on occurs as a derivational element in two Progressive Verb Bases. Other examples are not available. -K'i- (unlike -k'í-) is not a bound postpositional prefix so it functions very loosely in merging with the Progressive (bik'i + [y]iisdził > bik'iisdził).

PERSON

| Sgl | | Dpl |
|---|---|---|
| 1. | bik'iisdził | bik'iildził |
| 2. | bik'iyíldził | bik'iołdził |
| 3. | yik'iildził | |
| 3a. | bik'ijooldził | |

bik'i#-(yl)--ldzlł: support them (one's family)
'ák'i#-(yi)--ldził: support oneself; be self-supporting ('ák'iisdził: I'm self-supporting)

Cí-: Position 1b + Extended Base

Table 10

The bound postpositional prefix -í-: against, in contact with, of Position 1b appears in the Verb Base P-í#(yi)--Øyił: be pushing O along (as a wheelbarrow).

PERSON

| Sgl | | Dpl |
|---|---|---|
| 1. | bééshhił | bíigił |
| 2. | bííyił | bóohił |
| 3. | yíyooyił | |
| SP. | bóogił | |
| 3a. | bíjooyił | |

Có-: Position 1b + Extended Base

Table 11

Kó-: Position 1b contracts with yi-7 to produce kwáá- in 1st person sgl, 3rd person sgl/dpl and Simple Passive, and 2nd person dpl, as in:

PERSON

| Sgl | | Dpl |
|---|---|---|
| 1. | kwááshniił | kwíi'niił |
| 2. | kwáániił | kóohniił ~ kwáahniił |
| 3. | kwáániił | |
| 3a. | kójooniił | |
| 3o. | kóyooliił | |

'ąą kó#-(yi)--Øniił: increase in size, expand, inflate
náás kó#-(yi)--Øliił: increase O (as one's flock of sheep)

## 2. THE DA-YÍ-(NI)-PROGRESSIVE

When the number of actors is 3 or more (3+) they are conceived as acting individually and their plurality is marked by distributive plural da- (each of 3+) in Position 3. The distributive plural requires a special Progressive Base derived with an unidentified yí-prefix, arbitrarily assigned to Position 6. It is conjugated in a Ni-Imperfective pattern.

Number-specific verbs of locomotion distinguish between group action in the Progressive Mode, and individual (scattered) action. Thus the stems kah/káah: 3+ go, walk yield:

Simple Yi-Progressive: yiikah: we 3+ are going along in a group
Da-yí-(ni)-Progressive: deíníikááh: we 3+ are going along in a scattered group

The Yi-Progressive and the Da-yí-(ni)-Progressive are contrasted in the following examples:

'Ashkii 'atiingóó yiltł'ééł: the boy is trotting along the road.
'Ashiiké ndilt'éego 'atiingóó yiltł'ééł: a couple of boys are trotting along the road.
'Ashiiké tált'éego 'atiingóó deíltł'ééh: three boys are trotting along the road.

'Ashkii télii 'atiingóó yoolóós: the boy is leading the burro along the road.
'Ashiiké tált'éego télii 'atiingóó deílóós: three boys are leading a burro/burros along the road.

'Ashiiké' ndilt'éego dibé yázhí 'atiingóó yootéél: a couple of boys are going along on the road, each carrying a lamb.
'Ashiiké 'ashdlalt'éego dibé yázhí 'atiingóó deíłteeh: five boys are each carrying a lamb along on the road.

'Ashiiké 'ashdlalt'éego télii yázhí daaztsą́ą́ léi' 'atiingóó deíłteeh: five boys are carrying a little dead burro along on the road.

Tł'éédą́ą́' nahóółtą́. K'ad cháshk'eh góyaa tó yigoh: last night it rained. Water is running down in the wash.
Tł'éédą́ą́' nahóółtą́. K'ad chádaashk'eh góyaa tó deígeeh: it rained last night. Water is now running down in the 3+ washes.

'Ana'í t'óó 'ahayóí nihich'į' 'adah deílch'ą́ąłgo yiiłtsą́: I spotted a lot of enemies parachuting down on us.

'Ashkii be'at'ééd yił yi'ash: the boy is walking along with his girl friend.
'Ashiiké dį́įt'éego be'at'ééd yił deí'aash: four boys are walking along with their girl friends (a total of 4 pairs, as indicated by -'aash: dual go).

### Base Paradigm

The Da-yí-(ni)-Progressive is derived with elements that lie outside the Base markers of Position 7-8. However, the simple da-yí-(ni)- paradigm provides the foundation for a number of Verb Bases derived with prefixes of Positions 6 and 1.

In the Ni-Imperfective (Momentaneous) ni- is replaced by a (y)i-prefix in 3rd persons (exclusive of 3s. person), and (y)i- absorbs ni-7 as a high tone to take the shape (y)-í- with Ø/Ł-Class Themes. Thus:

3. yílyeed (< yi- + ni-7 > yí + lyeed): it's in the act of arriving running

3i. 'ílyeed (< '[i]-5 + [y]i- + -ni-7 > 'í- + lyeed): something unspecified is in the act of arriving running (as in shił 'ílyeed: I'm in the act of arriving by fast moving vehicle)

3a. jílyeed (< j[i]-5 + [y]i- + -ni-7 > jí- + lyeed): he/she is in the act of arriving running

3. yíłteeh (< y[i]-4 + [y]i- + -ni-7 > yí- + lteeh): he's in the act of arriving carrying it (an AnO)

3s. ch'íhóghááh (< ch'í-1b + ho-5 + [y]i- + -ni-7 > hó- + Øghááh): event starts

This pattern is also followed by da-yí-(ni)-Progressive in Simple 3rd person constructions, because the (y)í-derivational prefix appears to delete in these environments, producing Progressive and Imperfective constructions that converge in shape, as:

| | |
|---|---|
| Da-yí-(ni)-Progressive: | deí'nééh: they 3+ are crawling along<br>dají'nééh: 3a person subjects are crawling along |
| Ni-Imperfective: | deí'nééh: they 3+ are in the act of arriving crawling<br>dají'nééh: 3a person subjects are in the act of arriving crawling |
| Da-yí-(ni)-Progressive: | deí'aah; they 3+ are carrying a SRO along<br>dají'aah: 3a person subjects are carrying a SRO along |
| Ni-Imperfective: | deí'aah: they 3+ are in the act of arriving carrying a SRO<br>dají'aah: 3a person subjects are in the act of arriving carrying a SRO |

In the model paradigm there is a category identified as singular. These are components of comitative constructions, in which a singular subject is the focal actor within a group of three or more. These singular forms have limited use.

'Ashiiké daniidlínígíí dziłghą́ą'di bił deíníshkááh (or bił yishkah) ńt'éé' shash léi' nihich'į' ńdiilwod: I was walking along with the boys in the mountains when we were attacked by a bear.

## Table 12

T = any Verb Theme

| PERSON | Prefix Position | | | | | | | | | | | |
|---|---|---|---|---|---|---|---|---|---|---|---|---|
| Sgl | 3 | + | 4 | + | 5 | + | 6 | + | Base | | | as in: |
| 1. | de- | + | Ø | + | --- | + | (y)í- | + | nish-T | > | deíních-T | deíníshkááh |
| 2. | de- | + | Ø- | + | --- | + | (y)í- | + | ní-T | > | deíní-T | deíníkááh |
| 3. | de- | + | Ø | + | --- | + | --- | + | (y)í-T | > | deí-T | deíkááh |
| 3a. | da- | + | Ø | + | -j- | + | --- | + | (y)í-T | > | dají-T | dajíkááh |
| Dist. Pl | | | | | | | | | | | | |
| 1. | de- | + | Ø | + | --- | + | (y)í- | + | níí(d)-T | > | deíníí(d)-T | deínííkááh |
| 2. | de- | + | Ø | + | --- | + | (y)í- | + | nó(h)-T | > | deínó(h)-T | deínóhkááh |
| 3. | de- | + | Ø | + | --- | + | --- | + | (y)í-T | > | deí-T | deíkááh |
| 3o. | de- | + | (y-) | + | --- | + | --- | + | (y)í-T | > | deí-T | deí'aah |
| 3a. | da- | + | Ø | + | -j- | + | --- | + | (y)í-T | > | dají-T | dajíkááh<br>dají'aah |

da#-yí-(ni)--(d)kááh: 3+ subjects are going along
da#-yí-(ni)--Ø'aah: 3+ subjects are carrying a SRO along

When a Ni-Imperfective Verb Base includes a derivational-thematic prefix of Position 6 (di-, ni-, hi- ~ yi-), ni-7 takes the shape -ee- in 3rd person and Passive constructions, producing:

di-6 + ni-7 > dee- as in:

yaa yidee'aah: he's turning it over to him
baa deet'aah: it's being turned over to him
yaa deidee'aah: they 3+ are turning it over to him
baa dazhdee'aah: 3+ 3a subjects

ni-6 + -ni-7 > nee- as in:

yigháneelne': he's in the act of butting his head through it
yighádaneelne': they 3+ are butting their heads through it
bighádazhneelne': 3+ 3a subjects are butting their heads through it

hi-6 + -ni-7 > hee- as in:

heet'e': it's in the act of arriving hopping
daheet'e': they 3+ are arriving hopping

ho-4 (3s/thematic) + -ni-7 > hó- - as in:
hózíid: he's in the act of arriving groping

In da-yí-(ni)-Progressive constructions a Position 6 derivational-thematic element contracts similarly with ni-7 to produce C-ee-, but yí- does not entirely delete; it remains in the form of its high tone, and -ee- takes the shape -ée- in 3rd person constructions.

da- + di- + yí- + (ni)- > dadée-:
dadéedzééh: they 3+ are staggering along
dazhdéedzééh: 3+ 3a subjects are staggering along
deidéeyóód: they 3+ are driving them along
dazhdéeyóód: 3+ 3a subjects are driving them along

da- + ni- + yí- = (ni)- > danée-:
danéechééh: they 3+ are fleeing (along)
dazhnéechééh: 3+ 3a subjects are fleeing along
deinéełkaad: they 3+ are driving them along
dazhnéełkaad: 3+ 3a subjects are driving them along

da- + hi- ~ yi- + yí- + (ni)- > dahée- ~ dayiyée-:
dahéet'e': they 3+ are hopping along
dajiyéet'e': 3+ 3a subjects are hopping along
dayiyée'aah: they 3+ are tugging a SRO along
dajiyée'aah: 3+ 3a subjects are tugging a SRO along

da- + dzi- + yí- + (ni)- > dadzée-:
yídadzéełtaał: they 3+ are kicking it along
bídeijéełtaał: 3+ 3a subjects are kicking it along

da- + ho-4 (3s/thematic)- + yí- + (ni)- > dahwée-:
dahwée'aah: they 3+ are planning
dahojée'aah: 3+ 3a subjects are planning

Di-6a/ni-6b Derivational-Thematic Prefixes + Extended Base

Table 13

T = any Verb Theme

| PERSON | Prefix Position | | | | | | | | | | | | | |
|---|---|---|---|---|---|---|---|---|---|---|---|---|---|---|
| Dist. Pl | 3 | + | 4 | + | 5 | + | 6a/b | + | 6 | + | Base | | | as in: |
| 1. | da- | + | Ø | + | --- | + | Ci- | + | (y)í- | + | nîí(d)-T | > | daCíínîí(d)-T | dadíínîídzééh |
| 2. | da- | + | Ø | + | --- | + | Ci- | + | (y)í- | + | nó(h)-T | > | daCíínó(h)-T | dadíínóhdzééh |
| 3. | da- | + | Ø | + | --- | + | C- | + | \ ´ / | + | \ ´ /-T | > | daCée-T | dadéedzééh |
| 3o. | de- | + | (-i-) | + | --- | + | C- | + | \ ´ / | + | \ ´ /-T | > | deiCée-T | deidéełdą́ą́sh |
| 3a. | da- | + | Ø | + | -zh- | + | C- | + | \ ´ / | + | \ ´ /-T | > | dazhCée-T | dazhdéedzééh |

da#-di-yí-(ni)--(d)dzééh: be staggering along (deesdzah: I'm staggering along)
da#-di-yí-(ni)--łdą́ą́sh: be jerking O along (a recalcitrant)(dadíínííldą́ą́sh: we're jerking it along; deeshdąsh; I'm jerking it along)
da#-ni-yí-(ni)--Øchééh: be fleeing along (daníínííchééh: we're fleeing, we're in flight; danéechééh: they're fleeing)

## Hi- ~ yi-6a / 6c-Seriative + Extended Base

### Table 14

The hi-Seriative follows the same pattern as that described in Table 13, and its yi-allomorph is required in the presence of a preceding Conjunct Prefix.

| PERSON | Dist. Pl. | as in: |
|---|---|---|
| 1. | dahíínii(d)-T | dahíínííIghaał |
| 2. | dahíínó(h)-T | dahíínółghaał |
| 3. | dahée-T | dahéelghaał |
| 3a. | **dajiyée-T** | dajiyéelghaał |
| 3o. | **dayiyée-T** | dayiyée'aah |

da#-hi-yí-(ni)--lghaał: be wriggling along on back or belly (heeshghał: I'm wriggling along)
da#-hi-yí-(ni)--Ø'aah: be tugging a SRO along (first one side, then the other - as a heavy refrigerator)(dahíínííit'aah: we're tugging it along; dayiyée'aah: they're tugging it along

## 'A- ~ -'i- ~ -'-: Position 4 + Extended Base

### Table 15

The 3i object pronoun of Position 4 takes the form of its -'i-allomorph in 1st and 2nd person distributive plural, and reduces to -'- in 3rd persons. Thus:

| PERSON | Dist. Pl. | as in: |
|---|---|---|
| 1. | da'íínii(d)-T | da'íínííIkǫ́ǫ́h |
| 2. | da'íínó(h)-T | da'íínółkǫ́ǫ́h |
| 3. | da'í-T | da'íłkǫ́ǫ́h |
| 3a. | da'jí-T | da'jíłkǫ́ǫ́h |

da#-'(a)-(y)i-(ni)--łkǫ́ǫ́h: be swimming along ('eeshkǫ́ǫ́ł: I'm swimming along)

### Ho- ~ hw-: Position 4 + Extended Base

The 3s object pronoun of Position 4 behaves like a prefix of Position 6, producing -hwée- rather than -ho- in 3rd persons; and j(i)-: the 3a subject pronoun of Position 5 appears as -jée- in 3rd person when it is a constituent of a Verb Base that contains ho-4. Thus;

Table 16

| PERSON | Dist. Pl. |
|---|---|
| 1. | dahwííníídlááh |
| 2. | dahwíínóhłááh |
| 3. | **dahwéełááh** |
| 3a. | **dahojéełááh** |

da#-ho-yí-(ni)--ł(l)ááh: be carrying on a ceremony (hweeshłááł: I'm carrying on a ceremony)

## RECAPITULATION

## YI-PROGRESSIVE

### 1. Extended Base Paradigm

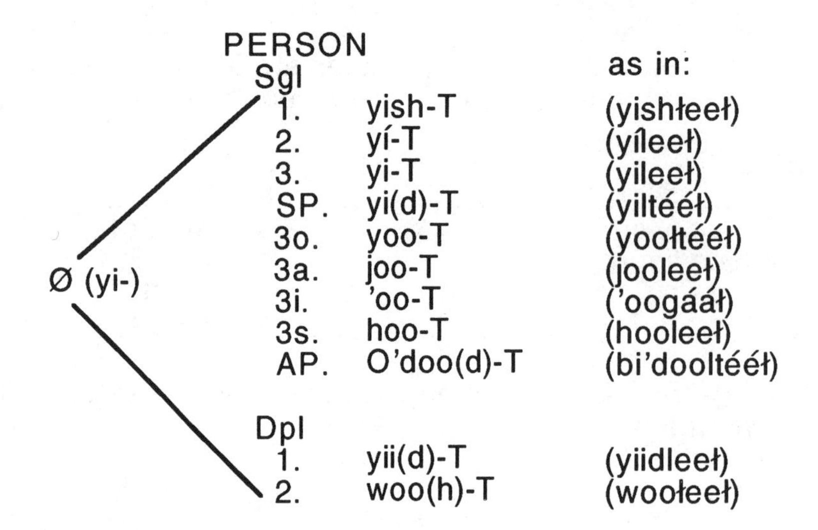


(yi)--Øleeł: be becoming
(yi)--ltééł: be being carried along (An O)
(yi)--łteeł: carry an AnO along
(yi)--Øgááł: be going along; be coming (ła' 'oogááł: someone is coming)

## Conjunct Prefixes

### 2. Ci-: Position 6a/6b + Extended Base

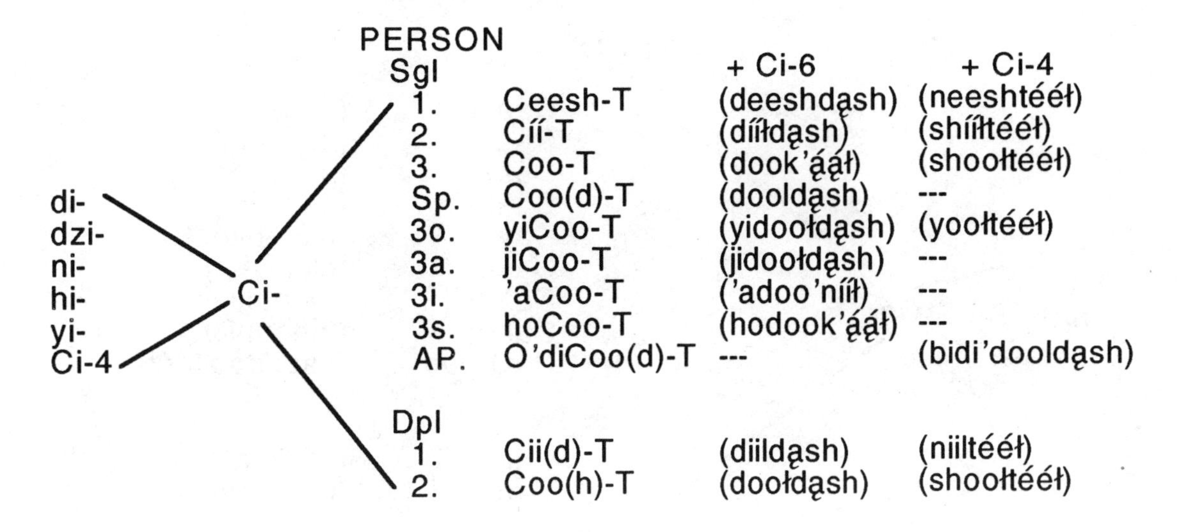

Prefixes: di-, dzi-, ni-, hi-, yi-, Ci-4 → Ci-

| PERSON | | + Ci-6 | + Ci-4 |
|---|---|---|---|
| Sgl | | | |
| 1. | Ceesh-T | (deeshdąsh) | (neeshtééł) |
| 2. | Cíí-T | (dííłdąsh) | (shííłtééł) |
| 3. | Coo-T | (dook'ą́ą́ł) | (shoołtééł) |
| Sp. | Coo(d)-T | (dooldąsh) | --- |
| 3o. | yiCoo-T | (yidoołdąsh) | (yoołtééł) |
| 3a. | jiCoo-T | (jidoołdąsh) | --- |
| 3i. | 'aCoo-T | ('adoo'nííł) | --- |
| 3s. | hoCoo-T | (hodook'ą́ą́ł) | --- |
| AP. | O'diCoo(d)-T | --- | (bidi'dooldąsh) |
| Dpl | | | |
| 1. | Cii(d)-T | (diildąsh) | (niiltééł) |
| 2. | Coo(h)-T | (doołdąsh) | (shoołtééł) |

di-(yi)--łdąsh: be jerking O along (a recalcitrant)
di-(yi)--Øk'ą́ą́ł: be burning
di-(yi)--(d)'nííł: be rumbling along (thunder)
ni-(yi)--łtééł: be carrying you along

### 3. 'A ~ 'i- ~ -'-/ho- ~ hw-: Position 4 + Extended Base

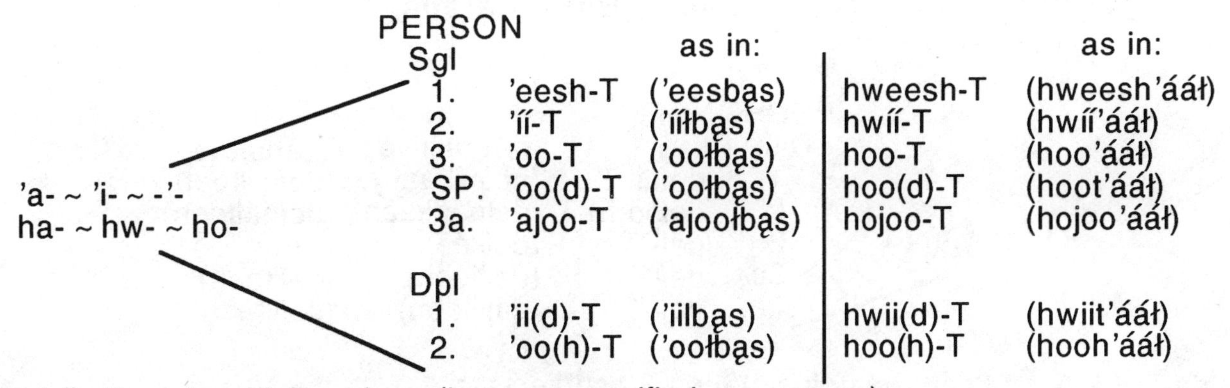

Prefixes: 'a- ~ 'i- ~ -'- / ha- ~ hw- ~ ho-

| PERSON | | as in: | | as in: |
|---|---|---|---|---|
| Sgl | | | | |
| 1. | 'eesh-T | ('eesbąs) | hweesh-T | (hweesh'ááł) |
| 2. | 'íí-T | ('ííłbąs) | hwíí-T | (hwíí'ááł) |
| 3. | 'oo-T | ('oołbąs) | hoo-T | (hoo'ááł) |
| SP. | 'oo(d)-T | ('oołbąs) | hoo(d)-T | (hoot'ááł) |
| 3a. | 'ajoo-T | ('ajoołbąs) | hojoo-T | (hojoo'ááł) |
| Dpl | | | | |
| 1. | 'ii(d)-T | ('iilbąs) | hwii(d)-T | (hwiit'ááł) |
| 2. | 'oo(h)-T | ('oołbąs) | hoo(h)-T | (hooh'ááł) |

'a-(yi)--łbąs: be driving along (in an unspecified car, wagon)
ho-(yi)--Ø'ááł: be planning, administering

## Disjunct Prefixes

### 4. Cá-: Position 1b + Extended Base

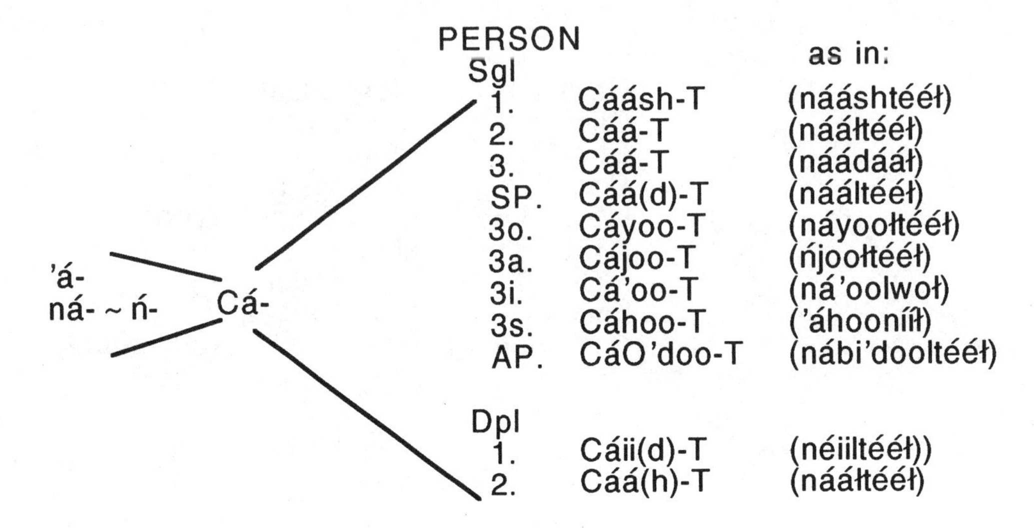

| | | PERSON | | as in: |
|---|---|---|---|---|
| | | Sgl | | |
| 'á-<br>ná- ~ ń- | Cá- | 1. | Cáásh-T | (náíshtééł) |
| | | 2. | Cáá-T | (náá**ł**tééł) |
| | | 3. | Cáá-T | (náádááł) |
| | | SP. | Cáá(d)-T | (náá**l**tééł) |
| | | 3o. | Cáyoo-T | (náyooł**t**ééł) |
| | | 3a. | Cájoo-T | (ńjooł**t**ééł) |
| | | 3i. | Cá'oo-T | (ná'oolwoł) |
| | | 3s. | Cáhoo-T | ('áhoonííł) |
| | | AP. | CáO'doo-T | (nábi'dooltééł) |
| | | Dpl | | |
| | | 1. | Cáii(d)-T | (néiiltééł)) |
| | | 2. | Cáá(h)-T | (náá**ł**tééł) |

'á-(yi)--Øliił: be making O ('ááshłiił: I'm making it)
ná-(yi)--łtééł: be carrying an AnO back
'á-ho-(yi)--Ønííł: be happening (an event)

## DA-YÍ-(NI)-PROGRESSIVE

### 1. Extended Base Paradigm

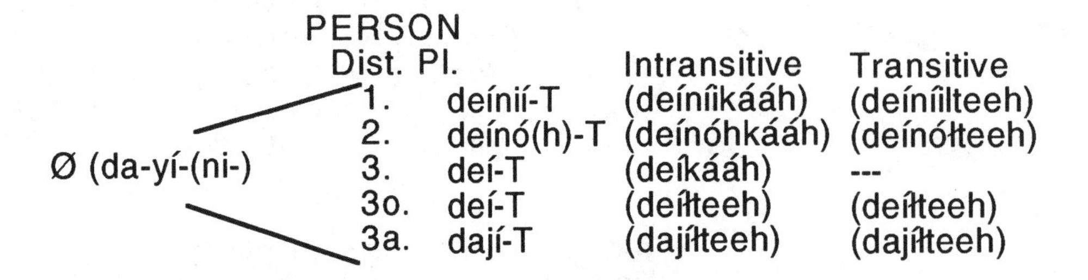

| | PERSON<br>Dist. Pl. | | Intransitive | Transitive |
|---|---|---|---|---|
| Ø (da-yí-(ni-) | 1. | deínií-T | (deíníikááh) | (deínííilteeh) |
| | 2. | deínó(h)-T | (deínóhkááh) | (deínółteeh) |
| | 3. | deí-T | (deíkááh) | --- |
| | 3o. | deí-T | (deíłteeh) | (deíłteeh) |
| | 3a. | dají-T | (dajíłteeh) | (dajíłteeh) |

da-(y)í-(ni)--(d)kááh: be going along - 3+ subjects
da-(y)í-(ni)--łteeh: be carrying an AnO along

## Conjunct Prefixes

### 2. Prefixes of Positions 6a/6b + Extended Base

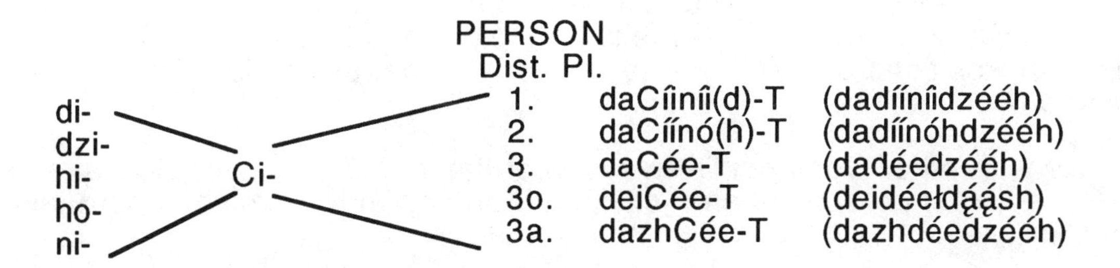


da-di-(y)í-(ni)--(d)dzééh: be staggering along (deesdzah: I'm staggering along)
da-di-(y)í-(ni)--łdą́ą́sh: be jerking O along (deeshdąsh: I'm jerking O along)
bí-da-dzi-(y)í-(ni)--łtaał: be kicking O along (bídadzíínííltaał: we're going along kicking them; bíjeeshtał: I'm kicking O along)
da-hi-(y)í-(ni)--lghaał: be wriggling along on back or belly (dahííníílghaał: we're wriggling along; heeshghał: I'm wriggling along)
da-ni-(y)í-(ni)--Øchééh: be fleeing (danéechééh: they're fleeing; noochééł: he's fleeing)
da-ho-(y)í-(ni)--ł(l)ááh: be conducting a ceremony / ceremonies (hweeshłááł: I'm conducting a ceremony)(Thematic ho-Position 4 behaves like a prefix of Position 6a/6b in 3rd person: dahwée'aah)

# CHAPTER SIX: THE FUTURE

Although classified as a Mode, the Future is basically a tense form, concerned with future time. It is a derived construction, produced by combining the di[13]-inceptive marker of Position 6a with the Yi-Progressive Base to yield the Future Base. This derived Base is then extended by incorporation of the prefixes of Positions 5, 4 and 3, and the derivational-thematic elements of Positions 6, 3 and 1.

As with other Conjunct Derivatives of the Yi-Progressive, yi-7 takes the shape -ee- in 1st person sgl and -oo- in 3rd person and Passive constructions. Compare:

Future

deeshłeel (< di[13]-6a + Progressive): I'll become
dooleeł (< di[13]-6a + Progressive): it will become

Progressive

deesht'ą́ą́ł (< di[5]-6a: fire + Progressive): I'm carrying it along (fire, a lighted torch)
yidoołt'ą́ą́ł (< di[5]-6a: fire + Progressive): he's carrying it along (fire, a torch)

Although many Verb Bases lack a Progressive, all fully conjugated verbs include a Future. Semantic constraints prevent Progressives of the type *yishbish: I'm boiling it along, or *yisk'ą́s: I'm straightening it along, but both of these non-functional Progressives provide the foundation for Future derivatives: deeshbish: I'll boil it, and deesk'ą́s: I'll straighten it.

The Simple Future Base paradigm provides the foundation for derivation of a full range of Future constructions produced by incorporating Conjunct and / or Disjunct modifying elements.

## Base Paradigm

Table 1

T = any Verb Theme

PERSON

| Sgl | di[13]-6a | + | Progressive Base | | | as in: |
|---|---|---|---|---|---|---|
| 1. | d(i)- | + | (y)ish-T | > | deesh-T | deeshłeeł |
| 2. | di- | + | (y)í-T | > | díí-T | dííleeł |
| 3. | d(i)- | + | (y)i-T | > | doo-T | dooleeł |
| Dpl | | | | | | |
| 1. | d(i)- | + | (y)ii(d)-T | > | dii(d)-T | diidleeł |
| 2. | d(i)- | + | (w)oo(h)-T | > | doo(h)-T | doohłeeł |

(di-yi)--Øleeł: become
(di-yi)--Øcha: cry

## Extended Base Paradigm

Table 2

The deictic subject pronouns of Position 5 and the direct object pronoun prefixes of Position 4 are simply added to the Future Base to extend the Base Paradigm.

T = any Verb Theme

| PERSON | Prefix Position | | | | | | Transitive | |
|---|---|---|---|---|---|---|---|---|
| Sgl | 4 | + | 5 | + | Base | Intransitive | +Ø-4 | + Ci-4 |
| 1. | Ø/Ci- | + | --- | + | -deesh-T | deeshłeeł | deesdlóós | nideesłóós |
| 2. | Ø/Ci- | + | --- | + | -díí-T | dííleeł | díílóós | shidíílóós |
| 3. | Ø/Ci- | + | --- | + | -doo-T | dooleeł | --- | shidoolóós |
| SP. | Ø/-- | + | --- | + | -doo(d)-T | --- | doodlóós | --- |
| 3o. | --/yi- | + | --- | + | -doo-T | --- | --- | yidoolóós |
| 3a. | Ø/Ci- | + | ji--zh- | + | -doo-T | jidooleeł | jidoolóós | shizhdoolóós |
| 3i. | --- | + | 'a- | + | -doo-T | 'adooleeł | --- | --- |
| 3s. | --- | + | ho- | + | -doo-T | hodooleeł | --- | --- |
| AP.O | | + | -'(a)di- | + | -doo(d)-T | --- | --- | shidi'doodlóós |
| Dpl | | | | | | | | |
| 1. | Ø/Ci- | + | --- | + | dii(d)-T | diidleeł | diidlóós | nidiidlóós |
| 2. | Ø/Ci- | + | --- | + | doo(h)-T | doohłeeł | doohłóós | shidoohłóós |

(di-yi)--Ølóós: lead O (deesłóós: I'll lead him; shidíílóós: you'll lead me)
(di-yi)--Øleeł: become ('áłah 'adooleeł: there'll be a meeting - i.e. unspecified subjects will come together; yá'át'ééh náhodoodleeł: the weather will be[come] good again – i.e. it will revert to good weather)

## 1. Conjunct Prefixes

Ci-prefixes of Position 6 + Extended Base

Most of the Ci- prefixes of Position 6 occur in the Future Mode. Those in Position 6a precede the Future Base, while those in Position 6b and 6c (with certain exceptions) take position between the Base constituents (i.e. between inceptive $di^{13}$- and the Progressive).

### 1. Prefixes of Position 6a:

Derivatives of this type involve little more than prefixation of a derivational-thematic element to the Future Base – most commonly a di-prefix with neutral tone; if its tone is inherently high, however, that of the Future Base becomes high also, by assimilation. Thus:

dideesłóós (< $di^{13}$-6a: start + -deesłóós): I'll start to lead it along

dídéesh'į́į́ł (< dí-6a: thematic + -deesh'į́į́ł): I'll look

(Note: high tone Disjunct Prefixes do not affect the tone of the Future Base – ch'ídeesłóós: I'll lead it out; ńdeeshdááł: I'll return.)

Table 3

T = any Verb Theme

| PERSON Sgl | di-6a | | dí-6a | |
|---|---|---|---|---|
| 1. | di-deesh-T | (dideesłóós) | dí-déesh-T | (dídéesh'įįł) |
| 2. | di-díí-T | (didíílóós) | dí-díí-T | (dídíí'įįł) |
| 3. | di doo T | (didoo'nah) | dí-dóo-T | (dídóo'įįł) |
| SP. | di-doo(d)-T | (didoodlóós) | --- | --- |
| 3o. | yidi-doo-T | (yididoolóós) | --- | --- |
| 3a. | jidi-doo-T | (jididoolóós) | jidí-dóo-T | (jidídóo'įįł) |
| AP. | Odi'doo(d)-T | (dibidi'doodlóós) | --- | --- |
| Dpl | | | | |
| 1. | di-dii(d)-T | (didiidlóós) | dí-díí(d)-T | (dídíít'įįł) |
| 2. | di-doo(h)-T | (didoohłóós) | dí-dóo(h)-T | (dídóoh'įįł) |

di[3]-(di-yi)--Ølóós: start to lead O along (one object)
dí-(di-yi)--Ø'įįł: look
na--b-í-#-dí-(di-yi)--łkił: ask him about it (nabídídéeshkił: I'll ask him about it; neídídóołkił: he'll ask him about it)
taah di[1]-(di-yi)--lchił stick hand into the water (taah dideeshchił)
P-aa di[2]-(di-yi)--Ø'ááł: relinquish O to P (baa dideesh'ááł: I'll turn it over to him)
hi-(di-yi-)--Ønish: pick O (as flowers)(hideeshnish)

## 2. Prefixes of Position 6b:

Table 4

The ni-prefixes of Position 6b appear between di[13]- and the Progressive constituent of the Future Base, and the tone of the resulting prefix cluster becomes high/falling, as:

| PERSON Sgl | ni-6b | |
|---|---|---|
| 1. | dí-néesh-T | (dínéesh'įįł) |
| 2. | dí-níí-T | (díníił'įįł) |
| 3. | dí-nóo-T | (dínóodaał) |
| SP. | dí-nóo(d)-T | (dínóol'įįł) |
| 3o. | yidí-nóo-T | (yidínóoł'įįł) |
| 3a. | jidí-nóo-T | (jidínóoł'įįł) |
| AP. | Odidí'noo(d)-T | (bididí'nóol'įįł) |
| Dpl | | |
| 1. | díníí(d)-T | (díníil'įįł) |
| 2. | dí-nóo(h)-T | (dínóoł'įįł) |

(dí)-ni-(yi)--ł'įįł: look at it
(dí)-ni-(yi)--Ødaał: sit down (one subject)(dínéeshdaał: I'll sit down)

## Prolongative Constructions

Many Verb Bases include a compound prefix di-ni- (<di$^{3}$-6a inceptive: start + ni$^{1}$-6b terminal: stop, finish), connoting prolongation of the verbal action.

Such Future Verb Bases may include as many as two or three di-prefixes of Position 6a and / or as many as two ni-prefixes of Position 6b, as:

didínéeshtłóół (< di$^{13}$-6a + di$^{3}$--ni$^{1}$-: 6 a/b + [yi]--łtłóół): I'll slacken O (as a taut rope or wire)

biih dididínéeshnih (< biih: into it + di$^{13}$-6a + di-thematic: action involving arms or legs + di$^{3}$--ni$^{1}$-: 6 a/b + [yi]--lnih): I'll stick my hand into it and get it stuck (as into a jar) (Prefix positional identification is speculative.)

biih didínínéesht'ááł (< biih: into it + di$^{13}$-6a + di$^{3}$--ni$^{1}$- + ni$^{2}$-: generic classifier for round shape + ni$^{1}$-6b [di$^{3}$- ni$^{1}$-: prolongative] + [yi]--[d]t'ááł): I'll stick my head into it and get it stuck (Prefix positional identification is speculative.)

However, the conjugational pattern remains essentially that described in Table 4 above, as:

Table 5

| PERSON | | |
|---|---|---|
| Sgl | di-di-ni- + Base | |
| 1. | didi-dínéesh-T | (biih dididínéeshnih) |
| 2. | didi-díníí-T | (biih dididíníílnih) |
| 3. | didi-dí-nóo-T | (biih dididínóolnih) |
| 3a. | dizhdi-dínóo-T | (biih dizhdidínóolnih) |
| Dpl | | |
| 1. | didi-díníi(d)-T | (biih dididíníilnih) |
| 2. | didi-dínóo(h)-T | (biih dididínóołnih) |

| PERSON | | |
|---|---|---|
| Sgl | di-ni-ni- + Base | |
| 1. | di-dí-ní-néesh-T | (biih didínínéesht'ááł) |
| 2. | di-dí-ní-níí-T | (biih didíníníít'ááł) |
| 3. | di-dí-ní-nóo-T | (biih didínínóot'ááł) |
| 3a. | -shdi-dí-ní-nóo-T | (biishdidíninóot'ááł) |
| Dpl | | |
| 1. | di-dí-ní-níi(d)-T | (biih didíníníit'ááł) |
| 2. | di-dí-ní-nóo(h)-T | (biih didínínóoht'ááł) |

biih di-di-di-ni-(yi)--lnih: stick hand into it and get it stuck
biih di-di-ni-ni-(yi)--(d)t'ááł: stick head into it and get it stuck

## 3. Prefixes of Position 6c

Included are:

yi$^{3}$- the allomorph of hi-6a-Seriative, required in the presence of a preceding prefix of Position 4 or 5, or when preceded by dzi-6a;

yi$^{4}$- the allomorph of si$^{1}$-6a: thematic prefix in the Verb Base for "kill one object."

yi$^{1}$- the marker of Transitional Aspect.

Yi$^{3}$- and yi$^{4}$-, like ni-6b, take position between the constituents of the Simple Future Base (i.e. between di$^{13}$- and the Progressive).

### Table 6

| PERSON<br>Sgl | yi$^{3/4}$- + Base | as in: | |
|---|---|---|---|
| 1. | di-yeesh-T | (yisdánihidiyeesdzį́į́s) | (I-you 3+) |
| 2. | di-yíí-T | (yisdánihidiyíídzį́į́s) | (you - us 3+) |
| 3. | di-yoo-T | (yisdánihidiyoodzį́į́s) | (he-us 3+) |
| SP. | di-yoo(d)-T | (yisdáhidoodzį́į́s) | (they 3+ will be) |
| 3o. | yidi-yoo-T | (yisdáyidiyoodzį́į́s) | (he-them 3+) |
| 3a. - | -zhdi-yoo-T | (yisdánihizhdiyoodzį́į́s) | (he-us 3+) |
| AP. | Odi'diyoo(d)-T | (yisdánihidi'diyoodzį́į́s) | (us/you 3+ will be) |
| Dpl | | | |
| 1. | di-yii(d)-T | (yisdánihidiyiidzį́į́s) | (we-you 3+) |
| 2. | di-yoo(h)-T | (yisdánihidiyoohdzį́į́s) | (you-us 3+) |

yisdá#-(di)-yi$^{3}$-(yi)--Ødzį́į́s: drag O to safety one after another (yisdánihidiyíídzį́į́s: you will drag us to safety one after another)
(di)-yi$^{4}$-(yi)--łhééł: kill O (one object)(Here the yi$^{4}$- allomorph appears throughout the paradigm although there need be no preceding Conjunct Prefix.) (diyeeshhééł: I'll kill it; yidiyoołhééł: he'll kill it; diyoolyééł: it will be killed; bidi'diyoolyééł: he'll be killed)

### TRANSITIONAL FUTURE

A yi-prefix, identified as yi$^{1}$-Position 6c, marks Transitional Aspect, and a prefix of similar shape and position, identified as yi$^{2}$-, marks Semelfactive Aspect. Of these, yi$^{1}$- occurs in the Transitional Future, but yi$^{2}$- does not appear in the Semelfactive Future.

Transitional (Imperfective) yiishch'íįł: I'm curling it / (Future) yideeshch'įł: I'll curl it
Semelfactive (Imperfective) yiishtał: I'm giving it a kick / (Future) deeshtał: I'll give it a kick

## Yi$^{1}$-: Position 6c - Transitional Aspect

### Table 7

Yi$^{1}$- - the marker of Transitional Aspect behaves like a prefix of Position 6a in the Future paradigm, appearing to the left of the Future Base forms. Thus:

| PERSON | | | |
|---|---|---|---|
| Sgl | yi$^{3}$- + Base | as in: | |
| 1. | yideesh-T | (yideeshch'ił) | (hwiideestsééł) |
| 2. | yidíí-T | (yidííłch'ił) | (hwiidííłtsééł) |
| 3. | yidoo-T | (yidoogah) | (hwiidoołtsééł) |
| SP. | yidoo(d)-T | (yidoolch'ił) | (hwiidooltsééł) |
| 3o. | yiidoo-T | (yiidoołch'ił | --- |
| 3a. | jiidoo-T | (jiidoołch'ił) | (hwiizhdoołtsééł) |
| Dpl | | | |
| 1. | yidii(d)-T | (yidiilch'ił) | (hwiidiiltsééł) |
| 2. | yidoo(h)-T | (yidoołch'ił) | (hwiidoołtsééł) |

yi-(di-yi)--łch'ił: curl O (as hair)
yi-(di-yi)--Øgah: turn white (yidoogah: it will turn white)
yi-(di-yi)--łdił: hatch O (as eggs)
hwi-(y)i-(di-yi)--łtsééł: see a place, visit a place (hwiideestsééł: I'll see it)
ná#-hi-(y)i-(di-yi)--(d)'naał: regain consciousness, come back to life (náhiideesh'naał: I'll come to)
ya#-(y)i-(di-yi)--Øyééł: dump O (as a load) (yeideeshhééł: I'll dump it; yeidooyééł: he'll dump it)
yé<ya-ná#-(y)i-(di-yi)--łne': toss a SRO up into the air (yéideeshniił: I'll toss it up into the air; yéidoołniił: he'll toss it up into the air)

## -'Ni-: The Inchoative

The Inchoative is marked by -'nii- in the Imperfective, Perfective and Optative Modes but, in the Future, -i-: the marker of Transitional Aspect is omitted.

As in other Modes, Future Inchoative constructions usually include a null postpositional prefix of Position 1a, which functions:

(10 as a direct object of transitive verbs;
(2) as subject in certain intransitive constructions; and
(3) as a thematic prefix in certain intransitives.

## Table 8a

### Type (1)
### Transitive - Null Postposition = direct object

| PERSON Sgl | | | Dist Plural | |
|---|---|---|---|---|
| 1. | P-dí'néesh-T | (bidí'néeshdlish) | P-dadí'nii(d)-T | (bidadí'niidlish) |
| 2. | P-dí'níí-T | (bidí'níídlish) | P-dadí'nooh-T | (bidadí'nóohdlish) |
| 3o. | yidí'nóo-T | (yidí'nóodlish) | yi-dadínóo-T | (yidadí'nóodlish) |
| 3a. | P-dízh'nóo-T | (bidízh'nóodlish) | P-dadízh'nóo-T | (bidadizh'nóodlish) |
| Dpl | | | | |
| 1. | P-dí'nii(d)-T | (bidí'niidlish) | | |
| 2. | P-dí'nóo(h)-T | (bidí'nóohdlish) | | |

P-di-'n(i)-(yi)--Ødlish: start to paint P (yiskąągo shikin bidí'néeshdlish: I'll start to paint my house tomorrow)
'ádi-di-'n(i)-(yi)--lzhih: start to shave self ('ádidí'néeshzhih: I'll start to shave)
so-di-di-'n(i)-(yi)--lzįįł: start to pray (sodidí'nóolzįįł: he'll start to pray)
'á-P-di-'n(i)-(yi)--Ølííł: start to make O ('ábidí'néeshłííł: I'll start to make it)

## Table 8b

### Type (2)
### Intransitive - Null Postposition = subject

| PERSON Sgl | | | Dist Plural |
|---|---|---|---|
| 1. | shidí'nóo-T | (shidí'nóodlóół) | (nihidadí'nóodlóół) |
| 2. | nidí'nóo-T | (nidí'nóodlóół) | (nihidadí'nóodlóół) |
| 3. | bidí'nóo-T | (bidí'nóodlóół) | (bidadí'nóodlóół) |
| 3s. | hodí'nóo-T | (hodí'nóodlóół) | (hodadí'nóodlóół) |
| Dpl | | | |
| 1. | P-dí'nii(d)-T | (nihidí'nóodlóół) | |
| 2. | P-dí'nóo(h)-T | (nihidí'nóodlóół) | |

P-di-'n(i)-(yi)--Ødlóół: get cold (shidí'nóodlóół: I'll get cold;nidí'nóodlóół: you'll get cold))
bidí'nóotsaał: he'll get sick, fall ill (lit. start to die)
'atsį' bidí'nóochxǫǫł: the meat will start to spoil

## Table 8c

### Type (3)
### Intransitive - Null Postposition = thematic

| PERSON | | | |
|---|---|---|---|
| Sgl | | | Dist Plural |
| 1. | 'idí'néesh-T | ('idí'néeshchah) | ('idadí'nííchah) |
| 2. | 'idí'níí-T | ('idí'nííchah) | ('idadí'nóohchah) |
| 3. | 'idí'nóo-T | ('idí'nóochah) | ('idadí'noochah) |
| 3s. | 'idízh'nóo-T | ('idízh'nóochah) | ('idazhdí'nóochah) |
| Dpl | | | |
| 1. | 'idí'níi(d)-T | ('idí'níichah) | |
| 2. | 'idí'nóo(h)-T | ('idí'nóohchah) | |

'idí'néeshchah: I'll start to cry
'idí'nííłtsą́ął: you'll get pregnant
'idí'nóołhą́ą́ł: he'll start to snore
'idí'nóóchxííł: it will start to snow
'idí'nóohah: it will start to become winter

### Na³-1b + -'(i)-6a + di-6a

## Table 9

| PERSON | | | | |
|---|---|---|---|---|
| Sgl | | | + Seriative hi-/yi- | |
| 1. | ndi'deesh-T | (ndi'deesh'ááł) | nahidi'deesh-T | (nahidi'deesh'ááł) |
| 2. | ndi'díí-T | (ndi'díí'ááł) | nahidi'díí-T | (nahidi'díí'ááł) |
| 3. | ndi'doo-T | (ndi'doogááł) | nahidi'doo-T | (nahidi'dookah) |
| SP. | ndi'doo(d)-T | (ndi'doot'ááł) | nahidi'doo(d)-T | (nahidi'doot'ááł) |
| 3o. | na'iididoo-T | (na'iididoo'ááł) | neidi'diyoo-T | (neidi'diyoo'ááł) |
| 3a. | ndizh'doo-T | (ndízh'doo'ááł) | nahizhdidoo-T | (nahizhdi'doo'ááł) |
| Dpl | | | | |
| 1. | ndi'dii(d)-T | (ndi'diit'ááł) | nahidi'dii(d)-T | (nahidi'diitááł) |
| 2. | ndi'doo(h)-T | (ndi'dooh'ááł) | nahidi'doo(h)-T | (nahidi'dooh'ááł) |

ndi'deesh'ááł: take a SRO down (hat from a peg, book from a shelf)
nahidi'deesh'ááł: take SRO down one at a time in succession; pick SRO one at a time in succession (melons)
ndi'doogááł: it will break loose and get away (as a tethered goat)
nahidi'dookah: they 3+ will break loose and get away (as tethered animals)
ndi'doolts'id: it (SRO will get loose (detached) and fall (as a hanging hat)

### 'A ~ 'i- ~ -'-: Positions 4 and 5 + Extended Base

With intransitive verbs 'a- and its allomorphs represent a 3i subject: "someone, something" unspecified; and with transitive verbs it represents a 3i object, with the same meaning. The shape and position taken by this morpheme are determined by the phonological environment. Thus:

1. 'A- ~ 'i- reduces to its initial consonant ('-) when it is preceded by another prefix, as in:

ha'doosoł (<ha-1b: up out + -'[a]-5 + -doosoł): they'll swarm up out (as flies from a garbage can)

'i'doo'ááł (< 'i-1b: away out of sight + -'(a)-5 + -doo'ááł): the sun will set (literally, SRO will move away out of sight)

da'dooyį́įł (< da-3: dist. pl. + -'[a]-4 + -dooyį́įł): they 3+ will eat (something)

bi'deeshłííł (< bi-1a: null postposition "at it" + ='[a]-4 + -deeshłííł): I'll copy it (literally I'll make something at [like] it)

2. 'A- metathesis: The 3i subject/object pronoun moves out of its base positional slot in certain environments, as:

a) When the Verb Base includes two or more derivational-thematic prefixes, of which one is a di-prefix of Position 6a. 'A- reduces to its initial consonant (-'-) and moves to the right of di-:

ch'éédi'doołdlał (< ch'éé- < ch'íná-: returning back out + di$^{5}$-6a: thematic: fire, light + -'[a]-4 + -doodlał): the sun will come back out (literally, it will rip something back out)

bídi'deeshłił (< b-í-1b: against it + di$^{5}$-: thematic for fire + -'[a]-4 + -deeshłił): I'll brand it (literally, I'll burn something against it - move fire against it)

didi'deesh'ááł (< di$^{6}$-6a: thematic for oral noise + di$^{3}$-6a: start + '[a]-4 + -deesh'ááł): I'll start a song (literally I'll start to move oral noise)

b) When the Verb Base includes 'a-4 + yi$^{3}$-6c (the allomorph of hi-Seriative required in the presence of a preceding prefix of Position 4/5), 'a-reduces to its initial consonant (-'-) and moves to the right of di$^{13}$-, taking position between di$^{13}$- and the Progressive Base.

ńdi'yeeshłah (<ń- < ná$^{4}$-1b + di$^{13}$- + '[a]-4 + yi$^{3}$-6c + -eeshłah): I'll pick pinyon nuts - literally, I'll gather unspecified objects.

c) When a Verb Base includes a ni-prefix of Position 6b, 'a-5 reduces to its initial consonant (-'-) and moves to the right of di-, taking position between di$^{13}$- and ni-, as:

nihił dí'nóodaał (< nihił: with us + di$^{13}$- + -'[a]-5 + ni$^{1}$-6b + -oodaał): we will land (in a plane) (literally something will sit down with us)

But 'a-4, representing a 3i <u>object</u>, usually remains in Position 4 <u>in the absence</u> of a preceding prefix, as:

'adínéesh'į́įł (< 'a-4 + di$^{13}$- + ni$^{1}$- + -éesh'į́įł): I'll steal (something)

<u>In the presence</u> of a preceding prefix 'a- moves to the right of di$^{13}$-, as in:

ndí'néeshkał (< n- < ná$^{1}$-1b: about + di$^{13}$- + ni$^{1}$-: thematic + -eeshkał): I'll go herding hadí'néeshchał (< ha-1b: up out + di[13]- + '[a]-4 + ni[2]-: generic classifier for round shape + -éeshchał): I'll do the carding (of wool) (literally, I'll cause something to swell out ball-shaped)

Ji- ~ -zh-: Position 5 + Extended Base

The 3a (4th person) subject pronoun of Position 5: he, she, one, they, takes variable position. Generally, in the absence of a preceding prefix it appears in its base form and slot, as:

jidooleeł: he will become
jidooyį́į́ł: he will eat it

But in the presence of a preceding prefix the -zh- allomorph is required, as in:

nízhdoodleeł: he/she will revert
'azhdooyį́į́ł: he will eat (something)

Ci- + 'a-4 + -zh-: When the 3i object pronoun of Position 4 cooccurs with the Position 5 subject pronoun -zh-, in a prefix cluster that includes a preceding Disjunct Ci- Prefix, 'a-4 reduces to its initial consonant (-'-) and moves to the right of -zh-5, as in:

dazh'dooyį́į́ł (< da-3: distributive plural + -zh-5 + '[a]-4 + -dooyį́į́ł): they 3+ (3a persons) will eat (something)

When 'a-4 and -zh- cooccur as constituents of a cluster that includes a prefix of Position 6a or 6b, 'a- and -zh- may exchange positions, appearing as -zh'(a)-, and they take position to the right of the Position 6 prefix, as in:

didizh'doo'áál (< di[3]-6a: start + di[6]-6a: thematic "oral noise" + -zh-5 + -'[a]-4 + -doo'áál): he (3a subject) will start a song (or di'dizhdoo'áál)
hadízh'nóołchał (< ha-1b + di[13]- + -zh-5 + -'[a]-4 + ni[2]-: generic classifier for round shape + -noołchał): he'll do the carding (of wool) (literally, he'll cause something to swell out ball-shaped)(or ha'dízhnóołchał)

## 2. Disjunct Prefixes

Ci-Position 1a + Extended Base

The null postpositions of Position 1a appear in a few Transitional verbs in which the subject is represented as a causative agent and Ci- represents an animate object that is caused to perform an action such as (be caused to) stand up = be placed on his/her/its feet, be righted (as an overturned car). Of the positionals only "stand up" is expressed as a Transitional - "sit down" and "lie down" are not viewed as Transitional.

## Table 1

T = any Verb Theme

| PERSON | Prefix Position | | | | | | | |
|---|---|---|---|---|---|---|---|---|
| Sgl | 1a | + | 5 | + | Base | > | as in: | |
| 1. | Ci- | + | --- | + | -ideesh-T | > | Ciideesh-T | biideessįįł |
| 2. | Ci- | + | --- | + | -idíí-T | > | Ciidíí-T | biidíísįįł |
| 3o. | yi- | + | --- | + | -idoo-T | > | yiidoo-T | yiidoosįįł |
| 3a. | Ci- | + | (-zh-)* | + | -i-zh-doo-T | > | Ciizhdoo-T | biizhdoossįįł |
| SP. | Ci- | + | --- | + | -idoo(d)-T | > | Ciidoo(d)-T | biidoolzįįł |
| AP. | Ci- | + | -di'- | + | -idoo(d)-T | > | Cidi'doo(d)-T | bidi'doolzįįł |
| Dpl | | | | | | | | |
| 1. | Ci- | + | --- | + | -idii(d)-T | > | Ciidii(d)-T | biidiilzįįł |
| 2. | Ci | + | --- | + | -idoo(h)-T | > | Ciidoo(h)-T | biidoosįįł |

bi#-i-(di-yi-)--sįįł = -łzįįł: stand him/her/it up, put O on feet, right it (as an overturned car)(chidí ná biideessįįł: I'll right your car - "put it back on its feet")(náníideessįįł: I'll stand you back up; łį́į́' sání bideidiilzįįł: we 3+ will stand the old horse up; ńdabiidiilzįįł: we 3+ will stand it back up)
bi#-i-(di-yi)--Ødaał: leave him/her behind to guard the place (biideeshdaał)

With few exceptions the entire gamut of Disjunct Prefixes of Position 3 and 1 occur in determinant position in the Future Mode. The Base Paradigm of the Future is "regular" and highly predictable, and so also are the Disjunct derivational elements in direct juncture with the Future Base and its Position 5 and 4 Extensions. The prefixes listed below illustrate:

'a-: away
'á-: thematic
'ada-: down
'ahá-: in two
'atí-: harm
ch'í-: out
da-: dist. pl.
da-: one S dies
di-: near fire
P-ghá-: through P
Pi-: null postposition
P-í-: against P
P-k'í-: onto P
P-ná-: around P
P-ní-: into P
P-níká-: through P
P-ts'á-: away from P
P-za-: into P's mouth

ha-: up; out
k'í-: in two; straight
na-: around about
na-: downward
ná-: encircling
ná-: upward
ná-: reversion
náá-: once again
naaná-: reverse
ni-: cessative
ntsi-: thought
tsístł'a-: cornered
tsídza-: into fire
wo'ą-: over edge
ya-: down
yá-: talk
yisdá-:save

Extended Future Base

1. -deesh-T
2. -díí-T
3. -doo-T
SP. -doo(d)-T
3. -idoo-T
3a. -zhdoo-T
3i. -'doo-T
3s. -hodoo-T
AP. -O'doo(d)-T

Dpl
1. -dii(d)-T
2. -doo(h)-T

## CHAPTER 7: THE OPTATIVE

The Optative serves to express a wish or desire – positive or negative; it functions as a negative imperative; and it marks an action as potential (usually in the negative sense).

wóchííł́ laanaa: I wish it would snow
wóchííł́ lágo: I hope it doesn't snow
t'áá ká ńdoóǫłtééł́: don't pick it up! (an AnO)
doo bee dósha'í da: I have no transportation (i.e. I have nothing with which I might go)
doo jóołta' 'ánéelą́ą́': they're countless (i.e. they're not-that-one-might-count-them many)

The Optative is marked by -ó- ~ -o- in Position 7. In the absence of a preceding prefix the Optative marker appears with peg w- (wó- ~ wo-) to maintain syllable integrity. With exception of yi[1,2]-Position 6c and ní[1]-Position 6b, the Conjunct Prefixes take -ó-. Yi[1,2]-Position 6c and ní[1]-, along with the Disjunct Prefixes, take -o-.

The Optative usually takes the same stem as the corresponding Imperfective.

wósha' (< wó-7 + -Øya'): that I might go
dósha' (< d[i]-6a + Øya'): that I might start to go
nóshdaah (< ni-6b + -ó- + -Ødaah): that I might sit down
nóosh'į́į́' (< ní[1]-6b + -o- + -ł́'į́į́'): that I might look at it
woostsééĺ (< wo- + [y]i[1]-6c + łtsééĺ): that I might glimpse it
ch'óosh'nééh (< ch'í-1b: out + -o- + [d]'nééh): that I might crawl out
noossił (< ni-4 + -o- + -sił < łził): that I might catch/grab you

### Base Paradigm

Table 1

In 2nd person sgl wó- ~ -ó- + -ni-8: you contract to produce -óó-; in 1st and 2nd persons dpl tone becomes low and -o- + -ii(d)- > -oo(d), -o- + -o(h)- > -oo(h).

T = any Verb Theme

| PERSON | Prefix Position | | | | | |
|---|---|---|---|---|---|---|
| Sgl | 7 | + | 8 | | | as in: |
| 1. | wó- | + | -sh- | > | wósh-T | wóshłe' |
| 2. | wó- | + | -ó- | > | wóó-T | wóóle' |
| 3. | wó- | + | Ø | > | wó-T | wóle' |
| SP. | wó- | + | Ø | > | wó(d)-T | wók'ą́ąs |
| Dpl | | | | | | |
| 1. | wo- | + | -oo(d)- | > | woo(d)- | woodle' |
| 2. | wo- | + | -o(h)- | > | woo(h)- | woołe' |

(wó--Øle': become
(wó)--Øcha: cry
(wó)--Øk'ą́ąs: straighten

## Extended Base Paradigms

### 1. Conjunct Prefixes

Ci-Prefixes of Position 4 and 5 + Base

Table 2

T = any Verb Theme

| PERSON | Prefix Position | | | | | | as in: | |
|---|---|---|---|---|---|---|---|---|
| Sgl | 4 | + | 5 | + | Base | Intransitive | + Ø-4 | + Ci-4 |
| 1. | Ø/Ci- | + | --- | + | (w)ósh-T | wóshłe' | wóshch'id | nóshch'id |
| 2. | Ø/Ci- | + | --- | + | (w)óó-T | wóóle' | wóóch'id | shóóch'id |
| 3. | Ø | + | --- | + | (w)ó-T | wóle' | --- | shóch'id |
| SP. | Ø/-- | + | --- | + | (w)ó(d)-T | --- | wóch'id | --- |
| 3o. | y- | + | --- | + | (w)ó-T | --- | --- | yóch'id |
| 3a. | Ø/Ci- | + | j- | + | (w)ó-T | jóle' | jóch'id | shijóch'id |
| 3i. | --- | + | '(a)- | + | (w)ó-T | 'óle' | --- | --- |
| 3s. | --- | + | h(w)- | + | (w)ó-T | hóle' | --- | --- |
| AP. | O | + | -'(a)d- | + | (w)ó(d)-T | --- | --- | shi'dóch'id |
| Dpl | | | | | | | | |
| 1. | Ø/Ci- | + | --- | + | (w)oo(d)-T | woodle' | wooch'id | nooch'id |
| 2. | Ø/Ci- | + | --- | + | (w)oo(h)-T | woohłe' | woohch'id | shoohch'id |

(wó)--Øle': become
(wó)--Øch'id: scratch O (shóóch'id lágo: don't scratch me; nóshch'id lágo: I hope I don't scratch you; shi'dóch'id lágo: I hope I'm not going to get scratched)

'A- ~ '-: Position 4 + Extended Base

Table 3

'A-: Position 4, the 3i object pronoun "someone, something unspecified" reduces to its initial consonant ('-) when in determinant position before the Optative marker (-ó-).

T = any Verb Theme

| PERSON | Prefix Position | | | | | | | as in: |
|---|---|---|---|---|---|---|---|---|
| Sgl | 'a-4 | + | 5 | + | Base | | | |
| 1. | '(a-) | + | --- | + | (w)ósh- | > | 'ósh-T | 'óshą́ą́' |
| 2. | '(a-) | + | --- | + | (w)óó- | > | 'óó-T | 'óóyą́ą́' |
| 3. | '(a-) | + | --- | + | (w)ó- | > | --- | 'óyą́ą́' |
| SP. | '(a-) | + | --- | + | (w)ó(d)- | > | 'ó(d)-T | 'ódą́ą́' |
| * 3a. | 'a- | + | -j- | + | (w)ó- | > | 'ajó-T | 'ajóyą́ą́' |
| Dpl | | | | | | | | |
| 1. | '(a-) | + | --- | + | (w)oo(d)- | > | 'oo(d)-T | 'oodą́ą́' |
| 2. | '(a-) | + | --- | + | (w)oo(h)- | > | 'oo(h)-T | 'oohsą́ą́' |

* 'a- reduces to -'- in the presence of a preceding prefix, as: ń'jółt'oh (< ná#-'[a]-jółt'oh): that one might smoke

'a-(-ó-)--Øyą́ą́': eat

## Ho- ~ h(w)-: Position 4 + Extended Base

### Table 4

Ho- ~ h(w)-: Position 4, the 3s object pronoun for "space, area, things" takes the shape h(w)- before the Optative marker (-ó-). (Hw- is written h- before -o-.)

T = any Verb Theme

| PERSON | Prefix Position | | | | | |
|---|---|---|---|---|---|---|
| Sgl | ho-4 | + | 5 | + | Base | as in: |
| 1. | h(w)- | + | --- | + | (w)ósh-T | hóshdééh |
| 2. | h(w)- | + | --- | + | (w)óó-T | hóółdééh |
| 3. | h(w)- | + | --- | + | (w)ó-T | hółdééh |
| 3a. | ho- | + | -j- | | (w)jó-T | hojółdééh |
| Dpl | | | | | | |
| 1. | h(w)- | + | --- | + | (w)oo(d)- | hooldééh |
| 2. | h(w)- | + | --- | + | (w)oo(h)- | hoołdééh |

h(w)-(-ó-)--łdééh: clear or clean up an area
h(w)-(-ó-)--lne': tell (bił hóółne' lágo: don't tell him)
h(w)-(-ó-)--Øtaał: sing (hóshtaał: that I might sing)

## Ci-prefixes of Positions 4, 6a/6b + Extended Base

### Table 5

These include the di-, hi- (~ yi-6c), dzi- ~ ji--prefixes of Position 6a and the ni-prefixes of Position 4. The prefix vowel elides before the Optative marker (-ó-). (Hi-Seriative is replaced by its yi3-6c allomorph when preceded by a Conjunct Prefix.)

T = any Verb Theme

| PERSON | Prefix Position | | | | | | | | | | |
|---|---|---|---|---|---|---|---|---|---|---|---|
| Sgl | 4 | + | 5 | + | 6a/b | + | Base | as in: | | | |
| 1. | Ø/Ci- | + | --- | + | C(i)- | + | (w)ósh- | dóssáás | jóshhaał | hóshnizh | nóstsééś |
| 2. | Ø/Ci- | + | --- | + | C(i)- | + | (w)óó- | dóósáás | dzóółhaał | hóónizh | nóółtsééś |
| 3. | Ø/Ci- | + | --- | + | C(i)- | + | (w)ó- | dóya' | dzółhaał | hónizh | nótsééś |
| SP. | Ø/-- | + | --- | + | C(i)- | + | (w)ó(d)- | dólzáás | --- | hó'nizh | nóltsééś |
| 3o. | --/yi- | + | --- | + | C(i)- | + | (w)ó-T | yidósáás | --- | yiyónizh | yinółtsééś |
| 3a. | Ø/Ci- | + | -j- | + | C(i)- | + | (w)ó- | jidósáás | jijółhaał | jiyónizh | jinółtsééś |
| AP. | O | + | -di'(a)- -d(i)- | + | C(i)- | + | (w)ó(d)-T | --- | --- | --- | --- |
| Dpl | | | | | | | | | | | |
| 1. | '(a-) | + | --- | + | C(i)- | + | (w)oo(d)- | doolzáás | dzoolghaał | hoo'nizh | nooltsééś |
| 2. | '(a-) | + | --- | + | C(i)- | + | (w)oo(h)- | doosáás | dzoołhaał | hoohnizh | noołtsééś |

di-(-ó-)--sáás < łzáás: dribble O along in a line (as sand)
ji-(-ó-)--łhaał, taah ---: tumble into the water
hi-(-ó-)--Ønizh: pluck or pick O (as herbs)

ni-(-ó-)--Øtséés: go out (a fire)
ni-(-ó-)--łtséés: extinguish O (a fire)

## Yi[1]-6c: Seriative + Extended Base

### Table 6

Yi[1]-6c is the allomorph of hi-6a: Seriative, required when immediately preceded by a prefix of Position 4 or 5, or by dzi-: Position 6a.

T = any Verb Theme

| PERSON | Prefix Position | | |
|---|---|---|---|
| Sgl | yi3 + -ó- | + Ci-4 | + dzi-6a |
| 1. | -yósh- | yisdá-nihi-yósłóós | 'a-dzi-yóshtaał |
| 2. | -yóó- | yisdá-nihi-yóólóós | 'a-dzi-yóótaał |
| 3. | -yó- | yisdá-nihi-yólóós | 'a-dzi-yótaał |
| 3o. | -yó- | yisdá-yi-yólóós | --- |
| 3a. | -yó- | yisdá-nihi-ji-yólóós | 'i-i-ji-yótaał |
| AP. | --- | | |
| Dpl | | | |
| 1. | -yoo(d)- | yisdá-nihi-yoodlóós | 'a-dzi-yootaał |
| 2. | -yoo(h)- | yisdá-nihi-yoohłóós | 'a-dzi-yoohtaał |

yisdá# + Ci-4 + yi[3]-(-ó-)--Ølóós: lead O to safety (yisdánihiyóólóós: that you might lead us to safety)
'a#-dzi-yi[3]-(-ó-)--Øtaał: let fly a series of kicks

## Dí-ní-: Positions 6a/6b + Extended Base

### Table 7

The compound prefix dí-ní, composed of di[3]-6a: start + ni[7]-6b: thematic, takes high tone. Similarly, di[11]-6a: slant, tilt + ni[2]-6b: generic classifier for round shape take the shape díní-.

T = any Verb Theme

| PERSON | Prefix Position | | |
|---|---|---|---|
| Sgl | dí + ní-- | dí[3]- + ní[7]- | dí[11]- + ní[2]- |
| 1. | dínósh-T | dínóshkaad | yaa dínósht'ááł |
| 2. | dínóó-T | dínóółkaad | yaa dínóót'ááł |
| 3. | dínó-T | dínóchééł | yaa dínót'ááł |
| SP. | dínó(d)-T | dínóolkaad | --- |
| 3o. | yidínóo-T | yidínóołkaad | --- |
| 3a. | dízhnó-T | dízhnółkaad | yaa dízhnót'ááł |
| Dpl | | | |
| 1. | dínóo(d)-T | dínóolkaad | yaa dínóot'ááł |
| 2. | dínóo(h)-T | dínóołkaad | yaa dínóoht'ááł |

di[3]-ni[7]-(-ó-)--łkaad: start to drive O (a herd); take a herd out
yaa di[11]-ni[2]-(-ó-)--(d)t'ááł: hang one's head

## Di-ni: Prolongative + Extended Base

### Table 8

The prefix compound di-ni, composed of di[3]-6a: start + ni[1]-6b: terminal, produces the Prolongatives. Di-ni- does not take high tone.

T = any Verb Theme

| PERSON | Prefix Position | | |
|---|---|---|---|
| Sgl | di + ni- | dí[1]-6a + + di-ní- | as in: |
| 1. | dinósh-T | biih didinóshnííh | biih dininóshtʼááł |
| 2. | dinóó-T | biih didinóólnííh | biih dininóótʼááł |
| 3. | dinó-T | yiih didinólnííh | yiih dininótʼááł |
| 3a. | jidinó-T | biishdidinólnííh | biih dinizhnótʼááł |
| Dpl | | | |
| 1. | dinoo(d)-T | biih didinoolnííh | biih dininootʼááł |
| 2. | dinoo(h)-T | biih didinoołnííh | biih dininoohtʼááł |

biih di-di-ni-(-ó-)--lnííh: stick hand into it and get it stuck
biih di-di-ni-(-ó-)--lʼéés: stick foot into it and get it stuck
biih di-ni-ni-(-ó-)--(d)tʼááł: stick head into it and get it stuck (ʼásaaʼ biih dininóótʼááł: donʼt get your head stuck in the jar!)

## Yi[1/2]-6c: Transitional/Semelfactive + Extended Base

### Table 9

Yi[1/2]-: Position 6c combines with the Optative marker to produce -oo-. Peg -w- is required in the absence of a preceding prefix, to maintain syllable integrity. Yi[1/2]- takes a low tone Optative marker (-o-) with the result that, in 2nd person sgl, yi- (> wo-) + ni-8: you + -o- > woó-, with rising tone.

T = any Verb Theme

| PERSON | Prefix Position | | | |
|---|---|---|---|---|
| Sgl | Base | as in: | + di-6a | + ni-6b |
| 1. | woosh-T | woostséét | dah doosłóós | nooshcháád |
| 2. | woó-T | woółtséét | dah doólóós | noócháád |
| 3. | woo-T | --- | dah dooyaʼ | noocháád |
| SP. | woo(d)-T | wooltséét | dah doodlóós | nooldóóh |
| 3o. | yoo-T | yoołtséét | dah yidoolóós | yinoołdóóh |
| 3a. | joo-T | joołtséét | dazhdoolóós | jinoocháád |
| AP. | Oʼdoo-T | biʼdooltséét | dah bidiʼdoodlóós | --- |
| Dpl | | | | |
| 1. | woo(d)-T | wooltséét | dah doodlóós | noocháád |
| 2. | woo(h)-T | woołtséét | dah doohłóós | noohcháád |

yi-(-o-)--łtséét: catch sight of O
dah di-yi-(-o-)--Ølóós: start off leading O
ni-yi-(-o-)--Øcháád: swell up
biʼn(i)-(-o-)--Øchʼíid: start to scratch O
dah di-yi-(-o-)--Øyaʼ: start off

## Ní-6b: thematic + Extended Base

### Table 10

Ní-thematic, a Conjunct Prefix of Position 6b, occurs in a Verb Base meaning "look at O." Like yi[1]-6c: Transitional Aspect marker, ní- takes a low tone Optative prefix (-o-). Ní- takes the shape nó- by assimilation when joined with -o-. In 1st and 2nd person dpl nó- + -oo(d)- and nó- + -oo(h)- > nóo(d)-/nóo(h)- respectively.

T = any Verb Theme

| PERSON | Prefix Position | | | | | | | as in: | |
|---|---|---|---|---|---|---|---|---|---|
| Sgl | 4 | + | 5 | + | 6b | + | Base | + Ø-4 | + Ci-4 |
| 1. | Ø/Ci- | + | --- | + | ní- | + | -osh- | nóosh'į́į́' | ninóosh'į́į́' |
| 2. | Ø/Ci- | + | --- | + | ní- | + | -óó- | nóół'į́į́' | shinóół'į́į́' |
| SP. | Ø/Ci- | + | --- | + | ní- | + | -oo- | nóol'į́į́' | --- |
| 3o. | --/yi- | + | --- | + | ní- | + | -oo- | yinóoł'į́į́' | shinóoł'į́į́' |
| 3a. | Ø/Ci- | + | ji-/-zh- | + | ní- | + | -oo- | jinóoł'į́į́' | shizhnóoł'į́į́' |
| AP. | O | + | -di'(a)- | + | ní- | + | -oo(d) | --- | bidi'nóol'į́į́' |
| Dpl | | | | | | | | | |
| 1. | Ø/Ci- | + | --- | + | n´- | + | -oo(d)- | nóol'į́į́' | ninóol'į́į́' |
| 2. | Ø/Ci- | + | --- | + | n´- | + | -oo(h)- | nóoł'į́į́' | shinóoł'į́į́' |

ní-(-ó-)--ł'į́į́': look at O (shinóół'į́į́': that you might look at me; don't look at me!

## Ci-4 + di-6a + yi[1]-6c + yi[3]-6c + Extended Base

### Table 11

A direct object pronoun of Position 4 or a deictic subject pronoun of Position 5 each require the yi[3]-6c allomorph of the Seriative (hi-6a) in a complex Verb Base that also includes di-6a + yi[1]-6c: transitional. Yi[1]- + -o-7 > -oo-.

T = any Verb Theme

| PERSON | Prefix Position | | | | | | | | | | | |
|---|---|---|---|---|---|---|---|---|---|---|---|---|
| Sgl | 4 | + | 5 | + | 6a | + | yi[3]- | + | yi[1]- | + | Base | as in: |
| 1. | Ci- | + | --- | + | -di- | + | -y- | + | (-yi-) | + | (w)oosh-T | dah nidiyooshłeeh |
| 2. | Ci- | + | --- | + | -di- | + | -y- | + | (-yi-) | + | (w)oó-T | dah shidiyoóleeh |
| 3o. | yi- | + | --- | + | -di- | + | -y- | + | (-yi-) | + | (w)oo-T | dah yidiyooleeh |
| 3a. | Ci- | + | ji-/-zh- | + | -di- | + | -y- | + | (-yi-) | + | (w)oo-T | dah shizhdiyooleeh |
| AP. | O | + | -'(a)di- | + | -di- | + | -y- | + | (-yi-) | + | (w)oo(d)-T | dah shidi'yoodleeh |
| Dpl | | | | | | | | | | | | |
| 1. | Ci- | + | --- | + | -di- | + | -y- | + | (-yi-) | + | (w)oo(d)-T | dah nidiyoodleeh |
| 2. | Ci- | + | --- | + | -di- | + | -y- | + | (-yi-) | + | (w)oo(h)-T | dah shidiyoohłeeh |

dah hi-di-yi[1]-(-o-)--Øleeh: hang O up with a cord or rope (O represented by Ø-4), BUT

dah Ci-di-y(i)[3]-yi[1]-(-o-)--Øleeh: hang O up (O represented by Ci-4)(dah nidiyooshłeeh: that I might hang you)

dah hi-di-yi-(-o-)--Ø'ááł: hang a SRO up (dah hidoosh'ááł: that I might hang a SRO up; dah yidiyoo'ááł: that he might hang a SRO up)

## The Inchoative

The Inchoative is derived with the compound prefix -'nii-, which combines with the Optative marker (-o-) to produce -'noo-. Inchoative constructions usually include a null postposition of Position 1a. In transitive verbs the null postposition represents the direct object; in one type of intransitive it represents the subject and, in still another type it functions, in 3i form (-'i-), as a thematic prefix.

Table 12a

Type (1) - Null Postpostion = direct object

| PERSON Sgl | | | Dist Plural | |
|---|---|---|---|---|
| 1. | P-'noosh-T | (bi'nooshbíísh) | P-da'noo(d)-T | (bida'noobíísh) |
| 2. | P-'noó-T | (bi'noóbíísh) | P-da'noo(h)-T | (bida'noohbíísh) |
| 3o. | yi'noo-T | (yi'noobíísh) | yida'noo-T | (yida'noobíísh) |
| 3a. | P-izh'noo-T | (bizh'noobíísh) | P-dazh'noo-T | (bidazh'noobíísh) |
| Dpl | | | | |
| 1. | P-'noo(d)-T | (bi'noobíísh) | | |
| 2. | P-'noo(h)-T | (bi'noohbíísh) | | |

bi'nooshbíísh: that I might start to braid it
bi'nooshdleesh: that I might start to paint it

Table 12b

Type (2) - Null Postposition = subject

| PERSON Sgl | | Dist Plural |
|---|---|---|
| 1. | shi'noogan | nihida'noogan |
| 2. | ni'noogan | nihida'noogan |
| 3. | bi'noogan | bida'noogan |
| 3s. | ho'noogan | hoda'noogan |
| Dpl | | |
| 1. | nihi'noogan | |
| 2. | nihi'noogan | |

shi'noogan: that I might become emaciated (dried up)
bi'noogan: that he might become emaciated
bi'nootsaał: that he might fall ill (start to die)

Table 12c

Type (3)
Null Postposition = thematic

| PERSON Sgl | Dist Plural | | | |
|---|---|---|---|---|
| 1. | 'i'noosh-T | ('i'nooshchééh) | 'ida'noo(d) T | ('ida'noochééh) |
| 2. | 'i'noó-T | ('i'noóchééh) | 'ida'noo(h)-T | ('ida'noohchééh) |
| 3. | 'i'noo-T | ('i'noochééh) | 'ida'noo-T | ('ida'noochééh) |
| 3s. | 'izh'noo-T | ('izh'noochééh) | 'idazh'noo-T | ('idazh'noochééh) |
| Dpl | | | | |
| 1. | 'i'noo(d)-T | ('i'noochééh) | | |
| 2. | 'i'noo(h)-T | ('i'noohchééh) | | |

'i'nooshchééh: that I might start to cry
'i'noółhą́ą́': that you might start to snore

Na3-1b + '(i)-6a + di-6a

The prefix cluster na3-'(i)- + (y)i-6c Transitional has the unitary meaning "break loose or become detached and fall or get free, take O down, pick O (as a melon. '(i-) is an unidentified prefix assigned to Position 1a.

Table 13

| PERSON Sgl | Dist Plural | | | |
|---|---|---|---|---|
| 1. | n'doosh-T | (n'doosh'ááł) | nahi'doosh-T | (nahi'doosh'ááł) |
| 2. | n'doó-T | (n'doó'ááł) | nahi'doó-T | (nahi'doó'ááł) |
| 3. | n'doo-T | (n'dooya') | nahi'doo-T | (nahi'dookááh) |
| 3o. | na'iidoo-T | (na'iidoo''ááł) | neidi'yoo-T | (neidi'yoo'ááł) |
| 3a. | nizh'doo-T | (nizh'doo'ááł) | nahizh'doo-T | (nahizh'doo'ááł) |
| Dpl | | | | |
| 1. | n'doo(d)-T | (n'doot'ááł) | nahi'doo(d)-T | (nahi'doot'ááł) |
| 2. | n'doo(h)-T | (nd'ooht'ááł) | nahi'doo(h)-T | (nahi'dooht'ááł) |

nahi'doosh'ááł: that I might take SRO down (hats from a peg, books from a shelf) one after another, one at a time
n'doosh'ááł: that I might take SRO down (hat from a peg, book from a shelf)
n'dooya': that he/it might break loose and get free (as a tethered goat)

## 2. Disjunct Prefixes

The Optative marker takes low tone when preceded by a Disjunct conjugational determinant (prefix of Position 1,3).

## 'A: Position 1b + Extended Base

### Table 1

'A-: Position 1b: away out of sight takes the shape -oo- by assimilation in combination with -o-7 . -oo-, reducing to '- before a vowel in 1st and 2nd persons dpl.

'A-('o-) retains its low tone in 2nd person sgl: 'a- + -o- + (ni)-8 > 'oó-.

T = any Verb Theme

| PERSON | Prefix Position | | | | | | | | | | |
|---|---|---|---|---|---|---|---|---|---|---|---|
| Sgl | 1b | + | 4 | + | 5 | + | Base | | | as in: | |
| 1. | 'o- | + | Ø | + | --- | + | (w)osh- | > | 'oosh-T | yah 'ooshtééł |
| 2. | 'o- | + | Ø | + | --- | + | (w)(ó)ó- | > | 'oó-T | yah 'oółtééł |
| 3. | 'o- | + | Ø | + | --- | + | (w)o- | > | 'oo-T | yah ooya' |
| SP. | 'o- | + | Ø | + | --- | + | (w)o(d)- | > | 'oo(d)-T | yah 'ooltééł |
| 3o. | 'a- | + | Ø | + | --- | + | (w)ó- | > | 'ayó-T | yah 'ayółtééł |
| 3a. | 'a- | + | Ø | + | -j- | + | (w)ó- | > | 'ajó-T | yah 'ajółtééł |
| AP. | 'a- | + | O | + | -'(a)d- | + | (w)ó- | > | 'aO'dó(d)-T | yah 'abi'dóltééł |
| Dpl | | | | | | | | | | |
| 1. | '(o)- | + | Ø | + | --- | + | (w)oo(d)- | > | 'oo(d)-T | yah 'ooltééł |
| 2. | '(o)- | + | Ø | + | --- | + | (w)oo(h)- | > | 'oo(h)-T | yah 'oołtééł |

yah 'a#-(-o-)--łtééł: carry an AnO inside
yah 'a#-(-o-)--Øya': enter inside (1 subject) (yah 'oosha': that I might go in; yah 'oóya' lágo: don't go in!)

## Ca-/Cá-: Position 1b + yi1,2-Transitional/Semelfactive + -o-7 Optative + Extended Base

### Table 2

T = any Verb Theme

| PERSON | Prefix Position | | | |
|---|---|---|---|---|
| Sgl | ya-1b + (y)i1,2-6c | | ya-1b + ná-- + (y)i1,2-6c | |
| 1. | yaosh- | (yaoshtaał) | yanáosh- | (yanáoshne') |
| 2. | yaóó- | (yaóótaał) | yanáóó- | (yanáóółne') |
| 3o. | yao- | (yaotaał) | yanáo- | (yanáotłíísh) |
| SP. | yao(d)- | (yaogééł) | yanáo(d)- | (yanáolne') |
| 3o. | yayoo- | (yayooyééł) | yanáyoo- | (yanáyoołne') |
| 3a. | yajoo- | (yajootaał) | yańjoo- | (yańjoołne') |
| AP. | yaO'doo | (yabi'doogééł) | yanáO'doo(d)- | (yanábi'doolt'e') |
| Dpl | | | | |
| 1. | yaoo(d)- | (yaoogééł) | yanáoo(d)- | (yanáoolne') |
| 2. | yaoo(h)- | (yaoohhééł) | yanáoo(h)- | (yanáoołne') |

ya-ná#-(yi)-(-o-)--łne': toss a SRO up into the air
ya-ná#-(yi)-(-o-)--Øtłíísh: bounce up into the air (one animate subject)
ya#-(yi)-(-o-)--ltaał: dash off
ya#-(yi)-(-o-)--Øyééł: dump O (a load)

## Cí-1b + yi[1,2]-6c + -o-7 Optative + Extended Base

### Table 3

Cí- + yi[1]-6c: Transitional + -o-7 take the shape Cóo- (= Có-o-o-). Cí- appears as Có-, by assimilation to -o-.

T = any Verb Theme

| PERSON | Prefix Position | | | |
|---|---|---|---|---|
| Sgl | bí-1b + -o- | | bí-1b + (y)i[1]-6c + -o- | |
| 1. | bóosh- | (bóoshjoł) | bóosh- | (bóostsóód) |
| 2. | bóó- | (bóółjoł) | bóó- | (bóółtsóód) |
| 3. | --- | --- | yóo- | (yóoya') |
| 3o. | yíyó- | (yíyółjoł) | yíyoo- | (yíyoołtsóód) |
| 3a. | bíjó- | (bíjółjoł) | bíjoo- | (bíjoołtsóód) |
| Dpl | | | | |
| 1. | bóo(d)- | (bóoljoł) | bóo(d)- | (bóolne') |
| 2. | bóo(h)- | (bóołjoł) --- | bóo(h)- | (bóołtsóód) |

bí#-yi-(-o-)--łjoł: rub O against it (as a rag against a window)(Cf. béshjoł: I'm rubbing it against it)
bí#-yi-(-o-)--łtsóód: hold O against it (bíiłtsood: I held it against it)
bí#-yi-(-o-)--Øya': join it (1 subject - as a church, party)(bóosha': that I might join it)(Cf. bíiyá: I joined it)

## 'A- ~ 'i- ~ 'o-: Position 1b + '(a)-: Position 4 + Extended Base

### Table 4

'A-: away out of sight takes the shape 'o- by assimilation to the following -ó-, and '(a)-4 (the 3i object pronoun) reduces to its initial consonant.

T = any Verb Theme

| PERSON | Prefix Position | | | | | | | | | |
|---|---|---|---|---|---|---|---|---|---|---|
| Sgl | 1b | + | 4 | + | 5 | + | Base | | | as in: |
| 1. | 'o- | + | '(a)- | + | --- | + | -ósh-T | > | 'o'ósh-T | 'o'óshkǫ́ǫ́ł |
| 2. | 'o- | + | '(a)- | + | --- | + | -óó-T | > | 'o'óó-T | 'o'óółkǫ́ǫ́ł |
| 3. | 'o- | + | '(a)- | + | --- | + | -ó-T | > | 'o'ó-T | 'o'ółkǫ́ǫ́ł |
| 3a. | 'i- | + | '(a)- | + | -j- | + | -ó-T | > | 'i'jó-T | 'i'jółkǫ́ǫ́ł |
| Dpl | | | | | | | | | | |
| 1. | 'o- | + | '(a)- | + | --- | + | -oo(d)- | > | 'o'oo(d)-T | 'o'oolkǫ́ǫ́ł |
| 2. | 'o- | + | '(a)- | + | --- | + | -oo(h)- | > | 'o'oo(h)-T | 'o'oołkǫ́ǫ́ł |

'a#-'(a)-(-ó-)--łkǫ́ǫ́ł: swim away
'a#-'(a)-(-ó-)--ł'eeł: paddle away (in a boat) ('o'ósh'eeł)
'ádaa 'a#-'(a)-(-ó-)--lgéé d: stab oneself ('ádaa 'o'óshgééd)

## Ca-: Position 1b + Extended Base

### Table 5

T = any Verb Theme

| PERSON | Prefix Position | | | | | | | | | |
|---|---|---|---|---|---|---|---|---|---|---|
| Sgl | 1b | + | 4 | + | 5 | + | Base | | | as in: |
| 1. | Ca- | + | Ø | + | --- | + | (w)-osh- | > | Caosh-T | bąąh haosh'nééh |
| 2. | Ca- | + | Ø | + | --- | + | (w)-óó- | > | Caóó-T | bąąh haóó'nééh |
| 3. | Ca- | + | Ø | + | --- | + | (w)-o- | > | Cao-T | yąąh hao'nééh |
| SP. | Ca- | + | Ø | + | --- | + | (w)-o(d)- | > | Cao(d)-T | haoltééł |
| 3o. | Ca- | + | y- | + | --- | + | (w)-ó- | > | Cayó-T | hayółtééł |
| 3a. | Ca- | + | Ø | + | -j- | + | (w)-ó- | > | Cajó-T | hajółtééł |
| 3i. | Ca- | + | --- | + | -'- | + | (w)-ó- | > | Ca'o-T | bąąh ha'ó'nééh |
| 3s. | Ca- | + | --- | + | -h(w)- | + | (w)-ó- | > | Cahó-T | hahóya' |
| AP. | Ca- | + | O | + | -'(a)d- | + | (w)-ó- | > | CaO'dó-T | habi'dóltééł |
| Dpl | | | | | | | | | | |
| 1. | Ca- | + | Ø | + | --- | + | (w)-oo(d)- | > | Caoo(d)-T | bąąh haoo'nééh |
| 2. | Ca- | + | Ø | + | --- | + | (w)-oo(h)- | > | Caoo(h)-T | bąąh haooh'nééh |

bąąh ha-(-o-)--(d)'nééh: climb it (as a tree)
ha-(-o-)--łtééł: take an AnO out (as from a box)
ha-h(w)-(-o-)--Øya': start (an event)
na-(-o-)--Øne': play
'ada#-(-o-)--ltééł: carry an AnO down from a height
tsídza#-(-o-)--Ø'ááł: put a SRO into the fire

## Cá-: Position 1b + Extended Base

### Table 6

T = any Verb Theme

| PERSON | Prefix Position | | | | | | | | | |
|---|---|---|---|---|---|---|---|---|---|---|
| Sgl | 1b | + | 4 | + | 5 | + | Base | | | as in: |
| 1. | Cá- | + | Ø | + | --- | + | (w)-osh- | > | Cáosh-T | yáoshti' |
| 2. | Cá- | + | Ø | + | --- | + | (w)-óó- | > | Cáóó-T | yáóółti' |
| 3. | Cá- | + | Ø | + | --- | + | (w)-o- | > | Cáo-T | yáołti' |
| SP. | Cá- | + | Ø | + | --- | + | (w)-o(d)- | > | Cáo(d)-T | 'aháogéésh |
| 3o. | Cá- | + | y- | + | --- | + | (w)-ó- | > | Cáyó-T | 'aháyógéésh |
| 3a. | Cá- | + | Ø | + | -j- | + | (w)-ó- | > | Cájó-T | yájółti' |
| 3i. | Cá- | + | --- | + | -'- | + | (w)-ó- | > | Cá'o-T | yá'óti' |
| 3s. | Cá- | + | --- | + | -h(w)- | + | (w)-ó- | > | Cáhó-T | náhódle' |
| AP. | Cá- | + | O | + | -'(a)d- | + | (w)-ó- | > | CáO'dó(d)-T | nábi'dóltééł |
| Dpl | | | | | | | | | | |
| 1. | Cá- | + | Ø | + | --- | + | (w)-oo(d)- | > | Cáoo(d)-T | yáoolti' |
| 2. | Cá- | + | Ø | + | --- | + | (w)-oo(h)- | > | Cáoo(h)-T | yáoołti' |

yá#-(-o-)--łti': talk
'ahá#-(-o-)--Øgéésh: cut O in two
ná#-(-o-)--łtééł: bring an AnO back
yisdá#-(-o-)--Ødzį́į́s: drag O to safety

ná#-h(w)-(ó)--d-le': that conditions might revert to a previous state (k'énáhódle' laanaa: I wish peace would return)

## Ci-: Position 1b + Extended Base

### Table 7

Ni-1b: cessative-terminative is the only Disjunct Prefix with the shape Ci- that appears in determinant position; where ni- + -o-7 > noo-. Ni- (no-) retains its low tone in 2nd person sgl.

T = any Verb Theme

| PERSON | Prefix Position | | | | | | | | | |
|---|---|---|---|---|---|---|---|---|---|---|
| Sgl | 1b | + | 4 | + | 5 | + | Base | | | as in: |
| 1. | no- | + | Ø | + | --- | + | (w)-osh- | > | noosh-T | nooshníísh |
| 2. | no- | + | Ø | + | --- | + | (w)(o)ó- | > | noó-T | noólníísh |
| 3. | no- | + | Ø | + | --- | + | (w)-o- | > | noo-T | noolníísh |
| SP. | no- | + | Ø | + | --- | + | (w)-o(d)- | > | noo(d)-T | ni'nooltééł |
| 3o. | ni- | + | -y- | +--- | | + | (w)-ó- | > | niyó-T | 'ąąh niyó'ááł |
| 3a. | n- | + | Ø | + | -j- | + | (w)-ó- | > | njó-T | njólníísh |
| 3i. | ni- | + | --- | + | -'- | + | (w)-ó- | > | ni'o-T | shił ni'óltłáád |
| AP. | ni- | + | O | + | -'(a)d- | + | (w)-ó- | > | niO'dó(d)-T | ni'nibi'dóltééł |
| Dpl | | | | | | | | | | |
| 1. | n- | + | Ø | + | --- | + | (w)-oo(d)- | > | noo(d)-T | noolníísh |
| 2. | n- | + | Ø | + | --- | + | (w)-oo(h)- | > | noo(h)-T | noołníísh |

ni-(-o-)--lníísh: stop working; quit work
ni' ni-(-o-)--łtééł: set an AnO down (ni' noółtééł: don't set it down! ni' nishóółtééł: don't set me down!

## RECAPITULATION

### 1. Extended Base Paradigm

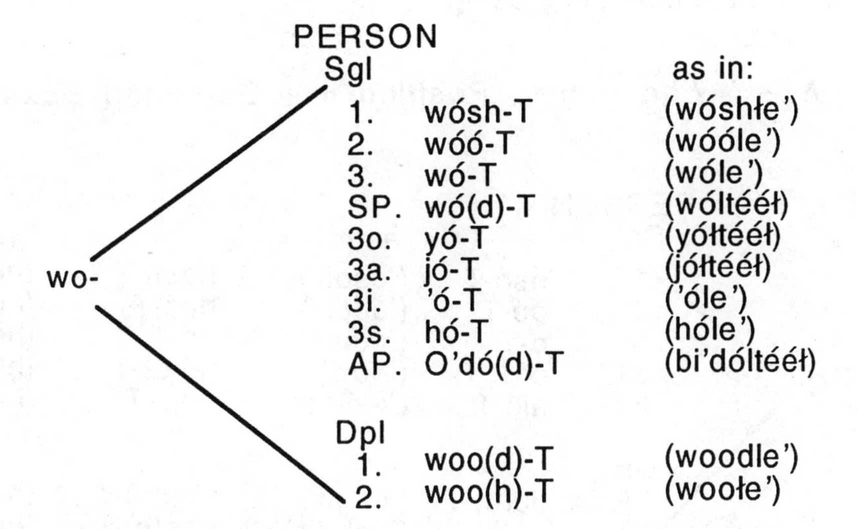


(wó)--Øle': become
P-aa (wó)--ltééł: be brought to P (an AnO)

## Conjunct Prefixes

### 2. Ci-: Position 6a/6b + Extended Base

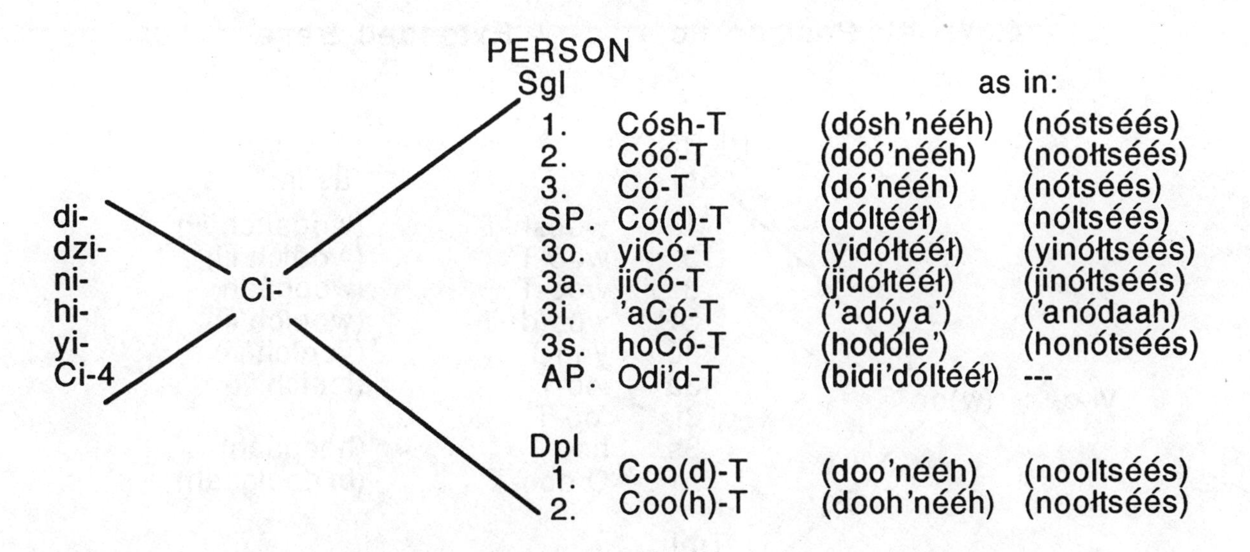


di-(-ó-)--(d)'nééh: start to crawl along
di-(-ó-)--Øya': start to go (shił 'adóya': wish I could start --- to go by unspecified conveyance)
ni-(-ó-)--Ødaah: sit down - one subject
ni-(-ó-)--Økeeh: sit down - two subjects
ni-(-ó-)--Øtsées: go out (fire)

ni-(-ó-)--łtsééś: put O out (fire)
'a-ni-(-o-)--Ødaah: unspecified subject sits down (shił 'anódaah laanaa: I wish I could land - in a plane)
ho-di-(-ó-)--Øle': start to come into being

### 3. 'A- ~ '- / ho- ~ hw-: Position 4 + Extended Base

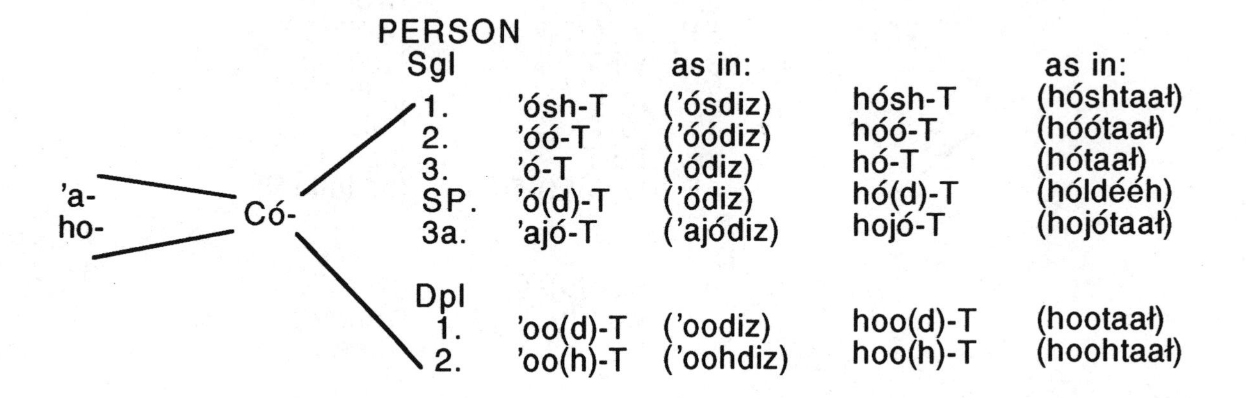


'(a)-(-ó-)--Ødiz: spin yarn; do the spinning
hw-(-ó-)--Øtaał: sing
hw-(-ó-)--łdééh: clean up/clear an area
'a#-'(a)-(-ó-)--łkǫ́ǫ́ł: swim away (yóó' 'o'óshkǫ́ǫ́ł: that I might swim away and disappear)

### 4. Yi[1,2]-: Position 6c + -o- + Extended Base

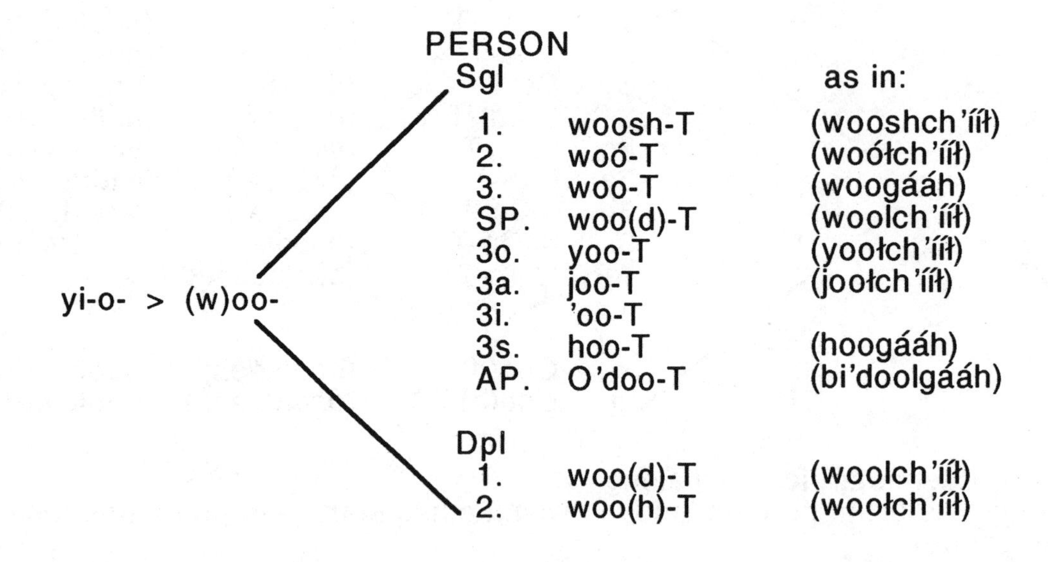


yi-(-o-)--łch'íił: curl O (hair)
yi-(-o-)--Øgááh: turn white (hoogááh: that the area might turn white)

## Disjunct Prefixes

### 5. Ca-: Position 1b/3 + Extended Base

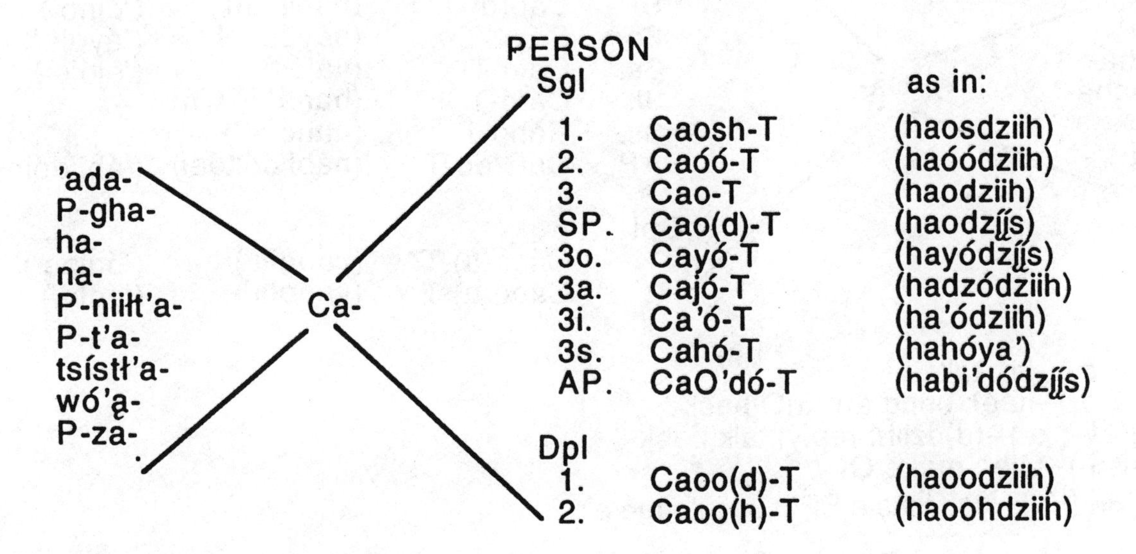


ha#-(-o-)--(d)dziih: speak
ha#-(-o-)--Ødzį́į́s: drag O out
ha#-ho-(-o-)--Øya': start (an event)
ha-da-(–o-)--(d)dziih: distributive plural subjects speak (hadaoodziih: that we 3+ might speak)
ya#-(-o-)--Øyeeh: dump O
ya#-(-o-)--ltaał: dash off

## 6. Cá-: Position 1b + Extended Base

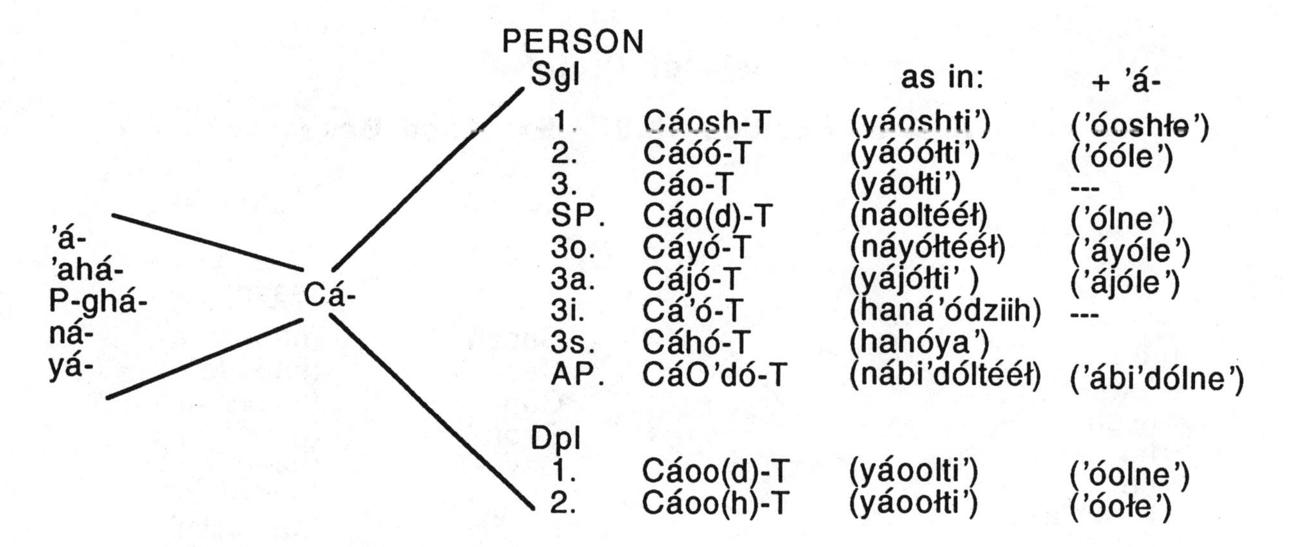


yá#-(-o-)--łti': talk
ná#-(-o-)--łtééł: bring an AnO back
ha-ná#-(-o-)--(d)dziih: reply; talk back
'á#-(-o-)--Øle': make O
ya-ná#-(-o-)--łne': toss a SRO up into the air

## 7. Ci-: Position 1b + Extended Base

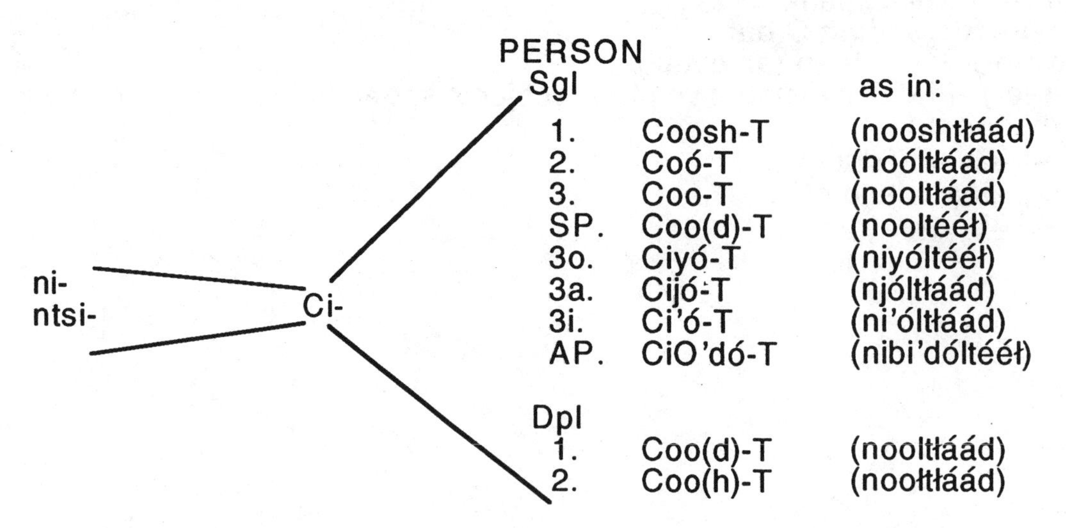


ni#-(-o-)--ltłáád: stop, halt
ni#-Ci-(-o-)--łtłáád: stop O (nibóshtłáád: that I might stop him; nibóółtłáád: that you might stop him; niyółtłáád: that he might stop him)
ntsi#-(-o-)--(d)dza': become worried, concerned: be sick (of it) (bá ntsoosdza': be worried for him; bik'ee ntsoosdza': be fed up with it)

## 8. Cí-: Position 1b + Extended Base

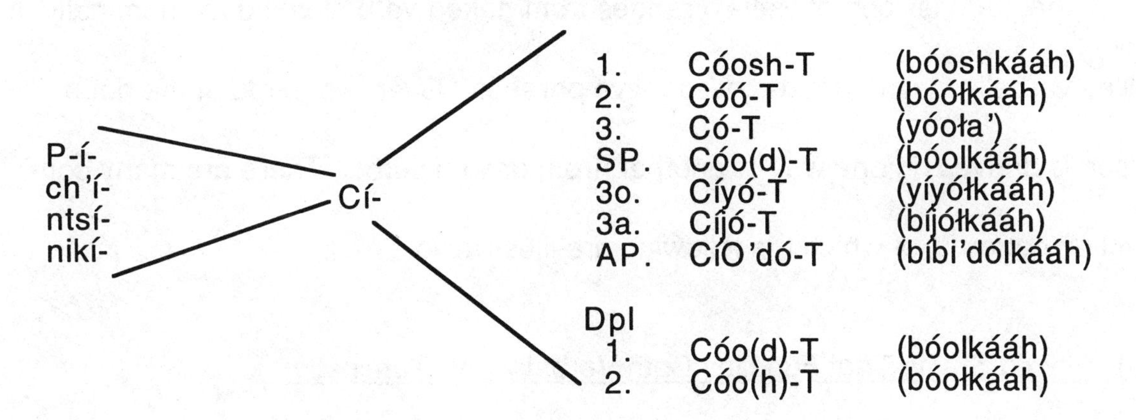


P-í#-(-o-)--ła' overtake him; catch up with him

P-í#-(-o-)--łkááh: track it down

ch'í#-(-o-)--łtééł: carry an AnO out

ntsí#-(-o-)--Økees: think

# THE VERBAL NOUN

The noun lexicon of Navajo ranges from naked verb stems used nominally as well as verbally to nominalized descriptive phrases. Over two thirds of the noun lexicon is derived, in one way or another, from or with verbs. There are many construction patterns, of which the following are illustrative.

1. <u>Naked Stems That Function Both Verbally and Nominally:</u>

   siil: vapor, steam / niiziil: it became warm (as heated milk)

   séí: sand, crumb / díízéí: it crumbled

   cha: weeping / yicha: it is crying

   chííl: snowstorm / níchííl: it's snowing

   jooł: ball / na'ajooł: it billows, floats about (as smoke)

   shéé': saliva / díízhéé': I spit, expectorated

2. <u>Verbal Noun Derivation</u>

   *<u>Impersonal Verbs (3i or 3s subject) Used Nominally:</u>

   'ólta' (< ' (a) - : something unspecified + -ólta' : is counted or read) : school

   'iiná (< ' i - ) : someone unspecified + - (y) i - ~ hiná : lives) : life

   názbąs (< ná- : around encircling + - zbąs : it is circular) : circle

   naaltsoos (< na- : about + - ltsoos: FFO is carried) : paper, book, document (lit. FFO that is carried around)

   na'ní'á ( < na- : across + - '(a) - : something unspecified + -ní'á : rigid object extends horizontally) : bridge

   na'al'eeł ( < na- : about + -'a- : something unspecified + -l'eeł : is caused to move floating) : navigation

níyol (lit. blowing arrived) : wind.

na'a'né (< na- : about + -'a- : someone unspecified + -'né : plays) : play, recreation

hadoh (< ha- : area, space, "things", impersonal "it" + -doh : warm) : heat, warmth

hootso (< ho- : area + -tso : is yellow, yellowish-green) : meadow

*Nominalized 3rd Person verb:

'ółta'í (< ' (a)- : something unspecified + -ółta' : he counts, reads + -í : the one) : student, pupil (lit. the one who reads or counts)

'ani'įįhii (< 'a- : something unspecified + -ni'įįh- : he steals + -ii : the particular one) : thief (lit. the one who steals things)

'azáát'i'í (< 'a- : something's + -za- : mouth + -át'i' < yít'i' - : it extends in a slender line + -í : the one) : bridle (lit. the thing that extends into something's mouth in a thin line)

'ashchíinii (< 'a- : someone unspecified + -shchį́- : they gave birth to + -(n)ii : the particular ones) parents (lit. they who gave birth to someone)

bááh łikanígíí (< bááh : bread + łikan- : it is sweet + -ígíí : kind) : sweet roll, cake (lit. the sweet kind of bread)

baa náhódóot'įįłígíí (< baa : about it + náhódóot'įįł : it will be discussed + -ígíí : that which will be discussed) : agenda

*Stem Noun + Descriptive Neuter Adjectival Verb: (derives nouns on the basis of appearance or other physical attributes)

'azeedích'íí' (< 'azee' : medicine, herb + dích'íí' : it is bitter, piquant, stinging) : chile, pepper

łeejin (< łee(zh)- : soil, dirt + -jin : black) : coal

ch'il łigaaí (< ch'il : plant + łigai- : it is white + -í : the one) : cabbage gałbáhí (< ga(h): rabbit + -łbá- < łibá: it is gray): cottontail rabbit

’áshįįh łikan (< ’áshįįh: salt + łikan: it is sweet) : sugar

béésh łigai (< béésh: metal + łigai: it is white): silver

*Instrumental Nouns (derived by combining a nominalized 3rd person verb and the postposition bee: with it, by means of it)

bee ’atsidí: (< bee: with it + ’atsid-: something is pounded + -í: the one): hammer (lit. the thing with which pounding is done)

bee ’ádích’idí ( < bee: with it + ’ádích’id-: self is scratched + -í: the one): back scratcher

bee da’ahijigánígíí (< bee: with it + da’ahijigą́-: distributive plural people kill one another + (n) ígíí: the kind of thing): weapon (lit. the kind of thing with which people kill one another).

bee ha’al’eełí (< bee: with it + ha’al’eeł: something unspecified is caused to float out + í: the one): strainer, sieve

bee ’ótsa’í (< bee: with it + ’ótsa’-: something is grasped as in beak or teeth + -í: the one): pliers (lit. the thing with which something is grasped)

*Nouns of Purpose or Benefit (usually constructed with the postposition bá: for it, for its benefit)

bá’ólta’í (< for him/her + ’ólta’-: something is read or counted + -í: the one): teacher (lit. the person for whose benefit reading or counting takes place)

sodizin bá hooghan (< sodizin: prayer + bá: for it + hooghan: home, place): church (lit. place for prayer)

’azee’ál’į bá hooghan (< ’azee’-: medicine + -’ál’į: it is made + bá: for it + hooghan: home, place): hospital (lit. place for medical treatment)

’aahwiinít’į bá hooghan (< ’aa-: about something unspecified -hwiinít’į: there is discussion + bá: for it + hooghan: home, place): courthouse (lit. place for the holding of trials)

*Nouns Based on Location (i.e. place or facility where the action denoted by the verb takes place)

bááh 'ál'į́įgi (< bááh: bread + 'ál'į́-: it is made + -gi: at, place where): bakery (lit. place where bread is made)

bii' da'njahí (< bii': inside of it + da'njah-: distributive plural unspecified people lie down - sleep + -í: the place): dormitory (lit. place where people sleep)

bii' tá'áńdazdigisígíí (< bii': inside of it + tá'áńdazdigis-: distributive plural people wash themselves + -ígíí: the kind of thing): wash bowl, wash basin (lit. the kind of thing in which people wash themselves)

bii' ndajibéhígíí (< bii': inside it + ndajibé-: distributive plural people bathe or swim around + -ígíí: the kind of thing): swimming pool (lit. the kind of thing in which people bathe or swim around)

*Nouns Based on a Tool or Apparatus (the apparatus or tool is usually represented by the stem noun béésh: metal)

béésh ná'iiláhí (< béésh: tool + ná'iilá-: it gathers or collects unspecified things + -(h)í: the one): magnet (lit. the tool that collects things)

béésh hataałí (< béésh: apparatus + hataał-: it sings + -í: the one): phonograph (lit. the apparatus that sings)

béésh bii' 'iigisí (< béésh: metal, apparatus + bii': inside of it + 'iigis-: something permeable but unspecified is washed + -í: the one): laundry tub

béésh bee 'í'diidlidí (< béésh: tool + bee: with it + 'í' diidlid-: something is burned against something + -í: the one): branding iron (the tool with which branding is done)

*Nominalized Descriptive Phrases

bee 'ádít'oodí bąąh dah náhidiiltsosí (< bee: with it + 'ádít'ood-: self is wiped + -í: the one ( =towel) + bąąh: alongside it + dah: up at an elevation + náhidiiltsos-: FFO is customarily hung + -í: the one): towel rack (lit. the thing on which a towel is hung) 'azee'íił'íní 'achí ye'eniihí (< 'azee-: medicine + 'íił'į-: he makes it + -(n)í: the one (=doctor) + 'achí: someone is born, there is birth + ye'eniih-: he is expert in it + -í: the one): obstetrician (lit. the doctor who is expert in birthing)

tsinaa'eeł biyaadi náábałgo yee naagháhígíí bá ní'áii (< tsinaa'eeł: ship + biyaadi: at a location under it + náábałgo: it spinning around rapidly + yee: it with it + naagháhígíí: it goes about - the one (= ship's propeller) bá: for it + ní'á-: slender rigid object extends horizontally + -ii: the particutar one): ship's propeller shaft (lit. slender rigid object that extends for the whirling thing under a ship with which it goes about)

tsiighá bił dah nátįhí dootł'izhii bii' sinilígíí (< tsiighá: hair + bił: in company with it + dah: up at an elevation + nátįh-: rigid flat or slender object is placed + -í: the one (= hairclip) + dootł'izh-: it is blue/green + -í: the one (=turquoise) bii': in it + sinil- plural objects lie + -í: the one): turquoise hairclip (lit. the kind of hairclip in which there are turquoise sets)

---

Pueblo, Spanish and Anglo-American contacts led historically to widespread cultural borrowing by the Navajo, and the language responded by generating necessary terminology to meet new communicational requirements. Borrowed terminology included a few nouns and no verbs during the early contact period. From the beginning the Navajo preferred to draw upon the internal lexicon of their own lenguage, including its own grammatical processes and lexical generative system to produce new labels for new items and concepts. Some of the generative processes involved are reflected in the foregoing examples.

Analysis of the verbal noun class points to the descriptive nature of the terms, and to the obvious fact that their successful generation presupposes full understanding of the concepts involved. It is a process that stands in sharp contrast to that of a language such as English, where new vocabulary is often borrowed from another speech system, including a "dead" language. Speakers of English read and hear many words that are vague or meaningless to them, e.g. "electron," "hydrogenated," whereas Navajo equivalents - if such were generated with the old formula - would be in the nature of descriptive definitions. "Lack of a word for it" (=unfamiliarity with an alien concept) has often had an adverse effect on cross-cultural communications.

---

REFERENCES


Hoijer, Harry. 1949. The Apachean Verb, V: The Theme and Prefix Complex. IJAL 15: 15-22

Kari, James. 1976. Navajo Verb Prefix Phonology. Garland Press.

Krauss, Michael E. 1964, Proto-Athapaskan-Eyak and The Problem of Na-Dene: The Phonology. IJAL 30:118-132

Leer, Jeff. 1979. Proto-Athabascan Verb Stem Variation I: Phonology. ANLC.

Young, Robert W. & Morgan, William. 1987. The Navajo Language, UNM Press.

__________ 1992. Analytical Lexicon of Navajo, UNM Press.

SAUK VALLEY CC LIBRARY
3 1516 00077 5732